출제 순위 파트 5&6

지은이 **구원**

시나공 토익

출제 순위 파트 5, 6 (신토익 개정판)

초판 발행 · 2015년 7월 1일
초판 7쇄 발행 · 2020년 5월 4일

지은이 · 구원
발행인 · 이종원
발행처 · ㈜도서출판 길벗
출판사 등록일 · 1990년 12월 24일
주소 · 서울시 마포구 월드컵로 10길 56(서교동)
대표전화 · 02) 332-0931 | **팩스** · 02) 322-6766
홈페이지 · www.gilbut.co.kr | **이메일** · eztok@gilbut.co.kr

기획 및 책임 편집 · 고경환(kkh@gilbut.co.kr) | **디자인** · 박행아 | **제작** · 이준호, 손일순, 이진혁
영업마케팅 · 김학흥, 장봉석 | **웹마케팅** · 이수미, 최소영 | **영업관리** · 심선숙 | **독자지원** · 송혜란, 홍혜진

편집진행 및 전산편집 · 기본기획 | **본문 디자인** · 김여진 | **CTP 출력 및 인쇄** · 북토리 | **제본** · 신정문화사

- 잘못된 책은 구입한 서점에서 바꿔 드립니다.
- 이 책에 실린 모든 내용, 디자인, 이미지, 편집 구성의 저작권은 ㈜도서출판 길벗과 지은이에게 있습니다.
  허락 없이 복제하거나 다른 매체에 옮겨 실을 수 없습니다.

- 이 도서의 국립중앙도서관 출판예정도서목록(CIP)은 서지정보유통지원시스템 홈페이지(http://seoji.nl.go.kr)와
  국가자료공동목록시스템(http://www.nl.go.kr/kolisnet)에서 이용하실 수 있습니다.(CIP제어번호: CIP2016015323)

ISBN 979-11-5924-051-5 03740
(길벗 도서번호 300906)

정가 15,000원

독자의 1초까지 아껴주는 정성 길벗출판사
㈜도서출판 길벗 | IT실용, IT/일반 수험서, 경제경영, 취미실용, 인문교양(더퀘스트) www.gilbut.co.kr
길벗이지톡 | 어학단행본, 어학수험서 www.eztok.co.kr
길벗스쿨 | 국어학습, 수학학습, 어린이교양, 주니어 어학학습, 교과서 www.gilbutschool.co.kr

머리말

이 책을 통해 여러분의 토익 점수가
가장 빨리, 가장 효과적으로 향상되기를 바랍니다.

토익을 준비하는 수험자들이 한 권의 기본서를 끝내고, 또 다른 기본서를 끝내는 방식으로 공부하는 사람들은 거의 없다. 공부할 자료들이 수없이 많기 때문에 기본서 한 권을 완벽하게 마스터한다는 것은 어려운 일이다. 또한, 토익 고득점을 필요로 하는 수험자들은 장기적인 계획을 세워 준비하기보다는 두세 달 내에 고득점을 얻기를 원하지만 이는 쉽지않다. 그렇다면 토익 고득점을 달성할 수 있는 최적의 공부 방법은 무엇일까? 그것은 자주 출제된 문제들을 가능한 많이 풀어보는 것이다.

필자는 학생들과 함께 매달 토익 시험을 치르고, 출제된 문제들을 모두 분석해 왔다. 그렇게 분석한 출제빈도가 높은 문제와 10년 동안 실강으로 학생들을 만나며 전했던 암기법과 문제풀이 방식을 이 책에 그대로 담았다. 특히 신토익 파트 5, 6도 문제 없도록 철저한 분석을 바탕으로 개정판을 만들었다.

이 책은 필히 앞 장부터 공부해야 한다. 각 법칙들은 주어진 문제를 통해 이 문제가 무엇을 묻는 것인지 스스로 찾을 수 있게 하는 것에서부터 시작한다. 어떠한 순서로 문제를 풀지 알려주는 강사의 노하우를 포함했고, 학습을 마친 후에 이를 실제 적용해 볼 수 있는 실전문제까지 제공한다.

이 책의 큰 특징은 함정 문제가 포함돼 있다는 점이다. 함정 문제는 토익 시험에서 단순히 요령만을 익혀 풀 때 틀리기 쉬운 문제를 말한다. 고득점을 원하는 수험자들이라면 꼭 해결해야 하는 것이 이 함정 문제이다. 저자는 다년간의 강의 경험을 바탕으로 학생들이 꼭 틀리는 함정 문제들을 정리했다. 또한 책의 후반부로 가면서 앞에서 소화하지 못한 법칙들이 다시 등장할 경우 앞으로 다시 돌아가 확인해 볼 수 있게 했으므로 순서대로 차근차근 공부하면 된다.

필자의 단골 식당 간판에는 '조미료 안 넣은 집 못 찾아서 직접 차린 집'이라고 적혀 있다. 시중에 나온 많은 교재들은 사실 실제 강의에 활용하기에는 과하거나 부족한 부분들이 많았다. 토익을 혼자서 공부하는 것 역시 토익 강의에서 알려주는 것과 마찬가지로 순서와 방법이 있어야 한다. 일반적인 토익 교재를 이용해 공부할 경우 문법에 대한 지식을 자세히 알 수는 있지만, 실제 시험을 치르는데 꼭 필요한 중요한 포인트들까지 알려주지는 않는다.

이 책은 토익 강의 교재로 더할 나위 없이 적합하며, 혼자서 토익을 공부하는 수험자들에게도 매우 효과적인 공부 방식을 제시해 줄 것임을 확신한다.

이 책이 나오기까지 도움을 주신 한국외대 일반대학원 테솔학과 대니 샘과 수 리, 구원 토익의 조교들에게 감사의 말을 전한다.

2016년 여름
저자 구원

목차

머리말 · 003
목차 · 004
Part 5, 6 출제경향과 대책 · 008
이 책의 특징 · 010
진단 고사 · 011
진단 고사에 따른 학습가이드 · 018

첫째 마당 어형 및 문법 편

Chapter 01 매월 출제되는 문제
이번 토익 시험에 반드시 나온다.

법칙 1	부사절 접속사는 양보, 이유, 시간, 조건 순	022
법칙 2	'관소전타' 뒤는 명사	025
법칙 3	주어와 동사, 조동사와 동사원형, have와 p.p., 어구 사이는 부사	028
법칙 4	명사 앞 소유격, 동사/전치사 뒤 목적격, 동사 앞 주격	031
법칙 5	시제 부사가 보기에 있으면 동사를 확인	034
법칙 6	빈칸 앞뒤 단어만 봐도 풀리는 시점과 기간 전치사	037
법칙 7	완전한 문장 다음에는 부사	040
법칙 8	의미로 풀어야 하는 명사 자리 문제는 수식어나 동사를 보고 판단	043
법칙 9	'관소전타' 뒤 명사 앞은 형용사	046
법칙 10	기본 형용사와 분사가 함께 나올 때는 기본 형용사	049
법칙 11	빈칸 앞뒤 단어만 봐도 풀리는 위치, 방향 전치사	052
법칙 12	'------ + the/a 명사' 문제, 보기 중 전치사가 1개면 그것이 정답	055
법칙 13	either A or B, both A and B, neither A nor B	058

Chapter 02 2개월에 한 번 출제되는 문제
토익 시험 2회에 반드시 한 번은 나온다.

법칙 14	2형식 또는 5형식 문장의 보어 자리는 형용사	062
법칙 15	전체 문맥을 알아야 풀리는 추가, 포함, 제외 및 for(이/용/대/목) 전치사	065
법칙 16	목적어가 있으면 능동, 없으면 수동	068
법칙 17	비교/최상급의 단서가 있으면 비교/최상급, 그렇지 않으면 원급	071
법칙 18	동사가 2개면 접속사가 답	074
법칙 19	부정대명사는 동사 개수, 명사 자리, 단수, 복수 확인	077
법칙 20	'a(an) + 형용사' 뒤는 단수 명사, a(an)이 없으면 복수 명사	080
법칙 21	주격, 목적격 보어 자리에 오는 분사는 주로 p.p.	083
법칙 22	이럴 땐 재귀대명사	086
법칙 23	명사를 앞에서 수식해 주는 분사는 주로 p.p.	089

법칙 24	전체 문맥을 알아야 풀리는 양보, 이유 전치사	092
법칙 25	단수 주어 뒤는 단수 동사-, 복수 주어 뒤는 복수 동사	095
법칙 26	문맥을 알아야 풀 수 있는 주제, 범위, 근거 전치사	098

Chapter 03 3개월에 한 번 출제되는 문제
토익 시험 3회에 반드시 한 번은 나온다.

법칙 27	빈칸 앞뒤 단어만 봐도 풀리는 동반, 수단, 수동 전치사	102
법칙 28	조동사, 명령문, 그리고 요구, 주장, 의무, 명령, 제안 뒤는 동사원형	105
법칙 29	덩어리로 외워야 하는 복합명사 문제	108
법칙 30	전명구 앞에 잘 오는 부사	111
법칙 31	문장, 형용사(혹은 -ing/p.p.), 부사 앞은 부사 자리	114

Chapter 04 4개월에 한 번 출제되는 문제
토익 시험 4회에 반드시 한 번은 나온다.

법칙 32	과거 시점(yesterday, last, ago, when 과거)이 보이면 과거시제	118
법칙 33	before[after, when, while]에는 -ing, as[once, unless, if]에는 p.p.	121
법칙 34	등위접속사(and, but, or, yet)가 답이면 같은 것은 버려라	124
법칙 35	미래 시점 단서(tomorrow, next, future)가 보이면 미래시제 또는 현재진행시제	127
법칙 36	'사람 선행사 + ------ + 동사'는 who	130
법칙 37	명사를 뒤에서 수식해 주는 분사는 목적어가 있으면 -ing, 없으면 p.p.	133

Chapter 05 5개월에 한 번 출제되는 문제
토익 시험 5회에 반드시 한 번은 나온다.

법칙 38	문장에 정동사 1개는 필수	138
법칙 39	'전치사와 a, the, 소유격 – 명사' 사이에는 동명사	141
법칙 40	명사절이 완전하면 that, 불완전하면 what, 선택은 whether	144
법칙 41	숫자 앞에는 숫자 수식 부사	147
법칙 42	'사물 선행사 + ------ + 주어, 목적어가 없는 문장'은 which 혹은 that	150

Chapter 06 6개월에 한 번 출제되는 문제
토익 시험 6회에 반드시 한 번은 나온다.

법칙 43	'(in order) to + 동사원형'은 문장 전체를 수식	154
법칙 44	빈칸 앞에 한정사가 없고, 뒤에 단수 명사가 있으면 불가산명사가 답	157
법칙 45	원급, 비교급, 최상급을 수식해 주거나 비교급, 최상급을 만들어 주는 부사	160
법칙 46	앞뒤 내용이 상반되면 but, 순차적이면 and나 or, 인과관계면 so	163
법칙 47	of가 답이 되는 주격, 목적격, 소유격, 동격	166

Chapter 07 7~8개월에 한 번 출제되는 문제
언제든 대비하고 있어야 하는 문제

| 법칙 48 | 희망, 요청, 설득, 허락 동사가 오면 to 부정사 | 170 |

법칙 49	감정분사는 '사물잉, 사람을 패?'	173
법칙 50	완전한 문장 뒤에는 '(in order) to 동사원형'이 동사를 수식	176
법칙 51	과거 시점보다 이전은 과거완료	179
법칙 52	시간[조건] 부사절 또는 반복[습관]적 사실의 단서가 보이면 현재시제	182
법칙 53	'since + 과거 시점, over/for+기간'이 보이면 현재완료시제	185
법칙 54	'선행사 + ------ + 명사 + 동사'는 whose	188
법칙 55	recent, past는 과거, current는 현재, upcoming, near, next는 미래	191

Chapter 08 평균 2년에 한 번 출제되는 문제
언제든 대비하고 있어야 하는 문제

법칙 56	복합관계사절은 형용사절이 아니다	196
법칙 57	plan[opportunity, way, effort, right]+to 부정사	199
법칙 58	to 부정사만 목적어로 취하는 동사	202
법칙 59	동명사만 목적어로 취하는 동사	205
법칙 60	완전한 문장 뒤에 오는 콤마는 -ing(분사구문)	208
법칙 61	완료시제에 have만 있다면 p.p.	211
법칙 62	'Those + 형용사' 류는 '~하는 사람들'	214
법칙 63	무조건 동명사	217
법칙 64	'번지점프' to 동사원형	220
법칙 65	무엇을 가리키는지 알 수 있을 때는 소유대명사	223
법칙 66	보기에 미래완료시제나 would have p.p.가 오면 주로 오답	226
법칙 67	고득점을 위한 기타 명사절 접속사	229
법칙 68	고득점을 위한 기타 형용사절 접속사	232
법칙 69	고득점을 위한 기타 전치사	235
법칙 70	목표[계획] is to 부정사	238

둘째 마당 어휘 편 및 파트 6

Chapter 09 동사 어휘 문제
매월 4문제

법칙 71	특정 명사를 목적어로 쓰는 3형식 동사	244
법칙 72	특정 전치사와 잘 어울리는 3형식 동사	247
법칙 73	to 부정사나 동명사, 명사절을 목적어로 하는 3형식 동사	250
법칙 74	'자동사 + 전치사' 묶음	253
법칙 75	'------ + 목적어 + 목적 보어'이면 5형식 동사	256
법칙 76	목적어가 없으면 1형식 동사	259
법칙 77	목적어가 2개면 4형식 동사	262
법칙 78	보어 자리에 형용사나 동격의 명사가 있으면 2형식 동사	265
법칙 79	보기 중 1개라도 오답 처리해라	268
법칙 80	제대로 해석해야 풀리는 동사 어휘 문제	270

Chapter 10 명사 어휘 문제
매월 4문제

- 법칙 81 특정 전치사와 잘 어울리는 명사 … 274
- 법칙 82 특정 명사와 잘 어울리는 명사 … 277
- 법칙 83 '사람 명사 및 -o 부정사'와 잘 어울리는 명사 … 280
- 법칙 84 특정 단어와 잘 어울리는 기타 명사들 … 283
- 법칙 85 올바른 해석으로 풀어야 하는 명사 어휘 문제 … 286

Chapter 11 형용사 어휘 문제
매월 3문제

- 법칙 86 특정 명사와 잘 어울리는 형용사 … 290
- 법칙 87 특정 전치사와 잘 어울리는 형용사 … 293
- 법칙 88 사람에 답이 되는 형용사 … 296
- 법칙 89 가주어, 진주어에 잘 어울리는 형용사 … 299
- 법칙 90 올바른 해석으로 풀어야 하는 형용사 어휘 문제 … 302

Chapter 12 부사 어휘 문제
매월 3문제

- 법칙 91 특정 시제와 잘 어울리는 부사 … 306
- 법칙 92 특정 형용사와 잘 어울리는 부사 … 309
- 법칙 93 전명구와 잘 어울리는 부사 … 312
- 법칙 94 특정 동사와 잘 어울리는 부사 … 315
- 법칙 95 올바른 해석으로 풀어야 하는 부사 어휘 문제 … 319

Chapter 13 빈칸 문장만으로는 풀 수 없는 파트 6 문제
매월 7문제

- 법칙 96 알맞은 문장 넣기 문제는 앞뒤 흐름을 파악 … 322
- 법칙 97 시제 문제는 나중에 푼다 … 326
- 법칙 98 연결어 문제는 밑줄 앞뒤를 요약하라 … 332
- 법칙 99 대명사 문제는 문법적으로 소거 후 가리키는 말을 확인 … 339
- 법칙 100 어휘 문제는 논리적 근거로 마무리한다 … 346

실전테스트

Actual Test 01 … 353
Actual Test 02 … 홈페이지 다운로드
Actual Test 03 … 홈페이지 다운로드
추가 5회분 실전테스트(본문 문제 재구성) … 홈페이지 다운로드
정답 및 해설 … 홈페이지 다운로드

> Actual Test 2, 3 문제, Actual Test 1, 2, 3의 해설 그리고 추가 5회분 실전테스트는 모두 홈페이지에서 내려받을 수 있습니다. (WWW.GILBUT.CO.KR)

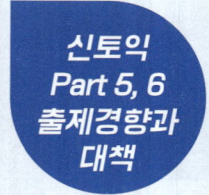

신토익 Part 5, 6 출제경향과 대책

토익이 10년만에 개정되었다. 파트 5, 6은 개정폭이 매우 적다. 파트 5는 40문제에서 30문제로 줄어들었고, 파트 6 역시 기존에 출제되었던 유형에서 신유형 문제가 지문당 하나씩 추가되었다.

따라서 신토익 파트 5, 6은 구토익 유형을 충분히 학습하고 추가된 신유형 문제까지도 파악해야 한다.

매달 꾸준히 10~12문제에서 8~10문제로 감소	주로 빈칸 앞뒤만 보고 푸는 품사 문제 (명사 자리, 동사 자리, 접속사 자리, 전치사 자리, 형용사 자리, 부사 자리, 대명사 격 확인)
매달 꾸준히 10문제에서 8문제로 감소	동사의 수, 태, 시제를 확인하는 문제와 준동사 문제
매달 5문제 이상에서 4문제로 감소	등위[상관]접속사, 명사절, 형용사절, 부사절 접속사 문제
평균 5문제 정도 유지	각종 품사 자리의 상위 문제들(가산/불가산, 복합명사, 비교/최상, 재귀대명사, 지시/부정대명사)
평균 3~4문제 정도에서 2~3문제로 감소	어휘 문제 (동사, 명사, 형용사, 부사, 전치사)
총 4문제의 신유형추가	문맥에 알맞은 문장 고르기 문제

파트 5문제를 보면 품사문제, 문법문제에 비해 어휘문제가 더 큰 폭으로 감소한 것을 알 수 있다. 파트 6와 7의 문제가 늘어났지만 전체적으로 동일한 난이도를 유지하기 위해 ETS는 상대적으로 시간이 더 많이 소요되는 파트 5의 어휘문제 수를 더 낮추었을 것이다.

하지만 기존의 수험생은 신토익에 더 어려움을 느낄 수밖에 없다. 일반적으로 기존 토익에서는 파트 5, 6에 20분, 파트 7에 55분을 계획하고 푼다. 그러나 파트 7이 여섯 문제 늘면서 이제 파트 5, 6을 적어도 15분 이내에 풀어야한다. 문맥을 확실히 알아야 하는 파트 6 신유형에도 시간이 상당히 걸리므로 파트 5, 6을 15분 안에 푸는 것이 쉽지 않다. 결국, 파트 7에 대한 부담을 없애려면 파트 5에서 시간을 더 단축하고, 파트 6의 신유형에 대한 연습을 철저히 하는 수밖에 없다.

단 한번도 기출 된 적이 없는 완전한 새로운 문제는 주로 어휘 문제에서 나오는 편이며 그 수는 매월 1~2문제 정도인데, 그 중 한 문제는 오답을 잘 제거하면 풀리는 수준에서 출제 된다.

신토익으로 개정되기 전까지도 토익은 조금씩 변해왔다. 특히 최근 2년 동안은 만점 방지용 고난도 어휘가 감소했다. 특히 파트 5의 마지막, 혹은 바로 그 전 문제로 고득점자를 좌절 시키던 고이도 어휘문제는 이제 문법 문제로 대체됐다. 심지어 품사문제가 나오기도 한다. 이렇게 전반적으로 파트 5의 난이도가 하락했다고 볼 수 있지만 대신, 뻔한 요령으로 풀면 틀리는 문법 문제가 많이 줄어들었다. 예를 들어 be동사 뒤는 형용사가 답이라고 외운 학생들은 틀리도록 명사가 답이 되는 문제가 출제되었다. 한편, 여전히 새로 개발되는 어휘문제는 매달 1~2문제가 나오고 있으나 확실히 이전보다 오답의 난이도가 낮아 새로 보는 어휘라도 풀 수 있을 수준으로 출제된다.

파트 6는 지문의 길이가 점점 짧아지고 있다. 그러나 지문의 길이가 짧을 수록 문제는 더 어렵게 나온다는 사실에 주의 해야 한다. 시제 문제가 파트 6 위주로 정착한 것은 한참 전의 일이지만, 첫 번째 문제로 나온 시제 문제가 마지막까지 다 봐야 하는 경우도 여러 번 있었고, additionally와 for example을 구분해야 하는 고 난이도 문제, this year인지, every year인지를 구분해야 하는 문제 등 섣불리 답을 고른다면 틀리기 쉬운 문제가 많아졌다. 결국 꼼꼼히 문맥을 따져야 하는 문제들이 짧은 지문 안에 단서가 압축되어 들어가 있으므로 짧은 지문이지만 문제를 푸는 데에는 오히려 시간이 더 소비된다. 특히 신유형 문제가 추가되면서 파트 6 지문은 결국 꼼꼼히 제대로 읽고 들어갈 말을 미리 예상한 후 대입해가며 앞뒤 흐름과 논리관계를 꼭 따져야 한다.

파트 7의 지문이 길이가 길어지고, 지문 개수가 많아지고 추론 문제가 많아진 것은 오래 전이지만 최근에는 추론의 정도가 더 심해지고 있다. 첫 지문부터 추론 문제가 들어가거나 기사문이 다수 출제되거나 그 기사문이 이중지문, 삼중지문의 유형으로 나오는 등, 파트 7은 이미 더 빠른 독해력, 더 명확한 논리력을 요구할 대로 요구하고 있다. 신토익에서는 의도파악 문제, 문장 삽입 문제 등의 새로운 문제 유형과 메시지 대화문, 인터넷 채팅, 삼중지문 등의 새로운 지문 유형이 추가되어 다양한 비즈니스 상황에 필요한 의사소통 능력을 요구하고 있다.

종합적으로 정리해보자면 ETS가 고득점과 그렇지 않은 사람들을 구분 짓기 위한 변별력의 수단으로 과거에는 파트 5에서 어려운 문법이나 어려운 어휘 문제를 사용했다고 한다면, 최근에는 파트 5는 쉽고 보편적으로 출제하는 대신, 파트 6에서는 논리력을, 파트 7에서는 논리력과 한정된 시간 안에 해결해야 하는 다량의 독해 능력을 테스트하는 문제들을 사용하고 있다.

그렇다면 어떻게 대비해야 할까? 파트 7이 어려우니 파트 7부터 대비하기 위해서 논리력을 키우고 독해실력을 키워야 할까? 논리력이나 독해실력은 하루아침에 느는 것이 아니다. 오히려 파트 7을 풀기 위해 시험장에서 좀더 시간을 확보하려는 노력이 빠르고 실질적이다. 충분한 시간이 확보되어야 독해를 좀 더 정확히 할 수 있고, 좀 더 논리적으로 생각할 수 있다. 결국 파트 5가 쉬울 수록 더 빠르고 정확하게 풀어, 남는 시간으로 파트 6와 7에 더 많은 시간을 할당할 수 있도록 해야 한다. 이 책을 통해서 파트 5의 정확도와 속도를 끌어올리고, 파트 6에 대한 논리력을 끌어올릴 수 있다. 이 책은 특히 최근에 많이 출제되는 함정문제를 다루었다. 이 책에 실린 문제들로 단문 직독직해 속도를 끌어올릴 수 있다. 단문 직독직해가 되지 않으면 장문 직독직해도 되지 않는다. 이 책을 통해서 쌓은 직독직해 능력과 논리력을 바탕으로 파트 5는 빠르고 정확하게, 파트 6는 논리적으로 빠르게 풀어서 파트 7을 위한 시간을 확보하기 바란다.

이 책의 특징

지난 8년간의 출제율을 완벽히 분석했다!
출제율 별로 우선 순위 학습이 가능하다!

풀이 기술로 부족한 부분을 채워주는 '함정을 피해 봐'!

토익 시험은 분명 기술적인 부분으로 상당 부분을 해결할 수 있다. 현재 시중에 판매되고 있는 수많은 책에 실린 내용들이 이를 반증한다. 하지만 기술로서 해결되지 않는 부분도 분명 존재한다. 특히 오답을 유도하는 함정 보기는 단기간 고득점을 목표로 하는 수험생들에게 큰 장애물이다. 저자는 '함정을 피해 봐'에서 수년 간 직접 쓰고 지우며 만든 함정을 피하는 법을 공개한다.

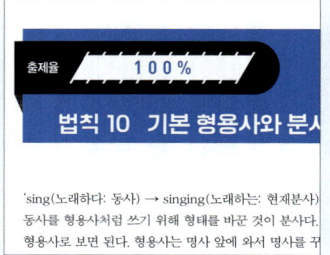

8년간 출제 문제 완벽히 분석, 출제율 순으로 학습!

지난 8년 동안 출제된 문제를 철저히 분석해서 유형별로 출제율을 뽑았다. 파트 5, 6에 출제되는 문법, 어휘 문제 유형을 모두 분석했고, 시간이 없는 수험생들을 위해 효율적인 학습이 가능하도록 출제율이 높은 유형부터 실었다. 사전식 구성으로 필요한 유형만 학습할 수 있어 맞춤형 학습도 가능하게 구성했다.

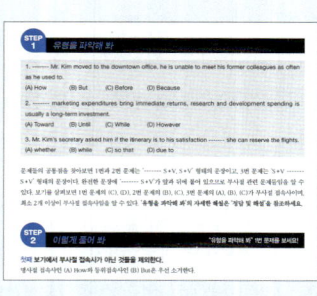

10년 간의 강의 노하우가 담긴 암기법과 풀이법!

저자는 수년 간 단 한 번도 거르지 않고 토익 시험을 봤고, 그 출제경향을 완벽히 분석해 수강생들의 머리속에 넣어 주고 있다. 시험을 보고, 가르치는 과정에서 발견한 변하지 않는 토익의 흐름과 풀이법, 그리고 저자 만의 암기법 등을 이 책에 담았다. 이 책에 실린 내용은 저자가 오랜 기간에 걸쳐 도출해 낸 '토익 공식'이다!

실전 적응력을 길러주는 실전 8회분 테스트 수록!

모든 유형 학습이 끝났지만, 실전 적응력을 높이려면 실전테스트가 필요하다. 그래서 책의 뒷부분에 파트 5, 6 실전테스트를 3회분 제공하여 실전을 앞두고 실전 감각을 기를 수 있도록 했다. 또한 본문에 나오는 문제도 재구성하여 5회분 실전테스트를 추가로 제공한다. 실전을 앞두고 실전 감각을 높이며, 배운 내용을 다시 한번 확인할 수 있도록 총 8회분 실전테스트를 제공한다. 실전테스트 1회만 책에서 제공하고 실전테스트 2, 3회 문제와 해설, 추가 실전 테스트 5회분도 www.gilbut.co.kr에서 내려받을 수 있다.

진단 고사

법칙 49-6
101. Mr. Bean was ----- when he entered the classroom twenty minutes after the lecture had already begun.
 (A) embarrassed
 (B) embarrass
 (C) embarrassing
 (D) embarrasses

법칙 4-2
102. Speakers are requested to hand in ------ presentation materials at least 2 hours before their talk.
 (A) they
 (B) them
 (C) their
 (D) theirs

법칙 2-1
103. The ------ of the new restaurant in the Sebu area has helped it grow between some larger restaurants that have moved into the area.
 (A) popularity
 (B) popularizes
 (C) popular
 (D) popularly

법칙 46-4
104. As Mr. Hague's résumé was reviewed ----- his work experience was recognized, he was asked to come for a job interview at the Jennings Company.
 (A) but
 (B) yet
 (C) and
 (D) that

법칙 3-8
105. In the metropolitan area, smoking is ----- prohibited outdoors and only allowed in designated areas.
 (A) strictness
 (B) stricter
 (C) strictly
 (D) strict

법칙 29-8
106. In case you experience an equipment ----- with our product, please call us and explain the problem you have with it before you send it back for a refund or exchange.
 (A) malfunctioning
 (B) malfunction
 (C) malfunctioned
 (D) malfunctions

법칙 17-8
107. The store manager ordered that store clerks serve their customers ----- during the peak hours of the day.
 (A) attentions
 (B) attentive
 (C) more attentively
 (D) most attentive

법칙 19-1
108. The CAB Group, the London Baguette bakery company, increased the number of its chain stores in ------ region of the country.
 (A) all
 (B) every
 (C) second
 (D) several

법칙 81-8
109. At the annual job fair, many visitors who had a great amount of ----- in overseas employment signed up to get information about the requirements of the jobs.
 (A) authority
 (B) opportunity
 (C) effort
 (D) interest

법칙 71-6
110. The farewell party for Mr. Lim, who is retiring from Lean, Inc., will be ----- next Saturday at a restaurant near the company building.
 (A) held
 (B) expected
 (C) supported
 (D) maintained

111. We ----- check every computer in our company for viruses to avoid a failure in its system.
    (A) originally
    (B) recently
    (C) significantly
    (D) regularly

112. The well-known Deluxe Entertainment Group, now ----- its business overseas, was once a small company in Lithuania.
    (A) expanding
    (B) has been expanding
    (C) will be expanding
    (D) expands

113. We give a sincere apology to you, Ms. Adams, ----- the CEO of the HK Corporation, who is currently unavailable to take your call.
    (A) instead
    (B) on behalf of
    (C) due to
    (D) notwithstanding

114. If ------ completes the budget proposal by this Friday, the budget meeting will have to be rescheduled for next week.
    (A) few
    (B) some
    (C) each another
    (D) no one

115. You should get a ticket from one of the staff members who ----- free tickets to the event at the moment.
    (A) provide
    (B) is provided
    (C) providing
    (D) is providing

116. Your salary will ----- increase in proportion to the number of years you are employed at this company.
    (A) carefully
    (B) thoroughly
    (C) gradually
    (D) hardly

117. Whitfield Consulting, which is working closely with government officials, will be closed next Monday ----- a national holiday falls on the weekend.
    (A) until
    (B) in spite of
    (C) by
    (D) because

118. All passengers for Flight 307 should proceed to the departure gate 30 minutes ----- the departure time.
    (A) but
    (B) before
    (C) then
    (D) during

119. If there are any ----- items, that fact must be indicated on the boxes to notify the deliverymen of the need to take special care of them.
    (A) suspicious
    (B) fragile
    (C) innovative
    (D) thorough

120. The New York City Center offers both cooking classes and hands-on training to residents completely free of charge ------ the year.
    (A) between
    (B) near
    (C) toward
    (D) throughout

법칙 39-6
121. Analyzing customer feedback is strongly recommended as a means of ----- the service quality.
(A) improve
(B) improves
(C) improving
(D) improvement

법칙 74-10
122. The manager is responsible for training the new construction workers to ----- with the safety rules.
(A) comply
(B) refer
(C) oppose
(D) endorse

법칙 16-1
123. Due to unexpected technical problems, the launch of the new smartphone -----.
(A) has delayed
(B) are delaying
(C) has been delaying
(D) will be delayed

법칙 8-1
124. The government ----- will visit one of our facilities in China to conduct an audit next Thursday.
(A) inspecting
(B) inspector
(C) inspected
(D) inspection

법칙 90-6
125. Although the candidate put a considerable effort into delivering his speech, the audience remained ----- to his pledges, which they did not find convincing.
(A) unresponsive
(B) excited
(C) attentive
(D) obligatory

법칙 83-7
126. Mr. Dobb is undoubtedly a desirable candidate for the position in the international division as he possess the ----- to speak 4 languages fluently.
(A) tendency
(B) ability
(C) interest
(D) property

법칙 41-10
127. In an effort to increase the sales of its beauty products, the Everlast Cosmetics Shop offered discounts ----- 30% off the regular prices.
(A) just as
(B) quickly
(C) as much as
(D) alike

법칙 12-9
128. ----- displaying instant messages and playing music from a smartphone, the Smart Watch functions as a fashion accessory.
(A) Just as
(B) Now that
(C) Furthermore
(D) In addition to

법칙 84-9
129. Ms. O'Connell, a council coordinator, cancelled all of her appointments for this Thursday to attend the ----- held in honor of 50th anniversary of the Local Aboriginal Land Council.
(A) tuition
(B) ceremony
(C) mark
(D) venue

법칙 18-8
130. ----- there are no further changes in raw material prices, we will not increase the prices of any of our products.
(A) Assuming
(B) Except
(C) Nevertheless
(D) Otherwise

Questions 131-134 refer to the following notice.

Attention, All Employees:

We learned that some employees have not gotten their ------ employee ID cards yet.
                                                           131.
If you have not picked yours up yet but need to have it ------ next week, please visit the
                                                        132.
Human Resources office during business hours to pick it up. ------, all the remaining cards
                                                              133.
will be sent to each department next Wednesday, so you can get yours then.

Please also note that the reissuance of an ID card is provided for free upon first request only, and it will cost $10 the next time you request one. You will need to complete a brief request form before being reissued an ID card as well. ------.
                                                                                134.

131. (A) extra
(B) printed
(C) online
(D) reissued

132. (A) before
(B) during
(C) after
(D) while

133. (A) Consequently
(B) Therefore
(C) Otherwise
(D) In addition

134. (A) Again, the end of this week is the latest possible time to receive your ID card.
(B) We hope this will help you find your missing ID card.
(C) Therefore, it is always advisable that you be careful not to lose your ID card.
(D) Thank you for your cooperation in returning ID cards to their respective owners.

Questions 135-138 refer to the following notice.

We are sorry to inform our customers that the item Blooming Flower Cushion (item no. 67542) is currently ------. Even though we have doubled the production of the item, the cushions sell out rapidly.
135.

The delivery of orders placed before April 8 will be made starting tomorrow, but those placed after that date will be ------, and the customers will be given a full refund.
136.

To apologize for this, we will give discount coupons to customers who made ------ orders.
137.

------. If you wish to be informed when the item is restocked, please contact us at 883-3333.
138.
Again, we are sorry for the inconvenience that we caused you and thank you for your understanding in advance.

135. (A) available
(B) malfunctioning
(C) out of stock
(D) irreplaceable

136. (A) sent
(B) allowed
(C) forwarded
(D) canceled

137. (A) their
(B) any
(C) all
(D) those

138. (A) We're holding a huge clearance sale on household items.
(B) The orders placed will be delivered by the end of the week.
(C) They are valid for 10% off any purchase.
(D) Customers are requested to report any defective items.

Questions 139-142 refer to the following memo.

From: Chris Bentley, Production Supervisor

To: All Plant Employees

Date: September 24

Subject: Reminder about the Executive's Visit

As you already know, Mr. Cyrus, an executive at Carson Auto, will make his ------ visit to
139.
the manufacturing plant next Monday to boost our morale.

Accordingly, all employees are ------ to gather in the seminar room by 5 P.M. on Monday.
140.
------.
141.

After the executive's brief speech of ------, a banquet will be held in the cafeteria. Please
142.
also note that this year's visit has been delayed by 4 days, and the next visit is scheduled

for September 20 next year.

See you all in the seminar room next Monday.

---

139. (A) informal
(B) abrupt
(C) annual
(D) allowed

140. (A) advising
(B) advisory
(C) advised
(D) advisable

141. (A) The room can't accommodate all the participants.
(B) You are supposed to discuss the problems in the room.
(C) Those who are assigned the night shift are to participate as well.
(D) A lecture about self-development will be delivered.

142. (A) farewell
(B) encouragement
(C) apology
(D) gratitude

Questions 143-146 refer to the following article.

The City of Cherryville Announces the Grand Opening of Supreme Techno Plaza

March 15 ------ the grand opening of a new cultural space in Cherryville. A special ceremony was
      143.
held at 10 A.M. and was followed by the official plaza opening at 11 A.M. Over 1,000 guests,

mainly local residents, attended the ceremony. ------.
                                     144.

The ------ of Supreme Techno Plaza is the first step in the plan to develop the region into
   145.
a multicultural hub and is managed by the Department of Cultural Affairs (DCA).

"The city of Cherryville is thrilled to introduce its own cultural space to the citizens -----,"
                                                                                     146.
said the director of the DCA at the opening. "Supreme Techno Plaza will provide local residents

with plenty of opportunities to enjoy a rich and varied cultural life."

143. (A) will mark
(B) is marking
(C) marks
(D) marked

144. (A) In other words, the number of guests is 10 on average each day.
(B) Those guests are proud that this space is globally acknowledged.
(C) Many of these guests plan to enter the plaza right after the ceremony.
(D) Community leaders and officials also visited to share a few remarks.

145. (A) establish
(B) established
(C) establishing
(D) establisher

146. (A) at last
(B) though
(C) however
(D) yet

진단고사 정답 (해설은 각 문제 앞에 적힌 법칙 번호를 따라 해당 단원의 해설을 참고)										
101. (A)	102. (C)	103. (A)	104. (C)	105. (C)	106. (B)	107. (C)	108. (B)	109. (D)	110. (A)
111. (D)	112. (A)	113. (B)	114. (D)	115. (D)	116. (C)	117. (D)	118. (B)	119. (B)	120. (D)
121. (C)	122. (A)	123. (D)	124. (B)	125. (A)	126. (B)	127. (C)	128. (D)	129. (B)	130. (A)
131. (D)	132. (A)	133. (C)	134. (C)	135. (C)	136. (D)	137. (D)	138. (C)	139. (C)	140. (C)
141. (C)	142. (B)	143. (D)	144. (D)	145. (C)	146. (A)				

진단 고사에 따른 학습가이드

진단 고사를 15분 동안 시간을 정해 잘 풀어보았나요? 1분이라도 초과해서 풀었다면 이미 진단의 정확도는 떨어지게 되므로 15분을 기준으로 그 이후에 풀게 된 문제들은 모두 오답으로 간주한 후, 아래 진단 및 학습 방향을 참고하세요.

1. 오답 개수로 가늠해 보는 현재 예상 점수대와 그에 맞는 학습법

토익 Reading은 틀린 개수에 따라 점수 변화가 심하고, 그에 따라 학습법도 달라져야 합니다. 필자는 그 동안 많은 수험생들을 가르치면서 점수대에 맞는 학습법을 정리했습니다. 수험생마다 상황이 조금씩 달라 이 학습법이 완전히 옳다고 할 수는 없지만, 직접 수험생에게 검증해 보고 90% 이상 효과를 거둔 학습법이므로 참고하면 좋은 결과를 얻을 것입니다.

오답 개수	예상 점수	학습법
0~5개	800 이상	파트 5, 6 시간 단축 연습, 파트 7 문제 유형 및 지문 유형 연습, 장문 독해
6~7개	750~800	파트 5, 6 시간 단축 연습, 함정 문법, 어휘, 파트 6 위주의 장문 독해 연습
8~10개	700~750	함정 문법, 어휘, 파트 6 위주의 장문 독해 연습
11~15개	600~700	세부 적인 문법을 포함한 전반적인 문법 및 단문 독해 연습
16~20개	500~600	아래 내용 + 준동사, 전치사, 접속사 등의 상위 문법 및 단문 독해 연습
20~25개	400~500	품사 자리, 정동사 등의 기본 문법 및 필수 요소 독해 연습
26개 이상	400 미만	기본서와 병행하여 이해 위주의 학습

2. 틀린 문제의 유형으로 파악할 수 있는 자신의 취약한 부분과 해결 가능한 법칙
★ 찍어서 맞춘 문제는 틀린 것으로 간주합니다.

파트 5, 6에는 다양한 유형의 문제가 출제됩니다. 이 책에는 모든 유형의 문제가 실려 있어 분량이 방대해 보일 수 있습니다. 하지만 틀린 문제에 따른 자신의 취약한 부분과 이를 다룬 법칙을 따로 정리해 효율적으로 학습할 수 있게 했습니다.

문제 번호	문제 유형	취약한 부분 및 해결 가능한 법칙
102, 103, 105, 109, 107, 128	품사 자리	명사(법칙 2), 동사(법칙 38), 접속사(법칙 18), 전치사(법칙 12), 형용사(법칙 9, 10, 14), 부사(법칙 3, 7, 30, 31) 자리 및 대명사 격확인(법칙 4), 부사 기능의 재귀대명사(법칙 22)
112, 115, 123	정동사	정준 확인(법칙 28, 38), 단복 확인(법칙 25), 수능 확인(법칙 16), 시제 확인(법칙 32, 35, 51, 52, 53, 61, 66)
101, 121	준동사	동명사(법칙 39, 59, 63), to부정사(법칙 43, 48, 50, 57, 58, 64, 70), 분사(법칙 21, 23, 33, 37, 49, 60, 61)
104, 117	연결어	등위 접속사(법칙 34, 46), 상관접속사(법칙 13), 명사절 접속사(법칙 40, 67), 형용사절 접속사(법칙 36, 42, 54, 68), 부사절 접속사(법칙 1), 복합관계사(법칙 56)
106, 124, 127	품사 상위	가산/불가산(법칙 20, 44), 의미 구분 명사(법칙 8), 복합명사(법칙 29), 비교급(법칙 17), 시간 관련 형용사/부사(법칙 5, 55), 숫자 수식 부사(법칙 41), 비교 최상급 수식 부사(법칙 45)
108, 114	대명사	부정대명사, 부정형용사(법칙 19), 지시대명사, 형용사(법칙 62), 재귀대명사(법칙 22), 소유대명사(법칙 65)
110, 122	동사 어휘	문장의 5형식(법칙 71 ~ 80)
109, 126, 129	명사 어휘	동사와의 어울림, 전치사와의 어울림 등(법칙 81 ~ 85)
119, 125	형용사 어휘	명사와의 어울림, 전치사와의 어울림 등(법칙 86 ~ 90)
111, 116	부사 어휘	동사와의 어울림, 형용사와의 어울림 등(법칙 91 ~ 95)
113, 118, 120	전치사 어휘	빈칸 앞뒤만 보고 푸는 전치사(법칙 6, 11, 27) 전체 문맥을 보고 푸는 전치사(법칙 15, 24, 26) 기타 전치사(47, 69)
143	파트 6, 시제	주변 문맥을 보고 푸는 시제 문제(법칙 97)
133	파트 6, 연결어	주변 문맥을 보고 푸는 연결어 문제(법칙 98)
137	파트 6, 대명사	주변 문맥을 보고 푸는 대명사 문제(법칙 99)
131, 135, 136, 139, 142	파트 6, 어휘	주변 문맥을 보고 푸는 어휘 문제(법칙 100)
134, 138, 141, 144	파트 6, 신유형	문맥에 맞는 문장을 고르는 신유형 문제(법칙 96)
132, 140, 145, 146	파트 6, 기타	파트 5처럼 푸는 문제들(법칙 1 ~ 95)

첫째 마당

어형 및 문법 편

Chapter 01

매월 출제되는 문제

출제 1순위

이번 토익 시험에 반드시 나온다.

출제율 196%

법칙 1 부사절 접속사는 양보, 이유, 시간, 조건 순

주절의 앞이나 뒤에서 문장 전체를 수식해 주는 것을 부사절이라고 한다. "Although he is bad, I like him."에서 although he is bad는 부사절이고, although는 부사절 접속사이다. 부사절 접속사의 종류에는 양보(although, though, even though), 이유(because, since), 시간(when, before, after, while), 조건(if, once) 목적, 결과(so that, in order that) 등이 있다.

STEP 1 유형을 파악해 봐

1. ------- Mr. Kim moved to the downtown office, he is unable to meet his former colleagues as often as he used to.
(A) How   (B) But   (C) Before   (D) Because

2. ------- marketing expenditures bring immediate returns, research and development spending is usually a long-term investment.
(A) Toward   (B) Until   (C) While   (D) However

3. Mr. Kim's secretary asked him if the itinerary is to his satisfaction ------- she can reserve the flights.
(A) whether   (B) while   (C) so that   (D) due to

문제들의 공통점을 찾아보면 1번과 2번 문제는 '------- S+V, S+V' 형태의 문장이고, 3번 문제는 'S+V ------- S+V' 형태의 문장이다. 완전한 문장에 '------- S+V'가 앞과 뒤에 붙어 있으므로 부사절 관련 문제들임을 알 수 있다. 보기를 살펴보면 1번 문제의 (C), (D), 2번 문제의 (B), (C), 3번 문제의 (A), (B), (C)가 부사절 접속사이며, 최소 2개 이상이 부사절 접속사임을 알 수 있다. '유형을 파악해 봐'의 자세한 해설은 '정답 및 해설'을 참조하세요.

STEP 2 이렇게 풀어 봐

"유형을 파악해 봐" 1번 문제를 보세요!

첫째 보기에서 부사절 접속사가 아닌 것들을 제외한다.
명사절 접속사인 (A) How와 등위접속사인 (B) But은 우선 소거한다.

둘째 양보, 이유, 시간, 조건 순으로 대입해 해석한다.
양보의 부사절 접속사(although, though, even though, even if 등)가 보기에 없으므로 이유의 부사절 접속사

(because, since, now that 등)를 대입하면, 'Mr. Kim이 시내 사무실로 옮겼기 때문에, 그는 예전만큼 자주 이전 동료들을 만날 수가 없다.'라는 자연스런 문장이 되므로 (D) Because가 정답이 된다.

PLUS

부사절이 현재시제, 주절이 미래시제인 경우에는 양보나 이유보다는 시간, 조건의 부사절 접속사를 먼저 대입하는 것이 좋다.

> 시간의 부사절 접속사: when, as soon as, before, after, while, until 등
> 조건의 부사절 접속사: if, once, provided that, providing that 등

부사절 안에 can, may, will, would, could가 있으면 대부분 so that이나 in order that이 정답이 되며, 주절에 not이 있으면 until이 주로 정답으로 제시된다.

함정을 피해 봐 — 실제 강의에서만 알려주는 풀이 노하우!

1. 여러 가지 뜻의 접속사로 쓰이는 단어에 유의한다.

while	~동안에 – 시간의 부사절 접속사	반면에 – 양보의 부사절 접속사
since	~이래로 – 시간의 부사절 접속사	~때문에 – 이유의 부사절 접속사
as	~함에 따라서, ~할 때 – 시간의 부사절 접속사	~하기 때문에 – 이유의 부사절 접속사

2. 접속사처럼 보이지 않는 단어들을 조심한다.

the moment ~할 때   at the time ~할 때   provided ~라면   providing ~라면   assuming ~를 가정하면

3. 부사절 접속사와 부사를 구별한다.

	부사절 접속사	부사
양보	although though even though even if whereas while	however nevertheless(= nonetheless) even so despite that on the other hand on the contrary
이유	because since now that as seeing that	accordingly therefore consequently thus as a result
시간	when by the time after as soon as before while until as	meanwhile in the meantime at the same time
조건	if providing (that) once as long as unless in case (that) in the event (that) given that on condition (that) considering (that)	otherwise if so if not in that case then
목적, 결과/기타	so that in order that so 형/부 that S V	furthermore moreover in addition besides as always likewise

단, however는 뒤에 형용사나 부사가 바로 올 경우 부사절 접속사의 역할도 한다.
(However/Seldom) uncomfortable it is, protective gear should be worn in the factory.

3. However

STEP 3 실전에 적용해 봐

1. Best Buy shoppers can get free shipping ------- they purchase more than 5 items or the total amount they purchase exceeds $300.
   (A) than
   (B) that
   (C) just
   (D) if

2. Registration for the workshop will not be completed ------- all of the required documents are received.
   (A) until
   (B) just
   (C) only
   (D) what

3. Several projects for which Nobel Laboratories has received funding are scheduled to begin next month ------- a sufficient amount of space is available.
   (A) as if
   (B) provided that
   (C) in reality
   (D) other than

4. ------- the board of directors has addressed the need for an aggressive advertising campaign, nothing has been done to improve the situation.
   (A) Because of
   (B) Whether
   (C) As always
   (D) Although

5. Hotel guests are advised to keep their valuables secure in the safe ------- they leave their rooms.
   (A) whenever
   (B) whomever
   (C) whatever
   (D) whichever

6. Whitfield Consulting, which is working closely with government officials, will be closed next Monday ------- a national holiday falls on the weekend.
   (A) until
   (B) in spite of
   (C) by
   (D) because

7. To ensure customer satisfaction, make sure you know how this new system works ------- you can clearly answer any customer's questions.
   (A) whereas
   (B) so that
   (C) as if
   (D) neither

8. Dr. Jacky Mason will have worked as a physician for the World Health Organization for 20 years ------- she retires.
   (A) by the time
   (B) in order for
   (C) as much as
   (D) now that

9. New recruits should contact the personnel manager immediately ------- they cannot attend the orientation program designed for them.
   (A) why
   (B) due to
   (C) if
   (D) regarding

10. ------- he hired an assistant to help him, Mr. Lee still handles all client-related issues himself.
    (A) So that
    (B) Even though
    (C) When
    (D) Until

출제율 169%

법칙 2 '관소전타' 뒤는 명사

'관소전타'는 관사, 소유격, 전치사, 타동사를 줄인 말이다.
- 관사: 명사 앞에 붙는 the와 a를 말한다
- 소유격: my, your, his, her 등을 말한다.
- 전치사: in the room, on the table에서 in, on 등을 말한다.
- 타동사: like(~를 좋아하다)처럼 목적어를 가지는 동사를 말한다.

STEP 1 유형을 파악해 봐

1. Farmers in the Rayburn Valley region have started growing a wider variety of organic vegetables in ------- to consumer demand.
(A) responded   (B) responsible   (C) response   (D) respond

2. Deadlines listed in this contract are subject to change at the ------- of the project manager.
(A) discreetly   (B) discreet   (C) discretion   (D) discretionary

3. Contact the attending physician to obtain ------- for any prescription refill requests.
(A) approved   (B) approves   (C) approve   (D) approval

보기를 살펴보면 세 문제의 보기가 모두 같은 단어의 변형 형태로 왔다. 이럴 경우 문제의 빈칸 위치를 파악해 보는 것이 좋다. 1번 문제는 빈칸 앞이 전치사, 2번 문제는 관사, 3번 문제는 타동사가 왔으며, 빈칸 뒷부분은 모두 전명구(전치사와 명사의 구)가 위치해 있다.

STEP 2 이렇게 풀어 봐
"유형을 파악해 봐" 1번 문제를 보세요!

첫째 빈칸 앞에 '관소전타'가 있는지 확인한다.
빈칸 앞에 위치한 in은 전치사임을 알 수 있다.

둘째 보기 중 명사를 답으로 고른다.
(A) responded와 (B) responsible은 형용사, (C) response는 명사, (D) respond는 동사이므로 답은 (C)가 된다.

함정을 피해 봐

실제 강의에서만 알려주는 풀이 노하우!

1. 명사라고 생각하지 못했던 단어들을 조심한다.

change 변경, 잔돈	charge 요금	contact 연락	graduate 졸업생
leave 휴가	pay 급료	permit 허가증	produce 농산물
raise 인상	request 요청	review 검토, 평론	alternative 대안
individual 개인	objective 목적	original 원본	potential 잠재력
representative 직원, 대표자	initiative 솔선 운동, 새로운 계획		

2. 형용사의 최상급에서는 명사를 생략한 경우가 많다.

Mr. Gu is considered the most (qualified/qualification) of the 10,000 candidates.

➜ qualified 다음에는 candidate가 생략되었다. 따라서 명사인 qualification(자격 요건)을 고르면 오답이 되고, 해석도 맞지 않게 된다.

3. 복합명사(2개의 명사가 덩어리로 묶여있는 형태)에서는 항상 뒤쪽 명사가 기준이 된다.

GWF Bank has four branch (located/locations) in Japan.

➜ four와 branch만 언뜻 보고 형용사를 고르면 오답이다. Four(4개의) 뒤에는 복수 명사가 와야 하므로 branch locations(지점들)라는 복합명사가 정답이 된다.

4. 빈칸 앞 '관소전타'만 보고 명사를 고르지 않도록 한다.

With the (flexibility/flexible) pricing policy being applied, passengers have the opportunities to buy tickets at reasonable prices.

➜ 앞에 있는 관사만 보고 바로 명사를 고르면 안 되며, 괄호 뒤에 pricing policy(가격 정책)라는 명사가 있으므로 형용사를 답으로 골라야 한다.

2. qualified 3. locations 4. flexible

STEP 3 실전에 적용해 봐

1. The ------- of the new restaurant in the Sebu area has helped it grow between some larger restaurants that have moved into the area.

   (A) popularity
   (B) popularizes
   (C) popular
   (D) popularly

2. Mr. Williams earned a ------- from the award committee for his work in improving employee benefits.

   (A) commendably
   (B) commendation
   (C) commendable
   (D) commend

3. In order to make a better impression on your potential employer, specify your work-related ------- such as professional certifications, publications, awards, and military service.

   (A) accomplishes
   (B) accomplished
   (C) accomplishing
   (D) accomplishments

4. The personnel director at Whitehouse Electric stressed hard work and ------- as the most vital qualities for a successful candidate.

   (A) dedication
   (B) dedicate
   (C) dedicated
   (D) dedicatedly

5. The readership of *East and West*, a cooking magazine with an impressive international -------, has improved this year.

   (A) circulation
   (B) circulate
   (C) circulatory
   (D) calculatedly

6. The GW Language Institute is dedicated to helping college students find ------- in their academic goals.

   (A) success
   (B) successfully
   (C) successful
   (D) succeed

7. Before receiving ------- to use Wigerly Hall, you should ask the event coordinator to confirm its availability.

   (A) authoritative
   (B) authorized
   (C) authorize
   (D) authorization

8. Representatives from the STV Group's five subsidiaries will meet one another to discuss plans to increase ------- between separate subsidiaries.

   (A) cooperation
   (B) cooperative
   (C) cooperate
   (D) cooperated

9. The city council's Web site is currently unable to be accessed due to the ------- errors.

   (A) temporarily
   (B) temporary
   (C) temporality
   (D) temporalize

10. ------- for the company's meeting room must be made 24 hours prior to the start of the meeting.

    (A) Reserved
    (B) Reservations
    (C) Reserve
    (D) Reservable

출제율 **147%**

법칙 3 주어와 동사, 조동사와 동사원형, have와 p.p., 어구 사이는 부사

1. 부사의 역할
- 동사 수식: speak loudly 시끄럽게 말하다
- 형용사 수식: really happy 매우 행복한
- 다른 부사 수식: really loudly 매우 시끄럽게
- 문장 전체 수식: Happily, he didn't die. 다행스럽게도, 그는 죽지 않았다.

2. 부사의 특징
부사는 생략해도 문장에 영향을 미치지 않으며, 필수 요소(주어, 동사, 목적어, 보어)의 앞과 뒤, 또는 사이에 위치한다. 단, 동사와 목적어 사이에는 올 수 없다.

STEP 1 유형을 파악해 봐

1. The board of directors must ------- review and assess the company's progress in carrying out long-term plans.
   (A) regular   (B) regularly   (C) regularity   (D) regulate

2. After noticing a serious error in the next year's business plan, the CEO ------- called a meeting of all those concerned.
   (A) prompt   (B) promptness   (C) prompts   (D) promptly

3. Our heaters have ------- proven to be 25% more efficient than heaters manufactured by our competitors.
   (A) consistently (B) consistency   (C) consistent   (D) consist

보기를 살펴보면 같은 단어의 변형 형태들이 왔으므로 빈칸의 앞과 뒤를 먼저 살핀다. 1번 문제는 조동사와 동사원형 사이에, 2번 문제는 주어와 동사 사이에, 3번 문제는 have와 p.p. 사이에 빈칸이 위치해 있다. 세 문제 모두 빈칸 부분이 없어도 문장을 구성하는데 지장이 없음을 알 수 있다.

STEP 2 이렇게 풀어 봐

"유형을 파악해 봐" 1번 문제를 보세요!

첫째 빈칸의 위치를 먼저 확인한다.
빈칸의 위치가 주어와 동사, 조동사와 동사원형, have와 p.p., be와 -ng/p.p., to와 동사원형, 전치사와 동명사, 덩어리동사(agree with와 같은 형태)의 사이에 있는지를 확인한다. must는 조동사, review는 동사원형이므로 빈칸은 부사가 와야 하는 자리임을 알 수 있다.

둘째 보기 중 부사를 답으로 선택한다.
(A) regular는 형용사, (B) regularly는 부사, (C) regularity는 명사, (D) regulate는 동사이므로 (B)를 답으로 선택한다.

함정을 피해 봐
실제 강의에서만 알려주는 풀이 노하우!

1. 주어와 동사 사이의 부사 자리를 파악할 때, 동사를 명사로 착각하지 않도록 한다.

The amended policy on employee benefits (effectively/effective) addresses concerns regarding health insurance and pensions.

→ addresses를 명사로 착각해 형용사 effective를 선택하면 오답이다. addresses는 동사이며, 이 동사를 수식하는 부사 effectively가 정답이 된다.

2. 명령문, 제안문의 앞은 주어 자리가 아니고 부사 자리이다. (주어 You 생략)

(Simplicity/Simply) fill out this form.

3. -ly 형태에 속지 않도록 한다.

-ly 형태지만 부사가 아닌 단어들

| assembly 집회, 모임 | friendly 친근한 | lovely 사랑스러운 |
| likely 있을 법한 | timely 시기 적절한 | |

-ly 형태가 아니지만 부사인 단어들

| always | often | sometimes | still | yet | already | soon | best | better |
| fast | once 등 | | | | | | | |

1. effectively 2. Simply

STEP 3 실전에 적용해 봐

1. Please reply ------- to the invitation for the 10th anniversary party at Anderson Industries.

   (A) prompt
   (B) promptness
   (C) promptly
   (D) prompted

2. Applicants should ------- mark the position title they are applying for on the envelope.

   (A) clear
   (B) clearly
   (C) cleared
   (D) clears

3. Those who are interested in the position are advised to ------- check the company's Web site for details and updates.

   (A) regular
   (B) regularly
   (C) regulars
   (D) regulated

4. Should you have any questions regarding gardening, ------- call the company's hotline at 555-6072.

   (A) simple
   (B) simplify
   (C) simpler
   (D) simply

5. Ms. Kwon thanked the company's customer service representative for ------- responding to her complaints.

   (A) quick
   (B) quickly
   (C) quickness
   (D) quicker

6. Over the last decade, Delta, Inc. has ------- changed its business model to diversify from just selling PCs.

   (A) significantly
   (B) significant
   (C) significance
   (D) signify

7. Environmentalists claim that the use of fossil fuel is most ------- the main cause of global warming, which is likely to induce substantial costs on the global economy.

   (A) like
   (B) likely
   (C) likeness
   (D) liking

8. In the metropolitan area, smoking is ------- prohibited outdoors and only allowed in designated areas.

   (A) strictness
   (B) stricter
   (C) strictly
   (D) strict

9. Employees at the SJ Company are ------- in favor of reducing working hours on weekdays even if they have to work on Saturdays.

   (A) overwhelms
   (B) overwhelmed
   (C) overwhelming
   (D) overwhelmingly

10. Libratone, Inc. is ------- appreciative of the strong support from the local community and aims to provide more job opportunities for the residents.

    (A) true
    (B) truly
    (C) truth
    (D) trueness

출제율 130%

법칙 4 명사 앞 소유격, 동사/전치사 뒤 목적격, 동사 앞 주격

대명사는 명사를 대신해 사용하는 품사를 말하며, I나 you가 아닌 경우 보통 대명사가 가리키는 말이 문장 내에 위치한다. 사람을 가리키는 인칭대명사에는 다음과 같은 것들이 있다.

- 주격대명사: I, you, he, she, we, they, it
  '~는'으로 해석하며, 주어나 보어 자리에 위치한다.
- 목적격대명사: me, you, him, her, us, them, it
  '~를'로 해석하며, 목적어나 보어 자리에 위치한다.
- 소유격대명사: my, your, his, her, our, their, its
  '~의'로 해석한다.

STEP 1 유형을 파악해 봐

1. Visitors to the Central Art Museum are advised to periodically check ------- belongings during the tour.
(A) they   (B) their   (C) them   (D) themselves

2. The company's automated systems became more efficient as ------- began using the latest technology.
(A) themselves (B) them   (C) their   (D) they

3. Please let ------- know as soon as you arrive at the airport so that we can pick you up on time.
(A) we   (B) our   (C) us   (D) ourselves

보기를 살펴보면 세 문제 모두 격만 다를 뿐 모두 인칭대명사들이 왔으며, 문장 내용을 파악해 알맞은 격의 형태를 찾는 문제들이다.

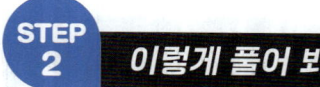

이렇게 풀어 봐

"유형을 파악해 봐" 1번 문제를 보세요!

첫째 빈칸의 위치를 확인한다.
빈칸이 명사 앞이면 소유격, 동사 앞이면 주격, 타동사나 전치사 뒤면 목적격 자리이다. 빈칸 뒤에 belongings(소지품들)이라는 명사가 있으므로 빈칸은 소유격대명사가 와야 한다.

둘째 보기들을 대입해 확인한다.
(A) they는 주격, (B) their는 소유격, (C) them은 목적격, (D) themselves는 재귀대명사로 목적격 또는 부사로 쓰인다. 따라서 정답은 소유격인 (B)가 된다.

 **함정을 피해 봐** 실제 강의에서만 알려주는 풀이 노하우!

1. 빈칸 앞과 뒤 단어의 품사를 혼동하지 않도록 주의한다.
Mr. Kim says (his/he) plans to be one of the best managers at the company.
→ says는 동사, plans는 명사라고 생각해 소유격을 정답으로 고르면 안 된다. says 뒤에는 that이 생략되었다고 볼 수 있으므로 plans는 동사가 된다. 따라서 빈칸에는 주격인 he가 와야 한다.

2. 빈칸 앞 동사의 주체와 대상이 목적어와 같은 경우, 목적격 자리에는 재귀대명사가 온다.
The manager asked his assistant to conduct (him/himself) in a hospitable manner.
→ 'conduct(행동하다)'가 동사이므로 뒤는 목적어 자리이다. conduct의 주체와 대상이 모두 his assistant이므로 재귀대명사인 himself가 정답이다.

3. 목적격 관계사가 생략된 문장에서는 격 확인에 주의한다. 고득점용
Mr. Gu must first get approval from his manager for any leave (he/his) requests.
→ request는 명사뿐 아니라 동사로도 쓰인다. 앞 부분의 get만 보고 request를 명사로 판단해 소유격을 선택하면 오답이다. 빈칸 앞 any leave는 '휴가'라는 명사이므로 뒤에 requests가 명사일 경우에는 충돌이 발생한다. 따라서 requests는 동사이며, any leave와 he 사이에는 목적격관계대명사 which가 생략된 것으로 봐야 한다.

1. he   2. himself   3. he

STEP 3 실전에 적용해 봐

1. If you do not want to receive direct mail or phone calls from us, you may send ------- request to the postal address above.
   (A) you
   (B) your
   (C) yourself
   (D) yours

2. Speakers are requested to hand in ------- presentation materials at least 2 hours before their talk.
   (A) they
   (B) them
   (C) their
   (D) theirs

3. Mr. Andoranti will lead the seminar, so any questions and requests should be directed to -------.
   (A) he
   (B) his
   (C) himself
   (D) him

4. The manager informed me that he has sent a complimentary booklet regarding the information ------- requested.
   (A) me
   (B) my
   (C) mine
   (D) I

5. The Shin Hwa Company requests that its staff be responsible for ------- development.
   (A) they
   (B) them
   (C) themselves
   (D) their own

6. Mr. Gu asked his two assistants to help ------- set up the projectors in the meeting rooms.
   (A) he
   (B) his
   (C) him
   (D) himself

7. It is strongly suggested that employees keep records of the hours ------- work and what they have been paid.
   (A) they
   (B) those
   (C) them
   (D) their

8. After ------- review additional surveillance tapes, the police officers are hoping to get a better description of the suspect.
   (A) their
   (B) theirs
   (C) they
   (D) them

9. Brenda said having the opportunity to work at overseas branches made ------- interested in the position.
   (A) she
   (B) her
   (C) hers
   (D) herself

10. The membership card will allow ------- to take advantage of all of the benefits the company offers.
    (A) we
    (B) our
    (C) ours
    (D) us

정답 및 해설은 006페이지에

Chapter 01 _ 매월 출제되는 문제 33

출제율 118%

법칙 5 시제 부사가 보기에 있으면 동사를 확인

동사를 수식하는 부사는 특정 시제와 어울리는 경우가 있는데, 예를 들면

I will visit your office **shortly**. (O)
내가 곧 너의 사무실을 방문할게.

I will visit your office **previously**. (X)
내가 전에 너의 사무실을 방문할게.

이렇게 동사의 시제를 보고 부사를 결정하거나 부사를 보고 시제를 결정할 수 있는 경우가 있다.

유형을 파악해 봐

1. Previously deleted files are ------- stored in the following locations on the computer hard disk.
   (A) usually   (B) relatively   (C) slightly   (D) vaguely

2. The weather conditions are not very favorable today, but they will improve -------.
   (A) openly   (B) nearly   (C) urgently   (D) shortly

3. We are about to investigate a complaint one of our customers has ------- filed against you.
   (A) noticeably   (B) friendly   (C) recently   (D) exactly

보기들이 모두 부사 형태로 왔으며, 3문제 모두 보기 중 1개는 시제 부사이다. 1번에서는 usually, 2번에서는 shortly, 3번에서는 recently가 시제 부사이다.

이렇게 풀어 봐   "유형을 파악해 봐" 1번 문제를 보세요!

첫째 대부분의 보기가 부사 형태라면, 시제 부사가 있는지 확인한다.
usually는 빈도부사이므로 시제 부사에 해당한다.

둘째 동사의 시제에 어울리는 부사를 찾는다.

현재시제	빈도부사와 주로 어울린다.
	regularly, frequently, always, usually, often, typically, routinely, periodically, occasionally, normally, customarily, every month, each month, these days

미래시제	soon, shortly
과거시제	previously, once, recently
현재완료	just 막, since 그 후에, recently, yet (→ 부정문일 때만)
현재진행	currently, presently

문장의 시제가 현재이므로 빈도부사인 (A) usually가 정답이 된다.

함정을 피해 봐 — 실제 강의에서만 알려주는 풀이 노하우!

1. will이 없어도 미래시제 부사와 어울리는 경우에 유의한다.

미래시제 부사와 어울리는 동사들

can, may, need, should, must, be expected to, be scheduled to, be supposed to, be about to, be going to 등

2. 시제 부사가 예외적으로 다른 시제으로 사용되는 경우에 유의한다.

During the last month, all line workers at the Denver facility (formerly/often) worked overtime to fill the order.

→ 과거시제만 보고 formerly를 바로 답으로 하면 안 된다. 앞에 이미 during the last month가 있으므로 formerly를 쓰는 것은 어색하다. often은 주로 현재시제와 쓰지만, 과거에 반복, 습관적으로 일어난 일을 묘사할 때도 사용할 수 있다.

	일반적인 경우	예외적인 경우
soon, shortly	미래시제	soon after, shortly after는 주로 과거시제에 사용됨
currently, presently	현재진행시제	현재시제: He currently has 5 employees. Currently, there are 5 employees.
always	현재	현재완료
already	현재완료	현재
once	과거, 현재완료	once again, once a week, once a year 등은 모든 시제와 사용 가능

3. recently는 과거 또는 현재완료시제와 사용되지만 구체적인 기간을 나타내는 문장과 어울려 쓰지는 않는다.

The prices of raw materials have (clearly/recently) risen in the last 5 years.

→ 현재완료시제만 보고 recently를 답으로 선택해서는 안 된다. '지난 5년간에'라는 구체적인 기간이 포함되어 있으므로 recently는 어울리지 않는다.

2. often   3. clearly

STEP 3 실전에 적용해 봐

1. The renowned journalist Glenn Greenwald will ------- publish his biography after 5 years of experience working for New York Daily News.

   (A) what
   (B) soon
   (C) ever
   (D) quite

2. The personnel manager has ------- to receive enough applications to proceed with job interviews even though he posted job openings several weeks ago.

   (A) several
   (B) if
   (C) yet
   (D) already

3. Employees who haven't ------- returned their performance evaluation forms to the Personnel Department should do that by June 3.

   (A) yet
   (B) then
   (C) still
   (D) shortly

4. The effort that Dr. Takayashi put in his research project ------- won him a research grant.

   (A) finally
   (B) frequently
   (C) especially
   (D) preferably

5. The endangered historic house has ------- reopened to the public after eight years of extensive repairs and restoration.

   (A) closely
   (B) finally
   (C) soon
   (D) quarterly

6. Most of our employees are avid supporters of the local art community and ------- volunteer their time.

   (A) frequently
   (B) since
   (C) previously
   (D) hardly

7. In compliance with company regulations, all factory workers must ------- wear protective gear beyond the facility's main gate.

   (A) always
   (B) nearly
   (C) highly
   (D) almost

8. Representatives from Jeil Advertising ------- met with a potential client about some marketing strategies for the company's new health beverage series.

   (A) recently
   (B) yet
   (C) soon
   (D) shortly

9. Mr. Kim has to turn down the job offer from GW International because he has ------- accepted another job offer from a rival company.

   (A) already
   (B) nearly
   (C) more
   (D) very

10. We at Hwawei, Inc. are ------- seeking highly qualified professionals who have more than five years of experience working in managerial positions.

    (A) considerably
    (B) currently
    (C) previously
    (D) simply

출제율 **109%**

법칙 6 빈칸 앞뒤 단어만 봐도 풀리는 시점과 기간 전치사

전치사는 명사 앞에 와서 시간, 장소, 방향, 위치, 목적을 나타낸다. 그 중 시각, 날짜, 요일 등 특정 시점을 나타내는 시점 전치사(at 3 o'clock, on Monday 등)와 일정 기간을 나타내는 기간 전치사(within a week, throughout the week 등)는 빈칸 앞뒤 단어를 파악하면 어렵지 않게 문제를 풀 수 있다.

STEP 1 유형을 파악해 봐

1. Employees are advised to submit their receipts for reimbursement ------- a week of returning from a business trip.
(A) under　　(B) within　　(C) directly　　(D) onto

2. The breathtaking ocean cruise will be offered every Sunday ------- October only when weather conditions are favorable.
(A) with　　(B) along　　(C) while　　(D) until

3. A complimentary breakfast available for all guests is served ------- 8:30 A.M. in our dining room.
(A) in　　(B) on　　(C) at　　(D) to

각 문제들의 보기에는 전치사가 2개 이상 포함되어 있다. 문제를 살펴보면 1번 문제는 빈칸 뒤에 a week가, 2번 문제는 October가, 3번 문제는 8:30라는 시점이나 기간 명사가 위치해 있다. 따라서 시점 및 기간 전치사를 고르는 문제임을 알 수 있다.

STEP 2 이렇게 풀어 봐

"유형을 파악해 봐" 1번 문제를 보세요!

첫째 빈칸 뒤가 시점 명사인지 기간 명사인지를 확인한다.
빈칸 뒤에 a week(일주일)가 왔으므로 기간 명사이다.

시점 명사	시각(3:30), 날짜(6월 3일), 요일, ago(3 days ago), last week, last month, last year와 년도 등
기간 명사	시간(hours), 날(days), 달(months) 등

'~의 말'을 뜻하는 end는 주로 시점으로 사용된다. (at the end of the year)

둘째 시점, 기간과 어울리는 전치사를 고른 후, 동사와 어울리는지를 확인한다.

기간에 어울리는 (B) within을 고른 후, 동사인 submit와 어울리는지 확인한다. '일주일 이내에 제출하다'로 잘 어울리므로 정답이 될 수 있다.

시점과 어울리는 전치사	at + 정확한 시각 on + 날짜, 요일 in + 달, 계절, 연도, 세기 since + 과거시점 before + 시점 1회성 동작 + by 지속적 동작 + until from + 출발 시점 등
기간과 어울리는 전치사	during + 기간 명사 within + 숫자 기간 for + 숫자 기간 throughout + 기간 명사 over + 숫자 기간, 기간 명사 등

PLUS

- after는 시점과 기간 모두 사용된다.
- in이 기간과 함께 사용되면 '~후에'라는 뜻을 갖는다. (in two days)
- in이 현재완료시제와 사용되면 '~의 기간 동안에'라는 뜻이 된다.
- from의 동의어로는 as of, starting, beginning, effective (from) 등이 있다.

함정을 피해 봐

실제 강의에서만 알려주는 풀이 노하우!

1. over는 기간 앞에 오는 전치사뿐 아니라 숫자 수식 부사의 기능을 포함한다.

GWF has been serving customers for (over/within) ten years now.
→ 이미 전치사 for가 있으므로 within은 올 수 없다. over는 여기서 숫자 ten을 수식하는 부사로 사용되었다.

2. before와 after는 접속사로도 쓰인다.

Employee benefits should be taken into consideration (before/prior to) employees' duties are discussed.
→ before와 after은 접속사와 전치사로 동시에 쓰이지만, 각각의 동의어인 prior to와 following은 전치사로만 쓰인다.

3. by는 1회성, until은 지속적인 상태를 나타낸다.

- by와 어울리는 동사: submit, return, inform, finish 등
- until과 어울리는 동사: stay, last, wait, remain, postpone 등

4. since는 현재완료시제와 쓰일 때만 '~이래로'라는 뜻이 된다.

(Since/Although) she dedicated her entire life to the company, Ms. Lee deserves the award.
→ since는 '~때문에'라는 뜻의 접속사로 사용되기도 한다. since가 '~이래로'의 뜻을 갖는 경우는 주절에 현재완료시제(have + p.p.)가 등장하며, since 뒤에는 과거시점이나 동사의 과거형이 온다.

1. over 2. before 4. Since

STEP 3 실전에 적용해 봐

1. We will have a short break ------- the first part of the presentation.
   (A) above
   (B) except
   (C) among
   (D) after

2. ------- the staff meeting, Ms. Choi will address some issues regarding the recent customer complaints.
   (A) Within
   (B) Below
   (C) During
   (D) Between

3. As soon as we receive a receipt, a refund will be issued ------- five business days according to our return policy.
   (A) now that
   (B) in front of
   (C) around
   (D) within

4. If the marketing director fails to submit the marketing data ------- the specified date, the budget committee will have to postpone the meeting.
   (A) in
   (B) from
   (C) between
   (D) by

5. All passengers for Flight 307 should proceed to the departure gate 30 minutes ------- the departure time.
   (A) but
   (B) before
   (C) then
   (D) during

6. The opening ceremony of the museum's art wing will not start ------- the arrival of keynote speaker Mr. Washington.
   (A) when
   (B) until
   (C) since
   (D) under

7. The New York City Center offers both cooking classes and hands-on training to residents completely free of charge ------- the year
   (A) between
   (B) near
   (C) toward
   (D) throughout

8. Due to the renovation work on the underground parking area, employees are advised to park their cars outside the building ------- the next two weeks.
   (A) as
   (B) greatly
   (C) for
   (D) when

9. Overall sales at Bright Digital Ltd. have increased significantly ------- last April, which is a result of its aggressive advertising campaign.
   (A) along
   (B) onto
   (C) in addition to
   (D) since

10. In preparation for the peak season, you should reserve your flight tickets several weeks ------- time.
    (A) ahead of
    (B) on top of
    (C) far from
    (D) apart from

출제율 108%

법칙 7 완전한 문장 다음에는 부사

필수어가 모두 있으면 완전한 문장이다.

- 1형식: 주어+동사 (I go.)
- 2형식: 주어+동사+보어 (I am happy.)
- 3형식: 주어+동사+목적어 (I love you.)
- 4형식: 주어+동사+간접목적어+직접목적어 (I gave you a pen.)
- 5형식: 주어+동사+목적어+목적보어 (I made him happy.)

필수어를 모두 포함하고 있다면 수식어들이 더 붙어도 여전히 완전한 문장이 된다.
* 부사가 기억나지 않으면 '법칙 3'으로!

STEP 1 유형을 파악해 봐

1. Any inquiries about the new time-reporting system should be directed to tech support -------.
(A) prompt   (B) promptness   (C) prompts   (D) promptly

2. Various departments work ------- to reduce energy expenses and to stay within the tight budget this month.
(A) collaboration   (B) collaborates   (C) collaboratively   (D) collaborated

3. The awards committee rewarded Mr. Kim for figuring out a way to cut the company's operating costs -------.
(A) effect   (B) effectively   (C) effectiveness   (D) effected

보기를 살펴보면 같은 단어의 변형 형태들이며, 따라서 적절한 품사를 고르는 문제임을 알 수 있다. 빈칸의 위치를 살펴보면, 1번 문제의 빈칸 앞 to tech support는 전명구이므로 수식어이고, 앞에는 be+p.p.의 형태로 목적어가 없는 완전한 상태이다. 2번 문제는 빈칸 앞이 work로 1형식 동사이므로 완전한 문장이고, 3번 문제는 빈칸 앞이 cut과 목적어인 the company's operating costs가 왔으므로 역시 완전한 문장의 형태이다.

STEP 2 이렇게 풀어 봐 "유형을 파악해 봐" 1번 문제를 보세요!

첫째 빈칸 앞의 문장이 완전한지 확인한다. (1형식 동사 뒤, be + p.p. 뒤, 타동사의 목적어 뒤)
빈칸 앞의 to tech support는 전명구로 수식어이므로 그 앞의 동사를 확인한다. 앞의 동사 형태가 be directed 이므로 완전한 문장이며, 따라서 빈칸에는 부사가 와야 한다.

둘째 완전한 문장이면, 빈칸에는 수식어가 온다.
(A) prompt는 형용사, (B) promptness는 명사, (C) prompts 단수 동사 또는 명사, (D) promptly는 부사이다.

함정을 피해 봐   실제 강의에서만 알려주는 풀이 노하우!

1. 문장의 맨 뒤라고 무조건 부사 자리는 아니다.

Mr. Kim advised me to keep the classroom (clean/cleanly).
→ clean은 to 다음의 5형식 동사 keep의 목적보어이다. 따라서 형용사가 목적보어로 온다. advise를 수식하는 자리라고 생각해서 cleanly를 답으로 고르지 않도록 한다.

2. 전치사로 끝나도 완전한 문장인 경우가 있다.

The problem was dealt with (caution/cautiously).
→ 덩어리 동사 deal with의 p.p.가 dealt with이다. 따라서 be + p.p. 다음은 부사인 cautiously가 와야 한다.

3. 부사를 끌어당기는 how를 조심한다.

We know how (quick/quickly) they can run.
→ quickly는 원래 run 다음에 오는 부사지만 how가 앞으로 끌어당기는 역할을 해 how 뒤에 부사가 오게 된다.

1. clean   2. cautiously   3. quickly

STEP 3 실전에 적용해 봐

1. Job applicants to the company should remember their interview times and locations ------- in order to be at their interviews on time.

   (A) accurate
   (B) accuracies
   (C) accurately
   (D) accuracy

2. The number of visitors at the Lincoln Memorial Park has increased ------- since the TV program about historical figures was broadcast last week.

   (A) significantly
   (B) significant
   (C) signifying
   (D) signified

3. All personal information and data provided by users can be accessed ------- by authorized personnel in the Service Department.

   (A) either
   (B) very
   (C) outer
   (D) only

4. The board of directors at the JYP Corporation was surprised by how ------- the profits of its rival, Electron Ltd., rose during the fourth quarter.

   (A) drastical
   (B) drastically
   (C) more drastic
   (D) drastic

5. Please make sure that your application form is filled out ------- so that the interviewer can get a better understanding of you before the interview.

   (A) complete
   (B) completely
   (C) competed
   (D) completing

6. Political and religious issues should be dealt with ------- because everyone has his or her own view of them.

   (A) caution
   (B) cautiously
   (C) cautions
   (D) cautioning

7. Since Mr. Shin cannot be at the trade fair on June 3 due to a scheduling conflict, he asked his assistant to represent the company -------.

   (A) wherever
   (B) that
   (C) them
   (D) there

8. The Human Resources director tried to distribute the company's resources more ------- and didn't concentrate solely on a specific department.

   (A) evens
   (B) evenly
   (C) evened
   (D) evenness

9. The Avion Water Company strongly recommends that customers get their water filters replaced -------.

   (A) frequently
   (B) frequent
   (C) frequency
   (D) frequentness

10. When hiking in the mountains, it is important to leave nothing behind on the trail and to walk ------- so as not to disturb other hikers.

    (A) quiet
    (B) quietly
    (C) quietest
    (D) quieted

법칙 8 의미로 풀어야 하는 명사 자리 문제는 수식어나 동사를 보고 판단

앞의 '법칙 2'의 '관소전타 뒤는 명사'를 다시 한 번 살펴보면, '관소전타'는 관사, 소유격, 전치사, 타동사를 줄인 말이다.

- 관사: 명사 앞에 붙는 the와 a를 말한다.
- 소유격: my, your, his, her 등을 말한다.
- 전치사: in the room, on the table에서 in, on 등을 말한다.
- 타동사: like(~를 좋아하다)처럼 목적어를 가지는 동사를 말한다.

STEP 1 유형을 파악해 봐

1. According to the ------- issued by the company, it expects that its mobile phone sales will exceed $1 billion this quarter.
   (A) state   (B) statement   (C) stating   (D) stated

2. All ------- for the assistant position are advised to send in all the necessary documents to the personnel director by June 3.
   (A) applicants   (B) applications   (C) apply   (D) applied

3. ABC Pharmaceuticals makes every effort to maintain the ------- of all participants in its clinical studies.
   (A) confidences   (B) confidentially   (C) confidential   (D) confidentiality

보기들이 모두 같은 단어의 변형 형태로 주어졌다. 빈칸에 알맞은 적절한 품사를 고르는 문제이므로 빈칸의 앞뒤를 살핀다. 1번 문제는 빈칸 앞에 관사, 2번 문제는 all이 형용사, 빈칸 뒤는 전명구, 3번 문제는 관사 뒤에 빈칸이 왔으므로 빈칸은 모두 명사 자리임을 알 수 있다. 보기에는 명사가 2개 이상 있으므로 명사들의 각 의미를 알아야 정답을 고를 수 있다.

STEP 2 이렇게 풀어 봐   "유형을 파악해 봐" 1번 문제를 보세요!

첫째 빈칸이 명사 자리인지 확인한다. ('법칙 2' 참조)
(A) state는 명사, (B) statement도 명사 (C) stating은 현재분사 혹은 동명사, (D) stated는 과거분사 혹은 동사의 과거시제이므로 (C), (D)는 정답이 될 수 없다.

둘째 빈칸 주변 수식어나 동사와의 어울림으로 결정하고, 그래도 안 되면 문맥을 파악해 고른다.

빈칸 뒤 issued(발급된, 발표된)의 수식어와 어울리는 것은 state(상태, 주)가 아닌 statement(성명서)이므로 (B)가 정답이 된다.

PLUS

문장을 해석하기 전에 아래 내용을 점검하면 문제의 답을 쉽게 고를 수 있다.

- 주어와 동격 관계인지 확인한다. Mr. Kim will be the keynote (speaker / speech).
- '사람 and 사람, 사물 and 사물' 관계를 살핀다. We need to purchase silverware and other (supplies / suppliers).
- 사람을 주로 수식하는 형용사를 확인한다. qualified, experienced, considerate, proficient, confident, eager 등
- 사람 명사와 사물 명사 구분 문제는 동사를 확인한다.
  Any (applications / applicants) should be submitted in person.

시험에 자주 나오는 사람/사물 명사

사람 명사		사물 명사	
attendee 참석자	attendant 도우미	attendance 참석	
applicant 지원자		application 신청서	
employee 직원	employer 고용주	employment 고용	
assistant 보조자		assistance 도움, 원조	
interviewer 면접관	interviewee 피면접인	interview 면접	
advisor 조언자		advice 충고	
professional 전문가	professor 교수	profession 직업	professionalism 전문적 기질
enthusiast 열성팬		enthusiasm 열정	

 함정을 피해 봐 실제 강의에서만 알려주는 풀이 노하우!

1. 회사나 기관도 사람이 모인 집단이므로 사람처럼 취급하기도 한다.

For more information, contact GWF, Inc., the leading (provider / provision) of compact electric products.

→ contact는 사람을 목적어로 취하는 동사지만 회사도 사람이 모여 있는 집단이므로 이 문장에서 GWF Inc.라는 회사를 가리키는 provider를 목적어로 취한다.

2. 단어의 모양과 의미가 유사한 명사들끼리 혼동하지 않도록 한다.

advancement 승진	advance 진보	character 인물 성격	characteristic 특징
effect 효과	effectiveness 효율성	location 지점, 지역	locality 지방
entrance 입장, 입구	entry 출품(물)	profession 직업	professional 전문가
potential 잠재능력	potentiality 가능성	quality 특징	qualification 자격요건

1. provider

STEP 3 실전에 적용해 봐

1. The government ------- will visit one of our facilities in China to conduct an audit next Thursday.

   (A) inspecting
   (B) inspector
   (C) inspected
   (D) inspection

2. ------- Tanaka had to go through many applications to fill the position due to the unexpected popularity of the open position.

   (A) Recruiter
   (B) Recruit
   (C) Recruits
   (D) Recruited

3. If you have any questions regarding our programs and guest lecturers, e-mail our education ------- at educoodi@naver.com.

   (A) coordinator
   (B) coordination
   (C) coordinate
   (D) coordinated

4. During a one-hour ------- at the Detroit facility, Mr. Good talked about how much the working environment could positively impact overall worker productivity.

   (A) lecture
   (B) lecturer
   (C) lecturers
   (D) lectured

5. Mr. White will be the key ------- for a $5 million contract with Avalon Technology, one of the leading manufacturers in the field.

   (A) negotiate
   (B) negotiates
   (C) negotiator
   (D) negotiation

6. The final ------- of the record-breaking series by British author J.K. Rowling has sold more than three million copies in Japan.

   (A) installing
   (B) installer
   (C) installment
   (D) install

7. Office ------- are stocked next to the copy machine in the copy room.

   (A) supplies
   (B) suppliers
   (C) supply
   (D) supplied

8. Since its ------- two years ago, Big Tree Co. has focused on designing office furniture, such as tables, desks, and chairs.

   (A) founder
   (B) found
   (C) foundation
   (D) founded

9. A fluent command of a language is the ------- of at least two years of intensive practice in the environment where it is spoken.

   (A) product
   (B) producer
   (C) produced
   (D) producing

10. In the university's library, it takes longer to borrow a book if the book is a recently published one and by an award-winning -------.

    (A) writing
    (B) writer
    (C) written
    (D) wrote

출제율 103%

법칙 9 '관소전타' 뒤 명사 앞은 형용사

형용사는 명사를 꾸며주는 역할을 하는데, 주로 '~인, ~한, ~의'의 형태로 해석되며 -ive, -ful, -ble, -less, -ous 와 같은 어미가 붙는다. 형용사는 주로 명사 앞에 위치하고, 명사는 관소전타('법칙 2' 참고) 뒤에 위치하기 때문에 '관소전타 ------- 명사'에서 빈칸에는 형용사가 와야 한다.

STEP 1 유형을 파악해 봐

1. A trip to Seongsan Ilchulbong Tuff Cone in Jeju Island will leave tourists excited about its ------- scenery.
   (A) dramatically   (B) dramatize   (C) dramatic   (D) drama

2. Due to the need for ------- checks on chemicals, the technicians work on a three-shift basis in the Fitch laboratory.
   (A) frequent   (B) frequently   (C) frequency   (D) frequents

3. To ensure a ------- refund, please bring the receipt you were issued when you purchased the product.
   (A) prompts   (B) prompt   (C) promptly   (D) promptness

모든 보기가 같은 단어의 변형 형태로 주어졌으므로 적절한 품사를 고르는 문제이다. 빈칸의 위치를 살펴보면 1번 문제는 소유격 뒤, 명사 앞, 2번 문제는 전치사 뒤, 명사 앞, 3번 문제는 관사 뒤, 명사 앞이다.

STEP 2 이렇게 풀어 봐
"유형을 파악해 봐" 1번 문제를 보세요!

첫째 빈칸 앞 '관소전타'를 확인한다.
부사가 있다면 수식어로 처리하고, 빈칸 뒤에 명사가 있는지 확인한다. 빈칸 앞은 its로 소유격, 빈칸 뒤는 scenery(장면)이므로 명사이다.

둘째 보기들을 대입해 확인한다.
(A) dramatically는 부사, (B) dramatize는 동사, (C) dramatic은 형용사, (D) drama는 명사이다. 따라서 빈칸에는 명사를 꾸며줄 수 있는 형용사 (C)가 와야 한다.

PLUS

분사도 형용사 자리에 올 수 있는데, 그 중에서도 특히 과거분사가 형용사를 대신해서 자주 등장한다. 만일 형용사가 보기에 없다면 분사를 답으로 선택해도 된다.

I like the (revise/revised) plan.

 함정을 피해 봐 실제 강의에서만 알려주는 풀이 노하우!

1. 형용사라고 생각하지 않았던 단어들을 조심한다.

| secure 안전한 | complete 완성된, 완전한 | timely 시기 적절한 |
| friendly 친근한 | lovely 사랑스러운 | likely 있을 법한 |

2. 형용사 두 개가 하나의 명사를 수식하는 경우를 조심한다.

Mr. Kim will become a (professional ✓/professional) financial advisor.
→ 전문적으로 재정고문(X), 전문적인 재정고문(O). 이 문장에서는 professional과 financial이 모두 advisor를 수식한다.

3. -ing 형태의 명사 앞에도 역시 형용사가 온다.

Due to (carefully/careful) planning, the renovation project was complete in a timely manner.
→ planning은 동명사가 아니고 명사이다. 따라서 형용사의 수식을 받는다.

4. 복합명사 앞에도 역시 형용사가 온다.

The company's (recently/recent) sales figures show that it is financially sound.
→ sales figures는 '판매 수치'라는 뜻의 복합명사이며, 하나의 명사로 취급한다. 따라서 형용사의 수식을 받는다.

2. professional   3. careful   4. recent

STEP 3 실전에 적용해 봐

1. Mr. Kim reported that the hotel room he stayed in last week was in good condition and showed ------- signs of wear.

   (A) minimally
   (B) minimize
   (C) minimizes
   (D) minimal

2. In order for your purchase to be covered by our 5-year worldwide warranty program, it is recommended that you purchase our product from an ------- dealer.

   (A) authorized
   (B) authorization
   (C) authority
   (D) authorize

3. Since seeing ------- increases in revenues last year, the Legolos Company has seen its stock price reach a record high.

   (A) sharply
   (B) sharp
   (C) sharpness
   (D) sharpen

4. Personnel director Rick Olmert was asked about the company's extended benefits program and gave a ------- response.

   (A) length
   (B) lengthy
   (C) lengthily
   (D) lengthen

5. Most of the accidents on the assembly line can be prevented by a ------- understanding of safety measures.

   (A) correctly
   (B) correct
   (C) correctness
   (D) corrects

6. Passengers traveling to and from Beijing are entitled to take up to 32kg at ------- additional charge.

   (A) no
   (B) not
   (C) none
   (D) never

7. Employees should avoid the main entrance while the maintenance work for the ------- door there is underway.

   (A) revolving
   (B) revolves
   (C) revolutions
   (D) revolve

8. The factory manager requested that employees wear a helmet and ------- gear all the time while working.

   (A) protected
   (B) protective
   (C) protect
   (D) protection

9. The address and phone number are accurately written on the order form so that the delivery of your order can be made in a ------- manner.

   (A) time
   (B) timing
   (C) timely
   (D) times

10. The city subway is the most ------- mode of transportation available today from Incheon Airport to the Merit Hotel.

    (A) conveniently
    (B) convenient
    (C) convene
    (D) convenience

출제율 100%

법칙 10 기본 형용사와 분사가 함께 나올 때는 기본 형용사

'sing(노래하다: 동사) → singing(노래하는: 현재분사), hire(고용하다: 동사) → hired(고용된: 과거분사)'처럼 동사를 형용사처럼 쓰기 위해 형태를 바꾼 것이 분사다. 현재분사나 과거분사는 사실 동사의 시제와는 관계 없는 형용사로 보면 된다. 형용사는 명사 앞에 와서 명사를 꾸며주거나('법칙 9' 참고), 보어 역할을 할 때는 주로 be동사 뒤에 온다. ('법칙 14' 참고)

STEP 1 유형을 파악해 봐

1. Despite our efforts to offer ------- information to our clients, errors may appear at times.
(A) use　　(B) used　　(C) useful　　(D) usefully

2. As an officially bilingual country, all government Web sites are ------- in both French and English.
(A) access　　(B) accessible　　(C) accessibility　　(D) accessing

3. The success of a team is ------- on the concerted efforts of individual members.
(A) depend　　(B) dependable　　(C) dependent　　(D) dependence

보기가 한 단어의 변형 형태들로 주어져 있으므로 품사 관련 문제임을 알 수 있다. 빈칸의 위치를 살펴보면 1번 문제는 명사 앞에, 2번과 3번 문제는 be동사 뒤와 전명구 앞이므로 보어가 되는 형용사를 찾는 문제이다. 그러나 보기에 형용사가 2개 이상 있으므로 역시 의미를 파악해 정답을 골라야 한다.

STEP 2 이렇게 풀어 봐   "유형을 파악해 봐" 1번 문제를 보세요!

첫째 빈칸이 명사 앞에 있거나, 보어 자리('법칙 14' 참고)인지 확인한다.
빈칸 뒤에 information이라는 명사가 왔으므로 빈칸은 명사를 수식하는 형용사 자리이다. (A) use는 동사, (B) used 형용사, (C) useful도 형용사, (D) usefully는 부사이므로 (B)와 (C)중 하나를 답으로 고른다.

둘째 의미를 파악하되 의미 파악이 어려울 경우에는 기본 형용사가 정답이다.
'used information(사용된 정보), useful information(유용한 정보)'으로 구분이 어렵다면 문장의 의미를 좀더 파악해 본다. 문장을 해석해 보면 '------- 정보를 제공하려는 우리의 노력에도 불구하고, 가끔 오류가 발생할 수 있다.'이므로 정답은 (C) useful이 된다.

PLUS

'be + 형용사 + 전치사' 형태의 숙어들이 등장해도 기본 형용사를 답으로 한다.

be hesitant to 동사원형 (O)	be hesitated to (X)
be dependent on (O)	be depended on (X)
be adaptable to 동사원형 (O)	be adapting to (X)
be indicative of 명사 (O)	be indicated of (X)

함정을 피해 봐
실제 강의에서만 알려주는 풀이 노하우!

1. 기본 형용사가 아닌 분사가 답이 되는 경우를 조심한다.

limited access 한정된 접속	challenging job 도전적인 일
extended hours 연장된 근무시간	promising candidates 유망한 후보자들
contributing author 투고 작가	intended accident 의도된 사건

2. 보기에 기본 형용사가 2개 이상 나오면 의미상으로 구분해 판단한다.

confident 자신하는	confidential 기밀의	weekly 매주마다의	weeklong 일주일간에 걸친
advisory 자문의	advisable 권할 만한	favorable 우호적인, 유리한	favorite 가장 좋아하는

3. 형용사보다 우선적으로 봐야 할 5형식 동사의 수동태 표현에 주의한다.

be allowed to 동사원형 (~하도록 허락되다)
be expected to 동사원형 (~하도록 기대되다)
be intended to 동사원형 (~하도록 의도되다)
be advised to 동사원형 (~하도록 권고되다)

STEP 3 실전에 적용해 봐

1. Marketing manager Greg Peterson was ------- to start his marketing campaign for the product since he was not given the results of the feasibility study.

   (A) reluctant
   (B) reluctance
   (C) reluctantly
   (D) reluctanted

2. The total research and development spending this year will not exceed the previous year's due to ------- restraints executed by the committee.

   (A) budgeted
   (B) to budget
   (C) budgetary
   (D) budgets

3. Beautiful Landscapes, a Seoul-based company, provides ------- designs and installations to enhance any landscape.

   (A) innovate
   (B) innovation
   (C) innovative
   (D) innovating

4. After ------- consideration, we will notify the person whose experience is the best match for the position.

   (A) care
   (B) cares
   (C) cared
   (D) careful

5. You are invited to attend the awards ceremony followed by a celebration ------- with cake and refreshments.

   (A) completion
   (B) completing
   (C) completes
   (D) complete

6. Because the tickets last year sold out even before the show started, it is highly ------- to purchase those for this year's show in advance.

   (A) advising
   (B) advisable
   (C) to advise
   (D) advisably

7. KJ Solutions, a venture that is ------- of economic cooperation between the two countries, will start operation next month.

   (A) representative
   (B) represented
   (C) representation
   (D) represent

8. Not only her experience at the overseas branches but also her excellent marketing ability made her an ------- candidate for international sales director.

   (A) attracted
   (B) attraction
   (C) attract
   (D) attractive

9. The manager reported that the response from our clients to the ------- office hours at our branches had been overwhelmingly positive.

   (A) extensive
   (B) extension
   (C) extended
   (D) extensively

10. In addition to teaching at the university, Ms. Kwon is also a ------- artist herself with a large following of admirers around the world.

    (A) respects
    (B) respect
    (C) respective
    (D) respected

정답 및 해설은 015페이지에

Chapter 01 _ 매월 출제되는 문제 51

출제율 81%

법칙 11 빈칸 앞뒤 단어만 봐도 풀리는 위치, 방향 전치사

위치 전치사는 움직임이 없이 위치를 표현하며, 방향 전치사는 움직임의 방향이 내포되어 있다.

위치 전치사	방향 전치사
in, on, at, next to, behind, in front of 등	to, from, into, out of 등
예 in the room 방안에 on the desk 책상 위에 in front of the house 집 앞에	예 to the hotel 호텔 쪽으로 from the door 문에서부터 out of the house 집 밖으로

STEP 1 유형을 파악해 봐

1. Several employees proposed making a smoking area ------- the main gate and the cafeteria on the first floor.
(A) from   (B) between   (C) until   (D) onto

2. In order to achieve our sales goals for this year, we have to find ways to boost our sales ------- the country.
(A) throughout   (B) during   (C) widely   (D) where

3. Audience members should routinely check their personal belongings while ------- the outdoors concert area.
(A) in   (B) through   (C) with   (D) along

보기들 중 2개 이상이 전치사라면 전치사 관련 문제라고 볼 수 있다. 1번 문제는 모두 전치사, 2번 문제는 (A), (B)가 전치사, 3번 문제는 모두 전치사 보기로 주어졌다. 빈칸 뒤에 공통적으로 '관사+명사'가 왔으므로 전치사의 위치를 묻는 문제로 볼 수 있다.

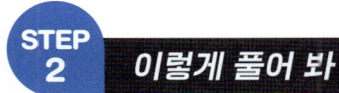

STEP 2 이렇게 풀어 봐
"유형을 파악해 봐" 1번 문제를 보세요!

첫째 빈칸 뒤에 장소를 의미하는 명사가 있는지 확인한다.
빈칸 뒤에 the main gate and the cafeteria on the first floor(1층의 정문과 카페테리아)가 왔다.

둘째 빈칸 뒤와 어울리는 위치, 방향 전치사를 선택한다. 고르기 어려울 경우 동사와의 어울림으로 판단한다.
빈칸 뒤가 'A and B' 형태로 왔기 때문에 (B)가 정답이다. 시점 앞에 쓰는 전치사 (C)는 오답이다. (A)는 '출처, 출발점'을 나타내는 동사들과 어울린다. (D)는 말이나 버스 탈 때 사용하는 전치사이며, 정답으로 기출된 적이 없다.

PLUS

특정 동사와 어울리는 방향 전치사 (더 많은 동사들은 '법칙 72' 참고)

submit A to B	obtain A from B	expand (A) into B
take A out of B	leave for 장소 명사	walk past 장소 명사
walk through 장소 명사		

위치 전치사와 방향 전치사

위치 전치사(정적인 느낌)	방향 전치사(동적인 느낌)
in, on, at, near, next to(= by, beside), over, above, under(= beneath, below), opposite(= across from), throughout, between, among	for(= toward), to, into, from, out of, onto, through, past, around, along, across, down, up, beyond, within

◎ 함정을 피해 봐
실제 강의에서만 알려주는 풀이 노하우!

1. 모양이나 뜻이 혼동되거나 용례가 다양한 전치사들이 있다.

besides, in addition to ~이외에도	beside ~옆에
down ~를 따라서	under ~아래에
between (두 개의) 사이	among(= amid) (3개 이상의) 가운데
throughout + 기간 명사	past + 시점
toward ~경, ~무렵	for + 방향/기간/목적/용도/대상 등
beyond (한계/기대치/능력/국경선)을 넘어	within ~이내에

STEP 3 실전에 적용해 봐

1. The person ------- the sales managers who makes the most sales in a month will be awarded a bonus.

   (A) among
   (B) above
   (C) about
   (D) up

2. The retirement ceremony for the company's vice president will be held ------- a secure location without any press in attendance.

   (A) at
   (B) between
   (C) during
   (D) out

3. Illustrations of dogs and cats are used ------- the book and provide visual interest, particularly to young readers.

   (A) regarding
   (B) from
   (C) besides
   (D) throughout

4. The schedule for next month's events is hanging ------- the bulletin board at the back of conference room.

   (A) in
   (B) for
   (C) on
   (D) to

5. The convention center at 40 Main Street is located ------- a bank and the post office and is easy to find.

   (A) among
   (B) between
   (C) down
   (D) into

6. Speedy Cargo is highly regarded for delivering packages ------- its business customers in the Seoul area within 24 hours.

   (A) unlike
   (B) with
   (C) on
   (D) to

7. All visitors at the Sagong facility must carefully read and follow the safety guidelines posted ------- the factory entrance.

   (A) from
   (B) among
   (C) next to
   (D) throughout

8. Consultant Peter Lee played a crucial role in turning our company ------- an ailing company to a profitable business.

   (A) about
   (B) from
   (C) for
   (D) with

9. Dr. Hamilton was a little late for the seminar because he mistakenly went ------- the HY Convention Center while thinking that he had not arrived at the center yet.

   (A) during
   (B) up
   (C) past
   (D) next to

10. Lincoln Hall, ------- which a number of meetings are often held, is scheduled to undergo renovations to accommodate more people.

    (A) in
    (B) from
    (C) until
    (D) down

출제율 80%

법칙 12 '------ + the/a 명사' 문제, 보기 중 전치사가 1개면 그것이 정답

전명구는 전치사와 명사로 이루어진 구를 말한다. 전치사('법칙 6' 참고)는 보통 단독으로 움직이지 않고 명사와 함께 덩어리로 움직이는데, 이것을 전명구라고 한다. 전명구의 위치와 역할은 다음과 같다.

- 문장의 맨 앞에서 문장 전체를 수식한다.
  In my opinion, he is bad
- 명사 바로 뒤에서 앞의 명사를 수식한다.
  The book **on the desk** is mine.
- 완전한 문장 뒤에서 동사를 수식한다.
  He was standing **on the desk**.

STEP 1 유형을 파악해 봐

1. You can take our shuttle, which departs ------ the hotel's front entrance every hour on the hour.
   (A) where   (B) whenever   (C) from   (D) then

2. ------ its limited budget, the Marketing Department couldn't increase its spending on advertising.
   (A) Due to   (B) Still   (C) Because   (D) Moreover

3. For general information ------ the benefits package, please refer to your employee handbook.
   (A) once   (B) pertaining to   (C) although   (D) likewise

각 보기들이 전치사, 접속사, 부사 등이 혼합돼 있어 공통점을 찾기가 어려우므로 문제의 공통점을 찾아야 한다. 빈칸의 위치로 보아 빈칸 뒤에 공통적으로 the 명사(복합명사 포함)의 형태가 존재한다는 것을 알 수 있다.

STEP 2 이렇게 풀어 봐
"유형을 파악해 봐" 1번 문제를 보세요!

첫째 보기에 전치사, 접속사 등이 섞여 있으면 연결어 문제이다. '동사의 개수 − 접속사 = 1'이면 접속사는 탈락한다.
동사: take, departs − 접속사 which = 1이므로 (A)와 (B)는 답이 될 수 없다.

둘째 전치사 자리인지 확인한다.

전명구가 문장의 맨 앞 또는 명사 뒤에 왔거나 완전한 문장에 왔는지를 확인한다. which가 주어, departs가 1형식 동사인 완전한 문장이므로 빈칸은 전치사 자리이며, 따라서 답은 (C) from이 된다.

------- the hotel's front entrance: 전명구

PLUS

전치사를 구별하는 방법에 대해 살펴본다.

- 전치사는 주로 길이가 짧은 편이다.
  in, on, at, to, for, from, as 등

- 전치사로 시작해 전치사로 끝나면 전치사이다.
  in spite of, in case of, in the event of 등

- 전치사로 끝나도 주로 전치사이다.
  because of, due to, owing to, thanks to 등

함정을 피해 봐
실제 강의에서만 알려주는 풀이 노하우!

1. 전치사라고 생각하기 쉬운 부사를 조심한다. (nevertheless, otherwise, in addition, as a result 등)

(Nevertheless/Despite) our limited workforce, our team managed to finished all the preparation work on time.
→ 전치사 자리이므로 부사인 Nevertheless는 올 수 없다.

2. 전치사와 접속사로 함께 쓰이는 단어에 유의한다. (after, before, until, since 등)

(After/Since) a series of unfavorable reviews by customers, the company terminated the distribution of the product.
→ 빈칸은 전치사 자리이며, since가 전치사라면 뒤에 과거시점이 와야 한다.

3. -ing 혹은 p.p. 형태의 전치사에 주의한다.

including ~를 포함하여	excluding ~를 제외하고
following ~후에	regarding ~에 관해
concerning ~에 관하여	pertaining to ~에 관하여
starting ~부로	beginning ~부로
considering ~를 고려할 때	given ~를 고려할 때
notwithstanding ~에도 불구하고	

1. Despite 2. After

STEP 3 실전에 적용해 봐

1. In order to qualify for their first promotion, all new recruits must finish the necessary training courses ------- six months of the day they start their employment.

    (A) while
    (B) within
    (C) unless
    (D) wherever

2. Nearly 4,000 students attended the job fair as scheduled ------- the poor weather conditions.

    (A) because
    (B) despite
    (C) although
    (D) when

3. ------- employee wages, employees can get very competitive salaries and bonuses based on their performances.

    (A) In terms of
    (B) For instance
    (C) Where
    (D) Although

4. Applicants for the dance instructor positon should have experience in many types of dances ------- salsa, swing, tango, rumba, and ballroom dancing.

    (A) likewise
    (B) such as
    (C) even so
    (D) as long as

5. If you renew your subscription this month, you are entitled to the current rate for 3 months ------- the price change as of next month.

    (A) nevertheless
    (B) insofar as
    (C) at the same time
    (D) regardless of

6. ------- the third-quarter financial statement issued last week, GW Industries reported a 15 percent gain in value.

    (A) As soon as
    (B) Providing that
    (C) According to
    (D) In case

7. For the last decade, the Cayenne Corporation has consistently ranked ------- the nation's ten leading manufacturers in the field of office supplies.

    (A) due
    (B) among
    (C) selective
    (D) belong

8. Your recent inquiries ------- company benefits have been directed to Ms. Blackwell in the personnel office.

    (A) regard
    (B) regarded
    (C) regarding
    (D) regards

9. ------- displaying instant messages and playing music from a smartphone, the Smart Watch functions as a fashion accessory.

    (A) Just as
    (B) Now that
    (C) Furthermore
    (D) In addition to

10. Dr. Masahiro Sato ------- the R&D team has been chosen to receive the technology award.

    (A) as a result
    (B) on behalf of
    (C) on the contrary
    (D) even though

출제율 72%

법칙 13 either A or B, both A and B, neither A nor B

상관접속사는 서로 관련이 있으므로 항상 함께 쓰인다.

- both A and B A와 B 둘 다
- either A or B A나 B 둘 중 하나
- neither A nor B A와 B 둘 다 아닌
- not only A but also B A뿐만 아니라 B도
- B as well as A A뿐만 아니라 B도

STEP 1 유형을 파악해 봐

1. The hotel guests can enjoy either a continental breakfast in the cafeteria ------- a full breakfast at the restaurant.
(A) neither   (B) nor   (C) or   (D) both

2. Our consultants are available for free consultations throughout the day by both phone ------- e-mail.
(A) but   (B) also   (C) either   (D) and

3. Neither flash photography ------- the touching of artifacts is allowed in the exhibit area.
(A) or   (B) nor   (C) and   (D) either

보기에 상관접속사의 접속사 부분(or, nor, and)과 그 짝(either, neither, both)이 함께 제시되었다. 문제에서도 상관접속사의 접속사 부분과 그 짝을 찾아 볼 수 있는데, 1번 문제에서는 either가, 2번 문제에서는 both가, 3번 문제에서는 Neither가 그것들이다.

STEP 2 이렇게 풀어 봐   "유형을 파악해 봐" 1번 문제를 보세요!

첫째 상관접속사의 접속사 부분(or, nor, and)과 그 짝(either, neither, both)이 문제에 있는지 확인한다.
문제에 either가 있다.

둘째 상관접속사의 접속사 부분(or, nor, and)과 그 짝(either, neither, both)이 보기에 있는지 확인한다.
보기에 either와 함께 쓰여 상관접속사를 구성하는 or가 있으므로 이것이 정답이다.

PLUS

기타 상관접속사

not A but B(= B but not A) A가 아니라 B
not only A but also B A뿐만 아니라 B도 • also는 생략 가능

함정을 피해 봐 실제 강의에서만 알려주는 풀이 노하우!

1. or만 보고 either를 답으로 고르거나 and만 보고 both를 답으로 고르면 위험하다. [고득점용]

(Whether/Either) I will go or not depends on the situation.

→ 위 문장에서 depends가 동사이기 때문에 앞에는 주어의 역할을 하는 명사절이 와야 한다. 접속사 Whether가 와야 명사절이 될 수 있으며, Either가 오게 되면 하나의 문장이 되기 때문에 주어의 자리에 올 수 없다.

(Both/Between) he and I will attend the conference.

이 문장 역시 attend가 동사이므로 앞이 주어가 되어야 한다. Both he and I는 덩어리 대명사로 주어가 될 수 있지만, Between he and I는 전명구로 수식어이기 때문에 주어가 될 수 없다.

2. either, neither, both가 단독으로 사용되는 경우를 조심한다.

Either (man) is scheduled to walk home.

Both (men) are scheduled to walk home.

→ either, neither, both 모두 단독으로 사용하면 대명사나 형용사 기능을 한다. Both는 이 경우에도 복수 취급한다.

1. Whether, Both

STEP 3 실전에 적용해 봐

1. The Miller Catering Company offers a wide range of menu options for both lunch ------- dinner.
   (A) and
   (B) or
   (C) so
   (D) including

2. ------- speaking loudly nor taking photographs is allowed during the factory tour.
   (A) Whether
   (B) Neither
   (C) Not only
   (D) With

3. Admission tickets can be purchased either online ------- at the ticket office beside the entrance.
   (A) but
   (B) yet
   (C) or
   (D) and

4. Ms. Imamura is not only a critically acclaimed poet ------- also an accomplished painter and sculptor.
   (A) furthermore
   (B) and then
   (C) whether
   (D) but

5. The purchasing contract has not been signed by both parties yet ------- has already been confirmed by phone.
   (A) but
   (B) both
   (C) which
   (D) or

6. AK Telecom customers are invited to upgrade to premier calling plans from basic calling plans that include text message service ------- not Internet service.
   (A) also
   (B) but
   (C) and
   (D) or

7. Passengers should present ------- their tickets and passports when boarding an airplane.
   (A) both
   (B) either
   (C) between
   (D) why

8. We are sorry to inform you that neither the marketing director ------- his assistant is available to conduct an interview today.
   (A) and
   (B) nor
   (C) but
   (D) either

9. Mr. Lopez travels regularly for business and uses the corporate account at hotels ------- car rental agencies.
   (A) rather
   (B) as well as
   (C) even if
   (D) if only

10. Those interested in making a difference in their careers may ------- contact us or visit our office for a free consultation.
    (A) whether
    (B) neither
    (C) both
    (D) either

Chapter 02

2개월에 한 번 출제되는 문제

출제 2 순위

토익 시험 2회에 반드시 한 번은 나온다.

출제율 65%

법칙 14 2형식 또는 5형식 문장의 보어 자리는 형용사

2형식 문장	S(주어)+V(동사)+C(보어)	I am happy. 나는 행복하다.
5형식 문장	S(주어)+V(동사)+O(목적어)+O.C.(목적보어)	I made him happy. 나는 그를 행복하게 만들었다.

문장이 완전하지 못할 때 이를 보충해 주는 것이 보어다. I am을 happy가 보충해 줘 문장을 완성시켜 주며, 5형식에서는 목적어 him을 happy가 보충해 주는 역할을 한다.

STEP 1 유형을 파악해 봐

1. If you have any inquiries regarding the updated employee handbook, they can be ------- to the personnel manager.
(A) directed (B) director (C) direction (D) directs

2. The employees at the Nielsen Company are easily ------- by the uniforms and badges they are wearing.
(A) identity (B) identifies (C) identify (D) identifiable

3. The business development specialist will be ------- for identifying and developing new business opportunities in East Asia.
(A) responsibility (B) responsibilities (C) responsibly (D) responsible

보기를 살펴보면 같은 단어의 변형 형태들이며, 형용사나 형용사 역할을 하는 분사(-ing 또는 p.p.)가 제시되었다. 빈칸의 위치를 보면 빈칸 앞에 be동사가 왔다. 2번 문제 역시 부사 easily를 제외하면 빈칸 앞에 be동사가 존재하는 것을 알 수 있다.

STEP 2 이렇게 풀어 봐
"유형을 파악해 봐" 1번 문제를 보세요!

첫째 빈칸의 위치가 보어 자리인지 확인한다.
2형식 동사(be, become, remain 등) 뒤, 그리고 5형식 동사(make, keep, find, consider 등) 뒤에 온 목적어(명사) 뒤가 빈칸이라면 보어 자리로 봐야 한다. 여기서도 빈칸 앞에 be가 위치해 있으므로 빈칸은 보어 자리이다.

둘째 형용사의 역할을 하는 보기를 찾는다.

(A)의 directed(지시된)는 p.p., (B) director(관리자)는 명사, (C) direction(방향)은 명사, (D) directs(지도하다)는 동사 3인칭 형태이므로 형용사 역할을 하는 (A)가 정답이 된다.

함정을 피해 봐
실제 강의에서만 알려주는 풀이 노하우!

1. be동사 다음에 부사가 답인 경우를 조심한다.

The company is (financially/financial) sound.
→ 빈칸 다음에 이미 형용사(sound)가 있으므로 오히려 부사가 답이다.

The manager is (probably/probable) in favor of the new renovation project.
→ 전명구(in favor of)가 이미 보어 기능을 하고 있으므로 그 앞에는 부사가 와야 한다.

Mr. Kim is (currently/current) our marketing manager.
→ 명사(our marketing manager)가 이미 보어 기능을 하고 있으므로 부사가 답이다.

2. be동사 다음에 명사가 답인 경우를 조심한다.

The most important characteristic that job candidates should have to get a job is (confident/confidence).
→ '지원자들이 갖추고 있어야 할 자질 = 자신감'의 관계이므로 명사가 답이 된다. confident는 주어가 사람일 때 어울린다.

3. 형용사 앞에 more나 most가 있어도 여전히 형용사이다.

Mr. Kim is more (capable/capably) than any other members in his team.
→ capable도 형용사, more capable도 형용사이다.

1. financially, probably, currently   2. confidence   3. capable

STEP 3 실전에 적용해 봐

1. After critics commented that the flavor of the Chikan Chinese restaurant's cuisine is very -------, the number of diners doubled there.

   (A) authenticates
   (B) authenticity
   (C) authentically
   (D) authentic

2. The preparation committee for the corporate outing was especially ------- for the work done by volunteers.

   (A) grate
   (B) grateful
   (C) gratefulness
   (D) gratefully

3. A report in *Trend Journal* suggests that consumers are most likely ------- on Internet advertising these days.

   (A) dependently
   (B) dependent
   (C) dependency
   (D) depend

4. The factory manager at the London facility considers it ------- to halt the production process until the causes and solutions of the defects are identified.

   (A) necessity
   (B) necessary
   (C) necessitate
   (D) necessarily

5. The recently released G-phone is lightweight, -------, and reasonably priced.

   (A) durable
   (B) durability
   (C) durably
   (D) durableness

6. The first opened unmanned post office in Korea is ------- for people who are unable to get to the post office during business hours.

   (A) idealism
   (B) idealist
   (C) idealize
   (D) ideal

7. Among the three routes to the convention center, Route 5, the recently repaved one, is the least ------- with traffic.

   (A) crowded
   (B) crowd
   (C) crowdedly
   (D) crowdedness

8. Employees' complaints about the company's benefits are no longer ------- directly to the CEO but to the department head first.

   (A) submitted
   (B) submission
   (C) submit
   (D) submissive

9. For their views to sound ------- to the public, politicians usually provide biased views on most pending issues.

   (A) plausibly
   (B) plausibility
   (C) plausible
   (D) plausibleness

10. In order to effectively keep track of their inventory, store managers should become ------- with the stock management software system.

    (A) familiar
    (B) familiarly
    (C) familiarity
    (D) familiarize

출제율 57%

법칙 15 전체 문맥을 알아야 풀리는 추가, 포함, 제외 및 for(이/용/대/목) 전치사

'추가, 포함, 제외 전치사와 이유, 용도, 대상, 목적 전치사인 for에 대해 알아 보기로 한다.

추가	in addition to ~에 덧붙여서	besides 게다가	on top of ~이외에도
	aside from ~이외에도	apart from ~이외에도	plus ~에 더하여
포함	including ~를 포함하여	such as 이를테면 ~와 같은	like ~와 같은
제외	instead of ~대신에	except ~를 제외하고	other than ~가 아닌, 다른
대상, 목적	for ~때문에, ~용으로, ~에 대해서, ~를 위해서		

STEP 1 유형을 파악해 봐

1. All employees at Blueone, Inc., ------- the ones working in the Maintenance Department, should attend the information session on facility regulation.
(A) among   (B) concerning   (C) on   (D) except

2. ------- a degree in management, the position requires at least 2 years of working experience in the related field.
(A) In addition to   (B) Unlike   (C) As   (D) On behalf of

3. Please let us know whether you want standard or express delivery ------- your company.
(A) at   (B) through   (C) for   (D) above

보기가 모두 전치사들로 구성되어 있으므로 전치사 어휘 문제임을 알 수 있다. 1번 문제는 보기 (D)가 제외 전치사 except, 2번 문제는 보기 (A)가 포함 전치사 in addition to, 3번 문제는 보기 (C)가 이유, 용도, 대상, 목적을 나타내는 for로 제시되었다.

STEP 2 이렇게 풀어 봐

"유형을 파악해 봐" 1번 문제를 보세요!

첫째 전치사 문제일 때는 보기에 '추가, 포함, 제외, 그리고 이/용/대/목(for)'이 있는지 확인한다.
(A)는 복수 명사를 취하는 전치사, (B)와 (C)는 주제(~에 관하여)와 어울리는 전치사, (D)는 제외 전치사이다.

둘째 일단 '제외' 전치사를 답으로 염두에 두고 해석으로 답을 판단한다.

포함, 제외, 추가 전치사나 이/용/대/목 전치사 for를 먼저 확인하는 이유는 가장 자주 출제되는 전치사이기 때문이다. 제외 전치사 (D) except를 넣어 해석해 보면 '관리부에서 근무하는 직원들(the ones)을 제외한 모든 직원들은 시설 규정에 관한 안내 세미나에 참석해야 한다.'로 자연스럽게 해석이 되므로 정답은 (D)가 된다.

PLUS

except 앞에는 주로 all이나 every가 많이 등장하며, in addition to 다음에는 동명사가 오거나 부사 also가 오는 경우가 많은데, in addition, apart, aside는 부사이며, besides는 전치사와 부사가 둘 다 가능하다.

함정을 피해 봐
실제 강의에서만 알려주는 풀이 노하우!

1. 의미가 비슷해 혼동되는 전치사들을 조심한다.

Everyone in the Marketing Department (without/except) Mr. Kim should attend the weekly seminar.
→ except는 '~를 제외하고'의 뜻이며, '~를 포함하고(including)'의 반대말이다.

Anyone (without/except) a visitor pass is not allowed to enter the facility.
→ without은 '~가 없이'라는 뜻이며, '~를 가지고(with)'의 반대말이다.

2. except의 다양한 쓰임새에 유의한다.

(Except/Unlike) the other employees, Mr. Kim works hard even on weekends.
→ except는 문두에 오지 않는데, 단 except for는 문두에 올 수 있다.

Employees can talk with their fellow workers (during/except) on the assembly line.
→ except 다음에는 전명구, to 부정사, 명사절 등이 올 수 있다.

Employees can work except the room. (X)
→ except는 앞에 명사가 없으면 뒤에 명사를 쓸 수 없다.

1. except, without   2. Unlike, except

STEP 3 실전에 적용해 봐

1. ------- detecting misspellings, the OCR 1 software also suggests alternative words for misspelled ones.

   (A) Except
   (B) Besides
   (C) However
   (D) Unless

2. The official duties of the secretary, ------- answering multiple phone lines, filing important documents, and scheduling the CEO's meetings, can be changed when necessary.

   (A) such as
   (B) through
   (C) now that
   (D) apart

3. Glass containers can be used ------- storing chemical and chemical solutions as long as they are labeled at all times.

   (A) to
   (B) for
   (C) with
   (D) upon

4. Those employees who would like to do part-time jobs at the community outreach program ------- their day jobs should contact Ms. Park in Personnel.

   (A) beforehand
   (B) furthermore
   (C) on top of
   (D) as long as

5. Because of the room availability, the opening ceremony will be held in the ballroom ------- the conference room.

   (A) in addition
   (B) without
   (C) instead of
   (D) except for

6. All employee at Cameroon Systems, ------- the recently hired part-timers, should participate in the company-wide recycling initiative.

   (A) between
   (B) together
   (C) including
   (D) since

7. Pineapple, Inc. has discontinued using one of the components supplied by Digitec because it found a substitute which has the same processing capability ------- better reliability.

   (A) both
   (B) though
   (C) together
   (D) plus

8. Mr. White's presentation on sales strategies during the board meeting yesterday was perfect ------- that it was too long.

   (A) except
   (B) when
   (C) so
   (D) now

9. This year, the selection committee is having a hard time nominating several people to be honored ------- their hard work and dedication to the company.

   (A) on
   (B) around
   (C) over
   (D) for

10. The proceeds from the book sale will go directly ------- the library's maintenance project, including the renovations on the main entrance.

    (A) toward
    (B) next to
    (C) onto
    (D) along

출제율 54%

법칙 16 목적어가 있으면 능동, 없으면 수동

'I love you.'라는 '주어+동사+목적어'를 갖춘 능동태 문장에서 목적어를 주어로 바꾸면 'You are loved (by me).' 형태의 수동태 문장이 된다. 수동태 문장은 '주어+be+p.p.'의 형태로 목적어가 없는 문장이다.

STEP 1 유형을 파악해 봐

1. Applications for the managerial position must ------- by the week of June 3.
(A) to receive   (B) receive   (C) received   (D) be received

2. Through a company-wide recycling initiative, Jason Paper ------- its overall operating expenses considerably last quarter.
(A) reduced   (B) were reduced   (C) was reduced   (D) reducing

3. Ms. Brown is very pleased that she ------- to department manager and received a pay increase.
(A) will promote   (B) was promoting   (C) has been promoting   (D) has been promoted

보기를 살펴보면 동사의 수동태 표현(be+p.p.)과 능동태 표현이 섞여 있으며, 준동사(-ing, p.p., to 부정사) 등이 함께 제시되었다. 빈칸의 위치를 보면 1번 문제는 must 조동사 뒤, 2번과 3번 문제는 주어 뒤에 위치해 모두 동사 자리임을 알 수 있다.

STEP 2 이렇게 풀어 봐

"유형을 파악해 봐" 1번 문제를 보세요!

첫째 먼저 동사 자리를 확인한 후, 주어와의 수일치도 확인한다.
보기에 정동사와 준동사가 섞여 있으므로 빈칸의 위치를 확인한다. 빈칸 앞에 조동사 must가 있으므로 빈칸은 동사원형이 와야 한다.

둘째 빈칸 뒤에 목적어가 있는지 확인한다.
빈칸 뒤에 목적어 역할을 할 수 없는 전명구가 있으므로 이 문장은 수동태 문장이다. 수동태는 be p.p.가 포함되어야 하므로 (D)가 정답이다.

PLUS

5형식 문장의 수동형은 뒤에 부사가 아닌 '형용사, -ing, p.p., to 부정사, 명사, as+명사' 등이 온다.

5형식 문장의 능동태	5형식 문장의 수동태
I kept him happy.	He was kept **happy**.
I found him hired by a renowned company.	He was found **hired** by a renowned company.
I allowed him to go.	He was allowed **to go**.
I made him go.	He was made **to go**.
I call him David.	He was called **David**.
I considered him (as) a teacher.	He was considered **(as) a teacher**.

함정을 피해 봐
실제 강의에서만 알려주는 풀이 노하우!

1. 목적어로 착각하기 쉬운 단어들을 조심한다.

The meeting will (be held/hold) tomorrow.
The rare book can (be purchased/purchase) online.
The initiative will (be implemented/implement) downtown.
→ tomorrow, online, downtown은 목적어가 아닌 부사이다. 다라서 수동태가 와야 한다.

2. 1, 2형식 동사인 자동사는 목적어를 갖지 않으므로 수동태가 없다.

He (has/is) disappeared.
→ disappear가 1형식 동사이므로 수동태가 없다. 따라서 be disappeared는 존재하지 않는다.

3. 목적어가 없어도 능동태인 경우를 조심한다.

We found several errors you (should be corrected/should correct) before the publication date.
→ errors와 you 사이에 목적격 관계대명사 that이 생략되어 있다. 따라서 목적어가 없어도 능동태이다

4. 목적어가 있어도 수동태인 경우를 조심한다.

Any library patrons who fail to return their books by the due date will (be charged/charge) a 5-dollar late fee.
→ charge는 여기서 4형식 동사이며, 수동태로 사용되어 '도서관 이용자에게 5달러의 연체료가 부과된다.'는 의미이다.

빈출 4형식 수동태 표현	빈출 5형식 수동태 표현
be charged a fee 비용을 부과 받다	be considered (as)+명사 ~로 간주되다
be issued a refund 환불 받다	be elected (as)+명사 ~로 선출되다
be told the news 뉴스를 듣다	be named (as)+명사 ~로 임명되다
be assigned a job 업무를 배당 받다	be appointed (as)+명사 ~로 임명되다

1. be held, be purchased, be implemented   2. has   3. should correct   4. be charged

STEP 3 실전에 적용해 봐

1. Due to unexpected technical problems, the launch of the new smartphone -------.

   (A) has delayed
   (B) are delaying
   (C) has been delaying
   (D) will be delayed

2. If you have any problems using your computer, you may refer to the following possible solutions that ------ by our service representatives.

   (A) are suggested
   (B) have suggested
   (C) was suggested
   (D) had been suggesting

3. Printing supplies such as paper, ink cartridges, and staplers can ------- in the file cabinet placed next to the copy machine.

   (A) finds
   (B) be finding
   (C) found
   (D) be found

4. In the decade since it was founded, SY Co. Ltd. ------- a legend in creative marketing approaches.

   (A) has become
   (B) are becoming
   (C) to become
   (D) was become

5. Every month, the Abelon Company ------- 1% of its earnings to local charities.

   (A) has been contributed
   (B) is contributed
   (C) was contributed
   (D) contributes

6. We regret to ------- you that your order had already been shipped before we received your e-mail requesting a change in the quantity.

   (A) inform
   (B) informing
   (C) be informed
   (D) be informative

7. If you can demonstrate proof of ownership, you ------- an interim pass which can be used anywhere in the amusement park.

   (A) being issued
   (B) to be issuing
   (C) will be issued
   (D) have issued

8. Employees at Peatrock, Inc. ------- to attend the healthy living seminar completely free of charge.

   (A) invited
   (B) had invited
   (C) are invited
   (D) to be invited

9. As project coordinator, Ms. Wong should ------- accountable for the progress of the company's recent renovation project.

   (A) be held
   (B) be holding
   (C) were held
   (D) have held

10. The energy-saving initiative must be publicized by means of television advertisements so that it can ------- nationwide.

    (A) have implemented
    (B) be implemented
    (C) implementing
    (D) implementation

출제율 54%

법칙 17 비교/최상급의 단서가 있으면 비교/최상급, 그렇지 않으면 원급

원급	He is tall. 그는 키가 크다.
비교급	He is taller than I. 그는 나보다 키가 크다.
최상급	He is the tallest of the three students. 그는 세 명의 학생 중에서 가장 키가 크다.

STEP 1 유형을 파악해 봐.

1. Mr. Lee may be ------- to work at the office in Busan than Seoul because his hometown is in Busan.
(A) willingly   (B) more willing   (C) willingness   (D) willing

2. The revised safety regulations will be reviewed extremely ------- by senior executives.
(A) care   (B) careful   (C) carefully   (D) more carefully

3. Rachel, the office manager, agreed that purchasing a new copier would be ------- than fixing the old one.
(A) cheap   (B) cheaper   (C) cheapest   (D) more cheaply

보기에는 비교급이나 최상급 형용사, 그리고 부사가 하나 이상 제시되었다. 빈칸의 위치를 보면 1번 문제와 3번 문제는 be동사 뒤이므로 보어가 되는 형용사 자리이고, 2번 문제는 빈칸 앞이 완전한 문장이므로 빈칸은 부사 자리이다.

STEP 2 이렇게 풀어 봐   "유형을 파악해 봐" 1번 문제를 보세요!

첫째 빈칸의 위치가 형용사, 부사 자리인지 확인한다.
빈칸이 be동사 뒤이므로 보어가 되는 형용사 자리, 따라서 부사인 (A)와 명사인 (C)는 소거한다.

둘째 비교 단서를 보고 답을 결정한다.
문장에 than이 있으므로 비교급이 와야 하며, 따라서 (B)가 정답이다.

PLUS

단서가 되는 단어

비교급	than
최상급	among of in possible available ever 등

정관사(the)나 소유격은 최상급 형용사와 어울리며, 비교급 앞에는 일반적으로 the를 쓰지 않는다.

원급, 비교급, 최상급을 수식하는 표현들

원급 수식	extremely	very	quite	pretty	so	too
비교급 수식	even	still	a little	a lot		
최상급 수식	single	only	by far			
비교급, 최상급 수식	far	much				

함정을 피해 봐
실제 강의에서만 알려주는 풀이 노하우!

1. than이 없어도 비교급이 정답인 경우에 주의한다.

The new vacation policy proved to be (more effective/most effective) according to the survey results.

→ effective 뒤에 than old vacation policy 부분이 생략되었다. 따라서 than이 없어도 비교급이 정답이다.

2. 비교급만 보고 than을 답으로 생각하면 안 되는 경우에 주의한다.

The man wearing the hat is junior (than/to) me.

→ 라틴어를 어원으로 하는 senior, junior, inferior, superior 등을 라틴비교라고 하며, 뒤에는 than 대신에 to를 쓴다.

3. the만 보고 최상급을 골라서는 안 된다.

He is the (more/most) qualified of the two candidates.

→ 문장 뒤에 of the two가 형용사의 비교급인데도 the를 붙인다.

4. 형용사의 최상급뿐만 아니라 부사의 최상급 앞에도 the를 쓸 수 있다.

He works the (hardest/harder) of his team members.

→ 부사의 최상급 앞에는 일반적으로 the를 쓰지 않지만 부사와 형용사로 모두 사용되는 단어가 부사의 최상급으로 쓰이면 the를 쓰기도 한다.

5. 형용사의 최상급 앞에 형용사가 오는 경우를 조심한다.

the (single/singly) largest 단일 규모로는 가장 큰   the (second/secondly) largest 두 번째로 가장 큰

1. more effective   2. to   3. more   4. hardest   5. single, second

STEP 3 실전에 적용해 봐

1. To select the most qualified applicant for the position, the personnel director reviewed the applicants' resumes ------- than ever.

   (A) thorough
   (B) more thorough
   (C) most thoroughly
   (D) more thoroughly

2. Of the ten members of the Marketing Department, Ms. Gupta is the ------- at using the new database software.

   (A) proficient
   (B) proficiency
   (C) more proficient
   (D) most proficient

3. By providing more reliable and affordable items, Minton Electronics could secure the ------- position in the industry.

   (A) highly
   (B) highest
   (C) higher
   (D) high

4. A ------- study indicates that high blood pressure and obesity have become major public health problems in China.

   (A) recent
   (B) more recently
   (C) recentness
   (D) more recent

5. The Well Designs T55 has been rated the ------- ergonomic chair available for purchase on the market today.

   (A) more lightweight
   (B) lightweight
   (C) lightweightly
   (D) most lightweight

6. Visitors to the library are asked to speak ------- in the reading room than at the entrance of the library.

   (A) more quietly
   (B) most quietly
   (C) more quiet
   (D) most quiet

7. Copy editors for *L.A. Press* are to proofread the manuscripts from staff writers to the ------- extent possible.

   (A) most fully
   (B) more fully
   (C) fullest
   (D) fuller

8. The store manager ordered that store clerks serve their customers ------- during the peak hours of the day.

   (A) attentions
   (B) attentive
   (C) more attentively
   (D) most attentive

9. The new T47 lawnmower will help gardeners complete their jobs much -------.

   (A) efficient
   (B) efficiently
   (C) more efficiently
   (D) most efficiently

10. Dr. Steven was honored for having performed the ------- of all the staff members at the general hospital this month.

    (A) well
    (B) better
    (C) best
    (D) good

출제율 53%

법칙 18 동사가 2개면 접속사가 답

'I love her, so I am happy.'라는 문장에서 동사는 love와 am이다. 기본적으로 한 문장에 동사는 하나이다. 만약 동사가 이렇게 두 개 이상이 온다면 접속사로 문장이 연결되어야 한다. 따라서 '동사의 수 – 접속사 = 1'이 항상 성립한다.

STEP 1 유형을 파악해 봐

1. ------- the budget for renovating the office is approved within a week, we can't meet the deadline for the completion of the project.
(A) Unless   (B) Moreover   (C) Furthermore   (D) Besides

2. ------- we receive the results of the survey, the advertising campaign for the new product will not proceed.
(A) Without   (B) Until   (C) Onto   (D) Within

3. It remains to be seen ------- Samdasu, Inc. will open a new branch office in Jeju.
(A) would   (B) whether   (C) on   (D) to

보기가 접속사, 전치사, 부사 등으로 구성되어 있으며, 문제는 모두 동사의 수가 2개, 즉 두 문장이 연결되어 있음을 알 수 있다.

STEP 2 이렇게 풀어 봐   "유형을 파악해 봐" 1번 문제를 보세요!

첫째 동사의 수가 2개인지 확인한다.
문제에서 is와 can't meet이 동사이다. 한 문장에서 '동사의 수 – 접속사 = 1'이라는 공식이 성립하려면 빈칸에는 접속사가 와야 한다.

둘째 보기에서 접속사를 찾는다.
주로 wh-, though, if나 that이 포함된 단어들이 접속사이다. (A) Unless(~가 아니라면)는 접속사, (B)와 (C), (D)는 부사이다.

PLUS

등위접속사	FANBOYS(for, and, nor, but, or, yet, so) S – V, _____ S + V.	
종속접속사	명사절 접속사	that, whether 으 관대명사: who, whom, which, what 으 관형용사: whose, what, which 으 관부사: when, where, why, how 복합관계대명사: whoever, whomever, whichever, whatever 복합관계형용사: whosever, whatever, whichever
	형용사절 접속사	관·계대명사: who, whom, which, whose, of which, that 관·계부사: when, where, why, how
	부사절 접속사	양보, 이유, 시간, 조건, 목적, 결과 접속사 ('법칙 1' 참조) 복합관계대명사, 복합관계형용사 복합관계부사: whenever, wherever, however

함정을 피해 봐 실제 강의에서만 알려주는 풀이 노하우!

1. 접속사가 생략된 문장에 유의한다.

The product you ordered (earlier/which) will be made available to you within a week.

→ product와 you 사이에 목적격 관계 대명사 which가 생략되어 있다.

We hope you (will patronize/to patronize) our services.

→ hope와 you 사이에 명사절 접속사 that이 생략되어 있다.

2. 과거분사와 과거시제를 구분해야 한다.

The plan proposed (while/during) the meeting includes the company's budget for next year.

→ proposed는 형용사 기능을 하는 과거분사이며, 동사가 아니다.

3. 명사로도 동사로도 사용되는 단어를 조심한다.

(When/On) employees request vacation time, the request form should be turned in on a weekend.

→ 앞의 request는 동사이며, 뒤의 request는 명사이다. 따라서 앞의 request와 뒤의 be가 동사이다.

4. 전치사, 부사로 익숙하지만 접속사로도 쓰이는 단어를 조심한다.

The presentation will not start (by/until) all presenters are ready to speak.

→ until은 전치사뿐 아니라 접속사로도 쓰인다. 동사의 수가 2개(start, are)이므로 until이 정답이다. 접속사로도 쓰이는 until, since, before, after, once 등을 기억하자.

5. 분사 구문은 동사가 없어도 접속사가 올 수 있다.

Be sure to get approval from your manager (so that/when) ordering office supplies.

→ when ordering은 when you order의 줄임 형태이며, 이것을 분사구문이라고 한다.

1. earlier, will patronize 2. during 3. When 4. until 5. when

STEP 3 실전에 적용해 봐

1. At tonight's awards ceremony, the CEO will deliver his speech ------- 90% of the invited guests arrive at the banquet hall.

   (A) still
   (B) less
   (C) once
   (D) apart

2. ------- people tend to prefer short-term investments, they value the benefits of long-term investments.

   (A) Somewhat
   (B) Including
   (C) With
   (D) Even though

3. The annual conference will be held in the head office as scheduled ------- all regional managers will be able to attend it.

   (A) whether or not
   (B) in favor of
   (C) regardless of
   (D) despite of

4. Having your body regularly checked is highly recommended ------- without a sound body, you can't have a sound mind.

   (A) out of
   (B) prior to
   (C) even
   (D) because

5. Mr. Baek will assume his new position, ------- he will be in charge of supervising all the interns who were hired last month.

   (A) in which
   (B) not only
   (C) in case of
   (D) along with

6. It hasn't been decided ------- the community gathering will take place indoors at the community center or outdoors in GW Park.

   (A) whether
   (B) about
   (C) near
   (D) either

7. This quarter, the company's revenues surpassed its goal, ------- its net profits were still below the target due to increases in manufacturing costs.

   (A) but
   (B) past
   (C) as always
   (D) otherwise

8. ------- there are no further changes in raw material prices, we will not increase the prices of any of our products.

   (A) Assuming
   (B) Except
   (C) Nevertheless
   (D) Otherwise

9. You will be able to fly directly to Israel ------- Vanilla Airlines starts providing customers with nonstop flights there.

   (A) instead
   (B) around
   (C) after
   (D) past

10. ------- you renew your subscription within a week of receiving this e-mail, you are still entitled to get one issue of our magazine at no cost.

    (A) As long as
    (B) In spite of
    (C) Following
    (D) In order for

출제율 53%

법칙 19 부정대명사는 동사 개수, 명사 자리, 단수, 복수 확인

부정대명사의 부정(不定)은 정해지지 않았다는 뜻이다. 따라서 부정대명사는 어떤 특정한 사람이나 사물을 가리키는 것이 아니라, 막연한 대상이나 정해지지 않은 수량을 나타낼 때 사용하는 대명사이다. 부정대명사로는 some, any, one, another, other, every, all, each, both, either, neither, none 등이 있다. 또한 some apples(몇 개의 사과들)처럼 부정대명사가 명사 앞에 오면 형용사로 사용되는데, 이것을 부정형용사라고 한다.

STEP 1 유형을 파악해 봐

1. ------- attendees at the educational seminar are advised to reserve a hotel room well in advance of their arrival next month.
(A) All　　(B) Each　　(C) Every　　(D) Whichever

2. ------- inquiries regarding the return policy should be directed to the Service Department.
(A) Whoever　　(B) Anything　　(C) Each　　(D) All

3. Many commuters in this area use the company shuttle bus instead of ------- forms of transportation because of high oil prices these days.
(A) other　　(B) another　　(C) one another　　(D) each other

보기에는 부정대명사와 부정형용사들이 섞여 있다. 이럴 경우 빈칸이 대명사의 자리인지, 형용사의 자리인지를 먼저 확인해야 한다. 문제 1, 2, 3번 모두 빈칸 뒤에 명사가 왔으므로 형용사 자리임을 알 수 있다.

STEP 2 이렇게 풀어 봐

"유형을 파악해 봐" 1번 문제를 보세요!

첫째 보기에 있는 접속사부터 소거한다.
동사의 수를 확인하여 빈칸이 접속사 자리인지 아닌지를 확인한다. 문장에서 동사는 are 한 개이므로 접속사인 (D) Whichever는 오답이다.

둘째 형용사 자리인지, 명사 자리인지는 수일치를 확인해 해석으로 마무리한다.
빈칸 뒤 attendees가 복수 명사이므로 앞은 복수와 어울리는 부정형용사 (A) All이 와야 한다.

PLUS

- 대부분은 부정대명사와 부정형용사가 모두 가능하지만, every와 other는 부정형용사로만 사용된다. every 뒤는 단수 명사가, other 뒤는 복수/불가산명사가 온다.
- one, each, either, neither는 단수 명사와 어울리며 few, a few, both, several, many는 복수 명사와 어울린다.
- little, a little, much는 불가산명사와 어울리며, 단수 동사로 받는다.
- all, most, some, any는 복수 명사와 불가산명사 모두 다 가능하다.
- no는 형용사, none은 명사, not은 부사, never도 부사이다.
- 대부분을 뜻하는 most는 형용사 혹은 명사이다. almost는 '거의'라는 뜻의 부사이다.

 함정을 피해 봐 실제 강의에서만 알려주는 풀이 노하우!

1. 비슷한 뜻이기 때문에 품사가 같다고 생각하는 경우에 유의한다.

(Anyone/Whoever) needing the CEO's approval should contact the secretary first.
→ anyone은 부정대명사, whoever는 접속사이다. 동사의 수가 1개이므로 접속사인 whoever는 오답이다. either(부정대명사/부정형용사)와 whichever(접속사) 역시 혼동하기 쉽다.

2. '서로서로'라는 뜻의 each other나 one another를 조심한다.

The group worked (each other/together) to meet the tight goal.
→ each other나 one another는 부사로 착각하기 쉽지만 명사이다.

(One another/Each) of the students received a $5 gift certificate.
→ each other나 one another는 주어 자리에 쓰지 않는다.

3. few는 복수 취급한다.

(Little/Few) has been reported about the future of our economy.

4. none의 쓰임새를 조심한다.

(None/Nothing) of the attempts we made were found to be effective.
→ none은 사람, 사물을 모두 가리킬 수 있다. 또, of the 뒤에 불가산명사가 오면 단수로 받지만 복수 명사가 오면 단수, 복수 모두 가능하다. nothing은 단수로 받는다.

5. any와 some의 예외 용법을 조심한다. 고득점용

Would you like some soup? (긍정의 답을 예상하거나, 권유, 부탁 시는 의문문에도 사용)

Any plan will do. (긍정문에 사용하면 '어떤 ~든지'라는 뜻)
→ any와 some 뒤는 복수 명사뿐 아니라 단수 명사도 올 수 있다. 또한 any도 긍정문에, some도 의문문에 사용하기도 한다.

1. Anyone 2. together, Each 3. Little 4. None

STEP 3 실전에 적용해 봐

1. The CAB Group, the London Baguette bakery company, increased the number of its chain stores in ------- region of the country.

   (A) all
   (B) every
   (C) second
   (D) several

2. According to the customer survey, ------- of the two products released recently attracted young consumers.

   (A) however
   (B) one another
   (C) where else
   (D) neither

3. If ------- completes the budget proposal by this Friday, the budget meeting will have to be rescheduled for next week.

   (A) few
   (B) some
   (C) each other
   (D) no one

4. Group members at the workshop helped ------- to find solutions to the questions raised by the host.

   (A) each
   (B) one another
   (C) altogether
   (D) along

5. ------- of the attendees were satisfied with the inspiring speech by the featured speaker.

   (A) Most
   (B) Almost
   (C) Little
   (D) Other

6. ------- of Ms. Kim's current colleagues expressed very favorable views on her performance and work ethic.

   (A) One other
   (B) Both
   (C) Everybody
   (D) Those

7. ------- who wants to volunteer his or her time to the charity event should contact Olga Maksymenko at (044) 428-7010.

   (A) Those
   (B) Every
   (C) Whoever
   (D) Anyone

8. ------- of the students who enrolled in the daytime computer class suggested that there be classes available even in the evenings.

   (A) Some
   (B) Much
   (C) A Little
   (D) Other

9. Employees at Jay's Lumberyard have recently worked late at night because they have to keep track of ------- orders during this peak season.

   (A) some of
   (B) each
   (C) all
   (D) every

10. Several efforts, ------- of which have been effective, have been made to relieve heavy traffic congestion on North Bridge.

    (A) nothing
    (B) nonetheless
    (C) none
    (D) nobody

출제율 50%

법칙 20 'a(an) + 형용사' 뒤는 단수 명사, a(an)이 없으면 복수 명사

명사에는 셀 수 있는 가산명사와 셀 수 없는 불가산명사가 있다. 가산명사라면 단수와 복수를 a나 an, 또는 명사 뒤에 s 등을 붙여 구분해 주어야 하는데, a와 명사 사이에 다른 단어들이 있거나 a가 표시되지 않은 경우에는 단수, 복수를 주의해서 확인해야 한다.

유형을 파악해 봐

1. Vivigo Cafe offers ------- to employees of Samuel Industries.
   (A) discounted   (B) discount   (C) discountable   (D) discounts

2 If you fill out the survey form, you will automatically participate in a special ------- to win $100 gift certificates.
   (A) contest   (B) contests   (C) contested   (D) contestant

3. To reduce -------, salespeople normally prefer to use public transportation for long distance trips.
   (A) expense   (B) expenses   (C) expensive   (D) expensively

보기를 보면 단어 앞 부분이 같은 단어의 변형 형태이며, 명사가 두 개 제시되었다. 빈칸의 위치를 살펴보면, 2번 문제는 앞에 'a + 형용사'가 있는 명사 자리, 1번과 3번 문제는 a가 없는 명사 자리이다.

이렇게 풀어 봐
"유형을 파악해 봐" 1번 문제를 보세요!

첫째 명사 자리인지 확인한다. ('법칙 2' 참고)
'관소전타 뒤 전준형 앞'은 명사 자리이다. 따라서 타동사 offers와 전명구(to employees) 사이는 명사 자리이다.

둘째 빈칸 앞에 a/an이 있으면 단수 명사, 없으면 복수 명사가 온다.
앞에 a가 없으므로 복수 명사인 (D)가 답이다.

PLUS

- one[each, either, neither] of the 다음에는 복수 명사가, of the가 없으면 단수 명사가 온다.
- every + 단수 명사, all + 복수 명사/불가산명사
- few, a few, several, both, many + 복수 명사
- 시험에 주로 나오는 가산 명사는 다음과 같다.

1. 사람	designer, architect, expert, contestant, representative
2. 시간	a day, a week, a month, a year
3. 규칙	regulations, rules, codes, directions
4. 증가/감소	an increase, a jump, a hike, a rise, a decline, a decrease, a drop, a reduction
5. 돈	a cost, a price, a refund, a bonus, an incentive, an account, a budget, a discount, a coin, funds
6. 시도/노력/결과	problems, ideas, reasons, alternatives, solutions, suggestions, efforts, attempts, results, decisions

함정을 피해 봐
실제 강의에서만 알려주는 풀이 노하우!

1. 단수 명사가 -s로 끝나는 경우를 조심한다.

Neither of the (business/businesses) showed an intention to give up.

→ neither of the + 복수 명사, business가 사업체라는 뜻으로 사용되면 가산명사이며, 이 경우 businesses라고 해야 복수 명사가 된다.

2. -s로 끝나도 단수 동사로 받는 경우를 조심한다

| access 접속 → 불가산명사 | freshness 신선함 → 불가산명사 | economics 경제학 → 불가산명사 |
| Jones 사람 이름 | success 성공 | The United States 미국 등 |

1. businesses

STEP 3 실전에 적용해 봐

1. The financial consultant recommended that ------- regarding office supplies be reduced significantly.

   (A) expensive
   (B) expenses
   (C) expense
   (D) expensively

2. Eating and drinking are banned inside the exhibit areas in the museum under all -------, but you can use the cafeteria next to the main entrance.

   (A) circumstantial
   (B) circumstances
   (C) circumstance
   (D) circumstanced

3. The attendance at Dr. Kim's retirement ceremony after 30 years of service reached nearly 1,000 as he has not only lots of colleagues but also many friends and ------- in the medical industry.

   (A) acquaintance
   (B) acquaintances
   (C) acquainted
   (D) acquainting

4. Following the discussion on our renovation project, the construction company sent an ------- reflecting our needs.

   (A) estimate
   (B) estimates
   (C) estimated
   (D) estimating

5. The UAB medical facility is looking for an alternative ------- of energy as oil prices are expected to continuously rise for the time being.

   (A) sources
   (B) sourcing
   (C) source
   (D) sourced

6. Our marketing director plans to take part in a weeklong conference where he can meet with various advertising ------- to discuss online advertising strategies.

   (A) professionals
   (B) profession
   (C) professional
   (D) profess

7. One of the ------- of the company-wide recycling initiative is to promote the importance of recycling which, in turn, reduces expenses for office supplies.

   (A) aim
   (B) aimed
   (C) aims
   (D) aiming

8. Located within a five-minute ------- from the main subway lines, the Lenoir Hotel provides the best convenience to tourists visiting the city.

   (A) walk
   (B) walks
   (C) walked
   (D) walking

9. With a record high ------- in sales, the company's stock price also reached the highest level in 5 years of operation.

   (A) to increase
   (B) increase
   (C) increases
   (D) increased

10. The marketing presentation made by Mr. Lu was a huge ------- due mainly to the support from the Graphics Department.

    (A) success
    (B) successes
    (C) succeeding
    (D) succeeded

출제율 47%

법칙 21 주격, 목적격 보어 자리에 오는 분사는 주로 p.p.

주격 보어	S(주어) + V(동사) + C(주격보어) I am hired. 나는 고용되어 있다.
목적격 보어	S(주어) + V(동사) + O(목적어) + O.C.(목적격 보어) I made him hired. 나는 그가 고용되게 했다.

문장이 완전하지 못할 때 이를 보충해 주는 것이 보어이다. 주격 보어는 주어인 I를 보충해 주고, 목적격 보어는 목적어 him을 보충해 주는 역할을 한다.

STEP 1 유형을 파악해 봐

1. While your flight is taking off and landing, your seatbelt should be firmly -------.
   (A) security   (B) secured   (C) securely   (D) securing

2. Airplane service has been temporarily ------- due to maintenance work on the runways.
   (A) suspended   (B) suspends   (C) suspend   (D) suspending

3. The book is also out of print and can no longer be ------- from the publisher.
   (A) order   (B) orders   (C) ordered   (D) ordering

보기가 같은 단어의 변형 형태들로 제시되었으며, -ing 형태와 p.p. 형태도 제시되어 있다. 1번 문제는 수식어인 부사 firmly를 제거하면 앞에 be동사가, 2번 문제 역시 부사 temporarily 앞에 been이, 3번 문제도 빈칸 앞에 be가 있다.

STEP 2 이렇게 풀어 봐
"유형을 파악해 봐" 1번 문제를 보세요!

첫째 빈칸이 보어 자리인지 확인한다.
빈칸 앞 부사 firmly를 제거하면 빈칸 앞 be동사가 있으므로 빈칸은 보어 자리이다.

둘째 목적어가 있으면 -ing, 목적어가 없으면 p.p.가 온다.
빈칸 뒤에 목적어가 없으므로 p.p. 형태를 보기에서 찾는다. 따라서 정답은 (B)가 된다.

 **함정을 피해 봐**   실제 강의에서만 알려주는 풀이 노하우!

1. 빈칸 뒤에 to 부정사가 있을 경우 목적어인지 아닌지 구분한다.

Employees are not (allowed/allowing) to enter the facility after 9 P.M.
→ allow는 to 부정사를 목적어로 취하는 동사가 아니다. 따라서 p.p.가 필요하다.

2. 빈칸 뒤에 'that S+V'가 있을 경우 목적어인지 아닌지 구분한다.

Please be (assuring/assured) that no charges will be applied to my account.
→ 이 경우 assure는 4형식 동사이며, 목적어가 있어도 수동태를 쓴다.

3. 덩어리 동사의 경우 전명구 앞이라고 p.p.를 답으로 하면 안 된다.

The company will be (dealt/dealing) with the issue.
→ deal with가 하나의 덩어리 동사로 사용된다. the issue가 목적어이므로 능동태 형태인 dealing이 와야 한다.

4. 감정 동사로 만든 분사는 목적어가 없어도 -ing가 가능하다.

All of the employees found the CEO's speech long and (boring/bored), though it ended 5 minutes earlier than planned.
→ 감정 동사로 만든 분사는 목적어를 생략한다. 따라서 목적어 유무와 상관없이 보충해 주는 주어나 목적어가 사람이면 p.p., 그렇지 않으면 -ing 형태가 돼야 한다. 위 문장에서 speech는 사람이 아니므로 -ing가 와야 한다.

1. allowed   **2.** assured   **3.** dealing   **4.** boring

STEP 3 실전에 적용해 봐

1. In compliance with factory regulations, smoking is not ------- anywhere in the perimeter of the facility.

   (A) allow
   (B) allows
   (C) allowed
   (D) allowing

2. As a part of the company's renovation project, a new stairwell will be ------- to connect the first and the second floor, and the building's sprinkler system will be replaced.

   (A) install
   (B) installation
   (C) installing
   (D) installed

3. If the personnel director is not available to conduct the interview due to a scheduling conflict, it will be ------- for a later time.

   (A) rescheduled
   (B) reschedules
   (C) reschedule
   (D) rescheduling

4. The board of directors will explain the details on the company's future strategy to all the shareholders who are ------- about the upcoming merger.

   (A) concerning
   (B) concerned
   (C) concerns
   (D) concern

5. The increase in profits this quarter is ------- to result in employees being given bonuses and incentives at the end of the year.

   (A) expectation
   (B) expected
   (C) expecting
   (D) expectant

6. To celebrate its 10th anniversary, Best Appliance store is ------- to announce that it will offer up to 50-percent discounts on all items in the store.

   (A) pleasing
   (B) please
   (C) pleasure
   (D) pleased

7. Many individuals who have been ------- in the so-called ice bucket initiative have been instrumental in raising public awareness of Lou Gehrig's disease all over the world.

   (A) participating
   (B) participate
   (C) participates
   (D) participated

8. You will be ------- that the workshop provides an excellent opportunity for your employees to broaden their knowledge.

   (A) convinced
   (B) convincing
   (C) convince
   (D) convinces

9. Factory workers are ------- from smoking outside designated smoking areas during their break times.

   (A) prohibit
   (B) prohibitions
   (C) prohibiting
   (D) prohibited

10. Vacation requests during the busy season should be ------- by each department manager and submitted to the personnel director to maintain productivity.

    (A) approving
    (B) approve
    (C) approved
    (D) approval

출제율 46%

법칙 22 이럴 땐 재귀대명사

myself, yourself, himself, herself, ourselves, yourselves, themselves 처럼 '~자신'이란 뜻의 대명사를 재귀대명사라고 한다.

 STEP 1 유형을 파악해 봐

1. Unlike her predecessor, the new secretary, Ms. Park, likes to handle appointment scheduling -------.
(A) hers   (B) her   (C) herself   (D) her own

2. The new hires are advised to familiarize ------- with the employee handbook detailing how to file an expense report.
(A) they   (B) their   (C) theirs   (D) themselves

3. To submit the budget report on time, Shawn collected all the data necessary for the report by -------.
(A) he   (B) him   (C) himself   (D) his own

보기에는 모두 재귀대명사와 목적격대명사, 소유격대명사가 왔으며, 1번 문제는 완전한 문장, 2번 문제는 타동사의 목적어 자리, 3번 문제는 전치사의 목적어 자리이다.

 STEP 2 이렇게 풀어 봐   "유형을 파악해 봐" 1번 문제를 보세요!

첫째 보기에 재귀대명사가 있으면 완전한 문장인지 확인한다.
unlike her predecessor는 전명구이며, 수식어 the new secretary = Ms. Park는 동격으로 주어, likes가 동사, to ~ scheduling이 목적어로 완전한 문장이다.

둘째 문장 구조에 영향을 미치지 않는 부사, 재귀대명사를 답으로 고른다.
(A), (B), (D)는 대명사로 부사의 기능이 없다. 재귀대명사만이 부사의 기능을 하는데 이것을 강조용법이라고 한다.

PLUS

- 문장이 불완전하면 해석을 통해 동작의 주체와 대상이 같은지를 확인한 후 주체와 대상이 같으면 재귀대명사가 답이다.
- 빈칸 앞에 by나 for가 왔을 때, '혼자 힘으로, 홀로'의 의미로 해석이 되면 재귀대명사가 답이다. on one's own 도 by oneself와 같은 뜻이다.

 함정을 피해 봐   실제 강의에서만 알려주는 풀이 노하우!

1. by의 뒤가 무조건 재귀대명사 자리는 아니다.

Mr. Gu is in charge of the project, so any changes to the projects budget should be approved by (him/himself).

→ any changes(변경 사항)가 스스로 approved(승인)될 수는 없고, Mr. Gu에 의해 승인되어야 하기 때문에 Mr. Gu를 가리키는 him이 정답이다.

2. '그 자신'으로 해석된다 해도 himself가 아닌 경우가 있다.

The manager asked his team members to help (him/himself) to finish the team project.

→ him은 the manager를 가리킨다. 해석상으로는 '그 자신을 도와서'가 어색하지 않지만 자세히 살펴보면 빈칸은 help의 목적어이다. help의 주체는 members이므로 주체와 목적어가 같지 않기 때문에 himself는 오답이다.

3. 재귀대명사는 단독으로 주어가 될 수 없다.

(You/Yourself) should inform my assistant Joan of your estimated arrival time.

1. him   2. him   3. You

STEP 3 실전에 적용해 봐

1. Passengers must carry their belongings with ------- or secure them in a safe place.

    (A) they
    (B) themselves
    (C) them
    (D) their

2. Although the factory manager called in sick, the workers at the Nagoya facility ------- successfully finished their daily work without him.

    (A) their
    (B) themselves
    (C) they
    (D) theirs

3. Companies use professional advertising agencies because it costs less and performs better than doing the work by -------.

    (A) themselves
    (B) their
    (C) they
    (D) them

4. Having served as a science professor for 6 years, Dr. Jang gave ------- some time off to be in his extended family at his hometown.

    (A) whose
    (B) his
    (C) him
    (D) himself

5. All newly appointed managers are invited to complete a leadership class to familiarize ------- with how to lead their teams efficiently.

    (A) yourself
    (B) itself
    (C) ours
    (D) themselves

6. Mr. Gu agreed to work on the renovation project -------, which is expected to be completed by the end of this May.

    (A) he
    (B) him
    (C) himself
    (D) his

7. Both part-time and full-time employees are required to attend an information session on facility safety regulations -------.

    (A) himself
    (B) him
    (C) themselves
    (D) theirs

8. After 10 years of experience working in public relations, Mr. Yamada finally founded an advertising company on -------.

    (A) himself
    (B) his own
    (C) his
    (D) he

9. The software was designed easily enough to use, so even home users could install it by -------.

    (A) theirs
    (B) themselves
    (C) them
    (D) their own

10. Among the best ways for workers to refresh ------- is to get some rest on a regular basis after working for many hours.

    (A) they
    (B) them
    (C) theirs
    (D) themselves

출제율 45%

법칙 23 명사를 앞에서 수식해 주는 분사는 주로 p.p.

'singing bird'에서 singing은 명사 앞에서 명사를 수식해 준다. 이러한 기능을 하는 singing을 분사라고 하며, 분사에는 singing처럼 -ing로 끝나는 현재분사와, hired처럼 주로 -ed로 끝나는 과거분사(p.p.)가 있다.

STEP 1 유형을 파악해 봐

1. Due to there being a ------- number of tickets for the music awards show, those who want to participate should make reservations in advance.
(A) limiting   (B) limited   (C) limit   (D) limitation

2. The design team will have a meeting to follow up on the ------- design following a discussion with the marking manager.
(A) proposer   (B) propose   (C) proposed   (D) proposing

3. The company outing scheduled for June 3 was canceled because of the ------- weather conditions.
(A) unexpect   (B) unexpecting   (C) unexpected   (D) unexpectation

보기가 모두 한 단어의 변형 형태들로 제시되었으며, 보기에 현재분사(-ing)와 과거분사(p.p.)가 제시되었다. 빈칸의 위치를 살펴보면 모두 '관사 뒤 명사 앞'으로, 명사를 앞에서 수식해 주는 형용사 자리임을 알 수 있다.

STEP 2 이렇게 풀어 봐 "유형을 파악해 봐" 1번 문제를 보세요!

첫째 형용사 자리에 어울리지 않는 보기를 소거한다.
빈칸의 위치가 '관사 뒤 명사 앞'이므로 명사를 수식하는 형용사 자리이다. 분사는 형용사 기능이 있으므로 분사가 아닌 (C)나 (D)는 탈락한다.

둘째 p.p. 형태의 보기를 빈칸에 대입해 본다.
limited를 빈칸에 넣어 보면 '제한된[한정된] 숫자'라는 의미로 뜻이 통하므로 (B) limited가 정답이 된다.

PLUS

- -ing가 답이 되는 경우는 주로 수식을 받는 명사가 의미상 주어가 되는 경우이다. singing bird에서 '새가 노래하다'의 관계가 가능하다. p.p.가 답이 되는 경우는 주로 수식을 받은 명사가 의미상 목적어가 되는 경우이다. revised law에서 '법을 수정하다'의 관계가 가능하다. 때로는 이러한 의미관계와 상관없이 무조건 ing 혹은 p.p.를 쓰는 경우도 있으니 아래의 표현들을 익숙하게 하도록 한다.

- 의미상 주어 관계

aspring man 대망을 품은 사람	demanding supervisor 까다로운 상관
participating store 참여하는 상점	following year 다음 해
revolving door 회전문	upcoming year 내년
leading company 선도하는 회사	preceding years 이전 해들
contributing author 기고 작가	challenging work 고된 일
increasing[rising] demand 증가하는 수요	existing law 현행법

- 무조건 ing, 무조건 p.p.

asking price 호가 (부르는 가격)	qualified candidate (자격이되는 후보자)
missing belongings (분실된 소지품)	distinguished guests (귀빈)
experienced manager (경험이 많은 매니저)	detailed instructions (상세한 설명서)
complicated process (복잡한 절차)	informed decision (현명한 결정)

 함정을 피해 봐   실제 강의에서만 알려주는 풀이 노하우!

1. 수식해 주는 명사를 동명사의 목적어로 착각하지 않도록 조심한다.

The customer didn't receive the (estimating/estimated) costs.
→ 빈칸은 costs를 수식하는 분사 자리이다.

2. 복합명사를 조심한다.

We are going to hold a (retired/retiring/retirement) party for our vice president.
→ 복합명사의 N1 자리에는 분사가 오지 못한다. ('법칙 29' 참고)

1. estimated   2. retirement

STEP 3 실전에 적용해 봐

1. The Accounting Department currently located on the second floor will move to the newly ------- third floor due to the increasing number of employees.

   (A) renovation
   (B) renovating
   (C) renovated
   (D) renovate

2. In order to reduce manufacturing costs due to recent rising oil prices, Ogata Industries, an ------- firm, has implemented a company-wide energy conservation initiative.

   (A) establishment
   (B) establishing
   (C) established
   (D) establish

3. If you spend more than $100 at Jane's Home Appliances, we can give you the newest blender at a ------- price.

   (A) reduced
   (B) reduce
   (C) reducing
   (D) reduction

4. As we are expecting an ------- number of attendees at the next meeting, we need to reserve a spacious venue for it.

   (A) overwhelmed
   (B) overwhelming
   (C) overwhelmingly
   (D) overwhelm

5. Those who want to rent a brand-new car are strongly recommended to send in a ------- rental form within the 30-day promotional period.

   (A) completely
   (B) completed
   (C) completion
   (D) completing

6. Prime Jack has been the city's ------- design firm in the clothing industry since it was founded a decade ago.

   (A) led
   (B) lead
   (C) leading
   (D) leader

7. Attached is the list of candidates with the ------- writing skills who passed the first step.

   (A) specializing
   (B) specialized
   (C) specialize
   (D) specialization

8. Taking his young age into account, Allen Jue is already a widely ------- architect in the resort construction field.

   (A) to recognize
   (B) was recognized
   (C) recognizing
   (D) recognized

9. Following a heated discussion, researchers at Havors Laboratory finally came to a ------- conclusion about renewable energy.

   (A) satisfying
   (B) satisfaction
   (C) satisfied
   (D) satisfyingly

10. Artee Publishing rated Jeju Island one of the ------- destinations in its travel magazine.

    (A) features
    (B) featured
    (C) featuring
    (D) to feature

출제율 **45%**

법칙 24 전체 문맥을 알아야 풀리는 양보, 이유 전치사

양보와 이유 전치사들을 접속사와 구분해 알아 보기로 한다.

	전치사	접속사
양보: ~에도 불구하고	despite, in spite of, notwithstanding ~에도 불구하고 regardless of ~와 상관없이	although, though, even though, even if ~라 할지라도
이유: ~때문에	because of, due to, owing to ~때문에 thanks to ~덕택에 in response to ~에 대한 응답으로 on account of ~때문에	because, since, now that, as

STEP 1 유형을 파악해 봐

1. ------- the construction on 7th Street, drivers must take a detour on 9th Street.
(A) In spite of   (B) Since   (C) Because of   (D) Besides

2. ------- the rainy and stormy weather, the football association announced that the FA Cup final will take place on schedule.
(A) Among   (B) Within   (C) Except   (D) Despite

3. ------- the time constraint, the marketing director managed to finish his presentation briefly and to the point.
(A) Prior to   (B) From   (C) Until   (D) Despite

3문제 모두 보기가 전치사로 왔기 때문에 전치사 어휘 문제임을 알 수 있다. 1번 문제의 보기에서는 (A), (C)가 각각 양보와 이유 전치사이며, 2번 문제는 (D)가 양보 전치사이고, 3번 문제는 (D)가 양보 전치사이다.

STEP 2 이렇게 풀어 봐   "유형을 파악해 봐" 1번 문제를 보세요!

첫째 '추가, 포함, 제외 전치사와 이유, 용도, 대상, 목적 전치사('법칙 15' 참고)를 확인한다.
(D)가 추가 전치사므로 가장 먼저 대입해 확인해 본다. '7번 가의 공사 이외에도, 운전자들은 9번 가로 우회해야 한다.'라는 해석은 어색하므로 (D)는 오답이다.

둘째 양보와 이유 전치사가 있는지 확인해서 그 중 양보 전치사를 우선 대입해 본다.
(A)는 양보 전치사, (C)는 이유 전치사이다. 양보와 이유 중에서는 양보 전치사가 우선이 된다. 양보 전치사 (A) In spite of를 넣어 해석해 보면 '7번 가의 공사에도 불구하고 운전자들은 9번 가로 우회해야 한다.'이므로 의미가 어색하다. 이유 전치사 (C)는 '7번 가의 공사 때문에 운전자들은 9번 가로 우회해야 한다.'로 해석이 자연스러우므로 (C)가 답이 된다. 양보나 이유 전치사를 해석하는 이유는 역접 관계인지, 인과 관계인지를 정확히 판단하기 위해서이다.

 **함정을 피해 봐**   실제 강의에서만 알려주는 풀이 노하우!

1. since의 다양한 쓰임새와 뜻에 주의한다.

(Because of / Since) the economic downturn, most industries saw low earnings last quarter.
→ since를 이유 전치사라고 생각해 둘으로 고르면 안 된다. since는 접속사일 때 '~때문에'로 해석되고, 전치사일 때는 '~이래로'의 뜻이 된다.

2. 양보나 이유 전치사처럼 보이는 부사들을 조심한다.

(Nevertheless/Despite) a 2-month delay, the new shopping complex was finally completed this month.
→ '그럼에도 불구하고'의 뜻을 가진 nevertheless는 부사이므로 전치사 자리에 올 수 없다.

1. Because of   2. Despite

STEP 3 실전에 적용해 봐

1. Mr. Brown called the manager to ask him to postpone the meeting by half an hour ------- the traffic jam.

   (A) in spite of
   (B) while
   (C) thanks to
   (D) due to

2. ------- the lack of time, the renovations at Riley's restaurant must be done by next week before the holiday.

   (A) Despite
   (B) In case of
   (C) Because of
   (D) Unless

3. ------- the increased costs of manufacturing pipes, GK, Inc. may exclude the pipes from the list of the items it sells.

   (A) Otherwise
   (B) Because of
   (C) In spite of
   (D) In contrary to

4. TOP Tech may decide to terminate its contract with ELP, Inc. ------- the increased contract fee ELP, Inc. has demanded.

   (A) except for
   (B) besides
   (C) due to
   (D) except

5. HM Pasta & Pizza is the most popular restaurant due to its excellent food and friendly service ------- there being a lot of competing dining establishments nearby.

   (A) despite
   (B) above
   (C) inside
   (D) around

6. ------- Mr. Leckon's effort to ensure the safe shipment of the products, the client company was very satisfied with the service and asked for the contract to be renewed.

   (A) Regarding
   (B) Because
   (C) Thanks to
   (D) Without

7. With demand at a record high, Martin Auto is striving to meet the production deadline for the KR5 sedan ------- the recent increase in production costs.

   (A) through
   (B) besides
   (C) following
   (D) despite

8. The charity funds reached almost $300,000, the same amount that was raised last year as well ------- the economic downturn this year.

   (A) following
   (B) besides
   (C) on behalf of
   (D) in spite of

9. As Ryan, Inc. has partnered with Fab, Inc. for 7 years and been satisfied with the service provided by Fab, Inc., it is willing to accept the deal ------- the types of services Fab, Inc. offers.

   (A) over
   (B) apart from
   (C) regardless of
   (D) throughout

10. Mr. Dennis bought his new camera from Leo Cam other than any other nearby stores ------- the attention to detail of its service representative, Ms. Morgan.

    (A) regardless of
    (B) due to
    (C) ahead of
    (D) across

출제율 43%

법칙 25 단수 주어 뒤는 단수 동사, 복수 주어 뒤는 복수 동사

동사는 주어가 단수인지 복수인지에 따라 모양이 변한다. 주어가 3인칭 단수면서 동사가 현재일 때는 동사 뒤에 s가 붙는다. 동사에 s가 붙은 형태를 편의상 단수 동사라고 한다.

주어	동사(현재시제)	동사(과거시제)
an apple (단수 명사)	is (단수 동사)	was (단수 동사)
apples (복수 명사)	are (복수 동사)	were (복수 동사)
a worker (단수 명사)	works (단수 동사)	worked
workers (복수 명사)	work (복수 동사)	worked
I, You	work	worked

STEP 1 유형을 파악해 봐

1. Even after the oil shock, Wing Air still ------- that more than 2 million customers will use its services.
   (A) expect   (B) expecting   (C) expects   (D) expectedly

2. The application for the engineer position at both JP, Inc. and Black Tech ------- the applicant's resume be attached.
   (A) requiring   (B) requirement   (C) requires   (D) require

3. The dinner show which will be hosted by BK, Inc. tonight ------- a special guest.
   (A) featuring   (B) to feature   (C) features   (D) feature

제시된 보기들은 모두 한 단어의 변형 형태이며, 동사가 아닌 것과 단수 동사, 복수 동사가 섞여 있다. 빈칸을 살펴보면 1번 문제는 앞에 주어와 뒤에 목적어가 있는 동사 자리이고, 2번 문제는 The application의 동사 자리이고, 3번 문제는 The dinner show의 동사 자리이다.

STEP 2 이렇게 풀어 봐   "유형을 파악해 봐" 1번 문제를 보세요!

첫째 동사 자리인지부터 확인한다. (법츠 38번 참고)
빈칸의 앞뒤를 살펴보면 Wing Air가 주어, still은 부사, that 이하가 목적어 역할을 하므로 빈칸은 동사 자리임을 알 수 있다.

둘째 수식어를 제거한 후, 주어가 단수이면 단수 동사, 주어가 복수이면 복수 동사가 답이다.

수식어 still을 제외하면, Wing Air는 단수이므로 정답은 단수 동사 (C) expects가 된다.

PLUS

동사 바로 앞의 단어와 수일치해서는 안 되며, 주어와 동사 사이에 자주 들어가는 수식어인 부사, 전명구, 분사구, 형용사절 등을 빼고 수일치를 시켜야 한다.

Workers **hardly** (commute/commutes) to work on time.
Workers **at the Detroit facility** (work/works) three shifts.
Workers **doing repetitive work** (have to/has to) take regular breaks.
Workers **informed of the new schedule** (are/is) to meet the deadline.
Workers **that were recently hired by the company** (need/needs) to attend an orientation session.

여기서는 'hardly(부사), at the Detroit facility(전명구), doing repetitive work(현재분사구), informed of the new schedule(과거분사구), that were recently hired by the company(형용사절)' 등이 수식어이다.

동명사는 단수로 취급한다.

Estimating sales figures (require/requires) a lot of energy and research.

함정을 피해 봐
실제 강의에서만 알려주는 풀이 노하우!

1. 주어가 s로 끝나는 단어지만 단수 동사로 받아야 하는 경우를 조심한다.

 • 불가산명사 중 s로 끝나는 단어들: access 접근   freshness 신선함   happiness 행복   economics 경제학
 • 가산명사 중 s로 끝나는 단어들: a success 성공   a business 회사
 • 고유명사 중 s로 끝나는 단어들: the United States 미국   Jones 사람 이름

2. 주어가 없는 것처럼 보이는 경우 수일치에 주의한다.

Ms. Lee played a crucial role finding potential customers and truly (deserve/deserves) a pay raise.
→ 수식어 truly를 빼내면 동사 앞의 주어인 Ms. Lee는 생략된 것으로, 주어가 단수이므로 단수 동사가 와야 한다.

The book which (outlines/outline) the procedure is very good.
→ which는 여기서 주격관계대명사이며, 이것이 가리키는 것이 선행사 book이다. 이 경우 선행사와 수일치를 시켜야 한다.

3. 목적격관계대명사가 생략된 경우 수일치에 주의한다.

Mr. Gu managed to finish the project by the deadline although some of the assistants he works with (was/were) on vacation.
→ he works with가 형용사절이다. he 앞에는 목적격관계대명사 that 또는 whom이 생략되었다. 따라서 he works with를 빼고 some of the assistants와 수일치를 시켜야 한다.

2. deserves, outlines   3. were

STEP 3 실전에 적용해 봐

1. The printer on the first floor ------- to have been occupied for the whole day.
   (A) seem
   (B) seeing
   (C) seems
   (D) being seem

2. The employees recently hired by the HJ Company ------- to be instructed by the manager.
   (A) need
   (B) needs
   (C) needing
   (D) had needed

3. Hanna Chen has been very strict with her time management and never ------- late for the meetings.
   (A) come
   (B) coming
   (C) to come
   (D) comes

4. The deposits for the construction ------- sent to the JB Company by next week as requested.
   (A) to be
   (B) being
   (C) is
   (D) will be

5. The employees who work the eight-hour shifts in the day ------- the keys to the staff room every Sunday.
   (A) returning
   (B) return
   (C) returns
   (D) has returned

6. You should get a ticket from one of the staff members who ------- free tickets to the event at the moment.
   (A) provide
   (B) is provided
   (C) providing
   (D) is providing

7. The CEO of King Motors ------- the merger offer from Beckon Motors after reviewing Beckon Motor's financial status.
   (A) accept
   (B) accepting
   (C) accepted
   (D) acceptance

8. Ms. White's concerns about the company's profits last quarter ------- clearly stated in the e-mail she sent.
   (A) was
   (B) were
   (C) being
   (D) will be

9. These products have recently become very popular with young customers and ------- out of stock soon.
   (A) been
   (B) was
   (C) will be
   (D) to be

10. Taint Motors promised to provide full compensation and free service until every customer ------- fully repaid.
    (A) being
    (B) to be
    (C) are
    (D) is

출제율 43%

법칙 26 문맥을 알아야 풀 수 있는 주제, 범위, 근거 전치사

주제 전치사: ~에 관하여	about with regard to relating to	regarding in regard to related to	concerning pertaining to over	as to pertinent to on
범위 전치사	within	beyond		
근거 전치사	according to	based on	in accordance with	

STEP 1 유형을 파악해 봐

1. The meeting will address the issue ------- the retirement party plans.
(A) after　　　(B) whichever　　　(C) regarding　　　(D) plus

2. The companies received approval that allows them to build manufacturing plants ------- the boundaries of the development area.
(A) within　　　(B) against　　　(C) as to　　　(D) without

3. ------- the research conducted by Richard Raymond, every 2 in 5 employees working at the construction site has gotten injured or witnessed an accident.
(A) According to　　　(B) In case of　　　(C) Given that　　　(D) When

보기의 공통점을 살펴보면 3문제 모두 보기 중 전치사가 2개 이상이므로 전치사 어휘 문제임을 알 수 있다. 1번 문제는 (C)가 주제 전치사, 2번 문제는 (A)가 범위 전치사, (C)가 주제 전치사이며, 3번 문제는 (A)가 근거 전치사이다.

STEP 2 이렇게 풀어 봐
"유형을 파악해 봐" 1번 문제를 보세요!

첫째 보기에 접속사가 있으므로 접속사 자리인지부터 확인한다.
'동사의 수 – 접속사의 수 = 1'인데, 동사는 will address 하나이므로 접속사는 필요 없다. 접속사와 전치사로 모두 사용 가능한 after와 복합관계사 whichever, 그리고 나머지는 전치사이므로 이 문제는 전치사 어휘 문제이다.

둘째 추/포/제/for(이, 용, 대, 목) → 양보와 이유 전치사 순서로 대입한다.
(D) plus가 추가 전치사이며, 해석해 보면 '은퇴 파티 계획에 덧붙여 문제를 다룰 것이다.'라는 뜻이 되어 자연스럽지 못하다. 양보와 이유 전치사는 보기에 없다.

셋째 주제, 범위, 근거 전치사를 대입하여 해석해 본다.
(C) regarding이 주제 전치사이며, 해석해 보면 '은퇴 파티 계획에 대한 문제를 다룰 것이다.'라는 뜻이 되어 해석이 자연스럽다. 따라서 (C)가 정답이다. (A) after는 시점 및 기간 전치사인데, 빈칸 뒤 명사가 시점, 기간과 관련이 없으므로 자연스럽게 탈락한다.

PLUS

- within은 범위뿐 아니라 기간과도 잘 어울린다.
- beyond는 한계, 기대치, 국경선, 능력 등을 넘어설 때 사용한다.
- according to 뒤는 뉴스, 조사, 보고, 연구 등이 오며, in accordance with 뒤는 규정, 법 등이 온다.
- over(~에 관하여)는 말다툼, 논쟁 등을 나타내는 말과 주로 쓰인다.

함정을 피해 봐 — 실제 강의에서만 알려주는 풀이 노하우!

1. as to, as of, as for를 구분한다.

as for : (주로 문두에 와서) ~에 한하여
As for me, I like summer much better.

as of : (시점 앞에서) ~부로
As of today, Mr. Kim will serve as our vice-president.

as to : ~에 관하여
Employees differ as to the solution to the problem.

STEP 3 실전에 적용해 봐

1. Customers should bring the items they want to return with the receipts to the nearest store ------- 2 weeks of ordering them to get a full refund.

   (A) for
   (B) throughout
   (C) within
   (D) during

2. The client has just called the office ------- the cancellation of her membership.

   (A) of
   (B) along
   (C) under
   (D) about

3. Until the company makes an official announcement ------- the layoff of its employees, Mr. Williams will feel uneasy about it.

   (A) within
   (B) along with
   (C) regardless of
   (D) regarding

4. ------- the Accounting Department, 60% of the firm's debt has been paid, and sales are gradually increasing.

   (A) As a result
   (B) According to
   (C) In comparison to
   (D) Providing that

5. The terms ------- the acquisition offer proposed by Wireless Tech were revised at Wireless Tech's request.

   (A) aside from
   (B) pertaining to
   (C) due to
   (D) in spite of

6. The researchers must be given a proper education ------- the proper ways to handle chemical substances before going into the lab.

   (A) over
   (B) beyond
   (C) from
   (D) on

7. It is also recommended that you look up other clients' cases ------- your case if you want to know the probable outcome.

   (A) belong to
   (B) available to
   (C) referring to
   (D) pertaining to

8. As far as Lob, Inc. is involved in the issue ------- environmental pollution in China, it is restricted to expanding its business to other countries.

   (A) relating
   (B) in relation
   (C) concerning
   (D) in regard

9. The decision ------- whether to move the headquarters to the northern city should be made and confirmed by the executive manager by Thursday.

   (A) up to
   (B) as to
   (C) referring
   (D) pertaining

10. ------- government policy, Felcons, Inc. had to revise its financial statement and clearly state the amount of its annual profits.

    (A) In addition to
    (B) Pertaining to
    (C) In order for
    (D) In accordance with

Chapter 03

3개월에 한 번 출제되는 문제

출제 3 순위

토익 시험 3회에 반드시 한 번은 나온다.

출제율 39%

법칙 27 빈칸 앞뒤 단어만 봐도 풀리는 동반, 수단, 수동 전치사

동반 전치사와 수단 전치사, 그리고 수동태 전치사에 대해서 알아 본다.

- 동반: with ~와 함께   alongside ~와 나란히   without ~없이
- 수단: with ~를 가지고   by ~에 의해서   through ~를 통해서
- 수동태: by ~에 의해서

STEP 1 유형을 파악해 봐

1. Mr. Brown was informed ------- his co-worker that there will be an important meeting next week.
(A) on   (B) of   (C) by   (D) during

2. Royal Electronics will compensate every customer ------- a full refund for their purchase of its malfunctioning products.
(A) with   (B) to   (C) in   (D) for

3. Customers who return the item within three days of the date of purchase may exchange the item for a new one ------- any penalties.
(A) without   (B) through   (C) until   (D) for

보기가 모두 전치사들로 제시된 것으로 보아 전치사 문제임을 알 수 있다. 위치와는 관계가 없으므로 빈칸의 위치와 같은 문제의 공통점은 찾지 않아도 된다. 1번 문제는 (C)가 수동태의 by, 2번 문제는 (A)에 동반[수단] 전치사 with, 3번 문제는 (A)에 with의 반대어인 without가 왔다.

STEP 2 이렇게 풀어 봐   "유형을 파악해 봐" 1번 문제를 보세요!

첫째 전치사 문제일 경우 추가, 포함, 제외(추/포/제), for(이유, 용도, 대상, 목적) → 양보, 이유 → 주제, 범위, 근거 전치사 순으로 확인한다.
보기에는 존재하지 않는다.

둘째 동반, 수단, 수동태 전치사 순으로 확인한다.
(C) by가 수동태 전치사이므로 먼저 대입해 본다. 또한 빈칸 앞에 be p.p.가 온 것으로 보아 수동태의 주체를 나타내는 전치사가 필요함을 알 수 있다. 해석해 보면 '중요한 미팅이 있을 것이라고 동료에 의해 통보 받았다.'는 내용이 자연스럽기 때문에 (C)가 정답이다.

PLUS

• with의 경우, 위탁이나 동시 상황을 나타낼 때도 사용하고, 단순한 숙어로 사용되기도 한다.

위탁	leave a message with ~에게 메시지를 남기다		
동시 상황	with the demand at an all-time high 수요가 가장 많은 상태인		
숙어	comply with ~를 준수하다		agree with ~에 동의하다
	deal with ~를 다루다		proceed with ~를 진행하다
	provide A with B A에게 B를 제공하다		in cooperation with ~와 협력하여

• without 뒤에는 보통 '영수증, 통행증, 허가, 허락, -ing' 등이 온다.
• by -ing도 많이 사용하며, '~함으로써'라는 뜻을 갖는다.
• through 뒤에는 주로 이메일이나 인터넷, TV 등의 수단, 매개체를 나타내는 명사가 온다.

함정을 피해 봐
실제 강의에서만 알려주는 풀이 노하우!

1. 동반의 with와 수동태의 by를 혼동하지 않도록 조심한다.

Books lent from the public library should be returned (by/with) students within two weeks.
→ 책은 학생들에 의해 반납되므로 수동태(be p.p.)의 주체를 나타내는 전치사 by가 와야 한다.

2. without과 except를 혼동하지 않도록 한다. ('법칙 15' 참고)

Nobody (without/except) a visitor pass is allowed to enter the facility.
Everyone in the Marketing Department (without/except) Mr. Kim should attend the weekly seminar.
→ without은 '~가 없이'라는 뜻이며, '~를 가지고(with)'의 반대말이다.
except는 '~를 제외하고'의 뜻이며, '~를 포함하고(including)'의 반대말이다.

3. 수동태 by 앞에 p.p.가 생략된 경우에 주의한다.

The newly released book, Get to Heaven (by/with) Mr. Gu was well received by a lot of readers.
→ by 앞에 written이 생략되었다.

1. by   2. without, except   3. by

STEP 3 실전에 적용해 봐

1. All application forms for the program are sealed ------- the pamphlets explaining its benefits in an envelope.

   (A) with
   (B) from
   (C) to
   (D) through

2. The executive manager has in fact confirmed and agreed to the project ------- asking for a budget to carry it out.

   (A) with
   (B) by
   (C) until
   (D) to

3. Permission to access the SG Co.'s private account is granted ------- the General Affairs Department.

   (A) on
   (B) to
   (C) by
   (D) in

4. The Human Resources Department cannot look through employees' personal documents ------- their approval.

   (A) without
   (B) with
   (C) between
   (D) upon

5. You can experience the all-new Brenda automobile ------- applying for a free seven-day trial offer.

   (A) at
   (B) by
   (C) in
   (D) over

6. Volca Tech does not let anyone access the laboratory ------- showing an employee ID card to the staff member on duty.

   (A) without
   (B) on
   (C) upon
   (D) over

7. Jazzy Salon has decided to attract more customers ------- online advertisements placed on some of the most-visited Web sites.

   (A) of
   (B) through
   (C) except
   (D) after

8. The timeless classic movie '50 Secrets about the Sea' ------- Liam Kidson was remade by another director, and both the movie and the director quickly gained international popularity.

   (A) upon
   (B) nearby
   (C) by
   (D) besides

9. The items delivered just now should be placed on the shelves ------- sales clerks before the store opens.

   (A) with
   (B) by
   (C) on
   (D) along

10. Imported products weighing under 10kg can directly pass the examination process ------- delay at the airport.

    (A) along
    (B) without
    (C) instead
    (D) except

출제율 **31%**

법칙 28 조동사, 명령문, 그리고 요구, 주장, 의무, 명령, 제안 뒤는 동사원형

조동사 can, may, will, should, must 등은 동사 앞에서 동사의 시제나 의미를 보충해 주는 기능을 한다. 조동사 뒤에는 동사원형이 오는데, 동사원형이란 s나 -ing가 붙지 않은 동사의 기본형을 말한다. 또한, 요구, 주장, 의무, 명령, 제안을 뜻하는 명사, 형용사, 동사를 줄여 '요번주의명제'로 알아 두도록 한다.

STEP 1 유형을 파악해 봐

1. Chad should ------- more staff members to distribute pamphlets to customers visiting the store.
(A) hirable   (B) hiring   (C) hire   (D) hires

2. Please ------- tuned for more news coming up soon.
(A) stay   (B) staying   (C) to stay   (D) will stay

3. Mr. Gratski has asked that his secretary ------- an appointment with his client at noon.
(A) arranged   (B) have arranged   (C) arrange   (D) will arrange

보기의 공통점을 살펴보면 같은 단어의 변형 형태들임을 알 수 있다. 빈칸의 위치를 보면 1번 문제는 조동사 뒤에, 2번 문제는 제안문 형태로 please 뒤에, 3번 문제는 has asked 뒤 that절의 동사 자리에 빈칸이 왔다.

STEP 2 이렇게 풀어 봐   "유형을 파악해 봐" 1번 문제를 보세요!

첫째 빈칸 앞에 조동사가 있으면 동사원형을 고른다.
should가 '~해야 한다'라는 뜻의 조동사이므로 동사원형인 (C)를 답으로 고른다.

둘째 제시된 보기들의 품사 형태를 파악한다.
(A)는 형용사, (B)는 준동사(동명사나 현재분사), (D)는 단수 동사이므로 동사원형이 아니다.

PLUS

- 명령문은 주어 you가 생략된 형태이며, 동사원형으로 시작한다.
- 제안문은 명령문 앞에 please가 온 형태이며, 역시 동사원형으로 시작한다.
- '요번주의명제' 뒤에는 should가 생략된 형태이므로 동사원형이 온다.

요구 : ask, request, advise
주장 : insist, prefer
의무 : necessary, mandatory, imperative, crucial, natural ⎫
명령 : order   ⎬ that S (should) 동사원형
제안 : suggest, recommend, advisable   ⎭

함정을 피해 봐
실제 강의에서만 알려주는 풀이 노하우!

1. please 바로 뒤가 동사원형이 아닌 경우를 조심한다.

Please (specify/specifying/**specifically**) note the date by which you can submit the proposal.
→ 이미 note 부분이 동사이므로 앞에는 동사를 수식하는 부사가 답이 된다.

2. '제안하다'의 뜻으로 사용되지 않는 suggest는 '요번주의명제'가 아니다.

Mr. Kim's comments suggest that he (**is**/be) in favor of the new benefits plan.
→ 여기서 suggest는 '의미하다, 나타내다'의 뜻이므로 정상적으로 is가 와야 한다.

3. to 부정사의 부사적 용법을 명령문으로 착각하지 않도록 주의한다.

(Summit/**To submit**) your proposal by the deadline, be sure to work at least eight hours a day.
→ 문장에 이미 동사 be가 있으므로 동사가 또 올 수 없다. 따라서 to 부정사의 부사적 용법인 To submit이 정답이다.

1. specifically   2. is   3. To submit

STEP 3 실전에 적용해 봐

1. To make a difference in your career, simply ------- for the managerial position at Alaska Co. by filling out the form.

   (A) apply
   (B) applies
   (C) applying
   (D) applied

2. Anyone whose budget report does not ------- the standard will be asked to revise and submit it again.

   (A) met
   (B) meet
   (C) meeting
   (D) have met

3. Before signing the contract, please ------- check the terms and conditions of the contract for any mistakes.

   (A) repeat
   (B) repeating
   (C) repeatedly
   (D) repetition

4. Although you will be rather free to wear whatever you want once you finally get accepted to work at Venom Co., the managers may ask that you ------- a formal suit at least to the interview.

   (A) will wear
   (B) wore
   (C) are wearing
   (D) wear

5. The health insurance plan provides you with $200 for hospital bills but does not ------- expenses for regular health checks.

   (A) covering
   (B) covered
   (C) cover
   (D) covers

6. When returning the equipment, ------- your signature with the date you return it on the sheet placed on the desk.

   (A) wrote
   (B) writing
   (C) writes
   (D) write

7. One of the job consultant's comments suggests that most mid-sized companies ------- reluctant to hire more employees.

   (A) are being
   (B) be
   (C) are
   (D) being

8. Before the shipment could ------- to Mr. Doe, the transport ship got into an accident, and part of the shipment was lost.

   (A) delivering
   (B) be delivered
   (C) delivers
   (D) being delivered

9. ------- the sixteenth year since the Alim Corporation was founded, several CEOs at its partner companies attended the event to deliver congratulatory messages.

   (A) Commemoration
   (B) Commemorate
   (C) Commemorated
   (D) To commemorate

10. Alison Motors recently decided to sell more automobiles next year and requested that the manufacturing plants ------- their speed of production.

    (A) increased
    (B) have increased
    (C) increase
    (D) will increase

출제율 31%

법칙 29 덩어리로 외워야 하는 복합명사 문제

복합명사는 'retirement party(은퇴 파티)'와 같이 두 개 이상의 단어가 한 단어처럼 사용되는 것을 말한다. 이렇게 복합명사는 지정된 형태를 사용하기 때문에 익혀두어야 한다.

유형을 파악해 봐

1. The Sales Department focused on stressing the product's quality to increase customer -------.
(A) satisfied　　(B) satisfaction　　(C) satisfactorily　　(D) satisfactory

2. Please have your ------- card with you when entering the restricted area.
(A) authorization　　(B) authorizer　　(C) authorized　　(D) authorizes

3. Employees of the McQueen Company are asked to go to the reception desk to get a security ------- to get inside the factory.
(A) pass　　(B) passed　　(C) passing　　(D) passes

보기가 한 단어의 변형 형태들로 왔음을 알 수 있다. 3문제 모두 보기에는 명사형이 1개 이상 제시되었으며, 빈칸 앞이나 뒤에도 명사가 있다.

이렇게 풀어 봐
"유형을 파악해 봐" 1번 문제를 보세요!

첫째 빈칸 앞이 가산명사인지 확인한다.
빈칸 앞 customer가 가산명사인데도 a customer나 customers로 오지 않았다.

둘째 N2 부분에 들어갈 명사를 결정한다.
N2가 가산/불가산을 결정하는데, 앞에 a가 없다면 N2는 복수 명사나 불가산명사이다. 따라서 불가산명사인 (B)가 답이다.

PLUS

- 복합명사의 단수, 복수는 N2를 기준으로 한다.
  EX) an application form, application forms
- N1이 -s로 끝나거나, 불가산명사인 경우는 복합명사의 형태를 알아야 풀 수 있다.

주요 기출 복합명사

N1이 복수형인 경우	N2가 가산명사인 경우	N2가 불가산명사인 경우
sales manager 판매부장	an application form 신청서	customer satisfaction 고객만족
sports complex 종합경기시설	a retirement party 은퇴파티	worker productivity 작업자 생산성
customs office 세관	office supplies 사무용품	workplace safety 작업장 안전
savings bank 저축은행	safety measures 안전조치	consumer access 소비자 접근
savings account 은행계좌	a building permit 건축허가증	address verification 주소지 확인
electronics company 전자회사	a marketing strategy 마케팅전략	heating equipment 난방 장비

 함정을 피해 봐 — 실제 강의에서만 알려주는 풀이 노하우!

1. N2 자리에 명사가 아닌 다른 품사를 넣지 않도록 조심한다.

There will be an information session on company (regulations/regulated).

→ '회사 규정에 대한 설명회가 있을 것이다.'로 해석되는 문장에서 regulated가 답이라면 먼저 '통제된, 조절된 회사'로 해석되어야 하므로 어색하다. 또한 company는 가산명사이므로 그 뒤에 N2가 복수형이나 불가산명사가 와야 관사나 소유격 없이도 쓸 수 있다. regulated는 과거분사.

2. N1 자리에 명사가 아닌 다른 품사를 넣지 않도록 조심한다.

All visitors are required to have their (identification/identical) card visible while in the building.

→ '모든 방문객들은 신분증이 보이도록 해야 한다.'는 내용의 문장에서 identical이 답이라면 '동일한 카드'로 해석되므로 내용이 어색하다.

1. regulations   2. identification

STEP 3 실전에 적용해 봐

1. The employees should have the workplace cleaned up and report any problems they find with the facilities during the regular ------- check.

   (A) maintained
   (B) maintaining
   (C) maintain
   (D) maintenance

2. Instead of making the ------- party for Mr. Tall open for everyone to attend, Mr. Gallery sent the invitations to only few employees upon Mr. Tall's request.

   (A) retire
   (B) retiring
   (C) retirement
   (D) retired

3. To carry out the ------- inspection in the manufacturing facility, all machines should be turned off temporarily.

   (A) safety
   (B) safely
   (C) safe
   (D) safable

4. Anyone looking for a new job or planning a job transfer is encouraged to come to the job ------- held at Mary Street this week.

   (A) fairness
   (B) fairy
   (C) fairly
   (D) fair

5. All new employees are required to submit their verification of ------- letter to the head of their department by the end of this week.

   (A) employ
   (B) employing
   (C) employed
   (D) employment

6. Innovation Electronics has expected that its profit ------- will exceed 30% this year.

   (A) margin
   (B) margining
   (C) margined
   (D) marginal

7. Please tell us your ------- account number, and the insurance fee will automatically be transferred at the end of every month.

   (A) savings
   (B) saving
   (C) saved
   (D) save

8. In case you experience an equipment ------- with our product, please call us and explain the problem you have with it before you send it back for a refund or exchange.

   (A) malfunctioning
   (B) malfunction
   (C) malfunctioned
   (D) malfunctions

9. The documents needed to be reviewed and submitted by a customs -------, who can be found on the second floor of this building.

   (A) officials
   (B) officially
   (C) official
   (D) officiality

10. All employees must carefully read the sheet explaining the workplace safety ------- during the orientation meeting on Tuesday.

    (A) regulated
    (B) regulations
    (C) regularity
    (D) regular

출제율 31%

법칙 30 전명구 앞에 잘 오는 부사

in the room처럼 전치사로 시작해 명사로 끝나는 덩어리를 전명구라고 하며, 형용사나 부사의 기능을 한다. 부사는 형용사나 부사, 동사를 수식하기 때문에 전명구를 수식하는 것도 부사라고 볼 수 있다.

STEP 1 유형을 파악해 봐

1. Mr. Wisby, who has plenty of experience in the relevant field, put on an outstanding performance ------- during the training period at his new workplace.
(A) more   (B) so   (C) even   (D) yet

2. All volunteers must come to the venue, where the buses heading to our destination will leave ------- at 7 P.M.
(A) internally   (B) frequently   (C) promptly   (D) greatly

3. Please make sure that you are using this self-adhesive tool ------- on objects and not on a person as it can be hard to detach it once glued.
(A) finally   (B) completely   (C) rarely   (D) only

보기가 주로 부사들로 구성되어 있다. 특히 1번 문제의 경우 보기들이 -ly로 끝나지 않는 부사들로 왔고, 빈칸은 완전한 문장의 뒤, 전명구 앞에 위치해 있다.

STEP 2 이렇게 풀어 봐
"유형을 파악해 봐" 1번 문제를 보세요!

첫째 보기들이 모두 부사인지 확인한다.
-ly로 끝나지 않았지만 보기가 모두 부사들로 제시된 것으로 보아 부사 문제임을 알 수 있다.

둘째 빈칸이 전명구 앞에 있는지 확인한다.
빈칸이 전명구 앞에 있으므로 전명구를 좋아하는 초점 부사 even을 우선 대입해 해석해 본다. '심지어 훈련 받기 전에도 탁월한 실적을 보여주었다.'는 내용으로 해석이 자연스럽기 때문에 (C)가 정답이다. (A)는 비교 단서 than이 있어야 가능하고, (B)는 형용사나 부사 앞에 오며, (D)는 부정문에 쓴다.

PLUS

• 부사 중에서 특히 전명구 앞에 잘 오는 부사들을 기억한다.

주로 전명구 앞에 오는 부사들		
초점 부사	only 단지 specifically 특히 exclusively 독점적으로 especially 특히	just 단지 exactly 정확히 even ~조차
방식	directly from ~로부터 직접 separately from ~와는 별도로	directly to ~쪽으로 직접
시간	sometime between A and B A와 B 사이 promptly at ~정각에 right after 직후에	later in the week 주 후반에 immediately after 직후에 soon after 직후에
기타	ideally from two supervisors 이상적으로 everywhere in the room 방안 어디든지 temporarily out of stock 일시적으로 재고가 바닥난	probably due to ~ 주로 ~때문에 consistently behind schedule 지속적으로 일정보다 늦은

함정을 피해 봐
실제 강의에서만 알려주는 풀이 노하우!

1. 초점 부사는 명사 앞에도 올 수 있다.

(Only/Entirely) those who have their identification badge are allowed to enter the facility.
→ those는 '사람들'이란 뜻의 명사이며, 명사 앞에 올 수 있는 부사는 초점 부사인 only이다.

2. 전명구 앞이 무조건 부사 자리가 되는 것은 아니다.

All questions should be (directed/directly) to the manager.
→ 'directly to 명사'에 익숙해져 있는 수험생들이 틀리기 쉬운 문제이다. be 동사가 빈칸 앞에 있다면 빈칸 뒤엔 보어가 필요하다. 부사 directly가 아닌 directed가 와야 보어가 될 수 있다.

1. Only 2. directed

STEP 3 실전에 적용해 봐

1. This fitness program, in which a professional trainer intensively manages the trainee for 3 months, is offered ------- to individuals who have been members for more than one year.

   (A) exclusively
   (B) beneficially
   (C) completely
   (D) mutually

2. The interviewer seemed to value the educational backgrounds of the applicants, ------- regarding their majors at their universities.

   (A) extremely
   (B) fully
   (C) promptly
   (D) particularly

3. As a production manager, Mr. Bail's job is to make sure that the products are ------- up to date with the current trends.

   (A) vaguely
   (B) consistently
   (C) gradually
   (D) consequently

4. We ensure that the goods we sell go for the lowest prices because we deliver them ------- from the providers to our customers.

   (A) directly
   (B) completely
   (C) steadily
   (D) frequently

5. Please note that a shipping fee will be charged ------- from the price of the products ordered.

   (A) separately
   (B) formerly
   (C) cooperatively
   (D) sharply

6. ------- those who have not paid the registration fee yet will be primarily restricted from using specific facilities at the gym.

   (A) Only
   (B) Entirely
   (C) Because
   (D) Either

7. It is the company's policy that ------- the night shift workers are allowed to use heating equipment while working.

   (A) widely
   (B) relatively
   (C) only
   (D) simply

8. The meeting will address the issue of the recent economic downturn, ------- its effect on the company's profits.

   (A) specifying
   (B) specifically
   (C) specify
   (D) specified

9. The former president of the Trent Corporation started his own business ------- after resigning.

   (A) immediately
   (B) formerly
   (C) completely
   (D) extremely

10. Ms. Glow will deliver a speech on the development of information technology, ------- in the field of e-commerce.

    (A) particularly
    (B) particular
    (C) particulars
    (D) particularity

출제율 30%

법칙 31 문장, 형용사(또는 -ing/p.p.), 부사 앞은 부사 자리

부사는 문장에서 다양한 자리에 위치한다. 필수요소(주어, 동사, 목적어, 보어)의 사이 또는 뒤에 위치하기도 한다. ('법칙 3, 법칙 7' 참고) 이번에는 문장의 가장 앞과 형용사, 부사 앞에 자리하는 부사에 대해서 알아 본다.

 유형을 파악해 봐

1. Innovative Tech introduced a mobile phone equipped with a ------- new technology.
(A) completely   (B) completing   (C) complete   (D) completion

2. The Anywhere Travel Agency believes that it will soon become the leading tour company because it provides a number of ------- priced package tours.
(A) competitive   (B) compete   (C) competition   (D) competitively

3. As a result of ------- advertising the latest car model released, Furious Auto earned profits triple the amount it earned last year.
(A) actively   (B) activeness   (C) active   (D) action

보기들이 모두 한 단어의 변형 형태로 왔다. 3문제 모두 '관소전타' 뒤에 빈칸이 존재하며, 1번 문제의 빈칸 뒤에는 '형용사+명사'가, 2번 문제는 'p.p.+복합명사,' 3번 문제는 '출시된 가장 최신 자동차 모델을 광고하는 것'이라는 동명사가 왔다.

 이렇게 풀어 봐   "유형을 파악해 봐" 1번 문제를 보세요!

첫째 빈칸 앞이 '관소전타', 빈칸 뒤가 형용사나 -ing, p.p.가 있으면 부사가 답이다.
빈칸 앞에 a가 있고, 빈칸 뒤에 형용사 new가 와서 technology를 수식하고 있다.

둘째 보기를 대입해 해석해 본다.
형용사를 수식하는 부사 (A)를 넣어 해석이 어울리는지 확인해 보면, '완전히 새로운 기술'이라는 뜻으로 자연스럽게 해석이 되는 (A)가 답이 된다.

PLUS

- 현재분사와 동명사 모두 -ing 형태를 하고 있지만 모두 부사의 수식을 받는다.

a pleasantly singing bird 기쁘게 노래하고 있는 새   singing → 현재분사
by pleasantly singing a song 기쁘게 노래 한 곡을 부름으로써   singing → 동명사

- 숫자는 형용사 취급한다. 따라서 앞에 부사가 온다.

함정을 피해 봐   실제 강의에서만 알려주는 풀이 노하우!

1. 형용사 앞에 부사가 아닌 형용사가 오는 경우를 조심한다.

The (impressively/impressive) new line of cars will soon be on sale.
→ 이 문장에서 impressive도 line of cars를 수식해, impressive and new line of cars의 뜻이 된다. confidential financial document(비밀 재무 문건), professional financial advisor(전문적인 재무 고문) 등도 같은 경우이다.

2. 명사로 굳어진 -ing 앞에는 형용사가 온다.

Thanks to (careful/carefully) planning, the construction of the new office will be completed ahead of schedule.
→ 이 문장에서 planning은 동명사가 아니고 명사이다. 따라서 그 앞에는 부사가 아니라 형용사가 와야 한다.

-ing 형태의 가산명사	a painting 그림 a covering 덮개	listings 목록 earnings 수입	findings 조사결과물 a meeting 회의	a showing 전시회
-ing 형태의 불가산명사	funding 자금지원 advertising 광고 processing 처리	planning 기획 seating 좌석, 좌석배치	cleaning 청소, 세탁 housing 주택	clothing 옷 widening 확장

1. impressive   2. careful

STEP 3 실전에 적용해 봐

1. The renovation of the parking lot was done to make its entrance more ------- accessible for car owners.

   (A) easily
   (B) easier
   (C) easy
   (D) ease

2. -------, Mr. Jacob thought his work was too demanding, but after two weeks of training, he felt confident enough to do it.

   (A) Despite
   (B) At first
   (C) Although
   (D) Nevertheless

3. The results of the evaluations on the new employees' performances were ------- off the usual results.

   (A) statistic
   (B) statistical
   (C) statistics
   (D) statistically

4. Central Library is visited by many local residents because it is ------- located by the apartment.

   (A) convenience
   (B) conveniences
   (C) conveniently
   (D) convenient

5. The contract should specify which products should be shipped every week to render it ------- understood.

   (A) clear
   (B) clearer
   (C) cleared
   (D) clearly

6. The Top Cosmetics Shop sells its fragrances and beauty products at ------- higher prices by emphasizing their brand value.

   (A) signifying
   (B) signified
   (C) significant
   (D) significantly

7. Best Tech Electronics recently introduced a new MP3 player and saw huge success, ------- increasing its market share.

   (A) substantially
   (B) substantial
   (C) substantiality
   (D) substantiate

8. Formost Electronics has been leading the computer program industry through its ------- technical developments, especially its hardware programs.

   (A) innovation
   (B) innovatively
   (C) innovate
   (D) innovative

9. Newstar Co., which was newly founded a couple of years ago, has been expanding its business ------- rapidly in the past few years.

   (A) even
   (B) very
   (C) with
   (D) any

10. Due to ------- handling, the customer no longer complained about the service she received and seemed rather satisfied with the compensation.

    (A) professional
    (B) professionally
    (C) profession
    (D) professioning

Chapter 04

4개월에 한 번 출제되는 문제

출제 4 순위

토익 시험 4회에
반드시 한 번은 나온다.

출제율 28%

법칙 32 과거시점(yesterday, last, ago, when 과거)이 보이면 과거시제

동사에는 현재, 과거, 미래 등의 시제가 있는데, 동사에 -d나 -ed를 붙이는 규칙 동사, went(go의 과거시제), ate(eat의 과거시제)와 같은 불규칙 동사가 있다. 영어의 과거시제는 과거 동사만 사용하지 않고, 문장 내에서 yesterday, last week, 3 days ago, when I was young과 같이 과거를 나타내는 표현들과 함께 사용된다.

유형을 파악해 봐

1. The expired contract ------- obsolete a month ago.
(A) become   (B) became   (C) becoming   (D) becomes

2. Last weekend, all employees at JTB Co. ------- at the venue for the retirement party of the president of the company.
(A) gathered   (B) gather   (C) gathering   (D) gathers

3. The announcement on the personnel arrangements ------- scheduled to be made yesterday, but it has not been posted on the Web site until now.
(A) was   (B) were   (C) is   (D) has been

보기는 모두 정동사와 준동사들로 구성되어 있다. 1번과 2번 문제에는 현재와 과거시제가, 3번 문제에는 현재, 과거, 현재완료시제가 섞여 있는 것으로 보아 시제를 묻는 문제임을 알 수 있다.

이렇게 풀어 봐

"유형을 파악해 봐" 1번 문제를 보세요!

첫째 빈칸의 위치를 확인한다. (정동사, 준동사, 그리고 단수와 복수)
한 문장에 동사는 1개 이상 있어야 한다. expired는 준동사이므로 빈칸은 정동사 자리이다. 복수 동사인 (A)와 준동사인 (C)는 탈락한다. contract는 단수 명사이므로 동사도 단수 동사가 와야 한다.

둘째 과거시제의 단서를 확인한다.
시제 문제에는 반드시 시제와 관련된 단서가 있다. 과거시점인 a month ago가 단서가 되어 (B)가 정답이다. 때로는 준동사가 답이 되거나 시제가 맞아도 수일치에서 잘못된 경우가 있기 때문에 시제를 먼저 확인하지는 않는다.

PLUS

- once, previously, those days 등도 과거시제의 단서가 될 수 있다.

- would는 과거의 습관을 나타낼 때 사용하기도 한다.

    Mr. Kim would take a nap after lunch. 김 씨는 점심 후에 낮잠을 자곤 했다.

 함정을 피해 봐   실제 강의에서만 알려주는 풀이 노하우!

1. 과거시제의 단서는 있지만 준동사가 답이 되는 경우를 조심한다.

Last week, the manager (will work/works/worked/working) on the project asked his assistant not to disturb him.

→ last week와 보기만을 보고 시제 문제로 판단해 worked를 답으로 고르면 안 된다. 이미 정동사 asked가 있으므로 준동사인 working이 답이다.

2. 과거시제의 단서는 있지만 다른 시제가 오는 경우를 조심한다.

KYK Solutions (has deemed/deemed) technological development as its highest priority since it was founded twenty years ago.

→ 20 years ago를 보고 과거시제를 답으로 선택하면 안 된다. 여기서 20 years ago는 was를 수식해 주고 있으며, 'since + 과거시점'이 단서가 되어 현재완료시제가 답이 된다.

3. 현재시제와 과거시제가 같은 형태인 동사들을 조심한다. (put, hit, cut 등)

When Mr. Kim was in high school, he (read/reads) magazine articles written in English.

→ 앞의 부사절이 과거시점이고, read는 여기서 과거시제이다. 수일치가 맞지 않는다고 생각해 reads를 선택하면 안 된다.

1. working 2. has deemed 3. read

STEP 3 실전에 적용해 봐

1. The Reborn Corporation ------- to be one of the major corporations that represents the country after overcoming financial difficulties last year.

   (A) will grow
   (B) grown
   (C) grew
   (D) growing

2. Mr. Pal ------- to conduct a survey on the customers and advised to reflect their feedback three weeks ago before the new model was launched.

   (A) to be asked
   (B) is asked
   (C) to ask
   (D) was asked

3. Ms. Pill ------- by her co-workers when she returned to the Hitsby Company after her 4-month-long maternity leave.

   (A) to be welcomed
   (B) will be welcomed
   (C) was welcomed
   (D) is welcomed

4. The manager ------- that an increasing number of employees have been promoted during the past few years.

   (A) has announced
   (B) was announced
   (C) announces
   (D) announcing

5. Mr. Carter ------- as a part-timer at the Joey Restaurant before he moved to Plenty Buffet to work 9-hour shifts each day in 2007.

   (A) work
   (B) working
   (C) works
   (D) worked

6. Last month, the program engineer ------- on the new project requested that the executive manager extend its due date.

   (A) takes
   (B) will take
   (C) taking
   (D) took

7. The number of customers at Fine Investment ------- when many companies went bankrupt due to financial difficulties.

   (A) decreasing
   (B) decreased
   (C) decrease
   (D) decreases

8. Robust Auto ------- by Mr. Raymond 50 years ago when there were only a few renowned automobile companies.

   (A) is founded
   (B) was founded
   (C) founded
   (D) found

9. Gloria Weddings ------- customer satisfaction as its primary goal since it was founded ten years ago.

   (A) has pursued
   (B) pursuing
   (C) pursued
   (D) is pursued

10. When it was announced that a safety inspection would be held soon, Mr. Corazon ------- his files away to clean up the place.

    (A) puts
    (B) putting
    (C) put
    (D) is put

출제율 28%

법칙 33 before[after, when, while]에는 -ing, as[once, unless, if]에는 p.p.

분사구문에 대해서 알아 보자.

원래 문장	분사 구문
When I entered the room, I saw Ms. Lee.	When entering the room, I saw Ms. Lee.
Once it is received, your order will be processed quickly.	Once (being) received, your order will be processed quickly.

분사구문은 부사절의 주어를 생략하고 동사를 현재분사로 바꿔 쓰는 형태를 말하며, 이때 접속사는 생략하기도 한다.

STEP 1 유형을 파악해 봐

1. Please make sure you turn off the power to all the appliances before ------- the room.
   (A) leaving   (B) left   (C) leave   (D) leaves

2. Customers of Breeze Air need to visit the Breeze Air Web site and check the flight schedule first when ------- a reservation for a flight.
   (A) make   (B) to make   (C) making   (D) are making

3. As ------- earlier in the morning, we will have a brief discussion about our project later this evening.
   (A) mentioned   (B) mention   (C) mentioning   (D) mentions

모든 보기에 정동사도 있고, 분사(-ing, p.p.)가 있기 때문에 분사 문제일 가능성이 높다. 1번과 2번 문제의 빈칸 앞에는 before와 when이 있고, 3번 문제의 빈칸 앞에는 as가 왔다.

STEP 2 이렇게 풀어 봐   "유형을 파악해 봐" 1번 문제를 보세요!

첫째 빈칸이 정동사 자리인지 확인한다.
before는 주로 전치사나 접속사로 사용하는데, 접속사로 쓰일 경우 뒤에 'S+V'가 와야 하지만 S가 없으므로 정동사 자리는 아니다. 따라서 (C), (D)는 탈락한다. -ing와 p.p. 중에서 선택해야 하므로 분사를 고르는 문제임을 알 수 있다.

둘째 빈칸 앞에 before, after, while, when이 있다면 -ing부터 먼저 대입해 본다.

빈칸 뒤에 있는 the room은 목적어이다. 그런데 p.p. 다음에는 목적어가 올 수 없으므로 -ing 형인 (A)가 답이 된다.

PLUS

- as, once, unless, if 뒤에는 p.p.가 와야 하며, 단 목적어가 없어야 한다.
- -ing나 p.p.가 제시되고 before, after, while, when 혹은 as, once, unless, if 등을 고르는 문제도 출제된다.
- as p.p.는 '~한대로,' once p.p.는 '일단 ~하면,' unless p.p.는 '~와는 달리,' if p.p.는 '~된다면'의 뜻이다.
- unless otherwise indicated(달리 통보된 바 없으면)란 숙어도 기억하자.
- 이유 접속사 계열(because)은 분사구문을 쓰지 않는다. 즉, because -ing/p.p.라는 표현이 없다.
- 접속사까지 생략하는 분사구문은 출제빈도가 매우 낮다. (Entering the room, I saw her.)
- 1형식 동사 다음에 보어(명사, 대명사, 형용사)가 오는 경우를 유사보어라고 하는데, 이것을 분사구문으로 보기도 한다. He died rich. (=He died when he was rich.)

함정을 피해 봐
실제 강의에서만 알려주는 풀이 노하우!

1. before, after, while, when 뒤에 -ing가 오지 않는 경우에 유의한다.

When (asked/asking) whether he would open his own restaurant, the chef avoided answering the question.

→ '요리사는 질문에 대답하기를 피했다.'라는 뒷부분 내용으로 보아, 앞의 내용으로는 '그의 식당을 열지에 대한 질문 받았을 때'라는 내용이 어울린다. 따라서 being asked에서 being이 생략된 asked가 답이다. (원래 문장은 When he was asked~)

2. before, after, while, when 뒤에 전명구만 남는 경우는 복원하여 해석한다.

Travelers should be careful not to lose their passports while (in/through) a foreign country.

→ while they are in a foreign country에서 they are가 생략된 분사구문이다. '외국에 있는 동안'이라는 말이 자연스러우므로 따라서 in이 답이다.

3. 분사 자리에 형용사가 올 때는 주어와의 어울림으로 판단한다.

Though not (expensive/extended), the new computer model isn't selling well due to lack of advertising.

→ the new computer model과 어울리는 형용사는 '비싼'이란 뜻의 expensive이다. extended는 '연장된'이란 뜻으로 보통 영업시간, 근무시간 등의 연장을 가리킨다.

1. asked   2. in   3. expensive

STEP 3 실전에 적용해 봐

1. The manager decided to hire more employees after ------- the increased workload, which was too much to handle with the current number of employees under his supervision.

    (A) consider
    (B) considering
    (C) consideration
    (D) considered

2. All the participants in the event need to have their invitation letters with them when ------- the event.

    (A) attending
    (B) attend
    (C) attended
    (D) attends

3. As ------- by the dermatologist, this facial care product works best when used 3 times a day.

    (A) recommend
    (B) recommending
    (C) recommendation
    (D) recommended

4. Due to lack of time to prepare the meeting beforehand, Mr. Lake thought about what he should discuss at the meeting while ------- to the designated place.

    (A) drive
    (B) driving
    (C) drove
    (D) driven

5. Before ------- the application form online, Mr. Gill should double-check the e-mail address of the program manager.

    (A) submit
    (B) submitted
    (C) submitting
    (D) submits

6. Mr. Nolan's new project, if -------, is likely to need more investment to be carried out.

    (A) approving
    (B) approval
    (C) approved
    (D) to approve

7. Please be aware that these customized items cannot be refunded or exchanged once -------.

    (A) ordering
    (B) order
    (C) orders
    (D) ordered

8. When ------- his whereabouts, Mr. Bee could not give a clear answer since he was in a completely new place while on his business trip.

    (A) asked
    (B) ask
    (C) asking
    (D) asks

9. Mr. Gibson asked Ms. Stuart to assume his jobs temporarily while ------- on his business trip.

    (A) away
    (B) in
    (C) over
    (D) throughout

10. Though not -------, the one-hour lecture by Professor Olsen was rather brief and to the point.

    (A) impressed
    (B) impressive
    (C) impression
    (D) impress

출제율 27%

법칙 34 등위접속사(and, but, or, yet)가 답이면 같은 것은 버려라

'I like him, and I like her.'의 and처럼 동등하게 두 문장을 연결해 주는 접속사를 등위접속사라고 한다. 이 문장은 'I like him and her.'로 줄여 사용할 수 있는데, 이러한 등위접속사에는 and, but, or, yet 등이 있다. 이처럼 '명사 and 명사, 동사 and 동사, 형용사 and 형용사, 부사 and 부사' 등으로 줄여 사용하는 유형을 병치(고르게 위치시킴)구조라고 한다.

STEP 1 유형을 파악해 봐

1. You can take the subway ------- bus to Central Park Station.
(A) but   (B) also   (C) or   (D) then

2. Ms. Pratt recorded the greatest number of sales among all employees this year ------- will receive an award.
(A) also   (B) or   (C) but   (D) and

3. We have thoroughly reviewed your resume ------- have to tell you that you will not be offered a job at our company.
(A) but   (B) then   (C) also   (D) or

보기들이 모두 병치가 가능한 등위접속사 and, but, or들로 제시되었다. 1번 문제는 빈칸 앞과 뒤에 모두 명사가, 2번과 3번 문제는 빈칸 뒤에 주어는 없고, 동사가 바로 나왔다.

STEP 2 이렇게 풀어 봐   "유형을 파악해 봐" 1번 문제를 보세요!

첫째 빈칸 앞뒤로 같은 품사가 있는지 확인한다.
빈칸 앞에 명사 subway가, 빈칸 뒤에는 bus가 있으므로 등위접속사 자리임을 알 수 있다. also나 then은 부사이므로 탈락한다.

둘째 등위접속사 and, but, or, yet 중 의미가 자연스러운 것을 선택한다.
지하철이나 버스를 탈 수 있다는 말이 자연스럽기 때문에 (C) or가 정답이다.

PLUS

- 상관 접속사('법칙 13' 참고)로 분류한 as well as도 병치 구조가 가능하다.
- and, but, or, yet과 달리 so나 for 뒤에는 완전한 문장이 온다.

I know him well, so I recommend him for the position.
→ so 다음에 I를 생략할 수 없다.

함정을 피해 봐 — 실제 강의에서만 알려주는 풀이 노하우!

1. and와 혼동되기 쉬운 also를 조심한다.

Employee handbooks can be found on the desk (and/also) in the cabinet.
→ and는 등위접속사이므로 전명구(on the desk)와 전명구(in the cabinet)를 연결할 수 있으나, also는 부사이므로 연결 기능이 없다.

2. 등위접속사 앞뒤로 일부가 생략되어 있는 경우에 조심한다.

Employees are encouraged (and/but) not required to attend the training session.
→ encouraged 뒤에는 to attend the training session이 생략되어 있고, not required 앞에는 employees are가 생략되어 있다. '장려되지만 필수조건은 아니다.'라는 내용이 자연스러우므로 but이 정답이다.

1. and 2. but

STEP 3 실전에 적용해 봐

1. Tickets for the play *Lost with the Macara* will be sold at the front gate ------- on the second floor of the building.

   (A) but
   (B) also
   (C) and
   (D) then

2. Whether the event will be held on Kensington Street ------- Blueberry Street, the event planner must give us the budget estimate for the event.

   (A) and
   (B) or
   (C) but
   (D) over

3. Promotional sales of KarlBay Clothing will be held at its main store ------- its store downtown.

   (A) but
   (B) over
   (C) then
   (D) and

4. Ms. Nielson has been in the field of computer programming for only 3 years ------- has been nominated as one of the outstanding employees at Carper Tech.

   (A) yet
   (B) so
   (C) then
   (D) or

5. Talbot Oil & Gas was one of the companies badly affected by the oil price boom ------- recovered quickly and stabilized its business.

   (A) and
   (B) also
   (C) but
   (D) or

6. Mr. Coy finished his report a while ago ------- is printing it to show to the manager.

   (A) but
   (B) and
   (C) or
   (D) yet

7. Ms. Young had a lot of work experience in accounting ------- had more interest in marketing.

   (A) and
   (B) or
   (C) also
   (D) but

8. Bank of Hemmington, with significantly low turnover rate of employees, is an institution where its employee welfare was ------- will be the top priority.

   (A) so
   (B) but
   (C) also
   (D) and

9. In order to attract more customers, it is important to improve customer satisfaction ------- the quality of our products.

   (A) but
   (B) except
   (C) and
   (D) also

10. The e-commerce Web site encourages, ------- does not make it mandatory, for its customers to verify their e-mail addresses.

    (A) and
    (B) if
    (C) but
    (D) also

출제율 26%

법칙 35 미래 시점 단서(tomorrow, next, future)가 보이면 미래시제 또는 현재진행시제

동사에는 현재, 과거, 미래 등의 시제가 있는데, 미래시제는 조동사 will 뒤에 동사원형을 사용한다. 미래시제는 문장에서 보통 tomorrow, next week, in the future 등과 같은 미래 시점을 나타내는 표현들과 함께 사용된다. 또한 현재 진행되는 일을 묘사하는 현재진행시제도 미래 시점과 함께 미래의 일을 나타낸다.

STEP 1 유형을 파악해 봐

1. The results of the consumer survey ------- next month.
   (A) will come out   (B) comes out   (C) came out   (D) has come out

2. The exhibition coming to New Uptown next Monday ------- for 2 weeks.
   (A) to being held   (B) was held   (C) has been held   (D) will be held

3. The company ------- an official retirement party for the vice president tomorrow morning.
   (A) holds   (B) had held   (C) was held   (D) will hold

1번 문제의 보기는 단수 동사와 복수 동사, 그리고 다른 시제들로 구성되었고, 2번 문제는 시제가 다른 정동사 3개와 준동사 1개, 그리고 3번 문제는 수동태 하나와 다른 시제 3개로 구성되어 있다. 이러한 유형의 문제가 수일치나 수동태로 풀리지 않을 경우에는 시제 문제임을 간파해야 한다.

STEP 2 이렇게 풀어 봐 "유형을 파악해 봐" 1번 문제를 보세요!

첫째 빈칸이 단수 동사 자리인지, 복수 동사 자리인지 확인한다.
results는 복수 명사이므로 동사도 복수 동사가 와야 한다. 단수 동사인 (B)는 탈락한다.

둘째 시제 문제의 단서를 확인한다.
next month가 단서가 되어 미래시제인 (A)가 답이다. 시제가 일치해도 수일치에서 오답이 나올 수 있기 때문에 시제부터 확인하는 것은 금물이다.

PLUS

- 시제를 살피기 전에 정동사, 준동사, 단수, 복수, 그리고 수동태, 능동태를 확인한다.
- soon, shortly도 미래시제와 잘 어울린다.
- 현재진행시제가 가까운 미래를 나타내는 경우는 보통 미래 시점과 같이 사용되는 경우이다.

함정을 피해 봐 *실제 강의에서만 알려주는 풀이 노하우!*

1. 미래시제를 만들 때 조동사 will만 사용하는 것은 아니다.

Mr. Kim (misses/has to miss) the marketing meeting tomorrow because of a scheduling conflict.

→ has to는 '~해야만 한다'는 뜻의 조동사로 미래시제를 만드는 기능도 포함하는데, 이것을 '미래상당어구'라고 한다.

미래상당어구	can need must be scheduled to be about to	may should be expected to be supposed to be going to 등

2. '요번주의명제'를 조심한다. ('법칙 28' 참고)

The manager has requested that the store clerks (report/will report) to work 30 minutes earlier next week.

→ next week만 보고 미래시제를 답으로 고르지 않도록 한다. 요번주의명제(request)를 먼저 생각해야 한다.

3. 시간과 조건부사절을 조심한다. ('법칙 52' 참고)

When you (meet/will meet) my manger tomorrow, please tell him.

→ tomorrow만 보고 미래시제를 답으로 고르지 않도록 한다. 주절이 명령문이나 미래시제이고, 부사절 (When ~ tomorrow) 부분이 시간부사절이므로 현재가 미래를 대신한다.

1. has to miss 2. report 3. meet

STEP 3 실전에 적용해 봐

1. Mr. Blonde ------- the employees on the revised safety guidelines instead of the work rules tomorrow.

   (A) instructs
   (B) will instruct
   (C) instructed
   (D) has instructed

2. In response to the growing demand for liquid soap, the Everyday Needs Company will develop a refillable liquid soap, which ------- introduced to the market in the near future.

   (A) was
   (B) being
   (C) will be
   (D) has been

3. The Comfy Furniture Company ------- to add more models to its line of wooden wardrobes within the next 3 years.

   (A) planning
   (B) is planning
   (C) to plan
   (D) planned

4. Mr. Down from headquarters ------- in town to meet officials at the regional office no later than tomorrow morning.

   (A) will arrive
   (B) arriving
   (C) to arrive
   (D) arrived

5. The executive officer at the Trenta Corporation has asked that the managers ------- the causes of the operational problems of the program in the future.

   (A) examined
   (B) to examine
   (C) will examine
   (D) examine

6. The Bad Kid Company's TV commercial ------- soon for its appropriateness for children under the age of 10.

   (A) reviewed
   (B) will be reviewed
   (C) have been reviewed
   (D) to review

7. Ms. Rose is currently copying the necessary documents and ------- distributing them to all of the attendees at the beginning of the tomorrow's meeting.

   (A) are
   (B) has been
   (C) will be
   (D) was

8. The board meeting ------- be held next Wednesday instead of this Thursday because some of the attendees are out of town on business.

   (A) is been to
   (B) is to
   (C) has been
   (D) was

9. If you ------- a reservation for the seminar tomorrow, please be sure to let me know the date and place right away.

   (A) made
   (B) will make
   (C) making
   (D) make

10. Sue recently ------- written notice regarding her absence due to her family trip planned for the near future.

    (A) gives
    (B) gave
    (C) is giving
    (D) will give

출제율 26%

법칙 36 '사람 선행사 + ------ + 동사'는 who

'The man who likes you is Mr. Kim.'에서 the man이 선행사이며, who likes you(너를 좋아하는) 부분이 형용사절 또는 관계사절이다. who는 주격관계대명사, the man은 사람을 가리키는 말이므로 사람 선행사라고 한다.

STEP 1 유형을 파악해 봐

1. The new employees ------- do not have their name cards yet must request them this week.
(A) whose　　(B) what　　(C) who　　(D) when

2. Anyone ------- submits a response to the customer survey will be given free samples of our new beauty products.
(A) whose　　(B) who　　(C) whom　　(D) which

3. Engineers ------- have not received a notice on their assigned task are required to report to the manager.
(A) those　　(B) who　　(C) whom　　(D) them

보기들이 모두 관계대명사(who, whom, which, what, whose), 관계부사(when, where, why, how), 그리고 지시대명사(those, these, that, this)로 구성되어 있다. 빈칸 앞 선행사가 사람인지 사물인지를 확인하고 빈칸 뒤에 무엇이 오는지를 살펴야 하는 관계대명사 문제이다.

STEP 2 이렇게 풀어 봐   "유형을 파악해 봐" 1번 문제를 보세요!

첫째 빈칸 앞에 선행사가 있는지, 사람 선행사인지, 사물 선행사인지를 확인한다.
선행사를 갖지 못하는 what과 선행사가 시간일 때 사용하는 when은 탈락한다.

둘째 빈칸 뒤가 동사인지, 명사인지를 확인한다.
동사 do not have가 빈칸 뒤에 왔으므로 주어 역할을 할 수 있는 (C) who가 답이 된다. (A) whose는 명사 앞에 사용한다.

PLUS

- 관계대명사를 고르기 전 동사의 수가 2개인지 확인한다. 동사의 수가 1개이면 일반대명사를 선택해야 한다.
- whom을 대신해 who를 쓸 수도 있다.

  The manager who employees like to work with is Mr. Kim.

- that도 who를 대신할 수 있으나 전치사 되나 콤마 뒤에는 올 수 없다.

  Coach James, (who/that) led the discussion last year, is in front of me.
  The clients with (whom/that) I spoke never smiled at me.

함정을 피해 봐 — 실제 강의에서만 알려주는 풀이 노하우!

1. 빈칸 뒤에 동사와 명사로 모두 사용되는 단어를 조심한다.

Workers (whose/who) plan to take time off during the peak season should inform their supervisors in advance.

→ plan은 명사도 되고 동사도 되는 단어지만 여기서는 동사가 should inform뿐이므로 plan은 동사이며, 따라서 빈칸은 주격 관계대명사가 와야 한다. 시험에 주로 나오는 명사와 동사로 모두 사용되는 단어들은 plan, file, work, permit, visit 등이 있다.

2. 명사라고만 알고 있었으나 동사로 사용되는 단어를 조심한다.

Any employees (who/whose) question their supervisors about a pay raise will be not be answered for the time being.

→ 여기서 question은 명사가 아니고 동사이므로 뒤에 목적어 their supervisors가 있다. 시험에 많이 나오는 명사로 알고 있지만 동사로도 쓰이는 단어에는 value(소중히 생각하다), function(기능을 하다), preorder(선주문하다) 등이 있다.

3. 사람 명사 중 -er이나 -or로 끝나지 않는 단어들을 조심한다.

| representative 대표자, 직원 | architect 건축가 | professional 전문가 |
| expert 전문가 | critic 비평가 | scientist 과학자 |

1. who 2. who

STEP 3 실전에 적용해 봐

1. The public seminar was held for anyone ------- was interested in gardening.

   (A) whom
   (B) whose
   (C) them
   (D) who

2. The staff manager has been reviewing the documents sent by the applicant ------- will be working at the regional office once hired.

   (A) who
   (B) whom
   (C) thoroughly
   (D) where

3. A number of tour programs were offered to Balloon Tour's customers ------- are planning trips during the holiday season.

   (A) who
   (B) whom
   (C) they
   (D) whose

4. Free refunds and exchanges are allowed for those ------- bought clothing in the wrong sizes and return them within 3 days of purchase.

   (A) whose
   (B) them
   (C) their
   (D) who

5. The increasing number of tourists ------- visited the Roam River had a positive effect on the regional economy of the town.

   (A) whose
   (B) whom
   (C) who
   (D) whomever

6. Only those customers ------- preorder Danny Ferenz's new album will have it delivered next Monday, the day before its release date.

   (A) whose
   (B) who
   (C) their
   (D) whom

7. The new model in Vagen Auto's automobile line was designed by several engineers ------- are renowned in the field.

   (A) who
   (B) whose
   (C) them
   (D) else

8. Mr. Twain is a medical professional ------- works at the Wellbeing Company to handle the employees' health care.

   (A) since
   (B) whose
   (C) who
   (D) what

9. Mr. Tale was asked to assume the duties of Michael Back, ------- was temporarily away on a business trip.

   (A) whose
   (B) that
   (C) he
   (D) who

10. Any facilities ------- function by making unusually loud noises are suspected of having broken down and must be reported for replacement.

    (A) what
    (B) whose
    (C) of which
    (D) which

출제율 **24%**

법칙 37 명사를 뒤에서 수식해 주는 분사는 목적어가 있으면 -ing, 없으면 p.p.

'한국에서 만들어진 제품'을 영어로는 the product made in Korea로 표현할 수 있다. 이때 made는 앞의 product를 수식하는 과거분사(p.p.)이다. 반면에 a singer singing a song에서 singing은 앞의 a singer를 수식하는 현재분사(-ing)이며, a song은 분사 singing의 목적어 역할을 한다.

STEP 1 유형을 파악해 봐

1. The real estate agent will come to evaluate the value of the site ------- the Hale Lake.
   (A) surround   (B) surrounds   (C) surrounded   (D) surrounding

2. In case of an accident, please refer to the emergency measures ------- on the bulletin board.
   (A) outlining   (B) outlined   (C) outline   (D) outlines

3. The owner of Jody's Restaurant, ------- part-time waitresses is going to interview three applicants this afternoon.
   (A) seeking   (B) seeks   (C) will seek   (D) seek

문제 보기들이 모두 정동사, 분사(-ing, p.p.)로 제시된 것으로 보아 빈칸에 알맞은 분사를 고르는 문제임을 알 수 있다. 빈칸이 뒤에 온 명사를 수식하려면 빈칸은 관사, 소유격, 전치사, 타동사 뒤, 그리고 명사 앞에 있어야 하는데, 1, 2번 문제는 '관소전타' 앞에 빈칸이, 3번 문제는 명사 뒤에 빈칸이 있으므로 빈칸이 뒤에 있는 명사를 수식하지 않는 것을 알 수 있다.

STEP 2 이렇게 풀어 봐
"유형을 파악해 봐" 1번 문제를 보세요!

첫째 빈칸이 정동사 자리인지 분사 자리인지 확인한다.
문장에서 will come이 정동사이다. 한 문장에 접속사 없이 정동사가 더 올 수 없으므로 정동사인 (A), (B)는 탈락한다.

둘째 빈칸이 수식하는 것을 찾는다.
빈칸이 뒤의 명사를 수식하려면 '관소전타 + ------- + 명사'의 구조여야 한다. 하지만 관사 the가 빈칸 뒤에 있으므로 빈칸은 앞의 명사를 수식하는 분사 자리로 봐야 한다.

셋째 빈칸 뒤에 목적어가 있으면 -ing, 없으면 p.p.가 온다.
빈칸 뒤에 목적어(the Hale Lake)가 있으므로 -ing가 정답이다.

PLUS

• 목적어가 있으면 -ing가 오므로 결국 '명사1과 명사2 사이에는 -ing'라는 공식이 성립한다.

 함정을 피해 봐   실제 강의에서만 알려주는 풀이 노하우!

1. 목적어로 착각하기 쉬운 단어들을 조심한다. ('법칙 16' 참고)

the meeting (held/hold) yesterday
the rare book (purchased/purchase) online
the initiative (implemented/implement) downtown
the reservation (made/make) 72 hours before departure

→ yesterday, online, downtown, 72 hours before departure는 목적어가 아닌 부사이므로 p.p.가 와야 한다.

2. 자동사(1, 2형식 동사)로 만들어진 분사는 목적어가 없어도 -ing를 쓴다.

Employees (working/worked) in the Delmont facility will receive a one-month paid vacation at the end of the year.
→ 수식어인 in the Delmont facility를 제외하면 work가 1형식 동사이기 때문에 목적어가 올 수는 없지만 p.p.를 쓰지 않고 -ing를 쓴다.

3. 목적어로 쓰인 명사를 수식하는 단어를 조심한다.

Being able to take a vacation (exceeding/excessively) more than 5 days requires the CEO's approval
→ more than은 숫자 수식 부사, 숫자는 형용사이다. more를 형용사로 보고 부사인 excessively를 답으로 선택하지 않도록 한다. days라는 목적어가 있으므로 -ing가 답이다.

1. held, purchased, implemented, made   2. working   3. exceeding

STEP 3 실전에 적용해 봐

1. There will be a brief inspection of the documents ------- that their publication date is the same as what we were informed.

   (A) verification
   (B) verifiably
   (C) verifies
   (D) verifying

2. Mr. Marr was concerned about his project ------- the required financial support of the Rabb Corporation.

   (A) lacked
   (B) lacking
   (C) lacks
   (D) lack

3. According to the statement ------- just a few hours ago, the managerial position which has remained empty will be filled by Mr. Johnson.

   (A) issue
   (B) to be issued
   (C) issued
   (D) was issued

4. The engineer position at Muffler Auto is ideal for those ------- in mechanics.

   (A) interesting
   (B) interests
   (C) interest
   (D) interested

5. This team project will be fairly easy for employees ------- with teams or partners on a regular basis.

   (A) work
   (B) working
   (C) are working
   (D) worked

6. The article ------- in News Daily last Monday dealt with issues related to low employment rate.

   (A) publish
   (B) to publish
   (C) published
   (D) publishing

7. Some of the items ------- downtown were reported to have technical defects that prevented them from working properly.

   (A) delivering
   (B) delivery
   (C) delivered
   (D) deliver

8. The shipping charge will be waived for all orders ------- more than $100 at Beauty Cosmetics Shop.

   (A) will total
   (B) totaling
   (C) being totaled
   (D) totaled

9. Please make sure you have the quality assurance of the product ------- in the envelope we sent you.

   (A) enclosed
   (B) enclosing
   (C) enclosure
   (D) enclose

10. The proposal ------- of specific steps to accomplish the goal received positive feedback from the executives.

    (A) consists
    (B) to be consisted
    (C) will consist
    (D) consisting

만점 강사가 알려주는 파트 7 팁 I

1. 파트 7 공부는 언제 시작하는 것이 가장 효과적인가?

토익 시험을 보면 대부분의 학생들이 시간 부족을 경험한다. 그리고 그 원인이 파트 7을 빠르게 풀지 못해서라고 생각하며, 자신에게 가장 시급한 것이 파트 7이라고 생각한다. 파트 5, 6를 제쳐두고 파트 7을 공부해 보지만 별로 효과를 얻지 못한다. 그러나 파트 7을 풀기 위해서는 장문 독해 능력이 있어야 한다. 또, 장문 독해를 하려면 단문 독해를 먼저 할 수 있어야 한다. 파트 5, 6을 15분 이내에, 오답 10개 이내로 푼다면 단문 독해가 어느 정도 되는 시기이며, 이때부터 파트 7을 공부하는 것이 효과적이다. 아직 이 수준에 도달하지 못했다면 파트 5, 6에 올인해야 한다. 대신 파트 5, 6를 풀고 리뷰할 때 각 문제를 정성껏 직독직해 해 본다. 이것은 파트 5, 6 공부뿐만 아니라 파트 7에 대한 대비가 된다. 파트 5, 6의 단문이 모여서, 파트 7의 장문이 되기 때문이다.

2. 파트 7 공부는 무엇부터 해야 하나?

"그냥 문제집 사서 죽도록 문제만 많이 풀면 늘지 않나요?"라고 학생들이 물어보면 필자는 "죽도록 풀면 죽을 수 있다"고 말한다. 파트 7 공부에도 우선순위가 있고, 전략이 있는데, 그것을 무시한 채로 어떻게 단기간에 점수가 오르겠는가? 당장 장문을 놓고 독해 연습만 해서 독해만 잘 한다고 점수가 많이 오르지 않는다. 독해 능력 이외에도 문제 유형, 지문 유형을 알면 확실히 빠르고 정확하게 풀린다. 해석된 문장을 보고도 이해 안 되는 경우는 논리력도 필요하다. 이 모든 것을 갖추고 있어도 시간 관리를 제대로 못하면 역시 점수가 잘 나오지 않는다. 이 5가지 요소는 문제를 많이 풀다 보면 저절로 배양되기도 하지만, 단기에 점수를 향상시키기 위해서 가장 우선순위로 할 것은 바로 문제 유형에, 그리고 그에 대한 풀이법에 익숙해 지는 것이다. 독해실력이나 논리력을 갖추는 것은 몇 달이 걸리는 작업이다. 시간 관리는 실제 토익을 최대한 많이 봐야 해결된다. 그러나 지문 유형은 하루만 공부해도, 특히 문제 유형과 그 유형에 맞는 풀이법은 한 시간만 공부해도 충분히 익숙해 질 수 있다.

3. 문제부터 먼저 읽어야 하나? 지문부터 먼저 읽어야 하나?

문제부터 읽되, 모든 문제를 다 읽지는 않도록 한다. 그렇지 않으면 후반부의 문제는 기억에 남지 않는다. 총 4문제짜리 지문이라면 첫 번째 문제는 보통 지문의 초반부, 즉 4분의 1 부분까지에 단서가 있는 편이다. 만약 그 부분까지 읽었는데도 단서가 없다면 더 지문을 그 이상 읽지 말고, 두 번째 문제를 읽는다. 두 번째 문제에 대한 단서는 지문의 절반까지에 있는 편이다. 두 번째 문제를 풀다 보면 그때서야 첫 번째 문제의 단서가 나오면서 첫 번째 문제까지 같이 풀리게 된다. 이렇게 해야 지문이나 문제를 두 번씩 읽는 번거로움을 줄일 수 있으며, 그래야 최소의 시간으로 풀 수 있다.

4. 지문을 다 읽어야 하나? 필요한 부분만 찾아서 읽어야 하나?

마지막 문제가 육하원칙 문제(키워드 문제)일 경우엔 필요한 부분만 찾아서 풀리는 문제도 일부 있으나 최근 출제 경향을 보면 추론 문제가 많아지고 있다. 추론을 하려면 지문에 대해 충분히 익숙해야 하므로 결국 지문을 다 읽는 것이 좋다. 이 경우, 글의 주제를 묻는 문제 풀기도 쉬워진다. 사실 단문 독해가 어느 정도 되는 단계라면 다 읽는데 소요되는 시간과 필요한 부분만을 찾기 위해 소요되는 시간이 큰 차이가 없다. 게다가 필요한 부분만 찾아서 풀면 함정에 빠지기 쉽다. 단, 정답의 단서가 없어 보이는 부분을 읽을 때는 주로 명사, 동사 위주로 신속히 독해를 한다.

Chapter 05

5개월에 한 번 출제되는 문제

출제 5 순위

토익 시험 5회에
반드시 한 번은 나온다.

출제율 22%

법칙 38　문장에 정동사 1개는 필수

'I loved you.'라는 문장에서 loved는 주어의 상태나 동작을 서술해 주는 역할을 하는 '동사'이며, 이것을 '정동사'라고 부르기도 한다. 영어 문장에서는 반드시 정동사가 1개 이상 와야 하며, 2개가 오려면 접속사가 필요하다. 이에 반해 'I am loved., I am going., I am to go.'에 등장하는 loved, going, to go와 같은 말들을 '준동사'라고 한다. 준동사는 동사가 아니며, 문장 안에서 명사, 형용사, 부사의 기능을 하면서 한 문장 안에 여러 개가 올 수도 있다.

STEP 1　유형을 파악해 봐

1. Luncheon vouchers ------- for free to the attendees of Mr. Brown's seminar from 11 A.M.
(A) will be provided　　(B) providing　　(C) to be provided　　(D) provision

2. Mr. Wiley used to have the best sales record, but his record ------- by Ms. Lowe.
(A) to surpass　　(B) to be surpassed　　(C) was surpassed　　(D) surpassing

3. GK Cloud's service ------- you to access and edit any of your files online no matter where you are.
(A) enabling　　(B) to enable　　(C) enablement　　(D) enables

보기들이 모두 정동사와 준동사들로 구성되어 있다. 1번 문제는 (A)만 정동사, (B)와 (C)는 준동사, (D)는 명사이며, 2번 문제는 (C)만 정동사, 나머지 보기들은 준동사, 3번 문제는 (D)만 정동사, (A)와 (B)는 준동사, (C)는 명사이므로 동사 문제 중에서도 정동사, 준동사를 구분하는 문제임을 알 수 있다.

STEP 2　이렇게 풀어 봐

"유형을 파악해 봐" 1번 문제를 보세요!

첫째 정동사의 개수를 확인한다.
정동사의 개수를 확인한다.

둘째 빈칸 뒤가 동사인지, 명사인지를 확인한다.
문장 안에 접속사가 없는 상태이다. 한 문장에 정동사 1개는 반드시 필요하므로 빈칸은 정동사 자리이며, 보기 중에 정동사는 (A)뿐이다.

PLUS

- been p.p., -ing 등도 준동사이며, 앞에 have가 있어야 정동사가 된다.

- 등위접속사는 동일 요소를 생략하므로 '동사의 개수 - 접속사가 = C'일 수 있다. 따라서 '단어+등위접속사+단어'를 함께 덩어리로 취급한다.

  I like him, and I like her. → I like him and her.
  → him and her를 덩어리로 하나의 목적어로 볼 것.

함정을 피해 봐

실제 강의에서만 알려주는 풀이 노하우!

1. 과거분사를 정동사로 착각하지 않도록 한다.

The building constructed downtown 30 years ago (overlooks/overlooking) a train station.
→ constructed는 건설했다는 정동사가 아니고, '건설된'이란 뜻의 과거분사 즉, 준동사이다. 한 문장에 정동사 1개는 반드시 있어야 하므로 overlooks가 답이다.

2. 접속사로 보이지 않거나 접속사뿐 아니라 전치사 혹은 부사인 단어를 조심한다.

접속사처럼 보이지 않는 접속사	the moment considering	at the time by the time	providing in case	provided
접속사, 전치사, 부사	since	before	after	
접속사, 전치사	as	until		
접속사, 부사	once			

3. 사역동사나 help 동사의 목적보어 자리를 정동사로 착각하지 않도록 조심한다.

Please have all computers (setting/set) up by the end of the week.
Please help our staff (finishing/finish) the project within the week.
→ 여기서 set이나 finish는 정동사가 아니다. set은 p.p.이며, finish는 앞에는 to가 생략된 것으로 준동사이다. 이미 정동사(have, help)가 있으므로 정동사가 또 와서는 안 된다.

1. overlooks   3. set, finish

STEP 3 실전에 적용해 봐

1. The exhibition was a huge success because the artwork displayed ------- many visitors.

   (A) interesting
   (B) interested
   (C) interest
   (D) to interest

2. The conference on the new expansion ------- will be discussed along with the renovation of the building.

   (A) projected
   (B) is projecting
   (C) will project
   (D) project

3. The well-known Deluxe Entertainment Group, now ------- its business overseas, was once a small company in Lithuania.

   (A) expanding
   (B) has been expanding
   (C) will be expanding
   (D) expands

4. The express train skipping a few stops on its way to Eastern Terminal has shortened the time it takes ------- to the terminal.

   (A) be get
   (B) has gotten
   (C) to get
   (D) will get

5. K-Watts Lights recently introduced a lamp allowing users to control the brightness for those who ------- different amounts of lighting for various purposes.

   (A) preferring
   (B) prefer
   (C) preference
   (D) preferential

6. Our store manager truly ------- a promotion and increased salary for his dedication to the Everyday Low Store.

   (A) deserving
   (B) deservedly
   (C) deserver
   (D) deserves

7. The number of items to be sold at the main store will ------- the same this month regardless of the market conditions.

   (A) remain
   (B) remaining
   (C) remained
   (D) remains

8. All employees, including sales -------, will convene at the Brookade Building for the retirement party.

   (A) represent
   (B) represented
   (C) representatives
   (D) represents

9. With technology constantly advancing, digital devices quickly ------- obsolete the moment they are released on the market.

   (A) become
   (B) becoming
   (C) to become
   (D) are become

10. Because the staff members ------- Mr. Weld with minor managerial problems began to handle more work, Mr. Weld was able to concentrate more on his business.

    (A) assist
    (B) assistance
    (C) assisted
    (D) assisting

출제율 **22%**

법칙 39 '전치사와 a, the, 소유격 + 명사' 사이에는 동명사

'I enjoy watching games.'에서 watching games는 동명사이며, 동명사는 전치사 뒤에 오기도 한다. 'I will study English by watching an American drama.'에서 watching 자리에 to watch나 watched는 올 수 없다. 이렇게 전치사 뒤에 오는 동명사를 전치사의 목적어가 되는 동명사라고 한다.

STEP 1 유형을 파악해 봐

1. The MP3 player has gained popularity for ------- a good balance between price and performance.
(A) keeping   (B) keep   (C) to keep   (D) kept

2. The committee members were asked to review the proposal about ------- the main office.
(A) relocate   (B) relocation   (C) to relocate   (D) relocating

3. For the purpose of ------- the number of loyal customers, Ellusion Cosmetics held a promotional event last week.
(A) increase   (B) to increase   (C) increasing   (D) increased

세 문제 모두 보기에 정동사가 1개 이상 있고, 준동사(-ing, p.p., to 부정사)와 명사가 보기에 섞여 있는 것으로 보아 준동사를 정답으로 골라야 하는 문제들일 가능성이 높다.

STEP 2 이렇게 풀어 봐

"유형을 파악해 봐" 1번 문제를 보세요!

첫째 빈칸의 자리를 확인한다. (정동사, 준동사)
한 문장에 접속사가 없는 상태에선 정동사가 2개 올 수 없다. has gained가 정동사이므로 빈칸에는 준동사가 와야 한다. 따라서 (B)는 탈락한다.

둘째 전치사의 목적어 자리인지 확인한다.
전치사 뒤에 빈칸이 있고, 이어서 관사와 명사가 나오므로 빈칸에는 동명사만 가능하다. 보기 (C)의 to 부정사는 전치사의 목적어 기능이 없고, (D) 과거분사는 관사 a를 건너뛰어 명사 good balance를 수식할 수 없다.

PLUS

- Step 1과 2를 정리하면 '전치사 + ------- + 관사/소유격 (형용사) + 명사'에서 빈칸은 -ing가 답이다.

- 관사, 소유격이 없는 경우에는 해석으로 판단해야 한다.
  Sales associates can learn various ways of (attractive/attracting) customers through the workshop.
  → customers 앞에 the가 있으면 공식처럼 -ing 형태가 답이 되지만 위와 같은 경우에는 customers 앞에 형용사인 attractive도 가능하다. attractive를 넣어 해석해보면 '매혹적인 고객의 방법'이 되어 어색하다.

> **동명사를 좋아하는 표현**
> way of -ing ~하는 방법
> for the purpose of -ing ~를 목적으로
> be in the process of -ing ~의 과정 중에 있다

함정을 피해 봐 — 실제 강의에서만 알려주는 풀이 노하우!

1. 동명사 자리라고 생각하기 쉬우나 형용사가 답인 경우를 조심한다.

The recently released mobile device comes with (complimentary/complimenting) software installed.
→ software 앞에 관사나 소유격이 없으므로 해석해 풀어야 하는데, '소프트웨어를 칭찬하는 것과 함께 온다.'라는 내용은 어색하다. '무료 소프트웨어가 딸려온다.'고 해야 자연스럽기 때문에 형용사가 답이 된다.

2. 빈칸 뒤 명사가 없어도 동명사가 답인 경우를 조심한다.

ICQ, a leading software company, is notable for (specializing/specialty) in creating innovative software.
→ 목적어가 없는 것을 보고 specializing이 오답이라고 생각하면 안 된다. specialize in은 '~를 전문으로 하다'라는 표현으로 덩어리로 취급하면 타동사가 되기 때문에 뒤에 목적어로 creating innovative software가 왔다. specialty는 가산명사이므로 앞에 관사나 소유격을 써야 한다.

1. complimentary   2. specializing

STEP 3 실전에 적용해 봐

1. The problem with ------- the automatic shutdown of the facilities was repeatedly pointed out.

    (A) prevent
    (B) preventing
    (C) prevention
    (D) prevented

2. Among the many employees in the Human Resources Department, Ms. Tomoya was talented at ------- the employees to work hard.

    (A) motivate
    (B) motivating
    (C) motivated
    (D) motivation

3. Mr. Cooper was headhunted by Exton Technologies as he was highly skilled at ------- the vehicles.

    (A) maneuver
    (B) maneuvered
    (C) maneuvering
    (D) to maneuver

4. The first step in ------- proper working rules is to analyze whether the employees are currently working in compliance with their supervisor's advice at all times.

    (A) establish
    (B) established
    (C) establishment
    (D) establishing

5. Our production manager is responsible for ------- the staff and each manufacturing process.

    (A) supervising
    (B) supervise
    (C) supervises
    (D) supervised

6. Analyzing customer feedback is strongly recommended as a means of ------- the service quality.

    (A) improve
    (B) improves
    (C) improving
    (D) improvement

7. Mr. Poll was surely a talented man, but the Sales Department wanted Mr. Back, who was better at ------- customer complaints at the office.

    (A) manage
    (B) managing
    (C) management
    (D) manager

8. Following his partner's advice, Mr. Chew decided to prepare for his retirement age by ------- in Forrester Co.

    (A) invest
    (B) investing
    (C) invested
    (D) investment

9. You have to consider beforehand how much you would pay for ------- housing if you had to rent it.

    (A) comparable
    (B) compare
    (C) to compare
    (D) comparing

10. Queen Newspapers verified the date the ruins were found prior to ------- the public of the new discovery.

    (A) notifying
    (B) notification
    (C) notify
    (D) notified

출제율 22%

법칙 40 명사절이 완전하면 that, 불완전하면 what, 선택은 whether

'절'이라고 불리는 문장 덩어리가 명사처럼 주어, 목적어, 보어 역할을 하는 것을 명사절이라고 한다.

He is bad. (문장) that he is bad (명사절)	I know **that he is bad**. 나는 알고 있다. 그가 나쁘다는 것을	명사절이 목적어
	That he is bad is true. 그가 나쁘다는 것은 사실이다.	명사절이 주어
	The fact is **that he is bad**. 사실은 그가 나쁘다는 것이다.	명사절이 보어

STEP 1 유형을 파악해 봐

1. The staff at the exhibition requested ------- all visitors remain silent.
   (A) what   (B) whether   (C) should   (D) that

2. The pamphlets explain ------- you need to bring to apply for membership.
   (A) who   (B) how   (C) what   (D) which

3. Mr. Neil should decide ------- or not to hire more employees at his company.
   (A) that   (B) either   (C) else   (D) whether

1번 문제는 (C)를 제외하고는 모두 접속사, 2번 문제는 모두 접속사, 3번 문제는 (A)와 (D)가 접속사이다. 1번 문제는 접속사 3개가 모두 명사절 접속사이며, 2번은 접속사 4개가 모두 명사절 접속사, 그리고 3번 문제는 (A)와 (D)가 모두 명사절 접속사이다.

STEP 2 이렇게 풀어 봐   "유형을 파악해 봐" 1번 문제를 보세요!

첫째 빈칸의 자리를 확인한다.

request와 remain이 동사이므로 빈칸은 접속사 자리이다. 따라서 조동사 (C)는 탈락한다. request는 3형식 동사이므로 빈칸은 명사절 접속사가 필요하다.

둘째 빈칸 뒤 문장이 완전한지, 불완전한지를 따진다.

빈칸 뒤 all visitors가 주어, remain이 2형식 동사, silent가 보어이므로 완전한 문장이다. (D) that은 이어지는 문장이 완전할 때 사용하므로 정답이 될 수 있다. (A) what은 뒤의 문장이 불완전할 때 사용하므로 탈락하고, (B) whether는 빈칸 앞 주절에 ask나 wonder 등 불확정적인 말들이 올 때 사용한다.

PLUS

- 'that S+V'를 좋아하는 동사들이 있는데, '생각하다, 말하다, 예측하다, 제안하다'의 뜻을 가진 동사들이 여기에 해당하며, 줄여서 '생말예제' 동사라고 한다. 이때 that은 생략되기도 한다.

생각하다	think	guess	assume	believe	
말하다	mention outline	state stress	indicate add	say caution	detail ensure
예측하다	predict	project	expect	anticipate	
제안하다	suggest	recommend	request	ask	

(that) S + V
이때 S + V는 완전한 문장

- wh-접속사 뒤의 주어와 조동사(will, should 등)는 to로 줄여 사용할 수 있으며, or not 부분도 생략 가능하다.
  I haven't decided whether I will buy a boat (or not). → I haven't decided whether to buy a boat (or not).
  I know what I should do. → I know what to do.

- whether가 3형식 동사 뒤에 오는 경우 if로 대체할 수 있다. 이때 if는 whether와 같이 '~인지 아닌지'라는 의미를 가지며, 이 경우 if는 or not이 바로 따라올 수 없다.
  I wonder if (= whether) he will be hired. (O)
  I wonder if or not he will be hired. (X)
  If he will be hired is not sure. (X)

함정을 피해 봐
실제 강의에서만 알려주는 풀이 노하우!

1. that 뒤가 불완전해도 답이 될 수 있는 경우를 혼동하지 않도록 한다.

Please refer to the tentative schedule (what/that) you can find in the enclosed packet.
→ you can find가 불완전한 문장이라고 해서 what을 답으로 고르면 안 된다. 선행사(schedule)가 있고, 문장이 불완전할 때 쓰는 that을 '관계대명사 that 혹은 형용사절 that'이라고 한다.

2. '자동사+전치사' 덩어리 동사를 조심한다.

Mr. Roberts said (what/that) his company specializes in ecological design.
→ specialize 뒤에 목적어가 없다고 해서 what을 선택하면 안 된다. specialize in이 덩어리로 3형식 동사이며, 이어서 ecological design이 목적어이므로 완전한 문장이다.

3. know 다음에 무조건 that만 오는 것은 아니다.

The manager would like to know (that/whether) his assistant wants a pay raise.
→ would like to know(알기를 원한다)는 아직 알고 있는 것이 아니므로 불확정적인 말이며, 따라서 that이 아니고 whether가 와야 한다.

1. that 2. that 3. whether

STEP 3 실전에 적용해 봐

1. Ms. Sun requests ------- you submit the reports that are due today as soon as possible.

    (A) that
    (B) what
    (C) with
    (D) for

2. ------- is interesting about the Glad Company is that every employee has worked there for at least 5 years.

    (A) What
    (B) That
    (C) Which
    (D) How

3. It is crucial ------- every employee immediately notify the manager if there are any operational problems with the facilities.

    (A) to
    (B) that
    (C) what
    (D) if

4. The committee members will determine ------- extending the contract will be beneficial to the Voltax Corporation.

    (A) however
    (B) whatever
    (C) whether
    (D) unless

5. The study shows ------- taking a five-minute break after every hour at work can increase a person's work efficiency.

    (A) what
    (B) that
    (C) them
    (D) which

6. The workshop on team leadership includes Mr. Tsubasi's lecture ------- provides specific know-how on improving the team performance.

    (A) what
    (B) that
    (C) should
    (D) this

7. Mr. Wiley ordered the employees to write ------- the boxes contain on their covers.

    (A) which
    (B) where
    (C) what
    (D) how

8. A survey conducted by National Research Institute shows ------- a growing number of new hires quit their jobs in less than one year.

    (A) that
    (B) what
    (C) which
    (D) should

9. It remains to be seen ------- this year's annual charitable event will be held in December as it was last year.

    (A) regards to
    (B) whether
    (C) because
    (D) what

10. All employees working at the Cameron Company should let their supervisors know ------- they want a pay raise or stock options by the end of the fiscal year.

    (A) than
    (B) what
    (C) whether
    (D) that

출제율 22%

법칙 41 숫자 앞에는 숫자 수식 부사

숫자를 수식하는 부사들은 주로 숫자 앞에 와서 형용사인 숫자를 꾸며준다. '거의, 대략, ~이상'이라는 뜻으로 해석되는 nearly, approximately, more than 등이 여기에 해당한다.

STEP 1 유형을 파악해 봐

1. It will take ------- two months for the shipments to arrive here.
(A) approximate   (B) approximately   (C) approximated   (D) approximating

2. Sales of home appliances have dropped ------- 20 percent this year.
(A) near   (B) nearing   (C) nearer   (D) nearly

3. ------- 70 percent of the employees at the McCoy Corporation say that they are satisfied with their salaries.
(A) Over   (B) Beyond   (C) More   (D) Most

빈칸 뒤에 숫자가 위치해 있는 문제들이다. 1, 2번 문제의 보기들은 같은 단어의 변형 형태들이므로 품사 문제이며, 3번 문제는 (A)가 부사 및 전치사, (B)는 전치사, (C)와 (D)는 형용사 및 부사이다.

STEP 2 이렇게 풀어 봐   "유형을 파악해 봐" 1번 문제를 보세요!

첫째 숫자 앞이 빈칸이면, 보기에 숫자 수식 부사가 있는지 확인한다.
two라는 숫자 앞에 빈칸이 존재하며, 보기는 같은 단어의 변형으로 이루어져 있다. (B) approximately가 숫자 수식 부사로 정답이다.

둘째 '관소전타 + ------- + 숫자(형용사) + 명사'로 확인한다.
숫자 수식 부사인 (B)가 정답일 확률이 높지만 실수를 방지하기 위해 빈칸 앞과 뒤의 구조를 확인한다. take는 3형식 동사이므로 타동사이고, 형용사인 숫자 two, 그 뒤를 명사인 months가 이어지는 순서로 되어 있다.

PLUS

- 숫자 수식 부사는 다음과 같다.

approximately	nearly	almost	more than	less than
over	at least	up to	roughly	around
about	just	a maximum of	a minimum of	as much as

 함정을 피해 봐 실제 강의에서만 알려주는 풀이 노하우!

1. 숫자 모양이 아니지만 의미상 숫자인 단어들(half, double, decade, triple, once, a 등)을 조심한다.

(Approximate/Approximately) half the employees at Goodwill, Inc. registered for the evening language classes.

→ half를 명사로 생각하여 형용사를 고르면 오답이다. half는 50%를 의미하므로 숫자의 의미를 가지고 있기 때문에 숫자 수식 부사가 정답이다.

2. over는 기간 앞에 오는 전치사뿐 아니라 숫자 수식 부사의 기능을 갖고 있다.

GWF has been serving customers for (over/within) ten years now.

→ 이미 전치사 for가 있으므로 within이 와서는 안 된다. over는 여기서 숫자 ten을 수식하는 부사 기능으로 사용되었다.

1. Approximately 2. over

STEP 3 실전에 적용해 봐

1. Apply for our annual membership now and receive discounts ------- 40% on all purchases.
   (A) much
   (B) on
   (C) up to
   (D) off

2. Please be present at the airport ------- half an hour before the arrival time so that you can pick him up right away.
   (A) lesser
   (B) less
   (C) a little
   (D) at least

3. Due to the various promotional activities, the amount of funds raised this year has ------- doubled compared to previous years.
   (A) after
   (B) almost
   (C) unless
   (D) while

4. At the meeting, the discussion on the employee training session continued for ------- 2 hours.
   (A) roughly
   (B) greatly
   (C) hardly
   (D) openly

5. The managerial position available at Reb Auto requires ------- 3 years of experience in the relevant field.
   (A) regards to
   (B) as though
   (C) more than
   (D) instead of

6. Guests who brought their cars and are staying at the Best Hotel for ------- two days must ask for a parking permit at the front desk.
   (A) during
   (B) until
   (C) now that
   (D) more than

7. In a survey conducted last week, ------- half of the attendees at the seminar answered that they were willing to attend the seminar again if it were held on the same subject.
   (A) approximate
   (B) approximately
   (C) approximating
   (D) approximates

8. After ------- 7 months of delays, the construction of the Harley Bridge will finally resume next week.
   (A) for
   (B) frequently
   (C) seldom
   (D) around

9. For ------- 13 years, the Veronica Jewel Company has been offering our customers the finest jewelry at the most reasonable prices.
   (A) about
   (B) during
   (C) until
   (D) still

10. In an effort to increase the sales of its beauty products, the Everlast Cosmetics Shop offered discounts ------- 30% off the regular prices.
    (A) just as
    (B) quickly
    (C) as much as
    (D) alike

출제율 19%

법칙 42 '사물 선행사 + ------- + 주어, 목적어가 없는 문장'은 which 혹은 that

사물 선행사일 때 사용하는 which에 대해 살펴 본다.

The car / which has a new system / is mine. 자동차, 새로운 시스템을 갖춘, 내 것이다.
사물 선행사 주격관계사

The car / which you bought / is over there. 자동차, 당신이 구입한, 저쪽에 있다.
사물 선행사 목적격관계사

이때 which 대신에 that을 쓸 수 있다.

유형을 파악해 봐

1. Mr. Pale recently bought a car ------- doesn't work very well, so he wants to sell it.
(A) what   (B) that   (C) how   (D) her

2. The new Lob Home Furnishings, ------- opened near Seventh Street Station, is very accessible.
(A) which   (B) where   (C) this   (D) whatever

3. Attached is the itinerary ------- you requested for your trip earlier.
(A) then   (B) what   (C) which   (D) while

1번 문제는 (D) her를 제외하고는 모두 접속사, 2번 문제는 (C) this를 제외하고는 모두 접속사, 3번 문제는 (A) then을 제외하고는 모두 접속사이다. 세 문제 모두 문장에 동사가 2개 있으므로 빈칸은 접속사 자리이며, 빈칸 앞에는 사물이 선행사로 등장한 것으로 보아 관계대명사(형용사절 접속사)를 고르는 문제임을 알 수 있다.

이렇게 풀어 봐   "유형을 파악해 봐" 1번 문제를 보세요!

첫째 보기에 접속사와 그렇지 않은 것이 섞여 있을 때는 동사의 개수를 확인한다.
so가 접속사이므로 이어서 문장이 왔고, 나머지 문장을 확인해 보니 동사의 개수가 bought와 work 2개이다. 따라서 밑줄에는 접속사가 필요하다. 접속사가 아닌 (D)는 탈락이다.

둘째 빈칸 앞 선행사를 확인하고, 빈칸 뒤에는 무엇이 부족한지 확인한다.

빈칸 앞에 사물 선행사 a car가 있고, 빈칸 뒤에는 동사가 바로 왔으므로 주격관계대명사 which가 필요한데, which 대신에 that을 쓸 수 있으므로 (B)가 정답이다. (A) what은 선행사를 갖지 않으며, (C) how 뒤에는 완전한 문장이 와야 한다.

PLUS

- that은 which를 대신해 쓸 수 있으나 콤마 뒤나 전치사 뒤에는 쓰지 않는다.

  Asahi Airline, (which/that) offers very reasonable prices to passengers, started a new service.

함정을 피해 봐   실제 강의에서만 알려주는 풀이 노하우!

1. 명사절 that을 관계대명사 that(형용사절 that)과 혼동하지 않도록 한다.

The mechanic thoroughly examined the car (that/what) Mr. Rue bought.

→ that 뒤는 완전한 문장, what 뒤는 불완전한 문장이 오므로 what이 정답이라는 식으로 풀어서는 안 된다. 빈칸 앞에 선행사가 있으므로 명사절 접속사 what은 올 수 없다. that 뒤의 문장이 주어나 목적어가 빠져있는 불완전 문장으로 보이는 것은 관계대명사로 쓰인 that(형용사절 that)이 주어나 목적어로 쓰였기 때문이다.

2. 동격의 that과 관계대명사 that(형용사절 that)을 혼동하지 않도록 한다.

We have to admit the fact (which / that) she will leave our company soon.

→ which 뒤는 불완전한 문장이 온다. 여기서 that은 형용사절 that이 아닌 동격의 that이며, 'fact = 그녀가 우리의 회사를 곧 떠날 것'의 관계이다. 동격의 that 뒤에는 완전한 문장이 온다.

1. that   2. that

STEP 3 실전에 적용해 봐

1. If this is the first time you are visiting Memorial Hall, please present your ID card to the staff to receive a permit ------- grants you free access for a week.

   (A) what
   (B) so
   (C) for
   (D) that

2. Safe Pharmaceuticals has been acknowledged for developing pills ------- have been proven effective without causing drowsiness.

   (A) them
   (B) they
   (C) which
   (D) who

3. Refunds or exchanges are available only when you bring the receipts ------- you received along with the purchased items.

   (A) what
   (B) them
   (C) that
   (D) those

4. The retirement party for Mr. Vogel will be held at Ronn Tower, the entrance of ------- can be found next to the fountain.

   (A) that
   (B) which
   (C) it
   (D) what

5. SecretX Security, ------- specializes in security services for large companies, is entrusted with the protection of BK Tech's private account.

   (A) because
   (B) that
   (C) what
   (D) which

6. Ms. Cole was asked to record the number of items ------- have been returned due to them having the wrong address.

   (A) and
   (B) them
   (C) where
   (D) that

7. Please find and complete the application form ------- is enclosed in the booklets and send it back to us by mail.

   (A) when
   (B) what
   (C) that
   (D) this

8. It seems that none of the stores near your place has the item ------- you ordered now.

   (A) that
   (B) then
   (C) what
   (D) where

9. Harbor Burger announced that it will soon open its next store, ------- will mark the company's 100th franchise.

   (A) so
   (B) which
   (C) also
   (D) this

10. Employees in the Sales Department suggested Exia Station as a great place in ------- to conduct a survey of their new product among a large number of daily visitors to the station.

    (A) where
    (B) that
    (C) there
    (D) which

Chapter 06

6개월에 한 번 출제되는 문제

출제 6 순위

토익 시험 6회에 반드시 한 번은 나온다.

출제율 18%

법칙 43 '(in order) to + 동사원형'은 문장 전체를 수식

To discuss the problem, all members will have a meeting.

위 문장에서 To discuss the problem(문제를 토론하기 위해)은 뒤에 오는 문장 전체를 수식하는 부사 기능을 하며, 이것을 문장 전체를 수식하는 to 부정사라고 한다. to 앞에 in order를 붙여도 같은 의미가 된다.

STEP 1 유형을 파악해 봐

1. ------ renew your membership, you will need to call the office and ask for a renewal.
(A) Instead   (B) In order to   (C) Since   (D) Otherwise

2. ------ prevent accidents from occurring, safety inspections should be regularly carried out.
(A) Unless   (B) Whereas   (C) In order to   (D) In regards to

3. ------ hand out all of the flyers by next week, we should be done making them no later than Tuesday.
(A) Since   (B) However   (C) In order to   (D) Prior to

문제들이 모두 빈칸 뒤에 동사원형이 왔다. 1번 문제의 보기 중 (A)와 (D)는 부사, (C) Since는 전치사/접속사이며, 2번 문제는 (A)와 (B)가 접속사, (D)는 전치사, 3번 문제의 경우 (B)는 부사/접속사, (D)는 전치사이다.

STEP 2 이렇게 풀어 봐

"유형을 파악해 봐" 1번 문제를 보세요!

첫째 빈칸이 문장 제일 앞에 있다면 빈칸 뒤 동사원형을 확인한다.
빈칸이 문장 제일 앞에 오고, 주어 앞에 콤마가 있는 경우, 빈칸이 속한 구는 문장 전체를 수식하는 부사 기능을 한다고 볼 수 있다. 1번 문제에서 빈칸 뒤에 동사원형 renew가 왔으므로 빈칸은 부사 기능을 한다. (C) Since는 전치사/접속사이기 때문에 전치사라면 뒤에 명사가, 접속사라면 뒤에 문장이 와야 하므로 탈락한다. (A)와 (D)는 자체가 부사이므로 구가 문장 전체를 수식하는 부사의 역할을 할 수 없다.

둘째 해석으로 확인한다.
문장 전체를 수식하는 부사 기능을 하는지를 확인하기 위해서는 해석해 보는 것이 필요하다. '당신의 회원권을 갱신하기 위해서, 당신은 전화를 할 필요가 있다.'로 해석되므로 정답은 (B) In order to가 된다.

PLUS

- so as to도 in order to와 같은데, 출제빈도는 in order to보다 낮다. so as만 써서 오답으로 종종 출제되기도 한다.
- in order to의 부정형은 in order not to이며, '~하지 않기 위해서'의 뜻이다.

함정을 피해 봐 — 실제 강의에서만 알려주는 풀이 노하우!

1. in order that, in order for와 혼동하지 않도록 한다.

In order that the new policy be implemented successfully, we hired an expert in the field.
      접속사
새로운 정책이 성공적으로 이행되기 위해서

In order for him to avoid heavy traffic in the morning, please advise Mr. Kim to get to work early.
for him 부분이 to 부정사의 의미상 주어
그(Mr. Kim)가 교통체증을 피하도록 하기 위해서

2. to 동사원형이라고 해서 무조건 in order to만을 답으로 하지 않도록 한다.

① (In order/Whether/How) to speed up and finish the current project on time, Mr. Kim hired several assistants.

② (In order/Whether/How) to speed up and finish the current project on time was taught by the lecturer.

③ I haven't decided (in order/whether/how) to accept the company's offer or not.

→ 문장의 제일 앞이 빈칸, 주어 앞에 콤마가 있으므로 1, 2번 문제는 문장 전체를 수식하는 부사의 자리이다. how to는 부사가 아닌 명사의 기능을 하므로 1, 2번 문제는 해석이 필요하다.

- 1번은 문장의 제일 앞이 빈칸, 주어 앞에 콤마가 있으므로 문장 전체를 수식하는 부사의 자리이다. How to 및 Whether to는 부사가 아닌 명사의 기능을 하므로 탈락한다.
- 2번은 빈칸부터 on time까지가 주어가 되어야 하므로 명사의 기능을 하지 않는 In order는 탈락. Whether to는 문장의 맨 앞에 오지 않으므로 탈락한다.
- 3번은 decide의 목적어 자리이므로 명사절 접속사가 아닌 in order는 탈락한다. 밑줄 뒤 or not으로 선택 사항이 제시되었으므로 whether가 정답이다.

2. In order, How, whether

STEP 3 실전에 적용해 봐

1. ------- have the newspaper delivered at your home every day, you can pay an annual subscription of $10.

   (A) Prior to
   (B) Instead of
   (C) By means of
   (D) In order to

2. ------- better serve you, we want you to fill out a brief questionnaire regarding the quality of our service.

   (A) Whether
   (B) Because
   (C) For
   (D) In order to

3. ------- the appointment of Jacob Nelson as the executive manager, the president silenced all of the employees at the venue.

   (A) To announce
   (B) Announcement
   (C) Announce
   (D) Announced

4. ------- the grand opening of the resort, all guests staying at the resort were given one extra day to stay for free.

   (A) To celebrate
   (B) Celebration of
   (C) Celebrated
   (D) Celebrate

5. ------- proceed with this project, please show this outline to the head of your department and get his approval first.

   (A) Prior to
   (B) Because
   (C) Unless
   (D) In order to

6. ------- a healthy image of the newly launched beverage, the Drizzle Beverage Company focused on advertising its positive effects on the body.

   (A) As a promotion
   (B) To promote
   (C) Promotion of
   (D) For the promotion

7. Ms. Stewart's personal counselor advised her to take a break from her work in order ------- her to relieve her stress.

   (A) that
   (B) to
   (C) for
   (D) because

8. We haven't decided ------- to directly head to the museum or stop by the restaurant to have lunch.

   (A) in order
   (B) whether
   (C) due
   (D) how

9. ------- to sound logical in one's own writing, especially in essays and reports, is a subject about which many employees have interest.

   (A) Owing
   (B) In order
   (C) In addition
   (D) How

10. ------- expect a positive outcome from his business plan, Mr. Ken should first consider the possibility of effectively carrying it out.

    (A) Although
    (B) Therefore
    (C) Whether
    (D) In order to

출제율 18%

법칙 44 빈칸 앞에 한정사가 없고, 보기에 단수 명사가 있으면 불가산명사가 답

명사는 apple처럼 셀 수 있는 명사, 즉 가산명사가 있고, water처럼 셀 수 없는 명사, 즉 불가산명사가 있다. 가산명사는 apples처럼 뒤에 s를 붙여 복수형을 만든다. 편의상 apple을 단수 명사, apples를 복수 명사라고 한다. 단수 명사는 단독으로 쓰지 않고, a(모음 앞에는 an), the, my, this, that 등을 붙여 사용하는데 이러한 것들을 한정사라고 한다.

STEP 1 유형을 파악해 봐

1. Customers who need ------- with the products they purchased can reach us by calling the toll-free number.
(A) assistance   (B) assist   (C) assisted   (D) assistant

2. Ms. Lake was seeking part-time ------- at the Gohl Corporation, where she got hired.
(A) employee   (B) employing   (C) employer   (D) employment

3. After passing the examination, Ms. Earnings received ------- as a professional hairstylist.
(A) certificated   (B) certification   (C) certify   (D) certificate

문제들의 보기가 모두 한 단어의 변형 형태들로 제시된 것으로 보아 품사 문제임을 알 수 있다. 먼저 빈칸의 위치를 살펴보면 3문제 모두 빈칸 앞에 '관소전타'가 있고, 빈칸 뒤에는 전명구가 왔다. 이는 '법칙 2'의 명사 자리에 해당한다. 1번 문제는 (A)와 (D)가 명사, 2번 문제는 (A), (C), (D)가 명사, (B)는 동명사, 3번 문제는 (B)와 (D)가 명사이므로 이를 풀기 위해서는 명사의 가산/불가산명사에 대한 개념을 알고 있어야 한다.

STEP 2 이렇게 풀어 봐

"유형을 파악해 봐" 1번 문제를 보세요!

첫째 품사 문제는 빈칸의 위치를 확인한다.
보기가 한 단어의 변형 형태라면 품사 문제이므로 빈칸을 확인한다. 빈칸 앞은 타동사, 빈칸 뒤는 전명구이므로 빈칸은 명사 자리이다. (B)는 동사, (C)는 형용사이므로 탈락한다.

둘째 가산명사 자리인지, 불가산명사 자리인지를 확인한다.
빈칸 앞에 한정사가 없으므로 빈칸에 복수 명사가 오거나 불가산명사가 와야 한다. (A) assistance는 '도움, 원조'의 뜻을 가진 불가산명사, (D)는 '조수'의 뜻을 가진 가산명사이다. 가산명사는 단수로 쓸 경우 앞에 한정사가 필요하므로 탈락한다.

PLUS

- 불가산명사는 앞에 부정관사(a, an)나 복수형(-s, -es)을 쓸 수 없으며, 동사와의 수일치는 단수로 받는다.

시험에 주로 나오는 불가산명사

equipment 장비	machinery 기계류	news 뉴스	information 정보
baggage/luggage 여행 가방	money/cash 돈/현금	furniture 가구	scenery 장면
advice 충고	mail 우편물	flair 솜씨	software 소프트웨어
access 접근	consent 허가, 허락	merchandise 제품	produce 농산물
assembly 조립	membership 회원제	resistance 저항	knowledge 지식
behavior 행동	bulk 부피, 용적	care 걱정, 근심, 주의	caution 주의, 경계

- 단수 명사와 어울리는 한정사는 아래와 같다.

a/an → 부정관사, the → 정관사　　　　　my, your, his, her → 소유격
this/that → 지시형용사　　　　　　　　　either, neither, each, every → 배분사

함정을 피해 봐
실제 강의에서만 알려주는 풀이 노하우!

1. 가산명사와 불가산명사가 모두 가능한 단어를 조심한다.

불가산명사		가산명사	
support 지지	business 사업	supports 지지대	a business 회사
condition 상태	room 공간	conditions 여건	a room 방
interest 관심, 이자	work 일, 작업, 직장	interests 흥미, 관심	works 작품들
spending 소비, 지출	receipt 수령	spendings 소비, 지출	a receipt 영수증

2. 불가산으로 착각하기 쉬운 가산명사를 조심한다.

delays 지연	approaches 접근법	costs 비용	expenses 비용
funds 자금	fines 벌금	proceeds 수익금	findings 조사 결과물
a covering 덮개	alternatives 대안	suggestions 제안사항	efforts 노력
attempts 시도	results 결과	decisions 결정	discounts 할인

3. 가산으로 착각하기 쉬운 불가산명사를 조심한다.

assistance 도움	help 도움	vocabulary 어휘	evidence 증거
software 소프트웨어	funding 자금지원	planning 기획	advertising 광고
seating 좌석배치	processing 처리	ticketing 발권	widening 확장
housing 주택	clothing 의류	heating 난방	speeding 과속

STEP 3 실전에 적용해 봐

1. The project is making steady progress under the supervisor's tight ------- to meet its deadline.

   (A) coordination
   (B) coordinate
   (C) coordinator
   (D) coordinates

2. Due to careful -------, the regular meeting could avoid being held on the same day as the annual employee appreciation dinner.

   (A) planner
   (B) plan
   (C) planning
   (D) planed

3. The attention to ------- and scheduling leads to what is probably the most useful feature of the GX software.

   (A) organized
   (B) organization
   (C) organizer
   (D) organize

4. Ms. Wang attended Mr. Khan's seminar held on Wednesday upon his -------.

   (A) invite
   (B) inviting
   (C) invitatory
   (D) invitation

5. In order to save more money this month, Ms. Yale decided to minimize her -------, especially on dining.

   (A) spend
   (B) spender
   (C) spending
   (D) spent

6. Entry to the building is restricted to those without ------- granted by the head official.

   (A) permit
   (B) permission
   (C) permitted
   (D) permitting

7. We ask you to answer the following questions honestly, and we guarantee that your ------- will be kept confidential.

   (A) corresponding
   (B) corresponds
   (C) correspondent
   (D) correspondence

8. The items you ordered will be shipped right away on ------- of payment.

   (A) receipt
   (B) recipient
   (C) receipts
   (D) received

9. Although the tools to repair the bikes were costly, Mr. Herrington purchased them because he had no other -------.

   (A) alternatives
   (B) alternation
   (C) alternative
   (D) alternate

10. Please put all your belongings, including your -------, onto the conveyer belt to have them go through the inspection for any illegal items.

    (A) luggages
    (B) luggaged
    (C) luggage
    (D) luggaging

출제율 18%

법칙 45 원급, 비교급, 최상급을 수식해 주거나 비교급, 최상급을 만들어 주는 부사

- 원급: He works efficiently.
- 비교급: He works more efficiently than I.
- 최상급: He works the most efficiently at the company.

위와 같이 부사의 비교급과 최상급은 more나 most를 붙여 만들고, 형용사가 3음절 이상일 때의 비교급과 최상급은 more나 the most를 붙여 만든다. 이때 more나 most는 부사 취급한다.

한편 원급, 비교급, 최상급을 수식해 주는 부사는 각각 따로 있는데, 예를 들어 very는 원급만 수식하기 때문에 very tall은 되지만, very taller, very tallest는 안 된다.

STEP 1 유형을 파악해 봐

1. The manager is ------- strict about meeting the deadlines for reports.
(A) nearly   (B) very   (C) among   (D) single

2. Commuting to work at 8 A.M. every day was ------- harder than expected.
(A) about   (B) over   (C) because   (D) much

3. The ------- largest employer in Europe is the retailer Mores Superstore.
(A) even   (B) single   (C) a little   (D) so

문제들의 빈칸이 모두 형용사 앞에 위치해 있다. 1번 문제는 (A)와 (B)가 부사, (C)는 전치사, (D)는 형용사이고, 2번 문제는 (A)와 (B)는 부사, 전치사, (C)는 접속사, (D)는 형용사, 부사이며, 3번 문제는 (A)와 (D)는 부사, (B)와 (C)는 형용사이다.

STEP 2 이렇게 풀어 봐

"유형을 파악해 봐" 1번 문제를 보세요!

첫째 빈칸의 품사 자리를 먼저 확인한다.
be동사 뒤, 형용사 앞이므로 빈칸은 형용사를 수식하는 부사 자리이다. (C)는 전치사, (D)는 형용사이므로 탈락한다.

둘째 부사 중에서 원급 형용사를 수식하기 좋은 부사를 고른다.

형용사의 정도를 강조해 주는 (B)가 자연스럽다. (A) nearly는 주로 숫자 앞에 오거나 '완성된'이란 표현 앞에 사용하는 부사이다.

PLUS

원급 수식, 비교급 수식, 최상급을 수식하는 표현들을 구분한다.

원급 수식	extremely	very	quite	pretty	so	too
비교급 수식	even	still	a little	a lot	considerably	
최상급 수식	single	only	by far			
비교급/최상급 수식	far	much				

함정을 피해 봐 — 실제 강의에서만 알려주는 풀이 노하우!

1. 최상급 형용사 앞에 부사가 아닌 형용사가 오는 경우를 조심한다.

the (single/singly) largest 단일 규모로= 가장 큰
the (second/secondly) largest 두 번째로 가장 큰

2. even은 비교급을 수식하는 기능 외에도 명사를 수식하는 기능이 있다.

Mr. Kim refused to eat (even/too) the most delicious food after 6 P.M. to keep in shape.
→ even이 비교급 수식만 가능하다고 생각해 오답처리하면 안 된다. 여기서 even은 명사 the most delicious food 앞에 오는 초점 부사이다. ('법칙 30' 참고)

1. single, second   2. even

STEP 3 실전에 적용해 봐

1. Mr. Dunken had to return the table he had purchased few days ago because it was ------- smaller than he had thought it would be.

   (A) single
   (B) a little
   (C) that
   (D) by far

2. The leakage of the clients' personal information is ------- problematic than Joan Holdings had expected as it is being sued for it.

   (A) a lot
   (B) because
   (C) more
   (D) that

3. Working on more than two projects at the same time was ------- difficult, and Ms. Fray was getting only 4 hours of sleep every day.

   (A) extremely
   (B) much
   (C) than
   (D) over

4. At The World's Best Noodles, we promise that we serve our customers ------- the finest cuisine cooked by Michelin-starred chefs.

   (A) that
   (B) over
   (C) extremely
   (D) only

5. Ms. Koy was assigned a new task which seemed ------- more confusing.

   (A) much
   (B) that
   (C) so
   (D) than

6. The Fluto Photo Exhibition impressed Ms. Knowles so much that she had no doubt it was by ------- the greatest exhibition she had ever seen.

   (A) so
   (B) extremely
   (C) far
   (D) that

7. The manager tried to encourage the new employees to participate in the discussion ------- actively by having an ice-breaking session.

   (A) that
   (B) more
   (C) but
   (D) than

8. Although Mr. West requested that the delivery of the products be made as soon as possible, the products were delivered ------- later than usual.

   (A) even
   (B) very
   (C) nearly
   (D) with

9. As there were no tables available at A Taste of India, Mr. Brown called Eddy's, which was the ------- largest restaurant in the city.

   (A) secondly
   (B) very
   (C) second
   (D) than

10. Photographer Naomi Jerome invited ------- the harshest art critics to her private exhibition because she had confidence in her work.

    (A) too
    (B) as well
    (C) along
    (D) even

출제율 **16%**

법칙 46 앞뒤 내용이 상반되면 but, 순차적이면 and나 or, 인과관계면 so

'I like him, but he dislikes me.'에서 but처럼 문장과 문장을 동등하게 연결해 주는 접속사를 등위접속사라고 한다. 등위접속사에는 for(왜냐하면 ~때문에), and(그리고), nor(~도 아니다), but(그러나), or(혹은, 그렇지 않으면), yet(그러나), so(그래서) 등이 있는데, 이것의 앞 글자를 딴 'FANBOYS'를 알아 두자. 앞 문장과 뒷문장의 의미 관계에 따라 적절한 등위접속사를 사용해야 한다.

STEP 1 유형을 파악해 봐

1. Installation instructions and product warranty information are included in the product package, ------- batteries are not.
(A) but   (B) or   (C) with   (D) either

2. Subscribe to *Regional Businessweek* ------- receive the newsletters that more than 10 million people are reading.
(A) so   (B) and   (C) that   (D) but

3. The renovations on the main gate will begin soon, ------- visitors are advised to use the rear door.
(A) nor   (B) because   (C) so   (D) except for

문제들이 모두 빈칸 앞과 뒤로 완전한 문장이 오고, 보기 중 2개 이상이 등위접속사들로 제시되었다. 1번 문제는 (A)와 (B)가, 2번 문장은 (A), (B), (D)가, 3번 문장은 (A)와 (C)가 등위접속사이다.

STEP 2 이렇게 풀어 봐   "유형을 파악해 봐" 1번 문제를 보세요!

첫째 접속사 자리인지부터 확인한다.
빈칸의 앞에도 문장, 그리고 콤마 다음에도 문장이 있으므로 접속사가 필요하다. (C) with는 전치사, (D) either 역시 대명사나 형용사 기능을 하므로 탈락한다. either A or B에서는 or가 접속사이다.

둘째 but부터 대입해 해석해 본다.
등위접속사를 고르는 문제이므로 but을 먼저 대입해 해석해 본다. '설치 설명서와 품질 보증 정보는 제품 패키지에 포함되어 있다. 그러나 배터리들은 그렇지 않다.'는 해석이 자연스러우므로 (A) but이 정답이다.

Chapter 06 _ 6개월에 한 번 출제되는 문제 153

PLUS

- nor 다음에는 도치된 문장이 온다.

  I can't go, nor **can you** go. 나는 갈 수 없다. 그리고 너도 갈 수 없다.

- 등위접속사 중 같은 말을 생략할 수 있는 등위접속사는 and, but, or, yet, as well as, than 등이다.
  ('법칙 34' 참고)

  I like him and her.
  → 'I like him, and I like her.'에서 반복되는 말인 I like을 생략한 것이다.

- 부사절 접속사 so that을 줄여 so로 쓰기도 한다.

  Please make a payment today **so** we can process your order as soon as we confirm receipt of it.
  → 여기서 so는 so that과 같은 기능이며, '그래야 ~하니까'의 뜻이다.

 함정을 피해 봐 실제 강의에서만 알려주는 풀이 노하우!

1. so와 because를 혼동하지 않도록 한다.

The copier on the third floor is not working, (so/because) employees should use the one on the second floor.

→ '3층에 있는 복사기가 작동하지 않는다.'가 원인이고, '직원들은 2층의 복사기를 사용해야 한다.'가 결과이다. because는 콤마 뒤에 오는 경우가 드물며, because 뒤에는 원인이 와야 한다.

1. so

STEP 3 실전에 적용해 봐

1. A $10 deposit must be submitted upon the reservation of a room, ------- you can have it returned when you check out.

   (A) with
   (B) that
   (C) even
   (D) and

2. The renovations on the building were scheduled to be done on Wednesday, ------- they will not be finished until next Friday.

   (A) even
   (B) that
   (C) either
   (D) but

3. The market conditions were rather unfavorable, ------- Sweet Home Furnishings' profits actually increased this year.

   (A) over
   (B) but
   (C) even
   (D) likewise

4. As Mr. Hague's resume was reviewed ------- his work experience was recognized, he was asked to come for a job interview at the Jennings Company.

   (A) but
   (B) yet
   (C) and
   (D) that

5. Please have your tickets prepared in advance to present them to the staff at the entrance ------- you can be let inside with no delay.

   (A) because
   (B) if
   (C) so
   (D) but

6. Analysts say that the region's economic growth has been stagnant over the past few years, ------- in fact, public spending increased by 5 percent.

   (A) but
   (B) and
   (C) or
   (D) if

7. Dr. Jones advised Ms. Riley to take the medicine when she experiences nausea ------- dizziness.

   (A) or
   (B) either
   (C) so
   (D) but

8. Ms. Kerr didn't bring the materials that are usually needed for a regular seminar, ------- did she remember to print extra copies of the document that Mr. Shin requested.

   (A) if
   (B) although
   (C) but
   (D) nor

9. Mr. Gilbert left his office earlier than usual today ------- he had a dinner appointment with a client.

   (A) so
   (B) if
   (C) or
   (D) because

10. When you see an item is running out of stock report it to the warehouse nearby ------- we can be sure to have it available any time.

    (A) yet
    (B) even
    (C) so
    (D) but

출제율 16%

법칙 47　of가 답이 되는 주격, 목적격, 소유격, 동격

of는 보통 명사와 명사를 연결하는데, 우리말로 '~의'라고 해석되는 of에는 총 4종류가 있다.

주격의 of	an outbreak of war 전쟁의 발발 → 전쟁이 발발하다
목적격의 of	a demonstration of the product 제품의 시연 → 제품을 시연하다
소유격의 of	legs of the desk 책상의 다리 → 책상다리는 책상의 일부임
동격의 of	the aim of fighting global warming 지구 온난화를 막기 위한 목표 → 지구 온난화 막기 = 목표

STEP 1　유형을 파악해 봐

1. The success of the project was attributable to the commitment ------- the team members involved.
(A) about　　(B) at　　(C) of　　(D) during

2. The assessment ------- the risks involved in business expansion is negative.
(A) by　　(B) at　　(C) from　　(D) of

3. You deserve compensation ------- a two-week vacation for your recent contribution to the Jamison Corporation.
(A) by　　(B) to　　(C) of　　(D) about

보기들이 모두 전치사로 구성되어 있다. 전치사 어휘 문제는 해석을 하거나 빈칸의 앞과 뒤를 확인해 정답을 고른다.

STEP 2　이렇게 풀어 봐
"유형을 파악해 봐" 1번 문제를 보세요!

첫째 빈칸 뒤를 확인한다.
전치사 어휘 문제는 전체 문맥을 보는 경우와 빈칸의 앞과 뒤를 확인하는 경우가 있다. 추가, 포함, 제외 전치사와

166　어형 및 문법 편

이유, 용도, 대상, 목적 전치사, 그리고 양보, 이유 전치사가 보기에 없으므로 빈칸 앞과 뒤만 보고도 풀 수 있는 문제이다. 빈칸 뒤에 the team members가 왔으므로 이와 어울리지 않는 전치사부터 제거한다. (D)는 기간 명사와 함께 사용하므로 탈락한다.

둘째 빈칸 앞을 확인한다.
빈칸 앞에 '헌신'이라는 명사가 있다. (B)는 앞의 동사나 명사가 at과 같이 쓰이는 경우만 가능하고, commitment는 to나 about과 어울리므로 탈락한다. (A)는 '팀 멤버에 대한 헌신'을 의미한다. (C)는 주격의 of가 되어 '팀 멤버들이 헌신'하는 것을 의미한다. 앞부분을 확인해 보면 '팀 멤버들의 헌신에 프로젝트의 성공 여부가 달려 있다'는 말이므로 (C)가 답이 된다.

PLUS

- 'of + 명사'가 형용사나 보어로 사용되기도 한다.

of importance 중요한	of use 유용한	of interest 재미있는

- 형용사 뒤에 of가 오는 경우는 숙어로 기억한다.

be representative of ~를 대표하다 (= represent)	be aware of ~를 알고 있다 (= know)
be indicative of ~를 나타내다 (= indicate)	be reminiscent of ~를 상기시키다 (= remind)

- 주격, 소유격, 목적격, 동격 of 이외에도 '관련, 한정의 of(~에 관한, ~에 대한)'가 있다.

a list of my past employers 나의 이전 고용주들의 목록 → 이전 고용주들이 나온, 그에 한정된 목록
stories of his travels 그의 여행담 → 그의 여행에 대한 이야기
an issue of housing 주택의 문제 → 주택에 관한 문제

함정을 피해 봐 — 실제 강의에서만 알려주는 풀이 노하우!

1. 해석상 of를 쓸 것 같지만 그렇지 않은 경우를 조심한다.

He has a passion (of/for) his work. 그는 일에 대한 열정을 가지고 있다.

He broke the record (of/for) eating food. 그는 음식을 먹는 것에 대한 기록을 깼다.

→ record of는 뒤에 구체적인 기록 자체나 기록의 주체가 나와야 한다.

1. for, for

STEP 3 실전에 적용해 봐

1. Mr. Fray, the founder ------- Elaska, Inc., will soon appoint a new CEO who is going to take his seat after he retires.

   (A) about
   (B) of
   (C) to
   (D) with

2. ------- all the applicants, Ms. Wozniak seems to have the most comprehensive understanding of our company and her job.

   (A) Of
   (B) Since
   (C) Even
   (D) But

3. Many analysts have predicted that the retirement ------- Mr. Jobs will be a great loss for the Innovation Corporation, which does not have an executive as talented as him.

   (A) by
   (B) from
   (C) of
   (D) with

4. The ultimate goal ------- the project is to raise global awareness of sweatshops in Indonesia.

   (A) at
   (B) to
   (C) within
   (D) of

5. Although the renovations ------- the venue will be done tomorrow, it will not open until next week.

   (A) about
   (B) with
   (C) of
   (D) to

6. Company policy requires at least two test-runs ------- automobiles before they are officially released.

   (A) of
   (B) within
   (C) during
   (D) about

7. Please assist those waiting in line who have inquiries about the price ------- tickets.

   (A) at
   (B) of
   (C) during
   (D) to

8. The lecture ------- entrepreneurship, which is a mandatory course for Sales Department employees, is scheduled to be held in room 780 every Thursday.

   (A) of
   (B) with
   (C) at
   (D) on

9. ------- all the possible career paths, accounting seems to be the most suitable one for Mr. Bedford, who has a great amount of interest in the field.

   (A) By
   (B) For
   (C) Of
   (D) Along

10. The R&M Research Institute has been conducting research on ways to motivate employees with the aim ------- enhancing the general working conditions at local companies.

    (A) at
    (B) on
    (C) by
    (D) of

Chapter 07

7~8개월에 한 번 출제되는 문제

출제 7 순위

언제든 대비하고 있어야 하는 문제

출제율 15%

법칙 48 희망, 요청, 설득, 허락 동사가 오면 to 부정사

5형식 동사 중 '희망, 요청, 설득, 허락'의 뜻을 가진 동사들을 편의상 '결혼승낙' 동사라고 하며, 목적어 뒤에 오는 목적 보어 자리에 to 부정사가 오는 것이 특징이다.

희망	want	wish	would like	+ 목적어 + 목적 보어
	expect			
요청	ask	require	request	명사 to 동사원형
	advise	remind	invite	
설득	convince	persuade	urge	
	encourage	drive		
허락	allow	permit	enable	

'I want you to go.'의 뜻은 '나는 너를 원한다, 가기 위해서'가 아니고, '나는 네가 가기를 원한다.'로 해석한다. 여기서 to go는 want의 목적 보어이다.

STEP 1 유형을 파악해 봐

1. The executive manager asked the head of the Sales Department ------- the sales record during the last quarter.
(A) to report (B) reported (C) will report (D) reporting

2. The CEO of Blooming Audio expects the company's profit margin this year ------- the rate predicted last year.
(A) exceed (B) be exceeding (C) to exceed (D) exceeded

3. These pills are advised ------- at least half an hour after a meal and three times a day.
(A) to be taken (B) take (C) taken (D) took

보기가 모두 정동사와 준동사들로 구성되어 있다. 1번 문제는 (C)만 정동사이고, (A)와 (D)는 준동사, (B)는 정동사와 준동사가 모두 가능하다. 2번 문제는 (B)와 (A)가 정동사, (C)는 준동사, (D)는 정동사와 준동사가 모두 가능하다. 3번 문제는 (B)와 (D)가 정동사, (A)와 (C)는 준동사이다. 준동사의 개수가 2개 이상 포함된 문제는 준동사를 고르는 문제일 가능성이 높다.

STEP 2 이렇게 풀어 봐

"유형을 파악해 봐" 1번 문제를 보세요!

첫째 빈칸이 정동사 자리인지 준동사 자리인지 확인한다.
asked가 정동사이므로 빈칸은 준동사 자리이므로 정동사인 (C)는 탈락한다.

둘째 준동사의 기능을 확인한다.
빈칸은 '결혼승낙' 동사인 ask의 목적 보어 자리이다. 따라서 to 부정사가 필요하다.

PLUS

- '결혼승낙' 동사와 '응큼쟁이'(to 부정사만 목적어로 취하는 동사)에 모두 해당하는 동사들이 있다.
  I want to go. (3형식 '응큼쟁이' 동사)
  I want you to go. (5형식 '결혼승낙' 동사)
  → want, need, hope, expect, ask가 여기에 해당한다.

- '결혼승낙' 동사와 '인어노리' 동사('법칙 71' 참고)에 모두 해당하는 동사들이 있다.
  I advised him to go. (5형식 '결혼승낙' 동사) → '권고하다'의 뜻
  I advised him of my arrival. I advised him that I had been wrong. (3, 4형식 '인어노리' 동사) → '알리다'의 뜻
  → advise, convince, remind가 여기에 속한다.

- '결혼승낙' 동사와 '생말예제' 동사('법칙 73' 참고)에 모두 해당하는 동사들이 있다.
  I requested him to go. (5형식 '결혼승낙' 동사)
  I requested that he go out. (3형식 '생말예제' 동사)
  → expect, ask, request, advise 등이 여기에 속한다.

🎯 함정을 피해 봐

실제 강의에서만 알려주는 풀이 노하우!

1. '결혼승낙' 동사와 '응큼쟁이' 동사를 혼동해서는 안 된다.
Even though he was late for the movie, Mr. Kim (wanted/allowed) to enter the theater.
→ allow가 to와 잘 어울릴 것 같다는 생각만으로 정답을 고를 경우 실수하기 쉽다. allow는 to 부정사를 목적 보어로 취하는 동사('결혼승낙' 동사)이지, to 부정사를 목적어로 취하는 동사('응큼쟁이' 동사)가 아니다.

2. help 동사, 사역동사, 준사역 동사를 조심한다.
Mr. Kim helped me (to) finish the project./Mr. Kim helped (to) finish the project.
→ 5형식뿐 아니라 3형식도 가능하다.
Mr. Kim let me go. → let, have, make는 to 동사원형 대신 동사원형을 쓴다.
Mr. Kim got me to wash his car. → get은 to 동사원형을 쓴다.

1. wanted

STEP 3 실전에 적용해 봐

1. Dailywear Outfitters allows its store staff ------- a 20% discount on every purchase when they purchase items at the store.

   (A) receive
   (B) receiver
   (C) will receive
   (D) to receive

2. As an employee training specialist, Mr. Hills was asked ------- basic etiquette at the workplace to the newcomers.

   (A) explain
   (B) to be explained
   (C) explaining
   (D) to explain

3. The employees are encouraged ------- online lessons on whistleblowing that are provided for free for all employees.

   (A) taking
   (B) to take
   (C) being taken
   (D) takes

4. The manager wants Mr. Doe ------- with Mr. Browne from the Accounting Department to work on the new project.

   (A) to pair up
   (B) will pair up
   (C) pair up
   (D) pairs up

5. All applicants are required ------- either online or offline payments before the end of this week; otherwise, their registrations will be cancelled.

   (A) making
   (B) to make
   (C) made
   (D) will make

6. The supervisor reminded the employees working at the construction site ------- with the safety guidelines at all times even when he is not around.

   (A) complying
   (B) complies
   (C) to comply
   (D) complied

7. JR Holdings lets its employees ------- its company automobiles for free for a maximum of three weeks.

   (A) to use
   (B) using
   (C) used
   (D) use

8. Since most of her friends at other companies were working under more favorable working conditions, Ms. Stephen was convinced ------- her job.

   (A) changing
   (B) will change
   (C) to change
   (D) changes

9. The manager got Ms. Dawson ------- all of the employees to deliver an announcement on the recent changes in the policy.

   (A) gathering
   (B) gather
   (C) to gather
   (D) gathers

10. Mr. Gohr sent an e-mail to the executive manager that he ------- to extend the time he was given for his presentation.

    (A) considered
    (B) finished
    (C) allowed
    (D) wished

출제율 **14%**

법칙 49 감정분사는 '사물잉, 사람을 패?'

'재미있는 영화'라고 말할 때 interested movie가 아니라 interesting movie라고 한다. 또한 지치고 피곤한 상태를 말할 때도 'I'm tiring.'이 아닌 'I'm tired.'라고 한다. interesting, interested, tiring, tired와 같은 말들을 감정동사로 만든 분사라고 하는데, 이를 '감정분사'라고도 한다.

감정동사의 종류

| satisfy | excite | bore | tire | disappoint | embarrass | frustrate |
| refresh | interest | exhaust | please | overwhelm | surprise | amaze |

STEP 1 유형을 파악해 봐

1. We are ------- to announce the grand opening of Shop n' More's 76th store in Maryland.
(A) pleasing   (B) pleasure   (C) pleased   (D) please

2. Although the exhibition had about a whole year to be prepared, the majority of the visitors said that it was -------.
(A) disappointment   (B) disappointing   (C) disappointed   (D) disappoint

3. Ms. Grin is looking forward to attending the show held next week because she heard that the scale of the show is -------.
(A) overwhelmed   (B) overwhelmingly   (C) overwhelming   (D) overwhelm

보기는 모두 정동사와 준동사들이 포함되어 있다. 1번 문제는 (D)가 정동사, (A)와 (C)는 분사, (B)는 명사, 2번 문제는 (D)가 정동사, (B)와 (C)는 분사, (A)는 명사, 그리고 3번 문제는 (D)가 정동사, (A)와 (C)가 분사 (B)는 부사이다. 세 문제 모두 분사들은 감정분사들이 왔다.

STEP 2 이렇게 풀어 봐

"유형을 파악해 봐" 1번 문제를 보세요!

첫째 빈칸이 분사 자리인지 확인한다.
보기에 감정분사가 있으므로 감정분사 관련 문제일 가능성이 높은 문제들이다. be동사 뒤에는 형용사 기능을 하는 분사가 필요하다. 따라서 동사인 (D)는 오답이고, 명사 (B)가 답이 되려면 주어와 동격이 되어야 하는데 '우리

= 기쁨'의 관계는 아니므로 역시 오답이다.

둘째 빈칸이 수식해 주는 명사가 사람인지 사물인지 확인한다.

빈칸은 주격 보어 자리이므로 주어인 we와의 어울림을 따져야 하는데, we는 사람이므로 p.p.를 쓴다. 따라서 (C)가 답이다. 감정동사는 '~하게 하다'의 뜻으로 사물이 사람을 기쁘게 하고, 사람은 그 사물에 의해 기쁘게 되는 관계이다. 따라서 감정분사를 고르는 문제가 출제될 경우 '사물잉(-ing), 사람을 패?(p.p.)' 즉, 사물은 -ing, 사람은 p.p.를 답으로 고르면 된다.

PLUS

- 감정분사는 형용사로 취급하므로 -ing의 경우 뒤에 오는 목적어를 생략할 수 있다.

  The movie interests us. → The movie is interesting (us).

  We are interested by the movie. → We are interested (in the movie).

함정을 피해 봐
실제 강의에서만 알려주는 풀이 노하우!

1. 감정분사를 결정할 때 엉뚱한 부분을 보지 않도록 한다.

The construction noise in the next door building has left the office workers (annoying/annoyed).
→ 빈칸은 5형식 동사 leave의 목적 보어 자리로, 주어인 noise가 아닌 목적어인 office workers와의 어울림을 따져야 한다.

2. 사람, 사물을 따질 때 혼동할 수 있는 부분에 조심한다.

Ace Hightech is (pleased/pleasing) to announce the merger with Westsoft.
→ 회사명을 보고 사물이라고 생각해서는 안 된다. 회사도 사람이 모인 집단이다.

1. annoyed 2. pleased

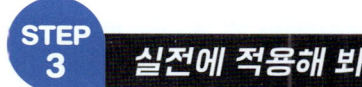

1. Please validate your e-mail address to receive our ------- tour program offers for free.
   (A) excited
   (B) exciting
   (C) excite
   (D) excitation

2. The book Ms. Brooklyn wrote contained a ------- story of life as a bag designer in New York that was based on her own experience.
   (A) fascinated
   (B) fascination
   (C) fascinator
   (D) fascinating

3. The executive manager was ------- when the rival firm had the same celebrity advertise its product as his own company.
   (A) startled
   (B) startling
   (C) startle
   (D) startles

4. You can take this medicine with relief as it does not have any ------- effects on your health.
   (A) worries
   (B) worried
   (C) worry
   (D) worrying

5. The workshop on managing e-commerce Web sites will be held for free for anyone -------.
   (A) interested
   (B) interesting
   (C) interestingly
   (D) to interest

6. Mr. Bean was ------- when he entered the classroom twenty minutes after the lecture had already begun.
   (A) embarrassed
   (B) embarrass
   (C) embarrassing
   (D) embarrasses

7. Power Auto Parts is ------- to announce that it has finally become a member of the Kansas City local business association.
   (A) honor
   (B) honored
   (C) honoring
   (D) honors

8. The short play *Dancing with Aria* did not receive much positive feedback from the audience, who thought it was -------.
   (A) bored
   (B) boringly
   (C) bore
   (D) boring

9. Ms. Plain is ------- that her proposal, which she had worked on for an entire month, was rejected by the executive manager.
   (A) frustration
   (B) frustrated
   (C) frustrate
   (D) frustrating

10. The recent news about the tragic accident that happened in Northeast Town left all of the residents ------- about the security of the town.
    (A) concerning
    (B) concern
    (C) concerned
    (D) concerns

출제율 12%

법칙 50 완전한 문장 뒤에서는 '(in order) to 동사원형'이 동사를 수식

'I go to stay.'에서 to stay 부분의 해석은 '머물기 위해서'이며, 앞의 동사인 go를 수식하는 부사 기능을 한다. 즉, 'I go in order to stay.'와 같은 뜻이다. 따라서 숙어 'in order to 동사원형'은 '~하기 위해서'로 해석한다. 'in order to 동사원형'은 부사의 기능을 하므로 앞의 문장이 '필수요소를 모두 갖춘 완전한 문장'일 때 올 수 있다.

STEP 1 유형을 파악해 봐

1. The free luncheon will be held in the cafeteria ------- the retirement of Mr. Guru.
(A) celebrate (B) to celebrate (C) celebrated (D) celebrates

2. Applicants must have their driver's license obtained ------- for a part-time bus driver position.
(A) to apply (B) applied (C) is applying (D) apply

3. Residents must show their resident identity card to the security guard ------- park their cars at the lot for free.
(A) in front of (B) when (C) for (D) in order to

1, 2번 문제의 보기는 모두 정동사와 준동사들로 구성되어 있다. 분사 문제(-ing, p.p.)와의 차이점은 준동사 중에서도 to 부정사가 보기에 등장한다는 점이다. 3번 문제는 동사원형(park) 앞에 빈칸이 있고, 보기는 전치사와 접속사, 그리고 in order to로 구성되어 있다.

STEP 2 이렇게 풀어 봐

"유형을 파악해 봐" 1번 문제를 보세요!

첫째 빈칸이 정동사 자리인지 준동사 자리인지 확인한다.
이미 정동사 will be가 있으므로 빈칸은 준동사 자리이다.

둘째 빈칸 앞에 완전한 문장이 있는지, 뒤에 목적어가 있는지 확인한다.
빈칸 앞에는 2형식의 완전한 문장이 있으므로 to 부정사인 (B)가 와야 뒤에 the retirement라는 목적어를 가질 수 있다. (C)는 p.p.로 볼 경우 뒤에서 앞의 명사 cafeteria를 수식할 수는 있으나 뒤에 목적어를 가질 수 없다. 해석을 해 보면 '은퇴를 축하하기 위해서'라는 말이 자연스럽다.

PLUS

- in order to는 문두에 오기도 한다. ('법칙 43' 참고)
- so as to도 in order to와 같은데, 출제빈도는 in order to에 비해 낮다. so as만 쓰여 오답으로 종종 출제되기도 한다.
- in order to의 부정형은 in order not to이며, '~하지 않기 위해서'의 뜻이다.

함정을 피해 봐 — 실제 강의에서만 알려주는 풀이 노하우!

1. in order that, in order for와 혼동하지 않도록 한다.

We hired an expert in the field <u>in order that the new policy be implemented successfully</u>.

새로운 정책이 성공적으로 이행되기 위해서

Please advise Mr. Kim to get to work early <u>in order for him to avoid heavy traffic in the morning</u>.
for him이 to avoid의 의미상 주어
그(Mr. Kim)가 아침에 교통체증을 피하도록 하기 위해서

STEP 3 실전에 적용해 봐

1. Free samples of beauty products were given to customers making purchases of $50 or more ------- them to buy more items.

   (A) encourage
   (B) to encourage
   (C) are encouraging
   (D) will encourage

2. We ship all products ordered within two days of payment being confirmed ------- guarantee our customers prompt delivery.

   (A) so that
   (B) because
   (C) even
   (D) in order to

3. Your responses to our customer survey questions will be carefully reviewed and reflected upon ------- improve the quality of our service.

   (A) will help
   (B) helped
   (C) to help
   (D) being helped

4. You should call the restaurant Friday Night at least two days in advance ------- a table for 15 people.

   (A) reserving
   (B) reserved
   (C) to reserve
   (D) reservation

5. Ms. Clarkson uses his company's vehicle ------- pick up important clients at the airport, and has never used it for other purposes.

   (A) so to
   (B) only to
   (C) unless
   (D) in order that

6. Mr. Toffler was asked to move all the stuff in the supply room to some other place to ------- room for the new printer.

   (A) make
   (B) be made
   (C) makes
   (D) making

7. The user guide for the audio player explains ------- to deal with temporary technical problems such as a sudden power shutdown in detail.

   (A) whether
   (B) how
   (C) in order
   (D) that

8. All sales staff at Deli Foods is required to come to the store by noon to ------- the facility prior to the sanitary inspection.

   (A) clean up
   (B) cleaning up
   (C) cleaned up
   (D) cleans up

9. Please assist the customers waiting in line to receive the service they want in order ------- them not to have to wait until the receptionist arrives.

   (A) that
   (B) to
   (C) for
   (D) of

10. Ms. Lam needs to decide ------- to register for an entry-level or intermediate swimming class before the deadline.

    (A) in order
    (B) how
    (C) that
    (D) whether

법칙 51 과거 시점보다 이전은 과거완료

'내가 방에 들어갔을 때쯤, 그녀는 이미 떠났다.'는 내용에서 내가 방에 들어간 것보다 그녀가 떠난 것이 먼저라는 것을 알 수 있다. 이렇게 똑같은 과거시제라도 더 먼저 일어난 과거시제가 있는데, 이것을 '과거완료시제'라고 하며, had p.p.로 나타낸다. 'By the time I entered the room, she had (already) left.'에서 By the time I entered the room 부분이 과거 시점인데, 과거완료시제는 과거 시점이 있어야 사용할 수 있다.

STEP 1 유형을 파악해 봐

1. Before Mrs. McGuire was promoted to store manager, she ------- part time at the store on weekdays.
(A) will work   (B) works   (C) had worked   (D) working

2. Mr. Krowski received an e-mail replying to his inquiries by Anywhere Travel after he ------- for details regarding his itinerary.
(A) had asked   (B) will ask   (C) asks   (D) asking

3. By the time Yum Bakery began to plan the expansion of its business overseas, more than one billion of its doughnuts ------- on the Chinese market.
(A) will be sold   (B) are sold   (C) had been sold   (D) has been sold

1, 2번 문제의 보기는 준동사 1개에 나머지는 정동사들로 구성되어 있고, 3번 문제는 보기 4개가 모두 정동사들로 구성되어 있다. 정동사들이 미래, 현재, 과거완료, 현재완료 등의 다양한 시제로 제시된 것으로 보아 시제를 묻는 문제임을 알 수 있다.

STEP 2 이렇게 풀어 봐   "유형을 파악해 봐" 1번 문제를 보세요!

첫째 정동사 자리인지 확인한다.
빈칸 앞이 주어이므로 정동사가 필요하다. 따라서 준동사인 (D)는 탈락한다.

둘째 시제의 단서를 확인한다.
시제 문제에는 반드시 시제의 단서가 있다. Before ~ manger 부분이 과거 시점이고, 과거보다 더 이전의 상황을 나타내야 하므로 과거완료시제가 필요하다. (A)는 미래, (B)는 현재시제라서 탈락한다.

PLUS

- 과거완료가 뻔한 경우에는 과거시제를 쓰기도 한다.

    Mr. Kim **washed** his hands before he ate lunch.
    → had washed를 써야 하지만 washed를 사용하는 것도 가능하다.

 함정을 피해 봐   실제 강의에서만 알려주는 풀이 노하우!

1. 과거시제가 없어도 과거완료를 쓰는 경우를 조심한다.

Mr. Kim (had worked / will work) as an assistant manager before his recent promotion to his current position.
→ 직접적으로 과거시제가 제시되진 않았으나 '최근의 승진'은 과거에 발생한 일임을 알 수 있다. 따라서 과거보다 더 이전의 일을 나타내야 하므로 과거완료시제가 필요하다.

1. had worked

STEP 3 실전에 적용해 봐

1. After Ms. Bourne ------- the skills to make garments, she was allowed to skip the rest of the training session and to work as a regular employee at Clothes 4 All.

   (A) has mastered
   (B) had mastered
   (C) is mastered
   (D) masters

2. A free delivery coupon was provided to Mr. Titus for his next purchase of items at SellForLess.com due to the delayed delivery of the items, which came later than he -------.

   (A) had anticipated
   (B) is anticipated
   (C) anticipating
   (D) anticipated

3. By the time the merger of Kolb Mobile with the major corporation Everywhere Network was announced, the stock price of Kolb Mobile ------- its peak.

   (A) reaches
   (B) will reach
   (C) is reaching
   (D) had reached

4. The project director ------- estimating the number of attendees at the seminar even before the date and place of the seminar were announced.

   (A) is beginning
   (B) has begun
   (C) begins
   (D) had begun

5. Ms. Kinsey ----- tickets for the opera *Haunted House* before fans bought all of them both online and offline.

   (A) will have purchased
   (B) had purchased
   (C) would be purchasing
   (D) purchasing

6. After the media ------- on the potential of the animation market, an increasing number of jobseekers applied for jobs at Joy Pictures.

   (A) had reported
   (B) to report
   (C) is reporting
   (D) will report

7. Mr. Martin ------- for jobs at over 50 mid-sized companies in France until he finally got hired by Branson Resources.

   (A) applies
   (B) had applied
   (C) is applying
   (D) will apply

8. Ms. Packer ------- the marketing team's project on analyzing the needs of local consumers before she was transferred to the international division.

   (A) will assist
   (B) is assisting
   (C) assists
   (D) had assisted

9. It was fortunate that Mr. Harrison ------- all the documents on his computer before the power went out.

   (A) saves
   (B) was saving
   (C) had saved
   (D) will save

10. Advanced Technologies had worked in a partnership with Bayfold Production until another manufacturing company ------- a deal with more benefits for the same conditions.

    (A) had offered
    (B) will offer
    (C) offers
    (D) offered

출제율 11%

법칙 52 시간[조건] 부사절 또는 반복[습관]적 사실의 단서가 보이면 현재시제

영어의 동사에는 현재, 과거, 미래 등의 시제들이 있는데, 현재시제는 3인칭 단수인 경우에는 동사에 –s나 –es를 붙여 만들고, 그렇지 않은 경우에는 동사원형을 쓴다. 'I work every day.'와 같이 반복[습관]적인 행동을 나타내는 문장과 'When(If) you come tomorrow, I will go.'와 같이 시간[조건] 부사절에서는 현재시제가 미래시제를 대신하기도 한다.

STEP 1 유형을 파악해 봐

1. When Mr. Talbot ------- North Cape, he will attend the regional conference.
   (A) was visiting   (B) visits   (C) visited   (D) visiting

2. Because of her children, Ms. Chad ------- pizza for dinner every Friday night.
   (A) ordering   (B) ordered   (C) orders   (D) to order

3. You may exit and reenter the theater 10 minutes before the play -------.
   (A) begins   (B) began   (C) begin   (D) to begin

보기들이 모두 정동사와 준동사들로 구성되어 있다. 정동사는 2개 이상 제시되었고, 그것들은 각기 다른 시제들로 구성되어 있으므로 시제를 묻는 문제임을 알 수 있다.

STEP 2 이렇게 풀어 봐
"유형을 파악해 봐" 1번 문제를 보세요!

첫째 정동사 자리인지 확인한다.
빈칸 앞이 주어이므로 빈칸에는 정동사가 필요하다. 따라서 준동사인 (D)는 탈락한다.

둘째 시제의 단서를 확인한다.
시제 문제에는 반드시 시제의 단서가 제시되기 마련이다. 콤마 다음 문장이 주절이며, 이 주절의 시제가 미래시제이다. 하지만 when으로 시작하는 부사절에서는 현재시제가 미래를 대신하므로 (B)가 정답이다.

PLUS

• 반복, 습관적인 사실을 나타내는 문장은 현재시제를 사용하므로 아래의 빈도부사들과도 잘 어울린다. ('법칙 5' 참고)

regularly	frequently	always	usually	often
typically	routinely	periodically	occasionally	normally
customarily	every month	each month	these days	

- 현재시제는 규정을 나타내는 내용과도 잘 어울린다.

  No one without a pass is allowed to enter the facility.

- 시간 및 조건 부사절 접속사에는 다음과 같은 것들이 있다.

  시간 부사절 접속사: when, by the time, after, as soon as, before, while, until S + V
  조건 부사절 접속사: if, provided (that), providing (that), once, as long as, unless S + V

- 시간 및 조건 부사절에서 현재가 미래를 대신하는 것은 주절이 미래일 때만 적용된다.

  When my brother came in, I was reading the newspaper.
  → 시간 부사절에 과거를 쓴 이유는 주절이 미래가 아니기 때문이다.

 함정을 피해 봐   실제 강의에서만 알려주는 풀이 노하우

1. 과거 시점은 과거 시점이 명확할 때 사용한다.

   You are entitled to a special program that (extended/extends) your warranty for another year.
   → 여기서 현재시제가 답이 되는 이유는 '보증을 추가로 한 해 더 연장해 준다.'는 것이 일종의 규정, 사실이기 때문이다.

2. 우리말 해석으로만 시제를 판단하지 않는다.

   I (am writing/write) to you to file a complaint.
   → 우리말의 현재시제를 생각하고 '불평을 제기하기 위해서 편지를 쓴다.'라고 생각해 현재시제를 선택하면 안 된다. 현재시제는 반복, 습관적 사실일 때 사용하는데, 불평을 반복, 습관적으로 제기한다는 것은 어딘지 어색하다.

3. 미래의 어감을 가진 단어에 유의한다.

   The warranty (expires/has expired) next week.
   → 미래 시점을 나타내는 next week가 문장에 있는데, 보기에 미래 동사가 없다고 생각해서는 안 된다. expire라는 동사 자체가 미래적인 어감을 가지고 있기 때문에 will expire 대신 현재를 쓰기도 한다.

1. extends   2. am writing   3. expires

STEP 3 실전에 적용해 봐

1. Mr. Kernings ------- weekly newspapers, which are delivered to his door every Sunday morning.

    (A) read
    (B) reading
    (C) was reading
    (D) reads

2. Visitors ------- not allowed to take photographs of any of the displayed paintings in the museum at any time.

    (A) are
    (B) will be
    (C) were
    (D) been

3. If the installed software program ------- to shut down randomly, please delete the program and reinstall it.

    (A) continue
    (B) will continue
    (C) was continuing
    (D) continues

4. It is advisable that you ------- the pills at least two times every day to relieve your chronic migraines.

    (A) taking
    (B) take
    (C) to take
    (D) are taking

5. Ms. Murray will begin working on the assigned paperwork, which needs to be done by next Wednesday, once she ------- from Paris this week.

    (A) will return
    (B) returned
    (C) returns
    (D) returning

6. As long as Erox Steel ------- partnered with Camp Quest, Inc., a global steel company, it will keep its lead in the industry.

    (A) remains
    (B) remained
    (C) remaining
    (D) was remaining

7. You are not authorized to access the database that ------- users to browse the personal profiles of the employees at the Gohr Corporation.

    (A) allowed
    (B) allowing
    (C) allows
    (D) will allow

8. The annual council ------- at the local conference hall during the first week of July every year.

    (A) convened
    (B) will convene
    (C) convening
    (D) convenes

9. I ------- to your inquiry regarding changing the date of the reservation you made for this Saturday.

    (A) reply
    (B) am replying
    (C) replying
    (D) have been replying

10. Your subscription to *Evon Magazine* ------- next Friday, so if you want to receive more issues, please send us the subscription renewal fee of $20.

    (A) expired
    (B) expires
    (C) expiring
    (D) was expiring

출제율 **11%**

법칙 53 'since + 과거 시점, over/for + 기간'이 보이면 현재완료시제

현재완료시제는 조동사 have나 has에 p.p.를 붙여 만드는데, 우리말로는 '~해 왔다, ~했다'로 해석되며, '~동안, ~이래로'라는 말과 잘 어울린다.

STEP 1 유형을 파악해 봐

1. Montana Food's Meals-to-Go ------- sold exclusively at Max Superstore for the last five years
(A) is   (B) should be   (C) has been   (D) may be

2. Ms. Ford ------- assisting Mr. Jones as his secretary for almost ten years.
(A) has been   (B) has   (C) may be   (D) should be

3. Since its merger with Wegner Tech ten years ago, Reality Games ------- the quality of graphic designs in its mobile games.
(A) improving   (B) improves   (C) will improve   (D) has improved

3번 문제의 (A)를 제외하면, 모든 보기들이 정동사로 구성되어 있고, 동시에 다양한 시제들로 제시된 것으로 보아 시제를 묻는 문제임을 알 수 있다.

STEP 2 이렇게 풀어 봐 — "유형을 파악해 봐" 1번 문제를 보세요!

첫째 주어의 단수, 복수를 확인한다.
보기가 모두 정동사이므로 정동사 자리인지 준동사 자리인지는 확인하지 않아도 된다. 그러나 빈칸이 단수 동사 자리인지 복수 동사 자리인지를 살피면 의외로 쉽게 답을 고를 수 있는 경우가 있는데, 여기서도 보기들이 모두 단수 주어와 함께 사용할 수 있는 동사들이 왔으므로 시제를 묻는 문제이다.

둘째 시제의 단서를 확인한다.
시제 문제에는 반드시 시제의 단서가 제시되기 마련이며, 여기서도 'for the last five years'가 단서가 되어 (C)가 답이 된다.

PLUS

- 현재완료시제가 '~했다'로 해석되는 경우도 있는데, 이러한 경우 과거 시점을 같이 쓸 수 없다.

    The receipt we issued you details our free delivery service. On the receipt, we've indicated the expected delivery date.

    → 우리가 당신에게 발급해준 영수증은 우리의 무료 배송 서비스에 대해 상세히 설명해 줍니다. 우리는 영수증에 예상 배송 날짜를 표기했습니다.

    We've indicated the expected deliver date yesterday. (X)

    → 현재완료시제는 '~했다'로 해석되는 경우에 과거 시점과 같이 사용할 수 없다.

- since 뒤에는 과거 시점이 오는데, 숫자뿐 아니라 시점 명사, 과거시제 문장이 올 수 있다.

    She has worked for the company since 2014. → 과거 연도
    She has worked for the company since the start of the project. → 시점 명사
    She has worked for the company since he left for Seoul. → 과거시제 문장으로, since는 접속사

 함정을 피해 봐　　　　실제 강의에서만 알려주는 풀이 노하우!

1. since가 보인다고 무조건 현재완료시제를 답으로 선택해서는 안 된다.

Since Mr. Kim will be transferring to the Chicago office, Ms. Lee (has taken/will take) his place as the interim CEO.

→ since 뒤에 과거시점이 이어지지 않으므로 since는 '~때문에'의 뜻으로 사용된 접속사이다.

1. will take

STEP 3 실전에 적용해 봐

1. BestGear Auto's repair service ------- provided for free to every customer since its foundation in 2010.

   (A) will be
   (B) has been
   (C) is
   (D) should be

2. Five years ------- passed since Ms. Bell was offered a sales manager position at the YM Company, and she still enjoys her job.

   (A) are
   (B) were
   (C) could be
   (D) have

3. Jennings Restaurant ------- our customers at more than 100 stores overseas over the last 17 years.

   (A) is served
   (B) serving
   (C) will serve
   (D) has served

4. Since Mr. Bloom left the company 3 days ago, the workload ------- for the rest of the employees.

   (A) has increased
   (B) is increased
   (C) will increase
   (D) increasing

5. Anyone who ------- for the yoga class at the Wellness Fitness Center during the last week is encouraged to attend the orientation class held for free next Wednesday.

   (A) will register
   (B) has registered
   (C) registers
   (D) registered

6. Mr. Hawk, a renowned researcher in the field of biology, ------- his entire life to studying the ways to increase human life expectancy over the past 50 years.

   (A) would dedicate
   (B) is dedicating
   (C) has dedicated
   (D) dedicates

7. Our production manager, who ------- responsible for supervising the manufacturing process of goods since last year, will be promoted to the head of the Manufacturing Department.

   (A) being
   (B) will be
   (C) was
   (D) has been

8. Since the recent financial audits of local companies, Plaque, Inc. ------- more shareholders willing to invest in the company, which is growing steadily.

   (A) has attracted
   (B) will attract
   (C) attracts
   (D) would attract

9. Since the annual seminar will have a limited budget this year, a smaller number of guest speakers ------- to the seminar.

   (A) has come
   (B) were coming
   (C) will come
   (D) came

10. According to a recent survey, most employees believe that the actual value of the salaries they get ------- in recent years when inflation is taken into consideration.

    (A) will drop
    (B) to drop
    (C) has dropped
    (D) had dropped

출제율 11%

법칙 54 '선행사+------+명사+동사'는 whose

'I like the man whose car is expensive.'에서 the man은 선행사, whose는 소유격 관계대명사, whose car is expensive는 형용사절 또는 관계사절이며, whose는 소유격 역할을 하므로 뒤에는 관사나 소유격이 없는 명사가 온다. 또한 whose는 선행사가 사람, 사물일 때 모두 사용 가능하다.

유형을 파악해 봐

1. The applicant ------- resume was reviewed by the Sales Department manager was contacted for a job interview.
(A) whose   (B) their   (C) that   (D) which

2. Please make a note of those companies ------- products may affect the sales of our company's products.
(A) that   (B) which   (C) whose   (D) who

3. Brian O'Neil is a fiction novelist ------- latest book has been a mega hit around the world.
(A) which   (B) that   (C) who   (D) whose

1번 문제의 (B)를 제외한 나머지 보기들은 모두 형용사절 접속사, 즉 관계대명사로 구성되어 있다. whose는 소유격 관계대명사, who는 주격 관계대명사이며, that은 주격 및 목적격 관계대명사이다. which는 선행사가 사물일 때만 사용하는 주격 및 목적격 관계대명사이다.

이렇게 풀어 봐
"유형을 파악해 봐" 1번 문제를 보세요!

첫째 접속사 자리인지 확인한다.
동사의 수가 2개이므로 빈칸은 접속사 자리이다. (B)는 소유격이며, 접속사가 아니므로 탈락한다.

둘째 빈칸 뒤 격을 확인한다.
빈칸 뒤 resume가 명사이므로 소유격이 필요하며, 따라서 (A)가 답이다. whose는 선행사가 사람/사물 모두 가능하다. (C)는 빈칸 다음에 주어나 목적어가 빠졌을 때 와야 하는데, 이 문장은 주어, 동사, 보어가 있는 완전한 문장이므로 탈락한다. (D)는 선행사가 사물일 때 사용하므로 탈락한다.

PLUS

- whose는 선행사가 사물일 때도 사용한다.
- whose는 소유격이므로 뒤에 대명사는 올 수 없다.

  Mr. Kim, (whom/whose) you work with, is one of my customers.

함정을 피해 봐 — 실제 강의에서만 알려주는 풀이 노하우!

1. 빈칸 뒤 단어가 명사와 동사 모두 가능한 경우를 조심한다.

It is necessary for employees (who/whose) work repetitively with their hands to take breaks on a regular basis.

→ 빈칸 뒤 work는 동사로 사용되었다. 따라서 주격인 who가 와야 한다.

1. who

STEP 3 실전에 적용해 봐

1. The exhibition presents the life of Riley Jones, ------- paintings have been appraised by many as masterpieces.
   (A) which
   (B) that
   (C) whose
   (D) their

2. Ms. Keys, the head of the Human Resources Department, remembers the employees ------- resumes she reviewed when they applied to the Nikka Corporation for jobs.
   (A) whose
   (B) which
   (C) that
   (D) who

3. BTB Design promised to give incentives to employees this year ------- performances contribute to the company's profits.
   (A) whose
   (B) who
   (C) that
   (D) whom

4. It is advisable that any individuals ------- plan to visit India during the next two months be vaccinated against measles before leaving.
   (A) anyone
   (B) which
   (C) who
   (D) whose

5. According to the statement issued yesterday, the Cloud, Inc. is searching for the new CFO ------- pay could range between $150,000 and $234,000 annually.
   (A) whom
   (B) whose
   (C) that
   (D) which

6. Arson Holdings, ------- customers used to complain about its services, was recently named the company with the top ratings in the customer satisfaction measurement.
   (A) who
   (B) that
   (C) whether
   (D) whose

7. Attached in the e-mail is a list of researchers ------- reports I found to be helpful in case you need more references for your project.
   (A) who
   (B) whose
   (C) that
   (D) their

8. The executive meeting will convene without Ms. Ford, ------- plans to read a report on the discussions held at the meeting once she returns from her business trip.
   (A) whose
   (B) whom
   (C) whether
   (D) who

9. Access to the conference room was denied to Mr. Collins, ------- pass to attend the conference turned out to be invalid.
   (A) who
   (B) whose
   (C) which
   (D) that

10. The head of the company requested that the project be supervised by Mr. Edward, ------- major was economics.
    (A) whose
    (B) who
    (C) that
    (D) whom

출제율 9%

법칙 55 recent, past는 과거, current는 현재, upcoming, near, next는 미래

형용사에는 시제와 관련된 형용사들이 있는데, recent, past는 과거나 현재완료와 어울리고, current, present는 현재, 그리고 upcoming, near, next는 미래시제와 어울린다.

STEP 1 유형을 파악해 봐

1. The Yoyo Gym will be relocated to 6th Avenue ------- year.
   (A) next   (B) last   (C) near   (D) recent

2. Ms. Sick will design our sportswear items so that they follow ------- trends.
   (A) former   (B) late   (C) current   (D) near

3. During the ------- few years, Goodwill Charity has substantially improved its reputation.
   (A) past   (B) near   (C) next   (D) following

보기들이 모두가 형용사들로 왔는데, 그 중에서도 시제와 관련이 있는 형용사들로 제시되었다.

STEP 2 이렇게 풀어 봐   "유형을 파악해 봐" 1번 문제를 보세요!

첫째 품사 자리를 확인한다.
빈칸은 year를 수식하는 형용사 자리이다. 보기 모두 형용사들이지만 빈칸 앞 문장이 완전하므로 빈칸은 year와 함께 부사 기능을 해야 한다. (C), (D)는 year와 함께 쓰일 경우 부사 기능을 하지 못하므로 탈락하고, (A), (B)는 가능하다.

둘째 시제를 확인한다.
will be는 미래시제이므로 next가 어울린다. last는 과거나 현재완료시제에 등장한다.

PLUS

- past나 recent는 보통 전치사 in이나 over와 같이 사용한다. → in[over] the past[last] year
- near는 year보다는 future를 수식할 때 사용한다. → in the near future
- former, previous는 주로 과거, current는 주로 현재와 어울리지만 항상 그런 것은 아니다.
- in recent years, in recent months, in recent weeks 등은 현재완료시제와 어울린다.
- following은 after와 같은 뜻으로 전치사로도 사용된다.

함정을 피해 봐
실제 강의에서만 알려주는 풀이 노하우!

1. following과 upcoming을 혼동하지 않도록 조심한다.

Although Mr. Kim wrote about the damaged goods last Friday, he was not replied to until the (upcoming/following) Monday.

➜ upcoming은 미래시제와 어울린다. 과거를 기준으로 이어서 일어나는 일은 following을 쓴다.

2. present는 비교, 최상급을 쓰지 않는다.

Based on the most (recent/present) inventory figures, board markers need to be ordered right away.

➜ '최신 재고량을 기준으로 볼 때, 보드마커가 당장 주문될 필요가 있다.'는 뜻이다. 현재보다 '더 현재' 또는 '가장 현재'라는 말은 존재할 수 없다.

1. following   2. recent

STEP 3 실전에 적용해 봐

1. Prior to the development of that new product, the production manager suggested that the team refer to a ------- consumer survey to analyze consumers' needs.

    (A) soon
    (B) late
    (C) before
    (D) recent

2. After the meeting, the board members and the CEO from the partner company promised to meet at the next meeting in the ------- future.

    (A) past
    (B) over
    (C) near
    (D) recent

3. Ms. Bufford finally returned the office supplies she borrowed a week ago because the supply room was locked the ------- time she came to return them.

    (A) over
    (B) last
    (C) next
    (D) few

4. The musical *Call of the Wind* will be performed for at least the ------- five months at the Northwest Arts Plaza.

    (A) past
    (B) next
    (C) recent
    (D) current

5. All required materials, including handouts, have been copied and prepared for the ------- seminar.

    (A) recent
    (B) frequent
    (C) upcoming
    (D) during

6. It is expected that Tranquil Medic will decide to hire more managerial staff because it is difficult to maintain its facilities with the ------- number of employees.

    (A) current
    (B) near
    (C) past
    (D) now

7. The price of pork significantly dropped due to the ------- news regarding the outbreak of swine fever.

    (A) upcoming
    (B) recent
    (C) next
    (D) possible

8. Borders, Inc.'s annual revenues this year heavily depend on the ------- economic conditions.

    (A) past
    (B) near
    (C) current
    (D) late

9. Your response to the following survey questions will be reflected in the main article of the ------- issue.

    (A) next
    (B) past
    (C) late
    (D) recent

10. Mr. Czar's ------- careers surprised the job interviewers because they had no relation to the Web page designer position that he was currently applying for.

    (A) following
    (B) beforehand
    (C) over
    (D) past

만점 강사가 알려주는 파트 7 팁 II

1. 101번부터 푸는 것이 좋은가? 거꾸로 푸는 것이 좋은가?

RC의 마지막 세트(195-200번)부터 시작하여 파트 6, 파트 5순으로 푸는 것이 좋다. 이는 사람의 심리상 '시험 종료 5분 전입니다'는 안내 방송을 들으면 심리적 압박으로 인해 깊이 생각해야 하는 파트 7 마지막 세트를 푸는 것은 거의 불가능하지만, 단순한 파트 5는 보통 심리적인 압박과 상관없이 5분내에도 충분히 정해진 수의 문제를 풀 수 있기 때문이다. 단, 파트 7은 평균 1문제당 1분 정도를 계산해야 하므로 그 이상 소비하면 결국 파트 5, 6을 풀 시간이 모자라게 되어 마찬가지로 전체적인 시간이 부족해진다. 단, 뒤에서부터 푸는 연습이 되지 않아 익숙하지 않다면 실제 시험장에서 오히려 시간관리에 실패하는 경우도 있으니 주의한다.

2. 추론 문제를 잘 푸는 방법은?

지금보다 독해 실력을 키워서 논리력을 키워야 한다는 말은 당장 시험을 봐야 하는 사람들에겐 너무 힘든 이야기일 수 있다. 추론 문제를 잘 푸는 방법은 최대한 지문을 조금만 읽고 보기 한 두 개와 대조하는 것이다. 추론 문제에서 오답이 자주 나오는 이유는 선택 보기가 지문 이곳저곳에서 사용된 단어로 구성되어 있기 때문이다. 지문 3줄 정도를 읽은 후 보기 한 두 개를 추론할 수 있는지 보고, 없다면 또 3줄을 더 읽고 다시 확인해 보는 식으로 풀면 함정에 빠지지 않는다.

3. 다중 지문 잘 푸는 방법은?

다중지문은 이중지문 유형과 삼중지문 유형이 있다. 이중지문은 단일 지문 두 개로 구성된 것이다. 3문제는 순차적으로 첫 번째 지문에 단서가, 나머지 2문제는 두 번째 지문에 단서가 있다고 생각하면 되나, 보통 나머지 2문제 중 최소 한 문제는 첫 번째 지문과 연계해서 풀어야 하는 문제가 나온다. 시간, 장소, 날짜 등의 변경되는 부분을 유의하며 표 등을 유심히 보면 분명 그 안에 연계 문제가 있다. 이상하게 잘 안 풀린다 싶으면 연계문제인지 의심하고, 너무 복잡한 계산이나 추론 없이 답을 결정한다. 연계문제는 보통 1문제이며, 2문제가 나오는 경우는 더 드물다. 삼중지문 역시 연계문제를 생각해가며 푸는 것이 핵심이며, 3개의 지문을 동시에 연계하는 문제는 나오지 않고, 두 지문을 연계시키는 문제가 2-3개 나온다. 삼중지문은 지문의 길이가 이중지문보다 짧고, 반드시 표나 목록으로 구성된 지문이 하나 나오므로 연계문제 찾기가 비교적 수월하다.

4. 한꺼번에 마킹을 하는 것이 좋은가?

필자의 경우는 파트 5는 각 문제별, 파트 6와 7은 각 지문별 마킹을 한다. 한꺼번에 마킹을 하면 분명 정답을 밀려 쓰는 경우가 발생할 수 있고, 그 경우 답을 다 지우거나, 답안지를 다시 교체하여 작성하면 5분 이상의 손실이 발생하기 때문이다. 특히 지문 별 마킹을 하는 이유는 한 지문을 풀고 마킹을 하면서 몇 초나마 휴식을 취하는 것이 다음 지문 풀이 시 집중력을 향상시켜 주기 때문이다.

5. 영자 신문, 영어 뉴스, 영어 소설, 미드 등을 많이 접하면 파트 7에 도움이 되나?

토익은 토익으로 공부하라. 외국에서 공부를 오래 한 영문학 박사도, 혹은 학사 이상의 학력을 가진 원어민도 준비하지 않은 상태에서 토익 시험을 보면 만점을 받지 못한다. 미드나 영어 소설은 영어 공부에 흥미를 줄 수 있고, 영어 뉴스나 영자 신문도 영어 실력을 키워줄 수는 있으므로 안 하는 것보다는 도움이 될 수 있을 것이라 생각하겠지만, 그것으로 효과를 보려면 정말 오랜 시간이 필요하고, 효과를 보기도 전에 포기하게 된다. 단기간에 고득점, 특히 만점을 원하는 학생이라면 토익 이론을 공부하고, 토익 문제를 풀면서 토익 시험 공부를 하기를 추천한다.

Chapter 08

평균 2년에 한 번 출제되는 문제

출제 8 순위

언제든 대비하고 있어야 하는 문제

법칙 56 복합관계사절은 형용사절이 아니다

출제율 8%

복합관계사는 의문사에 ever를 붙여 만드는데, 복합관계사에는 복합관계대명사, 복합관계형용사, 복합관계부사가 있다. 복합관계사는 형용사절 접속사가 아니므로 선행사를 갖지 않는다.

종류	이름	절 안쪽 모양새
명사절 접속사, 부사절 접속사	복합관계대명사(의문대명사+ever) whatever, whichever, whoever, whomever	주어나 목적어가 빠짐
	복합관계형용사(의문형용사+ever) whatever, whichever, whosever	필수요소를 모두 갖추고 있으나 어순이 틀어지거나 관사/소유격이 빠짐
부사절 접속사	복합관계부사(의문부사+ever) however, whenever, wherever	완전한 문장 단 'however + 형용사'나 부사가 바로 옴

STEP 1 유형을 파악해 봐

1. ------- can work on the weekend will have a higher chance of being hired than the other applicants.
(A) Whoever   (B) Someone   (C) That   (D) Everyone

2. Ms. Cook always does her best to do ------- job she is given.
(A) that   (B) whatever   (C) what   (D) when

3. Mr. Morrison calls the technical engineer ------- his computer does not work.
(A) however   (B) whenever   (C) whoever   (D) whichever

1번 문제는 보기가 모두 대명사들이다. 보기 중 (A)와 (C)는 접속사 기능이 있다. 2번과 3번 문제의 보기는 모두 접속사들로 구성되어 있다. 1, 2번은 보기에 복합관계사가 1개, 3번은 모두 복합관계사가 보기로 제시된 것으로 보아 접속사를 고르는 문제임을 알 수 있다.

STEP 2 이렇게 풀어 봐

"유형을 파악해 봐" 1번 문제를 보세요!

첫째 접속사 자리인지 확인한다.
보기에 접속사가 함께 있는 경우에는 먼저 동사의 수를 확인해 빈칸이 접속사 자리인지를 확인한다. 정동사가

can work, will have 모두 2개이므로 빈칸은 접속사 자리이며, 따라서 접속사가 아닌 (B)와 (D)는 탈락한다.

둘째 접속사의 종류를 확인한다.
빈칸부터 weekend까지는 will have의 주어가 될 수 있는 명사절이 필요하다. 또한 빈칸 다음에 바로 동사가 나오므로 빈칸은 명사절 안에서 주어의 기능도 갖고 있어야 한다. 따라서 (A)가 답이다. (C)는 명사절 접속사일 경우 이어서 완전한 문장이 와야 한다.

PLUS

• 복합관계사는 형용사절 접속사가 아니므로 선행사를 가질 수 없다.
  Anyone (who/whoever) is interested in the position should contact our HR manager.

• 복합관계사 중에서 답을 고르는 문제가 나올 경우 ever가 없다 생각하고 풀면 편하다.
  Please bring (whatever/whomever) you want if it's not a prohibited item.
  → ever를 무시하고 생각하면 what은 사물을 가리키는 말, whom은 사람을 가리키는 말이다. '금지된 항목들'이란 말은 사물을 가리키는 말이므로 what이 어울리며, 따라서 whatever가 맞다.

• 부사절로 사용되는 복합관계사는 'no matter + 의문사'로 바꿀 수 있다.
  Whatever you say, I won't be shocked. = No matter what you say, I won't be shocked.

함정을 피해 봐 — 실제 강의에서만 알려주는 풀이 노하우!

1. 접속사로도 부사로도 사용되는 however를 조심한다.
(However/Whatever) heavy the desk is, I can move it by myself. → However는 접속사
(However/Whatever), I think we should go out. → However는 부사
→ However가 접속사로 쓰이면 바로 뒤에 형용사나 부사가 와야 하며, '아무리 ~일지라도'로 해석하며, 부사로 쓰이면 '그러나'의 뜻이다.

2. 복합관계사 뒤 주어 동사가 생략되는 경우를 조심한다.
The reimbursement requests should be accompanied by receipts (whenever/whereas) possible.
The sales manager stressed that anything is possible, (however/whatever) remote.
→ 첫 번째 문장은 whenever 뒤에 it is가 생략되었고, 두 번째 문장은 remote 다음 it is가 생략되었다. 주어 동사가 없는 것처럼 보이지만 생략된 것이므로 복합관계사가 답이 될 수 있다.

3. whichever와 either를 혼동하지 않도록 한다.
We will issue our customers refunds or send replacements, (either/whichever) is necessary.
→ 문장에 정동사가 2개이므로 빈칸은 접속사가 와야 한다. either는 대명사이다.

1. However, However 2. whenever, however 3. whichever

STEP 3 실전에 적용해 봐

1. ------- patents the item first will have the right to use the new technology.

   (A) Whoever
   (B) Everyone
   (C) Someone
   (D) Other

2. Ms. Dawson is willing to accept ------- her boss at M&E, Inc. orders her to do as she desperately wants to get a promotion.

   (A) which
   (B) that
   (C) however
   (D) whatever

3. ------- purchases our new product will receive a discount of 30% when the product is introduced to the market next Wednesday.

   (A) Anyone
   (B) Each
   (C) Either
   (D) Whoever

4. Ms. Penning likes her new workplace because even the new employees are encouraged to say ------- comes to their minds at meetings.

   (A) however
   (B) whenever
   (C) whatever
   (D) everything

5. Safety helmets and jackets are placed ------- the employees can easily locate them at the construction site.

   (A) whatever
   (B) however
   (C) those
   (D) wherever

6. The Elvis Record Company will sell the copyrights of the songs to ------- other record companies offer the highest amount.

   (A) whichever
   (B) those
   (C) what
   (D) whoever

7. ------- becomes a member of Shoes 'n More will receive a 30% discount on his or her first purchase of shoes at the store.

   (A) Whatever
   (B) Whoever
   (C) Whichever
   (D) Wherever

8. Mr. Browne will buy a mobile phone made by Alan Electronics or Pabo, Inc., ------- sells a more portable one.

   (A) what
   (B) either
   (C) whichever
   (D) another

9. ------- costly it may be to purchase a new camera, Ms. Jennings will buy a new one because hers is not working.

   (A) Although
   (B) Recently
   (C) Whichever
   (D) However

10. ------- Mr. Fowler wished to purchase at the Mega Sale Store was also available at the new store that opened near his house.

    (A) However
    (B) Almost
    (C) Whatever
    (D) Nonetheless

법칙 57 plan[opportunity, way, effort, right] + to 부정사

'I have a plan to go.'는 '나는 갈 계획을 갖고 있다.'이다. 여기서 to go는 a plan을 수식하는데, plan처럼 to 부정사의 수식을 잘 받는 명사들을 plan, opportunity, way, effort, right의 앞 글자를 따서 'POWER'로 알아 두자.

STEP 1 유형을 파악해 봐

1. The internship program at MIC Media provides applicants an opportunity ------ as apprentice reporters.
   (A) working   (B) to work   (C) worked   (D) be working

2. Tell Mr. Blanski that the best way ------ computer programming is to participate in the workshop held every month.
   (A) to learn   (B) learning   (C) learn   (D) learned

3. In an attempt ------ more tourists, Anywhere Travel Agency decided to extend the period of its promotional event.
   (A) attracting   (B) to attract   (C) attracted   (D) attract on

문제의 보기들을 살펴보면 정동사가 1~2개, 준동사가 1~2개로 구성되었으며, 3번 문제의 경우는 명사가 한 가지 있다. 보기에 정동사와 준동사가 한 두 개씩 함께 나오면 이것은 준동사 문제라고 보면 되는데, 특히 세 문제 모두 보기에 to 부정사가 포함되어 있다.

STEP 2 이렇게 풀어 봐   "유형을 파악해 봐" 1번 문제를 보세요

첫째 빈칸이 정동사 자리인지 확인한다.
준동사 문제도 보기 중 1개는 보통 정동사가 포함되기 마련이며, 항상 정동사 확인이 1순위이다. 문장에 이미 provides가 있으므로 빈칸은 준동사 자리이다. 따라서 정동사인 (D)는 탈락한다.

둘째 준동사의 기능을 확인한다.
준동사 중에서도 어떤 준동사가 어떤 기능으로 오는지를 확인한다. 빈칸 앞에 완전한 문장이 있고, 빈칸은 뒤에서 앞에 있는 opportunity라는 명사를 수식해야 하는 자리이다. 뒤에서 앞의 명사를 수식할 수 있는 (A)와 (B) 중

opportunity는 to 부정사의 수식을 잘 받는 'POWER'에 속하므로 대입해 해석하면 '지원자들에게 일할 기회를 제공한다.'는 말이 자연스러우므로 (B)가 답이 된다. 이때 to 부정사를 '명사 수식 to 부정사'라고 한다.

PLUS

• ability, attempt도 'POWER'에 해당하며, a power로 기억하자.

• to 부정사의 의미상 주어는 'for 명사'로 나타낸다.
  I will tell you the way <u>for people to communicate</u> with one another.
  　　　　　　　　　　　　사람들이 의사소통하는 방법

• to 부정사가 수식하는 명사가 to 부정사의 목적어일 경우에는 목적어를 생략한다.

  a plan to meet the man 남자를 만날 계획 → to 부정사의 목적어(the man)가 있음
  a man to meet 만날 남자 → to 부정사의 목적어 (the man)을 생략함

함정을 피해 봐
실제 강의에서만 알려주는 풀이 노하우!

1. '명사 to 명사'를 조심한다.

The sales representative stressed that no changes to (order/orders), once shipped, can be made.
→ changes를 'POWER'로 생각하고 to 부정사를 답으로 선택해서는 안 된다. changes는 'to 명사'를 취한다. 시험에 자주 출제되는 'to 명사'에는 다음과 같은 것들이 같다.

solution to ~에 대한 해결책	transfer to ~쪽으로의 전근	contribution to ~에 대한 기여
commitment to ~에 대한 헌신	access to ~에 대한 접근	introduction to ~에 대한 소개
answer to ~에 대한 답변	solution to ~에 대한 해결	key to ~에 대한 열쇠/방법
transition to ~로의 이전/전환	changes to ~에 대한 변경	exposure to ~에의 노출
reaction to ~에 대한 반발		

2. 'power to 부정사'라고 해서 실제로 power를 답으로 선택해서는 안 된다.

Any employee should have a(n) (power/opportunity) to influence the making of company policies.
→ 실제로 'power to 부정사'라고만 기억했다가 power를 답으로 선택한 사례가 있었다. 공부는 했으나 power만 기억나고 각각의 글자가 무엇을 의미하는지 알아 두지 않았기 때문이다.

1. orders　2. opportunity

STEP 3 실전에 적용해 봐

1. The airport pickup service provides a convenient way for customers visiting Incheon International Airport ------- to their hotels.

   (A) proceeding
   (B) to proceed
   (C) proceeds
   (D) proceeded

2. In an effort to ------- the utility bills, Ms. Lesborne urged the employees to turn off the lights when they were not using them.

   (A) reduction
   (B) reducing
   (C) reduced
   (D) reduce

3. When Mr. Gibert heard that he was assigned to a team with Ms. Lowe, he believed that it was a good chance ------- to know her.

   (A) to get
   (B) getting
   (C) got
   (D) get

4. The manager explained several ways ------- customer complaints to the new part-timers at the store.

   (A) handling
   (B) handle
   (C) to handle
   (D) handled

5. Jobs assumed by the Legal Department include making sure that every employee is guaranteed the right ------- in safe conditions.

   (A) working
   (B) work
   (C) to work
   (D) works

6. As the meeting was postponed by an hour, Mr. Phillips was relieved that he had an opportunity ------- his proposal to explain at the meeting later.

   (A) revising
   (B) to be revised
   (C) to revise
   (D) revised

7. The new computer had the ability ------- more than two computer design tools at the same time.

   (A) operate
   (B) operating
   (C) to operate
   (D) operation

8. As a company policy, anyone who has a plan ------- the new antivirus program on their computer this week must report to the manager once the installation is done.

   (A) installed
   (B) installing
   (C) installation
   (D) to install

9. You will soon be able to hear from our customer service team, whose members are responsible of providing answers to ------- on our Web site regarding shipments.

   (A) inquiring
   (B) inquiries
   (C) inquire
   (D) inquired

10. Please make sure you save all your work on the computer to avoid losing it due to a sudden power -------.

    (A) failure
    (E) to fail
    (C) failing
    (D) failingly

출제율 7%

법칙 58 to 부정사만 목적어로 취하는 동사

'I want to go.'와 'I want going.' 중 어느 문장이 옳은 문장일까? want는 to 부정사만 목적어로 취하는 동사이며, 이와 같이 to 부정사만 목적어로 취하는 동사를 '응큼쟁이' 동사라고 한다.

나는 너와 여행 가기를 원하고(want), 바라고(wish), 희망하고(hope), 기대한다(expect).
네가 동의를 해도(agree) 상관 없고, 거절을 해도(refuse) 상관 없다.
그러나 가기를 결정하고(decide), 약속해 준다면(promise), 계획을 짤(plan), 작정이다(intend).

STEP 1 유형을 파악해 봐

1. Mr. Pope plans ------- revising his report by Wednesday.
(A) finish (B) finished (C) to finish (D) finishes

2. The project manager wants ------- the workshop on Wednesday.
(A) to attend (B) attended (C) attending (D) attends

3. Golden Holdings strives ------- the losses caused by the subprime mortgage crisis in 2008.
(A) recovering (B) to recover (C) recovered (D) to be recovered

세 문제 모두 보기에 정동사가 1~2개, 준동사가 1~2개가 포함돼 있고, 2번 문제는 명사도 하나 있다. 보기에 정동사와 준동사가 한 두 개씩 제시된 이러한 유형의 문제는 준동사 문제에 해당한다고 볼 수 있다.

STEP 2 이렇게 풀어 봐

"유형을 파악해 봐" 1번 문제를 보세요!

첫째 빈칸이 정동사 자리인지 확인한다.
준동사 문제도 보기 중 1개는 보통 정동사이므로 정동사 확인이 1순위이다. 이미 문장에 정동사인 plans가 있으므로 빈칸은 준동사 자리이다.

둘째 준동사의 기능을 확인한다.

준동사 중 어느 준동사가 어떤 기능을 하는지를 확인해야 한다. 빈칸은 3형식 동사 plan의 목적어 자리이다. (B)와 (C) 중에서 목적어로 가능한 것은 to 부정사 (C)뿐이다. plan은 to 부정사를 목적어로 취하는 '응큼쟁이' 동사이기도 하다. 이어지는 revising 이하 내용은 to 부정사인 finish의 목적어에 해당한다.

PLUS

• 자동사 중 to 부정사와 어울림이 좋은 것들이 있다.

fail to 동사원형 ~하지 못하다	wait to 동사원형 ~를 기다리다
strive to 동사원형 ~하려고 애쓰다	stop to 동사원형 ~하기 위해 멈추다
hesitate to 동사원형 ~하기를 주저하다	happen to 동사원형 우연히 ~하다

• to 부정사와 동명사를 모두 목적어로 취할 수 있는 동사들이 있다.

like	love	hate	prefer	attempt
continue	begin	start	propose	

함정을 피해 봐 — 실제 강의에서만 알려주는 풀이 노하우!

1. '응큼쟁이' 동사로 착각하기 쉬운 경우를 조심한다.

The architect objected to (change/changes) made to his building.

→ object를 '응큼쟁이' 동사로 착각하여 동사원형을 써서는 안 된다. object to 다음에는 명사나 동명사가 온다. change는 명사일 때는 가산명사로서 앞에 관사가 오거나 복수형을 써야 한다.

to로 끝나는 덩어리 동사들

refer to	reply to	react to	respond to
revert to	relocate to	subscribe to	lead to

1. changes

STEP 3 실전에 적용해 봐

1. Customers who purchased malfunctioning products may choose ------- cash refunds or discount coupons for their next purchase.

   (A) to receive
   (B) receiving
   (C) received
   (D) reception

2. The Newhope Charity Organization would like ------- all of our donors and everyone else who have contributed their time and money to making this event possible.

   (A) thanking
   (B) thanked
   (C) thanks
   (D) to thank

3. Kimko Audio Technologies hopes to ------- its new audio player this year.

   (A) launching
   (B) launcher
   (C) launch
   (D) launched

4. Megatech Co. Ltd. intends ------- more start-ups which specialize in manufacturing phone accessories to expand into the mobile market.

   (A) acquiring
   (B) being acquired
   (C) to be acquried
   (D) to acquire

5. In order to get information on the delivery of the items you ordered, please contact us at our toll-free number and ask ------- to someone in the customer service office.

   (A) speaking
   (B) spoke
   (C) to speak
   (D) speakers

6. Mr. Gore decided to ------- the schedule for his training sessions when he realized that he had to go on a business trip for a week.

   (A) rearranged
   (B) rearrange
   (C) rearranging
   (D) be rearranged

7. Since it was successfully installed, the program should run properly, but it consistently fails to ------- well.

   (A) operating
   (B) operate
   (C) operation
   (D) operated

8. Our CEO objects to ------- with Gwen Industries since many analysts claim that the merger will have no substantial effect on the company's profits.

   (A) merge
   (B) merger
   (C) be merged
   (D) merged

9. Those who wish ------- their purchases must present the receipt and the credit card which they used to buy the items.

   (A) to cancel
   (B) cancelling
   (C) cancellation
   (D) cancelled

10. Please read the guidelines on using the machine first since improper use of the machine may ultimately lead ------- production.

    (A) to interruption in
    (B) interrupting
    (C) to interrupt
    (D) interrupted

출제율 5%

법칙 59 동명사만 목적어로 취하는 동사

'I enjoy to go.'와 'I enjoy going.' 중 어느 문장이 옳은 문장일까? enjoy는 동명사만 목적어로 취하는 동사이며, 이와 같이 동명사만 목적어로 취하는 동사를 '회장아들' 동사로 알아 두자.

회장 아들이 인조이(enjoy)하겠다는 마인드를(mind) 포기(give up)하자
그 아들을 허락(admit)하고, 옹호(advocate)해 주었다.

이에 영업 상무가 된 회장 아들은
'우리 제품을 고려(consider)해 보세요, 귀사의 제품에 포함(include)시켜 보세요'라고
고객 업체에 제품을 제안하고, 추천(suggest/recommend)했으나

업체는 회장 아들을 피하기만(avoid)하여, 계약이 차일피일 연기되다(postpone)가
계약 체결이 끝나지도(finish) 않은 채 협상이 중단(stop/discontinue)되었다.

STEP 1 유형을 파악해 봐

1. Please avoid ------- the machines near water or any fluid as doing that can cause malfunctioning.
   (A) operate   (B) operating   (C) operated   (D) operation

2. Ms. Camora enjoys ------- camping with her family at the park near in her house on her spare time.
   (A) going   (B) to go   (C) go   (D) goes

3. According to rumors, the CEO is in fact considering ------- the regional office to Newtown.
   (A) relocation   (B) relocate   (C) will relocate   (D) relocating

문제들의 보기에 정동사가 1~2개, 준동사가 1~2개 왔으며, 1번과 3번 문제의 경우 명사도 한 개 제시되어 있음을 알 수 있다. 이렇게 보기에 정동사와 준동사가 한 두 개씩 등장할 경우, 이것은 준동사를 고르는 문제라고 볼 수 있다.

STEP 2 이렇게 풀어 봐   "유형을 파악해 봐" 1번 문제를 보세요!

첫째 빈칸이 정동사 자리인지 확인한다.
준동사 문제도 보기 중 1개는 보통 정동사가 오므로 항상 정동사 확인이 1순위이다. 이미 정동사인 avoid가 문장에 있으므로 빈칸은 준동사 자리이며, 따라서 정동사 (A)는 탈락한다.

Chapter 08 _ 평균 2년에 한 번 출제되는 문제 205

둘째 준동사의 기능을 확인한다.

준동사 중 어떤 준동사가 어떤 기능으로 온 것인지를 확인해야 한다. 빈칸은 3형식 동사 avoid의 목적어 자리이다. 목적어로 사용 가능한 (B)와 (D) 중에서 뒤에 the machines라는 명사를 수반할 수 있는 것은 동명사인 (B)이다. 동명사도 자신의 목적어를 갖기 때문에 the machines는 동명사의 목적어가 된다. (D)는 명사이므로 앞에 또 명사가 올 수 없다.

PLUS

- '회장아들' 동사를 mind, enjoy, give up, avoid, postpone, admit, stop, suggest, include, discontinue의 앞 글자를 따서 'MEGAPASS ID'로 알아 두도록 하자.

함정을 피해 봐
실제 강의에서만 알려주는 풀이 노하우!

1. 동명사를 쓸 때와 to 부정사로 쓸 때 뜻이 달라지는 경우가 있다.

Please don't forget (to secure/securing) the door when you leave.
→ 외출할 때는 문을 잠그는 것을 잊지 말아야 하므로 to 부정사를 쓴다. 동명사를 쓰게 되면 과거에 문을 잠그는 것을 잊었다는 의미이므로 어색하다.

stop -ing ~하는 것을 멈추다, 중단하다	stop to 동사원형 ~하기 위해서 멈추다
remember -ing ~했던 것을 기억하다	remember to 동사원형 ~할 것을 기억하다
forget -ing ~했던 것을 잊다	forget to 동사원형 ~할 것을 잊다
regret -ing ~했던 것을 후회하다	regret to 동사원형 ~하게 돼서 유감이다

1. to secure

STEP 3 실전에 적용해 봐

1. As 70% of the store's total sales are made on Saturdays, the manager suggested ------- later than usual on weekends.

   (A) closed
   (B) close
   (C) closing
   (D) to close

2. Delivering a presentation on a the new construction project must be challenging for a new employee, but never consider ------- as one of your options.

   (A) to give up
   (B) give up
   (C) gave up
   (D) giving up

3. Ms. Edmond called an engineer to look at her computer, which frequently froze and stopped -------.

   (A) to run
   (B) run
   (C) running
   (D) runs

4. Since the demand for portable cell phones quickly grew, Revo Tech began ------- the lightest phone on the market.

   (A) development
   (B) developing
   (C) develop
   (D) develops

5. Ask Mr. Kim if he is willing to pick you up after the conference because he probably will not mind ------- there as his house is nearby.

   (A) drivers
   (B) driving
   (C) to drive
   (D) drives

6. It is obvious that Mr. Gallos will soon be penalized now that he has admitted ------- on his promotion exam.

   (A) cheating
   (B) to cheat
   (C) cheats
   (D) cheated

7. While he was on his way back home, Mr. Daniels stopped ------- the weekly newspaper at a newsstand.

   (A) buying
   (B) buys
   (C) buyer
   (D) to buy

8. An announcement was made that headquarters will put off ------- all new employees at the company until further notice.

   (A) to train
   (B) training
   (C) trainer
   (D) trains

9. Ms. Hawkins forgot ------- a heavy coat before she left for a business trip to Russia, so she caught a cold there.

   (A) taking
   (B) to take
   (C) took
   (D) take

10. One of the main jobs of the Human Resources staff includes ------- the survey results of employee satisfaction to the CEC.

    (A) to report
    (B) reporter
    (C) report
    (D) reporting

출제율 5%

법칙 60 완전한 문장 뒤에 온 콤마는 -ing(분사구문)

'법칙 33'에서 분사구문에 대해 이미 배웠다. 분사구문에서 분사 부분이 문장 뒤에 올 경우, 예를 들면 'I found the room key, entering the room.'은 '나는 방에 들어갈 수 있는 키를 찾았다.'로 해석된다. 이때 entering the room 부분은 결국 I에 대한 이야기, 즉 I를 수식해 주는 분사이다. 이처럼 분사가 문장 뒤에 오는 경우도 일종의 분사구문이므로 잘 알아 두자.

STEP 1 유형을 파악해 봐

1. The recent flood has adversely affected the cafeteria as its walls began to crack, ------- renovation.
(A) necessarily   (B) necessitated   (C) necessaries   (D) necessitating

2. Mr. Chez moved all of the office supplies to another place to make room, ------- a new table to be set in the office.
(A) allowed   (B) allowing   (C) allows   (D) allowably

3. Ms. Horton's tour guide sent her the itinerary for the tour in Spain, ------- the schedule which had been revised.
(A) reconfirms   (B) reconfirmed   (C) reconfirming   (D) being reconfirmed

세 문제 모두 보기에 정동사도 있고, 분사(-ing/p.p.)도 있기 때문에 분사 문제일 가능성이 높으며, 빈칸 앞에는 완전한 문장이 있고, 빈칸 뒤에는 명사가 왔다.

STEP 2 이렇게 풀어 봐
"유형을 파악해 봐" 1번 문제를 보세요!

첫째 빈칸이 정동사 자리인지 확인한다.
빈칸 앞 부분에 정동사 affected가 있으므로 빈칸에는 준동사가 와야 한다.

둘째 빈칸 뒤 목적어가 있는지 확인한다.
빈칸 뒤에 목적어로 명사가 왔으므로 -ing형인 (D)만 올 수 있다. 부사인 (A)는 명사를 수식하지 못한다. (B) p.p.는 목적어를 갖지 않으며, 과거시제로 보면 정동사가 2개가 되므로 답이 될 수 없다.

PLUS

• 문장 뒤에 오는 -ing 앞에는 인과관계의 부사가 오기도 한다.

She started working at a company last month, **thereby** receiving a paycheck.
그녀는 지난 달에 입사했으며, **때문에** 급여를 받았다.

함정을 피해 봐 — 실제 강의에서만 알려주는 풀이 노하우!

1. -ing를 답으로 선택할 때는 목적어가 있는지 없는지 반드시 확인해야 한다.

You can visit our main office on Main Street, (directing/directed/directly) across from the post office.

→ 앞에 완전한 문장이 왔다고 해서 -ing를 답으로 고르면 안 되는데, 그것은 -ing는 뒤에 목적어가 있어야 하기 때문이다. '우체국 바로 맞은 편에'라는 말이 어울리므로 directly가 답이다. 한편 directed는 '유도된'이란 뜻으로 어울리지 않는다.

2. 완전한 문장 뒤의 콤마 뒤라도 p.p가 오는 경우가 있다. 단 목적어는 없다.

ABC Tech already employed 50 employees, (established/establishing) only 2 years ago.

→ 완전한 문장 뒤 콤마만 확인하고, -ing를 고르면 오답일 수 있다. 콤마 뒤에 목적어가 없다면 p.p가 답이 될 수 있다. only 2 years ago는 부사이며, 목적어가 될 수 없고, established는 ABC Tech를 수식한다.

1. directly   2. established

STEP 3 실전에 적용해 봐

1. The e-mail sent by Euros Air stated that the payment has been successfully received, ------- the reservation for the flight.

   (A) confirm
   (B) confirmed
   (C) confirmation
   (D) confirming

2. Lyson Electronics has recently introduced a new computer model equipped with highly advanced functions, thereby ------- its rival company's newly launched model uncompetitive.

   (A) to be rendered
   (B) rendering
   (C) rendered
   (D) will render

3. The CEO has named Mr. Harlen the outstanding employee of the year, ------- his contribution at successfully concluding the contract with Regina Pipelines.

   (A) will acknowledge
   (B) be acknowledged
   (C) acknowledging
   (D) acknowledged

4. The renovation of Mount National Monument has begun, ------- the parts that have been corroded by rust.

   (A) restoring
   (B) restored
   (C) restorable
   (D) will restore

5. When it was time to check out, Mr. Ming packed his luggage and returned the keys to the front desk, ------- the room.

   (A) vacating
   (B) to vacate
   (C) vacated
   (D) vacation

6. ABC Tech, established only 2 months ago, already ------- 50 employees.

   (A) to employ
   (B) employing
   (C) employ
   (D) employs

7. The Bodywell Fitness Center has been offering a special price for the hot yoga class for a limited time, ------- more people to register for the class.

   (A) encouraged
   (B) encourages
   (C) will encourage
   (D) encouraging

8. You can find our office located on the street next to Bright Bridge ------- adjacent to the Stars Building.

   (A) directed
   (B) directly
   (C) directing
   (D) direction

9. The manager of the Manufacturing Department has requested that the teams primarily focus on the painting job, ------- some redundant production processes.

   (A) eliminated
   (B) elimination
   (C) eliminating
   (D) will eliminate

10. The promotional event for the new show *Rain in Seattle* went viral on the Internet, ------- in a boost in ticket sales.

    (A) resulting
    (B) will result
    (C) is resulted
    (D) results

법칙 61 완료시제에 have만 있다면 p.p.

출제율 5%

'I have lived in Seoul for 5 years.'에서 have lived는 우리말로 '살아왔다'로 해석되는 '현재완료시제'이다. 이 때 조동사 have는 '가지다'의 의미가 아니고, lived는 과거분사이며 p.p.로 나타내기도 한다. have lived는 하나의 덩어리로 사용되어야 완료시제가 될 수 있다.

STEP 1 유형을 파악해 봐

1. Ms. Evans has ------- Mr. Holmes for more than 7 years.
 (A) knowing   (B) know   (C) known   (D) knew

2. The manager has ------- to finish the follow-up review by this week.
 (A) plan   (B) planned   (C) planning   (D) planner

3. Researchers have ------- the fact that 8 hours of sleep ensures that people will be in good condition.
 (A) verify   (B) verification   (C) verifiable   (D) verified

보기에는 정동사, 분사(-ing/p.p.)가 함께 제시되어 있기 때문에 분사 문제일 가능성이 많다.

STEP 2 이렇게 풀어 봐   "유형을 파악해 봐" 1번 문제를 보세요!

첫째 빈칸이 정동사 자리인지 확인한다.
준동사 문제도 보기 중 최소 1개는 정동사가 포함되는 것이 보통이므로 항상 정동사를 확인하는 것이 1순위이다. 문장에는 정동사인 has가 이미 있으므로 빈칸은 준동사 자리이다.

둘째 -ing와 p.p. 중 어울리는 것을 확인한다.
빈칸 앞에 have나 has가 있으면 이것이 본동사 have/has인지, 현재완료시제 have/has인지를 먼저 구분해야 한다. have/has가 본동사로 왔을 경우 뒤에 동명사를 목적어로 갖지 않는다. 조동사 have/has 뒤에 p.p.가 오면 현재완료시제가 되어 'Ms. Evans는 Mr. Holmes를 7년 동안 알아왔다.'로 자연스럽게 해석이 되므로 (C)가 정답이다.

PLUS

- 부정어나 only가 문두에 오면 도치가 돼, 조동사 have나 has가 주어 앞으로 나간다.

  Never have I (see/seeing/seen) such a beautiful resort in my life.

  → never가 문두에 오면서 조동사 have가 앞으로 도치되었으며, 따라서 have p.p.에서 seen이 답이 된다.

- Only recently I have visited his office. (X)

  Only recently have I visited his office. (O)

  → Only가 문두에서 recently를 강조하여 have I로 도치됐다.

 함정을 피해 봐   실제 강의에서만 알려주는 풀이 노하우!

1. have 다음에 -ing가 오거나 to 부정사가 오는 경우를 조심한다.

All of the members have (interesting/interested) books in their bags.

→ have p.p.로 외워서 문제를 풀려고 해서는 안 된다. 문맥상 재미있는 책들(interesting books)을 가지고 있다는 내용이 자연스럽다.

The team members have (to finish/finished) the project within the next week.

→ 다음 주 내로 프로젝트를 마쳐야 한다는 미래의 내용으로 보아 have finished는 시제가 일치하지 않는다.

1. interesting, to finish

STEP 3 실전에 적용해 봐

1. Mr. Kimberly had already ------- his paperwork when Ms. Gray came to offer him her help.

   (A) finishes
   (B) finished
   (C) finishing
   (D) finish

2. Ms. Simmons has ------- her co-workers to stay at her house until they find a house they can afford to move in to.

   (A) allow
   (B) allowed
   (C) allows
   (D) allowing

3. Most citizens agree that the city has ------- the amount of subsidies for low-income households in the coming year.

   (A) increased
   (B) increasing
   (C) to increase
   (D) increase

4. Since we will have ------- more than 500 customers by next week, we should analyze the results of the customer survey after then.

   (A) surveyed
   (B) surveys
   (C) surveying
   (D) survey

5. It was unfortunate that Mr. Butler had no money at all since he had ------- most of his salary in the stock market.

   (A) investing
   (B) investment
   (C) invests
   (D) invested

6. Only recently have people ------- to use wearable devices over mobile phones because of their portability.

   (A) preferring
   (B) preferred
   (C) prefer
   (D) preference

7. The executive manager was considering having Ms. Hudson lead the upcoming project because she had ------- above and beyond his expectations on the last one.

   (A) performing
   (B) performs
   (C) performingly
   (D) performed

8. Mr. Dunn had ------- at Jinko, Inc. for over 3 years before he moved to Revolution Tech.

   (A) working
   (B) work
   (C) worked
   (D) workingly

9. Never has Ms. Bailey ------- more than a day fixing her computer, which seemed to have been affected by a more serious virus than ever.

   (A) spending
   (B) spend
   (C) spent
   (D) spendable

10. Hardly had his client ----- out of his office when Mr. Walker called her back to give her phone that she left in the office.

    (A) walked
    (B) walk
    (C) walks
    (D) walking

출제율 5%

법칙 62 'Those + 형용사' 류는 '~하는 사람들'

'이것, 저것'을 의미하는 this, that은 지시대명사이며, this의 복수형은 these, that의 복수형은 those이다. 지시대명사 중 that과 those는 문장에서 언급된 명사의 반복을 피하기 위해 사용하기도 한다.

His appearance was **that** of a child.
그의 외모는 어린아이의 그것과 같았다.

His speech and behavior were **those** of an adult.
그의 말과 행동은 어른의 그것들과 같았다.

한편, 지시대명사 those는 뒤에 있는 형용사류의 수식을 받을 때 '~하는 사람들'이란 뜻이 된다.

	형용사류(~하는)	
Those (사람들)	available in the evening	can attend the evening language course.
	in the meeting room 16	have waited for 1 hour.
	interviewing the applicants	should prepare questions to ask in an interview.
	contacted by our HR manager	will be interviewed by our executives.
	who visit the facility	should receive a visitor's pass at the security desk.

STEP 1 유형을 파악해 봐

1. ------- who wish to get more information on the job fair being held next week should call the office.
(A) They   (B) Those   (C) These   (D) Them

2. The Inka Corporation provides free regular checkups to ------- over 35 years of age working full time at the company.
(A) who   (B) whose   (C) those   (D) them

3. Please refer to the customer surveys regarding brand preference except for ------- conducted last year.
(A) they   (B) that   (C) those   (D) them

보기가 모두 대명사들로 구성되어 있다. 1번 문제의 (A)와 (D)는 인칭대명사, (B)와 (C)는 지시대명사이다. 2번 문제의 (B)는 wh- 계열의 대명사로 접속사 기능을 갖고 있으며, (C)는 지시대명사, (D)는 인칭대명사이다. 3번 문제의 (A)와 (D)는 인칭대명사, (B)는 (C)는 지시대명사이다.

 STEP 2 이렇게 풀어 봐   "유형을 파악해 봐" 1번 문제를 보세요!

첫째 빈칸의 자리를 확인한다.
who부터 next week까지가 주어를 수식하는 형용사절이며, 따라서 빈칸은 주어 자리이다. 주어의 기능이 없는 them은 탈락하고, them은 목적어 자리에 쓴다.

둘째 형용사절의 수식을 받는 명사가 무엇인지 확인한다.
대명사 중에서 형용사절의 수식을 받아 '~하는 사람들'이란 뜻을 나타낼 수 있는 것은 (B)뿐이며, those는 those people를 줄인 말이다. (A)는 형용사절의 수식을 받지도 않고, 누구를 가리키는지도 불확실해 탈락한다. (C) 역시 형용사절의 수식을 받는 대명사가 아니다.

PLUS

- those와 같은 말은 anyone이다. 단 anyone은 단수 취급한다.

  (Anyone/Those) who wants to enroll in the evening course should let me know directly.

 **함정을 피해 봐**   실제 강의에서만 알려주는 풀이 노하우!

1. them과 those를 혼동하지 않도록 한다.

The employees at our company work harder than (them/those) of your firm.

→ 여기서 them을 답으로 하면 '우리회사의 직원들'을 가리키는 말이 된다. those는 employees라는 복수 명사의 반복을 피하기 위해 사용되었다.

2. 비슷한 의미라고 해서 품사가 같다고 생각해서는 안 된다.

(Anyone/Whoever) satisfied with our product is encouraged to fill out the questionnaire.

→ anyone은 부정대명사, whoever는 접속사. 동사의 수가 1개이므로 접속사인 whoever는 탈락한다. 여기서 satisfied는 동사가 아니고 분사이다. either(부정대명사/부정형용사)와 whichever(접속사) 역시 혼동하기 쉽다.

1. those   2. Anyone

STEP 3 실전에 적용해 봐

1. ------- who placed an order of items before Tuesday will be able to have the items delivered before the holiday, but items ordered after Tuesday will be delivered after the holiday.

    (A) These
    (B) Them
    (C) Their
    (D) Those

2. Mr. Wagner may be able to travel to Libya and Egypt as ------- countries have recently lifted the restrictions on visitors entering.

    (A) these
    (B) theirs
    (C) which
    (D) that

3. The topic of the discussion was ------- which was raised at the last meeting.

    (A) those
    (B) that
    (C) it
    (D) either

4. Only ------- with valid parking permits will be allowed to park their vehicles in the lot for free.

    (A) them
    (B) those
    (C) whose
    (D) whom

5. The seminar is ready to be held tomorrow thanks to the help of ------- who volunteered their time.

    (A) they
    (B) who
    (C) whose
    (D) those

6. The fundraising campaigns of 2015 collected more funds globally than ------- of last year.

    (A) them
    (B) that
    (C) which
    (D) those

7. Please immediately assist and escort ------- waiting to be seated to the empty tables.

    (A) they
    (B) theirs
    (C) those
    (D) whose

8. The annual seminar hosted by the R&S Research Institute allowed all visitors, including ------- who did not attend the seminar last year, to listen to the speech.

    (A) them
    (B) those
    (C) they
    (D) this

9. Feel free to provide cosmetic samples to customers visiting our store as there are plenty of ------- left in storage.

    (A) they
    (B) theirs
    (C) there
    (D) those

10. ------- interested in our latest-model car is encouraged to place a preorder to receive a free-trial offer and a discount of 10% upon purchase.

    (A) Those
    (B) Whoever
    (C) They
    (D) Anyone

출제율 

법칙 63 무조건 동명사

'나는 너를 보기를 기대해.'라는 말은 look forward to see you일까, look forward to seeing you일까? 정답은 후자이며, 여기서 to는 전치사이기 때문에 뒤에는 명사나 동명사가 와야 한다. 'look forward to -ing'와 같은 유형을 '동명사 관용어구' 혹은 '무조건 동명사'라고 한다.

STEP 1 유형을 파악해 봐

1. Ms. Laymore looks forward to ------- her family reunion during the upcoming holiday.
   (A) have   (B) having   (C) had   (D) will have

2. The executive manager had difficulty ------- the necessary resources the Sales Department requested.
   (A) allocate   (B) allocation   (C) allocated   (D) allocating

3. Mr. Hall attended the conference as a guest speaker in Ms. Gale's place because she was busy ------- a project.
   (A) supervise   (B) supervised   (C) supervising   (D) supervisor

세 문제 모두 정동사가 1~2개, 준동사가 1~2개로 보기들이 제시되었으며, 2, 3번 문제의 경우는 명사도 하나 있다. 따라서 이러한 유형의 문제들은 준동사 문제로 볼 수 있다.

STEP 2 이렇게 풀어 봐   "유형을 파악해 봐" 1번 문제를 보세요!

첫째 빈칸이 정동사 자리인지 확인한다.
준동사 문제도 보기 중 최소 1개는 정동사가 제시되므로 항상 정동사 확인이 1순위이다. 정동사인 looks가 이미 문장에 있으므로 빈칸은 앞의 to와 함께 사용되는 준동사 자리이다. 정동사인 (C)와 (D)는 탈락.

둘째 준동사의 기능을 확인한다.
준동사 중 어떤 준동사가 어떤 기능으로 오는지를 확인해야 한다. 빈칸 앞에 to가 있으므로 이 to가 전치사인지 to 부정사인지를 확인해야 한다. 'look forward to -ing'은 동명사 관용어구이므로 동명사인 (B)가 답이 된다.

PLUS

- 동명사 관용어구는 다음과 같은 연상법으로 암기할 수 있다. → eat를 대입해 볼 것

정준하는 먹는 것에 익숙하다.	be used(= accustomed) to -ing
정준하는 먹는 것에 헌신적이다.	be devoted(= dedicated, committed) to -ing
정준하의 어머니는 먹는 것에 반대한다.	object to -ing(be opposed to -ing)
정준하는 오늘도 먹기를 기대한다.	look forward to -ing
오늘도 먹고 싶은 생각이 든다.	feel like -ing
먹을 때, 먹자마자	in -ing, on -ing
'아! 먹을 가치가 있어!'라고 느낀다.	be worth -ing
먹으러 간다.	go -ing
먹지 않을 수 없다.	cannot help -ing
먹는데 바쁘다.	be busy (in) -ing
계속 먹는다.	keep (on) -ing
먹는데 시간과 돈을 몽땅 소비한다.	spend time[money] (on[in]) -ing
정준하도 결국 먹는데 어려움을 느낀다.	have difficulty[trouble, a hard time] (in) -ing

 함정을 피해 봐   실제 강의에서만 알려주는 풀이 노하우!

1. be used to를 조심한다.

The proceeds will be used to (establish/establishing) a new museum, an art center, and hotel.

➡ be used to는 동사원형이 올 경우 '~하기 위해서 사용되다'의 뜻이 되며, 'be used for 명사'와 같은 말이다. 참고로 be 없이 used to도 뒤에 동사원형이 오는데, 이때 used to는 조동사로 '~하곤 했다'는 뜻이 된다.

1. establish

STEP 3 실전에 적용해 봐

1. The Sharing Society is a charity organization which is committed to ------- to the public welfare by funding children from low-income families to be educated for free.

   (A) to be contributed
   (B) contribute
   (C) contributing
   (D) contributed

2. 3 years after she joined Arts Design, Ms. Cha became fully accustomed to ------- as a designer at the company.

   (A) working
   (B) worked
   (C) work
   (D) worker

3. Glorious Wedding Shop is dedicated to ------- you with the best quality service for your special occasion.

   (A) provide
   (B) providing
   (C) provided
   (D) provider

4. Dr. Bryant advised you to take the medicine that is used to ------- chronic migraines regularly.

   (A) treating
   (B) treats
   (C) treat
   (D) treated

5. Mountain Outdoors is an outdoor sports equipment retailer which encourages people to spend their spare time ------- outdoor activities.

   (A) do
   (B) does
   (C) done
   (D) doing

6. No matter how hard her co-workers tried to convince her to take a break, Ms. Rose kept ------- her plans to launch the new product.

   (A) pursuing
   (B) pursuit
   (C) pursue
   (D) to pursue

7. Since her house was two hours away from her work by car, Rhonda always had a hard time ------- to the office.

   (A) commuting
   (B) commute
   (C) commuted
   (D) commutable

8. Mr. Gratski, a renowned journalist, has devoted himself to ------- around the world to write articles on different cultures.

   (A) travel
   (B) traveled
   (C) traveler
   (D) traveling

9. These self-adhesive hooks are used to ------- materials — usually those that are not too heavy — on the wall.

   (A) hanging
   (B) hang
   (C) hanged
   (D) hanger

10. Since the company car broke down while he was in the middle of heading to the meeting place, Mr. Nielson had to spend all his money on ------- the car.

    (A) repaired
    (B) repairing
    (C) repairs
    (D) repair

출제율 4%

법칙 64 '번지점프' to 동사원형

'be able to 동사원형'은 '~를 할 수 있다'는 뜻인데, 이때 to 부정사는 앞의 형용사 able을 수식하는 부사 기능을 하며, 이러한 표현들에는 be likely to, be sure to, be eager to, be willing to, be ready to 등이 있으며, 이러한 표현들을 '번지점프 to 부정사'라고 알아 두도록 하자.

유형을 파악해 봐

1. The manager was able ------- the documents with the help of his secretary.
(A) revised   (B) to revise   (C) revising   (D) revise

2. After ten months of preparations, the director, John Hibbert, was ready to ------- the show to the public.
(A) revealing   (B) revealed   (C) reveal   (D) be revealed

3. Please make sure to ------- to the reports Mr. Shin gave you when you are working on your paper.
(A) refer   (B) be referred   (C) referring   (D) refers

보기에는 모두 정동사가 1~3개, 준동사가 1~2개가 제시된 것으로 보아 준동사 문제임을 쉽게 알 수 있다. 2, 3번 문제에는 빈칸 앞에 to가 왔는데, 이것이 전치사 to인지, to 부정사의 to인지를 구분해야 한다.

이렇게 풀어 봐   "유형을 파악해 봐" 1번 문제를 보세요!

첫째 빈칸이 정동사 자리인지 확인한다.
준동사 문제도 보기 중 최소 1개는 정동사가 오므로 항상 정동사를 확인하는 것이 먼저다. 문장에는 이미 정동사 was가 있으므로 빈칸은 준동사 자리이다.

둘째 준동사의 기능을 확인한다.
준동사 중 어떤 준동사가 어떤 기능을 하는지를 확인해야 한다. 빈칸 앞에 able이 있으므로 able과 잘 어울리는 '번지점프 to 부정사'가 필요하며 따라서 (B)가 답이 된다.

220 어형 및 문법 편

PLUS

번지점프 to 부정사

올라가기 전	I am hesitant[reluctant] to jump.	나는 번지점프 하기를 주저한다.
1층에서 보니	I am likely to jump.	나는 번지점프를 할 수 있을 것 같다.
2층에서 보니	I am sure to jump.	나는 번지점프에 대해 확신이 생긴다.
3층에서 보니	I am eager to jump.	나는 번지점프를 할 열망이 생긴다.
점프대에 올라서	I am willing to jump.	나는 번지점프를 기꺼이 할 수 있을 것 같다.
교관이 묻기를	Are you ready to jump?	뛰어 내릴 준비가 되어 있나요?
나는 대답했다.	I am able to jump.	나는 점프할 수 있습니다.

 함정을 피해 봐 실제 강의에서만 알려주는 풀이 노하우!

1. 'be 형용사 to 명사' 계열의 숙어를 구분한다.

A 5$ delivery fee will be added to (order / orders) received after the promotion ends.

The new banking service will be accessible to (work / workers).

→ 능동태일 때 'A to B'로 쓰는 '보내다, 덧붙이다' 계열의 3형식 동사들과 available to, entitled to 등을 주의한다. 이럴 경우에는 'to 동사'가 아닌 'to 명사'가 온다.

1. orders, workers

STEP 3 실전에 적용해 봐

1. Since it will rain next Thursday, the place for the luncheon is likely to ------- to somewhere inside the building.

   (A) be changed
   (B) being changed
   (C) been changed
   (D) changes

2. Although it was necessary to do so, Mr. Cruz was hesitant to ------- personal questions to his client as she might find them offensive.

   (A) ask
   (B) asking
   (C) asked
   (D) asks

3. Keep it out of direct sunlight as the state of this product is apt to ------- depending on the temperature.

   (A) altering
   (B) altered
   (C) being altered
   (D) alter

4. Those over 65 years of age are entitled ------- from being covered by the national pension plan.

   (A) benefited
   (B) to benefits
   (C) being benefited
   (D) been benefited

5. If Ms. Hail could get service as good as the last time, she would be willing to ------- more money.

   (A) paying
   (B) pay
   (C) be paid
   (D) payable

6. As the manager's job at Postop Software is known to be very demanding, Ms. Moon was reluctant to ------- her resume.

   (A) submitting
   (B) submit
   (C) be submitted
   (D) submission

7. Please note that in compliance with the customs law, additional taxes will be added to ------- for over $500.

   (A) order
   (B) orders
   (C) ordering
   (D) orderer

8. As Mr. Chad's performance has been among the best of the Sales Department employees, he was certain to ------- a promotion this time.

   (A) receiving
   (B) receipt
   (C) received
   (D) receive

9. A free shuttle bus is available to ------- upon request which should be made at least a week before arrival at the airport.

   (A) visited
   (B) visiting
   (C) visit
   (D) visitors

10. Since Mr. Vonin got accustomed to his job at the Kamore Corporation, he was not likely to ------- a job offer from the company he had previously applied to.

    (A) accepting
    (B) accepted
    (C) accept
    (D) acceptance

출제율 **4%**

법칙 65 무엇을 가리키는지 알 수 있을 때는 소유대명사

'He likes his car, but I like my car.'에서 my car는 mine으로 바꿀 수 있다. mine과 같은 단어를 소유대명사라고 하며, 소유대명사는 앞에 이미 이것을 가리키는 단어가 쓰였을 때 중복 사용을 피하기 위해 사용한다.

나의 것	너의 것	그의 것	그녀의 것	우리의 것	그들의 것	그것의 것
mine	yours	his	hers	ours	theirs	없음

STEP 1 유형을 파악해 봐

1. As almost every employee has already received an employee ID card, Ms. Eve requested -------.
   (A) her   (B) herself   (C) hers   (D) she

2. When Ms. Blue tried to pick up the bag on the table, Mr. Browning told her that the bag was -------.
   (A) himself   (B) he   (C) him   (D) his

3. Since I cannot find my purse anywhere, someone must have mistaken ------- as his.
   (A) my   (B) mine   (C) myself   (D) I

세 문제의 보기들이 모두 인칭대명사, 소유대명사, 재귀대명사들로 구성되어 있는 것으로 보아 인칭대명사를 고르는 문제일 가능성이 높은 문제들이다.

STEP 2 이렇게 풀어 봐

"유형을 파악해 봐" 1번 문제를 보세요!

첫째 격을 확인한다.
대명사 문제의 기본은 격을 확인하는 것이다. 해석을 하지 않고도 격을 확인하는 것으로 쉽게 답을 고를 수 있는 경우가 있다. 빈칸 앞에 3형식 동사가 있으므로 빈칸은 목적격 자리이며, 따라서 주격인 (D)는 탈락한다.

둘째 빈칸이 가리키는 말을 해석해 확인한다.
'모든 직원들이 직원 ID 카드들을 받았으므로, Ms. Eve도 그녀 자신의 카드를 요청했다.'는 의미이므로 빈칸은 '그녀 자신의 카드'를 가리키는 말, 즉 '그녀의 것'이라는 소유대명사 (C)가 와야 한다.

PLUS

- 소유대명사가 가리키는 말은 보통 '소유격+명사'나 'the+명사'로 제시된다.
- 이중소유격에서도 소유대명사를 사용한다.

| a friend of mine 나의 한 친구 | a friend of me (X) |
| a picture of his 그가 소유한 사진 | a picture of him 그가 찍힌 사진 |

 함정을 피해 봐　　　　실제 강의에서만 알려주는 풀이 노하우!

1. one's own의 용법에 주의한다.

Ms. Lee argued that the idea was (hers/her) own rather than her manager's.
➜ one's own은 '자기 자신의'라는 소유격도 되지만, '자기 자신의 것'이라는 명사로 사용될 수 있다.

After retiring from a big firm, Mr. Kim and his co-worker Ms. Lee will open a private business of (theirs/their own/them).
➜ of one's own은 '자기 자신의'라는 뜻이다. 일단 a private business 다음에는 이중소유격을 써야 하므로 them은 탈락하고, 대신 theirs를 쓰면 '그들 사업체 여러 개 중 하나의 사업체를 열 것이다.'라는 말이 돼 어색하다. '그들 자신의 사업을 처음 시작한다.'는 의미로 보는 것이 맞으므로 of their own이 답이다.

1. her, their own

STEP 3 실전에 적용해 봐

1. Everyone else has submitted his or her proposals on the project due tomorrow, but Mr. Will has not submitted ------- yet.

   (A) him
   (B) his
   (C) himself
   (D) he

2. Ms. Stoney returned the locker keys that she took from the changing room while thinking they were ------- to the front desk.

   (A) she
   (B) herself
   (C) her
   (D) hers

3. Most of the vehicles that the employees are driving are not ------- but are the property of Gear Auto.

   (A) they
   (B) them
   (C) theirs
   (D) their

4. Ms. Earning was surprised to hear that the new CEO's house is located right next to -------.

   (A) her
   (B) herself
   (C) hers
   (D) she

5. The executive manager limited the use of the company credit card and asked the employees to pay expenses not directly related to the business with ------- own.

   (A) them
   (B) they
   (C) theirs
   (D) their

6. Mr. Gale is suspected of plagiarizing his doctoral thesis as a number of researchers claim that it has many clauses and phrases copied from -------.

   (A) theirs
   (B) they
   (C) their
   (D) themselves

7. While most of the other proposals for the contract regarding the mining business focus only on its benefits, ------- mentions the disadvantages as well.

   (A) mine
   (B) myself
   (C) my
   (D) I

8. Joan's team was proud that the executive manager rejected all of the other proposals and decided to proceed with -------.

   (A) theirs
   (B) their
   (C) themselves
   (D) them

9. None of the wallets at the Lost and Found Office belonged to Mr. Penning, but he found ------- in the building near the office.

   (A) his
   (B) him
   (C) himself
   (D) he

10. Ms. Wells always had her co-worker drive her to her workplace because it was too costly to buy a car of -------.

    (A) her
    (B) her own
    (C) hers
    (D) herself

출제율 3%

법칙 66 보기에 미래완료시제나 would have p.p.가 오면 주로 오답

will have p.p.는 미래완료시제를 의미하는데, 예를 들면, '내가 회의 장소에 도착할 쯤에는 이미 미팅이 시작되었을 것이다.'와 같이 미래의 한 시점을 기준으로 그보다 전에 완료되는 일을 묘사할 때 사용한다. 가정법에는 다음과 같이 종류들이 있다.

가정법 이름	부사절	주절	의미
가정법 과거완료	If 주어 had p.p.	주어 would[should, could, might] have p.p.	과거를 반대: 내가 과거에 ~였더라면
가정법 과거	If 주어 과거동사/were	주어 would[shoud, could, might] 동사원형	현재를 반대: 내가 지금 ~라면
가정법 미래	If 주어 should 동사원형	주어 will 동사원형 혹은 Please 동사원형	가능성이 비교적 낮은 일: 혹시 ~라면
가정법 현재	If 주어 현재형 동사		가능성이 반반: 만약 ~라면

STEP 1 유형을 파악해 봐

1. If visitors were allowed, they ------- photographs of the ancient monument.
   (A) can take (B) have taken (C) could have taken (D) could be taking

2. If Ms. Hudson had known there was a meeting today, she ------- a meeting room in advance.
   (A) has reserved (B) had reserved (C) will reserve (D) would have reserved

3. By the time Mr. Wilson arrives at the airport, a limousine ------- to pick him up.
   (A) arrives (B) has arrived (C) would have arrived (D) will have arrived

보기들이 모두 정동사이고, 수일치나 태를 살필 필요 없이 각기 다른 시제들로 구성되어 있으므로 시제를 묻는 문제임을 알아차릴 수 있다. 파트 5에 시제 문제가 등장할 때는 반드시 문제 안에 시제의 단서가 등장하게 마련이다.

STEP 2 이렇게 풀어 봐

"유형을 파악해 봐" 1번 문제를 보세요!

첫째 시제 문제인지 확인한다.
시제 문제로 간주하고 단서를 찾았으나 의외로 정동사, 준동사를 확인하는 것으로 정답을 찾을 수 있거나, 수일치, 태 등으로 문제가 풀리게 될 경우 시제 문제가 아니라고 봐야 한다. 여기서는 보기들이 모두 they와 함께 사용 가능한 동사 형태이며, 모두 능동태이므로 시제 문제가 맞다.

둘째 시제의 단서를 찾아라.

시제 문제에는 반드시 시제의 단서가 포함되기 마련이다. 'If 주어 were'로 시작하는 문장이 등장하면 가정법 과거이며, 주절에는 'would[should, could, might] 동사원형'이 와야 한다. 따라서 (D)가 답이다.

PLUS

- 미래완료시제는 미래의 한 시점을 기준으로 더 먼저 일어나는 일에 사용한다. 미래완료시제가 답이 되려면 미래 시점이 등장해야 하고, 그 전에 일이 끝난다는 내용이 성립돼야 한다. 미래완료와 자주 쓰이는 미래 시점으로는 'by+미래 시점 명사'나 'by the time S+V(현재시제)' 등이 있다.

  The meeting will have already started by the time I arrive at the meeting room.
  내가 회의실에 도착할 때 쯤 미팅은 이미 시작되었을 것이다.

- would가 반드시 가정법에만 사용되는 조동사는 아니다. 주절이 과거시제일 때 시제를 맞추기 위해 명사절에 사용하거나 과거의 반복적인 습관 또는 주로 be동사와 함께 추정을 나타내기 위해서 쓴다.

  Mr. Kim said that he would go to the hospital tomorrow. → will을 대신하여 would를 사용한다.
  After lunch he would take a nap. → '낮잠을 자곤 했다.'로 해석되며, 과거의 습관을 나타낸다.
  That would be his mother. → '저 사람이 그의 어머니일 것이다.' 추정을 의미한다.

- 파트 6에서는 가정법과거완료나 미래완료시제가 정답으로 출제된 적이 없으며, 파트 5에서 조차도 출제율이 매우 낮은 편이다. 특히 would[should, might, could] have p.p.나 will have p.p.가 보기에 보이면 본 단원에서 확실히 배운 경우가 아니라면 주로 오답이라고 생각해도 무방하다. 특히 파트 6에서는 더욱 그렇다.

함정을 피해 봐
실제 강의에서만 알려주는 풀이 노하우!

1. 혼합 가정법을 조심한다.

If I had been born in America, I (would speak/would have spoken) English very well now.
→ 앞의 부사절에서는 가정법과거완료를 사용해 과거의 일을 반대로 가정했으나, 주절에서는 현재의 일을 말하고 있다. 이렇게 부사절에는 과거완료를, 주절에는 과거를 사용하는 것을 혼합가정법이라고 하며, 아직 뉴토익에서는 출제된 바가 없다.

2. 미래시제와 미래완료시제를 구분한다.

The meeting will (have started/start) when Mr. Kim arrives because he will preside at the meeting.
→ 미래시제는 미래 시점에 일이 발생할 때 쓰고, 미래완료시제는 미래 시점 이전에 일이 발생했을 때 쓴다. 'Mr. Kim이 회의를 주재할 예정이므로 그가 도착한 다음에 회의를 시작할 것이다.'라는 뜻이다.

1. would speak 2. start

STEP 3 실전에 적용해 봐

1. If Ms. Halland had finished her project before Mr. Raymond left for his business trip, she ------- his feedback on the project.

   (A) requests
   (B) could have requested
   (C) can request
   (D) has requested

2. Since her manager was not able to catch the flight on time, Ms. Lee told the manager that she ------- the seminar by herself tomorrow.

   (A) will be attended
   (B) is attended
   (C) would be attending
   (D) would have been attended

3. By the time the executive manager returns from his business trip, Marketing Department ------- customer survey to be submitted to him.

   (A) will have completed
   (B) would have completed
   (C) was completed
   (D) had completed

4. If Pioneer Bank successfully maintains its current profit margins, it ------- another branch in another city.

   (A) opens
   (B) opened
   (C) will open
   (D) could open

5. If the sales clerks ------- that they were running low on a few items, they would have notified the managers.

   (A) had known
   (B) knew
   (C) have known
   (D) know

6. The recent fluctuations in the price of gasoline ------- the price of every product transported from the port to the stores in each region.

   (A) should be affected
   (B) will have affected
   (C) have affected
   (D) would have been affected

7. Ms. Hall ------- over $4,000 by herself by the time she books a package tour to Guam.

   (A) is saving
   (B) will have saved
   (C) saved
   (D) saves

8. If Mr. Campbell had been informed about the increased benefits of the insurance he was interested in, he ------- it without hesitation.

   (A) will have bought
   (B) might have bought
   (C) might be bought
   (D) was bought

9. Had he ------- aware that the job would involve quite a few business trips every year, he would not have applied for the job.

   (A) be
   (B) being
   (C) were
   (D) been

10. The safety inspector reported the products whose dates of manufacture -------.

    (A) had been forged
    (B) will have been forged
    (C) would have been forged
    (D) should be forged

법칙 67 고득점을 위한 기타 명사절 접속사

출제율 2%

'법칙 40'에서 살펴본 명사절 접속사 what, that, whether에 비해 기타 명사절 접속사는 출제빈도가 높지는 않다. what뿐만 아니라 who, whom, which와 같은 의문대명사, what, which, whose와 같은 의문형용사, where, when, why, how와 같은 의문부사들도 명사절 접속사로 사용될 수 있다.

STEP 1 유형을 파악해 봐

1. The amount of incentives depends on ------- well your department performs over the year.
   (A) any   (B) how   (C) that   (D) if

2. The program manager should decide ------- project to give more funds to this week.
   (A) when   (B) whoever   (C) which   (D) why

3. The manager will decide ------- suggestions will be adopted for the next marketing plan.
   (A) them   (B) who   (C) whose   (D) their

모든 보기들이 2개 이상의 접속사들을 포함하고 있다. 1번 문제는 (A)가 대명사, (B), (C), (D)가 접속사이고, 2번 문제는 보기가 모두 접속사로 왔다. 그리고 3번 문제의 경우에는 (A)와 (D)는 대명사, (B)와 (C)는 접속사다. 따라서 이들 문제들은 접속사를 묻는 문제임을 알아차릴 수 있어야 한다.

STEP 2 이렇게 풀어 봐
"유형을 파악해 봐" 1번 문제를 보세요!

첫째 빈칸이 접속사 자리인지, 만약 그렇다면 무슨 절이 필요한지 확인한다.
일단 동사가 depends, performs로 2개이므로 빈칸은 접속사 자리이다. 대명사 (A)와 명사절 접속사가 아닌 (D)는 탈락한다.

둘째 빈칸 뒤 문장의 모양새를 확인한다.
that 뒤에는 정상적인 어순의 완전한 문장이 온다. 원래 부사인 well은 performs 뒤에 와야 하는데 지금은 빈칸 앞에 있으므로 well을 앞으로 가져올 수 있는 요소가 무엇인지 파악할 필요가 있다. how는 자신이 수식하는 형용사나 부사를 끌어당겨 사용하므로 (B)가 답이다.

PLUS

- who 뒤에는 주어가 빠진 문장, whom 뒤에는 목적어가 빠진 문장, which는 what과 같이 주어나 목적어가 빠진 문장이 오는데, 선택사항이 있는 경우 which를 사용한다.

  I know who loves you. → who 다음에는 주어가 없고 바로 동사가 온다.
  I know whom they like. → whom 다음에 like의 목적어가 없다.
  I know what you like. I know what is good. → what은 주어나 목적어가 빠진 문장이 온다.
  I have to choose which is good. → which는 선택사항이 있을 때 사용한다.

- where, when, why, how 다음에는 'I know where I should stay.'와 같이 완전한 문장이 온다.

- wh-접속사 뒤의 주어와 조동사(will, should 등)는 to로 줄일 수 있다.

  I know what I should do. → I know what to do. (I should가 to가 됨)
  I know who should go. → I know who to go. (who가 주어라 should만 to로 바뀜)

 함정을 피해 봐 실제 강의에서만 알려주는 풀이 노하우!

1. 의문형용사로 만든 명사절을 조심한다.

Customers should decide (which/that/where) car options to order when they buy a car.

→ to는 they will을 줄인 말로 볼 수 있다. car options가 목적어, they가 주어, will order가 3형식 동사로서 목적어가 주어보다 앞으로 도치되어 있다. 즉 어순이 비정상이다. 이렇게 자신이 수식하는 목적어를 앞으로 당겨 사용하는 것은 의문형용사로 만든 명사절 접속사 whose, what, which뿐이다. 한편 의문형용사 다음에는 대명사, 관사, 소유격이 오지 않고, 명사만 올 수 있다.

1. **which**

STEP 3 실전에 적용해 봐

1. The contract must clarify ------- the cost will be covered in case of a delay in the shipment of the goods.
   (A) what
   (B) how
   (C) about
   (D) which

2. Trust Investments can help you determine ------- investment program to choose to serve your interests the best.
   (A) that
   (B) about
   (C) whether
   (D) which

3. The managerial position at the Glam Company has remained unfilled for a long time because the CEO was still unsure ------- could handle the job the best.
   (A) what
   (B) when
   (C) which
   (D) who

4. A part of our sales team's policy describes ------- customer complaints should be handled so as not to cause any inconveniences to customers.
   (A) whom
   (B) any
   (C) about
   (D) how

5. When the last team is done with their presentation, the executive managers should decide ------- team will receive the award based on their evaluations.
   (A) in
   (B) which
   (C) on
   (D) why

6. Mr. Wilson sought advice on ------- to formulate appropriate team strategies for collaborative work from the workshop instructor.
   (A) how
   (B) which
   (C) whether
   (D) them

7. Once the contract with the operating system provider Ubiquitous, Inc. expires, our company needs to choose ------- software to install next.
   (A) which
   (B) these
   (C) how
   (D) among

8. The guest speaker at the conference talked about ------- the mobile phone market might change in the future.
   (A) that
   (B) because
   (C) any of
   (D) how

9. The executive officer asked Ms. Carr to order the office supplies that they were running out of online but did not specify ------- store to order them from.
   (A) another
   (B) neither
   (C) that
   (D) which

10. The head of the Marketing Department will soon determine ------- reports will be handed to the CFO to be reviewed.
    (A) whom
    (B) whoever
    (C) whose
    (D) whomever

출제율 2%

법칙 68 고득점을 위한 기타 형용사절 접속사

'법칙 36과 54'에서 이미 살펴본 형용사절 접속사 who, whose에 비해 나머지 형용사절 접속사들은 출제빈도가 낮은 편이다. 선행사가 사람이고 목적어 역할을 하는 목적격관계대명사 whom, 관계부사로 선행사가 장소, 시간, 이유, 방법일 때 사용하는 where, when, why, how 등은 출제빈도가 낮지만 오답으로는 자주 등장하는 형용사절 접속사들이므로 소홀히 해서는 안 된다.

유형을 파악해 봐

1. The government official to ------- the building permit must be shown will visit the construction site today.
(A) when   (B) whom   (C) where   (D) who

2. Ms. Clark called Mr. Shaw on Sunday afternoon, ------- he is usually at his home.
(A) which   (B) why   (C) when   (D) in case

3. Orlando, ------- one of the world's most famous tourist spots is located, is visited by many travelers.
(A) where   (B) which   (C) whether   (D) in that

보기가 모두 접속사로 구성되어 있는데, 1번 문제의 경우 모두 형용사절[명사절] 접속사들이고, 2번 문제는 (A)와 (B)가 형용사절[명사절] 접속사, (C)는 형용사절[명사절, 부사절] 접속사, (D)는 부사절 접속사이며, 3번 문제는 (A)와 (B)가 형용사절[명사절] 접속사, (C)는 명사절[부사절] 접속사, (D)는 부사절 접속사로 구성되어 있다.

이렇게 풀어 봐   "유형을 파악해 봐" 1번 문제를 보세요!

첫째 형용사절인지 명사절인지 확인한다.
보기들이 모두 형용사절 접속사, 명사절 접속사가 가능하므로 절의 종류를 확인해야 한다. 빈칸 앞 to 앞에 있는 official은 뒤에 to를 수반하는 명사가 아니다. 따라서 to는 shown 다음에 와야 하는 to이며, official은 선행사가 되므로 형용사절 접속사가 필요하다.

둘째 선행사가 사람인지 확인하고, 형용사절 안에 무엇이 빠져 있는지도 확인한다.
선행사는 official이므로 사람 선행사이고, the building permit ~ shown to까지가 형용사절인데, 전치사 to의 목적어가 빠져 있으므로 (B) whom이 답이 된다. 이때 to를 앞으로 보내면 to whom이 된다.

PLUS

- who는 whom을 대신해 사용할 수 있지만, 단 전치사 뒤에서는 불가능하다.

  I like the man whom(= who) I work with. (O)
  I like the man with whom I work. (O)
  I like the man with who I work. (X)

- 관계부사도 형용사절 접속사이며, 뒤에는 완전한 문장이 온다. 또한 관계부사는 언제든지 생략 가능하며, 선행사도 의미가 통할 경우 생략 가능하다.

  I know the place (where) I should stay. → I know where I should stay. → I know where to stay.
  I know the time (when) I should stay. → I know when I should stay. → I know when to stay.
  I know the reason (why) I should stay. → I know why I should stay. → I know why to stay.
  I know the way (how) I should stay. → I know how I should stay. → I know how to stay.

  * the way와 how는 같이 쓰지 않는다.

함정을 피해 봐 — 실제 강의에서만 알려주는 풀이 노하우!

1. 주어 자리지만 주격 관계대명사를 쓰지 않는 경우를 조심한다.

The major showed deep appreciation to the residents, all of (whom/who) had volunteered for community service.

→ 전치사의 목적격 자리이므로 whom이 답이다. whom이 꼭 선행사 바로 뒤에 와야 하는 것은 아니다. all of whom은 all of the residents를 가리키며 접속사 역할을 한다.

2. in which와 where를 혼동하지 않도록 주의한다.

For companies in Korea, Southeast Asia is an ideal place in (where/which) to reduce manufacturing costs.

→ 여기서 to는 주어와 조동사 will이나 should를 줄여 쓴 것이다. in을 costs 뒤로 보내면 where 뒤에는 완전한 문장이 와야 하지만, 전치사 in의 목적어가 없는 상황이 돼 불완전하며, 따라서 which가 답이다. in을 which 앞으로 보내면 where와 같은 뜻이 된다.

1. whom 2. which

STEP 3 실전에 적용해 봐

1. The recipe book received very positive feedback from readers, some of ------- were even professional cooks.

   (A) who
   (B) in order that
   (C) whether
   (D) whom

2. Mr. McKnight's presentation on his new invention explained the reasons ------- it will attract many young customers.

   (A) when
   (B) in that
   (C) of
   (D) why

3. Promotional giveaways are regularly held at Max Superstore on Saturday afternoons, ------- the most customers are visiting the store.

   (A) when
   (B) by
   (C) until
   (D) around

4. Please visit our offline store, ------- the items you are interested in can be purchased for 20% lower than from our online mall.

   (A) where
   (B) which
   (C) over
   (D) why

5. Mr. Morrison was in charge of purchasing office supplies, all of ------- could be purchased at a store near the company.

   (A) them
   (B) that
   (C) which
   (D) over

6. Movie director Derick Brown decided to shoot a film on Star Avenue at midnight, ------- there were not many people on the street.

   (A) why
   (B) which
   (C) when
   (D) how

7. The notice was sent to the attendees, all of ------- were asked to be on time for the seminar as late entrance is not permitted.

   (A) whom
   (B) who
   (C) them
   (D) those

8. Alkemi Manufacturing plans to locate its production plants in places near mines, ------- underground resources are abundant.

   (A) there
   (B) those
   (C) by which
   (D) where

9. No one knew ------- Mr. Hunt became the new CEO only 5 years after he started working at Murray, Inc., but his accomplishments were impressive.

   (A) while
   (B) the way
   (C) whom
   (D) who

10. For IT venture businesses, Central Valley is an ideal place in ------- to develop various technical devices.

    (A) which
    (B) where
    (C) how
    (D) any

출제율 2%

법칙 69 고득점을 위한 기타 전치사

출제빈도는 적지만 고득점을 위해서 꼭 필요한 전치사들에 대해 알아 본다.

in response to ~에 대한 응답으로	in advance 사전에, 앞서	in + 맛/색깔/치수
judging from ~로부터 판단하건대	given ~를 고려할 때	on behalf of ~를 대표하여
in terms of ~에 관하여	in favor of ~를 찬성하여	at + 가격/속도/비율
in the event of ~인 경우에	unlike ~와는 달리	off ~를 벗어나서
as ~로서		

STEP 1 유형을 파악해 봐

1. ------- inclement weather, the outdoor concert can be easily moved to an indoor hall.
(A) As opposed to   (B) In the event of   (C) Provided that   (D) For instance

2. Sound Electronics is a company producing high-quality audio players ------- competitive prices.
(A) after   (B) on   (C) at   (D) in

3. As office supplies often run out in a short amount of time, make sure that you order them ------- advance.
(A) at   (B) for   (C) of   (D) in

제시된 보기들의 공통점을 살펴보면, 세 문제 모두 보기에 전치사가 2개 이상이므로 전치사 어휘 문제로 볼 수 있다.

STEP 2 이렇게 풀어 봐
"유형을 파악해 봐" 1번 문제를 보세요!

첫째 보기에 접속사가 있으므로 접속사 자리인지부터 확인한다.
'동사의 수 – 접속사의 수 = 1'인데, 문장에서 동사는 can be 한 개이므로 접속사는 올 수 없어 접속사 (C)는 탈락. (D)는 부사이기 때문에 전치사 자리에 올 수 없으므로 (D) 역시 탈락한다.

둘째 빈칸 뒤가 시점 및 기간, 장소와 관련이 없으므로 추/포/제/for(이, 용, 대, 목) → 양보, 이유 → 주/범/근 → 동/수/수동 순으로 보기를 확인한다.

시점, 기간 관련 전치사나 양보, 이유, 주/범/근, 동/수/수동 모두 보기에 존재하지 않는다.

셋째 보기를 하나하나 대입해 해석한다.

(B)는 '~인 경우에'라는 뜻을 갖고 있는데, '날씨가 나쁠 경우에 야외 콘서트는 쉽게 실내로 옮겨 진행될 수 있다.'로 해석이 되므로 정답이 된다.

PLUS

- unlike 뒤에는 other나 previous 등이 온다.

함정을 피해 봐
실제 강의에서만 알려주는 풀이 노하우!

1. given의 쓰임에 주의한다.

(Given/Unlike) that there is enough time left, the project is sure to be complete before the deadline.

→ 여기서 given은 과거분사가 아닌 '~를 고려할 때'라는 뜻의 전치사로 사용되었다.

(Given that/Given which) I am older than him, this is a remarkable success.

→ 완전한 문장이 두 개 왔으므로 접속사가 필요하며, 따라서 Given that은 접속사로 사용되었다.

1. Given, Given that

STEP 3 실전에 적용해 봐

1. ------- the look on his face, the manager must have been satisfied with the employees' performances.

   (A) Due to
   (B) In contrary to
   (C) Despite
   (D) Judging from

2. ------- a sudden blackout, unplug all of the power cords and plug them back in after waiting at least 10 seconds.

   (A) In the event of
   (B) Given that
   (C) Unless
   (D) As an example

3. ABT Air offers a wide selection of channels, but ----- most other broadcasting companies, it also airs programs in other languages.

   (A) except
   (B) along
   (C) unlike
   (D) without

4. To visit Bleam, Inc., take the subway and get ------- at Bowrail Station, which is directly across from Bleam's building.

   (A) from
   (B) up
   (C) until
   (D) off

5. ------- that customers prefer items in small packages that are easy to carry, we will have to change the package designs.

   (A) Regarding
   (B) Given
   (C) In order
   (D) Since

6. You might also want to check out the item in a different color because it is currently available ------- blue, orange, and pink.

   (A) in
   (B) of
   (C) with
   (D) on

7. We give a sincere apology to you, Ms. Adams, ------- the CEO of the HK Corporation, who is currently unavailable to take your call.

   (A) instead
   (B) on behalf of
   (C) due to
   (D) notwithstanding

8. According to a recent survey, it seems that customers value quality ------- a cheap price when purchasing a product.

   (A) other than
   (B) as if
   (C) due to
   (D) rather than

9. ------- the working conditions, the Goodwill Company ensures that its employees receive benefits better than those offered by its rivals.

   (A) In terms of
   (B) In spite of
   (C) For instance
   (D) Owing to

10. ------- the growing demand for innovative designs of cars, Wheel Auto hired more car designers.

    (A) In response to
    (B) Since
    (C) In addition to
    (D) In contrary to

출제율 1%

법칙 70   목표[계획] is to 부정사

'Our goal is to go.'에서 our goal과 to go는 동격관계이다. 목표가 곧 가는 것, 가는 것이 곧 목표이다. 여기서 to go는 명사 보어 역할을 하는 to 부정사이며, 주어 자리에는 '목표나 목적, 계획'을 뜻하는 단어들이 오는데, goal, aim, purpose, objective, object, mission 등이 여기에 해당한다.

유형을 파악해 봐

1. The goal of Raymond Holdings ------- our customers' needs to the fullest.
(A) is to meet   (B) is met   (C) meet   (D) meeting

2. Please note that the purpose of this survey ------- only the customer satisfaction rate.
(A) is analyze   (B) analyze   (C) analyzing   (D) is to analyze

3. Our team's plan for the upcoming project ------- its outline on Wednesday and to finish the first draft by next week.
(A) discussion   (B) discussing   (C) is to discuss   (D) is discuss

보기들이 모두 정동사 2개 이상, 준동사 1개 이상으로 구성된 것으로 보아 준동사 문제임을 짐작할 수 있다. 그리고 세 문제 모두 보기에 to 부정사가 포함된 것이 특징이다.

이렇게 풀어 봐
"유형을 파악해 봐" 1번 문제를 보세요!

첫째 빈칸이 정동사 자리인지 확인한다.
준동사 문제도 보기 중 최소 1개는 정동사가 주어지므로 먼저 정동사를 확인해야 한다. 문장에 정동사가 없으므로 준동사인 (D)는 탈락한다.

둘째 주어 자리의 '목표, 목적, 계획'을 확인한다.
주어 자리에 '목표, 목적, 계획'을 나타내는 단어가 있으면 동격의 to 부정사가 필요한 경우이며, 여기서는 (A)가 답이 된다. (C)는 단수, 복수가 맞지 않고, (B)는 수동태이므로 뒤에 목적어를 가질 수 없다.

PLUS

- 주어가 사람인 경우에 'is to 부정사'는 ~해야 한다, ~할 것이다'로 해석된다. 이때 to 부정사는 형용사 보어 역할을 한다.

All managers are to attend the training session regarding facility safety.
→ '모든 매니저들은 참석해야 한다.'로 해석한다.

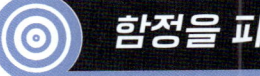 **함정을 피해 봐**   실제 강의에서만 알려주는 풀이 노하우!

1. 주어가 목표나 계획이 아닌 경우에도 to 부정사가 명사 보어로 올 수 있다.

This letter is (informing/to inform) you that your subscription to the car magazine expires next month.
→ 이 편지가 '통보하고 있는 중'이라는 뜻은 어색하며, '통보하기 위한 것'으로 해석하는 것이 맞다.

1. to inform

STEP 3 실전에 적용해 봐

1. The mission of this fundraising campaign ------- at least more than one million dollars to donate to the charity organization Hope Society.

    (A) is to raise
    (B) raising
    (C) is raised
    (D) raise

2. Carsons Technology Solutions is committed to achieving its objective, which ------- the leading company in the IT industry.

    (A) becoming
    (B) become
    (C) is became
    (D) is to become

3. Our team's goal for this project ------- some ways to maximize customer satisfaction of the services provided to them.

    (A) is to analyze
    (B) analyzes
    (C) analyzed
    (D) analyzing

4. The reason why Ms. Moreno chose to move to May Town ------- money by making her daily commute to work cheaper.

    (A) to save
    (B) was to save
    (C) was saving
    (D) saved

5. The nationwide campaign's ------- is to raise awareness of the need to preserve nature and wildlife.

    (A) permit
    (B) inquiry
    (C) objective
    (D) advice

6. This letter is ----- you that your car insurance will expire next week and requires renewal.

    (A) informing
    (B) to inform
    (C) informed
    (D) inform

7. The National Health Organization's ------- is to establish various norms and standards on health-related issues to promote public well-being.

    (A) preference
    (B) role
    (C) suggestion
    (D) advice

8. The goal of this training session ------- that all employees are comfortable working with CAD programs.

    (A) ensuring
    (B) ensures
    (C) is to ensure
    (D) ensured

9. At Delton Airlines, Mr. Nielson's ------- is to assist customers who have inquires about which gate to proceed to.

    (A) asset
    (B) attempt
    (C) consideration
    (D) job

10. The aim of viral marketing ------- customers highly dependent on social network services and to expose them to product advertisements online.

    (A) is to identify
    (B) identifying
    (C) identified
    (D) is identify

정답 및 해설은 102페이지에

둘째 마당

•

어휘 편 및 파트 6

Chapter 09

동사 어휘 문제

매월 4문제

출제율 55%

법칙 71 특정 명사를 목적어로 쓰는 3형식 동사

목적어가 필요한 3형식 동사들은 목적어 자리에 오는 명사들이 정해져 있는 경우가 대부분이다. attend는 '미팅에 참석하다, 시상식에 참석하다' 등과 같이 뒤에 행사를 나타내는 명사가 주로 오고, visit는 주로 장소를 나타내는 명사가 온다.

 유형을 파악해 봐

1. Ms. Elmore made a reservation to ------- the movie preview.
   (A) apply   (B) forward   (C) attend   (D) allow

2. The manager will be ------- resumes before the job interview.
   (A) operating   (B) directing   (C) reviewing   (D) offering

3. Please ------- your membership card to get discounts on your purchases.
   (A) enter   (B) allow   (C) observe   (D) show

보기가 모두 서로 다른 동사들로 왔으므로 동사 어휘 문제임을 알 수 있다. 빈칸 뒤에는 목적어가 왔고, 'A to B, A for B, A from B'처럼 특정 전치사와의 어울림을 보는 문제는 아니며, 이와 같은 유형의 문제들은 주로 목적어나 주어와의 어울림을 보고 풀어야 하는 문제들이다.

 이렇게 풀어 봐   "유형을 파악해 봐" 1번 문제를 보세요!

첫째 3형식 자리인지 확인한다.
뒤에 목적어가 있으므로 3형식 동사를 고르는 문제이며, 보기 역시 모두 3형식 동사들로 제시되었다.

둘째 목적어와의 어울림을 확인한다.
movie preview는 영화 시사회를 의미하므로 일종의 행사 관련 명사이다. 행사 관련 명사를 목적어로 취할 수 있는 동사는 attend, hold, host, organize 등이며, 따라서 (C)가 답이다. (A)는 적용시키다, (B)는 목적어로 'A to B' 형식을 취해 'A를 B로 전달하다'의 뜻으로 사용한다. (D)는 주로 흡연 등의 행위를 허락하거나, '사람 to 부정사' 형태를 취하는 5형식 동사로 사용된다.

PLUS

- 특정 명사를 목적어로 취하는 동사는 다음과 같다.

3형식 동사	목적어	예
attend, host, hold, organize, postpone	행사 명	meeting, seminar, session
inform, assure, notify, remind, advise, train	사람, 회사	Mr. Kim, GW, Inc., the company
attract, welcome	사람	customer, visitors
express 나타내다	감정, 견해	view, concern, thanks
show, present, produce 제시하다	티켓, 신분증	a visitor pass
release, launch, unveil	제품, 영화, 책	product, movie, book
conduct 수행하다	인터뷰, 견학	interview, tour
assume, take 떠맡다	자리	position, duty, responsibility
meet, fulfill, satisfy, accommodate	요구사항	needs, requirement
complete, fill out 채우다, 작성하다	과정, 신청서	application form, evaluation 평가
visit, enter, reach, contact	장소, 방, 회사	the office
announce	계획, 은퇴, 합병, 확장	plan, retirement, expansion
attain 달성하다, exceed, surpass 초과하다	목표	aim, goal
seek	충고, 사람	advice
take	조치	steps, measures
follow, comply with 준수하다	규정	rules, regulations

- 빈칸 앞에 be가 있고 보기들이 모두 p.p.일 경우는 주어와의 어울림을 따진다.

  The meeting will be (attended/expressed) by many participants.

  ➜ 주어인 meeting을 목적어라고 생각하고 대입한다. '미팅에 참석하다'가 어울리므로 attended가 답이다.

- 사람을 목적어로 취하는 '인어노리' 동사는 3, 4형식의 기능을 모두 갖는다.

  인어노리(inform, assure, notify, remind) 동사 + 사람 명사 + of 사물 명사 → 3형식

  ex) He informed me of his decision.

  인어노리(inform, assure, notify, remind) 동사 + 사람 명사 that S + V → 4형식

  ex) He informed me that he had decided.

함정을 피해 봐
실제 강의에서만 알려주는 풀이 노하우!

1. '말하다' 유형 동사의 쓰임에 조심한다.

Please (inform/say/talk/speak) me when I can find the book.

➜ 모두 '말하다'의 뜻이 있으나 talk나 speak는 주로 1형식 동사로 쓰이기 때문에 뒤에 목적어를 갖지 못한다. say는 3형식 동사이며, '주지를 나타내는 말'을 목적어로 갖는다. 위의 문장에서 me가 간접목적어, when ~ book이 직접목적어이므로 4형식 동사의 기능이 있는 inform이 답이다.

1. inform

STEP 3 실전에 적용해 봐

1. The city council has decided to do some advertising to ------- the nonsmoking campaign.

    (A) impose
    (B) admit
    (C) intervene
    (D) promote

2. Alpa Productions plans to ------- an experienced operations manager to increase its productivity.

    (A) hire
    (B) access
    (C) identify
    (D) enroll

3. To proceed to the platform, you must ------- your passport and ticket to the staff member near the gate.

    (A) present
    (B) confirm
    (C) analyze
    (D) place

4. The computer engineer ------- the software program which increased the amount of protection against viruses on the company's computers.

    (A) permitted
    (B) sustained
    (C) trained
    (D) installed

5. Because Shoppin' Spree announced it was having a clearance sale, it was packed with customers who came to ------- the items being sold at discounted prices.

    (A) fulfill
    (B) delay
    (C) purchase
    (D) replace

6. The farewell party for Mr. Lim, who is retiring from Lean, Inc., will be ------- next Saturday at a restaurant near the company building.

    (A) held
    (B) expected
    (C) supported
    (D) maintained

7. The charity National Support Foundation ------- its gratitude to the donors who helped raise the desired amount of funds this year.

    (A) expressed
    (B) allowed
    (C) encouraged
    (D) acknowledged

8. In preparation for the next concert, the New York Orchestra Club plans to ------- extra stage managers.

    (A) allow
    (B) recruit
    (C) submit
    (D) enlarge

9. In order to maintain the current margin, most retail stores had to ------- the cost of groceries, of which production has been largely affected by a recent flood.

    (A) build
    (B) sustain
    (C) increase
    (D) propose

10. The human resources manager will be ------- an orientation for the new employees on the company's policies and rules next week.

    (A) interacting
    (B) learning
    (C) leading
    (D) rejecting

출제율 33%

법칙 72 특정 전치사와 잘 어울리는 3형식 동사

add와 obtain 중 목적어 뒤에 from이 오는 동사는 obtain이다. add는 덧붙이는 것이므로 '~를 ~쪽으로 덧붙이다'가 된다. 이처럼 add는 'A to B'를 좋아하고, obtain은 'A from B'를 좋아하는데, 이와 같이 전치사와의 어울림을 확인하면 동사 어휘 문제를 보다 쉽게 풀 수 있다.

STEP 1 유형을 파악해 봐

1. It will require more funds to ------- a dirt road into the paved one in the city.
   (A) convert   (B) relocate   (C) produce   (D) construct

2. Heavy traffic should not ------- the items from being delivered on time.
   (A) commence   (B) rush   (C) prevent   (D) achieve

3. The opening of the exhibition will be ------- until further notice.
   (A) proposed   (B) suggested   (C) defined   (D) postponed

보기가 모두 서로 다른 동사들로 왔으므로 동사 어휘 문제임을 알 수 있다. 3번 문제의 보기들은 수동태지만 이것도 역시 동사 어휘 문제라고 할 수 있다. 빈칸 뒤 목적어에는 모두 전치사가, 즉 1번 문제는 into, 2번 문제는 from, 3번 문제는 until이 왔다. 이러한 경우 동사가 어떤 전치사를 좋아하는지 알면 문제의 정답을 보다 쉽게 고를 수 있다.

STEP 2 이렇게 풀어 봐   "유형을 파악해 봐" 1번 문제를 보세요!

첫째 3형식 자리인지 확인한다.
빈칸 뒤에 목적어가 왔으므로 3형식 동사를 고르는 문제이며, 보기들 역시 모두 3형식 동사들이다.

둘째 목적어와의 어울림을 확인한다.
목적어인 a dirt road 뒤에 into가 보이는 것으로 보아 'A into B'로 쓸 수 있는 동사를 고르는 문제이다. (A)가 오면 'A를 B로 바꾸다, 개조하다'의 뜻으로 자연스럽다. (B)는 'A to B'로 사용하며, 'A를 B로 이전시키다'의 뜻이 된다. (C)와 (D)는 딱히 전치사와의 어울림은 없으며, (C)는 제품을 목적어로, (D)는 건물을 목적어로 취하는 동사이다.

PLUS

• 특정 전치사와 친한 3형식 동사는 다음과 같다.

전치사 어울림	3형식 동사
A to B	덧붙이다: add, attach, affix 보내다: send, submit, return, donate, forward, direct (be directed to로 주로 사용) 기타: attribute A의 원인을 B로 돌리다, escort, limit, restore, transfer, apply
A from B	획득, 제거: obtain, collect, order, purchase, remove 막다: prohibit, prevent, keep, discourage A가 B하지 못하게 막다
A into B	진출: expand ('expand into 명사'로도 사용), load A를 B로 싣다 변환: convert, process 가공처리하다
A for B	이유: compensate, reimburse, reward, commend, congratulate, prefer A를 B 때문에 좋아하다 대상: substitute B 대신 A를 쓰다, exchange A for B A와 B를 교환하다, check (check for로도 사용), 　　　schedule A를 B로 일정 잡다
A with B	공급: replace A와 B를 교체하다, provide, equip A에게 B를 갖춰주다(= provide B to A) 　　　outfit, personalize 동반: take, bring B가 A를 지참하다, share A with B A를 B와 공유하다 기타: personalize A를 B로 자신의 기호에 맞추다
A on B	congratulate A on B A를 B에 대해 축하하다, base, focus (주로 수동태로 사용)
A until B	postpone A를 B까지 연기하다

함정을 피해 봐   실제 강의에서만 알려주는 풀이 노하우!

1. provide의 여러 용법에 주의한다.
   ➡ provide는 'A with B'로 뿐만 아니라, provide B to A로 쓸 수도 있는데, 이것이 수동태가 되면 'B is provided to A'이며, 'provided to A'는 'A에게 제공된'이란 뜻이다. equip은 'A with B'로만 쓰기 때문에 정답이 될 수 없다.

1. provided

STEP 3 실전에 적용해 봐

1. The flight attendants at Best Flight Air were ------- for taking appropriate measures during the emergency situation they recently had during a flight.

   (A) claimed
   (B) asked
   (C) entitled
   (D) commended

2. All customer inquiries about how to use the product should be ------- to the customer service office.

   (A) indicated
   (B) referred
   (C) directed
   (D) pointed

3. As Mr. Daniels kept receiving letters written for the previous owners of his house, he called them to have their old address ------- from various mailing lists.

   (A) removed
   (B) brought
   (C) forwarded
   (D) alternated

4. Please ------- the supplies to the supply room once you are done using them.

   (A) return
   (B) abandon
   (C) refer
   (D) inform

5. The CEO of Jerome, Inc., a venture company with over one billion dollars in net profits, ------- its success to the current era of IT.

   (A) explains
   (B) expects
   (C) predicts
   (D) attributes

6. Ms. Harrington will be ------- for Mr. Skully while he is away attending the council meeting for two weeks.

   (A) managing
   (B) reporting
   (C) substituting
   (D) appointing

7. All attendants at the upcoming Excel training courses will be required to ------- their own devices to the class to run the program on.

   (A) hold
   (B) bring
   (C) install
   (D) develop

8. Jane Beauty Parlor had broken stools, which should have been ------- with new ones.

   (A) called
   (B) gathered
   (C) replaced
   (D) proceeded

9. All of the employees are required to ------- their reports on their sales performances to their immediate supervisors every quarter.

   (A) submit
   (B) inform
   (C) receive
   (D) postpone

10. Those working overnight shifts this week have to ------- the staff room with the security guards.

    (A) permit
    (B) allow
    (C) relocate
    (D) share

출제율 21%

법칙 73 to 부정사나 동명사, 명사절을 목적어로 하는 3형식 동사

3형식 동사는 기본적으로 명사나 대명사를 목적어로 취하지만, 동명사를 목적어로 취하는 동사, to 부정사를 목적어로 취하는 동사, 명사절을 목적어로 취하는 동사는 따로 있다. 예를 들어 enjoy는 뒤에 동명사는 올 수 있으나 to 부정사나 명사절은 올 수 없다.

유형을 파악해 봐

1. Ms. Devon ------- to see her doctor immediately because of the pain in her back.
(A) requires   (B) wishes   (C) mind   (D) provides

2. The therapist ------- exercising for at least an hour every day.
(A) announced   (B) explained   (C) recommended (D) claimed

3. The CEO of Genome, Inc. ------- that the company is now in a critical situation.
(A) secured   (B) allowed   (C) announced   (D) occurred

보기가 모두 서로 다른 동사로 왔으므로 동사 어휘 문제이다. 1번 문제는 목적어로 to 부정사가 있고, 2번 문제는 동명사, 3번 문제는 명사절이 목적어로 왔다.

이렇게 풀어 봐   "유형을 파악해 봐" 1번 문제를 보세요!

첫째 3형식 자리인지 확인한다.
빈칸 뒤에 to 부정사가 있지만 이것이 수식어인지 목적어인지 혼동될 수 있으므로 보기를 확인한다. 보기들이 모두 3형식 동사들로 왔으므로 to 부정사는 목적어로 볼 수 있다.

둘째 목적어와의 어울림을 확인한다.
보기 중에 to 부정사를 목적어로 취하는 동사를 찾는다. (B)는 want나 would like to와 마찬가지로 to 부정사를 목적어로 취하는 동사이므로 정답이 된다. (A)는 to 부정사를 목적 보어로 갖는 5형식 동사로 사용되거나 'that S+V 명사절'을 목적어로 취하는 3형식 동사이다. (C)는 동명사를 목적어로 취하는 3형식 동사, (D)는 특정 전치사와의 어울림이 있는 3형식 동사이다. (A with B)

PLUS

- to 부정사나 동명사, 명사절을 목적어로 취하는 3형식 동사는 다음과 같다.

동명사를 목적어로	to 부정사를 목적어로
'회장아들' 동사 ('법칙 59' 참고) enjoy, mind, give up, admit, advocate, include, suggest, recommend, consider, avoid, postpone, put off, finish, stop, discontinue	'응큼쟁이' 동사 ('법칙 58' 참고) want, would like, wish, hope, expect, strive, agree, refuse, decide, promise, plan, intend

명사절을 목적어로	참고: to 부정사가 목적 보어 → 5형식 동사
'생말예제' 동사 생각하다: think, believe, assume, see, find 말하다: state, stress, indicate, announce, explain, add, point out, ensure, caution 예측하다: predict, project, expect, anticipate 제안하다: request, recommend, suggest	'결혼승낙' 동사 ('법칙 48' 참고) 희망: want, would like, expect 요청: ask, require, request, remind, instruct, invite 설득: persuade, force, urge, encourage 허락: allow, permit, enable

- '응큼쟁이' 동사와 '결혼승낙' 동사가 모두 가능한 동사들이 있다

want, expect, ask, intend → I want to go. I want you to go.
* help (to 생략 가능) → I help (to) go. I help you (to) go.

- 목적어로 둘 또는 세 가지 형태가 모두 가능한 동사들이 있다.

동명사와 to 부정사	love, hate, attempt, begin, start, like, need, continue
to 부정사와 명사절	hope, wish, expect, agree, decide, promise, ask, guarantee
동명사와 명사절	admit, suggest, recommend, require, anticipate, allow
to 부정사, 동명사, 명사절	regret, remember, forget, propose

함정을 피해 봐
실제 강의에서만 알려주는 풀이 노하우!

1. '결혼승낙' 동사와 '응큼쟁이' 동사를 혼동해서는 안 된다.
Even though he was late for the movie, Mr. Kim (wanted/allowed) to enter the theater.
→ allow가 to와 잘 어울릴 것 같다는 생각으로만 정답을 고를 경우 실수하기 쉽다. allow는 to 부정사를 목적 보어로 취하는 동사('결혼승낙' 동사)이지, to 부정사를 목적어로 취하는 동사('응큼쟁이' 동사)가 아니다.

1. wanted

STEP 3 실전에 적용해 봐

1. The board members ------- to make a deal with Flex Production, Inc. in order to let Flex Production produce their products.

   (A) decided
   (B) rejected
   (C) informed
   (D) reviewed

2. Ms. Miller will not ------- helping you with organizing the list of guests for the upcoming seminar because she has some time to spare now.

   (A) allow
   (B) follow
   (C) pursue
   (D) mind

3. Judging from reports, Graham, Inc. ------- to hire 10 more employees this year to fill vacancies in the Personnel Department.

   (A) relies
   (B) guarantees
   (C) regards
   (D) intends

4. After reviewing the reports on the business plans of other companies, the council members ------- that the competition on the market will become fiercer next year.

   (A) anticipated
   (B) requested
   (C) arranged
   (D) allowed

5. The unexpected job offer from Solutions Tech surprised Ms. Taylor, who never ------- working at another IT company.

   (A) allowed
   (B) considered
   (C) witnessed
   (D) ensured

6. In order to become a member, you must first ------- to pay the annual membership fee, which costs $10.

   (A) permit
   (B) reply
   (C) agree
   (D) ask

7. Ms. Browski needs to revise her report as she has been asked to ------- that her research was sponsored by Canol, Inc.

   (A) review
   (B) specify
   (C) allow
   (D) proceed

8. This business plan has to be reviewed by the Accounting Department to ------- that it will not exceed the budget.

   (A) ensure
   (B) expect
   (C) agree
   (D) recommend

9. Despite being a partner company with Royal, Inc., Genuine Solutions ------- to hand over its customer database information to Royal, Inc.

   (A) accepted
   (B) permitted
   (C) suggested
   (D) refused

10. Regardless of how much time has passed since the meeting began, the attendees ------- discussing the problems raised during the meeting.

    (A) confirmed
    (B) continued
    (C) reminded
    (D) organized

출제율 19%

법칙 74 '자동사+전치사' 묶음

'~를 다루다'라는 우리말 뜻은 영어로 deal with일까, handle with일까? handle은 전치사 with 없이도 deal with와 같은 뜻을 갖는다. 이처럼 전치사와 함께 덩어리로 쓰이는 동사들이 있는데, 이를 '자동사+전치사' 묶음 혹은 '덩어리 동사'로 부르기로 하자. 'I deal with the problem.'은 deal with가 덩어리이므로 3형식 문장이 된다.

STEP 1 유형을 파악해 봐

1. The total costs of office renovations are very roughly calculated, so you should ------- on improving the accuracy of the calculation.
   (A) focus   (B) quit   (C) determine   (D) join

2. The Instar Corporation will cover all of the expenses for employees who ------- in the workshop program.
   (A) record   (B) advise   (C) enroll   (D) explain

3. Those who ------- for the class this week will receive 30% discounts.
   (A) promise   (B) finish   (C) skip   (D) register

보기가 모두 서로 다른 동사들로 왔으므로 동사 어휘 문제이다. 보기들 중 일부는 전치사와 덩어리로 움직이는 동사들이다. 덩어리 동사들을 많이 알고 있는 수험생들이라면 쉽게 풀 수 있는 문제들이다.

STEP 2 이렇게 풀어 봐

"유형을 파악해 봐" 1번 문제를 보세요!

첫째 빈칸 뒤 전치사를 확인한다.
빈칸 뒤에 온 on과 함께 덩어리로 쓸 수 있는 (A) focus가 정답이다.

둘째 빈칸 주변의 해석으로 점검해 마무리한다.
세부사항에 집중해야 한다. focus on은 '~에 집중하다'는 의미로 자연스럽게 해석이 되므로 정답이다.

PLUS

• 빈출 '자동사+전치사' 묶음은 다음과 같다.

to	lead to ~한 결과를 낳다 react to ~에 반응하다 refer to ~를 참고하다 reply to ~에 응답하다 respond to ~에 응답하다 object to ~를 반대하다 subscribe to ~를 정기 구독하다 adhere to ~를 준수하다
with	deal with ~를 다루다 proceed with ~를 진행하다 interfere with ~를 방해하다 interact with ~와 상호작용하다 agree with ~에게 동의하다 comply with ~를 준수하다 contend with ~와 다투다 coincide with 동시에 일어나다, 일치하다, 부합하다 cope with ~에 대처하다, ~을 극복하다 negotiate with ~와 협상하다
for	account for ~를 설명하다 sign up for ~를 등록하다 register for ~를 등록하다 look for ~를 찾다 ask for ~를 요청하다 wait for ~을 기다리다 qualify for ~대해 자격이 되다
of	consist of ~로 구성되다 think of ~를 생각하다 dispose of ~를 처분하다
on	depend on ~에 의존하다 rely on ~에 의존하다 count on ~에 의존하다 rest on ~에 의존하다 comment on ~에 관해 말하다 focus on ~에 집중하다 concentrate on ~에 집중하다
in	result in ~한 결과를 낳다 enroll in ~에 등록하다 engage in ~에 종사하다 specialize in ~를 전공으로 하다 participate in ~에 참여하다 take part in ~에 참여하다 succeed in ~에 성공하다
into	look into ~를 찾다 expand into ~로 진출하다
about	think about ~에 관해 생각하다 inquire about ~에 관해 질문하다
from	result from ~로부터 결과가 오다 abstain from ~을 자제하다 refrain from ~을 자제하다 suffer from ~로부터 끙끙 앓다
around	look around ~를 둘러보다
against	compete against ~와 경쟁하다 fight against ~에 대항해 싸우다
by	come by ~에 잠깐 들르다 drop by ~에 잠깐 들르다 stop by ~에 잠깐 들르다 abide by ~을 따르다, 지키다
through	get through ~을 끝마치다 go through ~을 겪다 look through ~를 훑어보다
after	look after ~을 돌보다
at	look at ~을 보다 stare at ~를 보다 glance at ~를 힐끗 보다 gaze at ~를 보다 smile at ~에 대해 미소짓다
over	look over ~을 검토하다

함정을 피해 봐

실제 강의에서만 알려주는 풀이 노하우!

1. 덩어리 동사들은 수동태가 되어도 전치사가 남고, 이어서 부사나 전명구가 온다.

The knives are sharp object and should be (dealt/handled) with great care.
→ dealt가 답이 되려면 with 뒤에 부사나 전명구가 와야 한다. with great care는 '매우 조심해서'의 뜻.

2. 전치사 to와 to 부정사의 to를 혼동하지 않도록 한다.

The company will (decide/react) to changes in consumer demands.
→ decide to로만 기억한 경우 틀리기 쉬운 문제이다. 'decide to 동사원형, react to 명사'로 외워두자.

1. handled 2. react

STEP 3 실전에 적용해 봐

1. Since Mr. Reynolds is on vacation, he may not be able to ------- to your reply immediately.

   (A) respond
   (B) promise
   (C) send
   (D) submit

2. The annual city parade held on 7th Avenue ------- for the heavy traffic jam from 6th Avenue to 14th Street.

   (A) holds
   (B) accounts
   (C) delays
   (D) causes

3. If you change the address of the recipient, it may ------- in the delay of the delivery of the items ordered.

   (A) result
   (B) cause
   (C) complete
   (D) lead

4. Ms. Manning has to decide to attend either her co-worker's wedding or the seminar as their dates and times ------- with one another.

   (A) comply
   (B) change
   (C) coincide
   (D) interrupt

5. Reliable Investment has led the industry for 34 years as it ------- in investment counseling and customer management.

   (A) specifies
   (B) determines
   (C) nominates
   (D) specializes

6. Working as a project manager at the Grace Company provides an opportunity to ------- with people in various professions at different firms.

   (A) familiarize
   (B) respond
   (C) hire
   (D) interact

7. Mr. Rodriguez should finish his work and be ready to head to the conference room in order to ------- in the dinner meeting.

   (A) attend
   (B) participate
   (C) serve
   (D) join

8. Applicants with more than 3 years of experience in a relevant field ------- for the technical support engineer position.

   (A) dedicate
   (B) qualify
   (C) appoint
   (D) accept

9. Geneva, Inc. is still in the process of ------- with the contractor regarding the shipping costs of the supplies.

   (A) allocating
   (B) agreeing
   (C) negotiating
   (D) suggesting

10. The manager is responsible for training the new construction workers to ------- with the safety rules.

    (A) comply
    (B) refer
    (C) oppose
    (D) endorse

출제율 32%

법칙 75 '------ + 목적어 + 목적 보어'이면 5형식 동사

'I made him happy. (나는 그를 행복하게 만들었다.)'와 같은 문장을 5형식 문장이라고 하는데, 여기서 happy는 목적어인 him을 보충해 주는 역할을 하므로 목적 보어이다. 5형식 문장에서 목적 보어에는 형용사뿐만 아니라 '-ing, p.p., to 부정사, 동사원형, 명사, as + 명사' 등이 올 수 있는데, 어떤 형태의 목적 보어가 오느냐는 동사에 따라 달라질 수 있다.

STEP 1 유형을 파악해 봐

1. Mr. Grimes's improved performance ------ the manager pleased.
   (A) made   (B) become   (C) cause   (D) suggest

2. The company policy that outlines appropriate use of company vehicle ------ all employees safe.
   (A) prevents   (B) explains   (C) keeps   (D) states

3. The store's extended hours ------ customers to order meals 24/7.
   (A) accept   (B) request   (C) encourage   (D) allow

보기가 모두 서로 다른 동사들로 왔고, 각 문제의 보기에 5형식 동사가 섞여 있는 것으로 보아 어휘 문제임을 알 수 있다. 한편, 빈칸 뒤에는 목적어가 있고, 이어 목적 보어로 쓰일 수 있는 요소들이 함께 왔다. 1번 문제의 경우는 p.p., 2번 문제의 경우는 형용사, 3번 문제의 경우는 to 부정사가 목적 보어 역할을 하고 있다.

STEP 2 이렇게 풀어 봐

"유형을 파악해 봐" 1번 문제를 보세요!

첫째 목적어가 있는지 확인한다.
빈칸 뒤의 the manager가 목적어이므로 2형식 동사인 become은 탈락한다.

둘째 목적어 뒤에 있는 요소를 확인한 후 올바른 형태의 동사를 넣어 해석해 본다.
목적어 뒤의 pleased는 '기쁘게 된'이란 뜻의 p.p.(과거분사)이다. 5형식 문장에서는 목적어 뒤에 목적 보어로 p.p.가 올 수 있으므로 보기 중 5형식 동사인 (A)를 대입해 해석해 본다. '향상된 업무수행능력이 매니저를 기쁘게 했다.'는 해석이 자연스럽기 때문에 정답이 된다. (C)는 5형식 동사로 사용할 경우 목적 보어 자리에 to 부정사를 쓰는 동사이며, (D)는 동명사나 명사절을 목적어로 취하는 3형식 동사이다.

PLUS

• 자주 출제되는 5형식 동사는 다음과 같다. (기출 빈도 반영)

5형식 동사	목적어	목적 보어	대표 예문
'결혼승낙' 동사 ('법칙 48' 참고)	명사	to 동사원형	I want you to go.
help (※ assist는 to가 반드시 필요)	명사	(to) 동사원형	I help you (to) go.
'막가파' 동사: make, keep, find, hold, leave	명사	형용사, p.p., -ing	I found him happy[hired, sleeping].
consider, choose, name, elect	명사	(as) 명사	I consider him (as) a teacher.
regard, designate	명사	as 명사	I regard him as a teacher.
call, make	명사	명사	Please call me David.
사역동사: make, let, have	명사	동사원형, p.p.	I'll let you go.　I'll have my car fixed.
준사역동사: get	명사	to 동사원형, p.p.	I'll get you to go. I'll get the job done.
지각동사: see, hear, feel	명사	동사원형, -ing, p.p.	I saw him sleep[sleeping, hired].

• make는 목적 보어로 -ing 형태가 아닌 동사원형을 쓴다. 그러나 감정분사('법칙 49' 참고)는 -ing가 가능하다.

The manager made his assistant (working/work) harder by pushing him.　→ -ing는 안됨

The main actor's speech and behavior made the movie (interesting/interested).　→ interesting은 형용사 추급

➡ make는 -ing 대신 동사원형을 목적 보어로 취하는 반면, 감정분사는 형용사로 취급하므로 -ing도 가능하다.

 함정을 피해 봐　　실제 강의에서만 알려주는 풀이 노하우!

1. 다양한 형식으로 쓰이는 '인어노리' 동사에 주의한다.

The manager (reminded/recalled) his assistant to copy the agenda for the meeting.

➡ '인어노리' 동사('법칙 71' 참고) 중 remind, convince, advise는 '결혼승낙' 동사('법칙 48' 참고)도 가능하다. remind는 '결혼승낙' 동사도 가능하므로 목적보어에 to 부정사가 오면 5형식 문장이 된다.

1. reminded

STEP 3 실전에 적용해 봐

1. The express train ------- Mr. Kerning arrive in Kenmore on time so that he could attend the regional seminar.

   (A) appointed
   (B) transported
   (C) kept
   (D) helped

2. After careful consideration, the executive manager ------- Mr. Will as the executive manager who will take the job after he retires.

   (A) explained
   (B) appointed
   (C) requested
   (D) ordered

3. The Kashi Corporation ------- Mr. McKay use the company automobile to drive to the airport in order to pick up his foreign client.

   (A) let
   (B) kept
   (C) caused
   (D) accepted

4. Volume Music ------- its customers to use its streaming service for $10 per month.

   (A) rejects
   (B) accepts
   (C) enables
   (D) confirms

5. ------- a venue appropriate for the dean's retirement party is harder than expected since all the places I have called are fully booked.

   (A) Looking
   (B) Finding
   (C) Keeping
   (D) Allowing

6. Since the regular security check was scheduled to be held next Wednesday, the manager ------- all of the employees to be aware of it.

   (A) reminded
   (B) recalled
   (C) allowed
   (D) promised

7. Ms. Packard ------- Mr. Watanabi about the appointment that he wanted to reschedule.

   (A) allowed
   (B) called
   (C) permitted
   (D) designated

8. Ms. Jenkins had to receive a call from her boss, so she ------- Mr. Olson waiting at the door when he visited her house.

   (A) left
   (B) enabled
   (C) caused
   (D) rejected

9. After the votes were cast, Ms. Pill was ------- as the next member of the board.

   (A) arranged
   (B) allowed
   (C) elected
   (D) destined

10. Since the customer requested a consultation on the investment program, Bridge Solutions ------- David Kean to be his personal counselor.

    (A) encouraged
    (B) inspected
    (C) applied
    (D) designated

출제율 26%

법칙 76 목적어가 없으면 1형식 동사

'I go. I work. I live.'와 같이 주어와 동사만 있는 문장을 1형식이라고 한다. 1형식 문장 뒤에는 부사, 전명구, to부정사의 부사적 용법, 부사절과 같은 부사류만 올 수 있고, 목적어는 올 수 없다. 1형식 동사는 주로 '가다, 오다, 있다'의 뜻을 가진 동사들이 주를 이룬다.

STEP 1 유형을 파악해 봐

1. You should find the shortest way to the airport as your flight will ------- at 7 A.M.
   (A) transport   (B) appoint   (C) depart   (D) travel

2. Your membership needs to be renewed since it ------- next week.
   (A) rejects   (B) confirms   (C) assigns   (D) expires

3. Additional traveling expenses ------- after Mr. Bowman visited Norman Island, which was not included in his plan.
   (A) approved   (B) occurred   (C) involved   (D) encountered

보기가 모두 서로 다른 동사로 왔으므로 동사 어휘 문제들이다. 보기 중에는 1형식 동사들이 하나 이상 섞여 있고, 빈칸 뒤에는 부사류가 있다.

STEP 2 이렇게 풀어 봐
"유형을 파악해 봐" 1번 문제를 보세요!

첫째 빈칸 뒤 성분을 확인한다.
빈칸 뒤에 전명구가 있다. 전명구는 수식어이므로 이를 제외시키면 빈칸은 1형식 동사 자리이다. 3형식 동사인 (A)와 (B)는 탈락하고, (C)와 (D)는 1형식 동사이다.

둘째 주어와의 어울림을 확인한다.
your flight이 주어이며, '비행기가 출발하다'라는 말이 자연스러우므로 (C)가 정답이다. (D)는 '여행하다'라는 뜻으로 주어와 어울리지 않는다.

PLUS

- 1형식 동사는 다음과 같다.

가다	go, swim, fly, run, walk, proceed, depart, leave, emerge, disappear, rise, increase, peak, start, begin, commence	부사류: 부사: I go **quickly**. 전명구: I go **to the place**. to 부정사의 부사적 용법: I go **to meet her**. 부사절: I go **because you come**.
오다	come, arrive, get, appear, commute, fall, decrease, decline, drop, end, expire, happen, occur, take place	
있다	exist, stay, live, stand, sit, wait, last, work, collaborate, labor, serve, function, compete	

 **함정을 피해 봐**   실제 강의에서만 알려주는 풀이 노하우!

1. 1형식 동사로 생각하지 못했던 동사들에 유의해야 하며, 역시 뒤에 부사류가 온다.

act charitably 자비롭게 행동하다   fall behind considerably 상당히 뒤처지다
dress warmly 옷을 따뜻하게 입다   grow well 잘 성장하다
perform well 잘 기능하다   break down 고장이 나다   deliberate 숙고하다

2. 3형식으로도 쓰이는 1형식 동사와 전치사와의 어울림이 좋은 1형식 동사를 조심한다.

resume 다시 시작하다   reopen 다시 열다   double 두 배가 되다
take over 떠맡다   vary 다양하다   approach 접근하다

report to ~에게 보고하다   revert to ~로 돌아가다   return to ~로 복귀하다
relocate to ~로 이전하다   evolve into ~로 진화하다

STEP 3 실전에 적용해 봐

1. Please make sure you finish the first draft of your report today since the deadline for the submission of the final draft is quickly -------.

   (A) confirming
   (B) informing
   (C) declaring
   (D) approaching

2. The construction of the Riverside Bridge is scheduled to ------- on July 13 once the plans are approved by the city officials.

   (A) commence
   (B) expect
   (C) arrange
   (D) proceed

3. The sales director announced that the number of clients ------- after the company introduced its new counseling service.

   (A) regarded
   (B) released
   (C) doubled
   (D) provided

4. The renovations on the local convention center will be done a month later than planned since a problem with the drainage system has -------.

   (A) emerged
   (B) assisted
   (C) revealed
   (D) introduced

5. Although it took more than five years, a small group meeting on electronic engineering ------- into a startup technical support company.

   (A) encountered
   (B) evolved
   (C) arranged
   (D) allowed

6. Ms. Nevada is expected to ------- the CFO position as she received the highest number of votes in a recent poll.

   (A) retire from
   (B) take over
   (C) sign up
   (D) give up

7. The cost of delivery may ------- depending on your region, and an additional fee will be charged for delivery to remote areas.

   (A) charge
   (B) provide
   (C) arrange
   (D) vary

8. A written notice stating the approximate date when the office renovations will ------- is posted on the bulletin board next to the main gate.

   (A) offer
   (B) undergo
   (C) resume
   (D) plan

9. The amateur author ------- before making an announcement that he would welcome any criticism on his novels to improve his writing style.

   (A) rejected
   (B) allowed
   (C) offended
   (D) deliberated

10. To commemorate its 50th year in the automobile industry, Chez Auto introduced its new car model, ------- with Velocity Vehicles.

    (A) collaborating
    (B) supplying
    (C) providing
    (D) encountering

법칙 77 목적어가 2개면 4형식 동사

'I gave you a pen. (나는 너에게 펜을 주었다.)'와 같은 문장을 4형식 문장이라고 하며, 2개의 목적어를 갖는다. 4형식 동사들은 give, offer, send, bring 등 대부분 '주다'의 뜻을 가진 동사들이 주를 이룬다.

STEP 1 유형을 파악해 봐

1. Manning's Retail Shop has ------- Daisy Manufacturing a one-year contract.
(A) offered   (B) lent   (C) accessed   (D) produced

2. The manager ------- the customer management team access to the customer database.
(A) arranged   (B) induced   (C) granted   (D) allocated

3. Please ------- all staff members that the fashion show has been cancelled.
(A) inform   (B) note   (C) introduce   (D) refer

보기가 모두 서로 다른 동사들로 왔으므로 동사 어휘 문제이다. 보기들 중에는 4형식 동사들이 1개 이상 섞여 있고, 빈칸 뒤에는 목적어가 왔다.

STEP 2 이렇게 풀어 봐   "유형을 파악해 봐" 1번 문제를 보세요!

첫째 빈칸 뒤 성분을 확인한다.
빈칸 뒤에 온 Daisy Manufacturing과 a one-year contract는 둘 다 목적어이다. 목적어가 2개이므로 4형식 동사가 아닌 것은 탈락시킨다. (C), (D)는 3형식 동사이다.

둘째 보기들을 대입해 해석으로 어울림을 확인한다.
'1년짜리 계약을 제안하다.'가 자연스러우므로 (A)가 정답이다. '계약을 빌려주었다.'는 말은 어색하므로 (B)는 정답이 될 수 없다.

PLUS

- 4형식 동사는 다음과 같다.

give	offer	send	bring	grant	award	win	get	allow	assign
issue	cause	fax	show	tell	cost	lend	charge	make	

- 4형식은 3형식으로 전환이 가능하다.

  I gave him a pen. → I gave a pen (to him).

- '인어노리' 동사('법칙 71' 참고)는 직접목적어 자리에 명사절이 오기도 한다.

  I informed him **that I would leave soon**.

함정을 피해 봐 — 실제 강의에서만 알려주는 풀이 노하우!

1. 4형식 동사라고 생각하지 못했던 동사들을 조심한다.

Ms. Kim's exceptional sales performance last quarter (won/honored) her a paid vacation.

→ won을 win의 과거시제로 생각해 '이기다'라는 뜻의 1형식이나 '얻다'라는 뜻의 3형식 동사로만 알고 있는 경우가 많다. 그러나 위의 문장은 목적어가 2개이므로 4형식 동사이며, '그녀가 유급휴가를 받을 수 있게 해 주었다.'라는 뜻으로 사용되었다.

STEP 3 실전에 적용해 봐

1. It was Ms. Knight's report that ------- her a Nobel Prize and increased global public awareness of the fundraising campaign.

   (A) announced
   (B) achieved
   (C) distributed
   (D) won

2. Make sure you ------- Mr. Miller's client that he will not be in his office from tomorrow to next Tuesday because of his business trip.

   (A) ask
   (B) respond
   (C) notify
   (D) propose

3. If you are over 50 years of age with a record of disease, it will ------- you an additional 5% to purchase the insurance.

   (A) pay
   (B) cost
   (C) increase
   (D) allow

4. Upon the patient's request, the nurse ------- him more pain relievers.

   (A) appointed
   (B) brought
   (C) arranged
   (C) referred

5. Since the company's debt rate has been significantly low over the past few years, Local Industrial Bank ------- Prospect Energy more money than expected.

   (A) arranged
   (B) asked
   (C) announced
   (D) lent

6. The Embassy of Mexico ------- Mr. Azrek a work visa which allows him to stay in Mexico for 6 months.

   (A) issued
   (B) referred
   (C) arranged
   (D) received

7. After Ms. Frisen introduced herself to all of the employees around, she was ------- her seat in the marketing team office.

   (A) signed
   (B) seated
   (C) assigned
   (D) acquired

8. On his first day at the region's daily newspaper, Mr. Clark was ------- two articles he had to compare and told to find any misspelled words in them.

   (A) allowed
   (B) written
   (C) referred
   (D) shown

9. According to our company's policy, employees may be ------- a special leave during which they are excused from work for up to 15 days under certain circumstances.

   (A) excused
   (B) awarded
   (C) included
   (D) informed

10. Relish Dining ------- its customers that it serves only the finest cuisines made with the freshest ingredients.

    (A) assures
    (B) provides
    (C) grants
    (D) serves

출제율 4%

법칙 78 보어 자리에 형용사나 동격의 명사가 있으면 2형식 동사

'I am happy.'와 같은 문장을 2형식 문장이라고 하며, 여기서 happy는 주어인 I를 보충해 주기 때문에 보어이다. 'I am a boy.'에서 a boy도 보어인데, 이 경우 a boy는 주어인 I와 서로 같은 동격의 관계에 있다. 동사로 쓰인 am의 기본형은 be이고, be와 같은 동사를 2형식 동사라고 한다. 2형식 동사에는 become, remain 등이 있다.

STEP 1 유형을 파악해 봐

1. Film cameras ------- obsolete once digital cameras were introduced.
(A) managed (B) allowed (C) became (D) required

2. It was too late when Ms. Pope realized something ------- wrong with the operation.
(A) had proved (B) had answered (C) had questioned (D) had gone

3. The tangled power cords ------- to be problematic as they are causing the power supply to the entire building to be unstable.
(A) promise (B) seem (C) allow (D) require

보기가 모두 서로 다른 동사들로 왔으므로 동사 어휘 문제이다. 보기 중에는 3형식 동사뿐만 아니라 2형식 동사들이 1개 섞여 있으며, 빈칸 뒤에는 목적어는 없고 형용사가 있다.

STEP 2 이렇게 풀어 봐

"유형을 파악해 봐" 1번 문제를 보세요!

첫째 빈칸 뒤 성분을 확인한다.

빈칸 뒤에 온 obsolete는 형용사이므로 빈칸은 형용사를 보어로 취하는 2형식 동사 자리이다. (C)가 2형식 동사이므로 정답이다. (A)는 3형식 동사, (B)와 (D)는 3, 5형식 동사들이다.

둘째 동사를 대입해 해석으로 어울림을 확인한다.

'디지털 카메라가 도입되자 필름 카메라들은 쓸모 없는 상태가 되었다.'라는 해석이 자연스럽다.

PLUS

- 2형식 동사는 다음과 같다.

이다	be, remain, stay
되다	become, get, go, come, turn
숙어	seem (to be), appear (to be) ~인 것처럼 보이다 turn out (to be), prove (to be) 판명되다, remain (to be) seen 두고 볼 일이다
감각 동사	look, smell, taste, sound, feel

함정을 피해 봐
실제 강의에서만 알려주는 풀이 노하우!

1. 형용사 보어인데도 the와 같이 쓰는 경우를 조심한다.

When she revisited the restaurant, Ms. Evans was glad that its location (remained/surrounded) the same as it used to be.

→ the same을 목적어라고 생각해 3형식 동사인 surrounded를 답으로 선택하면 안 된다. the same은 '같은'이란 뜻의 형용사이며, 여기서는 보어로 사용되었다.

2. 명사가 보어로 오는 경우 5형식 동사와 혼동해서는 안 된다.

Attracting millions of visitors every year, Cancun (appears/elects) to be one of the top tourist destinations in Mexico.

→ 'Cancun이 최고의 휴양지로 꼽힌다.'라고 해석해 elects를 답으로 선택하면 틀리며, 'is elected (as)'로 써야 5형식 수동태가 가능해 진다. 여기서는 'Cancun = 최고의 휴양지 중 하나'의 관계이므로 2형식 동사 appears가 답이다.

1. remained 2. appears

STEP 3 실전에 적용해 봐

1. In the keynote speech, Mr. Khan stressed that to make the company's dream ------- true, every employee should have specific, achievable goals.

    (A) follow
    (B) see
    (C) come
    (D) approach

2. Mr. Johnson ------- well after being hospitalized for a broken leg for the past two weeks.

    (A) served
    (B) proceeded
    (C) got
    (D) received

3. It ------- to be seen whether sales during the holiday season this year will exceed those of last year.

    (A) prefers
    (B) decides
    (C) remains
    (D) stays

4. Notwithstanding many tempting merger offers by several other companies, Loyal, Inc. ------- partnered with the LOK Corporation.

    (A) found
    (B) stayed
    (C) terminated
    (D) called

5. The newly installed software has ------- effective at reducing the number of computers infected by viruses.

    (A) arrived
    (B) taken
    (C) proven
    (D) found

6. Ms. Sorenson ------- to be nervous about receiving feedback on her recent proposal from the executive manager.

    (A) returns
    (B) becomes
    (C) appears
    (D) asks

7. Recording over one million sales around the world, the novel *The Game of Swords* ------- one of the bestselling novels in recent times.

    (A) regarded
    (B) maintained
    (C) gained
    (D) became

8. Despite a few attempts to increase employee benefits, Harrisburg, Inc. ------- in the low ranks compared with other firms in terms of employee satisfaction.

    (A) remained
    (B) surrounded
    (C) located
    (D) directed

9. The recently discovered historical remains ------- to be examples of the oldest Roman pottery that had ever been discovered.

    (A) figured out
    (B) turned out
    (C) interested in
    (D) brought out

10. Peer evaluations ------- the essentials in employee performance evaluation.

    (A) remain
    (B) estimate
    (C) accessed
    (D) applied

출제율 168%

법칙 79 보기 중 1개라도 오답 처리해라

지금까지 알아 본 5형식 동사들을 충분히 숙지했다면 형식이 맞지 않는 동사, 예를 들어 빈칸 뒤에 목적어가 있고, 보기 4개 중 1개가 1형식 동사라면 1형식 동사는 바로 오답 처리하면 된다.

STEP 1 유형을 파악해 봐

1. You must ------- your name on the sheet to receive the item delivered to you.
(A) advise   (B) sign   (C) seem   (D) submit

2. Realm Manufacture will ------- the production of goods due to growing demand.
(A) grow   (B) work   (C) report   (D) increase

3. The guest speaker asked for some extra time during his lecture to ------- the audience member's question.
(A) answer   (B) reply   (C) support   (D) repeat

세 문제 모두 빈칸 뒤에 목적어가 있으므로 타동사(3, 4, 5형식 동사)를 필요로 한다. 1번 문제에는 2형식 동사가, 2번 문제에는 1형식 동사가, 3번 문제에는 1형식 동사가 최소 1개 등장하고 있으므로 이들 동사를 오답 처리한다.

STEP 2 이렇게 풀어 봐   "유형을 파악해 봐" 1번 문제를 보세요!

첫째 빈칸 뒤 성분을 확인한 후, 형식에 맞지 않는 동사는 오답 처리한다.
빈칸 뒤에 온 your name은 목적어이므로 목적어를 갖지 않는 1형식이나 2형식 동사는 오답이다. (C)는 2형식 동사이므로 탈락한다. 2형식 동사 뒤에 명사가 오는 경우는 you = your name의 관계일 때 가능하다.

둘째 목적어를 확인한 후, 해석해 답을 고른다.
(B)를 넣고 해석해 보면, '당신에게 배송될 물건을 받으려면 서식에 이름을 적어야 한다.'라는 해석이 자연스럽다. sign one's name은 '서명하다'의 뜻이다.

PLUS

• 동사의 형식은 의미가 결정하므로 한 동사가 여러 의미로 쓰이면 형식도 여러 가지가 된다.

He goes mad. 그는 미쳐 간다. → goes는 여기서 '변해가다'의 뜻이므로 2형식 동사이다.

He worked extended hours. 그는 초과 근무를 했다. → 여기서 work는 '근무하다'는 뜻의 3형식 동사이다.

STEP 3 실전에 적용해 봐

1. Mr. Schmitt requested that his secretary ------- the guest list for the retirement party of the vice-president before sending out invitations.

   (A) compile
   (B) appear
   (C) work
   (D) acknowledge

2. B2B Tech Solutions advised Baycom, Inc. to ------- a new employee benefits plan in order to increase the employees' morale.

   (A) restrict
   (B) confront
   (C) institute
   (D) look

3. To maintain the current safety level, G&W Electronics ------- safety inspections on a regular basis while under the strict supervision of an inspector.

   (A) extends
   (B) appoints
   (C) cancels
   (D) conducts

4. Mr. Kemp's past work experience at Gilson Ltd. where he ------- the managerial job has been acknowledged, and he was offered a better-paid job at Smith's Corp.

   (A) persuaded
   (B) organized
   (C) provided
   (D) assumed

5. The Central Bank of Lithuania announced its plans to ------- small local companies by reducing the interest rates on startup loans.

   (A) support
   (B) remain
   (C) refrain
   (D) announce

6. The information you provided on your membership registration form will be ------- confidentially and be used for informational purposes only.

   (A) approached
   (B) handled
   (C) regarded
   (D) assigned

7. General Pipelines, Inc. will hold a company-wide luncheon on Wednesday to commemorate its outstanding performance in ------- its sales targets.

   (A) attending
   (B) promising
   (C) achieving
   (D) arriving

8. We recommend that our guests make reservations for suites in advance as these rooms will be fully ------- during the upcoming holiday season.

   (A) appointed
   (B) permitted
   (C) reserved
   (D) arranged

9. Please note that we may not be able to ------- all our customers' requests for the delivery of items since we do not process the orders we receive manually.

   (A) respond
   (B) delay
   (C) encounter
   (D) fulfill

10. Having worked at Vox Motors for more than 10 years, Mr. Eliot is well aware that even small pieces of components are critical to ------- a car.

    (A) appeal
    (B) assemble
    (C) afford
    (D) wait

출제율 216%

법칙 80 제대로 해석해야 풀리는 동사 어휘 문제

지금까지 빈칸 주변 단어와의 어울림을 보고 풀어야 하는 동사 어휘 문제들에 대해 살펴보았지만, 매달 적어도 한 문제는 빈칸 주변 단어들의 어울림만으로 풀 수 없는 문제가 출제되는데, 이러한 경우에는 해석으로 풀어야 한다.

STEP 1 유형을 파악해 봐

1. Upon your request for renewal, the expiration date of your membership has been ------- to July 20.
   (A) shortened   (B) held   (C) extended   (D) remained

2. In order to increase sales, Dale, Inc. should ------- an effective marketing strategy.
   (A) continue   (B) implement   (C) inform   (D) discourage

3. The bright lighting in the jewelry shop ------- the glitter of the displayed jewelry.
   (A) enhanced   (B) seemed   (C) prevented   (D) switched

보기 모두 서로 다른 동사들로 왔으므로 동사 어휘 문제임을 알 수 있다. 위치상으로 보아 1번 문제는 주어와의 어울림을, 2, 3번은 목적어와의 어울림을 보는 문제이지만, 이들 문제 모두 단어들의 어울림만으로는 풀리지 않기 때문에 해석으로 논리적인 관계를 따져 정답을 골라야 한다.

STEP 2 이렇게 풀어 봐   "유형을 파악해 봐" 1번 문제를 보세요!

첫째 최대한 주변 단어들을 보고 오답을 소거한다.
2형식 동사인 (D)는 수동태가 불가능하고, 주어가 the expiration date이므로 (B) 역시 탈락한다.

둘째 전체 해석을 통해 논리관계를 확인한다.
(A)와 (C)는 서로 반대말이므로 둘 중 하나를 대입해 해석해 본다. '갱신에 대한 요구에 따라, 귀하의 멤버십 만기일이 연장되었다.'는 해석이 자연스러우므로 (C)가 정답이다. 갱신을 요구했는데, 만기일을 줄일 수는 없다.

PLUS

- 논리관계를 따질 때는 부정어구나 역접의 연결어(but, although, despite 등)에 주의한다.
- 보기에 서로 반대말이 있을 경우 둘 중 하나의 해석이 자연스러우면 다른 하나는 오답이고, 비슷한 말이 보기에 있을 경우 둘 다 오답인 경우가 많다.
- 정답을 찾는 논리적 근거는 반드시 문제 안에 있다는 생각으로 접근한다.

STEP 3 실전에 적용해 봐

1. The head chef on a TV show ------- the process of making a healthy meal without any artificial flavors.

   (A) delayed
   (B) left
   (C) appointed
   (D) demonstrated

2. Cescom Tech saw a sharp increase in its stock price after ------- its plan to acquire L&P Electronics.

   (A) allowing
   (B) announcing
   (C) appearing
   (D) enabling

3. If you missed the workshop last Tuesday, note that the activities we did are ------- in a 3-page-long handout, which will be distributed shortly.

   (A) attempted
   (B) placed
   (C) summarized
   (D) considered

4. In order to ------- a meeting room, you will be required to provide us with your ID card or driver's license, which will be returned to you on your way out.

   (A) reserve
   (B) lend
   (C) arrive
   (D) expand

5. The renovated convention hall was expanded prior to the summit to ------- up to 50,000 visitors.

   (A) apply
   (B) enter
   (C) count
   (D) accommodate

6. If this is your first time visiting the office, you can ------- a guest pass at the front desk to get access to the office inside.

   (A) obtain
   (B) allow
   (C) inform
   (D) grant

7. Prior to delivering a presentation on her proposal, Ms. Yamaguchi first distributed the handouts which ------- the main points of the proposal.

   (A) criticized
   (B) outlined
   (C) seemed
   (D) panned

8. Once we are done collecting all the employees' feedback on shortening the current work hours, we will try to get the CEO's approval to ------- the company policy accordingly.

   (A) reject
   (B) revise
   (C) call
   (D) reply

9. If you find the grand clock tower on Alton Street, you will be able to easily ------- our store, which is located nearby.

   (A) open
   (B) come
   (C) revisit
   (D) locate

10. It is recommended that you install the vaccine program to ------- your computer against viruses and worms.

    (A) upgrade
    (B) leave
    (C) protect
    (D) charge

뉴토익 빈도순 정답 어휘 정리 - 동사편

빈도	동사어휘	뜻	기출 collocation	빈도	동사어휘	뜻	기출 collocation
9	accept	받아들이다, 수락하다	제안, 도움, 지원서	3	develop	개발하다	아이디어, 계획, 쇼핑몰
9	announce	발표하다	승진, 공사, 예산	3	exceed	초과하다	한계, 목표, 수치
7	postpone	미루다, 연기하다	A(마감일, 행사) until B	3	expand	확장하다	회사
6	complete	완성하다	양식, 평가, 교육, 훈련	3	expire	만료되다	쿠폰, 보증, 구독
6	hold	개최하다	행사명	3	forward	전송하다, 회송하다	A to B
6	present	보여주다, 제시하다	신분증	3	intend	의도하다, 작정이다	~ to do
6	reserve	예약하다, 보유하다	장소, 좌석, 권리	3	preserve	보존하다, 지키다	자원, 특징, 꽃
5	accommodate	수용하다	고객, 단체, 수요	3	prevent	막다, 금지하다	목적어 from -ing
5	address	다루다	문제	3	process	처리하다	주문, 데이터
5	advise	조언하다, 충고하다	사람	3	release	발표하다, 출시하다, 개봉하다, 발간하다	보고서, 제품, 책, 영화
5	attract	끌다, 유치하다	고객, 참가자, 방문객	3	remind	상기시키다	사람
5	consider	고려하다, 간주하다	재배치, 명예, 지원자	3	renew	갱신하다	멤버십, 계약
5	express	표현하다	감정, 견해	3	set up	설치하다, 설정하다	장치
5	promote	홍보하다, 촉진하다	제품, 책자	3	waive	포기하다	권리
5	replace	대체하다	제품, 책자, A as B	2	attribute	탓(덕분)으로 돌리다	A to B
5	retain	유지하다, 보유하다	문서, 제도, 시스템	2	commend	칭찬하다	A for B
4	acquire	획득하다, 습득하다	티켓, 그림, 회사	2	designate	지정하다	주차공간, 흡연구역
4	extend	연장하다	시간, 마감일	2	evolve	발달하다, 진화하다	부산한 도시
4	implement	시행하다	프로그램, 시스템, 정책	2	feature	특징으로 삼다	공간, 자동차
4	reduce	줄이다	낭비, 양, 시간	2	settle	해결하다, 합의보다	논쟁, 미지급 계좌
4	seek	찾다, 구하다	지원자, 공간, 조언	1	conceive	생각해내다	줄거리
3	assemble	조립하다, 모이다	자동차, 자전거, 화물선	1	contend with	싸우다, 다투다	고장난 엘리베이터
3	conduct	수행하다, 안내하다	설문조사, 견학, 회의	1	gauge	평가하다, 측정하다	고객만족
5	confirm	확인하다	영수증, 예약, that S V	1	integrate	통합시키다	A with B
3	consult	상담하다, 참고하다	사람, 책자	1	personalize	표시하다, 개인화하다	A with B

Chapter 10

명사 어휘 문제

매월 4문제

출제율 27%

법칙 81 특정 전치사와 잘 어울리는 명사

우리말 '~에 대한 응답'에 해당하는 영어 표현은 answer about이 아닌 answer to이다. 그렇다면 increase는 to와 in 중 어느 것을 좋아할까? 정답은 in이다. 이처럼 명사 중에서 특정 전치사와 어울림이 좋은 명사들이 있는데, 예를 들어 agreement with, lack of, addition to, information on 등이 그것들이다.

유형을 파악해 봐

1. The recent ------- in the price of groceries caused a sharp drop in their sales.
(A) addition   (B) increase   (C) approach   (D) extension

2. We will not use your ------- to our survey questions for other purpose without your permission.
(A) answers   (B) access   (C) application   (D) consideration

3. The BLC Corporation made an ------- with the city council regarding the construction of Elga Bridge.
(A) agreement   (B) approach   (C) initiative   (D) expansion

보기가 모두 서로 다른 명사로 이루어져 있으므로 명사 어휘 문제이다. 그리고 빈칸 뒤에는 각각 다른 전치사들이 있는 것으로 보아 빈칸 뒤 전치사와의 어울림을 보고 풀어야 하는 문제들이다.

이렇게 풀어 봐
"유형을 파악해 봐" 1번 문제를 보세요!

첫째 빈칸 뒤 전치사를 확인한다.
빈칸 뒤에 있는 in과 자연스럽게 어울리는 (B)를 정답으로 고른다. (A)와 (C)는 주로 to와, (D)는 of와 사용한다.

둘째 빈칸 앞 형용사와의 어울림을 확인하고, 해석으로 점검한다.
'최근 식료품 가격 상승이 매출의 급격한 하락을 가져왔다.'라는 말이 자연스럽다.

PLUS
• 특정 전치사와 가까운 명사들은 다음과 같다.

명사 뒤 to	key, transition, exposure, reaction, subscription, promotion, attention to detail (세부적인 것에 대한 관심)
명사 뒤 in	error, increase, jump, hike, rise, decrease, decline, drop, advance, interest, growth, delay, fluctuation ~에 있어서의 변동 → '증감흥 in'으로 외워두자
명사 뒤 on	implications 으미, topic, seminar, demonstration, effect, impact, influence ~에 더한 영향
명사 앞 at	reception, arrival, request 요구대로
명사 뒤 with	problem, contact, agreement, compliance 준수, difficulty, cooperation, help
명사 뒤 about	inquiry, question, worry, detail, reservation ~에 대한 유보, 거리낌, information
명사 뒤 for	nomination, respect, advocate, cause, reason, passion, preference, demand
명사 뒤 from	result, permission, difference
명사 뒤 over	dispute ~에 대한 논쟁, concern ~에 대한 걱정
명사 뒤 of	lack, a list, knowledge, portion
명사 뒤 into	expansion, investigation, insight
명사 뒤 as	service ~로의 근무
명사 앞 along	border, street, river, way, line
명사 앞 under	pressure, warranty, construction, direction, supervision, guidance, control, consideration, discussion, review, policy 정책에 따라서
명사 앞 without	delay, a receipt, permission, consent 허락
명사 앞 upon	arrival 도착 즉시, receipt 수령 즉시, request 요청 즉시, delivery 배송 즉시, completion 완료 시에
명사 앞 on	schedule 일정대로 (cf. behind schedule, ahead of schedule)
명사 앞 across	street, river, border, road
명사 앞 according to	contract, factor, policy, survey
명사 앞 by	fax, bus, subway, mistake

함정을 피해 봐
실제 강의에서만 알려주는 풀이 노하우!

1. to 부정사의 to와 전치사 to를 구분해야 한다.

In a(n) (solution/effort) to respond to customers' inquires promptly, we have redesigned our Web site.

→ solution to로 알고 to 다음 내용을 확인하지 않으면 안 된다. respond는 동사이며, to는 to 부정사의 to이므로 effort가 답이다. effort은 같은 명사를 'POWER'라고 부른다. ('법칙 57' 참고)

1 effort

STEP 3 실전에 적용해 봐

1. If you write your basic personal information on the sheet provided and submit it to the reception desk, you will be given ------- to the building.

    (A) contribution
    (B) information
    (C) construction
    (D) access

2. The council members will hold an urgent meeting this morning to discuss the dramatic ------- in the price of oil imported from Iran.

    (A) possibility
    (B) donation
    (C) rise
    (D) accumulation

3. While you are working at the laboratory, you should make sure to be in full ------- with the safety guide.

    (A) credibility
    (B) compliance
    (C) contribution
    (D) specialty

4. In celebration of Kemore Publication's decennial year since its foundation, we would like to announce and honor those who have made great ------- to Kemore Publication.

    (A) approaches
    (B) cooperation
    (C) attempts
    (D) contributions

5. ------- about the exchange or return of items purchased should be made only by telephone within 7 days of purchase.

    (A) Problems
    (B) Inquiries
    (C) Solutions
    (D) Implications

6. Mr. Wales will move to other company after 20 years of ------- as the executive manager at Amerison, Inc.

    (A) reputation
    (B) treatment
    (C) reimbursement
    (D) service

7. The Aramax Corporation recruited a large number of employees for its international division upon its ------- into the European market.

    (A) inquiries
    (B) enrollment
    (C) expansion
    (D) permit

8. At the annual job fair, many visitors who had a great amount of ------- in overseas employment signed up to get information about the requirements of the jobs.

    (A) authority
    (B) opportunity
    (C) effort
    (D) interest

9. *The Story of Tom Carter*, which is to be published this weekend, will become the newest ------- to Jim Parker's latest series of novels.

    (A) operation
    (B) alternative
    (C) addition
    (D) pattern

10. If you have any urgent documents that need to be delivered immediately, send them through our express mail service, which ensures delivery without -------.

    (A) cause
    (B) delay
    (C) notice
    (D) help

출제율 18%

법칙 82 특정 명사와 잘 어울리는 명사

'은퇴 파티'는 retirement party, '고객 만족'은 customer satisfaction인데, 이처럼 명사 2개가 하나의 명사처럼 쓰이는 것을 복합명사라고 한다. 2개의 명사를 붙였다고 모두 복합명사가 되는 것은 아니며, 이미 지정된 복합명사만을 사용한다. 복합명사에서 앞의 명사를 N1, 뒤의 명사를 N2라고 하는데, N1이나 N2가 명사 어휘 문제의 단서로 사용된다.

STEP 1 유형을 파악해 봐

1. The Arium Convention Hall has been reserved for Belle, Inc.'s awards ------- on Tuesday.
(A) application　　(B) product　　(C) ceremony　　(D) development

2. A firm with an excellent benefits system has better employee -------.
(A) productivity　　(B) probability　　(C) feasibility　　(D) utility

3. It is a common procedure to submit your business ------- before requesting a budget.
(A) entry　　(B) merger　　(C) partnership　　(D) proposal

보기가 모두 서로 다른 명사들로 왔으므로 명사 어휘 문제이며, 동시에 빈칸 앞에 명사들이 주어져 있는 것으로 보아 복합명사를 묻는 문제들임을 알 수 있다.

STEP 2 이렇게 풀어 봐
"유형을 파악해 봐" 1번 문제를 보세요!

첫째 빈칸 앞이나 빈칸 뒤의 명사와 어울리는지 확인한다.
빈칸 앞에 명사 awards가 있기 때문에 빈칸은 awards와 함께 복합명사로 쓰일 단어가 필요하다. (C)가 빈칸에 오면 시상식이라는 복합명사 awards ceremony가 되어 자연스러운 뜻을 이룬다. (A)는 '적용, 신청'의 뜻이고, (B)는 '제품,' (D)는 '개발'이란 뜻으로 awards와는 어울리지 않는다.

둘째 복합명사가 전체 문맥에 맞는지 확인한다.
'화요일에 있을 벨 사의 시상식을 위해 아리움 컨벤션홀이 예약될 것이다.'로 해석되므로 의미가 자연스럽다.

PLUS

• 자주 출제되는 복합명사는 다음과 같다.

N1을 N2하다	address verification 주소지 확인 baggage allowance 수화물 중량 제한 building expansion 건물 확장 consumer[client] satisfaction 고객 만족 dress-code regulation 복장 규정 employee participation 직원 참여 hotel reservation 호텔 예약 money management 돈 관리 product recognition 제품인지도 project manager 프로젝트 매니저 budget proposal 예산 제안서 budget estimate 예산 견적서 meal preferences 식사 선호도 quality check 품질 점검 job offer 일자리 제안 expense reimbursement 비용 환급 retirement announcement 은퇴 발표 money transfer 송금
N1을 위한 N2	application form 신청서 complaint form 항의 문서 parking lot 주차장 advertising[marketing, sales] strategy 광고[마케팅, 판매] 전략 business sense 사업 감각 consumer loan 소비자를 위한 융자, 대부 heating equipment 난방 장치 replacement fee 교체 비용 retirement party 은퇴 파티 service desk 서비스 창구 safety regulations 안전 수칙 savings plan 저축 계획 training session 교육 시간 identification badge 신분 확인 명찰 contingency plan 비상 계획 travel itinerary 여행 일정
N1이 복수	sales manager 판매부장 sales representative 판매직원 customs office 세관 customs clearance 통관 electronics company 전자 회사 savings bank 저축 은행 savings account 보통예금계좌
기타	attendance record 출석률 expiration date 만기일 product availability 제품이 있음 profit margin 이윤 마진 worker productivity 직원 생산성 office supplies 사무용품 evening performances 저녁 공연 consumer access 고객 접근 consumer use 고객 사용 marketing approaches 마케팅 접근법

- 복합명사의 단수, 복수는 N2를 기준으로 하며, N1이 복수형인 복합명사도 N2를 기준으로 한다.

an application form → 단수	application forms → 복수	applications form (X)
a sales manager → 단수	sales managers → 복수	sale manager (X)

- 복합명사인지 몰라도 N1이 가산명사인데 한정사가 없거나 복수형이 아니면 N2가 필요하다.

Customer (satisfaction/satisfied) is our number-one priority.
→ customer는 가산명사인데 a customer나 customers라고 쓰지 않았으므로 복합명사 N1인 것을 알 수 있다. 따라서 N2가 필요하며, N2는 불가산명사나 복수 명사가 와야 한다.

함정을 피해 봐
실제 강의에서만 알려주는 풀이 노하우!

1. 복합명사의 N1자리에 형용사나 분사를 쓰지 않도록 한다.
For (safety/safe) reasons, all factory workers should wear protective gear.
→ 명사 앞은 형용사 자리라고 생각해 safe를 답으로 하기 쉽지만, '안전상의 이유'라는 복합명사이다.

2. 복합명사의 N2 자리에 형용사나 분사를 쓰지 않도록 한다.
There will be an information session on the facility (regulations/regulated) on Friday.
→ 뒤에서 앞의 명사를 수식하는 분사 자리라고 생각해 regulated를 답으로 하기 쉽다. '금요일에 규정된 설비'라는 해석은 어색하며, '설비 규정에 관한'이란 말이 어울린다.

1. safety 2. regulations

STEP 3 실전에 적용해 봐

1. The roads near the construction ------- will be closed until next Friday, when the restoration of the Gordon Bridge will be done.

   (A) management
   (B) workforce
   (C) site
   (D) institute

2. We will revise our safety ------- as we recently installed some new manufacturing equipment, which is highly functional but can be dangerous if mishandled.

   (A) awareness
   (B) measures
   (C) estimates
   (D) reasons

3. The number of bank loan ------- at Royal Bank has tripled compared to last year due to the increase in the monthly rent.

   (A) attendants
   (B) informers
   (C) applicants
   (D) presenters

4. You should rehearse your multimedia ------- in advance to make sure all the equipment works properly.

   (A) presentation
   (B) stance
   (C) policy
   (D) knowledge

5. The number of car owners using public transportation instead of their own vehicles to go to work has significantly increased due to high fuel -------.

   (A) costs
   (B) alternatives
   (C) receipts
   (D) necessity

6. If you have not received an e-mail containing the travel ------- we sent to you, please let us know.

   (A) equipment
   (B) holiday
   (C) tension
   (D) itinerary

7. Bell Airlines' TV commercial showing world-famous tourist spots in America has actually promoted the tourism -------.

   (A) description
   (B) industry
   (C) customer
   (D) maintenance

8. Our company's increased annual revenues are certainly attributable to the sales ------- who outsold all local companies.

   (A) jobs
   (B) employment
   (C) management
   (D) personnel

9. If you wish to buy Chinese spices one by one for each flavor, you may want to purchase them at a retail ------- rather than at a wholesale market.

   (A) meeting
   (B) supply
   (C) location
   (D) foundation

10. Wearing safety ------- can significantly increase one's level of protection against shock and physical damage in case of an accident.

    (A) equipment
    (B) guideline
    (C) caution
    (D) evidence

법칙 83 '사람 명사 및 to 부정사'와 잘 어울리는 명사

출제율 16%

hire나 contact처럼 사람을 주어나 목적어로 취하는 동사들이 있고, experienced와 같이 사람과 어울리는 수식어도 있다. 한편 to 부정사를 단서로 삼아 명사를 답으로 고르는 문제들이 있는데, 이들 문제들에 대해서는 '법칙 57'과 '법칙 70'에서 이미 배웠으므로 이 두 법칙을 다시 한번 복습해 보길 바란다.

STEP 1 유형을 파악해 봐

1. A ------- for Elevated Tech announced today that it will launch a state-of-the-art ergonomic chair next week.
(A) spokesperson   (B) reputation   (C) petition   (D) feedback

2. Customers participating in our promotional event will be given the ------- to win a prize.
(A) arrangement   (B) opportunity   (C) objection   (D) appointment

3. The ------- of the charity event are to improve self-sustainability and to eradicate extreme poverty.
(A) attitudes   (B) destinations   (C) goals   (D) managements

보기가 모두 서로 다른 명사로 왔으므로 명사 어휘 문제이다. 1번 문제는 빈칸이 주어 자리이므로 동사나 주어를 수식하는 전명구를 보고 단서를 찾아야 하며, 2번 문제는 빈칸 뒤 to 부정사와 빈칸 앞 동사를, 3번 문제는 빈칸이 주어 자리이므로 역시 동사나 이어지는 to 부정사와의 동격의 관계를 봐야 하는 문제이다.

STEP 2 이렇게 풀어 봐
"유형을 파악해 봐" 1번 문제를 보세요!

첫째 동사나 전명구와의 어울림을 확인한다.
announced는 생말예제('법칙 73' 참고) 동사이므로 주어 자리에 사람 명사가 온다. (B)는 평판, (C)는 청원, (D)는 '반응'이라는 의미이므로 일단 우선순위에서 제외한다. (A)의 spokesperson은 전명구와도 잘 어울린다.

둘째 사람 명사를 넣어 해석해 본다.
'that 이하의 내용을 Elevated Tech 대변인이 발표했다.'는 내용이 자연스럽다.

PLUS

- 사람 명사에 대한 단서는 다음과 같다.

1. 사람을 목적어로 취하는 동사가 앞에 있을 때 　채용 관련 동사들: hire, employ, interview 　연락 관련 동사들: contact, inform, assure, notify, remind 　기타: respect, invite
2. 사람을 주어로 취하는 동사가 뒤에 있을 때 　'생말예제' 동사('법칙 73' 참고), attend, participate in
3. 빈칸이 사람 주어와 동격인 경우 　Mr. Kim will be a factory manager.
4. who나 whom으로 시작하는 형용사절의 수식을 받는 경우 　who will be in charge of
5. 사람을 수식하는 형용사가 앞에 있을 때 　satisfied, pleased, interested, tired, disappointed 등의 감정동사 p.p.나 experienced, skillful, 　knowledgeable, considerate, responsible, aware, confident 등의 사람 수식 형용사
6. a team of, a group of 뒤

- 'POWER'는 to 부정사의 수식을 잘 받는 명사들이며, attempt, ability를 추가해 'A POWER'로 기억해 두자. ('법칙 57' 참고)

- '목표/계획 is to 부정사'는 'My purpose[aim, goal, objective, plan, mission] is to 부정사.' ('법칙 70' 참고)

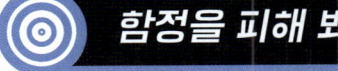 함정을 피해 봐　　　실제 강의에서만 알려주는 풀이 노하우

1. representative(직원), professional(전문가)처럼 사람 명사가 아닐 것 같은 명사들을 조심한다.

Mr. Kim was a welcome (addition/position) to any party.

→ Mr. Kim과 동격이어야 하므로 사람 명사가 필요하다. 여기서 addition은 '추가 인물'이란 뜻으로 '김 씨는 어느 파티에서든지 환영 받는 사람이었다.'로 해석된다.

1. addition

STEP 3 실전에 적용해 봐

1. *Exclusive Magazine* has reduced the price of a subscription in an ------- to retain its readers, who often complain about its high price.

   (A) approach
   (B) identity
   (C) application
   (D) effort

2. A majority of the board members are willing to accept the ------- for the sales director position because he already has 5 years of experience in a related field.

   (A) attendee
   (B) interviewer
   (C) application
   (D) candidate

3. Since Foster, Inc. has taken over control of Innovative Tech, Foster, Inc. reserves the ------- to use the touchscreen function that was initially devised by Innovative Tech on its mobile phones.

   (A) budget
   (B) right
   (C) inquiry
   (D) way

4. When you use First Security, Inc.'s recently developed security program on your computer, any unidentified ------- to access your bank account will be automatically blocked.

   (A) attempt
   (B) application
   (C) ability
   (D) question

5. According to a(n) ------- who was brought to our office to inspect the printer this morning, the printer needs to be replaced with a new one.

   (A) generator
   (B) accountant
   (C) estimate
   (D) technician

6. The ------- of judges for the annual world food contest was introduced to the audience at the opening of the event.

   (A) advantage
   (B) account
   (C) extent
   (D) panel

7. Mr. Dobb is undoubtedly a desirable candidate for the position in the international division as he possess the ------- to speak 4 languages fluently.

   (A) tendency
   (B) ability
   (C) interest
   (D) property

8. Wellbeing Food has introduced its new instant noodle meal targeting ------- who want to have quick meals.

   (A) supplies
   (B) instructions
   (C) locations
   (D) individuals

9. Among all of the individuals waiting in line at the Williams Convention Center, the staff only allowed invited ------- to enter the private show.

   (A) passengers
   (B) letters
   (C) guests
   (D) dinners

10. The Wellness Fitness Center provides newcomers with the ------- to sign up for a yoga class for free.

    (A) ability
    (B) information
    (C) opportunity
    (D) involvement

출제율 11%

법칙 84 특정 단어와 잘 어울리는 기타 명사들

명사 어휘 문제 중에서는 주변 단서만 보고도 바로 정답을 고를 수 있는 문제들이 있다.

meeting, ceremony, workshop, seminar 등	행사 관련 명사들로 attend, hold, host, organize와 같은 동사가 앞에 온다.
selection, collection, array, variety, number 등	'a ~ of 복수 명사' 형태로 자주 등장한다.
news, idea, opinion, claim, statement, fact, report 등	뒤에 이어지는 'that S + V'와 동격의 관계가 형성된다. I heard the news that the CEO will retire soon. 여기서는 '뉴스 = CEO가 곧 은퇴할 것'

STEP 1 유형을 파악해 봐

1. The general manager decided to hold a(n) ------- after the keynote speaker's presentation.
   (A) association   (B) construction   (C) population   (D) reception

2. At Home n' Shop, we provide a wide ------- of interior decorations.
   (A) variety   (B) merchandise   (C) approach   (D) allocation

3. It has been learned that the ------- that Mr. Mitch will resign is actually not true.
   (A) reason   (B) assessment   (C) news   (D) criticism

보기가 모두 서로 다른 명사들로 왔으므로 명사 어휘 문제임을 알 수 있고, 세 문제 모두 빈칸 앞이나 뒤에 문제를 풀기 위한 단서가 주어져 있다. 1번 문제는 hold가 행사 명사를 목적어로 취하는 동사이며, 2번 문제는 빈칸 앞 a wide, 빈칸 뒤 'of 복수 명사'가 단서로 제시되었고, 3번 문제는 빈칸 뒤에 'that S + V'가 온 것으로 보아 동격의 that을 생각해 볼 수 있는 상황이다.

STEP 2 이렇게 풀어 봐   "유형을 파악해 봐" 1번 문제를 보세요!

첫째 빈칸 앞과 뒤의 동사나 수식어를 확인한다.
빈칸 앞의 hold는 행사 명사를 목적어로 취하는 동사이므로 보기 중에서 행사 명사를 찾는다. (D)는 '리셉션'이라는 뜻으로 hold의 목적어로 적합하다. (A)는 '동료, 협회, 제휴,' (B)는 '건축,' (C)는 '인구'라는 뜻이므로 탈락한다.

둘째 전체 문맥에 맞는지 해석해 본다.

'부장은 기조연설이 끝난 후에 리셉션을 열기로 했다.'라는 해석이 자연스럽다.

PLUS

• 주변 단어들을 보고 답을 고를 수 있는 명사들은 다음과 같다.

단서	정답
빈칸 앞 attend, hold, host, organize, invited to와 '법칙 71'에 나오는 동사 어휘들	행사 명사(meeting, seminar, workshop, reception, ceremony)와 '법칙 71'에 나오는 동사 어휘와 어울리는 명사들
빈칸 앞 a wide[large, diverse], 빈칸 뒤 'of 복수 명사'	selection, collection, array, number, variety, series
빈칸 뒤 'that + 완전한 문장' (이것을 동격의 that이라고 한다.)	news, idea, opinion, claim, statement, fact, report, assurance, evidence
빈칸 뒤 'of 사람 복수 명사'	panel, delegation, committee, team, group
written 서면의	estimate 견적서, confirmation 확인서
additional, extra 추가의	charge, fee
unforeseen 예기치 않은	circumstances 상황
careful	planning 기획, evaluation 평가
minor	lapse 잘못, 과실, error 오류
highest 가장 높은	standard 기준, priority 최우선 고려사항
positive 긍정적인	review, feedback
ongoing 진행중인	effort 노력
after months of 수 개월의	negotiations 협상
staplers, pens, paper clips, and other	supplies 비품들
'법칙 86'에 나오는 형용사 어휘들	'법칙 86'에 나오는 형용사 어휘의 수식을 받는 명사들
숙어	in response to ~에 대한 응답으로 in conjunction with ~와 함께 in celebration of ~를 축하하여 in keeping with ~에 맞춰 in preparation for ~에 대한 준비로 as a consequence of ~에 대한 결과로써 make an arrangement 준비하다 make a recommendation 추천하다 make a decision 결정하다 make a reservation 예약하다 until further notice 추후 통지가 있을 때까지 take A into consideration [account] A를 고려하다 on a first-come, first-served basis 선착순으로 put A in jeopardy A를 위험에 빠뜨리다 in its entirety 전부, 온전히 keep records of ~를 기록하다 as is the case with A A가 그렇듯

함정을 피해 봐
실제 강의에서만 알려주는 풀이 노하우!

1. 명사 어휘 문제도 가산/불가산을 생각해 푼다.

To get the beverage you want, you need to prepare exact (coin/change) for the vending machine.

→ coin은 가산명사이므로 앞에 관사를 쓰거나 복수형으로 써야 한다. '잔돈'을 뜻하는 change가 답이다.

1. change

STEP 3 실전에 적용해 봐

1. Wagner IT, Inc. is organizing a ------- on multimedia computing which is mandatory for all new recruits to attend.

   (A) workshop
   (B) schedule
   (C) specialty
   (D) business

2. Mr. Loon requested that the architect provide a written ------- of the total costs involved in remodeling his house by one week before the scheduled date of the remodeling.

   (A) tender
   (B) relation
   (C) estimate
   (D) recommendation

3. Stationery Depot, which sells copy paper, memo pads, stamps, and other ------- in bulk, is an ideal place to shop for writing implements at affordable prices.

   (A) demands
   (B) missions
   (C) supplies
   (D) shipment

4. During his speech, Dr. Neilson attributed the positive ------- on his recent research findings to his assistants.

   (A) topic
   (B) advice
   (C) concern
   (D) feedback

5. If you plan to directly come to the Best Riverville Hotel once you arrive at the airport, a pickup service is available for an additional -------.

   (A) cash
   (B) opportunity
   (C) charge
   (D) estimate

6. As a result of unforeseen -------, a number of employees at Delipop Company were laid off last month.

   (A) circumstances
   (B) qualifications
   (C) categorizations
   (D) examples

7. Ms. Flora was glad when she received the ------- that she was selected as one of the employees that will be dispatched to the overseas branch.

   (A) promotion
   (B) idea
   (C) schedule
   (D) news

8. Home Service Support provides a broad ------- of housekeeping services, from cleaning homes to mowing lawns, for our customers.

   (A) range
   (B) point
   (C) chance
   (D) width

9. Ms. O'Connell, a council coordinator, cancelled all of her appointments for this Thursday to attend the ------- held in honor of 50th anniversary of the Local Aboriginal Land Council.

   (A) tuition
   (B) ceremony
   (C) mark
   (D) venue

10. It was fortunate that Ms. Spears received a light warning for a minor ------- she made in estimating the total revenues at her company on a financial statement.

    (A) recognition
    (B) tenure
    (C) concern
    (D) error

출제율 342%

법칙 85 올바른 해석으로 풀어야 하는 명사 어휘 문제

주변 단어와의 어울림을 보고 풀어야 하는 명사 어휘 문제 이외에도 문제를 해석해서 풀어야 하는 문제도 있다.

STEP 1 유형을 파악해 봐

1. In case of bad weather, we may not be able to follow all the routes indicated on the travel -------.
(A) itinerary   (B) guide   (C) agency   (D) destination

2. Due to the economic crisis, BC&M, Inc.'s shares sharply fell on the stock -------.
(A) industry   (B) analyst   (C) company   (D) market

3. Many people consider television to be the greatest modern ------- of the 20th century.
(A) times   (B) invention   (C) history   (D) technology

보기가 모두 서로 다른 명사들로 주어졌으므로 명사 어휘 문제이다. 1, 2번 문제는 위치상으로는 앞의 명사와의 어울림을 보는 문제이며, 3번 문제는 빈칸 앞 형용사와의 어울림을 보는 문제이다. 하지만 세 문제 모두 주변 단어와의 어울림만으로는 정확한 답을 고를 수 없다.

STEP 2 이렇게 풀어 봐
"유형을 파악해 봐" 1번 문제를 보세요!

첫째 주변 단어들을 파악한 후 오답을 소거한다.
보기들이 모두 여행이라는 말과 함께 사용할 수 있는 단어들로 제시되었다.

둘째 전체 해석을 통해 논리관계를 확인한다.
문장을 해석해 보면 '여행 일정에 제시된 대로 진행될 수 없을지도 모른다.'는 내용이 자연스럽다. guide는 '여행 안내자'라는 뜻 이외에도 '여행 안내 책자'라는 뜻도 있어 혼동될 수 있다. 그러나 논리적으로 생각해 보면 여행 안내 책에 나오는 내용을 모두 다 여행 일정에 포함시키지는 않으므로 (A)를 답으로 하는 것이 적합하다.

PLUS
- 논리관계를 따질 때는 부정어구나 역접의 연결어(but, although, despite 등)에 주의한다. 보어 자리의 명사가 주어와 동격 관계인지도 확인한다.
- 정답이 되기 위한 논리적 근거는 반드시 문제에 있다는 생각으로 접근한다.

STEP 3 실전에 적용해 봐

1. According to a recent study, a large ------- of the population lives in major cities while only 20% live either in suburban or remote areas.

   (A) scale
   (B) proportion
   (C) area
   (D) capacity

2. Revive Motors has been conducting a study on ways to enhance the ------- of its engines to produce engines with long-lasting power.

   (A) flexibility
   (B) complacency
   (C) durability
   (D) volatility

3. The development of a database where consumers' buying habits are automatically recorded has resulted in a significant ------- in traditional marketing methods.

   (A) shift
   (B) loss
   (C) amount
   (D) number

4. Mega Sales provides ------- for items with defects created during the production process but not for items that purchasers simply want to return.

   (A) support
   (B) refunds
   (C) receipts
   (D) supplies

5. Since a majority of the employees are still dissatisfied with the employee benefits program after its revision, the system needs a more thorough -------.

   (A) knowledge
   (B) process
   (C) effort
   (D) overhaul

6. Each ------- for the sales manager position was given a mission to conduct a brief mock product demonstration as a part of his or her job interview.

   (A) practitioner
   (B) judge
   (C) candidate
   (D) interviewer

7. Once the important decision-making process is done at headquarters, the ------- are responsible for following the orders sent from the executive board.

   (A) competitors
   (B) subsidiaries
   (C) creditors
   (D) customers

8. As the founder of the charity organization World Dream, Mr. Harper will take the initiative in funding the ------- center for the disabled.

   (A) city
   (B) research
   (C) amusement
   (D) rehabilitation

9. The credit ratings provided by Investment Watch are reliable ------- of a company's value.

   (A) indicators
   (B) markets
   (C) incomes
   (D) places

10. The executive rejected Mr. Harding's plan for the project because it required heavy ------- while the company had a limited budget.

    (A) fines
    (B) duties
    (C) expenditures
    (D) industries

명사 어휘 문제 (매월 4문제) 34.2%

뉴토익 빈도순 정답 어휘 정리 - 명사편

빈도	명사어휘	뜻	기출 collocation
7	estimate	견적서	written ~를 요청하다
5	requirement	요구 조건	~를 충족시키다
5	facility	편의시설	휘트니스센터와 같은 ~
5	contribution	공헌, 기여	~ to 명사
5	performance	공연, 성능, 성과, 실적	판매 ~ , 제품의 ~
4	productivity	생산성	작업자/직원 ~을 향상시키다
4	promotion	승진, 홍보	~ to a position
4	expansion	확장, 진출	~ into 해외시장
4	procedure	절차, 방법	표준 ~를 준수하다
4	initiative	주도적 계획, 솔선 운동	보여주다 ~ in -ing
4	reputation	명성, 평판	~ for
4	purchase	구매, 구매품	thank you for your ~ of our 제품
4	expertise	전문지식, 전문기술	~을 개발하다, 필요로 하다
4	variety	다양성	a ~ of + 복수명사 (다양한)
4	advantage	이점, 유리한 점	take ~ of (~를 이용하다)
4	charge	요금	추가의 ~
4	inquiry	문의, 문의사항	~ about
4	delay	지연, 연기	without ~
4	issue	문제, 사안	~을 다루다
4	opportunity	기회	~ to do
4	option	선택사항	~ of A or B
4	policy	정책	~를 수정하다
4	request	요청	on(upon) ~ (요구하는 즉시)
3	defect	결함	제품의 ~을 발견하다, 제거하다
3	review	평가	긍정적인, 훌륭한 ~
3	discount	할인	~을 제공하다
3	notice	공지	사전 ~, 추후 ~
3	preference	선호도	~를 보여주다, 표시하다
3	decline	감소	~ in 판매, 주가, 수익
3	presence	입지, 참석	~를 재확립하다
3	commitment	헌신, 전념	~ to 명사
3	transition	변이, 변화, 이전	~ to 명사
3	feedback	의견, 피드백	긍정적인
3	demand	수요	~가 절정에 달하다, 높은 ~
3	inconvenience	불편	~에 대해 사과하다
3	appointment	임명, 약속	~를 잡다
3	measures	조치, 수단	보안 ~
3	receipt	영수증, 수령	~을 제출하다, on(upon) ~ (수령 즉시)
2	interruption	중단, 방해	without ~
2	obligation	의무	~를 이행하다, ~가 없다
2	sequence	순서	적절한 ~를 따르다
2	consequence	결과	as a ~ of (~의 결과로서)
1	conjunction		in ~ of (~와 함께)
1	inception	시작, 개시	from its very ~ (시작부터)
1	contingency	우발 사건, 만일의 사태	~ plan (비상 계획)
1	sympathy	동정, 연민	~을 표현하다
1	eloquence	웅변, 능변	~ 때문에, 의장이 되었다
1	jeopardy	위험	put A in jeopardy (A를 위험에 빠뜨리다)
1	replica	모형, 복제품	19세기 가로등의 ~으로 조명되다
1	overhaul	점검	투자 전략에 대한 ~을 이끌다

Chapter 11

형용사 어휘 문제

매월 3문제

출제율 73%

법칙 86 특정 명사와 잘 어울리는 형용사

형용사 어휘 문제를 풀 때는 그 형용사가 수식하는 명사를 가장 먼저 살펴야 한다. 예를 들어 뒤에 단수 명사가 있다면 복수 명사를 수식하는 various는 정답에서 제외시키는 것과 같은 경우이다.

 유형을 파악해 봐

1. As competition in the PC industry grows more intensive, more computers are increasingly being offered at ------- prices.
(A) uncommon   (B) partial   (C) popular   (D) reasonable

2. Life Partner Insurance has remained at the top of the industry for over 20 years thanks to its ------- service.
(A) vague   (B) limited   (C) powerful   (D) outstanding

3. Please write your ------- information in the space provided to receive our special promotional offers for free.
(A) potential   (B) unfair   (C) dependent   (D) personal

보기가 모두 서로 다른 형용사들로 왔으므로 형용사 어휘 문제이다. 보기와 빈칸 주변만 봐서는 공통점이나 풀이 유형을 파악하기 쉽지 않을 경우에는 우선 수식을 받는 명사를 살펴야 한다.

 이렇게 풀어 봐 "유형을 파악해 봐" 1번 문제를 보세요!

첫째 빈칸의 수식을 받는 명사를 확인한다.
빈칸 뒤에 있는 명사 prices가 빈칸의 수식을 받는 명사이므로 뜻이 자연스럽게 어울리는 (D)가 정답이다.

둘째 해석상 자연스런 보기를 고른다.
'컴퓨터 업계의 경쟁이 치열해짐에 따라, 더 많은 컴퓨터들이 합리적인 가격으로 제공된다.'는 내용이 자연스럽다.

PLUS

• 수식 받는 명사만 보고 알 수 있는 형용사는 다음과 같다.

The price we offer is very reasonable. ➡ 주어인 price와의 어울림으로 정답을 고른다.

• 수식 받는 명사만 보고 알 수 있는 형용사는 다음과 같다. 기출 빈도순 대로 암기하자!

단서	정답으로 되는 형용사
time, amount, effort, money, growth	considerable, substantial, significant 상당한
복수 명사	various 다양한, numerous 많은, multiple
price	reasonable, affordable, competitive 경쟁력 있는
study, research	comprehensive 종합적인, extensive 폭넓은
information, report, review, proposal	detailed 상세한
service	outstanding 탁월한, exceptional 훌륭한
product, merchandise, items	defective 결함 있는
a ~ collection[selection, array, variety, number] of	wide, diverse 다양한, large
belongings 소지품, information	personal 개인의
time, period, access	limited 제한된
information, documents, data	confidential 비밀의
product, service, transportation 교통수단	dependable, reliable 신뢰할 만한
service, train, meeting, search	frequent 빈번한
weather conditions, market conditions, review	favorable, unfavorable
supplier, farmers, vendor 판매자, 납품업체	local 지역의
appreciation, gratitude, apology	sincere 진솔한
knowledge, familiarity 익숙함	broad 넓은
book, technology	latest 최신의
review, feedback	positive 긍정적인
change, error	minor 사소한
measures 조치, clothing 의류	protective 보호용의
manner 방식, fashion 방식	timely 시기 적절한, orderly 순서 정연한

 함정을 피해 봐 실제 강의에서만 알려주는 풀이 노하우!

1. 모양새나 의미가 비슷해 혼동하기 쉬운 형용사를 조심한다.

The factory's assembly line is (void/idle/null) and will not be operational until demand increases.
→ '공장 생산라인이 가동되지 않았고, 수요가 증가할 때까지 가동하지 않을 것이다.'라는 내용이므로 idle이 정답이다. void는 '공허한,' null은 '존재하지 않는'이란 뜻이므로 탈락한다.

unanimous 만장일치의   anonymous 익명의   competitive 경쟁력 있는
comparable 비교할 만한, 상당한   compatible 호환이 되는   accessible 접속 가능한
assessable 평가 가능한   prompt 즉각적인   short 짧은
adhesive 들러붙는   cohesive 결합력 있는   favorite 가장 좋아하는
favorable 우호적인   extended 연장된   extensive 광범위한

1. idle

STEP 3 실전에 적용해 봐

1. At the Sunrise Hotel, guests staying in suites are provided with ------- room service, which includes free meals upon request.

   (A) complimentary
   (B) permitted
   (C) applicable
   (D) relative

2. The sales manager sent an e-mail containing ------- information on the itinerary to each customer who recently purchased a package tour to Greece.

   (A) respectful
   (B) detailed
   (C) loyal
   (D) rare

3. The Human Resources Department prefers to have employees with ------- work experience on teams as they will not need much training.

   (A) potential
   (B) plausible
   (C) relevant
   (D) efficient

4. If there are any ------- items, that fact must be indicated on the boxes to notify the deliverymen of the need to take special care of them.

   (A) suspicious
   (B) fragile
   (C) innovative
   (D) thorough

5. The sales managers at We Fit Sporting Goods sent letters of apology to the customers who filed complaints about the ------- items being sold.

   (A) defective
   (B) regarded
   (C) demanding
   (D) avoidable

6. Before investing in Global Eco Energy, a more ------- review of the company's financial status is required.

   (A) diligent
   (B) extreme
   (C) comprehensive
   (D) utmost

7. Due to a lack of evidence, Dr. Birdman's research team came to a ------- conclusion that employees' personal characteristics have a correlation with a firm's overall productivity.

   (A) permanent
   (B) irreversible
   (C) tolerant
   (D) tentative

8. Ms. Combs is totally exhausted from doing the ------- training exercises ordered by her personal trainer.

   (A) spacious
   (B) rigorous
   (C) generous
   (D) single

9. The workshop attendants who plan to open their own venture businesses learned some key factors for success by analyzing some ------- cases.

   (A) permanent
   (B) reliant
   (C) aware
   (D) exemplary

10. The ------- market conditions have caused Watson Tech to delay the launch of its new computer model despite being in its final stage of development.

    (A) unfavorable
    (B) stable
    (C) encouraged
    (D) impartial

법칙 87 특정 전치사와 잘 어울리는 형용사

출제율 41%

형용사 중에서는 특정 전치와 잘 어울리는 형용사들이 있는데, 예를 들어 '~를 알고 있다'는 be aware of, '~를 잘 한다'는 be good at이 이에 해당한다. 따라서 형용사 어휘 문제가 출제되었을 때 aware와 good이 보기로 제시된다면 of나 at과 같은 전치사가 답이 될 수 있다는 점을 알아 두어야 한다.

STEP 1 유형을 파악해 봐

1. The sales staff is mainly ------- for managing the inventory.
   (A) explainable   (B) responsible   (C) reliable   (D) advisable

2. The employees are ------- to adopt the new company policy, which will ensure better working conditions.
   (A) susceptible   (B) prone   (C) eager   (D) tempt

3. Those new employees who are ------- with accounting terms may have difficulties with financial statements.
   (A) unfamiliar   (B) favored   (C) common   (D) comfortable

보기가 모두 서로 다른 형용사들로 왔으므로 형용사 어휘 문제이다. 빈칸 뒤에는 각각 다른 전치사들이 왔는데, 이러한 경우 빈칸 뒤에 있는 전치사와의 어울림을 보고 풀어야 한다.

STEP 2 이렇게 풀어 봐
"유형을 파악해 봐" 1번 문제를 보세요!

첫째 빈칸 뒤 전치사를 확인한다.
빈칸 뒤에 있는 for와 가장 잘 어울리는 보기를 답으로 고른다. '~을 책임지다, 담당하다'의 뜻을 가진 be responsible for가 정답이다.

둘째 빈칸 앞 주어와의 어울림을 확인하고, 최종 해석으로 점검한다.
'판매 직원은 주로 재고를 관리하는데 책임이 있다.'라는 내용이 자연스럽다. (A)는 주어가 사람일 때 쓰는 단어가 아니며, (C)는 사람과 함께 쓸 수 있으나 여기서는 의미가 잘 통하지 않고, (D)는 가주어, 진주어와 잘 쓰이는 형용사로 '~한 행위가 바람직하다'라고 할 때 사용한다.

PLUS

- 특정 전치사와 잘 어울리는 형용사들은 다음과 같다.

of	be aware of ~를 알고 있다 be representative of ~를 대표하다 be reminiscent of ~를 상기시키다	be appreciative of ~에 감사하다 be indicative of ~를 나타내다 be capable of ~를 할 수 있다
at	be good at ~에 능숙하다 be poor at ~에 능숙하지 않다 be aimed at ~를 겨누고 있다	be skilled at ~에 능숙하다 be present at ~에 참석하다
for	be responsible for ~를 책임지다 be notable for ~로 유명하다	be famous for ~로 유명하다 be eligible for ~할 자격이 있다
about	be optimistic about ~에 대해서 낙관적이다	be concerned about ~에 대해 우려하다
from	be exempt from ~로 부터 면제되다	
with	be familiar with ~에 익숙하다	
on	be based on ~에 기반을 두고 있다	
by	be accessible by ~에 의해 접속 가능하다	
to	be available to ~가 이용 가능하다 be entitled to ~에 대해 자격이 된다 be subject to ~에 좌우된다 be receptive to ~를 잘 수용하다	be accessible to ~가 접근 가능하다 be prone to ~하기 쉽다 be vulnerable to ~에 취약하다
to 동사원형	'번지점프' 형용사('법칙 64' 참고) be able to ~할 수 있다 be ready to ~할 준비가 되어 있다 be willing to ~할 의향이 있다 be eager to ~하기를 열망하다 be sure[certain] to 틀림없이 ~하다 be likely to ~일 것 같다 be reluctant to ~하기를 주저하다 be hesitant to ~하기를 주저하다 be about to ~할 예정이다		

- '결혼승낙' 동사('법칙 48' 참고)의 수동태도 to 동사원형이 온다.

be expected to	be asked to	be advised to	be reminded to	be required to
be requested to	be persuaded to	be forced to	be urged to	be encouraged to
be allowed to	be permitted to	be enabled to		

🎯 함정을 피해 봐
실제 강의에서만 알려주는 풀이 노하우!

1. to 부정사의 to와 전치사 to를 혼동하지 않도록 한다.

The new fitness facility will be (ready/available) to the apartment residents next week.

→ be ready to 뒤에는 동사원형이 온다. the apartment residents는 명사이므로 '명사에게 이용 가능하다'는 뜻을 가진 available이 답이다.

1. *available*

STEP 3 실전에 적용해 봐

1. These stated conditions regarding your insurance plan are ------- to change without notice.

    (A) subject
    (B) opt
    (C) willing
    (D) obvious

2. The novel *Seven Treasures*, which is considered one of the greatest masterpieces of all time, is the book that is ------- of the writer John Schouten.

    (A) exemplary
    (B) representative
    (C) proud
    (D) reliant

3. Jobseekers who are ------- in working at IT companies are encouraged to apply for a mock-job interview being held by E&T Solutions.

    (A) enclosed
    (B) concerned
    (C) interested
    (D) invited

4. As it was obvious that Mr. Decker's team had contributed to the total sales at the company less than the other teams had, his team was ------- to submit its sales report.

    (A) object
    (B) possible
    (C) reluctant
    (D) applicable

5. Employees who have worked for over 3 years without any absences are ------- for a vacation of up to one month.

    (A) exempt
    (B) variable
    (C) receivable
    (D) eligible

6. Having already taken the same session, Ms Parker was ------- from attending the required training workshop for the new employees.

    (A) liable
    (B) popular
    (C) applicable
    (D) exempt

7. Today's state-of-the-art IT technology is ------- on the industry developed in Silicon Valley.

    (A) based
    (B) agreed
    (C) delivered
    (D) placed

8. The staff rooms at the store are ------- only to full-time clerks who possess their own employee ID cards.

    (A) accessible
    (B) noticeable
    (C) replaceable
    (D) reliable

9. LM Electronics is ------- to add the recently released model to the series of portable devices for which the company is known.

    (A) apparent
    (B) proud
    (C) kind
    (D) incremental

10. Since it was her first day of work at Compa Design, Ms. Murray was ------- at working with the various designing tools that were all new to her.

    (A) confident
    (B) optimistic
    (C) poor
    (D) professional

출제율 12%

법칙 88   사람에 답이 되는 형용사

considerate과 considerable의 차이점은 전자는 '사려 깊은'이란 뜻으로 사람을 수식하는 반면, 후자는 시간, 양, 노력, 금액 등 사람이 아닌 것을 수식한다. 형용사 어휘 문제를 풀 때 빈칸이 수식하는 단어가 사람일 경우에는 사람을 수식하는 형용사를 답으로 골라야 한다. 반면에 빈칸이 수식하는 단어가 사람이 아닐 때 사람을 수식하는 형용사가 보기에 있다면 오답이다.

STEP 1   유형을 파악해 봐

1. Mr. Fowler is the most ------- applicant as he has 7 years of experience in a relevant field.
(A) pleasant   (B) acquired   (C) demanding   (D) experienced

2. The executive manager has decided to promote each highly ------- employee.
(A) mandatory   (B) qualified   (C) intentional   (D) probable

3. Kolm, Inc. promised to give more incentives to the employees ------ with their salaries.
(A) dissatisfied (B) interested (C) proceeded   (D) attached

보기가 모두 서로 다른 형용사들로 왔으므로 형용사 어휘 문제이다. 1번 문제는 빈칸 뒤 applicant와 어울림을 봐야 하고, 2번 문제는 빈칸 뒤 employee와의 어울림을, 그리고 3번 문제는 빈칸 앞 employees와의 어울림을 봐야 한다. 세 단어 모두 사람을 지칭하는 단어들이다

STEP 2   이렇게 풀어 봐   "유형을 파악해 봐" 1번 문제를 보세요!

첫째 빈칸 뒤 명사를 확인한다.
applicant는 '지원자'로 사람을 지칭하는 명사인데, 보기에서 사람을 수식할 수 있는 형용사는 (C)와 (D)이다. (A)는 날씨 등이 화창할 때 쓰는 말이며, (B)는 회사 등이 인수되었을 때 쓰는 말이므로 (A)와 (B)는 탈락한다.

둘째 해석으로 어울림을 점검한다.
demanding은 사람을 수식할 수는 있지만 보통은 customer나 supervisor 등을 수식하여 '까다로운'이란 뜻으로 쓰인다. (D)를 대입해 해석해 보면, '파울러 씨는 관련 분야에서 7년의 경험을 갖춘 가장 경험있는 지원자이다.'로 해석이 되어 자연스럽다.

PLUS

- 사람을 수식하는 형용사는 다음과 같다.

사람 수식	사물 수식
considerate, qualified, pleased, impressed, skilled, knowledgeable, experienced, responsible, aware, eligible, entitled, optimistic, able, capable, talented	considerable, significant, substantial, impressive, pleasant, convenient
감정 분사: interested, satisfied/dissatisfied, excited, overwhelmed, tired, bored, invigorated, embarrassed, disappointed, fascinated, startled, worried 등	감정 분사: interesting, satisfying/dissatisfying, exciting, overwhelming, tiring, boring, invigorating, embarrassing, disappointing, fascinating, startling, worrying 등

실제 강의에서만 알려주는 풀이 노하우!

1. 사람을 수식하는 형용사로 쓰이지만 사물도 수식 가능한 경우를 조심한다.
Cell phones are rapidly becoming more (versatile/impressed) and less expensive.
➔ '다재다능한'이란 뜻을 가진 versatile은 사람을 수식하기도 하지만, 제품 앞에 와서 '기능이 많은'이란 뜻을 갖기도 한다. impressed는 사람만을 수식하므로 탈락한다.

1. versatile

STEP 3 실전에 적용해 봐

1. Many financial analysts are ------- about the upward trend in the stock market due to the stabile economic conditions.

    (A) doubtful
    (B) optimistic
    (C) aware
    (D) common

2. KM Resources Design was named one of the 100 most desirable workplaces for providing a ------- working environment for its employees.

    (A) pleasant
    (B) challenging
    (C) fragile
    (D) cautious

3. As a receptionist at the Grand Royal Hotel, Ms. Tomoya is mainly ------- for assisting guests with checking in and out.

    (A) responsible
    (B) reliable
    (C) desirable
    (D) feasible

4. Because Mr. Pearson was ------- speaking both English and Spanish, he applied for a job as an interpreter.

    (A) confident
    (B) personal
    (C) exhaustive
    (D) practical

5. Although he is currently working as a project manager, Mr. Green is one of the most ------- employees we have at our company, so he can be assigned to any position.

    (A) varying
    (B) arguable
    (C) consistent
    (D) versatile

6. The board of directors at both companies, T&E Chemicals and Wells Energy, were ------- in their desire to extend the contract.

    (A) interesting
    (B) unanimous
    (C) obvious
    (D) speculative

7. In order to resolve these complicated problems with our software, we need to have a ------- engineer inspect the problem.

    (A) powerful
    (B) various
    (C) skilled
    (D) major

8. Mr. Roland has a good reputation among the new hires at his company as he is known to be very ------- of them even when they make minor mistakes.

    (A) dependent
    (B) detectable
    (C) considerate
    (D) informative

9. Although it was exhausting work to conceive a new business plan, the executive manager's positive feedback on their idea rendered the team feeling -------.

    (A) same
    (B) severe
    (C) invigorated
    (D) intricate

10. Since Ms. Nagoya started working at Turbo Auto, she has become ------- about the technology used to manufacture cars.

    (A) extensive
    (B) infrequent
    (C) knowledgeable
    (D) optimistic

출제율 36%

법칙 89 가주어, 진주어에 잘 어울리는 형용사

'It is necessary that employees attend the training session.'에서 It은 가주어, that 이하는 진주어이며, necessary는 가주어와 진주어에 어울리는 형용사다. 그리고 'I consider it necessary that employees attend the training session.'에서는 it이 가목적어, that 이하가 진목적어이며, necessary는 가목적어와 진목적어에 어울리는 형용사이다.

STEP 1 유형을 파악해 봐

1. It is ------- that you comply with the safety instructions at work.
   (A) accessible   (B) aware   (C) crucial   (D) intense

2. It became ------- that Ms. Jenson would be late for her appointment when the bus did not come on time.
   (A) essential   (B) obsolete   (C) prerequisite   (D) apparent

3. Young shoppers often find it much ------- to shop online than to go shopping at offline retail stores.
   (A) easier   (B) probable   (C) possible   (D) profound

보기가 모두 서로 다른 형용사들로 왔으므로 형용사 어휘 문제이다. 1, 2번 문제는 가주어, 진주어 문장이고, 3번 문제는 가목적어, 진목적어 문장으로 가주어, 진주어에 잘 어울리는 형용사를 고르는 문제라고 할 수 있다.

STEP 2 이렇게 풀어 봐   "유형을 파악해 봐" 1번 문제를 보세요!

첫째 가주어와 진주어, 그리고 잘 어울리는 형용사를 확인한다.
'It is ~ that S+V.' 형식의 완전한 문장으로 가주어, 진주어 문장이 확실하며, (C) crucial이 가주어, 진주어와 잘 어울리는 형용사이다. (A)는 전치사 to, by와 잘 어울리는 형용사이고, (B)는 사람을 수식하는 형용사이다. (D)는 딱히 어울림이 없다.

둘째 해석으로 어울림을 점검한다.
'당신이 직장에서 안전 사항을 준수하는 것이 중요하다.'로 해석돼 자연스럽다.

PLUS

- 가주어, 진주어와 잘 어울리는 형용사는 다음과 같으며, 특히 '요번주의 명제'('법칙 28' 참고)에 속하는 '이성판단의 형용사'는 that절 안에 should가 생략되어 있는 형태이므로 동사원형이 온다.

이성판단의 형용사	necessary, essential, important, urgent, mandatory, crucial
난이 형용사	easy, hard, impossible, possible
기타	advisable, desirable, true, strange, surprising, probable, common, helpful, beneficial

- 진주어는 'that S+V'만 오는 것이 아니고, to 부정사나 기타 명사절 모두 가능하다.

  It will be difficult for the new hires to finish the project on time.
  ➡ for the new hires가 의미상 주어이고, to 이하가 진주어다.

  It has not been decided whether the project will be launched.
  ➡ It가 가주어이고, whether 이하가 진주어다.

- 가주어, 진주어 문장과, 'It ~ that S+V.' 강조 구문은 다르다.

  It was yesterday that John met Sam in front of the church. → yesterday를 강조
  It was John that met Sam in front of the church. → John을 강조
  It was Sam that John met in front of the church. → Sam을 강조
  It was in front of the church that John met Sam yesterday. → in front of the church를 강조

 함정을 피해 봐 실제 강의에서만 알려주는 풀이 노하우!

1. 진주어는 사람이 아니므로 It is 뒤에 사람을 수식하는 형용사가 오면 오답이다.

   It is (advisable/proficient) that you wear protective clothing while working on the assembly line.
   ➡ proficient는 사람을 수식하는 형용사이다.

1. advisable

STEP 3 실전에 적용해 봐

1. It will be ------- for the meeting attendees to understand the data if the multimedia presentation contains more diagrams.

   (A) qualified
   (B) plausible
   (C) helpful
   (D) tangible

2. It is ------- that the Human Resources staff clearly understand our company's mission and goals to implement the appropriate HR policies.

   (A) competitive
   (B) vital
   (C) economic
   (D) responsible

3. It is ------- that the executive manager will notify us of the plans for the luncheon on Wednesday, the day he returns from his temporary leave.

   (A) probable
   (B) skilled
   (C) flexible
   (D) relative

4. Daily & Store has found it ------- to regularly hold promotional events at fixed times rather than at different times to attract more customers.

   (A) forcible
   (B) particular
   (C) abundant
   (D) beneficial

5. While car manufacturers once made their workers produce car parts manually, it is now more ------- for them to let facilities produce them.

   (A) offensive
   (B) efficient
   (C) convertible
   (D) outdated

6. It is relatively ------- for startup enterprises to receive subsidies from the government, which supports small-capital businesses.

   (A) positive
   (B) common
   (C) even
   (D) diverse

7. It is ------- to repair the heating system in this building because it frequently loses power.

   (A) apparent
   (B) absolute
   (C) obvious
   (D) necessary

8. It was ------- that shorts were being sold at discounts of up to 50% because the summer season was over.

   (A) reasonable
   (B) busy
   (C) sufficient
   (D) punctual

9. Most of the employees at Harold, Inc., which is located in a rural area, live in company housing as it is more ------- for them.

   (A) optional
   (B) convenient
   (C) various
   (D) comprehensive

10. It will be ------- to conduct the research once Dr. Harlan's team receives more funds to purchase research equipment.

    (A) significant
    (B) apparent
    (C) easy
    (D) volatile

정답 및 해설은 131페이지에

출제율 152%

법칙 90 올바른 해석으로 풀어야 하는 형용사 어휘 문제

대부분의 형용사 어휘 문제는 주변 단어와의 어울림을 보고도 풀 수 있지만 매회 한 문제는 빈칸 주변 단어와의 어울림만으로는 풀 수 없는 문제가 있는데, 이럴 경우에는 문제의 해석을 통해 답을 골라야 한다.

STEP 1 유형을 파악해 봐

1. The manager called on Ms. Lee to give a ------- comment on her proposal during the break time.
(A) dissatisfied   (B) brief   (C) unanimous   (D) lengthy

2. We need to order an extra shelf ------- enough to fit a bunch of books that cannot be placed on the current one.
(A) light   (B) strong   (C) old   (D) qualified

3. If the paper tray is -------, you should put a handful of A4 sheets in it for the next person to use.
(A) full   (B) stuck   (C) outdated   (D) empty

보기가 모두 서로 다른 형용사들로 왔으므로 형용사 어휘 문제이다. 1번 문제는 위치상으로는 빈칸 뒤 명사와의 어울림을 보는 문제이며, 2번 문제는 빈칸 앞의 shelf와의 어울림을 보는 문제인 반면에, 3번 문제는 주어와의 어울림을 보는 문제이다. 그러나 세 문제 모두 명사와의 어울림만으로는 정확한 답을 고를 수 없다.

STEP 2 이렇게 풀어 봐   "유형을 파악해 봐" 1번 문제를 보세요!

첫째 보기에 서로 반대되는 말이 있을 경우, 둘 중 하나를 대입해 해석해 본다.
의미상 서로 반대되는 말이 보기로 제시될 경우 둘 다 어울릴 수는 없다. (B)와 (D)가 반대의 의미를 갖고 있으므로 먼저 (B)를 대입해 해석하면, '매니저는 그녀의 제안에 대해 간단한 의견을 제시하려고 휴식 동안 Ms. Lee를 방문했다.'로 해석되어 자연스럽다.

둘째 나머지 보기를 대입해 해석해 보며 논리관계를 점검한다.
'매니저가 Ms. Lee에게 만장일치의 코멘트를 했다.'라는 내용은 어색하므로 (C)는 답이 될 수 없다.

PLUS
- 논리 관계를 따질 때는 부정어구나 역접의 연결어(but, although, despite 등)에 주의한다.
- 정답이 되기 위한 논리적 근거는 문제 안에 있다는 생각으로 접근한다.

STEP 3 실전에 적용해 봐

1. BNM International Air should set a(n) ------- amount of weight that each passenger can check in as luggage in order not to cause any confusion.

   (A) enormous
   (B) average
   (C) inaccurate
   (D) maximum

2. This month, the city council made it mandatory for local schools and companies to hold evacuation drills regularly due to the ------- earthquakes that had occurred.

   (A) rare
   (B) ancient
   (C) frequent
   (D) upcoming

3. Named one of the most prosperous companies in the world, Glory, Inc. has always maintained a ------- profit margin.

   (A) positive
   (B) rare
   (C) negative
   (D) limited

4. The CEO decided to launch the recently developed electronic device regardless of the ------- objections by the executives.

   (A) mere
   (B) strong
   (C) only
   (D) bearable

5. Dr. Moore advised the patient to include exercising for at least half an hour in his daily -------.

   (A) routine
   (B) visit
   (C) report
   (D) incident

6. Although the candidate put a considerable effort into delivering his speech, the audience remained ------- to his pledges, which they did not find convincing.

   (A) unresponsive
   (B) excited
   (C) attentive
   (D) obligatory

7. Considering that he has been at Spix Design for only a week, it was a ------- task for Mr. Davis to memorize the names of 50 employees sharing the office with him.

   (A) minimal
   (B) small
   (C) quick
   (D) formidable

8. At the awards ceremony, Ms. Jamison was praised for her ------- job managing the teams under her supervision.

   (A) trifling
   (B) insignificant
   (C) synthetic
   (D) superb

9. The restaurant, which is located just a block away from Exit 7, is the ------- venue to Almond Station that can hold a business luncheon.

   (A) largest
   (B) closest
   (C) widest
   (D) biggest

10. It happens quite often that Ms. Bacon skips meals because of her ------- schedule.

    (A) busy
    (B) empty
    (C) detailed
    (D) specific

뉴토익 빈도순 정답 어휘 정리 - 형용사편

빈도	형용사어휘	뜻	기출 collocation
7	additional	추가의	요금, 하루, 장려금
6	available	이용 가능한	서비스, 사람
6	eligible	~할 자격이 있는	사람 ~ for/to 할인, 지원, 계약
6	upcoming	다가오는	행사, 공사, 발표
5	accessible	접근[이용]가능한	장소, 정보
5	routine	일상의, 정기적인	업무, 검사
4	brief	간결한, 짧은	부재, 휴업
4	complimentary	무료의, 칭찬의	식사, 티켓, 쿠폰
4	comprehensive	포괄적인	연구, 데이터, 개발계획
4	convenient	편리한	서비스, 시간
4	current	현재의	규정, 숫자, 해(년)
5	defective	결함이 있는	기계, 제품
4	detailed	상세한	정보, 보고서, 평가
4	leading	선도하는	공급업체, 생산업체
4	limited	제한된	기간, 좌석, 지원
4	significant	상당한	승진, 저축, 성장
4	temporary	임시의, 일시적인	비밀번호, 할인, 해결책
4	unique	독특한	절차, 경우, 복장
3	complete	완성된, 완료된	주문, 절차, 일정
3	frequent	빈번한, 잦은	기차, 회의, 검색
3	innovative	혁신적인	광고, 방법, 웹 브라우저
3	reliable	믿을 수 있는, 신뢰할 만한	서비스, 교통수단
3	unfavorable	불리한, 비판적인	기상여건, 시장여건, 반응
3	beneficial	유익한, 이로운	~하는 것이
2	exempt	면제되는	from -ing

빈도	형용사어휘	뜻	기출 collocation
2	functional	기능을 하는	장비, 철도
2	outstanding	뛰어난	서비스, 판매실적
2	relevant	관련된	문서, 경력
2	tentative	잠정적인, 임시의	일정, 제안
2	versatile	다재 다능한	사람, 가구
1	administrative	관리상의, 행정상의	직책, 일자리
1	artificial	인공의	화초
1	compatible	호환되는	소프트웨어
1	consecutive	연속적인	날짜
1	depleted	고갈된	카트리지를 교체하다
1	exemplary	모범적인	업무수행
1	feasible	실현 가능한	계획
1	formidable	어마어마한, 가공할	도전과제, 어려움
1	idle	가동되지 않는	생산라인
1	immense	엄청난, 어마어마한	~ collection of (매우 다양한)
1	lingering	오래 끄는	근심, 걱정
1	mandatory	의무적인	검사, 점검
1	obsolete	쓸모 없는, 구식의	기계
1	optimal	최선의, 최상의	상태, 조건
1	pertinent	적절한, 관련 있는	문제
1	strenuous	몹시 힘든, 힘이 많이 드는	~하는 것
1	stringent	엄중한, 긴박한	조치
1	subsequent	차후의, 이 다음의	해(년)
1	unanimous	만장일치의	이사회
1	vulnerable	취약한, 연약한	~ to

Chapter 12

부사 어휘 문제

매월 3문제

출제율 119%

법칙 91 특정 시제와 잘 어울리는 부사

동사를 수식하는 부사들 중에는 특정 시제와 잘 어울리는 부사들이 있는데, 예를 들어 '정기적으로'라는 뜻의 regularly는 반복 습관적인 사실을 나타내는 현재시제와 잘 어울린다. 이렇게 특정 시제와 잘 어울리는 부사를 '시제 부사'라고도 하며, 현재시제와 잘 어울리는 '빈도부사'도 시제 부사의 한 종류이다.

STEP 1 유형을 파악해 봐

1. Voltech Solutions is ------- recruiting new employees for engineering positions.
(A) well   (B) now   (C) very   (D) even

2. The Host Hotel has ------- been renovated 30 years after its founding.
(A) primarily   (B) currently   (C) recently   (D) usually

3. The English version of the book will ------- be available.
(A) soon   (B) well   (C) yet   (D) even

보기가 모두 서로 다른 부사들로 왔으므로 부사 어휘 문제이며, 세 문제 모두 빈칸이 동사를 수식하는 부사 자리이다. 1번 문제는 현재진행시제, 2번 문제는 현재완료시제, 3번 문제는 미래시제이다. 보기에는 특정 시제와 잘 어울리는 부사들이 1개 이상 있으므로 이는 특정 시제와 잘 어울리는 부사를 묻는 문제라고 할 수 있다.

STEP 2 이렇게 풀어 봐

"유형을 파악해 봐" 1번 문제를 보세요!

첫째 동사의 시제를 확인한 후, 해당 시제와 어울리는 부사를 확인한다.
동사의 시제는 현재진행시제이며, 현재진행시제와 잘 어울리는 부사는 (B) now이다. 다른 부사들은 딱히 특정 시제와 어울리는 것이 없다.

둘째 부사를 넣어 해석해 확인한다.
'Voltech Solutions는 현재 엔지니어 직책에 필요한 새 직원들을 모집하고 있다.'로 자연스럽게 해석된다.

PLUS
• 시제 부사는 다음과 같다.

현재시제	빈도부사와 주로 어울린다 regularly, frequently, always, usually, often, typically, routinely, periodically, occasionally, normally, customarily, every month, each month, these days	
미래시제	soon, shortly	
과거시제	previously, once, recently	
현재완료	just, since, recently, yet (→ 부정문일 때만)	
현재진행 및 현재	now, currently, presently	

함정을 피해 봐 <small>실제 강의에서만 알려주는 풀이 노하우!</small>

1. will이 없어도 미래시제 부사와 어울리는 경우에 유의한다.

> 미래시제 부사와 어울리는 동사들
> can, may, need, should, must, be expected to, be scheduled to, be supposed to, be about to, be going to 등

2. 시제 부사가 예외적으로 다른 시제와 사용되는 경우에 유의한다.

During the last month, all of the line workers at the Denver facility (formerly/often) worked overtime to fill the order.

→ 과거시제만 보고 formerly를 바로 답으로 고르면 안 된다. 앞에 이미 during the last month가 있으므로 formerly를 쓰는 것은 어색하다. often은 주로 현재시제와 쓰지만, 과거에 반복, 습관적으로 일어난 일을 묘사할 때도 사용할 수 있다.

	일반적인 경우	예외적인 경우
soon, shortly	미래시제	soon after, shortly after는 주로 과거시제
currently, presently	현재진행시제	현재시제 He currently has 5 employees. Currently, there are 5 employees.
always	현재	현재완료
already	현재완료	현재
once	과거, 현재완료	모든 시제와 사용 once again, once a week, once a year

3. recently는 과거나 현재완료시제와 사용하나, 구체적인 기간과 어울려 쓰지 않는다.

The prices of raw materials have (clearly/recently) risen in the last 5 years.

→ 현재완료시제만 보고 recently를 답으로 선택해서는 안 된다. '지난 5년간'이라는 구체적인 기간이 있으므로 recently는 어울리지 않는다.

2. often 3. clearly

STEP 3 실전에 적용해 봐

1. We encourage our customers to choose a package tour to Australia during the summer season as the weather is ------- more favorable during this period.

   (A) possibly
   (B) exactly
   (C) usually
   (D) shortly

2. Employees who are ------- working under Mr. Dawson's supervision may be directed by the executive officer starting next Monday.

   (A) previously
   (B) significantly
   (C) recently
   (D) currently

3. After intensively interviewing the applicants one by one, the manager ------- decided whom he was going to hire.

   (A) meanwhile
   (B) finally
   (C) mostly
   (D) extremely

4. ------- a small domestic company, Genetic Auto has become a multinational company selling automobiles worldwide.

   (A) Newly
   (B) Upon
   (C) Formerly
   (D) Before

5. The products whose prices are subject to change after the promotion period is over should be announced ------- this week.

   (A) past
   (B) formerly
   (C) since
   (D) later

6. The ready-to-go meals were ------- intended to stimulate purchases by single households but also became popular with large households.

   (A) originally
   (B) smoothly
   (C) significantly
   (D) currently

7. Most of the garments sold at the store were ------- made by hand, but it is rare to find handmade ones among those produced by machines these days.

   (A) previously
   (B) currently
   (C) later
   (D) soon

8. We ------- check every computer in our company for viruses to avoid a failure in its system.

   (A) originally
   (B) recently
   (C) significantly
   (D) regularly

9. Although Ms. Miranda ------- lives downtown, she will soon move to company housing once she starts working at GK Design.

   (A) recently
   (B) once
   (C) quite
   (D) currently

10. Referring to these figures on the chart, you will see that the price of wheat has ------- increased over the past 3 years.

    (A) recently
    (B) clearly
    (C) monetarily
    (D) exactly

출제율 32%

법칙 92 특정 형용사와 잘 어울리는 부사

부사 중에는 특정 형용사와 잘 어울리는 부사들이 있는데, 예를 들어 형용사로 취급하는 숫자 앞에 잘 오는 숫자 수식 부사가 여기에 해당한다. ('법칙 41' 참고) 한편, somewhat, relatively, extremely, uncommonly, highly 등은 형용사를 주로 수식하는 부사들이다.

STEP 1 유형을 파악해 봐

1. The Hobb, Inc. Web site remained inaccessible for ------- two days.
(A) absolutely   (B) nearly   (C) frequently   (D) rarely

2. Mr. Song is already a(n) ------- successful author because his new book has made the bestseller list.
(A) elegantly   (B) mainly   (C) fortunately   (D) highly

3. Every year, the organization holds a weeklong workshop, and it is ---- attended by the area's businessmen.
(A) very   (B) enormously   (C) adversely   (D) well

보기가 모두 서로 다른 부사들로 왔으므로 부사 어휘 문제이며, 세 문제 모두 빈칸 바로 뒤에 형용사나 형용사 기능을 하는 p.p.가 있다. 보기에는 형용사와 잘 어울리는 부사들이 1개 이상 있으므로 형용사와 잘 어울리는 부사를 묻는 문제들이라고 할 수 있다.

STEP 2 이렇게 풀어 봐   "유형을 파악해 봐" 1번 문제를 보세요!

첫째 형용사와 잘 어울리는 부사를 확인한다.
빈칸 뒤에 형용사인 숫자가 왔는데, 숫자와 잘 어울리는 '숫자 수식 부사'는 (B)이다. (A)는 주로 impossible, correct, right 등의 형용사와 어울리며, (C)와 (D)는 동사의 빈도를 나타내는 빈도부사들이다. 특히 (D)는 준부정어라고 하며, 동사를 부정한다.

둘째 부사를 넣어 해석해 점검한다.
'거의 이틀 동안'이라는 해석이 자연스럽다.

PLUS

- 부사 중에서 특히 형용사 앞에 잘 오는 부사들을 기억한다.

형용사 앞에 오는 부사들				
숫자 수식 부사	approximately, nearly, almost, more than, less than, over, at least, up to, roughly, around, about, just, a maximum of, a minimum of, as much as			
정도 부사	somewhat 다소	relatively 비교적	extremely 매우	uncommonly 보통이 아니게
	highly 매우	slightly 약간	marginally 근소하게	heavily 심하게
	badly 심하게	well 잘	deeply 심히	so ~ that S + V 너무 ~해서 ~하다
기타	moderately successful 꽤 성공적인		unusually cold 유난히 추운	
	otherwise modern 반대로 현대적인		mutually beneficial 상호간에 혜택이 되는	
	nearly/almost complete 거의 완성된			

- 정도 부사 중 p.p.를 좋아하는 부사들도 있다.

highly recommended 적극 추천되는	highly regarded 매우 잘 알려진	well attended 참석률이 높은
well organized 잘 조직된	uncommonly found 드물게 발견되는	

함정을 피해 봐
실제 강의에서만 알려주는 풀이 노하우!

1. 숫자의 모양을 하고 있지 않아도 half, double, decade, triple, once, a처럼 의미상 숫자인 단어들을 조심한다.

(Entirely / Approximately) half the employees at Goodwill, Inc. registered for the evening language classes.

➡ half를 명사로 생각해 숫자 수식 부사를 오답 처리하지 않도록 한다. half는 50%를 의미하므로 숫자의 의미를 가지고 있기 때문에 숫자 수식 부사가 정답이다.

1. Approximately

STEP 3 실전에 적용해 봐

1. The interest rate at HB Bank is up by ------- 5%.

   (A) roughly
   (B) relatively
   (C) slightly
   (D) fairly

2. For our fundraising event, all kinds of support, whether it is in form of donations or volunteering, are ------- appreciated.

   (A) increasingly
   (B) gradually
   (C) deeply
   (D) carefully

3. The aptitude test for a professional CAD designer asks ------- 100 different questions.

   (A) for
   (B) up to
   (C) between
   (D) along with

4. After her proposal was turned down, Ms. Walter seemed ------- depressed and did not talk much at the meeting.

   (A) previously
   (B) once
   (C) somewhat
   (D) officially

5. Although Loonie Store is only a bridge away from Mr. Farrell's house, since there is always heavy traffic on the bridge, Farmers Shop, located a few miles away, is ------- more accessible.

   (A) relatively
   (B) severely
   (C) closely
   (D) barely

6. Because Ms. Tylor was a regular guest at the Sunpick Inn, she was given a special coupon which provided her with a one-night stay at a price discounted by ------- 30%.

   (A) regardless
   (B) alike
   (C) unless
   (D) as much as

7. The characteristic of luxury goods is to set their prices ------- high so that only a limited number of customers can own them.

   (A) extremely
   (B) accordingly
   (C) widely
   (D) finally

8. ------- 30 more staff members will be required for the upcoming event at the store.

   (A) Recently
   (B) Hardly
   (C) Commonly
   (D) Approximately

9. Consuming green food on a regular basis is undoubtedly a good habit, but depending ------- on it is likely to prevent the ingestion of proteins and other vital nutrients by your body.

   (A) sufficiently
   (B) heavily
   (C) well
   (D) reliably

10. Since the Maryland Annual Housing Fair has always been extremely popular, we encourage you to purchase tickets for the 17th fair ------- in advance.

    (A) well
    (B) eventually
    (C) beforehand
    (D) ahead

출제율 38%

법칙 93 전명구와 잘 어울리는 부사

'in the room'처럼 전치사로 시작해 명사로 끝나는 덩어리를 전명구라고 하며, 형용사나 부사의 기능을 한다. 부사는 형용사, 부사, 그리고 동사를 수식하기 때문에 전명구를 수식하는 것도 역시 부사이다.

STEP 1 유형을 파악해 봐

1. The registration period for Spanish class has been extended ------- for those who have not paid their fees yet.
   (A) noticeably (B) mutually (C) specifically (D) annually

2. Membership cards are offered ------- to customers who purchase over $500 every month.
   (A) firmly (B) exclusively (C) significantly (D) hopefully

3. Please forward this e-mail ------- to the director of the Personnel Department.
   (A) absolutely (B) directly (C) thoroughly (D) relatively

보기가 모두 서로 다른 부사들로 왔으므로 부사 어휘 문제이며, 세 문제 모두 빈칸 바로 뒤에 전명구가 있고, 보기에 전명구와 잘 어울리는 부사들이 1개 이상 있으므로 전명구와 잘 어울리는 부사를 묻는 문제라고 할 수 있다.

STEP 2 이렇게 풀어 봐   "유형을 파악해 봐" 1번 문제를 보세요!

첫째 전명구와 잘 어울리는 부사를 확인한다.
빈칸 뒤에 전명구가 왔고, 전명구와 잘 어울리는 부사는 초점 부사인 (C)이다. (A)는 증감 부사('법칙 94' 참고)이므로 증가나 감소의 뜻을 가진 동사와 어울리고, (B)는 beneficial과 같은 형용사를 수식하며, (D)는 현재시제와 함께 쓰이는 부사이다.

둘째 부사를 넣어 해석해 확인한다.
'스페인어 수업의 등록 기간은 특히 수업료를 납부하지 않은 사람을 위해 연장된다.'라는 해석이 자연스럽기 때문에 정답이다.

PLUS

• 부사 중에서 특히 전명구 앞에 잘 오는 부사들을 기억한다.

주로 전명구 앞에 오는 부사들				
초점 부사	only 단지	exclusively 독점적으로	just 단지	even ~조차
	specifically 특히	especially 특히	exactly 정확히	
방식	directly from ~로부터 직접	directly to ~쪽으로 직접	separately from ~와는 별도로	
시간	sometime between A and B A와 B 사이에		later in the week 주 후반에	
	promptly at 정각에		immediately after 직후에	
	right after 직후에		soon after 직후에	
기타	ideally 이상적으로		probably due to 주로 ~때문에	
	everywhere in the room 방안 어디든지		consistently behind schedule 지속적으로 일정보다 늦은	
	temporarily out of stock 일시적으로 재고가 바닥난			

• 초점 부사는 명사 앞이나 부사절 앞에도 올 수 있다.

Only those who have their identification badge are allowed to enter the facility.
→ those는 '사람들'이란 뜻의 명사이다.

Even before the meeting began, the attendees already started discussing the agenda.
→ before the meeting began은 부사절이다.

함정을 피해 봐 실제 강의에서만 알려주는 풀이 노하우!

1. only, alone, alike 등 명사 뒤에 오는 부사들을 조심한다.

The company announced that the sales of its shoe line (alone/apart) exceeded $5 million this quarter.
→ shoe line이라는 명사 뒤에서 수식할 수 있는 부사는 alone이다. 이번 분기 매출이 구두 단일 제품만으로 5백만 달러가 넘었다는 뜻이다.

1. alone

STEP 3 실전에 적용해 봐

1. Ms. Giambi addressed the issues which were repeatedly discussed by the employees, ------- those in the Accounting Department.

   (A) economically
   (B) approximately
   (C) randomly
   (D) particularly

2. The Sharp Corporation has decided to change its target customers to small company owners, ------- to individuals with startup businesses.

   (A) primarily
   (B) relatively
   (C) comparatively
   (D) temporarily

3. Ms. Mill ordered ------- the same dish she used to get at the restaurant she revisited after not having gone for five years.

   (A) exactly
   (B) approximately
   (C) timely
   (D) uncommonly

4. Of the applicants, those who are applying for the project manager position will be interviewed ------- from the others.

   (A) stably
   (B) recently
   (C) separately
   (D) nearly

5. For each survey on our customer satisfaction, we receive responses, ------- from more than 100 customers to yield reliable results.

   (A) abruptly
   (B) critically
   (C) rarely
   (D) ideally

6. Mr. Gill has not mentioned the reason for his absence at the last meeting, but it seems that he missed the meeting ------- due to his conflicting schedule with his doctor's appointment.

   (A) usually
   (B) conditionally
   (C) probably
   (D) exceptionally

7. Ms. Lace seems uncomfortable answering personal questions, ------- about her marriage, in front of her co-workers.

   (A) appropriately
   (B) particularly
   (C) significantly
   (D) unusually

8. Mr. Hall was given a final warning from his boss because he finished his paperwork ------- behind schedule.

   (A) consistently
   (B) rarely
   (C) appropriately
   (D) punctually

9. ------- after the flight attendant's announcement was delivered, the plane heading to Amsterdam departed from Istanbul International Airport.

   (A) Centrally
   (B) Immediately
   (C) Commonly
   (D) Usually

10. The job advertisement for an engineer at Maxx Tech states that the company hires ------- experienced applicants.

    (A) once
    (B) over
    (C) soon
    (D) only

출제율 22%

법칙 94 특정 동사와 잘 어울리는 부사

부사 어휘 문제 (매월 3문제)

부사 중에는 특정 동사와 잘 어울리는 부사들이 있는데, 예를 들어 '철저하게'라는 뜻을 가진 thoroughly는 test, inspect, read 등과 어울린다. 또한 '급격하게'라는 뜻을 가진 dramatically, sharply, drastically 등의 부사는 increase, decrease 등과 같은 '증가, 감소' 동사들과 잘 어울린다.

STEP 1 유형을 파악해 봐

1. The team's motivation ------- increased after sales reached their peak.
(A) aggressively   (B) eagerly   (C) dramatically   (D) currently

2. Mr. Trey ordered his secretary to review the e-mail ------- to filter out the spam.
(A) thoroughly   (B) firmly   (C) eagerly   (D) overly

3. As told by the manager, the sales staff member responded ------- to the customers' inquiries.
(A) firmly   (B) gradually   (C) deeply   (D) quickly

보기가 모두 서로 다른 부사들로 왔으므로 부사 어휘 문제이다. 1번 문제는 동사 앞에 빈칸이 있으므로 특정 동사와 잘 어울리는 부사를 묻는 문제이며, 2, 3번 문제는 문맥을 파악하지 못한 상태에서 보면 to 부정사나, 전명구와 잘 어울리는 부사 어휘 문제로 보일 수 있지만, 사실은 앞의 동사 즉 review, respond와의 어울림을 보는 문제이다.

STEP 2 이렇게 풀어 봐

"유형을 파악해 봐" 1번 문제를 보세요!

첫째 동사와 잘 어울리는 부사를 확인한다.
빈칸이 동사 앞에서 동사를 수식하는 자리이므로 increase와의 어울림을 살피면 증감 부사 (C)가 와야 하는 자리이다. (A)는 '적극적으로'라는 뜻으로 '반응하다' 류의 동사와 어울리고, (B)는 '열망하여'라는 뜻으로 '기대하다' 류의 동사와 어울린다. (D)는 현재진행시제나, 현재시제와 어울리는 부사이다.

둘째 부사를 넣어 해석해 점검한다.
'판매가 최고치를 기록한 후 팀의 동기부여가 급격하게 증가했다.'로 자연스럽게 해석된다.

PLUS

- 부사 중에서 특정 동사와 잘 어울리는 부사를 기억한다.

부사	어울리는 동사 (혹은 p.p.)
증감 부사: sharply, dramatically, drastically, remarkably, noticeably, increasingly, considerably, substantially, significantly, greatly, markedly, gradually, steadily	증가, 감소의 뜻을 가진 동사 increase, rise, decrease, drop, fall, reduce, raise 등
준부정어: hardly, scarcely, seldom, rarely, barely, rapidly, quickly, swiftly	조동사 뒤, 일반 동사 앞에 오며, not과 같이 쓸 수 없다. approach 접근하다, move, change 변화하다
thoroughly 철저하게, exhaustively 철저하게, carefully 주의 깊게	inspect, test, research, read, clean, wash, go through 검토하다
eagerly 갈망하여, 몹시	await 기다리다, anticipate 기대하다
adversely 역으로, 반대로	affect 영향을 끼치다
firmly 견고하게	hold 잡고 있다
conveniently, centrally	located, situated 위치된
extensively 광범위하게	research 연구조사하다
reasonably 합리적으로	priced 가격이 매겨진
eloquently 유창하게	speak 말하다
severely 심하게	damaged 손상된
prominently 눈에 띄게	post 게시하다, display 진열하다, place 위치시키다
deeply 심히	appreciate 감사하다
clearly 명백히, explicitly 명쾌하게	state 말하다, 서 있다
closely 면밀하게	look at ~를 보다
perfectly 완벽하게	suited 어울리는
cautiously 조심스럽게	predict 예측하다
meticulously 꼼꼼하게	plan 계획하다
particularly 특히	busy, stressful 스트레스가 많은
punctually 시간에 딱 맞춰	arrive 도착하다
tentatively 잠정적으로	scheduled 일정이 잡힌
generously 후하게, 관대하게	donate, offer 제안하다

- 부사 중에서 특정 단어와 잘 어울리는 부사를 기억한다.

not necessarily, not always 항상 ~인 것 만은 아니다; 부분부정   independently of ~와는 별개로
absolutely[completely] free of charge 완전히 공짜로   after ~ finally ~한 후에 마침내   after ~ still ~후에도 여전히
although ~ still ~에도 불구하고 여전히   as rapidly as possible 가능한 한 빨리   set forth ~를 제시하다, 발표하다
now 이제는 → 앞의 절이나 문장에 과거시제가 있을 때

 **함정을 피해 봐**   실제 강의에서만 알려주는 풀이 노하우!

1. 의미나 모양새가 비슷해 혼동하기 쉬운 부사를 조심한다.

❶ Patients at Stoke Hospital complained that they could only speak with the doctor (briefly/promptly) before being placed on hold for half an hour.

→ briefly는 shortly와 같은 뜻이고, promptly는 '즉시'라는 뜻으로 '연락하다, 통보하다, 도착하다' 등의 동사와 어울린다.

❷ The retirement ceremony can be (shortly/easily) moved to an indoor banquet hall if it rains tomorrow.

→ shortly는 현재를 기준해서 곧 일어날 일을 묘사할 때 사용한다. '내일 비가 온다면'이라는 말로 기준점이 내일로 바뀌었으므로 shortly는 어색하다. 비가 오면 쉽게 실내로 옮길 수 있다는 내용으로 easily가 답이다.

❸ Our team (recently/lately) finished the renovation project.

→ recently와 lately는 뜻은 같으나 lately는 주로 부정문이나 의문문에 등장하고 문두나 문미에 사용한다.

다른 모양		유사한 모양	
lastly 순서상으로 마지막에	finally 결국 마침내	high 높게	highly 매우
only 단지	fully 동사 앞	late 늦게	lately 요즘, 최근에
much too 형용사/부사	too much 불가산명사	right 정확히, 바로	rightly 바르게, 정당하게
merely 그 이상도 그 이하도 아닌, 별것 아닌		hard 열심히	hardly 거의 ~아니다
steadily 긍정적인 방향으로 꾸준히		near 가까이	nearly 거의; 숫자수식 부사
consistently 단순 지속적으로		low 낮게	lowly 비천하게
far 거리표시 숫자와 사용 불가		clear 완전히(completely)	clearly 의심의 여지가 없이
away 구체적인 숫자와 사용가능		pretty 꽤, 매우	prettily 귀엽게
prominently 배치, 위치 등이 눈에 띄게			
markedly 동작, 변화, 차이 등이 다르게			
enough 명사 앞, to 부정사 앞, 동사/형용사/부사 뒤			

1. briefly, easily, recently

STEP 3 실전에 적용해 봐

1. Please make sure you read the operating manual for the machine ------- before using it.
   (A) eagerly
   (B) carefully
   (C) formerly
   (D) extremely

2. Your salary will ------- increase in proportion to the number of years you are employed at this company.
   (A) carefully
   (B) thoroughly
   (C) gradually
   (D) hardly

3. The orders from headquarters required the store manager to conduct the inventory check as ------- as possible.
   (A) gradually
   (B) scarcely
   (C) inadvertently
   (D) rapidly

4. Because traffic is always bad around 7 P.M., Mr. Chang ------- leaves his office during this time and instead prefers to get off at 9 P.M.
   (A) seldom
   (B) recently
   (C) possibly
   (D) frequently

5. It is unfortunate that donations for low-income households have dropped ------- this year because of the recession.
   (A) sharply
   (B) timely
   (C) eloquently
   (D) desirably

6. The quality of the products produced by the Resil Manufacturing Company has been ------- improved after the company hired more employees.
   (A) firmly
   (B) indistinctively
   (C) typically
   (D) considerably

7. The Kelleher Furniture Shop ------- charges shipping fees on items ordered by customers who are VIP members.
   (A) then
   (B) rapidly
   (C) rarely
   (D) dominantly

8. Due to the unstable economic conditions, many of the companies are ------- downsizing their businesses to reduce their risks.
   (A) diversely
   (B) timely
   (C) availably
   (D) increasingly

9. The recent drought has ------- affected the production of barley, the amount of which reached only half of what had been expected.
   (A) favorably
   (B) valuably
   (C) adversely
   (D) positively

10. The 3-minute-trailer of the movie *Chicago Dance* made many moviegoers ------- anticipate its official release.
    (A) eagerly
    (B) lastly
    (C) regularly
    (D) abruptly

출제율 68%

법칙 95 올바른 해석으로 풀어야 하는 부사 어휘 문제

부사 어휘 문제(매월 3문제)

주변 단어와의 어울림을 보고 풀어야 하는 부사 어휘 문제 외에 빈칸 주변 단어와의 어울림 만으로는 정답을 고를 수 없는 문제가 적어도 매회 한 문제는 출제되는데, 이런 문제들은 해석을 통해 해결해야 한다.

STEP 1 유형을 파악해 봐

1. We use artificial flavors and preservations ------- in our dishes so that you can eat more healthily.
   (A) sparingly   (B) substantially   (C) frequently   (D) only

2. They were required to ------- answer the questions that were asked by the interviewers.
   (A) regularly   (B) reservedly   (C) clearly   (D) doubtfully

3. The play was ------- translated into English and received favorable reactions by audiences.
   (A) officially   (B) perfectly   (C) rarely   (D) manually

보기가 모두 서로 다른 부사들로 왔으므로 부사 어휘 문제이다. 1번 문제는 위치상으로는 동사와의 어울림을 보는 문제일 수도 있고, 뒤에 있는 전명구와의 어울림을 보는 문제일 수도 있다. 2번과 3번 문제는 동사와의 어울림을 보는 문제이긴 하지만 세 문제 모두 동사나 형용사의 어울림 만으로는 정확한 답을 고를 수 없다.

STEP 2 이렇게 풀어 봐
"유형을 파악해 봐" 1번 문제를 보세요!

첫째 보기에 서로 반대되는 단어가 제시되었을 경우 먼저 하나를 대입하여 해석해 본다.
내용상 서로 반대되는 말이 보기로 제시되는 경우 둘 중 하나가 어울리면 다른 하나는 오답이다. 비교적 뜻이 나머지와 반대인 (A)를 넣어 해석해 보면, '우리는 당신이 건강하게 먹을 수 있도록 요리에 인공감미료와 방부제를 드물게 사용했다.'라는 말이 자연스럽다.

둘째 나머지 보기를 대입하여 해석해 보면서 확인한다.
(B)는 '상당히,' (C)는 '빈번하게,' (D)는 '단지 요리에만'이라는 의미로 답이 되기에 어색하다.

PLUS

- 논리 관계를 따질 때는 부정어구나 역접의 연결어(but, although, despite 등)에 주의한다.
- 정답이 되기 위한 논리적 근거는 문제 안에 반드시 있다는 생각으로 접근한다.

STEP 3 실전에 적용해 봐

1. It is important to distribute the workload and to allocate tasks to the appropriate employees in order to do business more -------.

   (A) incrementally
   (B) efficiently
   (C) frequently
   (D) spontaneously

2. The CEO of the renowned company Bell, Inc. ------- donated half of his personal property to the Sharing Hope Society last month.

   (A) generously
   (B) indecisively
   (C) usually
   (D) consistently

3. These custom-made accessories can usually only be purchased on the company's Web site but will be ------- available at the offline store during the next week.

   (A) temporarily
   (B) extremely
   (C) permanently
   (D) accordingly

4. A private internal report was submitted ------- and claimed that a number of employees at GRT, Inc. had been involved in the wrongdoings.

   (A) respectfully
   (B) rarely
   (C) publicly
   (D) anonymously

5. The production manager at High-Tech Electronics ------- stressed the importance of the durability of the new wearable device, which was coated with three layers of titanium.

   (A) closely
   (B) uncertainly
   (C) continually
   (D) rarely

6. The policy ------- states that no returns or exchanges are permitted 30 days after the items were purchased.

   (A) ambiguously
   (B) indefinitely
   (C) explicitly
   (D) allegedly

7. Ms. Titus didn't know exactly what her manager meant when he ------- referred to beauty product shops.

   (A) clearly
   (B) broadly
   (C) obviously
   (D) directly

8. The urgent meeting, which took more than five hours, ------- affected her family trip, which had to be cancelled.

   (A) slightly
   (B) precisely
   (C) hardly
   (D) adversely

9. The Web site could not sustain the ------- large number of visitors and went down.

   (A) obviously
   (B) officially
   (C) sufficiently
   (D) unusually

10. You can trust the results of clinical trials on these cosmetics since the trials were ------- conducted by professional dermatologists.

    (A) meticulously
    (B) toughly
    (C) exactly
    (D) easily

Chapter 13

빈칸 문장만으로는 풀 수 없는 파트 6 문제

매월 9문제

출제율 100%

법칙 96 알맞은 문장 넣기 문제(신유형)는 앞뒤 흐름을 파악

신토익에서는 알맞은 문장 넣기 문제가 추가 되었다. 이러한 유형은 첫 번째 문제나 마지막 문제로 출제되기 보다는 두 번째나 세 번째 문제인 경우가 많다. 주로 앞뒤 문맥을 보고 풀어야 하므로 밑줄의 앞뒤 및 선택지를 정확히 독해하는 능력과 올바른 흐름을 분석하는 논리력이 요구된다. 아래의 134번이 신 유형 문제이다.

STEP 1 유형을 파악해 봐

Questions 131-134 refer to the following notice.

To: Project Leads
From: Clair Montgomery
Subject: Preliminary Meeting

To all Wills Technology project leaders:

We would like to inform you that a preliminary meeting for the upcoming training sessions will be held on Thursday. All project leaders are strongly ------ to attend the meeting. At the meeting,
131.
specific guidelines for each training session will be provided so that all members in charge of the training sessions clearly ------ the procedure of the sessions. We believe that a proper understanding
132.
of the entire procedure shared among all members is critical to the sessions' success. ------,
133.
should you not be able to attend the meeting, please let us know. ------.
134.

Thank you for your support.

131. (A) advise
(B) advises
(C) advised
(D) advising

132. (A) know
(B) claim
(C) plan
(D) suggest

133. (A) In addition
(B) After that
(C) Since
(D) However

134. (A) Doing so will help us find a better solution for the following reasons.
(B) We will contact you individually to discuss alternatives.
(C) The meeting will be preceded by the training sessions.
(D) Our clients will arrive in time for the meeting.

STEP 2 이렇게 풀어 봐
"유형을 파악해 봐" 134번 문제를 보세요!

첫째 밑줄 앞의 문장에 대한 정확한 독해 및 요약. 이어질 흐름 예상.
밑줄 앞의 내용은 '예비 미팅에 꼭 참석해야 한다. 참석하지 못하는 경우엔 알려달라'는 내용이므로 이어질 내용은 그에 대한 해결방책임을 알 수 있다.

둘째 선택지 4개를 독해한 후 예상과 일치하는 보기를 선택, 대입하여 밑줄 뒤의 흐름과 맞는지 확인.
선택지를 독해해 보면 (B) '우리가 너에게 개별적으로 연락을 취하겠다, 대안을 이야기 해보기 위해서'가 예상과 일치하므로 대입해보면 이어서 나오는 '당신의 지지에 감사한다'는 공지문의 마무리 문구와도 어울림이 좋으므로 정답.

PLUS

- 알맞은 문장 넣기 문제가 두번째나 세번째 문제로 나올 때 밑줄 앞만 봐도 풀리고, 뒤만 봐도 풀리는 경우가 있다. 앞뒤 어디를 봐도 풀리는 문제도 있다.

1. 밑줄 앞만 보고 바로 풀리는 경우

Thank you for doing business with Wendell Office Depot. We received your order placed yesterday afternoon. Some of the items you ordered are temporarily out of stock in our store, but we can get them from other branch locations in town or directly from the manufacturer. ------. You may cancel your order or change your order to other similar products in stock.
132.

132. (A) This will take about 2 business days.
    (B) We would appreciate it if you would return them.
    (C) You can purchase these in the coming year.
    (D) We refunded you the delivery fee.

→ 보기 중에 대명사가 사용되는 경우는 그 말이 가리키는 말을 잘 확인하면 바로 풀 수 있다. 밑줄 앞의 내용을 요약하면 '공장으로부터 직접, 혹은 다른 지점에서 얻어 줄 수 있다'는 말인데 이러한 행위가 곧 대명사 this를 받는 말이 되므로 굳이 이어지는 문장을 확인하지 않아도 (A)가 답이다.

2. 밑줄 뒤만 봐도 바로 풀리는 경우

Hello, everyone. I know that this is short-term notice, but I want to let everyone know that three new openings are available. ------ If we are unable to do so, then we will post them with a hiring agency.
132.

132. (A) I just received this information from the Personnel Department.
    (B) These positions require managerial experience in the field.
    (C) We would like to fill these internally first.
    (D) All staff members are already informed of their qualifications.

→ 밑줄 뒤에서 대명사가 사용되는 경우는 선택지에서도 그 대명사를 받을 수 있는 말이 있어야 한다. 밑줄 뒤에

서 '우리가 그렇게 할 수 없다면'이라는 말로 이어지므로 '그렇게 하다'는 부분의 내용은 이어서 나오는 '그 빈자리를 고용기관을 통해 고용한다'는 말과 반대되는 표현이 와야 한다는 것을 알 수 있다. 따라서 내부적으로 먼저 고용한다는 (C)가 답이다.

3. 밑줄 앞을 봐도 풀리고, 밑줄 뒤를 봐도 풀리는 경우

Our kitchen appliances must meet the highest standards for quality prior to being made available to you in our stores. We take extreme procedures in the development of the merchandise that we sell. ------ **133.** If this unfortunately is the case, we are happy to offer an exchange or a refund.

133. (A) In many cases, we offer 20% discount on our products.
(B) Even so, our dedication remains the same.
(C) Nevertheless, sometimes our product may not meet your expectations.
(D) From now on, we will take the product quality seriously.

➡ 선택지에 연결어(접속부사)가 있는 경우에는 앞을 봐도 풀리고 뒤를 봐도 풀리는 경우가 많다. 밑줄 앞을 요약하면 '품질 기준'에 대한 이야기인데, 보기들에 나오는 연결어와 문장을 보아도 품질에 대한 이야기를 하는 (C)가 어울린다. 한편, 밑줄 뒤만 본다고 하더라도 this라는 대명사를 사용, unfortunately라는 부정 표현이 나오므로 쉽게 부정 표현이 들어간 (C)를 답으로 선택할 수 있다.

4. 알맞은 문장 넣기 문제가 첫번째 문제로 나오는 경우 포괄적이거나 주제를 나타내는 문장이 정답이다.

------. **131.** As a result of the recent safety inspection, our main cafeteria will undergo renovations throughout this month to meet government requirements. During this time period, please be advised that you must use the second cafeteria near the east entrance. Normally, it is not allowed to use the employee lounge to eat your own food, but management decided to make an exception this month to ease any inconvenience the renovations may cause you.

131. (A) We are announcing lunch price increases.
(B) This is an important reminder for our cafeteria users.
(C) Note that the second cafeteria will close.
(D) New dining establishments are available on the premises.

➡ 글을 요약하면 주 구내식당이 보수공사를 할 것이며, 그 기간 동안에 주의해야할 내용을 공지하는 것이므로 글의 주제는 '주 구내식당 보수공사'라고 할 수 있다. 보기 중 가장 포괄적으로 주제를 나타낼 수 있는 '구내식당 사용자들에 관한 중요한 공지'라는 (B)가 정답이다.

5. 알맞은 문장 넣기 문제가 마지막 문제로 나오는 경우 전체를 요약하는 문장이 정답이 되기도 한다.

To Whom It May Concern,

We at the Avalon Corporation are planning to host a conference in Las Vegas next month and expect around 500 attendees this time. My friend Youngmin highly recommends your company, Wilson Manpower, to assist with conference and crowd-control issues. I am writing to inquire if you will be

able to assist us with our conference. We estimate that we will need about 45 individuals for the ticket counter, our merchandise booths, crowd control, and security. We hope that this will be an adequate number to meet our needs but may revise it as the conference date approaches. ------.
                                                                                                                                              134.

134. (A) I am very glad that you recruited us the last time.
　　　(B) I'm sorry to hear that you are understaffed.
　　　(C) Please let us know if you will be able to provide the staff we need at the conference.
　　　(D) Therefore, let's fix the number right now.

➡ 밑줄 앞의 내용을 요약하면 '행사에 필요한 인력 지원'이다. 선택 보기 중 (C)가 인력지원을 해달라는 내용이므로 앞의 내용을 요약하는 보기가 되며 정답이다.

함정을 피해 봐

실제 강의에서만 알려주는 풀이 노하우!

1. 앞의 내용과 내용상 모순되는 오답을 조심한다.

We would like to inform you that a preliminary meeting for the upcoming training sessions will be held on Thursday. All project leaders are strongly ------ to attend the meeting.
                                                                              131.
At the meeting, specific guidelines for each training session will be provided so that all members in charge of the training sessions clearly ------ the procedure of the sessions. We believe that
                                                                     132.
a proper understanding of the entire procedure shared among all members is critical to the sessions' success. ------ should you not be able to attend the meeting, please let us know. ------.
                      133.   134

134. (C) The meeting will be preceded by the training sessions.
➡ 앞의 내용에서 교육훈련을 위한 대비로 예비 미팅을 갖겠다고 하였다. 그러나 (C)는 교육훈련이 먼저 있고 미팅이 그 이후에 있다는 뜻이므로 앞의 내용과 모순된다. 내용상 모순이 되는 보기는 주로 첫번째 문제나 마지막 문제에 자주 등장한다.

2. 지문에 나오는 특정 단어와 연상되는 표현을 사용한 오답을 조심한다.

134. (D) Our clients will arrive in time for the meeting.
➡ 비행기 하면 공항, 승객, 이륙 등이 연상되고, 의사하면 병원, 환자 등이 연상되 듯 clients는 meeting 으로 연상되는 표현을 사용한 오답이 된다. 이는 토익의 전 파트 특히 파트1, 2에서 자주 사용되는 오답 기법이므로 주의한다.

3. 반쪽 흐름을 조심한다.

134. (A) Doing so will help us find a better solution for the following reasons.
➡ 반쪽 흐름이란 앞이나 뒤 어느 한쪽만 흐름이 일치하는 오답 보기를 말한다. (A)의 경우에는 앞의 흐름과는 맞으나 '다음의 이유로'라는 부분이 뒤의 흐름과 어울리지 않는다.

1. am seeking

출제율 **188%**

법칙 97 시제 문제는 나중에 푼다

파트 6은 파트 5와는 달리 시제 문제가 나올 때 해당 문장만으로는 정답을 고를 수 없게 출제된다. 예를 들면 첫 번째 문제가 시제 문제인 경우, 마지막 문제를 푸는 도중에 두번째 문제의 답을 찾게 되는 경우도 있다. 아래 문제의 경우 첫 번째 문제가 시제 문제이다.

STEP 1 유형을 파악해 봐

Questions 131-134 refer to the following notice.

We are pleased to announce that Dr. Dawson ------ Dr. Norris's research team this Tuesday.
                                              131.

Dr. Dawson had previously worked at the National Institute of Biotech Research but decided to ------
                                                                                           132.
Dr. Norris upon her request.

------. In light of his expertise and career, Dr. Dawson will be co-leading the team and its project with
133.
Dr. Norris until next year.

Under Dr. Dawson's supervision, the team is already making ------ progress as it recently discovered
                                                           134.
the possibility of replacing damaged human blood vessels with those from a healthy pig.

131. (A) joined
     (B) joins
     (C) is joined
     (D) will join

132. (A) inform
     (B) assist
     (C) keep
     (D) allow

133. (A) Unfortunately Dr. Dawson is leaving us to take on another project.
     (B) With the help of Dr. Dawson, the team has already completed the project.
     (C) Dr. Dawson has almost 15 years of experience in the biotechnology sector.
     (D) Considering his contributions to the team, Dr. Dawson is a great asset to us.

134. (A) slow
     (B) notable
     (C) limited
     (D) same

STEP 2 이렇게 풀어 봐
"유형을 파악해 봐" 131번 문제를 보세요!

첫째 밑줄이 포함된 문장 안의 단서만으로 오답을 최대한 소거.
밑줄은 동사자리이며, 뒤에 목적어가 있으므로 능동형의 동사가 필요하다. (C)가 들어오면 수동태가 되어 도전어를 가질 수 없기에 탈락.

둘째 두 번째 혹은 세 번째 문제까지 풀다가 단서를 잡아 답을 결정.
134번에서 Dr. Dawson의 관리하에, 팀이 이미 상당한 진척을 만들었다는 말이 나오므로 Dr. Dawson이 합류한 것이 과거의 일임을 알 수 있다. 따라서 131번은 과거시제인 (A)가 답.

PLUS

- 파트 6에서 주로 나오는 이메일/편지, 기사문, 공지글 등은 제목 근처에 날짜가 제시되는 경우가 많다. 그 날짜가 시제문제풀이의 단서가 되기도 한다.
- 시제 문제의 기출 순서는 미래나 미래진행 시제 → 현재나 현재 진행 시제 → 과거시제 → 현재완료시제 순이며, 미래완료시제나 가정법 (would/should/could/might have p.p., would/should/could/might 동사원형)은 아직까지 정답으로 나온 적이 없다.
- '나는 편지를 쓰고 있는 중이다, 우리 회사는 ~를 찾고 있는 중이다' 등의 표현은 주로 현재 진행시제를 사용하며, 현재시제는 반복, 습관적 사실이나 규정을 나타내는 문맥에서 사용된다.

함정을 피해 봐
실제 강의에서만 알려주는 풀이 노하우!

1. 현재 완료 시제는 과거에 발생한 일을 나타내기도 한다.

Last week, I moved to Shanghai and (am seeking / have sought) a new position in data management. As you can see by looking at the attached résumé, I think I am an excellent candidate for the positon.

➡ 지난 주에 이사를 왔고, 자신이 훌륭한 후보자라고 하는 것을 봤을때 아직 구직활동을 하고 있다고 볼 수 있다. 현재완료시제를 '~해왔다'라고 해석하면 답이 될 수 있을 것 같지만, 'since + 과거시점'이나 'for/over + 기간'과 같이 쓰지 않는 현재완료시제는 '~했다'라고 해석하며 과거에 발생한 일을 나타낸다. '계속 찾아왔고, 지금도 찾고 있는 중이다'의 뜻을 갖는 have been seeking이 더 좋은 말이겠으나 보기에 없으니 am seeking이 답이 된다.

1. am seeking

STEP 3 실전에 적용해 봐

Questions 131-134 refer to the following advertisement.

New Insurance for Startup Businesses

We understand that a startup business requires different coverage to protect against the unique risks it faces. Therefore, at Schmann Insurance, a new insurance policy ------ available
131.
for our clients to apply for.

The policy includes ------ benefits, including coverage of the initial startup costs. Therefore,
132.
the client is given a wide range of coverage to select and add. ------. Benefits such as
133.
discounts on employee health insurance fees are not found in any other policies.

Other unique benefits are also available in policies for businesses of different sizes and purposes. So ------ the type of business our client owns, we can recommend the right policy.
134.

If you are interested in being one of the 3,000 customers who are already covered by this insurance, call us today at 0888-330-3399.

131. (A) will become
 (B) has become
 (C) becomes
 (D) had become

132. (A) efficient
 (B) economical
 (C) enhanced
 (D) various

133. (A) Some of those benefits are also exclusive to this special policy.
 (B) We specialize in sourcing the right insurance plans for any businesses.
 (C) It is not the benefits that set this policy apart from other ones.
 (D) The client is considering whether to add more unique benefits or not.

134. (A) in addition
 (B) beside
 (C) regardless of
 (D) on top of

Questions 135-138 refer to the following letter.

To: Patrick Devon
From: Christine House
Date: December 28
Subject: Membership Expiry

Dear Mr. Devon,

It is our pleasure to have you as one of our loyal customers, and we are always ------ to
135.
providing you with the best service we can deliver.

Unfortunately, your annual membership ------ this Friday, and we are afraid that we cannot
136.
assist you any longer without an active membership.

If you wish to continue to be served by us, please fill out the brief request form attached to this
mail. ------. The address to send your form with the renewal fee is: Customer Service,
137.
Rendleman Bldg., Rm. 309, Box 776.

We sincerely hope to serve you for ------ year.
138.

Sincerely,
Christine House
Customer Service Coordinator

135. (A) dedicated
(B) interested
(C) tempted
(D) opt

136. (A) expired
(B) was expired
(C) expires
(D) will have expired

137. (A) You will be exempt from the renewal fee due to your permanent membership.
(B) Then, enclose the renewal fee of $20 and return the completed form.
(C) We were very glad that you promptly made your payment.
(D) Otherwise, you will have to visit us in person and pay your fine.

138. (A) every
(B) another
(C) this
(D) last

Questions 139-142 refer to the following letter.

To: All Employees
From: Daniel Jackson, Executive
Date: January 9
Subject: Comments on Retirement Party

Dear employees,

Thank you all for the great preparations you did at the ------ retirement party for Mr. Everett on
139.
his last day at Cenmora, Inc. He ------ enjoyed the party and wanted to thank each of you for
140.
making the day filled with unforgettable moments.

Mr. Everett was a very passionate and diligent man without whose dedication the company would not have been able to get to where it is now. ------. Cenmora, Inc. will always remember
141.
his service and contributions.

Although Mr. Everett ------ the company, his spirit will remain here. Let us encourage
142.
his ongoing support to Cenmora, Inc. as we strive for excellence.

139. (A) upcoming
(B) approaching
(C) past
(D) ultimate

140. (A) probably
(B) preferably
(C) gradually
(D) truly

141. (A) Thanks to his cooperation, we may be able to extend our partnership.
(B) Therefore, we would like everyone to attend the retirement party to say farewell.
(C) He will be gone for long periods of time until he resumes his work here.
(D) He sincerely served the company as a senior sales manager for 30 years.

142. (A) has left
(B) will leave
(C) is leaving
(D) was leaving

Questions 143-146 refer to the following article.

The City of Cherryville Announces the Grand Opening of Supreme Techno Plaza

March 15 ------ the grand opening of a new cultural space in Cherryville. A special ceremony
            143.
was held at 10 A.M. and was followed by the official plaza opening at 11 A.M. Over 1,000 guests, mainly local residents, attended the ceremony. ------.
                                                                144.

The ------ of Supreme Techno Plaza is the first step in the plan to develop the region into a
    145.
multicultural hub and is managed by the Department of Cultural Affairs (DCA).

"The city of Cherryville is thrilled to introduce its own cultural space to the citizens ------,"
                                                                                    146.
said the director of the DCA at the opening. "Supreme Techno Plaza will provide local residents with plenty of opportunities to enjoy a rich and varied cultural life."

143. (A) will mark
     (B) is marking
     (C) marks
     (D) marked

144. (A) In other words, the number of guests is 10 on average each day.
     (B) Those guests are proud that this space is globally acknowledged.
     (C) Many of these guests plan to enter the plaza right after the ceremony.
     (D) Community leaders and officials also visited to share a few remarks

145. (A) establish
     (B) established
     (C) establishing
     (D) establisher

146. (A) at last
     (B) though
     (C) however
     (D) yet

출제율 58%

법칙 98 연결어 문제는 밑줄 앞뒤를 요약하라

however, therefore를 접속부사 또는 연결어라고 하는데, 연결어 문제는 파트 6에서 자주 출제되는 문제 유형으로 연결어 앞과 뒤의 내용에 대한 명확한 이해와 논리적 관계 파악이 없으면 틀리기 쉬운 문제이다. 연결어의 종류로는 내용이 상반될 때 사용하는 however, 인과관계일 때 사용하는 therefore, 시간의 흐름을 연결할 때 사용하는 after that, 조건의 의미를 가지는 otherwise, 추가의 의미를 가지는 in addition, 예를 들어 설명할 때 사용하는 for example 등이 있다. 아래에서 136번 문제가 연결어 문제이다.

STEP 1 유형을 파악해 봐

Questions 135-138 refer to the following letter.

Dear readers,

Trends Magazine ------ to provide our readers with articles worthy to read at a reasonable price for
　　　　　　　　135.
the last 20 years.

Unfortunately, as most delivery companies have recently increased their delivery fees, we have found it hard to have the magazines delivered to you as they are now. ------, we had no choice but to
　　　　　　　　　　　　　　　　　　　　　　　　　　　　　　　　　　　136.
increase the price of an annual subscription effective as of next month.

------ on the increased subscription can be found on the sheet enclosed with this letter. ------.
137.　　　　　　　　　　　　　　　　　　　　　　　　　　　　　　　　　　　　　　**138.**

Thank you for your support over the years, and we hope to repay that loyalty for many more years to come.

With best wishes,
Kim Cooper
Editor-in-Chief

135. (A) strived
(B) was striving
(C) will strive
(D) has been striving

136. (A) In addition
(B) Therefore
(C) Unless
(D) On the contrary

137. (A) Suggestions
(B) Announcements
(C) Details
(D) Decisions

138. (A) We are very sorry and hope this will not affect your continued subscription.
(B) We appreciated your comments on our current subscription.
(C) The letter should explain reasons why you want to cancel your subscription.
(D) We are glad that we can now provide our magazine at a more affordable price.

STEP 2 이렇게 풀어 봐
"유형을 파악해 봐" 136번 문제를 보세요.

첫째 밑줄이 포함된 문장 안의 단서만으로 오답을 최대한 소거.
밑줄은 문장 전체를 수식하는 부사자리이다. (C)는 접속사이므로 탈락이다.

둘째 밑줄 앞의 문맥과 밑줄 후의 문맥의 논리적 흐름을 결정.
136번에서 밑줄 앞의 내용은 '대부분의 배송 업체들이 서비스 비용을 올렸고, 잡지를 지금처럼 계속 배송해주는 것은 어렵다'는 것이다. 밑줄 뒤의 내용은 '연간 구독료를 올리기로 결정했다'는 것이다. 이러한 관계는 '인과 관계'의 흐름이다. 인과 관계와 어울리는 연결어는 (B)이다. (A)는 '추가', (B)는 '역접'의 관계일 때 사용한다.

PLUS

• 파트 6에서 나오는 연결어 (접속부사)는 다음과 같다. 아래의 순서대로 대입하여 푸는 것이 정답을 맞힐 확률도 높고, 논리관계를 이해하기도 편하다.

논리관계	접속부사
역접	however (그러나), nevertheless (그럼에도 불구하고), nonetheless (그럼에도 불구하고), even so (심지어 그렇다 해도), on the other hand (반면에), on the contrary (반대로)
인과	therefore (그러므로), accordingly (때문에), as a result (그 결과로), thus (그리하여), consequently (결과적으로), for this reason (이러한 이유로)
시간	afterward (그 후에), at the same time (동시에), since then (그때 이후로), until now (지금까지), meanwhile (그러는 동안에), meantime (그러는 동안에), after that (그 후에), simultaneously (동시에), up until now (지금까지)
조건	alternatively (대안으로는), otherwise (그렇지 않으면), if so (그렇다면), if not (그렇지 않다면), in that case (그러한 경우에), then (그러면), instead (대신에)
추가, 강조	furthermore (게다가), in addition (게다가), plus (추가로), moreover (게다가), besides (게다가), in fact (사실상), actually (사실상)
예시	likewise (이와 유사하게), as always (항상 그렇듯이), for instance (예를 들어), for example (예를 들어)
요약, 결론	in short (요약하여 말하면), in conclusion (결과적으로)
기타	as usual (평상시대로), to that end (그러한 목적으로)

 **함정을 피해 봐** 실제 강의에서만 알려주는 풀이 노하우!

1. 단순한 시간의 흐름과 인과관계를 구분한다.

All line workers are advised to attend the information session this Friday morning. (Therefore / After that), everyone should be prepared for another session in the afternoon.

→ 이번 주 금요일 오전 안내시간에 참석해야 한다는 내용과 오후에 하나 더 참석해야 한다는 내용이 원인과 결과의 관계라고 볼 수 없다. 단순한 시간의 흐름이다.

2. 추가의 내용을 덧붙이는 것과 예를 들어 말하는 것을 구분한다.

Starting next week, we will have some special promotional offers. (For example / Additionally), we will start offering reduced-price flights to our customers.

→ 밑줄 앞 문장에서 '특별 판촉 행사'가 있을 것이라고 했고, 밑줄 뒤 문장에서 할인된 가격의 항공편을 제공하겠다고 했는데, 이는 특별 판촉 행사의 일부라고 할 수 있다. additionally가 답이 되려면 '특별 판촉 행사'에 포함되지 않는 다른 무엇인가를 추가로 언급할 때 써야 한다.

1. After that   2. For example

STEP 3 실전에 적용해 봐

Questions 131-134 refer to the following notice.

Attention, All Employees:

We learned that some employees have not gotten their ------ employee ID cards yet. If you
                                                          131.
have not picked yours up yet but need to have it ------ next week, please visit the Human
                                                  132.
Resources office during business hours to pick it up. ------, all the remaining cards will be sent
                                                       133.
to each department next Wednesday, so you can get yours then.

Please also note that the reissuance of an ID card is provided for free upon first request only, and it will cost $10 the next time you request one. You will need to complete a brief request form before being reissued an ID card as well. ------.
                                                                                              134.

131. (A) extra
(B) printed
(C) online
(D) reissued

132. (A) before
(B) during
(C) after
(D) while

133. (A) Consequently
(B) Therefore
(C) Otherwise
(D) In addition

134. (A) Again, the end of this week is the latest possible time to receive your ID card.
(B) We hope this will help you find your missing ID card.
(C) Therefore, it is always advisable that you be careful not to lose your ID card.
(D) Thank you for your cooperation in returning ID cards to their respective owners.

Questions 135-138 refer to the following e-mail.

To: All Council Members
From: George McQueen, General Manager
Date: May 14
Subject: Annual Regional Economic Forum

The annual regional economic forum ------ this Saturday in the same place where the last
                                    135.
forum was held: the 2nd floor of the Huntington Hall, Millsworth Town. ------ year, however,
                                                                        136.
since the forum will be held for full three hours from noon to 3 P.M., a free lunch will be

provided to every attendee during a short break. ------, we ask all council members to reply to
                                                 137.
this e-mail indicating whether you will attend the forum or not no later than this Thursday so

that the meals can be prepared beforehand according to the number of attendees. ------.
                                                                                138.

Thank you in advance for your prompt reply. We look forward to seeing you on Saturday.

135. (A) was held
 (B) has held
 (C) will be held
 (D) being held

136. (A) Once a
 (B) This
 (C) First
 (D) Each

137. (A) Accordingly
 (B) Otherwise
 (C) Ultimately
 (D) Nonetheless

138. (A) We also recommend that all members try the new dish at our restaurant.
 (B) Therefore, we will prepare extra meals in case you do not give us your reply.
 (C) Last year's forum lasted for two hours and did not have a lunch break.
 (D) Please also indicate in your reply if a vegetarian meal is required.

Questions 139-142 refer to the following notice.

Use of the Company Overhead Projector

Company-owned overhead projectors are available for use upon ------ but only for the purpose of in-office meetings. ------, usage for club meetings or small group meetings of fewer than three employees may be disapproved if there is another request to use one for a bigger official meeting. This ------ the limited number of projectors we have so that they can be used primarily to satisfy urgent needs. However, if you are in need of a projector and have a valid reason to borrow one, you may be allowed to use one regardless of the above-mentioned requirements as long as you get approval by the head of your department. To borrow a projector, fill out and submit a request form to Mr. Callaway in the General Affairs Department. ------.

139. (A) waiting
 (B) issuance
 (C) request
 (D) arrival

140. (A) Consequently
 (B) Likewise
 (C) In addition
 (D) Given that

141. (A) manageable
 (B) is managing
 (C) manages
 (D) is to manage

142. (A) However, your request may be rejected for the following reasons.
 (B) In addition, please allow at least two days for your request to be approved.
 (C) Therefore, you can talk to him about purchasing more projectors.
 (D) Please also get approval from him to borrow a projector for private meetings.

Questions 143-146 refer to the following notice.

Updates on the Construction of Abby Road

The construction of Abby Road ------ to be done by November 30. However, the annual
    143.
Thanksgiving Day festival, which was held from last Wednesday to Sunday, inevitably caused a

5 day ------ in the construction schedule. ------. Local access to businesses and residences
    144.   145.
will be permitted throughout the construction period. ------, Northbound Meiland Avenue
                                                        146.
will continue to be directed to Olympic Boulevard while the eastbound lanes on Southern

Bay Avenue will be permanently closed to all traffic between 7th Street and 8th Street. Other

updates on the project schedule are available and are kept current on the town's website at

www.cityoftrey.org.

Thank you for your patience and understanding during the construction period.

143. (A) will be scheduled
 (B) had scheduled
 (C) was scheduled
 (D) are being scheduled

144. (A) revision
 (B) notice
 (C) delay
 (D) advance

145. (A) Therefore, Abby Road will be permanently closed from this point.
 (B) As a result, Abby Road will be open on December 5, when the construction will be done.
 (C) Local residents are not allowed to attend the festival until further notice.
 (D) Please drive slowly while you pass the construction site.

146. (A) Meanwhile
 (B) Regrettably
 (C) At last
 (D) Alternatively

법칙 99 대명사 문제는 문법적 소거 후 가리키는 말을 확인

출제율 37%

명사를 대신하여 사용하는 말을 대명사라고 합니다. 대명사에는 I, she, he 등과 같은 인칭대명사, myself, herself, himself와 같은 재귀대명사, this, that, these, those와 같은 지시대명사, one, another, the other, some, others등과 같은 부정대명사가 있습니다. 이러한 대명사 문제가 파트 6에서 등장하면 같은 문장에서 답이 결정되지 않고 주변 문맥에서 그 대명사가 가리키는 말을 찾아야 합니다. 아래 문제에서는 두 번째 문제를 대명사 문제라고 합니다. 지시대명사나 부정대명사가 명사 앞에 올 땐 지시형용사, 부정형용사라고 부르기도 합니다.

STEP 1 유형을 파악해 봐

Questions 139-142 refer to the following letter.

December 21
Shelby Sheraton
52 Street, Central Valley
Newtown Land, CA

Dear Ms. McCarthy,

Thank you for your ------ about our rental service, which was launched recently.
                    139.
You asked us about the monthly rental fee for the model GX-780, which is offered from $100 to $130 a month with full options ------ year. ------.
                                                                                      140.   141.

If you are still interested in renting a GX-780, give us a reply for further assistance. ------, please note
                                                                                        142.
that the fees may vary next year as the price range mentioned above is being offered this year only as a promotional event.

Ana Sarkisova
Customer Service

139. (A) inquire
(B) inquirer
(C) inquired
(D) inquiry

140. (A) every
(B) future
(C) this
(D) first

141. (A) You will have a relaxing time soon.
(B) Our rental service will be available next week.
(C) Let me explain why we can provide free installation.
(D) We guarantee that this rental fee is the lowest in the area.

142. (A) Therefore
(B) Otherwise
(C) In addition
(D) For example

 STEP 2 이렇게 풀어 봐   "유형을 파악해 봐" 140번 문제를 보세요!

첫째 밑줄이 포함된 문장 안의 단서만으로 오답을 최대한 소거.
140번 문제 first와 future는 앞에 전치사 및 the를 써야 하므로 탈락. '올해에 제공되는 가격인지 매년 제공되는 가격인지'는 밑줄이 포함된 문장만으로는 알 수 없다.

둘째 대명사가 가리키는 말을 기준으로 답을 결정.
지문의 마지막 문장에서 '위에 언급된 가격이 올해에만 한정된 것이고, 내년에는 달라질 수 있다'는 말이 있으므로 140번 문제에서 제시되는 가격은 올해의 가격이라고 볼 수 있다. 따라서 this year가 답이 되어야 한다.

PLUS

- 대명사 문제의 보기 중 20% 가량은 wh-계열의 대명사(접속사)가 섞여 있으나 거의 정답이 되는 일이 없다. 접속사가 답이 되려면 동사의 개수가 접속사의 개수보다 1개 더 많아야 한다는 것을 명심한다.
  We will inform you as soon as (**one** / which) is available to pick up.
  → 동사의 개수가 2개, 접속사 1개가 있으므로 which는 탈락.

- 파트 6에서 정답으로 주로 나오는 대명사 문제. (정답 빈도 순!)

종류	주로 정답	정답의 단서
부정대명사/형용사	every, other, any, all, most, none, both, many, either, some, one, either 등	명사자리인지(other, every는 탈락), 형용사자리인지 (each other, one another는 탈락), 단수명사 앞인지 (many, few, a few, several 등은 탈락), 복수명사 앞(one, either, each, neither, every, another 등은 탈락)인지 등으로 문법적으로 먼저 해결. 모두를 가리키는 말이면 all, 대부분을 가리키고 여전히 나머지가 있다는 문맥이라면 most. 앞에 두 개의 고유명사 있으면 both나 either가 답.

소유격	our, your, her, his	앞에 가리키는 명사를 확인. 파트 6 특성상 our나 your가 답이 많이 되는 편이다. her나 his가 답이 되는 경우는 앞에 가리키는 사람 명사가 반드시 제시된다.
목적격	you, us, me, her, them	역시 파트 6 특성상 you나 us가 답이 많이 되는 편이다.
지시대명사/형용사	this, that, those, these접	앞에 바로 나온 내용을 받을 땐 주로 this나 these. 이번인지, 올해인지 등을 구분할 땐 뒤쪽 문맥을 본다.
주격	they, he	바로 앞에 복수/단수 명사를 받을 때 사용.

함정을 피해 봐
실제 강의에서만 알려주는 풀이 노하우!

1. 하나(혹은 한번)를 지칭하는지 모든 것(혹은 매번)을 지칭하는 지 구분한다.

In preparation for the upcoming government inspection, assembly line C will be shut down tonight. (Every / This) assembly line, which is used for packaging, will be inspected ahead of the other assembly lines.

→ 뒤에 다른 조립라인들 보다 앞서서 검사가 된다는 말이 있는 것으로 보아 조립라인 C를 가리키는 대명사가 와야 한다. Every를 쓰면 모든 생산라인을 가리키는 말이 되어 자연스럽지 못하다.

1. This

STEP 3 실전에 적용해 봐

Questions 131-134 refer to the following advertisement.

August 10
Breanne Chen
135 Greenville Avenue
Windsor, DM 32523

Dear Ms. Chen,

------. We successfully raised our targeted amount of money, which is one million dollars, an
131.
increased amount from ------ year.
                     132.

We would not have been able to reach our goal without your ------. The significant amount you
                                                            133.
contributed was a great help for our success in this fundraising.

The money raised for two years will be donated to Education for Children as we promised earlier. We sincerely hope to have you as a donor again for our next ------, which will be held
                                                                                    134.
by the beginning of next year.

Thank you again.

With regards,
Allen Parsons
Executive, One Hope Foundation

131. (A) I'm writing to inquire how I can receive research grants.
(B) Congratulations on winning the essay contest.
(C) Thank you for your contribution to our fundraiser.
(D) This is an important reminder regarding our charity funds.

132. (A) next
(B) this
(C) last
(D) second

133. (A) donation
(B) time
(C) permission
(D) distribution

134. (A) incident
(B) strategy
(C) session
(D) campaign

Questions 135-138 refer to the following notice.

We are sorry to inform our customers that the item Blooming Flower Cushion (item no. 67542) is currently ------. Even though we have doubled the production of the item, the cushions sell out rapidly.
                    135.

The delivery of orders placed before April 8 will be made starting tomorrow, but those placed after that date will be ------, and the customers will be given a full refund.
                              136.

To apologize for this, we will give discount coupons to customers who made ------ orders.
                                                                              137.
------. If you wish to be informed when the item is restocked, please contact us
138.
at 883-3333. Again, we are sorry for the inconvenience that we caused you and thank you for your understanding in advance.

135. (A) available
     (B) malfunctioning
     (C) out of stock
     (D) irreplaceable

136. (A) sent
     (B) allowed
     (C) forwarded
     (D) canceled

137. (A) their
     (B) any
     (C) all
     (D) those

138. (A) We're holding a huge clearance sale on household items.
     (B) The orders placed will be delivered by the end of the week.
     (C) They are valid for 10% off any purchase.
     (D) Customers are requested to report any defective items.

Questions 139-142 refer to the following notice.

Attention, all customers:

Recently, we discovered some ------ problems with the Web site for our online store.
                                139.

Some customers complained about not being able to access our Web site, and after analyzing the problem, we determined that the Web site was automatically blocking ------ access by
                                                                                                                        140.
visitors. ------.
         141.

We are currently doing our best to find out the cause of this, but ------ the Web site allows all
                                                                   142.
visitors access if they use the browser Plasm. So if you are having trouble accessing our Web site, please use a Plasm-based browser.

Thank you for your cooperation.

139. (A) multiple
(B) financial
(C) technical
(D) social

140. (A) any
(B) some
(C) other
(D) all

141. (A) None of the visitors had a hard time accessing our online store.
(B) We have placed new ads on our Web site.
(C) Online purchase is not available in your area.
(D) We apologize for any inconvenience this problem has caused.

142. (A) in advance
(B) accordingly
(C) so far
(D) once

Questions 143-146 refer to the following advertisement.

Return Your Old Phone to Get a New Moby Phone for Less!

In celebration of the 10th anniversary of our founding, Moby Electronics is now offering brand-new Moby phones at special prices for a ------ time.
                                                                                                             143.

If you bring a used phone—regardless of its manufacturer—you can get a discount of up to 20% on your purchase of one of the latest Moby Phones. ------ include the Moby 4 and the
                                                                                                             144.
Moby Mini. Be sure to hurry because the offer will end next week. ------.
                                                                                              145.

Visit our Web site at www.mobyphones.com to ------ detailed information on the models
                                                                                     146.
available for this special offer.

143. (A) less
 (B) remaining
 (C) limited
 (D) delayed

144. (A) What
 (B) There
 (C) These
 (D) Other

145. (A) This special offer may be extended for two more weeks.
 (B) Some of the models might sell out early.
 (C) Any inquiries regarding its availability should be directed to our personnel manager.
 (D) Our cutting-edge phones have attracted a lot of attention.

146. (A) share
 (B) get
 (C) provide
 (D) offer

법칙 100 어휘 문제는 논리적 근거로 마무리한다(동사/명사/형용사/부사 어휘)

출제율 47.3%

파트 6에는 보기가 다 같은 품사들로 구성된 문제가 나옵니다. 이를 어휘문제라고 합니다. 어휘 문제는 동사, 명사, 형용사, 부사 어휘 문제가 있는데 파트 5와는 다르게 밑줄이 포함된 문장만 봐서는 안 풀리는 경우가 대부분입니다. 어휘 문제도 쉽게는 그 다음 문장에서 어렵게는 한참 앞이나 뒤에서 단서가 제시되며, 그 단서를 찾지 못한 채 답을 결정하면 정답이 될 확률이 매우 낮습니다. 아래 문제의 경우는 두번째 문제가 어휘 문제, 그 중에서도 형용사 어휘 문제 입니다.

STEP 1 유형을 파악해 봐

Questions 143-146 refer to the following e-mail.

To: All Production Department Employees
From: David Maxwell, Production Coordinator
Date: July 20
Subject: Safety Inspection

------. In compliance with company policy, a ------ safety inspection will be conducted at the end of
143.   **144.**
the month. As you may be well aware, proper safety inspections help prevent workers from getting

injured at work, which negatively affects overall productivity.

Please make sure to leave the power to all machines on once you are done using them next

Wednesday as you ------ did for former inspections. The inspection will begin right after all
                145.
employees get off from work.

Additionally, ------ machines undergoing the inspection will be available for use after 9 P.M. on
            146.
Thursday.

---

143. (A) I'm writing to inform you of one thing you should bear in mind regarding the production line.
(B) This is to let you know that production has increased a lot.
(C) I'm writing to ask you to take part in a seminar on the newly installed machines.
(D) This is to remind all of you to follow the safety regulations.

144. (A) regular
(B) documentary
(C) first-time
(D) previous

346 어휘 편 및 파트 6

145. (A) previous
(B) previously
(C) prevision
(D) previousness

146. (A) other
(B) those
(C) their
(D) every

STEP 2 이렇게 풀어 봐
"유형을 파악해 봐" 144번 문제를 보세요!

첫째 밑줄이 포함된 문장의 단서만으로 오답을 최대한 소거.

안전점검을 수식할 수 있는 표현으로 (A) 정기적 안전점검, (C) 처음의 안전점검, (D) 이전의 안전점검을 생각할 수 있다. 안전점검이 문서상으로 이루어 질 수는 없으므로 (B)는 소거한다. 미래 시제와 어울리지 않는 (D)를 소거하면 밑줄이 포함된 문장으로만 더 이상 단서를 잡기에는 무리가 있는 상태이다. 다음 문맥으로 넘어간다.

둘째 특정 어휘를 답으로 만드는 논리적 근거를 확인.

145번 문제의 문장에서 '당신이 이전에 점검을 했었던 대로, 전원을 다 끄고 나가라'라는 말이 단서가 되어 이 점검이 한번 일어난 일이 아니고 정기적으로 일어나는 점검이라고 볼 수 있다. 따라서 (A)가 정답이다.

PLUS

• 파트 6 어휘문제는 밑줄이 포함된 문장 안에서 단서가 나오기 보다는 위나 아래의 문맥에서 단서가 나오지만 때로는 밑줄이 포함된 문장에서 바로 답이 나오거나, 최소한 그 문장만 봐도 오답 1~2개는 제거할 수 있도록 출제됩니다.

동사	목적어가 있으면 1, 2 형식 동사는 탈락한다. 주어나 목적어를 보고 특정 목적어를 취하는 동사를 고른다.
명사	동사, 형용사, 부사 어휘에 비해서 수식어를 보거나 동사 쪽을 보면 바로 풀리는 경우 많다. 실수, 오류, 사과, 불편함, 해결 등의 표현이 주로 정답이다
형용사	반의어가 보기로 같이 제시되는 경우는 긍정적인 표현이 주로 정답이다. 영구적인 것보단 임시적인 것이 답이 되는 경우가 많다. 사람을 수식하는 형용사인지, 사물을 수식하는 형용사인지를 확인할 것.
부사	특정 시제와 어울리는 부사가 등장하면 해당 시제 부사를 답으로 한다. '과거에 ~했었는데, 지금은 ~하다'라는 어울림이라면 과거 쪽은 once 지금쪽은 now를 답으로 한다. '실수로 ~ 했는데, 사실은 ~하다'라는 문맥이면 mistakenly와 actually를 답으로 한다.

함정을 피해 봐
실제 강의에서만 알려주는 풀이 노하우!

1. 의미가 비슷해 보이지만 사람의 성격을 묘사할 수 없는 표현에 조심한다.

Interviewers should be (optional / selective) so that the candidates they choose will be the most suitable for the job.

→ 밑줄은 면접관을 수식할 수 있는 형용사, 즉 사람을 수식할 수 있는 형용사가 필요하다. selective는 사람과 사용하면 '선택능력이 있는, 안목이 높은'이란 뜻이다. optional은 '임의의, 선택의'란 뜻으로 사람을 수식하지 않는다.

1. selective

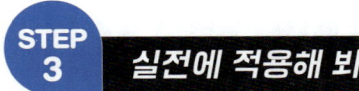

Questions 131-134 refer to the following memo.

From: Chris Bentley, Production Supervisor
To: All Plant Employees
Date: September 24
Subject: Reminder about the Executive's Visit

As you already know, Mr. Cyrus, an executive at Carson Auto, will make his ------ visit to the
131.
manufacturing plant next Monday to boost our morale.

Accordingly, all employees are ------ to gather in the seminar room by 5 P.M. on Monday.
132.
------.
133.

After the executive's brief speech of ------, a banquet will be held in the cafeteria. Please
134.
also note that this year's visit has been delayed by 4 days, and the next visit is scheduled for
September 20 next year.

See you all in the seminar room next Monday.

131. (A) informal
(B) abrupt
(C) annual
(D) allowed

132. (A) advising
(B) advisory
(C) advised
(D) advisable

133. (A) The room can't accommodate all the participants.
(B) You are supposed to discuss the problems in the room.
(C) Those who are assigned the night shift are to participate as well.
(D) A lecture about self-development will be delivered.

134. (A) farewell
(B) encouragement
(C) apology
(D) gratitude

Questions 135-138 refer to the following letter.

Date: January 25
Subject: Free Room Upgrade

Dear Ms. Lynn,

Thank you for being a regular guest at the Riverside Hotel. This letter is to inform you that you are ------ to get a room upgrade at no cost on your next visit. ------.
　　　　　135.　　　　　　　　　　　　　　　　　　　　　　　　　　136.

The free room upgrade is available if you get a deluxe room or something bigger. If you ------ a
　　　　　　　　　　　　　　　　　　　　　　　　　　　　　　　　　　　　　　137.
deluxe room, your room will be upgraded to a suite or business room.

If you ------ in this offer, please fill out the attached form and send it to us by the end of the
　　　　138.
month.

We look forward to seeing you soon and hope you have a great time with the upgraded room.

135. (A) likely
　　 (B) free
　　 (C) suitable
　　 (D) eligible

136. (A) Please be aware that our rates will increase next month.
　　 (B) The dining area has been renovated and will reopen soon.
　　 (C) Our hotel is well-known for its spectacular view of the Han River.
　　 (D) Please don't miss out on this great chance by checking the detailed information below.

137. (A) find
　　 (B) keep
　　 (C) reserve
　　 (D) browse

138. (A) will be interested
　　 (B) are interesting
　　 (C) interest
　　 (D) are interested

Questions 139-142 refer to the following announcement.

Regina Residences
IMPORTANT ANNOUNCEMENT

Lately, we have been receiving an increasing number of complaints about the ------ between floors from our residents.
                                                                                      139.

Please be aware that operating a washing machine may be a big disturbance to others and thus is not allowed after 10 P.M. Likewise, listening to a radio or watching TV at a high volume is ------ discouraged at night. ------.
     140.   **141.**

Regina Residence is an apartment building which is shared by more than 50 residents. We would appreciate it if you would ------ with us. Please make sure to follow the rules and
                                        142.
regulations, which you agreed to comply with when you moved in.

139. (A) crack
(B) noise
(C) privacy
(D) dispute

140. (A) probably
(B) relatively
(C) silently
(D) strongly

141. (A) Thus, the landlord will revise all the rules and regulations in this apartment.
(B) Moreover, no musical instruments should be played on the premises at any time.
(C) In addition, all trash has to be placed in the designated locations.
(D) Besides, the key deposit will not be returned before you move out.

142. (A) share
(B) cooperate
(C) stay
(D) encourage

Questions 143-146 refer to the following information.

The Arizona Natural Environment Foundation is a membership-based environmental organization which aims to resolve ------ issues on air, water, and soil pollution.
                                                                          143.

It is committed to conducting a wide range of research to find solutions to problems throughout the world. It ------ specifically in seeking solutions to the severe drought in Ghana
               144.
and the yellow dust in China since its foundation in 2007.

Although it is a ------ nonprofit organization, it has managed to form extensive alliances and
                 145.
cooperative ties with various institutions. ------.
                                            146.

143. (A) general
     (B) controversial
     (C) connective
     (D) international

144. (A) has been involved
     (B) has involved
     (C) will be involving
     (D) to be involved

145. (A) private
     (B) illegal
     (C) public
     (D) widespread

146. (A) By making these alliances, it will be converted to a public organization.
     (B) It has strived to find the causes of its internal problems.
     (C) Those institutions have established local offices throughout the world.
     (D) Through these alliances, it will be better able to achieve its aims to solve global environmental issues.

뉴토익 빈도순 정답 어휘 정리 - 부사편

빈도	부사어휘	뜻	기출 collocation
10	finally	마침내	~후에 마침내
10	regularly	정기적으로	현재시제
9	currently	현재	현재/현재진행시제
9	recently	최근에	과거/현재완료시제
8	already	이미, 벌써	현재완료/현재시제
8	immediately	즉시	제출/반환/통보하다
8	thoroughly	철저하게	읽다, 청소/조사/검토하다
7	carefully	주의 깊게	점검/검토/취급하다, 읽다
7	nearly	거의	숫자 앞, ~ 완성된
6	briefly	간략하게, 짧게	말하다, 다루다, 검토하다
6	exclusively	독점적으로	to 명사, for 명사
6	promptly	즉시	도착/응답/연락하다
6	still	여전히	불구하고/그러나 ~ 여전히
5	consistently	지속적으로	긍정적인 평가, 탁월한 기여
5	conveniently	편리하게	위치한
5	directly	즉시, 곧	directly from/to (~로부터/~로 직접)
5	highly	매우, 크게, 대단히	성공적인, 평가되는
5	now	지금, 이제, 즉시	~했었다, 그런데 지금은
5	only	오직	명사 앞, 전명구 앞
5	otherwise	달리, 그렇지 않으면	unless otherwise p.p (달리 ~된 바 없으면)
5	shortly	즉시, 곧	도착/재개/완성하다
4	accordingly	그에 따라서, 그에 맞춰	~할 때, 그에 따라 ~하다
4	also	또한, 게다가	~이외에도 또한
4	approximately	대략	숫자 앞
4	properly	올바르게	처분/보고/설치/고정하다

빈도	부사어휘	뜻	기출 collocation
4	separately	별도로	separately from (~와는 별도로)
4	yet	아직	have yet to do (아직 ~하지 못하다)
3	frequently	빈번하게	현재시제
3	gradually	점차적으로	증가/감소/움직임
3	ideally	이상적으로	2명, 6개월, 다음 주
3	once	한 번, 한때, 이전에	과거시제
3	periodically	정기적으로	점검하다, 업데이트하다
3	relatively	비교적으로, 상대적으로	작은, 새로운
3	specifically	특히, 분명히, 명확하게	전명구 혹은 명사 앞
2	explicitly	명쾌하게	언급하다, 설명하다
1	anonymously	익명으로	쓰여진
1	contractually	계약상으로	의무가 있다
1	customarily	습관적으로, 관례상	방문하다
1	eloquently	유창하게, 능변으로	말하다
1	marginally	미미하게, 아주 조금	성공적인
1	meticulously	꼼꼼하게	계획하다
1	momentarily	잠시, 잠깐	중단되다
1	ordinarily	보통, 정상적으로	제출되다
1	patiently	끈기 있게, 참을성 있게	답변하다
1	provisionally	일시적으로, 잠정적으로	임명되다
1	punctually	시간을 엄수하여	도착하다
1	sparingly	절약하여	사용하다
1	subsequently	그 후에, 뒤에	~했다, 그 후에 ~ 했다
1	systematically	조직적으로	검사하다
1	unbearably	참을 수 없을 정도로	습한 날씨

ACTUAL TEST 01

PART 5

Directions: A word or phrase is missing in each of the sentences below. Four answer choices are given below each sentence. Select the best answer to complete the sentence. Then mark the letter (A), (B), (C), or (D) on your answer sheet.

101. Please read carefully and follow the ----- posted on the board when working at the construction site.

    (A) guidelines
    (B) guided
    (C) guiding
    (D) guiders

102. ----- becomes a member will be given 30% discount coupons from Nice Shoes.

    (A) Whoever
    (B) Anyone
    (C) Some
    (D) Either

103. Mr. Browski delivered a speech about ----- latest research on renewable energy.

    (A) he
    (B) himself
    (C) his
    (D) him

104. Forrester Research required the staff to make a presentation on the research they ----- in last week.

    (A) participates
    (B) participated
    (C) will participate
    (D) participate

105. ----- the sudden car accident, Mr. Park had to cancel his appointment with his client.

    (A) Even
    (B) Although
    (C) After
    (D) If

106. All the employees were required to attend the meeting ----- the product demonstration.

    (A) prior
    (B) following
    (C) next to
    (D) by

107. Because the client has rejected almost all the terms of the contract, Mr. Chung had to make a ----- new contract.

    (A) completeness
    (B) completing
    (C) completely
    (D) completed

108. McKay Electronics has successfully developed a new technology which surpasses Java, a computer ----- that is widely used around the world.

    (A) industry
    (B) program
    (C) project
    (D) development

109. Alibaba, Inc. has signed a contract with a(n) ----- manufacturing firm in India to reduce its production costs.

    (A) local
    (B) impressed
    (C) accidental
    (D) profound

110. Both Bulls Auto and Miya Motors are expecting ----- sales to increase due to the falling price of gas.

    (A) them
    (B) themselves
    (C) they
    (D) their

111. Lepta, Inc. has ----- operations at several manufacturing plants since the demand for one of its beverages decreased.

(A) enlarged
(B) reduced
(C) indicated
(D) qualified

112. The contract explicitly stated that the ----- takes responsibility for paying the expenses involved in returning malfunctioning items.

(A) seller
(B) sells
(C) sold
(D) sellers

113. The sudden strike that occurred in the Mumbai facility ----- a month ago adversely affected the situation there.

(A) nearly
(B) partially
(C) shortly
(D) rigorously

114. Arson, Inc. offered to give more incentives to the employees ----- contributed to the sales increase last year.

(A) instead
(B) since
(C) either
(D) who

115. Loki, Inc. has successfully concluded a contract which will help the firm expand ----- the Chinese market.

(A) of
(B) by
(C) at
(D) into

116. Mr. Young was called to an urgent meeting to discuss the plans for the ----- event, which will be held next week.

(A) recent
(B) upcoming
(C) capable
(D) rough

117. It seems the contract will be signed soon since Bay, Inc. has been ----- pushing Plaque, Inc. to agree to the terms.

(A) continuously
(B) continuous
(C) continue
(D) continues

118. Piby Motors needs to improve the ----- of its latest model, which has been recalled for having a problem.

(A) quality
(B) qualified
(C) qualification
(D) qualifying

119. In order to meet the customers' desires for complex and different tastes, Eddie's has to focus on the ----- of its dishes.

(A) purchase
(B) selling
(C) variety
(D) disposal

120. The recent increase in sales at Auction Net is attributable mainly to the performance of the ----- workers at the company.

(A) talented
(B) talents
(C) talent
(D) to talent

▶ ▶ ▶ GO ON TO THE NEXT PAGE

121. The firm was responsible for providing compensation for the injured workers, two of ----- had to be hospitalized for 3 months.

    (A) whose
    (B) whom
    (C) other
    (D) both

122. Before today's meeting with her client, Ms. Yang should stop by her office to ----- some documents prepared by her assistant.

    (A) drop off
    (B) put off
    (C) call on
    (D) pick up

123. -----, Ms. Sorenson is not available to answer any phone calls because she is in an important meeting with a potential client.

    (A) Presently
    (B) Present
    (C) Presents
    (D) Most presently

124. Feel free to contact me at extension 277 ----- you have a problem with the service you are receiving.

    (A) however
    (B) although
    (C) so that
    (D) whenever

125. Please prepare the materials needed for the meeting scheduled for next week at least two days -----.

    (A) at each time
    (B) ago
    (C) in advance
    (D) finally

126. Due to the economic growth, the company expects its profits ----- greatly this year.

    (A) have grown
    (B) to grow
    (C) be grow
    (D) growing

127. Some Chinese consumers found Fit Earth's advertising rather ----- and began to boycott the firm's products.

    (A) offensive
    (B) offense
    (C) offended
    (D) offence

128. Mrs. Kwon and Mr. Raymond ----- were against making a deal with D-Mart because of its high asking prices.

    (A) well
    (B) alike
    (C) very
    (D) soon

129. More employees ----- to the headquarters, which is located in India, in the last two years.

    (A) will have been sent
    (B) to be sent
    (C) have been sent
    (D) send

130. We at Decent Auto offer free delivery upon request ----- of the amount of money a customer spends.

    (A) regardless
    (B) in the event
    (C) concerning
    (D) regarding

PART 6

Directions: Read the texts that follow. A word or phrase is missing in some of the sentences. Four answer choices are given below each of the sentences. Select the best answer to complete the sentence. Then mark the letter (A), (B), (C), or (D) on your answer sheet.

Questions 131-134 refer to the following article.

The annual Vancouver Post Photo Exhibition ------ to Saint Mary on April 1.
                                                131.
The exhibition that has been introduced to various media and praised by many will finally be held at Saint Mary this year after being held in Edmonton, Quebec, and Newfoundland. Usually, exhibitions are held at the Victoria Gallery, but since a large number of works are to be displayed for the show, the exhibition will be held at the Engria Gallery, which provides a ------ space.
                                132.

------. But if you preorder tickets for the exhibition now, you can receive a $1
133.
discount on each ticket and get a free chance to participate ------ our special event
                                                                    134.
at the show. So if you are interested, please call us at 388-8888 to preorder your tickets now.

131. (A) is coming
 (B) come
 (C) came
 (D) has come

132. (A) cleaner
 (B) larger
 (C) brighter
 (D) lower

133. (A) Changes to the venue will be posted on our Web site.
 (B) This decision has resulted in a reduction in entrance fees.
 (C) The entrance fee for the exhibition will be $5 for adults and $2 for children.
 (D) According to the event organizer, no tickets can be ordered in advance.

134. (A) on
 (B) by
 (C) in
 (D) onto

▶▶▶GO ON TO THE NEXT PAGE

Questions 135-138 refer to the following e-mail.

To: Morris Smith <m.smith@quickmail.net>
From: Customer Service <delphics@delphiinc.com>
Re: Answer to your inquiry
Date: March 21

Dear Mr. Smith,

Thank you for your ------ in our programs. We at Delphi, Inc. always try hard to offer
         135.
the best programs to our customers. You mentioned that you would like to sign up

for our new ------ program for your budget. However, we are very sorry to let you
            136.
know that the program is not available anymore. ------. And we cannot offer the
                                                   137.
program to more than 100 customers.

Instead, we have another program in which ------ can receive 10-percent discounts
                                            138.
for all orders over $50. If you are interested, please let us know. Then, we will send
you the details of this program.

We look forward to hearing from you soon.
Thank you.

135. (A) interest
(B) interesting
(C) interestingly
(D) interested

136. (A) savings
(B) cooking
(C) exercise
(D) supply

137. (A) I was unable to attend the program due to a family emergency.
(B) So there are not any alternatives that can make it up for you.
(C) You know that we tried our best to resolve this issue.
(D) 100 customers have already signed up for the program.

138. (A) you
(B) he
(C) we
(D) they

Questions 139-142 refer to the following e-mail.

To: Joseph Han <jhan@daymails.com>
From: David Choi <cutrel@dstour.com>
Subject: Survey
Date: August 20

Dear Ms. Han,

We sincerely hope that you enjoyed your trip ------ Turkey. To better serve you on
                                                139.
your future trips, we would like you to answer a few questions regarding your trip.

------ question should not take more than 2 minutes, and there are only 5 questions
  140.
for you to answer.

Please give us your responses to our questions and allow us to ------ our service for
                                                              141.
your future trips. As a reward, we will issue you a $5 gift certificate. ------. You may
                                                                         142.
find details about those stores on our Web site at www.dstour.com.

Thank you.

David Choi
Customer Relations
Dream Special Tour

139. (A) away
     (B) to
     (C) such
     (D) out

140. (A) This
     (B) Either
     (C) Each
     (D) Her

141. (A) improve
     (B) express
     (C) increase
     (D) verify

142. (A) You can purchase souvenirs at any time from the convenience of your home.
     (B) It is redeemable at any of the stores we are partnered with.
     (C) Your donation will be used to open more stores in town.
     (D) Several questions are enough to improve our service.

▶ ▶ ▶ GO ON TO THE NEXT PAGE

Questions 143-146 refer to the following notice.

143. ------.

The ------ on Stanleyford Avenue has been delayed due to the harsh weather
     144.
conditions, but it will resume this Friday.

The sidewalks along the Bay River ------ made first, and the road from the first block
                                    145.
of Twain Avenue to the second block of Pill Avenue will be repaved to mark
Stanleyford Avenue.

While Stanleyford Avenue is being made, a temporary road a block away from the
Bay River will be available, but as too much pressure on the road can affect the
pavement condition of Stanleyford Avenue, ------ vehicles exceeding the specified
                                           146.
limit will be restricted from using the road.

143. (A) We are happy to announce the opening of Stanleyford Avenue.
(B) Thank you for listening to today's weather update.
(C) This is a reminder regarding Stanleyford Avenue and other roads.
(D) This is to inform you of a change in our renovation project.

144. (A) construction
(B) installation
(C) assessment
(D) celebration

145. (A) would have been
(B) has been
(C) are to be
(D) were

146. (A) heavy
(B) lengthy
(C) outworn
(D) malfunctioning

파트 5, 6 문제 중
이 책에서 비껴나가는 문제는 없다!

출제순위
파트 5&6

지은이 **구원**

정답 및 해설

신(新)토익 완벽 반영!

정답 및 해설

매월 출제되는 문제

법칙 1 부사절 접속사는 양보, 이유, 시간, 조건 순

◎ 유형을 파악해 봐
1. (D) 2. (C) 3. (C)

1. 정답 (D)

해설 Mr. Kim이 이사를 했기 때문에 / 시내에 있는 사무실로 / 그는 만날 수 없다 / 그의 이전 동료를 / 그가 과거에 만났던 것만큼 자주

해설 빈칸은 완전한 문장 앞에서 완전한 문장을 이끄는 부사절 접속사 자리이다. (A)는 명사절 접속사, (B)는 등위접속사이므로 탈락하고, 나머지는 해석으로 판단한다. 이사를 했기 때문에 이전 동료를 자주 만나지 못한다는 원인과 결과의 관계이므로 이유를 나타내는 접속사 (D)가 정답이다.

표현 정리 move 이동하다, 이사하다 downtown 시내에 있는 be unable to+동사원형 ~할 수 없다 former 이전의 colleague 동료

2. 정답 (C)

해설 마케팅 비용이 즉각적인 수익을 낳는 반면 / 연구개발비는 보통 장기적인 투자이다

해설 문장에 정동사가 2개 왔으므로 빈칸은 접속사 자리이다. 따라서 전치사인 (A)는 탈락. (D)는 'However+형용사/부사+주어+동사' 구조로 쓰일 경우에만 접속사 기능을 하므로 역시 탈락. 주절과 부사절이 서로 대조되는 내용이므로 '~반면에'라는 의미로 쓰인 (C)가 정답이다.

표현 정리 expenditure 비용, 지출 bring 가져오다 immediate 즉각적인, 즉시의 return 수입, 수익 research and development 연구개발 spending 지출, 소비 long-term 장기적인 investment 투자

3. 정답 (C)

해설 Mr. Kim의 비서는 물었다 / 그에게 / 여행 일정이 만족스러운지 아닌지 / 그래야 그녀가 비행기를 예약할 수 있으니까

해설 정동사가 3개, 접속사가 1개이므로 빈칸은 접속사가 와야 한다. 따라서 전치사인 (D)는 탈락. 빈칸 다음 주어 뒤에 can이 있기 때문에 이와 잘 어울리는 so that을 우선 대입해 해석해 보면 문맥상 (C)가 정답이다.

표현 정리 secretary 비서 ask 묻다, 요청하다 itinerary 여행 일정(표) to one's satisfaction ~가 만족스럽도록, ~가 만족할 만큼 reserve 예약하다 flight 비행기, 비행편

◎ 실전에 적용해 봐
1. (D) 2. (A) 3. (B) 4. (D) 5. (A) 6. (D) 7. (B)
8. (A) 9. (C) 10. (B)

1. 정답 (D)

해설 Best Buy 구매자들은 받을 수 있다 / 무료 배송을 / 만약 그들이 구매한다면 / 5개 제품 이상을 / 또는 그들이 구매한 총액이 / 300달러를 넘는다면

해설 빈칸 앞뒤 문장이 완전하기 때문에, 빈칸은 부사절을 이끄는 부사절 접속사 자리이다. than은 비교급이 있을 때 쓰이므로 탈락하고, that은 명사절 또는 형용사절 접속사로 쓰이기 때문에 탈락한다. 그리고 just는 부사이므로 탈락. 따라서 부사절 접속사의 기능이 있는 (D) if가 정답이다.

표현 정리 shopper 구매자 shipping 선적, 운송, 배송 purchase 구매하다; 구매 more than ~이상 the total amount 총액 exceed 초과하다, 넘어서다

2. 정답 (A)

해설 등록은 / 워크숍을 위한 / 완료되지 않을 것이다 / 모든 필요한 서류들이 / 접수될 때까지

해설 빈칸 앞뒤 문장이 완전한 문장이므로 빈칸은 부사절을 이끄는 접속사 자리이다. just와 only는 부사이므로 탈락하고, what은 명사절 접속사이므로 탈락. 따라서 부사절 접속사인 (A) until이 정답이다.

표현 정리 registration 등록 complete 완료하다, 작성하다 required documents 필요한 서류들 not A until B B하고 나서야 A하다

3. 정답 (B)

해설 여러 프로젝트들이 / Nobel Laboratories가 받은 / 자금을 / 시작할 예정이다 / 다음 달에 / 만약 충분한 공간이 / 확보된다면

해설 for which부터 funding까지는 주어인 Several projects를 수식하는 형용사절이다. 빈칸 앞뒤 문장이 완전하므로 빈칸은 부사절을 이끄는 접속사 자리이다. in reality는 부사, other than은 전치사이므로 탈락. 부사절 접속사인 (A)와 (B) 중에서 해석으로 판단한다. 충분한 공간이 확보된다면 프로젝트를 시작할 것이라는 내용이므로 (B) provided that(~한다면)이 정답이다.

표현 정리 several 몇몇의, 일부의 receive 받다 funding 자금 be scheduled to ~할 예정이다 a sufficient amount of 충분한 양의 available 이용 가능한 as if 마치 ~인 것처럼 provided that ~한다면 in reality 실제로는, 사실은 other than ~외에, ~과 다른

4. 정답 (D)

해설 이사회가 필요성을 언급했음에도 불구하고 / 공격적인 광고의 / 아무 것도 실행되지 않았다 / 개선시키기 위해 / 상황을

해설 빈칸이 포함된 문장 뒤에 콤마가 있고, 완전한 문장이 나왔으므로 앞 문장은 부사절이며, 빈칸은 부사절 접속사 자리이다. (A)는 전치사이므로 탈락하고, (C)는 부사이므로 탈락. (B)와 (D) 중에서 해석으로 판단한다. 접속사 대입 우선순위인 although를 넣고 해석해 보면, 이사회가 언급했음에도 불구하고 아무것도 실행되지 않았다고 한 것으로 보아, 두 문장이 상반되는 내용임을 알 수 있다. 따라서 양보의 접속사인 (D) Although가 정답이다.

표현 정리 the board of directors 이사회 address 언급하다, 다루다 aggressive 공격적인 advertising 광고 improve 개선하다, 향상시키다 situation 상황, 상태 because of ~때문에(전치사) whether ~이든 아니든(부사절), ~인지 아닌지(명사절) as always 언제나처럼, 늘 그렇듯이 although ~에도 불구하고, 비록 ~일지라도

5. 정답 (A)

해설 호텔 손님들은 조언 받는다 / 그들의 귀중품을 안전하게 보관하도록 / 금고에 / 그들이 방을 떠날 때는 언제든지

2

해설 빈칸 앞 뒤에 완전한 문장이 있으므로 빈칸은 부사절 접속사 자리이다. 보기 모두 부사절 접속사가 될 수 있으나 (B), (C), (D)는 일반적인 부사절 접속사와는 달리 뒤에 불완전한 문장이 온다. 따라서 (A)가 정답이다.

표현 정리 be advised to+동사원형 ~하도록 조언 받다 valuables 귀중품 safe 금고 leave 떠나다 whenever ~할 때는 언제나 whomever ~하는 사람은 누구든 whatever ~하는 것은 무엇이든 whichever ~한 것은 어느 것이든

6. 정답 (D)

해설 Whitfield Consulting은 / 긴밀하게 일하는 / 정부 관리들과 / 문을 닫을 것이다 / 다음 주 월요일에 / 국경일이 겹치기 때문에 / 주말과

해설 빈칸 앞뒤 문장이 완전하므로 부사절 접속사 자리이다. (B)와 (C)는 전치사이므로 탈락. 국경일이 주말과 겹치기 때문에(원인) Whitfield Consulting이 다음 주 월요일에 닫을 것(결과)이라는 어울림으로 보아 이유의 접속사 (D) because가 정답이다.

표현 정리 closely 긴밀하게, 면밀하게 a national holiday 국경일 fall on (날짜가) ~에 해당되다, ~이다 in spite of ~에도 불구하고 (전치사) because ~때문에(접속사)

7. 정답 (B)

해설 고객 만족을 보장하기 위해 / 확실히 알도록 하시오 / 새로운 시스템의 작동법을 / 당신이 분명하게 답하기 위해 / 고객들의 질문에

해설 빈칸 앞뒤에 완전한 문장이 있으므로 빈칸은 부사절 접속사 자리이다. 대명사 혹은 형용사인 (D) neither는 탈락하고 나머지는 해석으로 판단한다. 빈칸 뒤 문장에 can이 있으므로 'so that ~ can'의 표현을 생각해 볼 수 있다. 질문에 확실하게 답하기 위해 새로운 시스템의 작동법을 확실히 알도록 하라는 의미이므로 (B) so that이 정답이다.

표현 정리 ensure 확실하게 하다, 보장하다 customer satisfaction 고객 만족 make sure 확실히 하다, 확인하다 clearly 명확하게, 분명하게 as if 마치 ~처럼

8. 정답 (A)

해설 Dr. Jacky Mason은 근무하게 된다 / 내과 의사로 / WHO에서 / 20년 동안 / 그녀가 은퇴할 때쯤이면

해설 빈칸은 부사절 접속사 자리이다. (B)는 전치사이므로 탈락. 미래완료 시제(will have worked)는 어떤 한 시점을 기준으로 그 전까지 완료되어 있을 것이라는 의미이기 때문에 문장에 미래시점이 필요하며, 미래완료시제와 함께 잘 쓰이는 접속사는 by the time(~할 때까지)이다. 그녀가 은퇴할 때쯤이면 Dr. Jacky Mason은 20년 동안 근무하게 될 것이라는 어울림으로 (A) by the time이 정답이다.

표현 정리 for+숫자 기간 ~동안 physician 내과의사 retire 은퇴하다, 퇴임하다 as much as ~만큼 많이

9. 정답 (C)

해설 신입 사원들은 연락해야 한다 / 인사 부장에게 / 즉시 / 만약 그들이 참여할 수 없다면 / 예비 교육 프로그램에 / 그들을 위해 계획된

해설 빈칸 앞뒤 문장이 완전하므로 빈칸은 부사절 접속사 자리이다. (B)와 (D)는 전치사이므로 탈락하고, why는 명사절이나 형용사절 접속사로 쓰이므로 탈락한다. (C) if가 정답이다.

표현 정리 recruit 구성원, 신입 사원 contact 연락하다 personnel manager 인사 부장 immediately 즉시, 바로 attend 참석하다 orientation 예비 교육, 오리엔테이션

10. 정답 (B)

해설 그가 고용했음에도 불구하고 / 그를 도울 비서를 / Mr. Lee는 여전히 다룬다 / 모든 고객 관련 문제들을 / 직접

해설 보기가 모두 부사절 접속사이므로 해석으로 판단해야 한다. 그는 그를 돕기 위한 비서를 고용했는데, 그는 여전히 직접 고객과 관련된 문제들을 처리한다는 상반되는 내용이므로 양보의 접속사 (B) Even though가 정답이다.

표현 정리 hire 고용하다 assistant 조수, 비서 handle 다루다, 처리하다 client-related 고객과 관련된 issue 문제, 사안 himself 스스로, 직접

법칙 2 '관소전타' 뒤는 명사

◎ **유형을 파악해 봐**
1. (C)   2. (C)   3. (D)

1. 정답 (C)

해설 Rayburn Valley 지역 농부들은 시작했다 / 재배를 / 다양한 유기농 채소들을 / 고객 수요에 대응해

해설 전치사 뒤, 전명구 앞이므로 빈칸은 명사 자리이며, (C)가 정답이다. (A)는 과거분사, (B)는 형용사, (D)는 동사이다.

표현 정리 farmer 농부, 농장주 region 지방, 지역 grow 재배하다, 자라다 a wider variety of+복수 명사 폭넓은, 다양한 organic 유기농의, 화학 비료를 쓰지 않는 vegetable 채소 in response to+명사 ~에 대한 응답으로, ~에 응하여 consumer demand 고객 수요

2. 정답 (C)

해설 계약서에 언급된 마감일은 변경될 수 있다 / 프로젝트 매니저의 재량에 따라

해설 관사 뒤, 전명구 앞이므로 빈칸은 명사 자리이며, (C)가 정답이다. (A)는 부사, (B)는 동사, (D)는 형용사이다.

표현 정리 deadline 마감일 list (리스트에) 작성하다, 언급하다 contract 계약, 계약서 be subject to+명사 ~하기 쉽다, ~에 좌우되다 change 변경하다, 바꾸다 at the discretion of ~의 재량대로

3. 정답 (D)

해설 연락하시오 / 참석하는 의사에게 / 승인을 얻기 위해서 / 처방전 자발 행을 위한

해설 타동사 뒤, 전명구 앞이므로 빈칸은 명사 자리이며, (D)가 정답이다. (A)는 과거분사, (B)와 (C)는 동사이다.

표현 정리 contact 연락하다, 접속하다 physician 의사, 내과의사 obtain 얻다, 구하다 approval 인정, 승인 prescription 처방전, 처방

refill 재발행, 재처방 request 요청

◎ 실전에 적용해 봐
1. (A) 2. (B) 3. (D) 4. (A) 5. (A) 6. (A) 7. (D)
8. (A) 9. (B) 10. (B)

1. 정답 (A)

해석 새 식당의 인기는 / 세부 지역에서 / 돋웠다 / 그것이 성장하도록 / 규모가 큰 식당들 사이에서 / 그 지역으로 옮겨 오픈한

해설 빈칸 앞에 관사 the가 있고, 뒤에 전명구가 있으므로 빈칸은 명사 자리이다. 보기 중 명사인 (A) popularity가 정답이다. (B)는 동사, (C)는 형용사, (D)는 부사이다.

표현 정리 popularity 인기 help 목적어 (to)+동사원형 목적어가 ~하도록 돕다 move into ~로 이동하다

2. 정답 (B)

해석 Mr. Williams는 받았다 / 상을 / 수상 위원회로부터 / 그의 업적에 대해 / 개선시킨 / 직원 복리후생을

해설 빈칸 앞은 관사, 뒤는 전명구이므로 빈칸은 명사 자리이다. 타동사인 earned의 목적어 자리이므로 명사인 (B) commendation이 정답이다. (A)는 부사, (C)는 형용사, (D)는 동사이다.

표현 정리 earn 벌다, 받다 commendation 상, 상장, 칭찬 award committee 수상 위원회 improve 개선시키다, 향상시키다 employee benefits 직원 복리후생

3. 정답 (D)

해석 더 나은 인상을 주기 위해 / 당신의 잠재적인 고용주에게 / 열거하시오 / 당신의 일과 관련된 업적을 / 전문 자격증, 출판물, 수상, 그리고 병역과 같은

해설 형용사(work-related) 뒤, 전명구 앞이므로 빈칸은 명사 자리이며, (D) accomplishments가 정답이다. (A)는 동사, (B)와 (C)는 분사 형태의 형용사이다.

표현 정리 in order to+동사원형 ~하기 위해 impression 인상, 감명 potential 잠재적인, 가능성 있는 employer 고용주 specify 명시하다, 열거하다 work-related 일과 관련된 accomplishment 업적, 성과 professional certification 전문 자격증 publication 출판물, 간행물 military service 병역, 군 복무

4. 정답 (A)

해석 Whitehouse Electric의 인사부장은 강조했다 / 노고와 헌신을 / 필수 자질로써 / 합격자들을 위한

해설 3형식 동사인 stress의 목적어 자리에 hard work가 왔고, 이어 and가 있으므로 빈칸은 and 앞의 명사와 동일한 구조가 와야 한다. 따라서 명사인 (A)가 정답이다. hard work and dedication은 '노고와 헌신'이라는 말로 함께 자주 등장한다.

표현 정리 personnel director 인사부장 stress 강조하다 hard work and dedication 노고와 헌신 vital 필수적인 quality 품질, 자질 successful candidate 합격자

5. 정답 (A)

해석 'East and West'의 구독률이 / 인상적인 국제 판매 부수를 자랑하는 요리 잡지인 / 증가했다 / 올해

해설 with는 전치사이며, impressive나 international은 명사를 수식하는 형용사이다. 결국 전치사 뒤에는 명사가 와야 하므로 (A) circulation이 정답이다. (B)는 동사, (C)는 형용사, (D)는 부사이다.

표현 정리 readership 구독률 impressive 인상적인, 감동적인 international 국제적인, 국제의 circulation (신문, 잡지의) 판매 부수 improve 증대하다, 높아지다(자동사)

6. 정답 (A)

해석 GW 어학원은 헌신적이다 / 돕는데 / 대학생들이 이루도록 / 성공을 / 그들의 학업의 목표에서

해설 빈칸 앞은 타동사, 뒤는 전명구이므로 빈칸은 find의 목적어 자리이며, 명사인 (A) success가 정답이다. (B)는 부사, (C)는 형용사, (D)는 동사이다.

표현 정리 language institute 어학원 be dedicated to -ing ~하는데 헌신[몰두]하다 college students 대학생 academic 학업의, 학교의 goal 목표, 목적

7. 정답 (D)

해석 승인을 받기 전에 / Wigerly Hall을 이용하기 위한 / 당신은 요청해야 한다 / 행사 진행자에게 / 그것의 이용 가능성을 확인하기 위해

해설 빈칸 앞에 동명사가 있고, 뒤에 전명구가 있으므로 빈칸은 동명사의 목적어 자리이다. 목적어가 될 수 있는 것은 명사인 (D) authorization이다. (A)는 형용사, (B)는 과거분사, (C)는 동사이다.

표현 정리 before -ing ~전에 receive 받다 authorization 승인, 허가 coordinator 진행자, 담당자 confirm 확인하다 availability 유용성, 유효성, 이용 가능성

8. 정답 (A)

해석 직원들이 / STV 그룹의 5개 자회사에서 온 / 서로 만날 것이다 / 계획을 논의하기 위해 / 협력을 증가시킬 / 독립된 자회사들 사이에서

해설 빈칸 앞에 타동사가 있고, 뒤에 전명구가 있으므로 빈칸은 명사 자리이다. increase의 목적어가 될 수 있는 명사인 (A) cooperation이 정답이다.

표현 정리 representative 직원, 대리인, 대표자 subsidiary 자회사 one another (셋 이상) 서로 discuss 논의하다, 토론하다 plan to+동사원형 ~할 계획 cooperation 협력, 협동 separate 분리된, 따로 떨어진

9. 정답 (B)

해석 시 의회 홈페이지는 현재 불가능하다 / 접속이 / 일시적인 오류 때문에

해설 빈칸 앞에 관사가 있고, 뒤에 명사가 있기 때문에 빈칸은 명사를 수식하는 형용사 자리이므로 (B)가 정답이다. (A)는 부사, (C)는 명사, (D)는 동사이다.

표현 정리 city council 시 의회 currently 현재, 지금 be unable to+동사원형 ~할 수 없다 access 접속하다, 접근하다 temporary 일시적인, 임시의 error 오류

10.   정답 (B)

해설 예약은 / 회사 회의실을 위한 / 이루어져야 한다 / 회의 시작 24시간 전에

해설 빈칸 뒤 for부터 room까지는 전명구이므로 must be가 동사이고, 빈칸은 주어 자리이다. 따라서 주어 자리에 올 수 있는 명사 (B)가 정답이다.

표현 정리 reservation 예약 meeting room 회의실 prior to ~이전에

법칙 3 주어와 동사, 조동사와 동사원형, have와 p.p. 어구 사이는 부사

◎ 유형을 파악해 봐
1. (B)   2. (D)   3. (A)

1.   정답 (B)

해설 이사회는 / 반드시 정기적으로 검토해야 한다 / 그리고 평가해야 한다 / 회사의 진척도를 / 수행하는데 있어 / 장기 계획을

해설 빈칸은 조동사와 동사원형 사이이므로 부사 자리이며, 따라서 부사인 (B)가 정답이다. (A)는 형용사, (C)는 명사, (D)는 동사이다.

표현 정리 the board of directors 이사회 regularly 정기적으로 review 검토하다 progress 과정, 진척도 carry out 수행하다 long-term plan 장기 계획

2.   정답 (D)

해설 발견한 후에 / 심각한 문제를 / 내년 사업 기획안에서 / CEO는 즉시 회의를 소집했다 / 모든 관련자들에 대한

해설 빈칸은 주어와 동사 사이이므로 부사 자리이며, 따라서 부사인 (D)가 정답이다. (A)는 형용사 혹은 동사, (B)는 명사, (C)는 동사이다.

표현 정리 after -ing ~한 후에 serious 심각한 error 문제점 promptly 즉시 call a meeting 회의를 소집하다 of all those concerned 모든 관련자들

3.   정답 (A)

해설 우리 히터들은 지속적으로 입증되어 왔다 / 25% 더 효율적이라고 / 제조된 히터들보다 / 우리 경쟁사에 의해

해설 빈칸은 have와 p.p. 사이이므로 부사 자리이며, 따라서 부사인 (A)가 정답이다. (B)는 명사, (C)는 형용사, (D)는 동사이다.

표현 정리 prove (to be) ~인 것으로 판명되다 efficient 능률적인 manufacture 제조하다 competitor 경쟁사 consistent 일관된

◎ 실전에 적용해 봐
1. (C)   2. (B)   3. (B)   4. (D)   5. (B)   6. (A)   7. (B)
8. (C)   9. (D)   10. (B)

1.   정답 (C)

해설 응답해 주세요 / 즉시 / 초대장에 / 10주년 기념 파티를 위한 / Anderson Industries 사에서 열릴

해설 빈칸은 덩어리 동사('법칙 74' 참고) 사이이므로 부사 자리이며, 따라서 부사인 (C)가 정답이다. (A)는 형용사 혹은 동사, (B)는 명사라서 탈락하고, (D)는 부사 자리에 쓸 수 없다.

표현 정리 reply to ~에 응답하다 promptly 즉시 invitation 초대장 anniversary 기념일

2.   정답 (B)

해설 지원자들은 분명하게 표시해야 한다 / 그들이 지원하는 직책 명을 / 봉투에

해설 빈칸은 조동사와 동사 사이이므로 부사 자리이며, 따라서 부사인 (B)가 정답이다. (A)는 형용사 혹은 동사, (D)는 동사, 그리고 (C)는 부사 자리에 쓸 수 없으므로 탈락한다.

표현 정리 applicant 지원자 mark 표시하다 clearly 분명하게 position title 직책 명 apply for ~에 지원하다 envelope 봉투

3.   정답 (B)

해설 직책에 관심이 있는 사람들은 / 조언을 받는다 / 정기적으로 검토하라고 / 회사 웹사이트를 / 세부사항과 업데이트된 내용을 위해

해설 빈칸은 to와 동사원형 사이이므로 부사 자리이며, 따라서 부사인 (B)가 정답이다. (A)는 형용사 혹은 동사, (C)는 동사, (D)는 부사 자리에 쓸 수 없으므로 탈락한다.

표현 정리 those who ~하는 사람들 be interested in ~에 관심이 있다 be advised to+동사원형 ~하도록 조언을 받다 regularly 정기적으로 details 세부사항

4.   정답 (D)

해설 만약 질문이 있다면 / 정원 가꾸기에 관한 / 전화 주세요 / 회사 직통 전화 555-6072로

해설 빈칸 앞은 가정법 미래 표현인 If you should have의 도치된 표현이고, 주절은 명령문이다. 빈칸은 동사 call 앞에서 수식해 주는 부사 자리이다. 따라서 부사인 (D)가 정답이다. (A)는 형용사, (B)는 동사라서 탈락하고, 형용사의 비교급인 (C)는 부사 자리에 쓸 수 없다.

표현 정리 regarding ~에 관련한 gardening 원예, 정원 손질 simply 그저 hotline 직통전화

5.   정답 (B)

해설 Kwon 씨는 고마워했다 / 회사 고객서비스 직원에게 / 빠른 응답을 해 준 것에 대해 / 그녀의 불만에

해설 빈칸은 전치사와 동명사 사이에서 동명사를 수식하는 부사 자리이다. 따라서 부사인 (B)가 정답이다. (A)는 형용사, (C)는 명사이고, 형용사 비교급인 (D)는 부사 자리에 쓸 수 없다.

표현 정리 thank 감사하다, 고마워하다 customer service representative 고객서비스 직원 quickly 빠르게 respond to ~에 응답하다, 반응하다 complaint 불만, 불평

6.
정답 (A)

해설 지난 10년 동안 Delta 사는 상당히 변화시켰다 / 회사의 사업 모델을 / 다양화하기 위해 / 단순히 컴퓨터를 판매하는 것에서

해설 빈칸은 has와 p.p. 사이이므로 부사 자리이다. 따라서 부사인 (A)가 정답이다. (B)는 형용사, (C)는 명사, (D)는 동사이다.

표현 정리 decade 10년 significantly 상당히 change 변화시키다 diversify 다양화시키다

7.
정답 (B)

해설 환경운동가는 주장한다 / 화석연료 사용이 / 아마도 주된 원인일 것이라고 / 지구온난화의 / 그것은 아마 초래하게 될 것 같다 / 상당한 비용을 / 세계 경제에

해설 that 절 안의 동사인 is와 보어인 the main cause 사이에 들어갈 수 있는 부사가 필요하다. most likely는 '~할 것 같은'이라는 의미의 덩어리 어휘이다. 따라서 (B)가 정답이다.

표현 정리 environmentalist 환경운동가 claim 주장하다 fossil fuel 화석연료 cause 원인 global warming 지구온난화 induce 초래하다 substantial 상당한 cost 비용 economy 경제

8.
정답 (C)

해설 대도시에서는 흡연이 엄격하게 금지되어 있다 / 거리에서 / 그리고 / 오로지 허용된다 / 지정된 구역에서만

해설 빈칸은 be 동사와 p.p. 사이이므로 부사 자리이다. 따라서 부사인 (C)가 정답이다. (A)는 명사, (D)는 동사이며, 형용사 비교급인 (B)는 부사 자리에 쓸 수 없다.

표현 정리 metropolitan area 수도권 strictly 엄격하게 prohibit 금지하다 allow 허락하다 designated 지정된

9.
정답 (D)

해설 SJ 사 직원들은 압도적으로 찬성하고 있다 / 근무 시간을 줄이는 것을 / 주중에 / 그들이 토요일에 일을 할지라도

해설 be 동사 다음이라고 바로 형용사를 답으로 고르면 안 되는 함정 문제이다. in favor of는 전명구지만 2형식 문장의 필수요소인 보어로 사용될 수 있다. 그러므로 빈칸은 be 동사와 in favor of 사이이므로 부사 자리이며, 따라서 부사인 (D)가 정답이다.

표현 정리 employee 직원 overwhelmingly 압도적으로 in favor of ~에 찬성하여 reduce 줄이다 working hour 근무시간 even if ~할지라도

10.
정답 (B)

해설 Libratone 사는 진심으로 고마워 한다 / 지역사회로부터의 강력한 지원에 대해 / 그리고 목표로 한다 / 제공하는 것을 / 더 많은 취업 기회를 / 지역 주민들을 위한

해설 빈칸은 be 동사와 보어인 형용사 사이이므로 부사 자리이며, 따라서 부사인 (B)가 정답이다. (A)는 형용사, (C), (D)는 명사이다.

표현 정리 truly 진심으로 appreciative 고마워하는 strong 강력한 support 지원 local 지역의 community 지역사회 aim to+동사원형 ~하는 것을 목표로 하다 provide 제공하다 job opportunity 취업 기회 resident 주민

법칙 4 명사 앞 소유격, 동사/전치사 뒤 목적격, 동사 앞 주격

◎ 유형을 파악해 봐
1. (B) 2. (D) 3. (C)

1.
정답 (B)

해설 방문자들은 / Central Art Museum의 / 조언을 받는다 / 정기적으로 확인하도록 / 그들의 소지품을 / 견학하는 동안

해설 빈칸 뒤에 명사가 왔으므로 빈칸은 명사를 수식하는 소유격 자리이다. 따라서 소유격인 (B)가 정답이다. (A)는 주격, (C)는 목적격, (D)는 재귀대명사로 목적격 혹은 부사로 쓰인다.

표현 정리 visitor 방문자 be advised to+동사원형 ~하도록 조언 받다 periodically 정기적으로 check 확인하다 belonging 소지품, 소유물 tour 견학

2.
정답 (D)

해설 회사의 자동화 시스템은 보다 효율화되었다 / 회사가 사용하기 시작했기 때문에 / 최신 기술을

해설 빈칸 앞에 접속사 as, 빈칸 뒤에 동사가 있으므로 빈칸은 주어 자리이며, 따라서 주격인 (D)가 정답이다. (A)는 재귀대명사로 목적격 혹은 부사로 쓰이고, (B)는 목적격, (C)는 소유격이다.

표현 정리 automated system 자동화 시스템 efficient 효율적인 the latest 가장 최근의

3.
정답 (C)

해설 우리에게 알려주세요 / 당신이 도착하자마자 / 공항에 / 그래야 우리가 당신을 제 시간에 데리러 갈 수 있어요

해설 문장에서 let은 사역동사로 쓰였다. 빈칸 뒤에 동사가 있으므로 빈칸은 목적어 자리이므로 (C)가 정답이 된다. (A)는 주격, (B)는 소유격이므로 탈락하고, 재귀대명사가 목적어 자리에 쓰일 때에는 동작의 주체와 대상이 같은 경우인데, 여기서 let 하는 주체는 'you'이고, 당하는 대상은 'we'이므로 (D) 역시 답이 될 수 없다.

표현 정리 as soon as ~하자마자 arrive at ~에 도착하다 airport 공항 so that ~하기 위해서, 그래야 ~하니까 pick up 태우다 on time 제때에, 제 시간에

◎ 실전에 적용해 봐
1. (B) 2. (C) 3. (D) 4. (D) 5. (B) 6. (C) 7. (A)
8. (C) 9. (B) 10. (D)

1.
정답 (B)

해설 만약 당신이 원하지 않는다면 / 수신하기를 / 우리로부터 직통 메일 또는 전화를 / 당신은 보낼 수 있다 / 당신의 요청서를 / 위의 우편 주소로

해설 빈칸 뒤의 request는 가산명사로 앞에 관사나 소유격을 써야 한다.

따라서 (B)가 정답이다.

표현 정리 receive 받다 direct 직통의 send 보내다 request 요청하다; 요청 postal address 우편 주소 above ~보다 위에

2. 정답 (C)

해석 연설자들은 요청 받는다 / 제출할 것을 / 그들의 발표 자료들을 / 최소한 2시간 전에 / 그들의 강연 시간

해설 빈칸 앞에 전치사, 빈칸 뒤에 명사가 있으므로 빈칸은 소유격이 와야 한다. 따라서 (C)가 정답이다. (D)를 소유대명사라고 하는데, 소유대명사도 명사 취급하므로 뒤에 명사와 함께 사용할 수 없다.

표현 정리 speaker 연설자 be requested to+동사원형 ~하기를 요청 받다 hand in 제출하다 presentation material 발표 자료 at least 최소한 talk 연설, 강연

3. 정답 (D)

해석 Mr. Andoranti는 주도할 것이다 / 세미나를 / 따라서 질문이나 요청 사항들은 / 그에게 보내져야 한다

해설 전치사 뒤는 목적격 대명사가 와야 하므로 목적격인 (D)가 정답이다. 주격인 (A)는 탈락하고, (B)는 소유격도 되지만 '그의 것'이라는 소유대명사도 되는데, 그의 것이 무엇인지 알 수 없으므로 탈락하고, 주어가 any questions and requests이므로 주체와 대상이 같을 때 사용하는 재귀대명사 (C) 역시 틀린다.

표현 정리 lead 이끌다 question 질문 request 요청 사항 be directed to ~에게 보내지다

4. 정답 (D)

해석 매니저는 알렸다 / 나에게 / 그가 보냈다는 것을 / 무료 소책자를 / 정보에 관한 / 내가 요청한

해설 여기서 requested는 동사이며, 빈칸은 주어 자격이다. 따라서 주격인 (D)가 정답이다. information과 I 사이에는 목적격관계대명사 that이 생략되었다. (C)도 주어 자리에 올 수는 있으나 '나의 것'이 '요청한 정보'가 될 수는 없다.

표현 정리 inform 알리다 complimentary 무료 booklet 소책자 regarding ~에 관해 information 정보 request 요청하다

5. 정답 (D)

해석 Shin Hwa 사는 요청한다 / 회사 직원들이 / 책임을 가질 것을 / 그들 스스로의 발전에

해설 빈칸 앞에 전치사, 빈칸 뒤에 명사가 있으므로 빈칸은 소유격 자리이며, 따라서 소유격인 (D)가 정답이다. own은 소유격을 강조할 때 사용할 수 있는 형용사로서 소유격과 함께 쓰여 소유격 또는 소유대명사 기능을 한다.

표현 정리 request 요청하다 be responsible for ~에 책임을 지다 development 발전

6. 정답 (C)

해석 Mr. Gu는 요청했다 / 그의 두 조수에게 / 그를 도와달라고 / 영사기를 설치하는 것을 / 회의실에 있는

해설 help는 5형식 동사로 to 부정사 또는 동사원형을 목적 보어로 취한다. 그러므로 빈칸 뒤는 목적어 자리이다. (A)는 목적어가 될 수 없어 탈락이다. (B)를 소유대명사로 볼 경우, '그의 것'을 도와줄 수는 없어 답이 될 수 없고, 결국 (C)와 (D)가 남는데, help라는 동작의 주체는 his two assistants이다. himself를 쓰려면 주체가 he가 되어야 하므로 (C) Him이 정답이다.

표현 정리 assistant 비서, 조수 set up 설치하다 projector 영사기 meeting room 회의실

7. 정답 (A)

해석 강력하게 권유한다 / 직원들이 기록하도록 / 그들이 일한 시간과 / 지불 받은 것을

해설 work는 주로 1형식 동사로 쓰이지만 hour나 shift 같은 목적어가 있으면 3형식 동사로 사용할 수 있다. 빈칸 뒤에는 동사가 있으므로 빈칸은 주어 자리이며, (A)가 정답이다. (B)는 지시대명사 혹은 지시형용사인데, work를 명사로 보면 앞의 hours도 명사이므로 명사와 명사를 연결해 줄 수 없다. work를 동사로 보면 those가 주어가 되어야 하는데, '그것들'이 무엇을 가리키는지 알 수 없고, (C)는 목적어 자리에 써야 하며, (D)가 오면 역시 work가 명사가 되어 앞의 hours와 연결이 안 된다. 이 문제는 work가 동사인지 명사인지 구분하고, 목적격 관계대명사의 생략, 그리고 work가 3형식 동사도 된다는 것을 알고 있는지를 묻는 고난이도 함정 문제이다.

표현 정리 strongly 강력하게 suggest 제안하다 keep records of ~을 기록하다

8. 정답 (C)

해석 그들이 검토한 후에 / 추가 감시 테이프를 / 경찰들은 더 좋은 인상착의를 기대하고 있다 / 용의자에 대한

해설 빈칸 앞에 접속사 after, 빈칸 뒤에 동사가 있으므로 빈칸은 주어 자리이며, 따라서 주격인 (C)가 정답이다. (A)는 소유격, (B)는 소유대명사 (D)는 목적격이다.

표현 정리 review 검토하다 additional 추가적인 surveillance 감시 description 묘사, 설명 suspect 용의자

9. 정답 (B)

해석 Brenda는 말했다 / 해외 지사에서 일할 기회를 갖게 된 것이 / 그녀를 그 직책에 흥미를 갖게 했다고

해설 빈칸 앞 made는 5형식 동사로 쓰였다. 빈칸은 목적어, 빈칸 뒤는 목적 보어다. interested는 사람을 수식해 주는 분사로 빈칸에는 사람을 나타내는 말이 와야 한다. (A)는 주격이라 탈락하고, (C)는 '그녀의 것'이란 뜻인데, 무엇을 가리키는지 알 수도 없고, 사물이라 탈락한다. (B)와 (D) 중 made라는 동작의 주체가 '기회를 가지는 것'이므로 대상과 동일하지 않아 재귀대명사 herself는 사용할 수 없다. 따라서 목적격 (B)가 정답이다.

표현 정리 opportunity to 동사원형 ~할 기회 overseas 해외의 branch 지사 position 직책

10. 정답 (D)

해석 멤버십 카드는 허용할 것이다 / 우리가 이용할 수 있도록 / 모든 혜택을 / 회사가 제공하는

해설 allow는 결혼승낙동사('법칙 48' 참고)이므로 목적어 다음에 목적 보어로 to 부정사를 취한다. 빈칸 앞에 동사가 있고, 뒤에 목적 보어로 to 부정사가 왔으므로 빈칸은 목적어 자리이며, 따라서 목적격인 (D)가 정답이다. (A)는 주격, (B)는 소유격이라 탈락한다. (C) '우리의 것'은 사물인데, 사물이 이용할 수는 없으므로 답이 될 수 없다.

표현 정리 allow 허용하다 take advantage of ~을 이용하다 benefit 혜택 offer 제공하다

법칙 5 시제 부사가 보기에 있으면 동사를 확인

◎ 유형을 파악해 봐
1. (A) 2. (D) 3. (C)

1. 정답 (A)

해설 이전에 삭제된 파일들은 대개 저장된다 / 컴퓨터 하드디스크의 다음 위치에

해설 보기 중 usually는 빈도부사이므로 시제 부사를 묻는 문제라고 볼 수 있다. 문장 시제가 현재시제이므로 빈도부사인 (A)가 정답이다. (B)와 (C)는 형용사나 부사의 정도를 수식한다.

표현 정리 previously ~이전에 deleted 삭제된 following ~후에, ~다음 location 장소 usually 보통, 대개 relatively 비교적 slightly 약간 vaguely 애매하게

2. 정답 (D)

해설 기상 상태는 매우 좋지 않다 / 오늘 / 하지만 상황이 호전될 것이다 / 곧

해설 보기 중 미래시제와 잘 어울리는 시제 부사는 shortly이므로 (D)가 정답이다. (B)는 주로 숫자 앞에 오거나 '완성된'이란 말과 어울린다.

표현 정리 weather conditions 기상 상태 favorable 호의적인 improve 개선되다, 개선시키다 openly 솔직하게, 공공연히 nearly 거의 urgently 급히 shortly 곧

3. 정답 (C)

해설 우리는 조사할 예정이다 / 불만 사항을 / 우리 고객들 중 한 명이 당신을 상대로 최근에 제기한

해설 보기 중 recently는 과거시제나 현재완료시제와 잘 어울리는 시제 부사이다. 문장의 시제가 현재완료이므로 (C)가 적절하다. (A)는 증가, 감소 등의 표현과 잘 어울리며, (B)는 형용사이고, (D)는 전명구 앞이나 명사절 앞에 잘 오는 부사이다.

표현 정리 be about to+동사원형 ~하려 하다, ~할 예정이다 complaint 불만, 항의 customer 고객 file against ~을 상대로 제기하다 noticeably 주목할 만하게 friendly 친근한 recently 최근에 exactly 정확하게

◎ 실전에 적용해 봐
1. (B) 2. (C) 3. (A) 4. (A) 5. (B) 6. (A) 7. (A)
8. (A) 9. (A) 10. (B)

1. 정답 (B)

해설 유명 언론인인 Glenn Greenwald는 곧 출판할 것이다 / 그의 전기를 / 'New York Daily News'에서 5년 동안 근무한 후

해설 조동사와 동사원형 사이이므로 빈칸은 부사 자리이다. 문장의 시제가 미래시제이므로 미래시제와 잘 어울리는 부사 (B)가 정답이다. 명사절 접속사인 (A)는 탈락하고, (C)를 긍정문에 사용하는 경우는 최상급이 있을 때이며, 주로 부정의문문과 사용한다. (D)는 주로 형용사나 부사를 수식한다.

표현 정리 renowned 유명한 journalist 기자, 언론인 soon 곧 publish 발행하다, 출판하다 biography 전기, 일대기 experience 경험

2. 정답 (C)

해설 인사 부장은 아직 받지 못했다 / 충분한 지원서들을 / 면접을 진행하기 위한 / 그가 공고했음에도 불구하고 / 직원 모집을 / 몇 주 전에

해설 정동사가 2개, 접속사가 1개 있으므로 빈칸에는 접속사가 또 올 수 없어 (B)는 탈락하고, has와 to 사이에 올 수 있는 것은 yet뿐이다. yet은 원래 부정문과 쓰지만, have yet to do는 '아직 ~하지 못하다'라는 뜻의 숙어이다. 모집 공고를 게시했음에도 불구하고 아직 충분한 지원서를 받지 못했다는 의미이므로 (C)가 정답이다.

표현 정리 personnel manager 인사 부장 has yet to 아직 ~하지 못하다 receive 받다 enough 충분한 application 지원, 지원서 proceed with ~를 진행하다 job interview 면접 even though 그럼에도 불구하고 post 공고하다, 게재하다 job opening 공석, 일자리

3. 정답 (A)

해설 아직 제출하지 않은 직원들은 / 그들의 실적 평가서를 / 인사과에 / 제출해야 한다 / 6월 3일까지

해설 현재완료시제와 잘 어울리는 부사는 (A)와 (C)인데, still은 not보다 앞에 온다. 따라서 (A)가 정답이다.

표현 정리 employee 직원 performance 실적 evaluation 평가 personnel department 인사과 still 여전히 shortly 곧

4. 정답 (A)

해설 노력은 / Dr. Takayashi가 그의 연구 프로젝트에 들인 / 마침내 그에게 안겨 주었다 / 연구 보조금을

해설 문장의 시제는 과거시제이다. 보기 중 finally는 현재완료나 과거시제와 잘 어울리는 부사이므로 (A)가 정답이다. (B)는 현재시제와 어울리고, (C)는 주로 전명구나 부사절 앞에 오는 초점 부사이다. (D)는 '되도록 ~이면'이란 뜻으로 전명구나 명사 앞에 주로 온다.

표현 정리 effort 노력 put in (시간을) 쏟다, 투자하다 research project 연구 프로젝트 win 획득하다 grant 보조금

5. 정답 (B)

해설 위기에 처한 전통 가옥은 마침내 다시 문을 열었다 / 대중들에게 / 8년 동안의 대규모 보수 및 복구 작업 후에

해설 문장의 시제는 현재완료시제이다. 보기 중 finally는 현재완료나 과거시제와 잘 어울리기도 하지만 특히 '~후에'라는 말이 포함될 때 자주 사용되므로 정답은 (B)가 된다. (A)는 무엇을 하거나 보는 동사와 사용하며, (C)

는 미래시제와 잘 어울리고, (D)는 '분기마다'라는 뜻으로 현재시제와 어울린다.

표현 정리 endangered 위기에 처한 historic 역사적인 reopen 다시 개방하다 public 대중 extensive 대규모의 repair 수리, 보수 restoration 복구

6. 정답 (A)

해석 대부분의 우리 직원들은 / 열렬한 지지자들이다 / 지역 예술 단체의 / 그리고 그들은 자원봉사를 자주 한다

해설 문장의 시제는 현재시제이다. 보기 중 frequently는 현재시제와 잘 어울리는 빈도부사이므로 (A)가 정답이다. (B)는 부사의 기능이 있는데, have p.p. 사이에 오며, (C)는 과거나 현재완료시제와 어울리는 부사이므로 탈락, (D)는 빈도부사의 기능이 있으나 '거의 ~하지 않다'는 뜻으로 앞의 내용과 상반된다.

표현 정리 most of 대부분 employee 직원 avid 열렬한, 열심인 supporter 지지자 local 지역의 community 단체 volunteer 지원하다; 지원자 frequently 자주 previously 이전에 hardly 거의 ~않다

7. 정답 (A)

해석 회사 규정에 따라 / 모든 공장 직원들은 반드시 항상 착용해야 한다 / 안전 장비를 / 공장 정문을 들어서면

해설 문장의 시제는 현재시제이다. 따라서 현재시제와 잘 어울리는 빈도부사인 (A)가 정답이다. 빈칸 앞뒤 내용을 보면 '항상' 보호 장비를 착용해야 한다는 의미이다. (C)는 주로 형용사나 부사를 수식하므로 탈락하고, (B)와 (D)는 숫자 앞이나 '완성된'이란 말을 수식한다.

표현 정리 in compliance with ~을 따라, ~을 준수해 regulation 규정 factory 공장 protective gear 안전 장비 beyond ~을 넘어 main gate 정문 always 항상 nearly 거의 highly 매우 almost 거의

8. 정답 (A)

해석 Jeil Advertising의 직원들은 최근에 만났다 / 잠재 고객과 / 마케팅 전략에 대해 / 회사의 새로운 건강음료 시리즈를 위한

해설 문장의 시제는 과거이다. (A)는 현재완료시제나 과거시제와 자주 사용하므로 정답이다. (B)는 부정문이나 의문문에 사용하고, (C)와 (D)는 미래시제와 잘 어울리는 부사이다.

표현 정리 representative 대표, 직원 potential 잠재적인 marketing strategy 마케팅 전략 health 건강 beverage 음료 recently 최근에

9. 정답 (A)

해석 Mr. Kim은 거절해야 한다 / 일자리 제안을 / GW International로부터 / 그는 이미 받아들였기 때문에 / 다른 일자리 제안을 / 라이벌 회사로부터의

해설 빈칸은 동사를 수식하는 부사 자리이다. 문장의 시제는 현재완료시제인데, 보기 중 현재완료와 잘 어울리는 부사는 (A)이다. (B)도 현재완료시제와 사용 가능하지만 문맥상 자연스럽지 못하다. (C)는 형용사나 부사를 수

식하며 비교의 단서(than 등)가 있어야 한다. (D)는 형용사나 부사를 수식하는 부사이므로 탈락한다.

표현 정리 turn down 거절하다 job offer 일자리 제안 accept 받아들이다 another 또 다른 rival 라이벌 already 이미 nearly 거의 more 보다 더 very 매우

10. 정답 (B)

해석 우리 Hwawei 사에서는 현재 찾고 있다 / 고도의 자격을 갖춘 전문가들을 / 5년 이상의 업무 경험을 가진 / 관리직

해설 문장의 시제는 현재진행형이다. 보기 중 현재진행시제와 잘 어울리는 부사는 (B)이다. (A)는 증감 부사이며 증가/감소/움직임이 있는 동사와 잘 어울린데, (C)는 과거시제와 잘 어울리고, (D)는 주로 명령문 앞에 쓰여 '단지 ~하기만 하면 되다'의 뜻으로 사용한다.

표현 정리 seek 찾다, 추구하다 highly 높은 qualified 자격이 있는 professional 전문가 managerial position 관리직 considerably 상당히 currently 현재 previously 이전에 simply 그저

법칙 6 빈칸 앞뒤 단어만 봐도 풀리는 시점과 기간 전치사

◎ 유형을 파악해 봐
1. (B) 2. (D) 3. (C)

1. 정답 (B)

해석 직원들은 제출하도록 권고된다 / 그들의 영수증을 / 환급을 위해 / 일주일 안에 / 출장에서 돌아와

해설 빈칸은 명사와 명사를 이어줄 수 있는 전치사 자리이다. 빈칸 뒤의 a week는 기간 명사이므로 기간에 어울리는 전치사인 (B)가 정답이다. 부사인 (C)는 탈락한다.

표현 정리 employee 직원 be advised to+동사원형 ~하도록 권고되다 receipt 영수증 reimbursement 환급 business trip 출장 within ~이내에

2. 정답 (D)

해석 숨이 멎을 듯한 유람선 여행이 제공될 것이다 / 매주 일요일 / 10월까지 / 날씨 조건이 좋을 경우에만

해설 빈칸 뒤에 명사가 왔으므로 전치사 자리이며, 빈칸 뒤의 October는 시점 명사이므로 시점에 어울리는 전치사 (D)가 정답이다. 문장에 접속사가 1개(when), 동사가 2개(will be, are) 있으므로 빈칸에 접속사는 올 수 없어 (C)는 답이 될 수 없다.

표현 정리 cruise 유람선 여행 offer 제안하다, 제공하다 until ~까지 October 10월 weather conditions 날씨 조건 favorable 우호적인

3. 정답 (C)

해석 무료 조식이 / 모든 손님들에게 이용 가능한 / 제공된다 / 아침 8시 30분에 / 우리의 식당에서

해설 보기가 모두 전치사이므로 빈칸 뒤의 명사를 살펴야 한다. 정확한 시각 앞에 올 수 있는 전치사인 (C)가 정답이다. 시점 앞에 쓰일 때 (A) on은

정답 및 해설 **9**

달, 계절, 년도, 세기 앞에, (B) on은 날짜, 요일 앞에 쓰인다.

표현 정리 complimentary 무료의 available 이용 가능한 serve 제공하다 dining room 식당

◎ 실전에 적용해 봐
1. (D) 2. (C) 3. (D) 4. (D) 5. (B) 6. (B) 7. (D)
8. (C) 9. (D) 10. (A)

1. 정답 **(D)**

해석 우리는 잠시 휴식 시간을 가질 것이다 / 첫 번째 발표가 끝난 후에

해설 보기가 모두 전치사이므로 빈칸 뒤의 명사를 살펴야 한다. 빈칸 뒤 '첫 번째 발표'는 시점도 될 수 있고, 기간도 될 수 있는데, 두 경우 모두에 쓸 수 있는 (D)가 정답이다. (A)는 위치를 나타내는 전치사이다. (B)는 제외 사항이 있을 때, (C)는 복수 명사 앞에 온다.

표현 정리 short break 휴식 시간 presentation 발표 except ~를 제외하고 among ~에 둘러싸인, ~중에

2. 정답 **(C)**

해석 직원 회의 동안 / Ms. Choi는 다룰 것이다 / 문제들을 / 최근에 제기 된 고객 불만에 관한

해설 보기가 모두 전치사이므로 빈칸 뒤의 명사를 살펴야 한다. 직원 회의는 기간의 개념이므로 기간 명사와 함께 사용하는 (C)가 정답이다. (A)는 범위나 기간을 나타내는 명사가 오고, (B)는 장소 명사가, (D)는 복수 명사나 A and B가 온다.

표현 정리 staff 직원 meeting 회의 address 다루다 issue 사안, 문제 regarding ~에 관하여 recent 최근 customer 고객 complaint 불만 within ~이내로

3. 정답 **(D)**

해석 우리가 영수증을 받자마자 / 환불이 이루어질 것이다 / 5 영업일 이내에 / 우리의 환불 정책에 따라

해설 빈칸 앞에 완전한 문장이 왔고, 빈칸 뒤에 명사가 왔으므로 전치사 자리이다. 빈칸 뒤의 five business days(5 영업일)은 기간 명사이므로 기간과 어울리는 전치사 (D)가 정답이다. (A)는 접속사이며, (B), (C)는 장소 명사가 온다.

표현 정리 as soon as ~하자마자 receive 받다 receipt 영수증 refund 환불 issue 발행하다, 지급하다 business day 영업일 return policy 환불 정책

4. 정답 **(D)**

해석 만약 마케팅 이사가 마케팅 데이터를 제출하지 못하면 / 명시된 날짜 까지 / 예산위원회는 연기할 것이다 / 회의를

해설 보기가 모두 전치사이므로 빈칸 뒤의 명사를 살펴야 한다. 빈칸 뒤의 the specified date(명시된 날짜)는 시점 명사이므로 1회성 동작의 시점과 어울리는 전치사 (D)가 정답이다. (A)는 시점과 쓸 경우 달, 계절, 년도, 세기 등이 오며, (B)는 출발 시점, (C)는 복수나 A and B 등이 온다.

표현 정리 marketing director 마케팅 이사 fail to ~하는데 실패하다 submit 제출하다 specified 명시된 budget committee 예산 위원회 postpone 연기하다 meeting 회의

5. 정답 **(B)**

해석 307편에 탑승하실 모든 승객들은 이동해야 한다 / 탑승구로 / 출발 시간 30분 전에

해설 빈칸 앞은 완전한 문장이 왔고, 빈칸 뒤엔 명사가 왔으므로 빈칸은 전 치사 자리이다. 빈칸 뒤의 the departure time(출발 시간)은 시점 명사이 므로 시점과 어울리는 전치사인 (B)가 정답이다. (A)는 전치사로 사용되면 '~를 제외하고'라는 뜻으로 앞에 부정어가 있을 때 사용하며, (C)는 부사이 고, (D)는 기간 명사와 사용한다.

표현 정리 passenger 승객 proceed 진행하다, 나아가다 departure 출발

6. 정답 **(B)**

해석 개막식은 / 미술관 별관의 / 시작되지 않을 것이다 / 기조 연설자인 Mr. Washington이 도착할 때까지

해설 빈칸 앞은 완전한 문장이 왔고, 빈칸 뒤는 명사가 왔으므로 빈칸은 전 치사 자리이다. 빈칸 뒤의 the arrival은 시점 명사이므로 시점과 어울리는 전치사인 (B)가 정답이다. (A)는 접속사이고, (C)는 시점에 쓰이지만 과거 시점이 와야 하며, (D)는 시점과 사용하지 않는다.

표현 정리 opening ceremony 개막식 wing 별관, 부속 건물 arrival 도착 keynote speaker 기조연설자 not A until B B할 때까지 A하지 않다(A하고 나서야 B하다)

7. 정답 **(D)**

해석 New York City Center는 제공한다 / 요리 수업과 실무 교육 모두 를 / 주민들에게 / 완전 무료로 / 연중 내내

해설 보기가 모두 전치사이므로 빈칸 뒤의 명사를 살펴야 한다. 빈칸 뒤의 명사 the year는 기간을 나타내며, (D)가 오면 '연중 내내'라는 말이 되어 정답이다. (A), (B)는 위치, (C)는 방향을 나타내는 전치사이다.

표현 정리 offer 제공하다 both A and B A와 B 둘 다 cooking class 요리 수업 hands-on 실무, 직접 해 보는 training 교육, 훈련 resident 주민 free of charge 무료로, 공짜로 throughout 내내, 동안

8. 정답 **(C)**

해석 지하 주차장 보수 작업 관계로 / 직원들은 주차하도록 권고 받았다 / 그들의 차들을 / 건물 바깥에 / 향후 2주 동안

해설 빈칸 앞에 완전한 문장이 왔고, 빈칸 뒤에 명사가 왔으므로 빈칸은 전 치사 자리이다. 빈칸 뒤의 명사 the next two weeks는 기간 명사이므로 기간과 어울리는 전치사인 (C)가 정답이다. (A)는 자격이나 신분을 나타내 는 전치사이고, (B)는 부사, (D)는 접속사이다.

표현 정리 renovation 수리, 혁신 underground 지하 parking area 주차 지역 employee 직원 be advised to+동사원형 ~하도록 권고 받다

9. 정답 (D)

해석 Bright Digital 사의 총 매출이 상당히 증가했다 / 지난 4월 이후 / 이것은 회사의 공격적인 마케팅 결과이다

해설 보기가 모두 전치사이므로 빈칸 뒤의 명사를 살펴야 한다. 빈칸 뒤의 last April은 과거 시점의 명사이므로 과거 시점과 어울리는 전치사인 (D)가 정답이다. (A)는 장소와 어울리는 전치사이고, (B)는 말이나 버스를 탈 때 어울리는 전치사이다.

표현 정리 overall 종합적인, 전체적인 significantly 상당히 aggressive 공격적인 adverting campaign 광고 활동

10. 정답 (A)

해석 성수기에 대비해 / 당신은 예약해야 한다 / 당신은 비행기 티켓을 / 몇 주 전에

해설 '일정보다 ~ 앞서'라는 표현을 알아야 풀 수 있는 문제이다. (A)가 오면 '일정보다 몇 주 전에'라는 말이 되어 정답이 된다. (B)와 (D)는 '~이외에도, 게다가'라는 뜻이 되어 의미가 다르고, (C)는 not과 같은 기능으로 사용한다.

표현 정리 in preparation for ~를 준비하여 peak season 성수기 reserve 예약하다 flight ticket 비행기 표 ahead of ~보다 먼저, 빨리 on top of ~위에, ~이외에 far from 결코 ~이 아닌 apart from ~외에는

법칙 7 완전한 문장 다음에는 부사

◎ 유형을 파악해 봐
1. (D) 2. (C) 3. (B)

1. 정답 (D)

해석 새로운 시간 기록 시스템에 대한 문의 사항은 / 보내져야 한다 / 기술 지원 팀으로 / 즉시

해설 be+p.p. 형태의 수동태로 완전한 문장과 전명구가 왔으므로 부사인 (D)가 정답이다. (A)는 형용사, (B)는 명사, (C)는 동사이다

표현 정리 inquiry 문의, 문의 사항 be directed to+장소 ~로 보내지다 tech support 기술지원 팀 promptly 즉시

2. 정답 (C)

해석 여러 부서들이 협력해 일한다 / 에너지 소비를 줄이기 위해 / 그리고 초과하지 않기 위해 / 이번 달의 빠듯한 예산을

해설 빈칸 앞 work는 1형식 동사이므로 목적어가 필요 없으며, 문장이 완전하므로 빈칸은 (C) 부사 자리이다. (A)는 명사, (B)는 동사, (D)는 동사의 과거형 또는 과거분사이다.

표현 정리 various 다양한 department 부, 부서 reduce 줄이다 energy expense 에너지 비용 stay within the budget 예산을 초과하지 않다 tight 빠듯한 budget 예산 collaboratively 협력적으로

3. 정답 (B)

해석 수상 위원회는 보상해 주었다 / Mr. Kim에게 / 방법을 생각해 낸 것에 대해 / 회사 운영비를 효과적으로 줄일

해설 빈칸 앞은 '주어+동사+목적어+to 부정사'의 부사적 용법 형태로 완전한 문장이 왔으므로 빈칸은 부사 자리이며, 따라서 (B)가 정답이다. (A)는 명사와 동사, (C)는 명사, (D)는 동사의 과거형 또는 과거분사이다

표현 정리 awards committee 수상 위원회 reward 보상하다 figure out 생각해 내다 operating cost 운영비

◎ 실전에 적용해 봐
1. (C) 2. (A) 3. (D) 4. (B) 5. (B) 6. (B) 7. (C)
8. (B) 9. (A) 10. (B)

1. 정답 (C)

해석 회사 취업 지원자들은 기억해야 한다 / 그들의 면접 시간과 장소를 / 정확하게 / 그들의 면접에 오기 위해 / 제 시간에

해설 빈칸 앞에 완전한 문장이 왔고, 빈칸 뒤에는 동사를 수식하는 수식어구가 왔으므로 빈칸은 부사자리이며, 따라서 (C)가 정답이다. (A), (D)는 명사, (B)는 형용사이다.

표현 정리 job applicant 취업 지원자 company 회사 remember 명심하다, 기억하다 interview 면접 location 장소 on time 제 시간에

2. 정답 (A)

해석 방문자 수는 / Lincoln Memorial 공원의 / 상당히 증가했다 / 역사적인 인물들에 관한 TV 프로그램이 방영된 후에 / 지난주

해설 빈칸 앞의 increase는 1형식 동사이므로 완전한 문장이 왔고, 뒤에는 전명구가 왔으므로 빈칸은 부사 자리이며, 따라서 (A)가 정답이다. (B)는 형용사, (C)는 동명사 또는 현재분사, (D)는 동사의 과거형 또는 과거분사이다.

표현 정리 the number of ~의 수 visitor 방문자 since ~이래 historical 역사적인 figure 인물 broadcast 방송하다, 퍼뜨리다

3. 정답 (D)

해석 모든 신상 정보와 데이터는 / 사용자들이 제공한 / 이용될 수 있다 / 오직 허가 받은 직원들만 / 서비스부의

해설 빈칸 앞에는 'be+p.p.' 형태의 수동태 문장이 왔고, 빈칸 뒤에는 수식어구인 전명구가 있다. 수동태 문장은 그 자체로 완전하므로 빈칸은 부사 자리이며, 전명구를 수식하는 초점 부사로 쓰인 (D)가 정답이다. (A)는 대명사 또는 형용사, (C)는 형용사이므로 탈락하고, (B)는 형용사와 부사를 수식하는 부사이다.

표현 정리 personal information 신상 정보 provided by+명사 ~에 의해 제공받은 access 접근하다, 이용하다 authorized personnel 허가 받은 직원 Service Department 서비스부

4. 정답 (B)

해석 GWF사의 이사회는 놀랐다 / 라이벌 회사인 Electron 사의 이익이 급격하게 증가한 것에 / 4분기에

해설 drastically가 1형식 동사인 rose를 수식하는 부사로 쓰였지만 how로 인해 부사가 앞으로 이동한 경우이다. 따라서 (B)가 정답이다. (A), (C), (D)는 모두 형용사이다.

표현 정리 board of director 이사회 corporation 기업 rival 라이벌 rose 증가했다(rise의 과거) quarter 분기 drastically 급격하게

5. 정답 (B)

해설 명심하세요 / 당신의 지원서가 완전하게 작성되도록 / 면접관이 잘 이해할 수 있도록 / 당신에 대해 / 면접 전에

해설 fill out을 하나의 동사 취급한다. 따라서 빈칸 앞까지 완전한 문장이고, 뒤에는 부사절이 있으므로 부사인 (B)가 정답이다. (A)는 형용사 또는 동사, (C)와 (D)는 준동사이다.

표현 정리 make sure 확실하게 하다 application form 지원서 fill out 채우다, 작성하다 interviewer 면접관 understanding 이해, 합의 interview 면접 completely 완벽하게

6. 정답 (B)

해설 정치적, 종교적인 문제들은 다루어져야 한다 / 조심스럽게 / 모든 사람들이 그것들에 대해 자신만의 관점을 갖고 있기 때문에

해설 빈칸 앞 문장은 'be+p.p.' 형태의 수동태로 완전한 문장이며, 따라서 빈칸은 부사인 (B)가 와야 한다. with를 보고 전치사 뒤에 오는 명사 자리로 생각했다면 함정에 빠진 것이다. deal with는 덩어리로 쓰이는 동사로 수동태로 쓰여도 전치사가 그대로 붙어 다닌다는 점을 알아두자.

표현 정리 political 정치적인 religious 종교적인 deal with ~을 다루다 view 시점, 관점 cautiously 조심스럽게 caution 조심, 경고

7. 정답 (D)

해설 Mr. Shin은 무역 박람회에 참가할 수 없었기 때문에 / 6월 3일에 / 일정이 겹쳐 / 그는 요청했다 / 그의 비서에게 / 회사를 대표할 것을 / 그곳에서

해설 접속사가 1개(since), 정동사가 2개(cannot be, asked) 왔으므로 빈칸은 접속사가 올 수 없어 (A), (B)는 탈락. 빈칸 앞까지 문장이 완전하므로 빈칸은 부사 자리이고, 따라서 (D)가 정답이다. (C)는 대명사이다.

표현 정리 since ~때문에 trade fair 무역 박람회 due to ~때문에 scheduling conflict 일정 충돌[겹침] assistant 조수, 비서

8. 정답 (B)

해설 인사 담당자는 분배하려고 노력했다 / 회사의 자원을 / 보다 균등하게 / 그리고 챙기지 않았다 / 특정 부서만을

해설 more는 형용사나 부사를 비교급으로 만들어 주는 부사이다. more 앞은 '주어+동사+목적어' 형태의 완전한 문장이 왔으므로 빈칸은 부사 자리이며, 따라서 (B)가 정답이다. evenly는 부사이고, more evenly도 부사가 된다. (A)는 동사, (C)는 동사의 과거형 또는 과거분사, (D)는 명사이다.

표현 정리 human resource director 인사 담당자 distribute 분배하다 resource 자원 concentrate on ~에 집중하다 solely 단독으로, 오로지 specific 특정한 evenly 균등하게

9. 정답 (A)

해설 Avion Water 사는 강력히 추천한다 / 고객들에게 / 그들의 정수 필터들을 자주 교체하라고

해설 빈칸 앞까지 5형식의 완전한 문장이 왔으므로 빈칸은 부사 자리이며, 따라서 (A)가 정답이다. (B)는 형용사, (C)와 (D)는 명사이다.

표현 정리 strongly 강하게 recommend 추천하다 customer 고객 water filter 정수필터 replace 교체하다 frequently 자주, 빈번하게

10. 정답 (B)

해설 등산을 할 때는 / 중요하다 / 산길에 아무것도 남기지 않는 것이 / 그리고 조용히 걷는 것이 / 다른 등산객들을 방해하지 않기 위해

해설 빈칸 앞에 온 to 부정사를 수식해 줄 부사가 필요하므로 빈칸에는 부사 (B)가 와야 한다. (A)는 형용사, (C)는 형용사의 최상급, (D)는 동사의 과거형 또는 과거분사이다.

표현 정리 hike 하이킹, 도보여행 important 중요한 leave behind 뒤에 남기다 trail 산길, 오솔길, 자국 so as to+동사원형 ~하기 위하여 disturb 방해하다 quietly 조용히

법칙 8 의미로 풀어야 하는 명사 자리 문제는 수식어나 동사를 보고 판단

◎ 유형을 파악해 봐
1. (B)   2. (A)   3. (D)

1. 정답 (B)

해설 회사가 발행한 보고서에 따르면 / 예상된다 / 회사의 휴대폰 매출액이 초과할 것이라고 / 10억 달러를 / 이번 분기에

해설 빈칸은 앞에 관사가 있고, issued의 수식을 받는 명사 자리이므로 (C)와 (D)는 탈락. 빈칸 뒤에 있는 'issued by the company'라는 수식어와 어울리는 것은 (B)이다.

표현 정리 according to+명사 ~에 따르면 statement 보고서, 진술서 issued 발표된 expect 예상하다 billion 10억 quarter 분기

2. 정답 (A)

해설 보조원 자리에 지원한 모든 지원자들은 조언 받는다 / 모든 필요한 서류들을 보내라고 / 인사 부장에게 / 6월 3일까지

해설 빈칸은 형용사 뒤, 전명구 앞 명사 자리이므로 (C)와 (D)는 탈락. (A)와 (B) 중에서 보내도록 조언을 받는 것은 사물이 아니라 사람이므로 '지원자들'이라는 의미의 (A)가 정답이다.

표현 정리 assistant position 비서직, 보조원 자리 be advised to+동사원형 ~하도록 조언 받다 necessary 필요한 document 서류 personnel director 인사담당자 applicant 지원자

3. 정답 (D)

해설 ABC 제약회사는 최대한 노력한다 / 유지하기 위해 / 모든 참가자들의 비밀을 / 회사의 의학 연구에

해설 빈칸은 관사 뒤, 전명구 앞 명사 자리이므로 (B)와 (C)는 탈락. (A)와 (D) 중에서 의학 연구에 참가한 사람들의 '비밀'을 유지하기 위해 노력한다는 내용이 문맥상 적절하므로 (D)가 정답이다.

표현 정리 pharmaceutical 제약의; 제약 make every effort to+동사원형 ~하기 위해 최대한 노력하다 participant 참가자 clinical study 의학 연구 confidence 믿음, 신뢰 confidentiality 비밀

◎ 실전에 적용해 봐

1. (B)　2. (A)　3. (A)　4. (A)　5. (C)　6. (C)　7. (A)
8. (C)　9. (A)　10. (B)

1. 정답 (B)

해석 정부 검사관은 방문할 것이다 / 중국에 있는 우리 시설들 중 한 곳을 / 감사를 진행하기 위해 / 다음 주 목요일

해설 빈칸은 명사 뒤, 동사 앞 명사 자리이므로 (A)와 (C)는 탈락. (B)와 (D) 중에서 동사인 visit를 보면 방문은 사물이 아니라 사람이 하는 것이므로 (B)가 정답이다.

표현 정리 government 정부　inspection 감사, 점검　facility 시설, 기관　conduct 진행하다, 지휘하다　audit 회계 감사　inspector 감사관

2. 정답 (A)

해석 신입 사원 선발자인 Tanaka는 살펴봐야 했다 / 많은 지원서들을 / 자리를 채우기 위해 / 예상치 못한 공석의 인기 때문에

해설 Tanaka와 동격인 명사가 와야 한다. 자격을 나타내는 명사는 관사를 생략할 수 있다. 따라서 (A)가 정답이다.

표현 정리 go through 살펴보다　fill 채우다　position 자리, 직책　due to+명사 ~때문에　unexpected 예상하지 못한　popularity 인기　open position 공석　recruiter 신입 사원 선발자

3. 정답 (A)

해석 만약 당신이 질문이 있다면 / 우리 프로그램과 초청 강사들에 대해 / e-mail을 보내주세요 / 교육 담당자에게 / educoodi@raver.com으로

해설 접속사가 1개(if), 동사가 2개(have, e-mail) 있으므로 빈칸에 동사는 올 수 없어 (C)는 탈락. e-mail의 목적어 자리에 our education이 있는데, 우리의 교육에 이메일을 보내란 말은 어색하므로 빈칸까지를 포함한 복합 명사를 생각해 볼 수 있다. 명사인 (A)와 (B) 중에서 이메일을 받는 대상은 사물이 아니라 사람이므로 (A)가 정답이다.

표현 정리 regarding ~관하여　guest lecturer 초청 강연자　education 교육　coordinator 조정관, 담당자　coordination 조직, 합동

4. 정답 (A)

해석 한 시간의 강연 동안 / Detroit 공장에서 / Mr. Good은 얘기했다 / 근무 환경이 얼마나 많이 긍정적인 영향을 미치는지에 대해 / 전체적인 직원 생산성에

해설 빈칸은 형용사 뒤, 전명구 앞의 명사 자리이므로 (D)는 탈락. 앞에 관사 a가 있으므로 복수 명사인 (C) 역시 탈락. 빈칸을 수식하는 one-hour(한 시간의)와의 어울림을 보면 '한 시간의 강연'이라는 의미로 (A)가 정답이다.

표현 정리 during ~동안　facility 시설, 공장　talk about ~대해 말하다　working environment 근무 환경　positively 긍정적으로　impact 영향을 미치다　overall 전반적인, 전체의　worker productivity 직원 생산성　lecture 강의, 강연

5. 정답 (C)

해석 Mr. White은 중요한 협상가가 될 것이다 / 5백만 달러의 계약을 위한 / Avalon Technology와의 / 이 분야의 선두 제조사 중 하나인

해설 빈칸은 명사 자리이므로 동사인 (A), (B)는 탈락하고 명사인 (C), (D) 중에서 주어(사람)와 동격 관계가 되어야 하므로 (C)가 정답이다.

표현 정리 key 가장 중요한　million 백만　contract 계약　leading 선두적인, 이끌고 있는　manufacturer 제조사　field 분야　negotiate 협상하다　negotiator 협상가　negotiation 협상

6. 정답 (C)

해석 기록적인 시리즈의 마지막 편은 / 영국 작가 J.K. Rowling이 쓴 / 판매되었다 / 300만 부가 넘게 / 일본에서

해설 빈칸은 형용사 뒤, 전명구 앞 명사 자리이므로 (A)와 (D)는 탈락하고, 명사인 (B), (C) 둘 중에서 선택하여야 한다. 문맥상 기록적인 시리즈의 마지막 편이 어울리므로 (C)가 정답이다.

표현 정리 record-breaking 기록적인　series 시리즈　British 영국인, 영국의　author 작가, 저자　million 백만　copy 부, 복사　installment 편, 회, 할부, 분납

7. 정답 (A)

해석 사무용품들은 채워져 있다 / 복사기 옆에 / 복사실 안에

해설 빈칸은 명사 자리(주어)이며, (D)는 동사 또는 과거분사라 탈락하고, 명사인 (A), (B), (C) 중에서 선택해야 한다. 동사가 복수이므로 단수 형태인 (C)는 탈락하고, 채워져 있다는 것은 용품이 채워져 있는 것이므로 빈칸 앞에 있는 office와 복합명사로 쓰일 수 있는 (A)가 정답이다.

표현 정리 office supplies 사무용품　stock 채우다　copy machine 복사기　copy room 복사실

8. 정답 (C)

해석 2년 전에 설립한 이후 / Big Tree 사는 항상 중점을 뒀다 / 사무용 가구들을 디자인 하는 것에 / 테이블, 책상, 그리고 의자들과 같은

해설 빈칸은 소유격 뒤 명사 자리이므로 (B)와 (D)는 탈락하고, 명사인 (A), (C) 둘 중에서 선택해야 한다. 전치사 since와 two years ago를 보고 판단해야 하는데, '2년 전에 설립한 이후'가 어울리므로 (C)가 정답이다.

표현 정리 since ~이래로　focus on ~에 중점을 두다　designing 디자인 하는 것　office furniture 사무용 가구　found 설립하다, 세우다　foundation 설립

9. 정답 (A)

해석 언어를 유창하게 구사하는 능력은 산물이다 / 최소 2년간의 집중적인 연습에 따른 / 언어를 사용하는 환경에서

해설 관사 뒤, 전명구 앞 명사 자리이므로 (C)와 (D)는 탈락. 빈칸은 주어인 fluent command of a language(유창한 언어 구사능력)와 동격이 되어야 한다. '최소 2년간의 집중적인 연습에 따른 산물'이라는 의미로 (A)가 정답이다.

표현 정리 fluent 유창한　command 능력　intensive 집중적인　practice 실천, 실행, 연습　environment 환경　product 산물, 생산물;

생산하다

10. 정답 (B)

해설 대학 도서관에서는 / 책을 빌리는데 더 오래 걸릴 수 있다 / 만약 책이 최근에 출판된 것이거나 / 상을 받은 작가의 책일 경우

해설 빈칸은 형용사 뒤, 명사 자리이므로 (C)와 (D)는 탈락하고, 명사인 (A), (B) 둘 중에서 선택해야 한다. '상을 받은'이라는 수식어에 어울리는 것은 '작가'를 뜻하는 (B)이다. (A)는 '작문, 문구'라는 뜻이다.

표현 정리 library 도서관 longer 더 오래 borrow 빌리다 recently 최근에 publish 출판하다 award-winning 상을 받은

법칙 9 '관소전타' 뒤 명사 앞은 형용사

◎ 유형을 파악해 봐
1. (C) 2. (A) 3. (B)

1. 정답 (C)

해설 제주도의 Seongsan Ilchulbong Tuff Cone 여행은 여행자들을 들뜨게 할 것이다 / 극적인 경치로

해설 빈칸 앞 소유격, 빈칸 뒤는 명사이므로 명사를 꾸며줄 수 있는 형용사가 와야 한다. 따라서 형용사인 (C)가 정답이다. (A)는 부사, (B)는 동사, (D)는 명사이다.

표현 정리 trip 여행 leave 남기다, 떠나다 tourist 여행자 excited 흥분한, 들뜬 dramatic 인상적인, 극적인

2. 정답 (A)

해설 화학물질의 빈번한 검사 필요성 때문에 / 기술자들은 일한다 / 3교대로 / Fitch 연구실에서

해설 빈칸 앞은 전치사, 빈칸 뒤는 명사이므로 명사를 꾸며줄 수 있는 형용사가 와야 한다. 따라서 형용사인 (A)가 정답이다. (B)는 부사, (C)는 명사, (D)는 동사이다.

표현 정리 due to ~때문에 need for 명사 ~위해서 필요하다 chemicals 화학물질 technician 기술자 three-shift 3교대 laboratory 연구실 frequent 빈번한

3. 정답 (B)

해설 즉각적인 환불을 보장하기 위해 / 영수증을 가져오세요 / 당신이 받은 / 물건을 구매했을 때

해설 빈칸 앞은 관사, 빈칸 뒤는 명사이므로 명사를 꾸며줄 수 있는 형용사가 와야 한다. 따라서 형용사인 (B)가 정답이다. (A)는 동사, (C)는 부사, (D)는 명사이다.

표현 정리 ensure ~을 보증하다 refund 환불 bring 가져오다, 데려오다 issue 발행하다 purchase 구매하다 product 상품, 생산물 prompt 즉각적인

◎ 실전에 적용해 봐
1. (D) 2. (A) 3. (B) 4. (B) 5. (B) 6. (A) 7. (A)
8. (B) 9. (C) 10. (B)

1. 정답 (D)

해설 Mr. Kim은 보고했다 / 그가 머물렀던 호텔 방이 / 지난주에 / 좋은 상태였고, 최소한의 마모 자국을 보여줬다고

해설 빈칸 앞은 타동사, 빈칸 뒤는 명사이므로 명사를 꾸며줄 수 있는 형용사가 와야 하며, 따라서 형용사인 (D)가 정답이다. (A)는 부사, (B)와 (C)는 동사이다.

표현 정리 report 알리다, 기록하다 stay 머무르다 be in good condition 좋은 상태이다 sign of wear 마모 자국 minimal 최소한의

2. 정답 (A)

해설 당신의 구매가 보장되기 위해 / 5년간의 세계적인 품질보증 프로그램에 의해 / 추천된다 / 당신이 구매할 것을 / 우리의 제품을 / 인가 받은 중개인으로부터

해설 빈칸 앞은 관사, 빈칸 뒤는 명사이므로 명사를 꾸며줄 수 있는 형용사가 와야 하며, 과거분사도 명사를 수식할 수 있으므로 (A)가 정답이다. (B), (C)는 명사, (D)는 동사이다.

표현 정리 in order for A to do A가 ~하기 위해 cover 보장하다, 보호하다, 덮다 worldwide 세계적인 warranty 품질 보증 recommend 추천하다 purchase 구매; 구매하다 product 제품, 상품 authorized 인증된 authorize 인정하다, 권한을 부여하다

3. 정답 (B)

해설 작년 수익이 뚜렷한 증가를 보인 이래로 / Legolos 사의 주가가 도달했다 / 최고치에

해설 빈칸 앞의 동명사에서 ing를 빼면 see는 타동사, 빈칸 뒤는 명사이므로 명사를 꾸며줄 수 있는 형용사가 와야 하며, 따라서 형용사인 (B)가 정답이다. (A)는 부사, (C)는 명사, (D)는 동사이다.

표현 정리 since ~이래로 revenue 수익, 수입 sharp 뚜렷한, 날카로운 increase 증가; 증가하다 stock 재고, 재고품 reach 도달하다 record high 최고치, 최고의 기록

4. 정답 (B)

해설 인사 부장 Rick Olmert는 / 질문을 받았다 / 회사의 향상된 복지 프로그램에 대해 / 그리고 긴 답변을 했다

해설 빈칸 앞은 관사, 빈칸 뒤는 명사이므로 명사를 꾸며줄 수 있는 형용사가 와야 하며, 따라서 형용사인 (B)가 정답이다. (A)는 명사, (C)는 부사, (D)는 동사이다.

표현 정리 personnel director 인사 부장 extended 늘어난, 연장된 benefit 이득 length 길이, 시간 lengthy 긴 lengthily 길게

5. 정답 (B)

해설 조립라인에서의 대부분의 사고는 예방될 수 있다 / 정확하게 이해함으로써 / 안전 조치에 대해

해설 빈칸 앞은 관사, 빈칸 뒤는 명사이므로 명사를 꾸며줄 수 있는 형용사

가 와야 하며, 따라서 형용사인 (B)가 정답이다. understanding은 -ing 형태의 명사이다. (A)는 부사, (C)는 명사, (D)는 동사이다.

표현 정리 most of ~의 대부분 accident 사고 assembly line 조립라인 prevent 예방하다 correct 정확한, 적절한

6. 정답 (A)

해석 베이징으로 여행을 오가는 승객들은 / 자격이 있다 / 32kg까지 가져갈 수 있는 / 추가 비용 없이

해설 빈칸 앞은 전치사, 빈칸 뒤는 '형용사+명사'가 왔다고 해서 형용사를 꾸며줄 수 있는 부사 자리로 오해하면 안 된다. 빈칸에는 charge를 수식해 줄 형용사가 와야 하며, 따라서 (A)가 정답이다. (C)는 명사, (B)와 (D)는 부사이다.

표현 정리 passenger 승객 traveling 여행하는 to and from A A로 오가는 be entitled to ~할 자격이 있다 at no additional charge 추가 비용 없이

7. 정답 (A)

해석 직원들은 피해야 한다 / 중앙 출입구를 / 회전문 유지보수 작업이 진행되는 동안

해설 빈칸 앞은 관사, 빈칸 뒤는 명사이므로 명사를 꾸며줄 수 있는 형용사가 와야 하며, 따라서 형용사의 기능이 있는 현재분사 (A)가 정답이다. (B), (D)는 동사, (C)는 명사이다.

표현 정리 employee 직원 avoid 피하다 main entrance 중앙 출입구 maintenance work 유지보수 업무 revolving door 회전문 underway 진행중인

8. 정답 (B)

해석 공장 관리자는 요청했다 / 직원들이 헬멧과 보호 장비를 착용할 것을 / 근무 시간 동안

해설 빈칸 뒤는 명사이므로 명사를 꾸며줄 수 있는 형용사가 와야 한다. (B)가 오면 protective gear(보호용 장비)가 돼 의미상 자연스러우므로 정답이다. (A)는 '보호된 장비'가 되어 장비가 보호받는다는 부자연스러운 말이 된다. (C)는 동사, (D)는 명사이다.

표현 정리 factory manager 공장 관리자 request 요청하다 employee 직원 wear 착용하다, 입다 helmet 헬멧 protective gear 보호 장비

9. 정답 (C)

해석 주소와 전화번호는 / 정확하게 작성돼야 한다 / 주문서에 / 당신이 주문한 제품이 배송되기 위해 / 제때

해설 빈칸 앞은 관사, 빈칸 뒤는 명사이므로 명사를 꾸며줄 수 있는 형용사 자리이다. timely는 부사처럼 생겼지만 품사는 형용사이다. 따라서 (C)가 정답이다. (A), (B), (D)는 모두 명사이다.

표현 정리 accurately 정확하게 order form 주문서 delivery 배송 timely 시기 적절한, 때맞춘

10. 정답 (B)

해석 도시 지하철은 가장 편리한 교통 수단이다 / 오늘날 이용 가능한 / 인천공항에서 Merit 호텔까지

해설 빈칸 뒤 명사를 수식하고, 빈칸 앞 the most와 최상급을 이루는 형용사 자리이므로 형용사 (B)가 정답이다. (A)는 부사, (C)는 동사, (D)는 명사이다.

표현 정리 subway 지하철 convenient 편리한 mode 방법 transportation 교통 수단 available 이용 가능한 from A to B A부터 B까지

법칙 10 기본 형용사와 분사가 함께 나올 때는 기본 형용사

◎ 유령을 파악해 봐
1. (C)   2. (B)   3. (C)

1. 정답 (C)

해석 우리의 노력에도 불구하고 / 유용한 정보를 제공하기 위한 / 우리의 고객들에게 / 오류들이 나타날지 모른다 / 때때로

해설 빈칸 뒤에 명사가 왔으므로 빈칸은 명사를 수식하는 형용사 자리이며, 형용사인 (B)와 (C) 중에서 선택해야 한다. 문맥상 '유용한 정보를 제공하려는 우리의 노력에도 불구하고'가 어울리므로 (C)가 정답이다. (A)는 동사, (D)는 부사이다.

표현 정리 despite ~에도 불구하고 effort 수고, 노력 offer 제공하다 useful 유용한 information 정보 client 고객 error 실수, 오류 appear 나타나다 at times 가끔, 때때로

2. 정답 (B)

해석 공식적으로 두 가지 언어를 사용하는 국가에서는 / 모든 정부 웹사이트에서 이용 가능하다 / 프랑스어와 영어 모두

해설 빈칸은 앞에 위치한 be 동사의 보어 자리이므로 형용사인 (B)와 (D) 중에서 선택해야 한다. 문맥상 '모든 정부 웹사이트에서 이용 가능하다'가 어울리므로 (B)가 정답이다. 명사인 (A)와 (C)는 주어인 '웹사이트'와 동격이 될 수 없어 탈락하고, (D)가 형용사의 기능으로 사용될 때는 뒤에 목적어가 있어야 한다.

표현 정리 officially 공식적으로 bilingual 두 가지 언어를 쓰는, 사용할 줄 아는 country 국가 government 정부 both A and B A와 B 둘 다 accessible 이용 가능한, 접근 가능한

3. 정답 (C)

해석 팀의 성공은 달려있다 / 각 멤버들의 혼신의 노력에

해설 빈칸 앞에 온 be 동사의 보어 자리이므로 형용사인 (B)와 (C) 중에서 선택해야 한다. 문맥상 '팀의 성공은 노력에 달려있다'가 어울리므로 (C)가 정답이다. (A)는 동사이고, 명사인 (D)는 주어인 '팀의 성공'과 등격이 되어야 하므로 답이 될 수 없다.

표현 정리 success 성공 dependent 의존하는 concerted 혼신의, 결연한 effort 노력 individual 개개인의

실전에 적용해 봐
1. (A) 2. (C) 3. (C) 4. (D) 5. (D) 6. (B) 7. (A)
8. (D) 9. (C) 10. (D)

1. 정답 (A)
해석 영업 부장인 Greg Peterson은 꺼려했다 / 그의 마케팅 캠페인을 시작하는 것을 / 상품에 대한 / 그가 받지 못했기 때문에 / 예비조사 결과를

해설 빈칸 앞에 온 be 동사의 보어 자리이므로 형용사인 (A)가 정답이다. (C)는 부사, 명사인 (B)는 주어(사람)와 동격이 되어야 하므로 탈락하고, (D)는 존재하지 않는 말이다.

표현 정리 marketing manager 영업 부장 product 제품 since ~때문에, ~이래로 result of ~의 결과 feasibility study 예비조사 reluctant 꺼리는

2. 정답 (C)
해석 전체 연구개발비는 / 올해의 / 초과하지 않을 것이다 / 전년도 연구개발비를 / 예산 규제 때문에 / 위원회가 취한

해설 빈칸 앞은 전치사, 빈칸 뒤는 명사가 왔으므로 명사를 수식하는 형용사 자리이며, 따라서 형용사인 (A)와 (C) 중에서 선택해야 한다. 문맥상 '예산 규제 때문에'가 어울리므로 (C)가 정답이다. (A)는 '예산이 짜진'이란 뜻이고, (B)는 형용사 기능이 있지만 명사 뒤에서 앞으로 수식하고, (D)는 명사이다.

표현 정리 total 총, 전체의 research 연구, 조사 development 개발, 발전 spending 비용, 지출 exceed 초과하다 previous 이전의 due to ~때문에 restraint 규제, 통제 executed 시행된, 취해진 committee 위원회 budgetary 예산의

3. 정답 (C)
해석 Beautiful Landscapes는 / 서울에 본사를 둔 회사인 / 제공한다 / 혁신적인 디자인과 / 향상시키기 위한 설비를 / 풍경을

해설 빈칸 뒤에 명사가 왔으므로 명사를 수식하는 형용사 자리이며, 따라서 형용사인 (C)와 (D) 중에서 선택해야 한다. 문맥상 '혁신적인 디자인을 제공한다'가 어울리므로 (C)가 정답이다. (A)는 동사, (B)는 명사이므로 또 명사가 올 수 없으므로 탈락하고, (D)는 '혁신하고 있는 중인'이란 뜻이다.

표현 정리 Seoul-based 서울에 본사를 둔 provide 제공하다 installation 설비, 장치 enhance 향상시키다, 높이다 landscape 풍경 innovative 혁신적인 innovation 혁신

4. 정답 (D)
해석 신중한 고려 끝에 / 우리는 알릴 것이다 / 경력이 가장 잘 맞는 사람에게 / 직책을

해설 빈칸은 전치사 뒤, 명사 앞이므로 형용사 자리이며, 문맥상 '신중한 고려 끝에'가 어울리므로 (D)가 정답이다. (A), (B)는 동사 혹은 명사라서 탈락하고, care는 자동사이므로 (C) cared라는 말은 형용사의 기능이 없다.

표현 정리 consideration 고려, 숙고 notify 알리다 match 아주 잘 어울리는 것 position 직책, 자리 careful 신중한, 주의 깊은

5. 정답 (D)
해석 당신은 초대 받았다 / 시상식에 참석하도록 / 기념행사에 이어 / 케이크와 다과들이 준비된

해설 빈칸은 명사 뒤, 전명구 앞이다. (A)는 명사이므로 또 명사가 올 수 없어 탈락하고, (B)는 현재분사로 뒤에서 명사를 수식하려면 자체의 목적어가 있어야 한다. (C)는 동사이며, (D)는 with와 함께 명사 뒤에서 '~이 준비된'이라는 뜻으로 명사를 수식한다. 따라서 (D)가 정답이다.

표현 정리 invite 초대하다 attend 참석하다 award ceremony 시상식 followed by 뒤이어 refreshment 다과, 가벼운 식사 celebration 기념행사 complete with+명사 ~이 준비된

6. 정답 (B)
해석 지난 해 티켓들이 매진되었기 때문에 / 공연이 시작되기도 전에 / 적극 권장된다 / 올해 공연 티켓을 구매하는 것이 / 미리

해설 빈칸 앞에 be 동사가 있으므로 빈칸은 보어 자리이며, 형용사인 (A)와 (B) 중에서 선택해야 한다. 문맥상 '구매하는 것이 적극 권장된다'가 어울리므로 (B)가 정답이다. (A)가 오려면 뒤에 사람 목적어가 있어야 하며, 가주어/진주어에 자연스럽게 어울리는 것도 (B)이다.

표현 정리 because ~때문에 ticket 표, 승차권 sold out 매진되다 highly 매우, 적극적으로 purchase 구매하다 in advance 미리, 이전에 advisable 권장되는

7. 정답 (A)
해석 KJ Solutions은 / 두 나라 사이의 경제 협력을 대표하는 벤처 기업인 / 운영을 시작할 것이다 / 다음 달에

해설 be 동사 뒤에 위치한 빈칸은 전명구의 수식을 받는 보어 자리이므로 형용사인 (A)와 (B) 중에서 선택해야 한다. '~를 대표하다'는 말은 be representative of = represent로 기억하자. represented는 전치사 of와 어울리지 않는다. (D)는 동사이다.

표현 정리 venture 벤처 기업 economic cooperation 경제 협력 operation 경영, 운영 representative 대표적인; 대표

8. 정답 (D)
해석 해외 지사에서의 경력뿐 아니라 / 그녀의 뛰어난 마케팅 능력도 만들었다 / 그녀를 / 매력적인 지원자로 / 해외 판매 담당 이사직을 위한

해설 빈칸 앞은 관사, 빈칸 뒤는 명사이므로 명사를 꾸며줄 수 있는 형용사 자리이며, 따라서 형용사인 (A)와 (D) 중에서 선택해야 한다. 문맥상 '매력적인 지원자'가 어울리므로 (D)가 정답이다. (A)는 '매혹된'이란 뜻이고, (B)는 명사, (C)는 동사이다.

표현 정리 not only A but also B A뿐만 아니라 B도 overseas 해외의 branch 지사, 지점 excellent 뛰어난, 훌륭한 candidate 지원자, 후보자 international 해외의, 국제적인 sales director 판매 담당 이사 attract 마음을 끌다

9. 정답 (C)
해석 부장은 보고했다 / 고객들로부터의 응답이 / 연장된 근무 시간에 대한 / 우리 지점의 / 압도적으로 긍정적이었다고

해설 빈칸 앞 관사, 빈칸 뒤는 명사이므로 명사를 꾸며줄 수 있는 형용사

16

가 와야 하며, 따라서 형용사인 (A)와 (C) 중에서 선택해야 한다. 문맥상 '연장된 근무 시간'이 어울리므로 (C)가 정답이다. (A)는 '폭넓은, 광범위한' 이란 뜻이고, (B)는 명사, (D)는 부사이다.

표현 정리 manager 관리자, 부장 report 보고하다, 기록하다 response 응답 client 고객 office hours 근무 시간 branch 지점 overwhelmingly 압도적으로 positive 긍정적인 extended 연장된, 길어진 extensive 아주 넓은, 대규모의

10. 정답 (D)

해설 대학에서 가르치는 것뿐 아니라 / Ms. Kwon은 또한 존경 받는 예술 가이다 / 그녀를 따르는 많은 팬들을 가진 / 세계적으로

해설 빈칸 앞은 관사, 빈칸 뒤는 명사이므로 명사를 꾸며 줄 수 있는 형용사 자리이며, 따라서 형용사인 (C)와 (D) 중에서 선택해야 한다. 문맥상 '존경 받는 예술가이다'가 어울리므로 (D)가 정답이며, (C) respective는 '각각의' 란 뜻이고, (A)와 (B)는 동사이다.

표현 정리 in addition to ~일뿐 아니라 teaching 가르치는 것 university 대학교 following of admirers 팬들, 추종자들 around the world 세계적으로

법칙 11 빈칸 앞뒤 단어만 봐도 풀리는 위치, 방향 전치사

◎ 유형을 파악해 봐
1. (B) 2. (A) 3. (A)

1. 정답 (B)

해설 일부 직원들은 / 제안했다 / 흡연 구역을 만들 것을 / 정문과 1층 구내 식당 사이에

해설 보기가 모두 전치사이므로 빈칸 뒤의 명사를 살펴야 한다. 빈칸 뒤가 A and B 형태로 왔고, A와 B가 장소이므로 (B)가 정답이다. (A)는 출처, 출발점을 나타내는 명사와 어울리고, (C)는 시점 앞에 쓰인다. (D)는 말이나 버스를 탈 때 사용한다.

표현 정리 several 몇몇의 employee 직원 propose 제안하다 smoking area 흡연 구역 main gate 정문 cafeteria 구내식당 between A and B A와 B 사이

2. 정답 (A)

해설 올해 우리의 매출 목표를 달성하기 위해 / 우리는 찾아야만 한다 / 방법들을 / 우리의 매출을 증가시킬 수 있는 / 전국적으로

해설 문장에는 정동사가 1개(have to fine) 있다. 접속사는 정동사가 2개 있을 때 오므로 접속사인 (D)는 탈락하고, 빈칸 앞 뒤에 명사가 있으므로 이 것을 이어줄 수 있는 전치사가 필요하다. 빈칸 뒤 the country는 장소이므로 (A)와 (B) 중에서 장소 앞에 쓸 수 있는 (A)가 정답이다. (C)는 부사이다.

표현 정리 in order to+동사원형 ~하기 위해서 achieve 달성하다 sales goal 매출 목표

3. 정답 (A)

해설 청중들은 일상적으로 확인해야 한다 / 그들의 소지품들을 / 야외 콘서트 장에 있는 동안

해설 정동사가 1개(should check), 접속사가 1개(while) 있다. 빈칸에 정 동사가 와야 할 것 같지만 보기에는 모두 전치사가 제시되었다. 주어가 주절의 주어와 같아 생략되었고, be 동사가 being으로 바뀌면서 생략되어 전명 구 보어만 남은 분사구문이다. 빈칸 뒤 the outdoors concert area는 장소이므로 장소 앞에 쓸 수 있는 전치사 (A)가 정답이다.

표현 정리 audience member 청중 routinely 일상적으로 check 확인하다 personal belonging 개인 소지품 outdoor 야외의 through ~을 통하여

◎ 실전에 적용해 봐
1. (A) 2. (A) 3. (D) 4. (C) 5. (B) 6. (D) 7. (C) 8. (B) 9. (C) 10. (A)

1. 정답 (A)

해설 영업 부장들 중 가장 많은 매출을 올린 사람은 / 한 달 안에 / 받을 것이다 / 보너스를

해설 보기는 모두 전치사이므로 빈칸 뒤에 있는 명사를 살펴야 한다. 빈칸 뒤에 복수 명사가 있으므로 (A)가 답이 된다. among은 복수 명사와 아주 친한 전치사이다. (B)와 (D)는 뒤에 장소 명사가 오며, (C)는 주로 주제를 나타내는 명사가 온다.

표현 정리 sales manager 판매[영업] 부장 award 보상하다, 수상하다 among ~중에, ~사이에

2. 정답 (A)

해설 회사 부사장님의 은퇴식이 열릴 것이다 / 보안 장소에서 / 기자들이 참석하지 않은 채

해설 보기는 모두 전치사이므로 빈칸 뒤에 있는 명사를 살펴야 한다. '보 안 장소'이므로 장소 앞에 쓸 수 있는 전치사 (A)가 정답이다. (B)는 뒤에 A and B가 오거나, 복수 명사가 오고, (C)는 기간 명사 앞에 쓰이며, (D)는 주로 부사로 사용된다.

표현 정리 retirement ceremony 은퇴식 vice president 부사장 secure 보안이 된, 안전한 location 장소 press 기자들, 언론

3. 정답 (D)

해설 강아지들과 고양이들의 삽화는 사용된다 / 책 전체에 / 그리고 제공한다 / 시각적 재미를 / 특히 어린 독자들에게

해설 보기가 모두 전치사이므로 빈칸 뒤 명사를 확인한다. 보기의 전치사는 모두 the book 앞에 올 수 있으므로 빈칸 앞 주어, 동사와의 어울림을 고려한다. 개와 고양이의 삽화가 이용된다고 했으므로 '책 전체에'라는 의미를 이룰 수 있는 (D)가 정답이다. throughout은 기간 명사 앞에서 '~동안 내내'라는 의미로도 쓰인다.

표현 정리 illustration 삽화 provide 제공하다 visual 시각의 interest 흥미, 재미 particularly 특히 regarding ~에 관하여 besides ~외에

4. 정답 (C)

해설 다음 달 행사들을 위한 일정이 / 게시판에 걸려 있다 / 휴게실 뒤에 있는

정답 및 해설 17

해설 보기가 모두 전치사이므로 빈칸 뒤에 있는 명사를 확인한다. 게시판은 벽에 걸려 있으므로 (C)가 정답으로 적절하다. (A)는 넓은 지역이나 범위에, (B)는 이유, 목적, 용도, 대상에, (D)는 동사가 움직임이 있을 때 사용하는 전치사이다.

표현 정리 schedule 계획, 일정 bulletin board 게시판 conference room 회의실

5. 정답 (B)

해설 40 Main Street에 있는 컨벤션 센터는 위치해 있다 / 은행과 우체국 사이에 / 그리고 찾기 쉽다

해설 보기가 모두 전치사이므로 빈칸 뒤에 있는 명사를 확인한다. A and B의 형태로 왔으므로 (B)가 가장 적절하다. (A)는 주로 3개 이상의 복수 명사 앞에 쓰이고, (C)와 (D)는 움직임이 있는 동사와 사용된다.

표현 정리 located 위치한 between A and B A와 B 사이

6. 정답 (D)

해설 Speed Cargo는 높이 평가된다 / 소포들을 배달하는데 있어 / 거래 고객들에게 / 서울 지역에 있는 / 24시간 안에

해설 보기가 모두 전치사이므로 빈칸 뒤에 있는 명사를 확인한다. 문맥상 '소포를 거래 고객들에게 보내다'라는 의미를 이루므로 (D)가 가장 적절한 정답이다.

표현 정리 highly 높이, 매우, 대단히 regard 간주하다, 여기다 deliver 배달하다 package 포장물, 소포 business customer 거래 고객 within ~이내에

7. 정답 (C)

해설 Sagong 공장을 방문하는 모든 사람들은 / 주의해서 읽고, 따라야 한다 / 안전 지침을 / 공장 입구 옆에 게시된

해설 보기가 모두 전치사이므로 빈칸 뒤 명사를 확인한다. 문맥상 '공장 정문 옆에 게시된'이라는 의미이므로 (C)가 정답이다. (A)는 움직임이 있을 때 사용하는데, posted는 '게시된'이란 뜻으로 정적인 느낌이다. (B)는 복수 명사 앞에 사용한다.

표현 정리 visitor 방문자 facility 공장, 시설 carefully 주의해서 safety guideline 안전 지침 entrance 입구, 문 next to+명사 ~옆에

8. 정답 (B)

해설 컨설턴트인 Peter Lee는 중요한 역할을 했다 / 회사를 바꾸는데 / 부실한 회사로부터 / 수익을 내는 회사로

해설 보기가 모두 전치사이므로 빈칸 뒤에 있는 명사를 확인한다. 문맥상 '부실한 회사를 수익을 내는 회사로 바꾸다'가 적절하므로 from A to B의 형태를 이룰 수 있는 (B)가 정답이다.

표현 정리 play a role 역할을 하다 crucial 중요한 turn A from B to C A를 B에서 C로 바꾸다 profitable business 수익을 내는 회사

9. 정답 (C)

해설 Dr. Hamilton은 조금 늦었다 / 세미나에 / 그가 실수로 지나쳤기 때문에 / HY Convention Center / 그가 아직 센터에 도착하지 않았다고 생각하고

해설 보기가 모두 전치사이므로 빈칸 뒤에 있는 명사를 확인한다. 컨벤션 센터 앞에 쓸 수 있는 (C)와 (D) 중에서 빈칸 앞에 went라는 동사가 있으므로 '~를 지나치다'의 의미를 이루는 (C)가 정답으로 적절하다. (A)는 기간 명사 앞에, (B)는 거리나 강 등의 길이가 긴 사물을 따라 위쪽으로 움직임이 있을 때 사용한다.

표현 정리 mistakenly 실수로 past ~를 지나서 ~옆에 arrive at+명사 ~에 도착하다 next to+명사

10. 정답 (A)

해설 Lincoln Hall은 / 많은 회의가 자주 열리는 / 예정되어 있다 / 보수를 하기로 / 더 많은 사람들을 수용하기 위해서

해설 보기가 모두 전치사이므로 빈칸 뒤 명사를 확인한다. 콤마와 콤마 사이의 절은 빈칸 앞 Lincoln Hall이라는 장소를 수식하는 형용사절이다. 원래는 전치사가 held 뒤에 와야 하지만 여기서는 형용사절 접속사 which 앞으로 나온 구조이다. 따라서 장소 앞에 쓸 수 있는 전치사 (A)가 정답이다.

표현 정리 a number of 많은 meeting 회의 undergo 받다, 겪다 renovation 수리 accommodate 수용하다, 공간을 제공하다

법칙 12 '_____+the/a 명사' 문제, 보기 중 전치사가 1개면 그것이 정답

◎ 유형을 파악해 봐
1. (C) 2. (A) 3. (B)

1. 정답 (C)

해설 당신은 우리 셔틀버스를 탈 수 있습니다 / 호텔 현관에서 출발하는 / 매시 정각에

해설 보기에 전치사와 접속사들이 섞여 있으므로 연결어 문제이다. 문장이 두 개이고, 접속사가 이미 존재하므로 접속사인 (A)와 (B)는 탈락한다. 빈칸 앞 1형식의 완전한 문장이 왔고, 빈칸 뒤에는 명사가 왔으므로 빈칸은 전치사 자리이며, 따라서 (C)가 정답이다.

표현 정리 shuttle 정기 왕복 버스 depart 출발하다 front entrance 현관 every hour on the hour 매시 정각

2. 정답 (A)

해설 제한된 예산 때문에 / 마케팅부는 늘릴 수 없었다 / 홍보비를

해설 보기에 전치사와 접속사들이 섞여 있으므로 연결어 문제이다. 빈칸 뒤에 명사가 왔으므로 빈칸은 전치사 자리이며, 따라서 (A)가 정답이다. (B)와 (D)는 부사, (C)는 접속사이다.

표현 정리 due to ~때문에 limited 제한된 budget 예산 spending 지출, 비용, 소비 adverting 홍보, 광고

3. 정답 (B)

해설 복리후생 제도에 관한 전반적인 정보를 위해 / 직원 안내서를 참고하시오

해설 보기에 전치사와 접속사들이 섞여 있으므로 연결어 문제이다. 빈칸 앞은 전명구이고, 빈칸 뒤는 명사이므로 전치사 자리이며, 따라서 (B)가 정답이다. (A)는 접속사 혹은 부사이고, (C)는 접속사, (D)는 부사이다.

표현 정리 general 전반적인, 일반적인 information 정보 pertaining to ~에 관하여(= regarding, concerning) benefit package 복리후생 제도 refer to+명사 ~을 참고하다

◎ 실전에 적용해 봐
1. (B) 2. (B) 3. (A) 4. (B) 5. (D) 6. (C) 7. (B)
8. (C) 9. (D) 10. (B)

1. 정답 (B)

해설 첫 승진에 필요한 자격을 얻기 위해서 / 모든 신입 사원들은 반드시 마쳐야 한다 / 필요한 교육 과정을 / 6개월 이내에 / 취직한 날로부터

해설 보기에 전치사와 접속사들이 섞여 있으므로 연결어 문제이다. '동사의 개수 - 접속사 = 1'이므로 접속사인 (A), (C), (D)는 탈락한다. 빈칸 앞은 완전한 문장이 왔고, 빈칸 뒤는 명사이므로 전치사 자리이며, 따라서 (B)가 정답이다.

표현 정리 in order to+동사원형 ~하기 위해 promotion 승진 recruit 신입사원 training course 교육 과정 employment 취업, 고용, 직장

2. 정답 (B)

해설 4,000명에 가까운 학생들이 참석했다 / 직업 박람회에 / 예정대로 / 궂은 날씨에도 불구하고

해설 보기에 전치사와 접속사들이 섞여 있으므로 연결어 문제이다. '동사의 개수 - 접속사 = 1'이므로 접속사인 (A), (C), (D)는 탈락한다. 빈칸 앞은 완전한 문장이 왔고, 빈칸 뒤는 명사이므로 전치사 자리이며, 따라서 (B)가 정답이다.

표현 정리 nearly 거의 attend 참석하다 job fair 취업 박람회 as scheduled 예정된 대로 despite ~에도 불구하고

3. 정답 (A)

해설 직원들의 급료에 관해 말하자면 / 직원들은 받을 수 있다 / 매우 높은 급여와 보너스를 / 그들의 성과에 따라

해설 보기에 전치사와 접속사들이 섞여 있으므로 연결어 문제이다. '동사의 개수 - 접속사 = 1'이므로 접속사인 (C)와 (D)는 탈락한다. 빈칸 뒤는 명사이므로 전치사 자리이며, 따라서 (A)가 정답이다. (B)는 부사이다.

표현 정리 in terms of ~에 관하여 wage 임금, 급료 competitive 상당한, 경쟁력 있는 salaries 급여, 연봉 performance 성과, 성취

4. 정답 (B)

해설 댄스 강사직 지원자들은 / 경험을 갖추고 있어야 한다 / 여러 분야의 댄스 / 살사, 스윙, 탱고, 룸바, 그리고 사교 댄스와 같은

해설 보기에 전치사와 접속사들이 섞여 있으므로 연결어 문제이다. '동사의 개수 - 접속사 = 1'이므로 접속사 (D)는 탈락한다. 빈칸 앞에 전명구, 빈칸 뒤에 명사가 왔으므로 빈칸은 전치사 자리이며, 따라서 전치사인 (B)가 정답이다. (A), (C)는 부사이다.

표현 정리 applicant 지원자 dance instructor 무용 강사 experience 경험 such as ~와 같은

5. 정답 (D)

해설 당신이 이번 달에 구독을 갱신할 경우 / 당신은 자격을 갖게 됩니다 / 현재 구독료의 / 3개월 동안 / 다음 달부터 변경되는 가격에 상관없이

해설 보기에 전치사와 접속사들이 섞여 있으므로 연결어 문제이다. '동사의 개수 - 접속사 = 1'이므로 접속사인 (B)는 탈락한다. 빈칸 앞에 전명구, 빈칸 뒤에 명사가 왔으므로 빈칸은 전치사 자리이며, 따라서 전치사인 (D)가 정답이다. (A)와 (C)는 부사이다.

표현 정리 renew 갱신하다 subscription 구독, 구독료 be entitled to ~할 자격이 있다 regardless of ~에 상관없이 as of ~부로 nevertheless 그럼에도 불구하고 insofar as ~하는 한 at the same time 동시에

6. 정답 (C)

해설 3쿼터 재무제표에 따르면 / 지난주에 발행된 / GW Industries 사는 보고했다 / 15퍼센트의 이익 증가를

해설 보기에 전치사와 접속사들이 섞여 있으므로 연결어 문제이다. '동사의 개수 - 접속사 = 1'이므로 접속사인 (A)와 (B)는 탈락한다. issued를 동사로 착각해 접속사를 답으로 유도하는 함정 문제이다. 빈칸 뒤에 명사가 왔으므로 빈칸은 전치사 자리이며, 따라서 전치사인 (C)가 정답이다. (D)는 접속사다.

표현 정리 financial statement 재무제표 issue 발행하다 report 보고하다, 기록하다 gain in value 이익이 늘다

7. 정답 (B)

해설 지난 10년간 / Cayenne 사는 계속해서 속했다 / 국내 10대 선두 제조회사들에 / 사무용품 분야에서

해설 보기에 전치사와 접속사들이 섞여 있으므로 연결어 문제이다. 문장의 정동사는 has ranked이므로 정동사인 (D)는 탈락한다. 빈칸 앞에 있는 rank는 자동사이므로 완전한 문장이고, 빈칸 뒤에 명사가 왔으므로 빈칸은 전치사 자리이며, 따라서 전치사인 (B)가 정답이다. (A)와 (C)는 형용사이다.

표현 정리 decade 10년 rank 자리 잡다, 지위를 차지하다 leading 선두적인 manufacturer 제조회사 office supplies 사무용품

8. 정답 (C)

해설 당신의 최근 문의들은 / 회사의 복리후생에 관한 / 보내졌습니다 / Ms. Blackwell에게 / 인사과에 있는

해설 빈칸 앞과 뒤에 명사가 왔으므로 빈칸은 전치사 자리이며, 따라서 전치사인 (C)가 정답이다. (A)와 (D)는 동사, (B)는 과거분사라 명사와 명사의 연결 기능이 없다.

표현 정리 inquiry 문의 regarding ~에 관해서 be directed to +명사 ~에게 보내지다, 안내되다 personnel office 인사과

9. 정답 (D)

해설 빠른 메시지를 보여주고, 스마트폰으로 음악을 재생시키는 것 외에도 / Smart Watch는 패션 액세서리 기능도 한다

해설 보기에 전치사와 접속사들이 섞여 있으므로 연결어 문제이다. '동사의 개수 - 접속사 = 1'이므로 접속사인 (A)와 (B)는 탈락한다. 빈칸 뒤에 명사가 왔으므로 빈칸은 전치사 자리이며, 따라서 전치사인 (D)가 정답이다. (C

는 부사이다.

표현 정리 in addition to ~외에도 function as+명사 ~의 기능을 하다

10. 정답 (B)

해설 Dr. Masahiro Sato는 / 연구개발 팀을 대표해 / 선정되었다 / 기술상 수상자로

해설 보기에 전치사와 접속사들이 섞여 있으므로 연결어 문제이다. '동사의 개수 - 접속사 = 1'이므로 접속사인 (D)는 탈락한다. 빈칸 앞과 뒤에 명사가 왔으므로 빈칸은 전치사 자리이며, 따라서 전치사인 (B)가 정답이다. (A)와 (C)는 부사이다.

표현 정리 on behalf of ~대표하여, 대신해서 as a result 결과적으로 on the contrary 그와는 반대로 even though 비록 ~일지라도

법칙 13 either A or B, both A and B, neither A nor B

◎ 유형을 파악해 봐
1. (C) 2. (D) 3. (B)

1. 정답 (C)

해설 호텔 손님들은 즐길 수 있다 / 식당에서 유럽풍의 아침식사를 / 또는 레스토랑에서 풀코스 아침식사를

해설 문장에 either가 있으므로 (C)가 정답이다. 상관접속사 either A or B.

표현 정리 hotel guest 호텔 손님 either A or B A와 B 중 하나 cafeteria 사내식당

2. 정답 (D)

해설 우리의 상담가들은 시간이 있습니다 / 무료 상담들을 위한 / 하루 종일 / 전화와 이메일로

해설 문장에 both가 있으므로 (D)가 정답이다. 상관접속사 both A and B.

표현 정리 consultant 상담가 available for+명사 ~을 위한 시간이 있는 consultation 상담, 협의 throughout 내내 both A and B A와 B 둘 다

3. 정답 (B)

해설 플래시를 이용한 촬영과 공예품들을 만지는 것 모두 / 허용되지 않는다 / 전시 공간 내에서

해설 문장에 neither가 있으므로 (B)가 정답이다. 상관접속사 neither A nor B.

표현 정리 neither A nor B A와 B 둘 다 아닌 artifact 공예품, 유물 exhibit area 전시 공간, 전시관

◎ 실전에 적용해 봐
1. (A) 2. (B) 3. (C) 4. (D) 5. (A) 6. (B) 7. (A)
8. (B) 9. (B) 10. (D)

1. 정답 (A)

해설 Miller Catering 사는 제공한다 / 다양한 메뉴들을 / 점심과 저녁 식사에

해설 문장에 both가 있으므로 (A)가 정답이다. 상관접속사 both A and B.

표현 정리 offer 제공하다, 제안하다 a wide range of+복수 명사 아주 다양한 both A and B A와 B 둘 다

2. 정답 (B)

해설 크게 말하는 것과 사진 촬영 둘 다 허용되지 않는다 / 공장을 견학하는 동안

해설 문장에 nor가 있으므로 (B)가 정답이다. 상관접속사 neither A nor B.

표현 정리 neither A nor B A와 B 둘 다 아닌 allow 허용하다, 용납하다 factory tour 공장 견학

3. 정답 (C)

해설 입장권들은 구입할 수 있다 / 온라인 / 또는 매표소에서 / 입구 옆에 있는

해설 문장에 either가 있으므로 (C)가 정답이다. 상관접속사 either A or B.

표현 정리 admission ticket 입장권 purchase 구매하다 either A or B A 또는 B 중 하나 ticket office 매표소 entrance 입구, 문

4. 정답 (D)

해설 Ms. Imamura는 매우 칭송 받는 시인일 뿐만 아니라 / 성공한 화가이자 조각가이다.

해설 빈칸 앞에 not only, 빈칸 뒤에 also가 보이므로 (D)가 정답이다. 상관접속사 not only A but also B.

표현 정리 not only A but also B A 뿐만 아니라 B도 critically 대단히 acclaimed 칭송을 받는 accomplished 기량이 뛰어난, 성공한 painter 화가 sculptor 조각가

5. 정답 (A)

해설 구매 계약은 아직 체결되지 않았지만 / 두 당사자들에 의해 / 이미 확인되었다 / 전화로

해설 문장에 not이 있으므로 (A)가 정답이다. 상관접속사 not A but B A가 아니라 B.

표현 정리 purchasing contract 구매 계약 sign 체결하다, 계약하다 party 당사자 confirm 확인하다, 확증하다

6. 정답 (B)

해설 AK Telecom 고객들은 / 요청 받는다 / 업데이트하도록 / 최신 전화 요금제들로 / 문자 서비스를 포함하는 / 하지만 인터넷 서비스는 포함하지 않는

해설 문장에 not이 있으므로 (B)가 정답이다. 상관접속사 not A but B = B but not A A가 아니라 B.

표현 정리 be invited to+동사원형 ~하도록 요청 받다 upgrade 업그레이드하다 calling plan 전화 요금제 include 포함하다

7. 정답 (A)

해석 승객들은 보여줘야 한다 / 그들의 티켓과 여권 모두를 / 비행기에 탑승할 때

해설 문장에 and가 있다. 상관접속사 both와 between 모두 A and B를 좋아하므로 함정에 빠질 수 있는 문제이다. between A and B는 전명구이므로 present의 목적어가 될 수 없으므로 (A)가 정답이다.

표현 정리 present 제시하다 both A and B A와 B 둘 다 ticket 티켓, 항공권 passport 여권 board 탑승하다

8. 정답 (B)

해석 우리는 알리게 되어서 유감입니다 / 당신에게 / 마케팅 이사 또는 그의 비서 모두 시간이 나지 않는다는 것을 / 면접을 진행하기 위한 / 오늘

해설 문장에 neither가 있으므로 (B)가 정답이다. 상관접속사 neither A nor B.

표현 정리 be sorry to+동사원형 ~하게 되어 유감이다 neither A nor B A와 B 모두 아닌 director 이사 assistant 비서, 조수 be available to+동사원형 ~할 수 있다 conduct 진행하다 interview 면접

9. 정답 (B)

해석 Mr. Lopez는 정기적으로 출장을 간다 / 그리고 법인 카드를 이용한다 / 호텔뿐 아니라 자동차 대여점에서도

해설 not only A but also B의 동의어로 B as well as A가 있다. '전명구 as well as 전명구'의 구조가 될 수 있으므로 (B)가 정답이다. (A)는 부사이고, 접속사인 (C)와 (D)는 이렇게 연결하는 기능(병렬이라고 한다)이 없다. '법칙 34' 참고)

표현 정리 travel 여행하다 regularly 정기적으로 business 사업 corporate 법인의, 회사의 account 계정 car rental agency 자동차 대여점

10. 정답 (D)

해석 관심 있는 사람들은 / 그들의 경력을 성공적으로 만드는데 / 우리에게 연락하거나 사무실을 방문할 수 있다 / 무료 상담을 위해

해설 either A or B와 whether A or B 사이에 혼동을 유도하는 함정 문제이다. or 이하가 없다고 생각하면 빈칸이 없어도 아무 문제가 없으며, 이럴 경우 either A or B가 정답이다.

표현 정리 those 사람들 make a difference 차별을 두다 career 경력, 직업, 이력 contact 연락하다 consultation 상담, 협의

Chapter 02 2개월에 한 번 출제되는 문제

법칙 14 2형식 또는 5형식 문장의 보어 자리는 형용사

◎ 유형을 파악해 봐
1. (A)   2. (D)   3. (D)

1. 정답 (A)

해석 만약 질문이 있다면 / 최신 직원 안내책자에 관해 / 그것들을 보내면 된다 / 인사 부장에게

해설 빈칸은 2형식 동사인 be 동사의 보어 자리이다. 명사인 (B), (C), 그리고 동사인 (D)는 탈락하고, 형용사인 (A)가 답이다.

표현 정리 if 만약 ~라면 inquiry 질문, 문의 regarding ~에 관한 personnel manager 인사 부장 direct 지도하다, 보내다 director 관리자, 감독 direction 방향, 지시, 길

2. 정답 (D)

해석 Nielsen Company 직원들은 / 쉽게 신원이 확인된다 / 유니폼과 배지에 의해 / 그들이 착용하고 있는

해설 easily는 부사이므로 수식어 처리해 제외하면 빈칸은 2형식 동사인 are의 보어 자리이다. 명사인 (A)와 동사인 (B)와 (C)는 탈락하고, 형용사인 (D)가 답이 된다.

표현 정리 employee 직원, 고용 easily 쉽게, 용이하게 identity 신원 identify 확인하다, 식별하다 identifiable 신원을 확인할 수 있는, 식별할 수 있는

3. 정답 (D)

해석 사업 개발 전문가는 책임질 것이다 / 확인하고 개발하는 것을 / 새 사업 기회를 / 동아시아에서

해설 빈칸은 2형식 동사인 be 동사의 보어 자리이므로 형용사인 (D)가 정답이다. (A), (B)는 명사, (C)는 부사이다. be responsible for는 숙어로 외워두자.

표현 정리 business 사업 development 개발 specialist 전문가 be responsible for ~을 책임지다, 담당하다 identify 확인하다 develop 개발하다 opportunity 기회 responsibility 책임, 의무 responsibly 확실히, 책임을 가지고 responsible 책임이 있는, 담당의

◎ 실전에 적용해 봐
1. (D) 2. (B) 3. (B) 4. (B) 5. (A) 6. (D) 7. (A)
8. (A) 9. (B) 10. (A)

1. 정답 (C)

해석 비평가들이 언급한 후에 / Chikan 중식당의 음식 맛이 매우 좋다고 / 식사하러 오는 손님 수가 두 배가 되었다 / 그곳에서

해설 수식어인 very를 빼내면, 빈칸은 2형식 동사인 is의 보어 자리이다. (A)는 동사, (B)는 명사, (C)는 부사이므로 탈락하고, 형용사인 (D)가 답이다. very는 주로 형용사나 부사를 수식하는 부사이다.

표현 정리 critic 비평가 comment 언급하다 flavor 맛 cuisine 요리, 요리법 the number of ~의 수 diner 식사하는 사람 double 두 배가 되다 authenticate ~이 진정한 것임을 증명하다 authenticity 확실성, 신뢰성 authentically 확실하게 authentic 정통의, 진정한, 실제의

2.   정답 (B)

해설 준비 위원회는 / 회사 야유회를 위한 / 특별히 고마워했다 / 일에 대해 / 자원봉사자에 의해서 진행된

해설 부사인 especially는 수식어이므로 빼내면 빈칸은 2형식 동사인 was의 보어 자리이며, 따라서 형용사인 (B)가 정답이다. (A)는 동사, (C)는 명사, (D)는 부사이다.

표현 정리 preparation 준비 committee 위원회 corporate 회사의, 기업의 outing 야유회, 소풍 especially 특히 grate 강판에 갈다; 화상 grateful 감사하는, 고마워하는 gratefulness 고마워 함, 감사해 함 gratefully 기꺼이, 감사하여

3.   정답 (B)

해설 보고서는 / Trend Journal의 / 보여준다 / 소비자들은 의존할 가능성이 높다고 / 인터넷 광고에 / 요즘에

해설 '동사의 개수 – 접속사의 수 = 1'이므로 빈칸에는 동사가 들어갈 수 없으며, 따라서 동사인 (D)는 탈락한다. 빈칸은 2형식 동사인 are의 보어 자리이므로 형용사인 (B)가 답이 된다. be dependent on은 숙어처럼 외워두자.

표현 정리 report 보고서, 보도 suggest 나타내다, 제안하다 consumer 소비자 most likely ~할 것 같은, 대부분 advertising 광고 these days 요즘, 오늘날에 dependently 의존하여 dependent 의존하는, 의지하는 dependency 종속물 depend 의존하다, 의지하다

4.   정답 (B)

해설 매니저는 / London 공장의 / 생각한다 / 생산 공정을 중단하는 것이 필요하다고 / 결함의 원인과 해결책이 확인될 때까지

해설 '동사의 개수 – 접속사의 수 = 1'이므로 빈칸은 동사가 들어갈 수 없어 (C)는 탈락한다. 여기서 consider는 5형식 동사로 사용되었다. it은 가목적어, to 이하가 진목적어이며, 빈칸은 목적보어 자리이므로 형용사인 (B)가 정답이다.

표현 정리 factory 공장, 회사 consider 생각하다, 고려하다 halt 중지하다, 멈추다 production 생산 process 공정 until ~까지 cause 원인 solution 해결책 defect 결함 identify 확인하다 necessity 필요성, 필수품 necessary 필요한, 필수적인 necessitate 필요로 하다, 필요하게 하다 necessarily 부득이, 필연적으로

5.   정답 (A)

해설 최근에 출시된 G-phone은 가볍고, 튼튼하고, 그리고 가격이 합리적으로 책정되었다.

해설 등위접속사 and는 앞뒤에 동등한 구조가 와야 한다. 2형식 동사 is의 보어로 빈칸 앞에는 형용사 lightweight가 왔고, and 뒤에 형용사의 기능인 reasonably priced가 왔으므로 빈칸도 형용사가 와야 하며, 이것이 곧 be 동사의 보어가 된다. 따라서 형용사인 (A)가 정답이다. (B)와 (D)는 명사, (C)는 부사이다.

표현 정리 recently 최근에 release 출시하다, 발매하다, 발표하다 lightweight 경량의, 가벼운 reasonably 합리적으로 priced 값이 붙은 durable 내구력이 있는, 튼튼한 durability 내구성, 내구력 durably 튼튼하게 durableness 오래감, 내구성이 있음

6.   정답 (D)

해설 최초로 문을 연 무인 우체국은 / 한국에서 / 이상이다 / 사람들에게는 / 우체국에 갈 수 없는 / 업무시간 동안

해설 '동사의 개수 – 접속사의 수 = 1'이므로 빈칸에는 동사가 올 수 없어 (C)는 탈락한다. 빈칸은 is의 보어 자리이므로 형용사인 (D)가 와야 한다. (A)와 (B)는 명사이다.

표현 정리 first 최초로, 처음으로 opened 연, 오픈한 unmanned 무인의 post office 우체국 be unable to ~ 할 수 없다 get to ~에 가다, 도착하다 during ~동안 business 업무, 사업, 경영 idealism 이상주의 idealist 이상주의자 idealize 이상화하다 ideal 이상적인, 이념적인

7.   정답 (A)

해설 세 가지 길 중에서 / 컨벤션 센터로 가는 / 5번 국도가 / 최근에 재포장된 국도인데 / 교통이 가장 덜 혼잡하다

해설 2형식 동사인 is의 보어가 필요하다. the least는 형용사의 최상급을 만들어주는 표현이며, 빈칸은 형용사 (A)가 와야 한다. 최상급 형용사 뒤에는 뒤에 수식 받는 명사가 생략되기도 하는데, 여기서는 빈칸 뒤에 route가 생략되었다. (B)와 (D)는 명사, (C)는 부사이다.

표현 정리 recently 최근에 repave 다시 포장하다 least 가장 적은, 최소의 traffic 교통, 통행, 차 crowded 붐비는, 혼잡한, 가득 찬 crowd 군중; 붐비다 crowdedly 붐벼서, 복잡하게, 가득하여

8.   정답 (A)

해설 직원들의 불평은 / 회사 복지에 대한 / 더 이상 CEO에게 직접 제출되지 않고 / 부서장에게 먼저 제출된다.

해설 빈칸 앞 no longer는 부사이므로 빈칸은 2형식 동사인 are의 보어가 와야 한다. 따라서 형용사의 기능이 없는 (B)와 (C)는 탈락한다. (D)가 들어가면 '직원들의 불평은 더 이상 순종적이지 않다.'라는 의미가 되므로 어색하다. 더 이상 사장에게 제출되지 않고 부서장에게 제출된다는 의미를 이루는 (A)가 답이다.

표현 정리 employee 직원, 고용인 complaint 불평, 고소 benefit 이익, 혜택 no longer 더 이상 ~이 아닌 directly 직접, 곧바로 department 부서, 부, 과 head 지도자, 우두머리 submission 제출 submit 제출하다, 복종하다 submissive 복종하는, 순종하는

9.   정답 (C)

해설 그들의 의견이 / 대중에게 그럴듯하게 들리기 위해서 / 정치가들은 보통 제공한다 / 편견을 가진 견해를 / 대부분의 미해결 문제들에 관한

해설 빈칸 앞 sound는 2형식 동사로 쓰였기 때문에 빈칸은 sound의 보어 자리이며, 형용사인 (C)가 정답이다. (A)는 부사, (B)와 (D)는 명사이다.

표현 정리 view 보기, 견해, 관점 sound 들리다; 소리 public 공공의;

대중, 국민 politician 정치가 usually 보통, 대개 provide 제공하다, 공급하다 biased 치우친, 편견을 가진 pending 미해결의, 미정의 issue 문제, 이슈; 발행하다 plausibly 그럴듯하게 plausibility 그럴듯함, 그럴듯한 일 plausible 그럴듯한, 외양만 좋은

10. 　　　　　　　　　　　　　　　　　　정답 (A)

해설 효율적으로 파악하기 위해 / 그들의 재고를 / 매장 매니저들은 익숙해야 한다 / 재고관리 소프트웨어 시스템에

해설 2형식 동사인 become의 보어 자리이므로 형용사가 필요하며, 따라서 (A)가 정답이다. (B)는 부사, (C)는 명사, (D)는 동사이다.

표현 정리 in order to ~하기 위해 effectively 효율적으로 keep track of ~을 추적하다, ~의 흔적을 쫓다 inventory 재고 stock management 재고 관리 familiar 익숙한, 친숙한 familiarly 친밀하게, 흉허물없이 familiarity 친밀함 familiarize 익숙해지게 하다, 일반화하다

법칙 15 전체 문맥을 알아야 풀리는 추가, 포함, 제외 및 for(이/용/대/목) 전치사

◎ **유형을 파악해 봐**
1. (D)　2. (A)　3. (C)

1. 　　　　　　　　　　　　　　　　　　정답 (D)

해설 Blueone 사의 전 직원들은 / 관리부에 근무하는 사람들을 제외한 / 참석해야 한다 / 정보 과정에 / 시설 규정에 관한

해설 전치사 어휘 문제로, 가장 자주 출제되는 전치사인 (D)부터 대입해 해석해 본다. '관리부에서 근무하는 직원들을 제외한 전 직원들은 ~'이라는 의미가 자연스러우므로 (D)가 정답이다. (A)는 복수 명사와 함께 쓰이고, (B)나 (C)는 주제와 어울리는 전치사이므로 탈락한다.

표현 정리 employee 직원들 maintenance department 관리부 attend 출석하다, 참석하다 facility 시설 regulation 규정 among ~중에, ~사이에 concerning ~에 관하여 except ~을 제외하고

2. 　　　　　　　　　　　　　　　　　　정답 (A)

해설 경영학 학위 외에도 / 그 직책은 요구한다 / 적어도 / 2년의 근무 경력을 / 관련된 분야에서

해설 보기가 모두 전치사로 구성되어 있는 전치사 어휘 문제로, 포함의 전치사인 (A)부터 대입해 해석해 본다. '그 직책은 경영학 외에 경력을 요구한다 ~'라는 의미가 자연스러우므로 (A)가 정답이다. (B)는 '경영학과 달리 그 직책은 ~'이라는 어색한 해석이 되므로 탈락하고, (C)는 전치사로 쓰였을 때 '~처럼, ~로서'라는 뜻으로 자격이나 수단을 나타내며, (D)는 '~를 대표하여, 대신하여'라는 뜻으로 주로 사람이나 회사가 온다.

표현 정리 management 경영, 관리 degree 학위, 등급 position 직책, 자리 require ~을 필요로 하다, ~을 요구하다 at least 적어도 working experience 근무 경력 related field 관련 분야 in addition to ~외에도, ~뿐 아니라 unlike ~와는 달리 on behalf of ~를 대표하여, 대신하여

3. 　　　　　　　　　　　　　　　　　　정답 (C)

해설 우리에게 알려주세요 / 당신이 원하는지를 / 일반 또는 등기 우송을 / 회사로 보내는

해설 보기가 전치사로 구성된 전치사 문제로, 이/용/대/목의 전치사인 (C)를 먼저 대입해 해석해 본다. '당신의 회사로 보내는 배송'이라는 의미가 자연스러우므로 (C)가 정답이다. 이 문장에서는 대상을 나타내는 전치사로 쓰였다. (A)는 장소나 시간 앞에, (B)는 통과의 의미 또는 시간이나 수단 같데, 그리고 (D)는 위치에 쓰인다.

표현 정리 let ~하게 하다, 시키다 standard 기준, 표준 express 고속의, 특별한 delivery 배달, 배송 through ~을 통하여, 지나서 above ~보다 위에

◎ **실전에 적용해 봐**
1. (B)　2. (A)　3. (B)　4. (C)　5. (C)　6. (C)　7. (D)
8. (A)　9. (D)　10. (A)

1. 　　　　　　　　　　　　　　　　　　정답 (B)

해설 오타를 감지하는 것 외에도 / OCR 1 소프트웨어는 또한 제시한다 / 대체 단어들을 / 철자가 틀린 단어들에 대한

해설 빈칸은 동명사를 목적어로 갖는 전치사 자리이므로 부사와 접속사인 (C)와 (E)는 탈락한다. 포함의 전치사인 (B)를 먼저 대입해 보면 '오타를 감지하는 것 외에도 ~'라는 의미가 자연스러우므로 (B)가 정답이다. (A)는 맨 두에 오지 않는다.

표현 정리 detect 감지하다, 발견하다 misspelling 틀린 철자, 오타 suggest 제안하다, 암시하다, 제시하다 except ~을 제외하고, ~외에는 besides ~외에, 게다가 however 그러나, 하지만 unless ~하지 않는다면, 제외하면

2. 　　　　　　　　　　　　　　　　　　정답 (A)

해설 비서의 공식 업무는 / 다양한 전화를 받고, 중요한 문서를 정리하고 CEO의 미팅을 잡는 것과 같은 / 변경될 수 있다 / 필요 시에는

해설 빈칸 뒤에 명사들이 나열되어 있으므로 빈칸은 전치사 자리이므로 접속사 (C)는 탈락한다. 빈칸 뒤는 업무에 대한 예들이 나열되어 있으므로 (A)가 정답이다. (B)는 통과의 전치사 또는 시간이나 수단의 전치사이고, (D)는 분리의 의미를 가진 전치사이다.

표현 정리 official duty 공식 업무 secretary 비서 multiple 다수의, 다양한 file 정리하다 important 중요한, 소중한 document 문서, 자료 schedule ~을 정하다 necessary 불가피한, 필수적인, 필요한 such as ~와 같은 now that ~이기 때문에 apart 떨어진, 분리된 구별도는

3. 　　　　　　　　　　　　　　　　　　정답 (B)

해설 유리 그릇들은 사용될 수 있다 / 화학물질 또는 화학용액을 저장하기 위해 / 그것들에 라벨이 붙어 있는 동안 / 항상

해설 전치사 어휘 문제로, 이/용/대/목의 전치사 (B)를 먼저 대입해 해석해 본다. '저장하는 것을 위해, 즉 저장을 위해 사용된다'라는 의미가 자연스러우므로 (B)가 정답이다. (A)는 방향이나 대상, (C)는 수단, (D)는 on과 같이 위치나 시간의 전치사이다.

표현 정리 container 용기, 그릇 be used for -ing ~하기 위해 사용되다 store 저장하다 chemical 화학물질, 화합물 chemical solution 화학용액 as long as ~하는 한, ~만큼 label 라벨을 붙이다 at all times 항상, 언제나

4. 정답 (C)

해석 직원들은 / 시간제 일을 하고자 하는 / 사회 봉사활동 프로그램에서 / 그들의 일상적인 업무 외에 / 연락해야 한다 / Ms. Park에게 / 인사부 직원인

해설 전치사 어휘 문제로 부사인 (B)와 접속사인 (D)가 먼저 탈락하고, (A) 역시 '사전에, 미리'라는 뜻의 부사이므로 탈락한다. '일상 업무 외에 시간제 업무'라는 의미를 이룰 수 있는 (C)가 정답이다.

표현 정리 those who ~하는 사람들 community 사회, 공동체, 집단 outreach 봉사활동 day job 일상적인 업무, 주된 업무 contact 접촉하다, 연락하다 Personnel 인사부 (직원)

5. 정답 (C)

해석 장소 이용 사정으로 인해 / 개회식은 개최될 것이다 / 무도회장에서 / 회의실 대신에

해설 빈칸은 앞의 명사와 뒤의 명사를 이어주는 전치사 자리이다. in addition은 to까지 있어야 전치사이며, '장소 이용 문제로 인해 회의실 대신 무도회장에서 개회식이 개최될 것이다'라는 의미가 자연스러우므로 (C)가 정답이다.

표현 정리 because of ~때문에 availability 이용 가능성, 유용성 opening ceremony 개막식, 개회식 be held 열리다 ballroom 무도회장 conference room 회의실 in addition 또한, 게다가 without ~없이 instead of ~대신에 except for ~을 제외하고

6. 정답 (C)

해석 Cameroon Systems의 전 직원들은 / 최근에 고용된 시간제 근로자를 포함한 / 참가해야 한다 / 회사 전체의 재활용 운동에

해설 빈칸부터 part-timers까지는 전명구가 되어야 빈칸 앞의 명사를 수식할 수 있고, 빈칸은 전치사 자리이다. since는 전치사로 쓰일 경우 과거 시점과 함께 쓰여 '~이래로'의 의미를 나타낸다. 모든 직원들이 참가해야 한다고 했으므로 최근에 고용된 시간제 근로자들 '사이에(between)' 보다는 '포함하여(including)'라는 말이 더 어울려 (C)가 정답이 된다. (B)는 부사이다.

표현 정리 employee 직원 recently 최근에 hired 고용된 part-timer 시간제 직원 participate in ~에 참여하다 company-wide 회사 전체의, 전사적인 recycling 재활용 initiative 활동, 계획 between ~사이에 including ~을 포함해 since ~이래로, ~이후

7. 정답 (D)

해석 Pineapple 사는 사용을 중단했다 / 부품들 중 하나의 / Digitec이 공급한 / 그들이 대체품을 찾았기 때문에 / 동일한 처리 능력을 가진 / 보다 나은 신뢰성뿐 아니라

해설 빈칸은 명사와 명사를 이어주는 전치사 문제로 대명사인 (A)와 부사인 (C)는 탈락하고, (B) 역시 접속사나 부사로 쓰이므로 탈락한다. 전치사인 (D)를 넣으면 '신뢰성뿐 아니라 처리 능력을 가진'이라는 자연스러운 해석이 되므로 (D)가 정답이다.

표현 정리 discontinue 중단하다, 취하다 using 사용 component 부품, 구성 요소 substitute 대체품 processing 가공, 처리 capability 능력, 재능 reliability 신뢰성 though 비록 ~일지라도, ~임에도 불구하고 plus 또한, 더욱이

8. 정답 (A)

해석 Mr. White의 발표는 / 판매 전략에 대한 / 중역 회의 동안 / 어제 / 완벽했다 / 너무 길었던 것을 제외하면

해설 보기 중 빈칸 뒤에 있는 접속사 (B)를 제외하고는 모두 that과 함께 사용할 수 있다. (A)가 오면 '길었던 것을 제외하면 완벽했다'로 해석되어 정답이 된다. (C)는 '완벽했다, 그래야 너무 길었으니까'라는 뜻이 되어 어색하고, (D)가 오면 '길었기 때문에 완벽했다'는 해석이 되어 역시 어색하다.

표현 정리 presentation 제출, 발표 sales strategy 판매 전략 board meeting 이사회 except that (that) 이하를 제외하면

9. 정답 (D)

해석 올해 / 선정 위원회는 / 어려운 시기를 겪고 있다 / 지명하는데 있어 / 사람들을 / 회사에 대한 그들의 노고와 헌신으로 상을 받을

해설 전치사 어휘 문제로, 가장 자주 출제되는 전치사 중 하나인 이/용/대/목의 전치사 (D)를 먼저 대입해 해석해 보면, '그들의 노고와 헌신으로 상을 받을'이라는 의미로 for 뒤에 이유가 나왔다. 따라서 이유의 전치사인 (D)가 정답이다. be honored for는 '~으로 상을 받다'로 알아 두자. (A)는 장소나 시간, (B)는 방향이나 장소, (C)는 시간이나 장소에 사용되는 전치사이다.

표현 정리 selection committee 선정 위원회 hard time 힘든 시간, 어려움 nominate 지명하다, 임명하다 dedication to ~에 대한 헌신

10. 정답 (A)

해석 책 판매로부터 얻은 수익금은 / 직접 쓰일 것이다 / 도서관 프로젝트에 / 수리를 포함한 / 정문

해설 전치사 어휘 문제로, 해석을 통해 빈칸 앞과 뒤의 관계를 살핀다. '수익금이 프로젝트에 직접 사용될 것이다'라는 내용이므로 (A)가 정답이다. (B)는 위치, (C)는 on과 함께 시간이나 장소, (D)는 운동이나 방향의 전치사로 주로 along the street, along the river와 같이 쓰인다.

표현 정리 proceeds 수익금, 수입 directly 직접적으로, 바로 library 도서관 maintenance 유지, 관리 including ~을 포함해 renovation 혁신, 수리 main entrance 정문 toward ~에 대한, ~쪽으로 next to ~옆에 onto ~위에 along ~와 함께, ~을 따라

법칙 16 목적어가 있으면 능동, 없으면 수동

◎ 유형을 파악해 봐
1. (D)　2. (A)　3. (D)

1. 정답 (D)

해석 관리직을 위한 지원서는 / 반드시 접수되어야 한다 / 6월 3일의 주까지는

해설 빈칸 앞에 조동사 must가 있으므로 빈칸은 동사원형이 와야 한다. 따라서 (A)와 (C)는 탈락한다. 빈칸 뒤에 오는 전명구는 목적어 역할을 할 수

24

없으므로 동사는 수동태가 되어야 한다. 따라서 be p.p 형태의 (D)가 정답이다.

표현 정리 application 지원, 신청 managerial position 관리직 receive 받다, 얻다

2.   정답 (A)

해석 회사 전체가 참여하는 재활용 운동을 통해 / Jason Paper는 감소시켰다 / 전체 운영비를 / 지난 분기에 상당히

해설 문장에 정동사가 없으므로 빈칸은 정동사 자리이며, 준동사인 (D)는 탈락한다. 주어(Jason Paper)가 단수이므로 복수 동사인 (B) 역시 탈락한다. 빈칸 뒤 its overall operation expenses가 목적어이므로 동사는 능동태가 되어야 하며, 따라서 (A)가 정답이다.

표현 정리 through ~을 통해 company-wide 회사 전체의 recycling 재활용 initiative 계획, 운동 overall 전체적인 operation 운영 expense 비용, 지출 considerably 상당히, 많이, 현저히 quarter 분기 reduce 줄이다, 감소시키다

3.   정답 (D)

해석 Ms. Brown은 / 매우 기쁘다 / 그녀가 승진해서 / 부서장으로 / 그리고 임금 인상을 받게 되어

해설 빈칸은 주어 she의 동사 자리이다. 빈칸 뒤 전명구는 목적어 역할을 할 수 없으므로 빈칸의 동사는 수동태가 돼야 하며, 따라서 (D)가 정답이다. 나머지는 모두 능동태이다.

표현 정리 be pleased that S+V ~하게 되어 기쁘다 department manager 부서장 receive 받다, 수상하다 pay increase 임금 인상 promote 홍보하다, 승진하다

◎ 실전에 적용해 봐

1. (D)   2. (A)   3. (D)   4. (A)   5. (D)   6. (A)   7. (C)
8. (C)   9. (A)   10. (B)

1.   정답 (D)

해석 예상치 못한 기술적인 문제로 인해 / 신형 스마트폰 출시가 지연될 것이다.

해설 빈칸은 주어인 the launch of the new smartphone의 동사 자리이다. 주어가 단수이므로 복수 동사인 (B)는 탈락하며, 빈칸 뒤에 목적어가 없으므로 (A), (C), (D) 중에서 수동태인 (D)가 답이다.

표현 정리 due to ~때문에, ~로 인해 unexpected 예상치 못한, 예기치 않은 technical problem 기술적인 문제 launch 시작하다, 출시하다 delay 지연시키다, 연기하다

2.   정답 (A)

해석 만약 어떤 문제가 있으면 / 컴퓨터를 사용하는데 있어 / 당신은 참고할 수 있다 / 다음 가능성 있는 해결책들을 / 우리 서비스 직원들이 제시한

해설 that부터 representatives까지는 solutions를 수식하는 형용사절이다. 형용사절 안의 동사는 선행사에 수일치를 시키므로 단수 동사인 (C)는 탈락한다. 빈칸 뒤 전명구는 목적어 역할을 할 수 없으므로 빈칸의 동사는 수동태가 되어야 한다. 따라서 능동태인 (B)와 (D)를 탈락시키면 답은 (A)가

된다.

표현 정리 problem 문제 refer to+명사 ~를 참조하다 following 다음의, ~후에 possible 가능한, 할 수 있는 solution 해결책, 방안, 해법 representative 직원, 대표자 suggest 제안하다, 제시하다

3.   정답 (D)

해석 인쇄 용품들은 / 종이, 잉크 카트리지, 그리고 스테이플러와 같은 / 찾아볼 수 있다 / 서류 캐비닛에서 / 복사기 옆에 있는

해설 빈칸 앞에 조동사 can이 있으므로 빈칸은 동사원형 자리이며, 따라서 (A)가 먼저 탈락한다. (B)와 (D) 외에 (C) found도 '설립하다'의 뜻 때는 동사원형이 된다. 빈칸 뒤에 목적어가 없으므로 (D) 수동태가 와야 한다.

표현 정리 printing supply 인쇄 용품 such as ~와 같은 paper 종이 ink-cartridge 잉크 카트리지 stapler 스테이플러 file cabinet 파일 캐비닛, 서류 캐비닛 place 놓다 next to ~의 옆에, 나란히 copy machine 복사기 found 설립하다, 세우다

4.   정답 (A)

해석 10년 동안 / 설립된 이래 / SY 사는 전설이 되었다 / 창조적인 마케팅 접근법으로

해설 '동사의 개수 - 접속사의 수 = 1'이므로 빈칸에는 정동사가 와야 하는데, (C)는 준동사이므로 탈락한다. 주어가 단수이므로 복수 동사인 (B) 역시 탈락하고, 2형식 동사인 become은 자동사이기 때문에 수동태로 쓸 수 없어 be p.p. 형태인 (D) 또한 탈락하면 남는 것은 (A) 뿐이다.

표현 정리 decade 10년 since ~이래로, ~한 후에 found ~을 설립하다 legend 전설 creative 창조적인, 창의적인 marketing 마케팅, 홍보 approach 접근, 접근법

5.   정답 (D)

해석 매달 / Abelon 사는 기부한다 / 수익의 1퍼센트를 / 지역 자선단체에

해설 문장에 정동사가 없으므로 빈칸은 정동사 자리이다. 빈칸 뒤에 목적어(1% of its earnings)가 있으므로 능동태가 와야 한다. 능동태는 (D)뿐이며, 나머지는 모두 수동태이다.

표현 정리 every month 매달 earning 수익 local charity 지역 자선단체 contribute 기여하다, 공헌하다, 기부하다

6.   정답 (A)

해석 우리는 알리게 되어 유감이다 / 당신에게 / 당신의 주문이 이미 배송되었음을 / 우리가 받기 전에 / 요청하는 당신의 이메일을 / 수량 변경을

해설 빈칸은 to 부정사의 동사원형 자리이므로 (B)가 먼저 탈락한다. 뒤에 you라는 목적어가 있으므로 수동태인 (C)와 형용사인 (D) 또한 답이 될 수 없고, 능동인 (A)가 정답이다.

표현 정리 regret to+동사원형 ~하게 되어 유감이다 order 주문; 주문하다 already 이미, 벌써 ship ~을 보내다, 선적하다 before ~전에 receive 받다, 수상하다 request 요청하다 change 변경, 변화 quantity 양, 수량 inform 알리다, 통보하다

7.   정답 (C)

해석 당신이 입증할 수 있다면 / 소유권 증명을 / 당신은 발급 받을 것이다

/ 임시 통행증을 / 놀이공원 어디에서나 이용할 수 있는.

해설 빈칸은 주어 you의 동사 자리이므로 준동사인 (A)와 (B)는 탈락한다. 빈칸 뒤에 목적어 an interim pass가 있다고 해서 능동태인 (D)를 고르지 않도록 한다. 소유권을 증명하는 사람은 발급을 받는 사람이지 발급을 해 주는 사람이 아니다. issue는 4형식 동사이므로 목적어를 2개 취하는데, 수동태로 쓰일 경우 목적어가 1개 남게 된다. 따라서 빈칸은 수동태인 (C)가 와야 발급받는다는 뜻이 된다.

표현 정리 demonstrate 증명하다, 입증하다 proof 증거, 증명, 입증 ownership 소유권 interim 임시의, 중간의 amusement park 놀이동산, 유원지 issue 발급하다, 발행하다

8. 정답 (C)

해설 Peatrock 사의 직원들은 초대된다 / 건강 생활 세미나에 참석하도록 / 전액 무료로

해설 문장에 정동사가 없으므로 빈칸은 정동사 자리이며, 준동사인 (D)가 먼저 탈락한다. invite는 5형식으로 쓰일 경우 목적 보어로 to 부정사를 취하는 '결혼승낙' 동사이다('법칙 48' 참고). 빈칸 뒤 목적어가 없이 바로 to 부정사가 나온 것으로 보아 수동태로 쓰였음을 알 수 있어 (C)가 정답이다. (A)와 (B)는 능동태이다. '결혼승낙' 동사의 수동태는 'be p.p. to+동사원형' 형태의 숙어로 알아두면 편리하다.

표현 정리 employee 직원, 고용인 attend 참석하다 completely 완전히, 전적으로 free of charge 공짜로, 무료로 invite 초대하다

9. 정답 (A)

해설 프로젝트 담당자로서 / Ms. Wong은 책임져야 한다 / 진척 상황에 대해 / 회사의 최근 보수 계획의

해설 빈칸 앞에 조동사 should가 있기 때문에 빈칸은 동사원형이 와야 하며, 따라서 (C)가 먼저 탈락한다. (D)가 오면 'should have p.p.' 구조가 되는데, 이것은 가정법에 쓰이는 구문이므로 역시 답이 될 수 없다. hold가 5형식으로 쓰일 경우 목적 보어로 형용사를 취할 수 있는데, 빈칸 뒤에 목적어가 없고 목적 보어인 형용사가 있는 것으로 보아 수동태로 쓰였음을 알 수 있다. 따라서 수동태인 (A)가 정답이다.

표현 정리 coordinator 책임자, 담당자 hold accountable 책임을 지다 progress 진전, 경과, 진행 recent 최근의 renovation 혁신, 수리, 보수

10. 정답 (B)

해설 에너지 절약 운동이 홍보돼야 한다 / TV 광고로 / 그것이 실행될 수 있도록 / 전국적으로

해설 빈칸 앞에 조동사 can이 있으므로 빈칸은 동사원형이 와야 하며, 준동사인 (C)와 명사인 (D)는 오답 처리한다. 빈칸 뒤에 있는 nationwide는 명사처럼 보이지만 형용사 또는 부사로 사용되는 단어로 이 문제에서는 부사로 사용되었다. 따라서 목적어가 없으므로 수동태인 (B)가 와야 한다.

표현 정리 initiative 주도적 계획, 솔선 운동 publicize 광고하다, 선전하다 by means of ~에 의해, ~을 수단으로 하여 so that A can A가 ~할 수 있게 nationwide 전국적으로; 전국적인 implement 실행하다, 실시하다

법칙 17 비교/최상급의 단서가 있으면 비교/최상급, 그렇지 않으면 원급

◎ **유형을 파악해 봐**
1. (B) 2. (C) 3. (B)

1. 정답 (B)

해설 Mr. Lee는 기꺼이 일할 것이다 / 서울보다는 부산에 있는 사무실에서 / 그의 고향이 부산이기 때문에

해설 빈칸은 be 동사의 보어 자리이므로 형용사가 와야 하며, 부사인 (A)와 명사인 (C)는 탈락한다. than은 비교급과 함께 쓰이므로 비교급인 (B)가 정답이다.

표현 정리 because ~때문에, 왜냐하면 hometown 고향 be willing to+동사원형 기꺼이 ~하다

2. 정답 (C)

해설 수정된 안전 규정들은 검토될 것이다 / 매우 신중하게 / 중역들에 의해

해설 빈칸 앞의 문장이 be p.p. 형태의 수동태와 부사가 왔으므로 빈칸은 부사 자리이며, 따라서 부사의 원급인 (C)가 정답이다. 빈칸 앞 extremely는 형용사나 부사의 원급을 수식하는 부사이므로, 비교급인 (D)는 올 수 없다.

표현 정리 revise 수정하다, 변경하다 safety regulations 안전 규정 review 검토하다 extremely 매우, 극도로, 굉장히 senior executive 중역, 임원 care 돌보다, 보살피다 careful 조심스러운, 주의 깊은, 철저한 carefully 신중하게, 주의하여, 세심하게

3. 정답 (B)

해설 Rachel 부장은 동의했다 / 새 복사기를 구입하는 것이 / 더 저렴할 것이라고 / 옛 것을 고치는 것보다

해설 빈칸이 be 동사 뒤에 있으므로 보어가 되는 형용사 자리이다. 빈칸 뒤에 than이 있으므로 비교급인 (B)가 정답이다. (A)는 원급, (C)는 최상급이고, (D)는 부사이다.

표현 정리 office manager 부장 purchase 구입하다, 구매하다 new copier 새 복사기 the old one 오래된 것, 옛 것 cheap 싼, 저렴한 cheaper 더 싼, 더 저렴한 cheaply 싸게, 쉽게

◎ **실전에 적용해 봐**
1. (D) 2. (D) 3. (B) 4. (A) 5. (D) 6. (A) 7. (C)
8. (C) 9. (C) 10. (C)

1. 정답 (D)

해설 선발하기 위해 / 그 직책에 가장 적격인 지원자를 / 인사 부장은 살폈다 / 지원자의 이력서들을 / 이전보다 더 철저하게

해설 빈칸 앞을 보면 '주어+동사+목적어' 구조의 완전한 문장이 왔으므로 빈칸은 부사 자리이다. 빈칸 뒤에 than이 있으므로 비교급인 (D)가 답이다. (A)와 (B)는 형용사이다.

표현 정리 select 선택하다, 선발하다 qualified 자격이 있는, 적임의

applicant 지원자, 신청자 position 직책, 위치 personnel director 인사 부장 review 살피다 thorough 철저한, 완전한 thoroughly 철저하게

2. 정답 (D)

해설 마케팅부에 근무하는 10명의 직원 중 / Ms. Gupta가 가장 능숙하다 / 사용하는데 / 새로운 데이터베이스 소프트웨어를

해설 관사 뒤, 전명구 앞이라고 해서 명사인 (B)를 골라서는 안 된다. 보어 자리에 명사가 올 수도 있지만 그럴 경우에는 주어와 동격이 성립되어야 한다. 주어인 Ms. Gupta가 proficiency(능숙함)와 동격이 아니기 때문에 명사는 올 수 없다. 문장 앞에 '10명의 직원 중'이라는 범위가 있고, 빈칸 앞에 the가 있기 때문에 최상급 표현인 (D)가 정답이다.

표현 정리 marketing department 마케팅부 proficient 능숙한, 숙달한 proficiency 능숙, 유창

3. 정답 (B)

해설 제공함으로써 / 더 믿을 만하고 저렴한 제품을 / Minton Electronics는 확보할 수 있었다 / 가장 높은 지위를 / 업계에서

해설 빈칸은 뒤에 있는 명사 position을 수식해 주는 형용사 자리이다. 빈칸 뒤 '업계에서'라는 범위도 있고, 빈칸 앞 정관사 the를 단서로 봤을 때, 최상급인 (B)가 정답이다. (A)는 부사이다.

표현 정리 provide 제공하다 reliable 신뢰할 만한, 믿을 만한 affordable 알맞은, 저렴한 item 물품, 품목 secure 보장하다, 확보하다 industry 산업, 업계 highly 매우, 높이, 가장 highest 가장 높은, 최고의 higher 높은, 더 ~한 high 높은, 많은

4. 정답 (A)

해설 최근 연구는 나타낸다 / 고혈압과 비만이 사회적인 건강 문제가 되었음을 / 중국에서

해설 빈칸은 명사를 꾸며주는 (A) 형용사 자리이다. (B)와 (C)는 부사와 명사이고, 비교급은 비교 대상이 있거나 than과 같이 단서가 되는 단어가 있을 때 쓸 수 있으므로 (D) 역시 오답이다.

표현 정리 study 연구, 조사 indicate 나타내다, 가리키다, 암시하다 high blood pressure 고혈압 obesity 비만 major 주요한, 중대한 public 대중의, 공공의 health problem 건강 문제 recent 최근, 최신 recently 최근에

5. 정답 (D)

해설 Well Designs T55는 평가되었다 / 가장 가벼운 인체공학 의자로 / 구매 가능한 / 마켓에서 / 오늘날

해설 빈칸이 정관사 뒤 형용사 앞에 위치해 있다고 해서 부사를 고르지 않도록 한다. 빈칸에 부사가 오게 되면 '가볍게 인체공학적 의자'라는 어색한 뜻이 되므로 ergonomic과 함께 chair를 꾸며주는 형용사 자리로 봐야 한다. 따라서 (C)는 탈락한다. 앞에 정관사가 있고, '오늘날 마켓에서 구입 가능한 것들 중 최고로 가벼운'이라는 범위가 있으므로 최상급인 (D)가 정답이다.

표현 정리 rate 평가하다 ergonomic chair 인체공학적 의자 available for purchase 구매 가능한 lightweight 가벼운, 경량의

6. 정답 (A)

해설 도서관 방문자들은 요청 받는다 / 조용히 말하도록 / 열람실에서 / 도서관 입구에서 보다

해설 빈칸 앞은 완전한 문장이므로 빈칸은 부사 자리이다. 뒤에 비교급 단서인 than이 있으므로 (A)가 정답이다.

표현 정리 visitor 방문자 be asked to ~하도록 요청 받다 reading room 열람실, 독서실 entrance 입구, 현관

7. 정답 (C)

해설 'L.A. Press' 교열 담당자는 / 원고를 교정해야 한다 / 작가들이 제출한 / 가능한 철저하게

해설 빈칸은 관사 뒤, 명사 앞인 형용사 자리이므로 (A)와 (B)는 탈락한다. 뒤에 최상급을 만들어주는 단서가 되는 단어인 possible이 있으므로 (C)가 정답이다. to the fullest extent는 덩어리 표현으로 '최대한으로'라는 뜻으로 알아두자.

표현 정리 editor 편집자 proofread 교정하다, 교정보다 manuscript 원고, 문서 writer 작가, 저자 extent 정도, 범위 to the fullest extent (possible) (가능한 한) 최대한으로 fully 충분히, 완전히 full 최대한, 가득한

8. 정답 (C)

해설 매장 관리자는 지시했다 / 직원들에게 서비스하라고 / 고객들을 / 더 정중하게 / 하루의 가장 바쁜 시간에

해설 빈칸 앞 '주어+동사+목적어'로 완전한 문장이 왔으므로 빈칸은 (C) 부사 자리이다. '평소보다 더 세심하게 서비스하라'는 뜻으로 '평소보다'라는 비교 대상이 생략된 형태이다.

표현 정리 order 명령하다 clerk 점원, 직원 serve 서비스하다, 봉사하다 peak hours 가장 바쁜 시간 attention 관심, 주의, 집중 attentive 주의 깊은, 세심한 attentively 주의 깊게, 정중하게

9. 정답 (C)

해설 새로운 T47 잔디 깎는 기계는 도와줄 것이다 / 정원사가 / 그들의 일을 완료하도록 / 훨씬 더 효율적으로

해설 빈칸 앞에 '주어+동사+목적어+목적 보어'로 완전한 문장이 왔으므로 빈칸은 부사 자리이다. 빈칸 앞에 비교급을 수식해 주는 표현인 much가 있으므로 (C)가 정답이다. (B)는 원급으로 extremely, very, quite 등이 수식할 수 있다. than이 없다고 최상급을 고르지 않도록 한다. 앞에 newly, newly가 보이는 경우 보통 'than the old ~' 부분이 생략된 것으로 보아야 하는데, 최상급을 답으로 선택하기에는 비교 대상이 불분명하다.

표현 정리 lawn 잔디, 정원 mower 잔디 깎는 기계 gardener 정원사 complete 끝내다, 완료하다 efficient 능률적인, 유능한, 효율적인 efficiently 효율적으로, 효과적으로

10. 정답 (C)

해설 Dr. Steven은 상을 받았다 / 업무 수행으로 / 모든 직원들 중에서 가장 뛰어난 / 이번 달 종합병원에서

해설 여기서 perform은 1형식 동사이며, 이어서 부사가 와야 한다. 빈칸 앞에 정관사 the가 있고, 뒤에 of all the staff라는 범위가 있으므로 부사

의 최상급인 (C)가 정답이다. (B)와 (C)는 형용사도 되고, 부사도 될 수 있다. the best는 형용사뿐 아니라 부사도 되며, 부사로 사용될 때 앞에 the를 붙여도 된다.

표현 정리 be honored for ~로 상을 받다, ~을 기리다 perform 수행하다, 공연하다 general hospital 종합병원 well 잘, 충분히 better 더 나은, 더 좋은 best 최고의, 가장 ~한, 최선의 good 좋은, 잘, 훌륭한

법칙 18 동사가 2개면 접속사가 답

◎ 유형을 파악해 봐

1. (A) 2. (B) 3. (B)

1. 정답 (A)

해석 사무실 보수를 위한 예산이 / 승인되지 않는다면 / 1주일 내에 / 우리는 맞출 수 없다 / 완공일을

해설 문장 안에 is와 can't meet 동사가 2개이므로, 빈칸은 (A) 접속사 자리이다. (B), (C)는 부사, (D)는 부사나 전치사이다.

표현 정리 budget 예산 renovate 수리하다, 개조하다 approve 승인하다, 동의하다, 허가하다 within ~이내에, ~안에 meet 충족시키다, 만나다 deadline 마감일, 최종 기한 completion 완공, 완성 unless ~이 아니면, ~하지 않는다면

2. 정답 (B)

해석 우리가 받을 때까지 / 설문조사 결과를 / 신제품에 대한 광고 활동은 진행되지 않을 것이다

해설 문장 안에 동사가 tend to prefer, value 2개 왔으므로 빈칸은 (D) 접속사 자리이다. 부사인 (A)와 전치사인 (B), (C)는 탈락한다.

표현 정리 receive 받다, 수상하다 result 결과 survey 설문조사; 조사하다 advertising campaign 광고 활동 product 제품, 상품 proceed 진행하다 without ~없이 until ~할 때까지, ~까지 onto ~위에, 위로에 within ~이내에, ~안에

3. 정답 (B)

해석 두고 봐야 한다 / Samdasu 사가 열 것인지 아닌지 / 새로운 지점을 / 제주에

해설 문장 안에 동사가 remains, will open 2개 왔으므로, 빈칸은 (B) 접속사 자리이다.

표현 정리 remain ~로 남다, ~이다 open 열다, 개방하다 branch 지점 whether ~인지 아닌지 on ~에, 위에 to ~에, ~까지

◎ 실전에 적용해 봐

1. (C) 2. (D) 3. (A) 4. (D) 5. (A) 6. (A) 7. (A)
8. (A) 9. (C) 10. (A)

1. 정답 (C)

해석 오늘밤 시상식에서, CEO는 연설할 것이다 / 초청된 하객들의 90퍼센트가 도착하면 / 연회장에

해설 문장 안에 동사가 will deliver, arrive 2개 왔으므로, 빈칸은 (C) 접속사 자리이다. 부사인 (A), (B), (D)는 탈락한다.

표현 정리 award ceremony 시상식 deliver one's speech 연설하다 invite 초대하다, 초청하다 guest 손님, 하객 arrive at ~에 도착하다 banquet hall 연회장 still 여전히, 아직도 less 더 적게, 덜한 once ~하자마자, 일단 ~하면 apart 떨어진, 분리된, 구별되는

2. 정답 (D)

해석 비록 사람들은 선호하는 경향이 있지만 / 단기 투자를 / 그들은 중시한다 / 혜택들을 / 장기간 투자의

해설 문장 안에 동사가 tend to prefer, value 2개 왔으므로 빈칸은 (D) 접속사 자리이다. 부사인 (A)와 전치사인 (B), (C)는 탈락한다.

표현 정리 tend to ~하는 경향이 있다 prefer 선호하다, 좋아하다 short-term investment 단기 투자 value 중시하다, 가치 benefit 이익, 혜택 long-term investment 장기 투자 somewhat 다소, 약간, 어느 정도 including ~을 포함해 even though 비록 ~지만

3. 정답 (A)

해석 연례회의는 열릴 것이다 / 본사에서 / 예정대로 / 모든 지사장들이 / 참석하든 못하든 / 회의에

해설 문장 안에 동사가 will be, will be 2개 왔으므로, 빈칸은 (A) 접속사 자리이다. 전치사인 (B), (C)는 탈락하고, (D)는 존재하지 않는 말이다. wh로 시작하는 단어들은 주로 접속사이다.

표현 정리 annual 연간의, 매년의 conference 회의 hold 열다, 잡다 head office 본사 as scheduled 예정대로 regional manager 지사장 be able to ~할 수 있다 attend 참석하다 whether or not 어떻든지 in favor of ~를 찬성하여, 지지하여 regardless of ~와 상관없이, ~에도 불구하고 despite ~에도 불구하고

4. 정답 (D)

해석 당신의 몸을 정기적으로 검진하는 것이 / 강력히 추천된다 / 건전한 신체 없이 / 당신은 건전한 정신을 가질 수 없기 때문에

해설 문장 안에 동사가 is, can't have 2개 왔으므로 빈칸은 (D) 접속사 자리이다. 전치사인 (A), (B)와 부사와 형용사인 (C)는 탈락한다.

표현 정리 regularly 정기적으로, 규칙적으로 highly 매우, 높이 recommend 추천하다, 권하다 without ~없이 sound 튼튼한, 건전한 mind 정신, 마음 out of ~없는, ~중에 prior to ~에 앞서, ~보다 전에 even 평평해지다; 같은 because ~때문에, 왜냐하면

5. 정답 (A)

해석 Mr. Baek은 맡을 것이다 / 새로운 직책을 / 그 직책에서 / 그는 담당할 것이다 / 모든 인턴들의 관리를 / 지난 달에 고용된

해설 문장 안에 동사가 will assume, will be, were hired 3개 왔으므로 접속사가 2개 필요하다. who가 이미 있으므로 빈칸에는 접속사인 (A)가 와야 한다. 부사인 (B), 전치사인 (C)와 (D)는 탈락한다.

표현 정리 assume 생각하다, 맡다 be in charge of ~의 책임을 맡다

28

supervise 감독하다, 관리하다 hire 고용하다 last month 지난 달 in case of ~의 경우에는, ~한 때에는 along with ~와 함께, 더불어

6. 정답 (A)

해석 결정되지 않았다 / 지역 사회의 모임이 / 열릴 것인지 / 실내에서 / 커뮤니티 센터 / 또는 외부 GW 공원에서

해설 문장 안에 동사가 hasn't been decided, will take place 2개 왔으므로 빈칸은 (A) 접속사 자리이다. 전치사인 (B)와 형용사, 전치사, 부사의 기능을 하는 (C), 그리고 대명사와 부사의 기능을 하는 (D)는 탈락한다. or를 보고 either를 답으로 고르지 않도록 한다. 상관접속사 either A or B에서 접속사는 or이다.

표현 정리 decide 결정하다 community gathering 지역 사회 모임 take place 열리다, 개최되다 indoors 실내에서 community center 문화 회관, 시민 회관 outdoors 외부에서 whether ~인지 아닌지 near 근처, 가깝게, 인접한 either 또한, 어느 쪽

7. 정답 (A)

해석 이번 분기에 / 회사 수익은 초과했다 / 회사 목표를 / 그러나 순이익은 여전히 낮았다 / 목표보다 / 제조비용 증가 때문에

해설 문장 안에 동사가 surpassed, were 2개 왔으므로 빈칸은 (A) 접속사 자리이다. (B)는 형용사, 명사, 부사, 전치사, (C)와 (D)는 부사이다.

표현 정리 quarter 분기 revenue 매출, 수익 surpass 넘어서다, 초과하다 goal 목표, 목적 net profit 순이익 still 여전히, 아직도 below 아래에, ~이하의 due to ~때문에 increase 상승, 증가 manufacturing costs 제작비, 제조 원가 past 지난 as always 늘 그렇듯 otherwise 그렇지 않으면

8. 정답 (A)

해석 추가 변화가 없다면 / 원자재 가격에 / 우리는 인상하지 않을 것이다 / 가격을 / 우리 모든 제품의

해설 문장 안에 동사가 are, will not increase 2개 왔으므로 빈칸은 (A) 접속사 자리이다. assuming은 '~라면'의 뜻으로 that이 생략된 접속사이다. (B)도 that이 생략되어 접속사 역할을 할 수 있으나 문두에 오지 않고, '추가 변화가 없다는 것을 제외하고 ~'라는 해석도 어색하다. (C)와 (D)는 부사이다

표현 정리 further change 추가 변경 raw material 원료, 원자재 increase 인상하다 assuming (that) ~라고 가정하면 except ~을 제외하고 nevertheless 그럼에도 불구하고 otherwise 그렇지 않으면

9. 정답 (C)

해석 당신은 직접 비행기로 갈 수 있을 것이다 / 이스라엘로 / Vanilla Airlines가 제공하기 시작하면 / 고객들에게 / 직항편을

해설 문장 안에 동사가 will be able to, starts providing 2개 왔으므로 빈칸은 (C) 접속사 자리이다. 부사인 (A), 전치사 부사인 (B)는 탈락한다. 그리고 (D)는 형용사, 명사, 전치사, 부사의 역할을 하지만 접속사의 기능이 없다.

표현 정리 be able to+동사원형 ~할 수 있다 directly 직접, 바로 fly to ~까지 비행기로 가다 provide 제공하다 customer 손님, 고객

nonstop flight 직행 비행기

10. 정답 (A)

해석 당신이 갱신할 경우 / 당신의 구독을 / 이메일을 받은 후 일주일 내에 / 당신은 여전히 받을 자격이 있다 / 우리 잡지 한 권을 / 무료로

해설 문장 안에 동사가 renew, are entitled to 2개 왔으므로 빈칸은 (A) 접속사 자리이다. (B), (C), (D)는 모두 전치사이다.

표현 정리 renew one's subscription to+명사 ~의 구독을 갱신하다 within a week 일주일 안에 receive 받다, 수상하다 be entitled to ~할 자격이 있다 at no cost 무료로 as long as ~하는 한, ~이기만 하면 in spite of ~에도 불구하고 following 다음의, ~후에

법칙 19 부정대명사는 동사 개수, 명사 자리, 단수, 복수 확인

◎ 유형을 파악해 봐
1. (A)   2. (D)   3. (A)

1. 정답 (A)

해석 교육 세미나에 참석한 모든 참가자들은 / 예약하도록 권고 받는다 / 호텔 객실을 / 그들이 도착하기 훨씬 전에 / 다음 달

해설 문장에 정동사가 1개뿐이므로 접속사인 (D)는 탈락하고, 빈칸 뒤에 명사가 있으므로 이를 수식할 수 있는 형용사 자리이다. 따라서 복수 명사와 함께 쓰일 수 있는 (A)가 정답이다. (B)와 (C)는 단수 명사와 쓰인다.

표현 정리 attendee 참석자 be advised to+동사원형 ~하도록 권고 받다 reserve 예약하다, 보유하다 well in advance 훨씬 미리 arrival 도착 next month 다음 달 all 모든, 모두 each 각, 각자 every 모든, 모두 whichever 어느 ~이든지

2. 정답 (D)

해석 모든 문의들은 / 환불 정책에 관한 / 보내져야 한다 / 서비스부로

해설 문장에 정동사가 1개뿐이므로 접속사인 (A)는 탈락하고, 빈칸 뒤에 명사가 있으므로 이를 수식하는 (D) 형용사 자리이다. (B)는 명사이고, (C)는 단수 명사와 쓰인다.

표현 정리 inquiry 조사, 문의 regarding ~에 대해, ~와 관련하여 return policy 환불 정책 be directed to ~로 보내지다 whoever 누구나 anything 무엇이든, 아무것도, 어느 것이든

3. 정답 (A)

해석 이 지역의 많은 통근자들은 이용한다 / 회사 셔틀 버스를 / 다른 형태의 교통수단 대신 / 비싼 연료비 때문에 / 요즘

해설 빈칸 뒤에 명사가 있으므로 형용사 자리이며, 복수 명사나 불가산명사와 쓰이는 (A)가 정답이다. (B)는 단수 명사 앞에, (C)와 (D)는 경사이므로 명사 앞에 또 올 수 없다.

표현 정리 commuter 통근자 instead of ~대신에 form 형태 transportation 교통 because of ~때문에 these days 오늘날, 요즘 other 다른, 그 밖의 another 또 하나의, 다른

◎ 실전에 적용해 봐

1. (B) 2. (D) 3. (D) 4. (B) 5. (A) 6. (B) 7. (D)
8. (A) 9. (C) 10. (C)

1. 정답 (B)

해설 런던 바게트 베이커리인 CAB Group은 / 전국에 있는 / 가맹점 수를 늘렸다

해설 빈칸 뒤 명사가 있으므로 형용사 자리이다. 단수 명사가 왔으므로 단수와 어울리는 (B)가 정답이다. (A)와 (D)는 복수 명사와 쓰이고, (C)는 정관사 the와 함께 쓰인다.

표현 정리 increase 증가시키다 the number of ~의 수 region 지역, 지방 country 나라, 국가, 지역 all 모든, 모두 every 전, 모든 second 두 번째의, 다음으로 several 여러 가지의, 몇몇의

2. 정답 (D)

해설 소비자 조사에 따르면 / 최근 출시된 두 제품 모두 호응받지 못했다 / 젊은 소비자들에게

해설 빈칸은 주어 자리이며, 주어가 될 수 있는 (D) 대명사가 정답이다. (A)가 접속사일 경우는 뒤에 형용사나 부사가 바로 따라온다. (B)는 명사지만 주어 자리에 쓰지 않고, (C)는 접속사인 where가 포함되어 탈락한다.

표현 정리 according to ~에 따르면, ~에 의하면 customer survey 소비자 조사 product 제품, 상품 release 발표하다, 출시하다 recently 최근에 attract 유치하다, 끌다 young consumers 젊은 소비자들 however 그러나, 하지만 one another 서로, 상호 neither 어느 것도

3. 정답 (D)

해설 아무도 제출하지 않는다면 / 예산안을 / 이번 주 금요일까지 / 예산안 의결을 위한 회의는 미뤄져야 할 것이다 / 다음 주로

해설 빈칸은 주어 자리인데, 동사가 단수로 왔다. (D)는 단수 동사로 받을 수 있어 정답이다. (A)와 (B)는 복수 취급하고, (C)는 주어 자리에 쓰지 않는다.

표현 정리 complete 완료하다, 끝내다 budget proposal 예산안 by ~까지 budget meeting 예산 회의 reschedule 예정을 다시 세우다, 재조정하다 next week 다음 주 no one 아무도 ~않다

4. 정답 (B)

해설 워크숍 그룹 멤버들은 / 서로 도왔다 / 해결책을 찾기 위해 / 호스트가 제기한 질문에 대한

해설 help를 5형식 동사로 보면 빈칸은 목적어 자리이다. (A)와 (B)는 대명사 기능을 하는데, each는 one과 성격이 같다. 그룹 멤버들이 하나를 돕는 것이 아니라, 서로 돕는다고 해야 자연스럽다. 따라서 서로의 뜻을 갖는 (B)가 정답이다. (C)는 부사로 help를 3형식 동사로 보고 이어지는 to 부정사를 목적어로 보면 가능하지만 '한꺼번에'라는 뜻이 어색하고, (D)는 전치사이다.

표현 정리 solutions to+명사 ~에 대한 해결책 raise 제기하다, 일으키다 host 호스트, 주인 each 각 one another 서로 altogether 전적으로, 모두 함께 along 함께, ~을 따라

5. 정답 (A)

해설 대부분의 참가자들은 만족했다 / 감동적인 연설에 / 특별 연사에 의한

해설 빈칸은 주어 자리이다. of the 다음에 단수, 복수, 불가산명사 모두 가능한 (A)가 정답이다. (B)는 부사이고, (C)는 of the 뒤에 불가산명사가 와야 하고, (D)는 형용사로만 쓰인다.

표현 정리 most of 대부분의 be satisfied with ~에 만족하다 inspiring 감동시키는, 고무하는 featured speaker 특별 연사 almost 거의, 대부분 little 좀, 조금, 작은 other 다른, 나머지의

6. 정답 (B)

해설 Ms. Kim의 현 두 동료들은 보였다 / 가장 호의적인 평가를 / 그녀의 실적과 직업 윤리에 대해

해설 빈칸은 주어 자리인데, 전치사 구와 복수 명사의 수식을 받을 수 있는 (B)가 정답이다. 형용사인 (A)는 단수 명사가 와야 한다. (C)는 대명사로 전치사구의 수식을 받지 못한다. (D)는 지시대명사로 앞에 있는 명사를 받을 때 쓰인다.

표현 정리 current 현재의, 현행의 colleague 동료 express 표현하다, 발표하다 favorable 호의적인, 우호적인 views 평가, 견해 performance 실적 work ethic 직업 윤리, 근면 one other 서로, 상호 both 둘, 양쪽의 everybody 모든 사람들, 모두

7. 정답 (D)

해설 원하는 누구든지 / 자선행사에 시간을 내 자원봉사하기를 / 연락해야 한다 / Olga Maksymenko에게 / (044) 428-7010로

해설 빈칸은 주어 자리인데, 이어지는 형용사절에 단수 동사 wants가 왔으므로 단수 명사인 (D)가 정답이다. (A)는 복수 취급하고, (B)는 형용사, 그리고 동사가 2개(want, should contact), 접속사가 1개(who)이므로 빈칸에는 접속사가 올 수 없어 (C)는 탈락한다.

표현 정리 those who ~하는 사람들 volunteer one's time 자진해 시간을 내다 charity event 자선행사 contact 연락하다 anyone who 누구든

8. 정답 (A)

해설 학생들 중 일부는 / 낮에 컴퓨터 수업에 등록한 / 제안했다 / 이용 가능한 수업이 있어야 한다고 / 저녁 시간에도

해설 빈칸은 주어 자리인데, of의 복수 명사의 수식을 받으며 명사 역할을 하는 (A)가 정답이다. (B)와 (C)는 of the 다음에 불가산명사가 와야 하며, (D)는 형용사로만 쓰인다.

표현 정리 some of ~중 일부는 enroll in ~에 등록하다 the daytime 낮 suggest 제안하다 available 이용할 수 있는, 시간이 있는

9. 정답 (C)

해설 Jay's Lumberyard 직원들은 / 최근에 일했다 / 밤늦도록 / 그들이 파악해야 하기 때문에 / 모든 주문들을 / 성수기 동안에

해설 빈칸은 명사인 orders를 꾸며주는 형용사 자리인데, 복수 명사를 취하면서 형용사 기능을 하는 (C)가 정답이다. (A)가 오려면 of 다음에 the가 필요하다. 단수 명사를 취하는 (B)와 (D)도 탈락한다.

표현 정리 recently 최근에 late at night 밤늦게 because ~때문에 keep track of ~을 추적하다, ~의 흔적을 쫓다 peak season 성수기 some of ~중의 조금 all 모든, 모두 every 모든, 매

10. 정답 (C)

해설 일부 노력들은 / 그 노력들은 아무런 효과가 없었지만 / 완화시키기 위해 이루어졌다 / 혼잡한 교통 체증 / North Bridge의

해설 빈칸은 주어 자리이며, 전명구 수식을 받으며 복수 취급할 수 있는 (C)가 정답이다. which는 several efforts를 가리킨다. (B)는 부사이다.

표현 정리 effort 노력, 활동 relieve 완화시키다, 해소시키다 heavy traffic congestion 혼잡한 교통 체증 effective 효과적인, 효율적인 none 아무도 ~않다 nonetheless 그럼에도 불구하고

법칙 20 'a(an)+형용사' 뒤는 단수 명사, a(an)이 없으면 복수 명사

◎ 유형을 파악해 봐
1. (D) 2. (A) 3. (B)

1. 정답 (D)

해설 Vivigo 카페는 제공한다 / 할인을 / Samuel Industries 직원들에게

해설 빈칸은 타동사 뒤, 전명구 앞이므로 명사 자리인데 관사나 소유격이 없으므로 복수 명사인 (D)가 답이다. p.p.가 올 수 없는 자리이므로 (A)는 탈락하고, (B)는 단수 명사로 관사가 필요하며, (C)는 혼용사이므로 탈락한다.

표현 정리 offer B to A A에게 B를 제공하다 employee 직원 discounted 할인된 discount 할인 discountable 할인할 수 있는

2. 정답 (A)

해설 만약 설문지를 작성한다면 / 당신은 자동으로 참가하게 될 것이다 / 특별 콘테스트에 / 100달러 상품권을 획득하기 위한

해설 빈칸은 '전치사+관사+형용사' 뒤 명사 자리이다. 참가하게 될 것이다'라고 했으므로 콘테스트에 참가하는 것이 가장 잘 어울리므로 (A)가 정답이다. 관사 a가 있으므로 복수 명사인 (B)는 탈락하고, (D)는 경쟁자라는 의미가 어울리지 않는다.

표현 정리 fill out 작성하다, 기입하다 survey form 설문지 automatically 자동으로 win 얻다, 획득하다 gift certificate 상품권 contestant 경쟁자, 논쟁자

3. 정답 (B)

해설 비용을 줄이기 위해 / 판매원들은 일반적으로 선호한다 / 대중교통 이용을 / 장거리 여행 동안

해설 빈칸은 준동사인 to 부정사의 목적어 자리이므로 명사 자리이다. 따라서 관사나 소유격이 없으므로 복수 명사인 (B)가 정답이다. (A)는 단수 명사, (C)는 형용사, (D)는 부사이다.

표현 정리 reduce expense 비용을 줄이다 normally 일반적으로, 보통 prefer to ~을 선호하다 public transportation 대중 교통 expense 비용 expensive 비싼, 고가의 expensively 비싸게

◎ 실전에 적용해 봐
1. (B) 2. (B) 3. (B) 4. (A) 5. (C) 6. (A) 7. (C)
8. (A) 9. (B) 10. (A)

1. 정답 (B)

해설 재무 상담가는 권고했다 / 사무용품 관련 비용을 / 상당량 줄여야 한다고

해설 빈칸은 that절의 주어 자리이자 전명구 앞 명사 자리이다. 관사나 소유격이 없으므로 복수 명사인 (B)가 정답이다. (A)는 형용사, (C)는 단수 명사, (D)는 부사이므로 탈락한다.

표현 정리 financial consultant 재무 상담가 regarding ~에 관한 significantly 상당히 reduce 줄이다, 감소시키다 expensive 비싼 expense 비용 expensively 비싸게

2. 정답 (B)

해설 먹는 것과 마시는 것은 금지된다 / 박물관 내 전시장에서 / 어떠한 경우에도 / 그러나 이용할 수 있다 / 구내식당은 / 현관 옆에 있는

해설 빈칸은 '전치사+형용사' 뒤에 온 명사 자리이다. 'all+복수 명사/불가산명사'이므로 (B)가 정답이다. (A)는 형용사, (C)는 단수 명사이므로 탈락한다.

표현 정리 ban 금지하다 inside 내부, ~안에 main entrance 현관 circumstantial 상황의 circumstance 상황, 정황 circumstanced 처지에 있는 under all circumstances 어떠한 경우에도

3. 정답 (B)

해설 Dr. Kim의 퇴임식 참석률은 / 30년 간의 근무 끝에 / 거의 1,000명에 달했다 / 그는 동료뿐 아니라 많은 친구들, 그리고 지인들이 있어 / 의료업계에

해설 빈칸 앞에 등위접속사 and가 있어 병치구조를 이루고 있고, and 앞이 명사이므로 빈칸도 명사 자리이다. 관사나 소유격이 없고, and가 복수 명사를 연결해 주고 있으므로 복수 명사인 (B)가 정답이다. (A)는 단수 명사, (D)는 뒤에 목적어가 있어야 하므로 탈락한다.

표현 정리 attendance 참석(률), 출석 retirement ceremony 퇴임식 reach 이르다, 도달하다 nearly 거의 not only B but (also) A B뿐만 아니라 A도 acquaintance 아는 사람, 지인 acquainted 알고 있는, 사귀게 된

4. 정답 (A)

해설 토론한 끝에 / 우리의 혁신 프로젝트에 관한 / 건설 회사는 보냈다 / 견적서를 / 우리의 요구를 반영한

해설 빈칸은 관사 뒤, 준동사구 사이에 위치해 있으므로 명사 자리이다. 관사 an이 있으므로 단수 명사인 (A)가 정답이다. (B)는 복수 명사이므로 탈락한다.

표현 정리 following ~후에 discussion 토론, 논의 renovation 개혁, 수리 construction company 건설회사 reflect 반영하다 estimate 견적서, 견적 need 요구, 필요

5. 정답 (C)

해설 UAB 의료 시설은 찾고 있다 / 대체 에너지원을 / 연료비가 계속해 오를 것으로 예상되기 때문에 / 당분간

해설 빈칸은 '전치사+관사+형용사' 뒤, 전명구 앞에 있으므로 명사 자리인데, 관사 an이 있으므로 단수 명사인 (C)가 정답이다. (A)는 복수 명사이므로 탈락한다.

표현 정리 look for ~을 찾다 alternative 대안 source of energy 에너지원 be expected to ~로 예상되다 continuously 계속해서, 지속적으로

6. 정답 (A)

해설 우리 마케팅 부장은 계획이다 / 참가할 / 1주일 동안의 회의에 / 그는 만날 수 있다 / 다양한 광고 전문가들을 / 온라인 광고 전략 토론을 위한

해설 빈칸 앞에 관사나 소유격이 없으므로 빈칸에는 복수 명사인 (A)가 와야 한다. (B)와 (C)는 단수 명사, (D)는 동사이므로 탈락한다.

표현 정리 take part in ~에 참가하다 discuss 토론하다, 논의하다 professional 전문의, 프로의; 전문가 profession 직업, 직종, 직위 profess 공언하다, 명언하다

7. 정답 (C)

해설 목표 중 하나는 / 회사 전체의 재활용 운동의 / 홍보하기 위함이다 / 재활용의 중요성을 / 그것이 결국에는 / 사무용품 비용을 줄여준다는

해설 빈칸은 관사 뒤, 전명구 앞이므로 명사 자리이다. one of the 다음에는 복수 명사가 와야 하므로 (C)가 정답이다. (A)는 단수 명사이므로 탈락한다.

표현 정리 aim is to+동사원형 목표는 to 동사원형이다 company-wide 회사 전체의 initiative 주도적 계획, 솔선 운동 in turn 결국에는 reduce 줄여주다 expense 비용 office supplies 사무용품 aim 목표, 목적 aiming 겨냥, 조준

8. 정답 (A)

해설 도보로 5분 이내에 위치한 / 지하철로부터 / Lenoir Hotel은 제공한다 / 최고의 편의를 / 이 지역을 방문하는 관광객에게

해설 빈칸은 '전치사+관사+형용사' 뒤, 전명구 앞이므로 명사 자리인데, 앞에 관사가 있으므로 단수 명사인 (A)가 정답이다. (B)는 복수 명사, (D)는 불가산명사이므로 탈락한다.

표현 정리 locate ~에 위치하다 provide 제공하다 convenience 편리, 편의 walk 보행, 도보

9. 정답 (B)

해설 기록적인 높은 매출 증가와 함께 / 회사 주가 역시 이르렀다 / 최고 수준에 / 가동 5년 만에

해설 '전치사+관사+형용사' 뒤, 전명구 앞이므로 명사 자리이며, 앞에 관사가 있으므로 단수 명사인 (B)가 정답이다. (C)는 복수 명사이므로 탈락한다.

표현 정리 record 기록적인; ~을 기록하다 stock price 주가 increase 증가하다, 확대하다

10. 정답 (A)

해설 마케팅 발표는 / Mr. Lu가 진행한 / 엄청난 성공이었다 / 주로 지원 때문에 / 그래픽 부서의

해설 빈칸은 앞에 제시된 be 동사 was의 보어 자리이자, '관사+형용사' 뒤, 전명구 앞이므로 명사가 와야 한다. 앞에 관사가 있으므로 단수 명사인 (A)가 정답이다. (B)는 복수 명사라 탈락한다.

표현 정리 huge 거대한, 엄청난, 막대한 success 성공, 성과 succeeding 이어서 일어나는, 다음의

법칙 21 주격, 목적격 보어 자리에 오는 분사는 주로 p.p.

◎ 유형을 파악해 봐
1. (B) 2. (A) 3. (C)

1. 정답 (B)

해설 당신의 비행기가 이착륙하는 동안, 안전벨트를 꼭 착용해야 한다.

해설 빈칸은 be 동사 뒤 보어 자리이다. 목적어가 있으면 -ing, 목적어가 없으면 p.p.가 와야 하는데, 목적어가 없으므로 (B)가 정답이다.

표현 정리 while ~동안에 taking off 이륙 landing 착륙 seatbelt 안전 벨트 firmly 확고하게, 강하게, 꽉

2. 정답 (A)

해설 여객기 운항이 일시적으로 중단되었다 / 활주로의 보수 작업 때문에

해설 빈칸은 has been 동사 뒤 보어 자리이다. 목적어가 있으면 -ing, 목적어가 없으면 p.p.가 와야 하는데, 목적어가 없으므로 (A)가 정답이다. (B)와 (C)는 정동사이므로 탈락한다.

표현 정리 temporarily 일시적으로, 임시로 due to ~때문에 maintenance work 보수 작업 runway 활주로 suspend 중단하다, 정지하다

3. 정답 (C)

해설 책 또한 절판되었다 / 그리고 더 이상 주문할 수 없다 / 출판사로부터

해설 빈칸은 be 동사 뒤 보어 자리이다. 목적어가 있으면 -ing, 목적어가 없으면 p.p.가 와야 하는데, 목적어가 없으므로 (C)가 정답이다. (A)와 (B)는 동사와 명사 둘 다 되는데, 문장에 정동사가 1개 있으므로 동사는 탈락하고, 명사일 경우 주어와 동격이어야 하므로 탈락한다.

표현 정리 order 주문하다, 명령하다, 주문 ordering 배열, 순서

◎ 실전에 적용해 봐
1. (C) 2. (D) 3. (A) 4. (B) 5. (B) 6. (D) 7. (A)
8. (A) 9. (D) 10. (C)

1. 정답 (C)

해설 공장 규정에 따라 / 흡연은 허용되지 않는다 / 공장 주변 어디서든

해설 be 동사 뒤 보어 자리이다. 목적어가 있으면 -ing, 목적어가 없으면 p.p.가 와야 하는데, 목적어가 없으므로 (C)가 정답이다. (A)와 (B)는 동사

이므로 탈락한다.

표현 정리 in compliance with ~에 따라, ~을 준수하여 smoking 흡연 anywhere 어디든지 perimeter 주변, 경계 allow 허용하다

2. 정답 (D)

해석 회사의 수리 프로젝트 일환으로 / 새 건물 내부에 계단이 설치될 것이다 / 1층과 2층을 연결하기 위해 / 그리고 건물 스프링클러 시스템은 대체될 것이다

해설 be 동사 뒤 보어 자리이다. 목적어가 있으면 -ing, 목적어가 없으면 p.p.가 와야 하는데, 목적어가 없으므로 (D)가 정답이다. (A)는 정동사이고, 명사인 (B)는 주어와 동격이어야 하므로 탈락한다.

표현 정리 as part of ~의 일환으로 stairwell 계단통 (건물 내부에 계단이 나 있는 공간) connect 연결하다, 이어지다 install 설치하다, 장착하다

3. 정답 (A)

해석 인사 부장이 시간이 없다면 / 인터뷰를 진행할 / 일정이 겹쳐 / 인터뷰는 재조정될 것이다 / 나중에

해설 be 동사 뒤 보어 자리이다. 목적어가 있으면 -ing, 목적어가 없으면 p.p.가 와야 하는데, 목적어가 없으므로 (A)가 정답이다. (B)와 (C)는 동사이므로 탈락한다.

표현 정리 available 시간이 있는, 이용할 수 있는 due to ~때문에 scheduling conflict 일정의 겹침, 중복 later time 나중에, 추후에 reschedule 일정을 다시 세우다, 재조정하다

4. 정답 (B)

해석 이사회는 설명할 것이다 / 회사의 미래 전략에 대한 세부 사항들을 / 모든 주주들에게 / 향후 합병을 걱정하는

해설 be 동사 뒤 보어 자리이다. 목적어가 있으면 -ing, 목적어가 없으면 p.p.가 와야 하는데, 목적어가 없으므로 (B)가 정답이다. (C)와 (D)는 명사이므로 주어와 동격이어야 하며, 동사로 보면 이미 동사가 있어서 탈락한다.

표현 정리 the board of directors 이사회 explain 설명하다 detail 세부사항, 세부 정보 upcoming 다가오는 merger 합병 be concerned about ~을 우려(걱정)하다 concern 우려, 걱정, 관심

5. 정답 (B)

해석 이익의 증가는 / 이번 분기 / 결과를 가져올 것으로 기대된다 / 직원들이 / 보너스와 장려금을 받는 / 연말에

해설 be 동사 뒤 보어 자리이다. 목적어가 있으면 -ing, 목적어가 없으면 p.p.가 와야 하는데, 목적어가 없으므로 (B)가 정답이다. expect는 '결혼승낙' 동사로 목적격 보어에 to 동사원형이 온다('법칙 48' 참고). (A)는 주어와 등격이어야 하고, (D)는 '기대하는, 출산을 앞둔'이라는 의미이므로 탈락한다.

표현 정리 result in ~을 야기하다, ~의 결과를 낳다 incentive 격려, 장려금 at the end of the year 연말에 be expected to ~이 예상되다

6. 정답 (D)

해석 10주년 기념을 축하하기 위해 / Best Appliance 매장은 알리게 되어 기쁩니다 / 제공하게 되었음을 / 최고 50퍼센트까지의 할인을 / 모든 제품에 대해 / 매장 내

해설 be 동사 뒤 보어 자리이다. 목적어가 있으면 -ing, 목적어가 없으면 p.p.가 와야 하는데, 목적어가 없으므로 (D)가 정답이다. please는 to 부정사를 목적어가 아닌 목적 보어로 취하는 5형식 동사로, 그것의 수동타형은 'be pleased to 동사원형'이다. (B)는 동사이고, (C)는 주어와 동격이어야 하므로 탈락한다.

표현 정리 celebrate ~을 기념하다, 축하하다 up to ~까지 discount 할인 be pleased to ~하게 되어 기쁘다

7. 정답 (A)

해석 많은 사람들은 / 참가해 온 / 이른바 아이스 버킷 운동에 / 주된 역할을 했다 / 대중의 인식을 확산시키는데 / 루게릭 병에 대한 / 전 세계로

해설 have been 동사 뒤 보어 자리이다. participate는 자동사로 수동태가 존재하지 않으므로 (D)는 탈락하고, (A)가 정답이다. 목적어가 없다고 p.p.를 답으로 고르지 않도록 한다.

표현 정리 individual 개인; 개인의 so-called 소위, 이른바 instrumental 주된 역할을 하는 all over the world 전 세계로

8. 정답 (A)

해석 당신은 확신할 것이다 / 워크숍이 제공한다는 것을 / 훌륭한 기회를 / 당신의 직원들이 / 그들의 지식을 넓히는데

해설 be 동사 뒤 보어 자리이다. 목적어가 있으면 -ing, 목적어가 없으면 p.p.가 와야 한다. that 이하가 목적어이기는 하지만, 여기서 convince는 4형식 동사로 목적어가 있어도 p.p.가 오기 때문에 (A)가 정답이다. -ing를 쓰려면 사람 명사가 먼저 목적어로 오고, 이어 that 이하의 내용이 와야 한다.

표현 정리 excellent 훌륭한, 최고의 opportunity 기회 broaden 넓히다, 넓게 하다 convince 납득시키다, 확신시키다

9. 정답 (D)

해석 공장 근로자들은 금지된다 / 흡연이 / 지정된 흡연 지역 외에서는 / 그들의 휴식 시간 동안

해설 be 동사 뒤 보어 자리이다. 목적어가 있으면 -ing, 목적어가 없으면 p.p.가 와야 하는데, 목적어가 없으므로 (D)가 정답이다. (A)는 동사이고, (B)는 주어와 동격이어야 하므로 탈락한다.

표현 정리 factory workers 공장 노동자들 outside ~외에, 외부의 designated 지정된 break times 휴식 시간 be prohibited 금지되다

10. 정답 (C)

해석 휴가 요청은 / 성수기 동안의 / 승인돼야 한다 / 각 부서장에 의해 / 그리고 제출돼야 한다 / 인사 부장에게 / 생산성을 유지하기 위해

해설 be 동사 뒤 보어 자리이다. 목적어가 있으면 -ing, 목적어가 없으면 p.p.가 와야 하는데, 목적어가 없으므로 (C)가 정답이다. (B)는 동사이고 (D)는 주어와 동격이어야 하므로 탈락한다.

표현 정리 during ~동안 busy season 성수기 maintain ~을 유지하다, 지속하다 productivity 생산성, 생산력 approve ~을 승인하다, 찬성하다

법칙 22 이럴 땐 재귀대명사

◎ 유형을 파악해 봐
1. (C) 2. (D) 3. (C)

1. 정답 (C)

해설 그녀의 전임자와는 달리 / 새 비서 Ms. Park는 다루는 것을 좋아한다 / 약속 일정을 / 그녀 스스로

해설 주어, 동사, 목적어, 모두 갖춘 완전한 문장이며, 따라서 완전한 문장에 영향을 미치지 않는 부사 자리이다. 강조 용법으로 쓰인 재귀대명사 (C)가 정답이다.

표현 정리 unlike ~와는 달리 predecessor 전임자 handle 다루다, 처리하다 appointment 약속, 임명

2. 정답 (D)

해설 신규 채용자들은 익숙해질 것을 권고 받는다 / 그들 자신이 / 직원 안내책자에 / 지출보고서를 제출하는 방법이 자세히 적힌

해설 빈칸은 familiarize의 목적어 자리이므로 주격인 (A)와 소유격인 (B)는 탈락한다. '그들 자신이 안내책자에 익숙해지는 것'이므로 (D)가 정답이다. familiarize oneself with 유형의 재귀용법으로 '~를 ~에 익숙하게 하다'라는 의미가 된다. (C)는 소유대명사로 '그들의 것'이라는 뜻인데, 무엇을 가리키는지 알 수 없다.

표현 정리 new hire 신규 채용자 be advised to+동사원형 ~하도록 권고 받다

3. 정답 (C)

해설 예산 보고서를 제출하기 위해 / 정시에 / Shawn은 수집했다 / 모든 데이터를 / 보고서에 필요한 / 혼자

해설 전치사 by의 목적어 자리이다. '데이터를 수집하는 것은 Shawn이 스스로 하는 것'이므로 (C)가 정답이다. by oneself는 on one's own과 같은 뜻이다.

표현 정리 budget report 예산 보고서 on time 정각에 collect 수집하다, 모으다 necessary 필수적인, 필요한 by himself 혼자서, 스스로

◎ 실전에 적용해 봐
1. (C) 2. (B) 3. (A) 4. (D) 5. (D) 6. (C) 7. (C)
8. (B) 9. (B) 10. (D)

1. 정답 (C)

해설 승객들은 소지해야 한다 / 그들의 소지품들을 / 그들이 / 또는 보관해야 한다 / 그것들을 / 안전한 장소에

해설 빈칸은 전치사 with의 목적어 자리로, 주격인 (A)와 소유격인 (D)는 탈락한다. (B)와 (C)중 동작(carry)의 주체는 passengers이고, 대상은 belongings이다. 밑줄이 belongings자리에 있는 것이 아니므로 동작의 주체와 대상이 같은 경우가 아니다. 따라서 이 문장에서 밑줄에 재귀대명사가 들어올 수 없다. passengers를 가리켜야 하므로 일반 대명사를 쓴다. 따라서 (C)가 답이다.

표현 정리 passenger 승객 carry 소지하다, 옮기다 belongings 소지품 secure 확보하다, 보장하다

2. 정답 (B)

해설 비록 공장장이 전화했지만 / 아파서 결근한다고 / Nagoya 공장 근로자들은 / 그들 스스로 / 성공적으로 마쳤다 / 그들의 업무를 / 그 없이

해설 빈칸은 주어 뒤, 동사 앞에서 주어를 강조해 주고 있다. 재귀대명사의 강조 용법으로 the workers를 강조해 주는 (B)가 정답이다. 소유격인 (A)나 주격인 (C), 소유대명사인 (D)는 탈락한다.

표현 정리 although 비록 ~지만 call in sick 아파서 결근한다고 전화하다 successfully 성공적으로 without ~없이 themselves 그들 스스로

3. 정답 (A)

해설 회사들은 이용한다 / 전문 광고 대행사를 / 비용이 덜 들고, 더 나은 성과를 내기 때문에 / 스스로 광고하는 것보다

해설 빈칸은 by의 목적어 자리로 (A)가 by와 함께 쓰이면 '그들 스스로'라는 뜻이 되고, 사용하는 주체와 대상이 같아져 자연스럽게 어울린다. 소유격인 (B)와 주격인 (C)는 탈락하고, (D)를 답으로 하면 them은 companies가 아닌 다른 것을 가리켜야 하는데 의미가 자연스럽지 않게 된다.

표현 정리 professional advertising agency 전문 광고 대행사 by themselves 자기들 스스로

4. 정답 (D)

해설 과학 교수로 종사해 온 / 6년 동안 / Dr. Jang은 주었다 / 스스로에게 / 휴식을 / 그의 대가족과 함께 하기 위해 / 그의 고향에서

해설 빈칸은 give의 간접목적어 자리이므로 소유격인 (B)는 탈락하고, 주절에 동사가 1개 있으므로 접속사 (A)도 역시 탈락한다. (C)는 Dr. Jang이 아닌 다른 사람을 받을 때 쓰므로 탈락한다. 주체와 대상이 동격이 되므로 재귀대명사 (D)가 정답이다.

표현 정리 serve as ~로 일하다, ~의 역할을 하다 professor 교수 extended family 대가족 hometown 고향

5. 정답 (D)

해설 새로 임명된 모든 매니저는 초대 받는다 / 받을 것 / 리더십 강의를 / 스스로를 익숙해지게 하기 위해 / 팀을 효과적으로 이끄는 방법에

해설 빈칸은 familiarize의 목적어 자리이다. (A)와 (C)는 문장 안에 you 또는 we라고 지칭할 수 있는 명사가 없으므로 탈락하고, (B)는 사물을 받는 명사이므로 역시 답이 될 수 없다. (D)는 주체와 대상이 동격이 되고, '그들 자신을(managers) 팀을 효과적으로 이끄는 방법에 익숙해지게 하다'라는 자연스러운 의미가 되므로 정답이다.

표현 정리 appointed 임명된, 지정된 be invited to+동사원형 ~하도록 초대받다 complete 완료하다, 마치다 familiarize oneself with ~를 ~에 익숙해지게 하다 leading 이끄는, 선도적인 efficiently

효율적으로

6. 정답 (C)

해설 Mr. Gu는 동의했다 / 진행하기로 / 보수 작업을 / 자신이 / 그런데 프로젝트는 예상된다 / 완성될 것으로 / 5월 말까지

해설 빈칸 앞은 '주어+동사+목적어'로 완전한 문장이 됐다. 따라서 빈칸은 문장 성분에 영향을 미치지 않는 부사 자리이다. 재귀대명사는 강조 용법으로 쓰일 때 부사 역할을 하므로 (C)가 정답이다.

표현 정리 agree to ~에 동의하다 renovation 수리, 보수 be expected to ~이 예상되다

7. 정답 (C)

해설 비정규직과 정규직 직원 모두 요구된다 / 참석하도록 / 정보 회의에 / 공장 안전 규정에 관한 / 그들 자신

해설 빈칸 앞에 '주어+동사+목적어'로 완전한 문장이 있으므로 빈칸은 문장 성분에 영향을 미치지 않는 부사 자리이다. 재귀대명사는 강조 용법으로 쓰일 때 부사 역할을 한다. (A)와 (C) 모두 재귀대명사지만, 문장의 주어가 복수이기 때문에 they로 받아야 한다. 따라서 (C)가 정답이다.

표현 정리 both A and B A, B 둘 다 be required to+동사원형 ~하도록 요구되다 attend 참석하다 safety regulations 안전 규정

8. 정답 (B)

해설 근무한지 10년 후 / 홍보 분야에 / Mr. Yamada는 마침내 설립했다 / 광고 회사를 / 스스로

해설 빈칸은 전치사 on 뒤의 목적어 자리이다. on one's own은 '스스로' 라는 뜻이므로 (B)가 정답이다. (A)는 by나 for와 함께 쓰일 때 '그 스스로' 라는 뜻이 있으나 on oneself라는 말은 없으므로 답이 될 수 없다.

표현 정리 public relation 홍보 finally 마침내 found 설립하다 on one's own 혼자 힘으로, 자기 스스로

9. 정답 (B)

해설 소프트웨어는 고안되었다 / 충분히 쉽게 사용할 수 있도록 / 때문에 일반 사용자들조차 설치할 수 있다 / 그것을 / 그들 스스로

해설 빈칸은 by의 목적어 자리이므로 목적격이 와야 한다. (B)는 by와 함께 쓰일 때 '스스로'라는 의미가 되므로 정답이다. 소유대명사인 (A), on과 함께 쓰여 '스스로'라는 뜻이 되는 (D)는 탈락한다. (C)가 오면 home users가 아닌 다른 복수 명사를 가리켜야 한다.

표현 정리 be designed to ~하도록 고안되다 easily 쉽게 enough 충분히 install 설치하다 by themselves 그들 스스로

10. 정답 (D)

해설 가장 좋은 방법 중 / 근로자들이 / 재충전하기 위한 / 그들 자신들을 / 휴식을 갖는 것이다 / 정기적으로 / 오랜 시간 작업 후에

해설 빈칸은 refresh의 목적어 자리이므로 주격인 (A)는 탈락한다. 의미상의 주어인 workers와 대상이 동격이 되므로 재귀대명사 (D)가 정답이다. (B)는 workers를 제외한 다른 복수 명사를 받기 때문에 답이 될 수 없고, (C)는 '그들의 것'이라는 뜻으로 사물을 지칭하는 명사가 앞에 명시되어야 한다.

표현 정리 among ~중에, ~사이에 refresh 재충전하다 on a regular basis 정기적으로

법칙 23 명사를 앞에서 수식해 주는 분사는 주로 p.p.

◎ 유형을 파악해 봐
1. (B) 2. (C) 3. (C)

1. 정답 (B)

해설 제한된 수의 티켓 때문에 / 뮤직 어워드 시상식을 위한 / 참가를 원하는 사람들은 예약해야 한다 / 사전에

해설 빈칸은 관사 뒤, 명사 앞으로 형용사 자리이다. p.p.를 먼저 대입해 해석하면 '제한된 수의 티켓 ~'이라는 자연스러운 의미가 되므로 (B)가 정답이다. (A)는 '숫자를 제한하는 티켓'이라는 어색한 해석이 되고, (C)는 동사, (D)는 명사이다.

표현 정리 a limited number of 제한된 수의 those who ~하는 사람들 make a reservation 예약하다 in advance 미리, 사전에 limiting 제한하는, 제한적인 limited 제한된, 한정된 limit 제한 limitation 한계, 제약

2. 정답 (C)

해설 디자인 팀은 회의를 할 것이다 / 후속 조치를 취하기 위해 / 제안된 디자인의 / 부장과 함께 한 토론 후에

해설 빈칸은 관사 뒤, 명사 앞이므로 형용사 자리이다. p.p.를 먼저 대입해 해석하면 '제안된 디자인'이라는 자연스러운 해석이 되므로 (C)가 정답이다. (D)가 오게 되면 design이 주체가 되어 무언가를 제안한다는 어색한 의미가 된다. (A)는 명사, (B)는 동사이다.

표현 정리 have a meeting 회의를 하다 follow up on ~에 대한 후속조치를 취하다 discussion 논의, 토론 proposed 제안된

3. 정답 (C)

해설 회사 야유회는 / 6월 3일로 예정된 / 취소되었다 / 예상치 못한 날씨 때문에

해설 빈칸은 관사 뒤, 명사 앞으로 형용사 자리이다. (C)만 사용 가능한 단어이다.

표현 정리 outing 야유회 because of ~때문에 weather conditions 기상 사태 unexpected 예상치 못한

◎ 실전에 적용해 봐
1. (C) 2. (C) 3. (A) 4. (B) 5. (B) 6. (C) 7. (E)
8. (D) 9. (A) 10. (B)

1. 정답 (C)

해설 회계부는 / 현재 / 2층에 위치한 / 이동할 것이다 / 새롭게 수리된 3층으로 / 직원 수가 증가해

해설 빈칸은 관사와 부사 뒤, 그리고 명사 앞으로 형용사 자리이다. 자주 출제되는 p.p.를 대입해 해석해 보면, '새롭게 수리된 3층'이라는 자연스러

운 문맥이 되므로 (C)가 정답이다. (B)가 오면 3층이 주체가 되어 무엇인가를 보수한다는 내용이 된다. 명사인 (A)와 동사인 (D)는 탈락한다.

표현 정리 newly 새롭게 due to ~때문에 the number of ~의 수 renovated 보수된, 개조된 renovation 혁신, 수리 renovate 보수하다, 개조하다

2. 정답 (C)

해석 줄이기 위해 / 제조 비용을 / 최근 증가하는 연료비 때문에 / Ogata Industries는 / 정착한 회사인 / 실시했다 / 회사 전체의 에너지 절약 운동을

해설 빈칸은 관사 뒤, 명사 앞으로 형용사 자리이다. established는 형용사로 '인정받은, 확실히 자리 잡은'이라는 뜻이 있어 firm이라는 명사와 잘 어울린다. 따라서 (C)가 정답이다. (B)는 '설립하는 회사'라고 해석되어 어색하고, 명사인 (A)와 동사인 (D)는 탈락한다.

표현 정리 in order to+동사원형 ~하기 위해 recent 최근, 최신 company-wide 회사 전체의 energy conservation 에너지 절약 establishment 설립, 설치 established 인정받는, 자리를 잡은 establish 설립하다, 확립하다

3. 정답 (A)

해석 만약 당신이 지출한다면 / 100달러 이상을 / Jane's Home Appliances에서 / 우리는 제공할 수 있다 / 당신에게 / 최신 믹서기를 / 할인된 가격에

해설 빈칸은 관사 뒤, 명사 앞이므로 형용사 자리이다. p.p.를 먼저 대입해 해석해 보면, '할인된 가격'이라는 자연스러운 해석이 되므로 (A)가 정답이다. (C)가 오면 가격이 주체가 되어 무엇인가를 줄이고 있다는 말이 되어 어색하고, 동사인 (B)와 명사인 (D)는 탈락한다.

표현 정리 newest 최신의 blender 믹서기 reduced 할인된, 감소된 reduce 줄이다, 감소시키다 reduction 감소

4. 정답 (B)

해석 우리는 예상하기 때문에 / 엄청난 참가자 수를 / 다음 미팅에서 / 우리는 예약을 필요로 한다 / 넓은 장소를 / 그에 대비한

해설 빈칸은 관사 뒤, 명사 앞으로 형용사 자리이다. overwhelm은 감정동사로 사람을 수식하면 p.p., 사물을 수식하면 -ing 형태를 쓴다. 숫자는 사물이므로 -ing (B)가 정답이다. 부사인 (C)와 동사인 (D)는 탈락한다.

표현 정리 the number of ~의 수 reserve 예약하다 spacious 넓은, 널찍한 venue 장소 overwhelming 압도적인, 굉장한 overwhelmingly 압도적으로, 대단히 overwhelm ~을 압도하다

5. 정답 (B)

해석 렌트하기를 원하는 사람들은 / 신형차를 / 강력하게 추천한다 / 보낼 것을 / 완성된 렌탈 양식을 / 30일 동안의 프로모션 기간 내에

해설 빈칸은 관사 뒤, 명사 앞으로 형용사 자리이다. p.p.를 먼저 대입해 해석해 보면, '완성된 렌탈 양식'이라는 자연스러운 문맥이 되므로 (B)가 정답이다. (D)는 임대 양식이 주체가 되어 무엇인가를 완성한다는 말이 되어 어색하다. 부사인 (A)와 명사인 (C)는 탈락한다.

표현 정리 those who 사람들 brand-new 완전 새로운 strongly 강력히 completely 완전히, 전적으로 completed 작성한, 작성된 completion 완공, 완성

6. 정답 (C)

해석 Prime Jack은 시의 선도적인 디자인 회사가 되었다 / 의류 업계에서 / 그것이 설립된 이래 / 10년 전

해설 빈칸은 관사와 소유격 뒤, 명사 앞으로 형용사 자리이다. leading은 '선도하는'의 뜻으로 -ing 형태만 가능한 단어이다. 따라서 (C)가 정답이다.

표현 정리 clothing industry 의류 업계 found ~을 설립하다 decade 10년 lead 이끌다, 선도하다 leading 선도적인, 주요한, 이끄는

7. 정답 (B)

해석 첨부되었다 / 지원자들의 목록이 / 전문화된 글쓰기 실력을 갖춘 / 통과한 / 첫 단계를

해설 빈칸은 관사 뒤 명사 앞으로 형용사 자리이다. 일단 p.p. 형태를 대입해 해석해 보면, '전문화된 기술'이라는 자연스러운 문맥이 되므로 (B)가 정답이다. (A)는 기술이 주체가 되어 무엇인가를 전문화시킨다는 말이 되어 어색하고, 동사인 (C)와 명사인 (D)는 탈락한다.

표현 정리 attach 부착하다, 첨부하다 candidate 지원자, 후보자 specialized 전문의, 전문화된 specialize 전문화하다, 특수화하다 specialization 전문화, 특수화

8. 정답 (D)

해석 그의 어린 나이를 고려할 때 / Allen Jue는 이미 널리 인정받은 건축가이다 / 리조트 건설 분야에서

해설 빈칸은 관사와 부사 뒤, 명사 앞의 형용사 자리이다. p.p.를 먼저 대입해 해석해 보면, '인정받은 건축가'라는 자연스러운 의미가 되므로 (D)가 정답이다. (C)는 건축가가 주체가 되어 무엇인가를 인정할 때 사용하는 말이다. to 부정사인 (A)와 과거동사인 (B)는 탈락한다.

표현 정리 take into account 고려하다 widely 널리, 광범위하게 architect 건축가 recognize 알아보다, 인정하다

9. 정답 (A)

해석 열띤 토론 후에 / 연구원들은 / Havors Laboratory / 마침내 도달했다 / 만족스러운 결론에 / 재생 가능 에너지에 대한

해설 빈칸은 관사 뒤, 명사 앞으로 형용사 자리이다. satisfy는 감정동사로 사람에게는 p.p.를 쓰고, 사물에는 -ing를 쓴다. '결론'은 사물이므로 (A)가 정답이다. 명사인 (B)와 부사인 (D)는 탈락한다.

표현 정리 heated discussion 격론, 열띤 토론 researcher 연구원 come to a conclusion 결론에 도달하다 renewable energy 재생 가능 에너지 satisfying 만족시키는 satisfaction 만족, 충족 satisfied 만족한, 납득한

10. 정답 (B)

해석 Artee Publishing은 평가했다 / 제주도를 / 특별한 목적지 중 하나로 / 여행 잡지에

해설 빈칸은 관사 뒤, 명사 앞으로 형용사 자리이다. 일단 p.p.를 먼저 대입해 해석해 보면 '특별한 목적지'라는 자연스러운 문맥이 되므로 (B)가 정

답이다. (C)는 목적지가 주체가 되어 무엇인가를 특집으로 다룰 때 사용하는 말이다. 명사인 (A)와 준동사인 (D)는 탈락한다.

표현 정리 rate 평가하다, 등급을 매기다 destination 목적지, 목표 features 특징, 용모 featured 특색으로 한, 특종의 feature 특징을 이루다, 특징으로 삼다

법칙 24 전체 문맥을 알아야 풀리는 양보, 이유 전치사

◎ 유형을 파악해 봐
1. (C) 2. (D) 3. (D)

1. 정답 (C)

해석 공사 때문에 / 7번 가의 / 운전자들은 우회해야 한다 / 9번 가로

해설 전치사 어휘 문제로, 양보와 이유 전치사인 (A)와 (C)를 먼저 대입해 해석해 본다. '공사 때문에 우회해야 한다'라는 인과 관계가 자연스러우므로 (C)가 정답이다.

표현 정리 construction 건설, 공사 take a detour 돌아서 가다, 우회하다 in spite of ~에도 불구하고 since ~이후, ~때문에 because of ~때문에 besides ~이외에, ~에 더하여

2. 정답 (D)

해석 비가 오고 험한 날씨에도 불구하고 / 축구 협회는 발표했다 / FA Cup 결승전이 열릴 것이라고 / 일정대로

해설 전치사 어휘 문제로 양보 전치사인 (D)를 먼저 대입해 해석해 보면, '험한 날씨에도 불구하고 결승전은 열린다'라는 자연스러운 해석이 되므로 (D)가 정답이다. (A)는 복수 명사 앞에, (B)는 기간이나 범위 앞에 쓰이는 전치사이다.

표현 정리 rainy 비가 오는 stormy 폭풍의, 험악한 announce 발표하다, 알리다 final 결승전 take place 열리다, 발생하다 on schedule 예정대로, 일정대로 among ~중에, ~사이에 within ~이내에, ~안에 except ~을 제외하고 despite ~임에도 불구하고

3. 정답 (D)

해석 시간 제약에도 불구하고 / 마케팅 부장은 가까스로 마쳤다 / 그의 발표를 짧게, 그리고 명료하게

해설 빈칸은 전치사 어휘 문제로 양보 전치사가 있으므로 (D)부터 대입해 해석해 본다. '제약에도 불구하고 발표를 마쳤다'라는 자연스러운 의미를 이루므로 (D)가 정답이다. 나머지는 시점과 어울리는 전치사들이다.

표현 정리 constraint 제약 manage to+동사원형 가까스로 ~하다 finish 끝나다, 마치다 briefly 간단히 to the point 명료한, 간결한 prior to ~전에 until ~할 때까지, ~까지 despite ~에도 불구하고

◎ 실전에 적용해 봐
1. (D) 2. (A) 3. (B) 4. (C) 5. (A) 6. (C) 7. (D)
8. (D) 9. (C) 10. (B)

1. 정답 (D)

해석 Mr. Brown은 전화했다 / 매니저에게 / 요청하기 위해 / 그에게 / 회의를 연기하라고 / 30분 동안 / 교통 체증 때문에

해설 전치사 어휘 문제로 양보와 이유 접속사인 (A), (C), (D)를 먼저 대입해 본다. '교통 체증에도 불구하고 전화했다'는 해석은 어색하기 때문에 (A)는 탈락한다. '교통 체증 때문에 전화했다'는 자연스러운 문맥이 되므로 (C)가 정답이다. (C)는 '~덕택에'라는 뜻이다.

표현 정리 postpone ~을 연기하다, 지연시키다 half an hour 30분 traffic jam 교통 체증, 교통 정체 in spite of ~에도 불구하고 while ~동안에 thanks to ~덕분에 due to ~때문에, ~로 인해

2. 정답 (A)

해석 시간 부족에도 불구하고 / 수리는 / Riley 식당의 / 끝나야 한다 / 하루 전인 다음 주까지

해설 전치사 어휘 문제로 양보와 이유 전치사인 (A)와 (C)를 먼저 대입해 해석해 본다. '시간 부족에도 불구하고 수리는 끝나야 한다'라는 문맥이 자연스러우므로 (A)가 정답이다.

표현 정리 lack 부족 renovation 수리, 개조 despite ~에도 불구하고 in case of ~의 경우에는 because of ~때문에 unless ~하지 않는다면

3. 정답 (B)

해석 증가된 비용 때문에 / 파이프 제작을 위한 / GK 사는 제외할지도 모른다 / 파이프를 / 회사가 판매하는 제품 목록에서

해설 전치사 어휘 문제로 양보와 이유 전치사인 (B)와 (C)를 먼저 대입해 해석해 본다. '증가된 비용 때문에 파이프를 제외시킨다'는 문맥이 자연스러우므로 (B)가 정답이다.

표현 정리 manufacture 제조하다 exclude 제외하다, 중단하다 otherwise 그렇지 않으면 because of ~때문에 in spite of ~에도 불구하고

4. 정답 (C)

해석 TCP Tech는 결정할 수 있다 / 계약을 해지하기로 / ELP 사와의 / 증가한 계약금 때문에 / ELP 사가 요구한

해설 문장에 정동사가 2개(may decide, has demanded) 있다고 해서 접속사인 (D)를 고르지 않도록 한다. ELP ~ demanded 부분은 fee를 수식하는 형용사절이다. 빈칸은 전치사 자리인데, 이유 전치사인 (C)가 있으므로 먼저 대입해 해석해 보면 '증가한 계약금 때문에 계약을 해지한다'라는 문맥이 자연스러우므로 (C)가 정답이다.

표현 정리 decide to+동사원형 ~하기로 결정하다 terminate 끝내다, 해지하다 contract 계약, 계약서

5. 정답 (A)

해석 HM 파스타 & 피자는 가장 인기 있는 레스토랑이다 / 훌륭한 음식과 친절한 서비스로 / 경쟁하는 많은 식당들이 있음에도 불구하고 / 인근에

해설 전치사 어휘 문제로 보기에 양보 전치사인 (A)가 있으므로 먼저 대입해 해석해 본다. '경쟁업체들이 있음에도 불구하고 가장 인기 있다'는 문맥이 자연스러우므로 (A)가 정답이다.

표현 정리 popular 인기 있는 excellent 훌륭한, 뛰어난 friendly 친절한, 우호적인 a lot of 많은 compete 경쟁하다 dining 식사 nearby 근처의, 인근의

6. 정답 (C)

해설 Mr. Leckon의 노력 덕분에 / 제품의 안전한 배송을 보장하기 위한 / 고객 회사는 매우 만족해 했다 / 서비스에 / 그리고 요청했다 / 계약이 / 갱신되도록

해설 명사 앞 전치사 자리이므로 접속사인 (B)는 먼저 탈락한다. 이유 전치사인 (A), (C), (D) 중 (C)를 넣고 먼저 해석해 보면, '노력 덕분에 회사는 만족해 했다'는 말이 자연스러우므로 (C)가 정답이다.

표현 정리 effort 노력 ensure 보장하다, 확실하게 하다 shipment 배송 be satisfied with ~에 만족하다 contract 계약, 계약서 renew 갱신하다 regarding ~에 관해 thanks to ~덕분에

7. 정답 (D)

해설 유례 없는 높은 수요로 / Martin Auto는 노력하는 중이다 / 맞추기 위해 / 제품 마감일을 / KR5 세단에 대한 / 최근 증가에도 불구하고 / 생산 비용의

해설 전치사 어휘 문제로 양보 전치사인 (D)를 먼저 대입해 해석해 보면, '최근 생산비 증가에도 불구하고 노력한다'라는 자연스러운 문맥이 되므로 (D)가 정답이다.

표현 정리 demand 수요 strive to+동사원형 ~하려고 노력하다, 애쓰다 deadline 마감일 recent 최근 production costs 생산비 besides ~을 제외하고, 게다가 following 다음의, ~후에

8. 정답 (D)

해설 자선모금이 도달했다 / 거의 300,000달러에 / 그것은 같은 금액이다 / 작년에 모금한 금액과 / 경제침체에도 불구하고 / 올해

해설 전치사 어휘 문제로 양보 전치사인 (D)를 먼저 대입해 해석해 보면, '침체에도 불구하고 모금은 작년과 같다'는 자연스러운 문맥이 되므로 (D)가 정답이다.

표현 정리 reach 도달하다, 이르다 almost 거의, 약 raise 모으다 as well 또한 economic downturn 경제 침체

9. 정답 (C)

해설 Ryan 사는 제휴해 왔다 / Fab 사와 / 그리고 만족해 왔기 때문에 / 제공한 서비스에 / Fab 사가 / 이 회사는 기꺼이 받아들일 것이다 / 계약을 / 서비스 유형에 상관없이 / Fab 사가 제공하는

해설 전치사 어휘 문제로 양보 전치사인 (C)를 먼저 대입해 해석해 보면, '제휴해 왔고, 만족해 왔기 때문에, 서비스 유형에 상관없이 받아들일 것이다'라는 자연스러운 문맥이 되므로 (C)가 정답이다.

표현 정리 partner ~와 제휴하다 be satisfied with ~에 만족하다 be willing to+동사원형 기꺼이 ~하다 accept 받아들이다, 수용하다 deal 거래, 계약 apart from ~을 제외하고 regardless of ~에 상관없이

10. 정답 (B)

해설 Mr. Dennis는 구입했다 / 새 카메라를 / Leo Cam에서 / 근처에 있는 다른 매장이 아닌 / 세부적인 설명 때문에 / 회사 서비스 직원인 Ms. Morgan의

해설 빈칸은 전치사 어휘 문제. 보기에 이유의 전치사인 (B)가 있으므로 먼저 대입해 해석해 본다. '서비스 직원의 세부적인 설명 때문에 카메라를 구입했다'는 문맥이 자연스러우므로 (B)가 정답이다.

표현 정리 nearby 근처의 attention to detail 세부적인 것에 대한 관심 representative 직원, 대표자

법칙 25 단수 주어 뒤는 단수 동사, 복수 주어 뒤는 복수 동사

◎ 유형을 파악해 봐
1. (C) 2. (C) 3. (C)

1. 정답 (C)

해설 석유 파동 이후에도 / Wing Air는 여전히 예상한다 / 2백만 명이 넘는 고객들이 / 서비스를 이용할 것으로

해설 빈칸의 앞뒤를 살펴보면 Wing Air가 주어, still은 부사, that 이하가 목적어 역할을 하므로 빈칸은 동사 자리이다. Wing Air는 단수이므로 정답은 단수 동사인 (C)가 정답이다.

표현 정리 even after ~후에도 shock 충격, 타격 more than ~이상 customer 고객, 소비자 expect 예상하다, 기대하다 expectedly 예상대로

2. 정답 (C)

해설 기술직을 위한 지원은 / JP 사와 Black Tech 양사의 / 필요로 한다 / 지원자들의 첨부된 이력서를

해설 빈칸 앞에 전명구인 for the ~ Black Tech를 수식어로 처리해 제외시키면 주어인 The application만 남는다. 따라서 빈칸은 동사 자리이다. 주어가 단수이므로 단수 동사인 (C)가 정답이다.

표현 정리 application 지원, 신청 both A and B A, B 둘 다 applicant 지원자, 신청자 resume 이력서 requirement 필요, 자격 require 필요로 하다, 요구하다

3. 정답 (C)

해설 디너 쇼는 / BK 사가 주최할 / 오늘 저녁 / 특별히 포함한다 / 특별 손님을

해설 빈칸 앞 형용사절인 which ~ tonight을 수식어로 처리해 제외하면 주어인 The dinner show만 남는다. 주어가 단수이므로 단수 동사인 (C)가 정답이다.

표현 정리 host 개최하다, 주최하다 feature 출연하다, 특별히 포함하다

◎ 실전에 적용해 봐
1. (C) 2. (A) 3. (D) 4. (D) 5. (B) 6. (D) 7. (C)
8. (B) 9. (C) 10. (D)

1. 정답 (C)

해설 프린터는 / 1층에 있는 / 사용 중이었던 것으로 보인다 / 온종일

해설 빈칸 앞에 전명구인 on the first floor를 수식어 처리해 빼내면, 주어인 The printer가 남는다. 주어가 단수이므로 단수 동사인 (C)가 정답이다.

표현 정리 occupy 차지하다, 사용하다 whole day 종일 seem to be ~한 모양이다, ~으로 보이다

2. 정답 (A)

해설 직원들은 / 최근에 고용한 / HJ 사가 / 교육이 필요하다 / 매니저에 의한

해설 빈칸 앞 hired는 뒤에 목적어가 없으므로 동사가 아닌 분사이다. recently hired ~ Company를 주어를 수식하는 수식구로 처리해 제외하면, 주어인 The employees만 남는다. 주어가 복수이므로 복수 동사가 필요해 (A)가 정답이다.

표현 정리 hire 고용하다 instruct 지시하다, 교육하다

3. 정답 (D)

해설 Hanna Chen은 매우 엄격했다 / 그녀의 시간 관리에 / 그리고 절대 늦게 오지 않는다 / 회의에

해설 빈칸 앞 never는 부사이며, 그 앞의 and는 등위접속사인데, 주어가 같기 때문에 주어가 생략된 것으로 볼 수 있다. 주어가 단수이므로 단수 동사 (D)가 답이다.

표현 정리 strict 엄격한, 철저한 time management 시간 관리

4. 정답 (D)

해설 보증금은 / 공사를 위한 / 보내질 것이다 / JB 사로 / 다음 주까지 / 요청대로

해설 빈칸 앞에 온 전명구인 for the construction을 수식어로 처리해 빼내면, 주어인 The deposits만 남는다. 주어가 복수이므로 (D)가 정답이다.

표현 정리 deposit 보증금 construction 공사 as requested 요청대로

5. 정답 (B)

해설 직원들은 / 하루에 8시간 교대조로 근무하는 / 반납한다 / 키들을 / 직원실에 / 일요일마다

해설 빈칸 앞에 온 형용사절인 'who work ~ in the day'를 수식어 처리해 빼내면 The employees가 주어로 남는다. 복수 주어이므로 복수 동사인 (B)가 와야 한다. (A)는 동사가 아니며, (C)와 (D)는 단수 동사이다.

표현 정리 return 돌려주다, 반납하다 shift 교대조, 근무조 employee 직원

6. 정답 (D)

해설 당신은 받아야 한다 / 티켓을 / 직원 중 한 사람으로부터 / 무료 티켓을 제공하고 있는 / 이벤트의 / 바로 지금

해설 빈칸 앞에 who가 있으므로 주어를 수식해 주는 형용사절이다. 접속사 who의 주어는 선행사인 one of the staff members인데, one이 단수이므로 (D)가 정답이다. 선행사를 staff members로 보아 복수동사인 (A)를 답으로 하면 시제가 맞지 않는다. at the moment는 현재진행시제와 어울린다.

표현 정리 staff members 직원들 provide 제공하다, 공급하다

7. 정답 (C)

해설 CEO는 / King Motors의 / 받아들였다 / 합병 제안을 / Beckon Motors로부터의 / 검토한 후에 / 그 회사의 재정 상태를

해설 빈칸 앞의 전명구인 of King Motors를 수식어로 처리해 빼내면, 주어인 The CEO만 남는다. 주어가 단수이므로 단수 동사를 골라야 하는데, 보기에 단수 동사가 없으므로 수의 영향을 받지 않는 과거시제인 (C)를 골라야 한다. (A)는 복수 동사, (B)는 준동사, (D)는 명사이다.

표현 정리 merger 합병 offer 제안 accept 받아들이다, 수용하다

8. 정답 (B)

해설 Ms. White의 염려가 / 회사 수익에 대한 / 지난 분기 / 분명하게 언급되었다 / 이메일에 / 그녀가 보낸

해설 빈칸 앞 전명구인 about the company's profits와 부사인 last quarter를 수식어로 처리하여 빼내면 복수 주어인 Ms. White's concerns가 남는다. 따라서 복수 동사인 (B)와 수의 영향을 받지 않는 미래시제인 (D)가 정답이 될 수 있는데, 문제 안에 last quarter라는 과거 시점이 언급되었으므로 (B)가 정답이다.

표현 정리 concern 우려, 염려, 관심 profit 이익, 수익 clearly 분명하게, 명확히 state 분명히 말하다, 언급하다

9. 정답 (C)

해설 O 제품들은 최근에 매우 인기를 끌었다 / 젊은 소비자들 사이에서 / 그리고 곧 품절될 것이다

해설 빈칸 앞에 and가 있으므로 복수 주어인 These products가 생략된 형태이며, 빈칸은 동사 자리이다. 주어가 복수이므로 단수 동사 (B)와 준동사인 (A)와 (C)도 탈락한다. 따라서 수의 영향을 받지 않는 미래시제 (C)가 정답이다.

표현 정리 recently 최근에 out of stock 재고가 없는, 품절된

10. 정답 (C)

해설 Taint Motors는 약속했다 / 제공하기로 / 전액 보상과 / 무료 서비스를 / 모든 고객이 전액 상환받을 때까지

해설 빈칸은 부사절의 동사 자리로 주어가 every customer로 단수이므로 단수 동사 (D)가 정답이다.

표현 정리 promise 약속하다 compensation 보상 repay 갚다, 상환하다

법칙 26 문맥을 알아야 풀 수 있는 주제, 범위, 근거 전치사

◎ 유형을 파악해 봐
1. (C) 2. (A) 3. (A)

1. 정답 (C)

해설 회의는 다룰 것이다 / 문제를 / 은퇴 파티 계획에 관한

해설 문장 안에 동사가 address 1개 있으므로 빈칸은 접속사 자리가 될 수 없다. 따라서 접속사인 (A)와 (B)는 탈락한다. (C)와 (D) 중에서 해석이 자연스러운 것을 답으로 골라야 한다. '은퇴 파티 계획에 관련한 문제'가 자연스러우므로 (C)가 정답이다. (A)가 전치사가 될 수 있지만, 해석이 어색하다.

표현 정리 address 다루다, 처리하다 retirement party 은퇴 파티 after ~후에 whichever 어느 ~이든지 regarding ~에 관해 plus ~을 더하여, 게다가

2. 정답 (A)

해설 회사들은 받았다 / 승인을 / 허락하는 / 그들이 제조 공장을 짓는 것을 / 개발 지역 내에

해설 보기가 모두 전치사로 구성된 전치사 어휘 문제이므로 해석을 통해 가장 자연스러운 전치사를 답으로 고른다. (A)를 대입해 해석하면, '개발 지역 내에 공장을 짓는 것'이라는 자연스러운 문맥을 이루므로 정답이다.

표현 정리 receive 받다, 수상하다 approval 승인, 동의 manufacturing plant 제조 공장 boundary 경계, 영역 within ~안에, ~이내에 against ~에 반대하여 as to ~에 관하여 without ~없이

3. 정답 (A)

해설 연구에 따르면 / 수행된 / Richard Raymond에 의해 / 직원 5명 중 2명은 / 근무하는 / 공사현장에서 / 부상을 당하거나 사고를 목격했다

해설 문장 안에 동사가 has gotten or witnessed 하나이므로 빈칸에 접속사는 올 수 없다. conducted는 뒤에 목적어가 없으므로 과거동사가 아닌 과거분사이다. 따라서 접속사인 (C)와 (D) 역시 탈락된다. 근거 전치사인 (A)를 먼저 대입해 해석해 보면, '연구에 따르면 ~'이라는 자연스러운 문맥을 이루므로 (A)가 정답이다.

표현 정리 research 연구, 조사 conduct 실시하다, 수행하다 construction site 공사 현장 witness 보다, 증언하다 accident 사고 according to ~에 따르면 in case of ~의 경우에는 given that ~라면 when ~때

◎ 실전에 적용해 봐
1. (C) 2. (D) 3. (D) 4. (B) 5. (B) 6. (D) 7. (D)
8. (C) 9. (B) 10. (D)

1. 정답 (C)

해설 고객들은 가져와야 한다 / 물품을 / 그들이 환불을 원하는 / 영수증과 함께 / 가장 가까운 지점으로 / 그것들을 주문한지 2주 이내에 / 전액 환불을 받기 위해서

해설 전치사 어휘 문제지만, 보기들이 모두 기간과 함께 사용 가능하므로 해석으로 풀어야 하는 문제이다. '전액 환불을 받기 위해서는 영수증을 가지고 가장 가까운 지점으로 가야 한다'는 내용으로 '2주 이내에'라고 해야 자연스러워 (C)가 정답이다.

표현 정리 full refund 전액 환불 throughout ~내내, ~동안 within ~이내에, ~안에 during ~동안

2. 정답 (D)

해설 고객은 전화했다 / 회사에 / 멤버십 해지에 관해 묻기 위해

해설 전치사 어휘 문제로 주제 전치사인 (D)를 먼저 대입해 해석해 보면 '해지에 관해 묻기 위해 전화했다'라는 내용이 자연스러우므로 (D)가 정답이다.

표현 정리 cancellation 취소, 해지 membership 멤버십, 회원 along ~을 따라

3. 정답 (D)

해설 회사가 공식 발표할 때까지 / 직원 해고에 관해 / Mr. Williams는 불안할 것이다 / 그것에 대해

해설 전치사 어휘 문제로 주제 전치사인 (D)를 대입해 해석해 보면, '직원 해고에 관해 공식 발표할 때까지 ~'가 자연스럽다. 따라서 (D)가 정답이다.

표현 정리 until ~할 때까지 make an announcement ~을 발표하다 layoff 해고 within ~이내에 along with ~와 함께, 더불어 regardless of ~에도 불구하고 regarding ~에 대해, ~에 관하여

4. 정답 (B)

해설 회계부에 따르면 / 회사 부채의 60퍼센트는 / 상환되었다 / 그리고 매출이 점차 증가하고 있다

해설 빈칸 뒤에 명사가 왔고, 동사의 수는 1개뿐이므로 접속사인 (D)는 탈락한다. (A)는 부사로 명사를 이끌 수 없다. 근거 전치사인 (B)를 먼저 대입해 해석해 보면, '회계부에 따르면 ~'이라는 자연스러운 내용을 이루므로 (B)가 정답이다.

표현 정리 firm 회사, 기업 debt 부채, 빚 gradually 점차, 점진적으로 as a result 그 결과 according to ~에 따르면 in comparison to ~와 비교하여 providing that 만일 ~라면

5. 정답 (B)

해설 계약 조건은 / 인수 제안에 관한 / Wireless Tech에 의해 제시된 / 수정되었다 / Wireless Tech의 요구로

해설 전치사 어휘 문제로 제외 전치사 (A)를 대입해 해석해 보면, '인수 제안을 제외하고 계약 조건 ~'이라는 말은 어색하다. 또 이유나 양보 전치사인 (C)와 (D)를 대입해 해석해 보면, '인수 제안 때문에, 또는 인수 제안에도 불구하고 계약 조건 ~'이라는 말 역시 어색하다. 결국 (B)가 남는데, 인수 제안에 관한 계약 조건들이 수정되었다는 내용이 가장 자연스럽다. 따라서 (B)가 정답이다.

표현 정리 term 조건 acquisition 취득, 획득 propose 제안하다, 제의하다 revise 개정하다, 수정하다 aside from ~을 제외하고, ~이외에 pertaining to ~에 관한, ~와 관련된 due to ~때문에 in spite of ~에도 불구하고

6. 정답 (D)

해설 연구원들은 받아야 한다 / 적절한 교육을 / 적절한 방법에 대해 / 화학 물질들을 다루는 / 들어가기 전에 / 연구실에

해설 전치사 어휘 문제로 주제 전치사인 (D)를 먼저 대입해 해석해 보면, '적절한 방법에 대한 적절한 교육을 받아야 한다'는 문맥이 자연스러우므로 (D)가 정답이다. (A)도 주제 전치사지만 주로 '말다툼'이나 '논쟁' 등을 나타

내는 말과 함께 쓰인다.

표현 정리 researcher 연구원 proper 적절한, 올바른 way 방법 handle 다루다, 처리하다 chemical substance 화학 물질 lab 실험실 over ~내내, ~위의 beyond ~을 넘어서, ~이상으로

7. 정답 (D)

해석 또한 권고된다 / 찾아 보는 것 / 다른 고객들의 경우를 / 당신의 경우와 관련된 / 당신이 알기를 원한다면 / 가능한 결과를

해설 전치사 어휘 문제로 주제 전치사인 (D)를 먼저 대입해 해석해 보면, '당신의 경우와 관련된 다른 고객들의 경우를'이라는 의미가 자연스러우므로 (D)가 정답이다. (A)는 동사이고, (B) 다음에는 보통 사람명사가 와서 '사람이 ~를 이용할 수 있다'는 식으로 사용된다. (C)도 주로 '사람이 ~를 참고하다'는 식으로 사용되는데, other clients' cases는 사람이 아니다.

표현 정리 recommend 추천하다, 권한다 look up 찾아보다 probable 가능한, 확실한 outcome 결과, 성과 belong to ~에 속하다, ~의 부속이다 pertaining to ~에 관한, ~와 관련된

8. 정답 (C)

해석 Lob 사가 문제에 연루되어 있는 한 / 환경 오염에 관한 / 중국에서 / 사업을 다른 국가로 진출하는 것이 제한된다

해설 전치사 어휘 문제로 주제 전치사인 (C)를 먼저 대입해 해석해 보면, '환경 오염에 관한 문제에 ~'로 해석이 자연스러우므로 (C)가 정답이다. (A), (B), (D)는 모두 뒤에 to가 있어야 전치사로 사용된다.

표현 정리 as far as ~에 관한 한 be involved in ~에 관련되다 issue 문제 environmental pollution 환경 오염 be restricted to ~하는데 제한되다 concerning ~에 관하여

9. 정답 (B)

해석 결정은 / 옮길 것인지에 대한 / 본사를 / 북부 도시로 / 이루어지고 확정되어야 한다 / 최고 관리자에 의해 / 목요일까지

해설 전치사 어휘 문제로 주제 전치사인 (B)를 걷어 대입해 해석해 보면, '옮길 것인지에 대한 결정'이라는 말이 자연스러우므로 (B)가 정답이다. (D)는 to가 있어야 전치사가 된다.

표현 정리 decision 결정 headquarter office 본사 executive 임원, 책임자 up to ~까지 as to ~에 관하여

10. 정답 (D)

해석 정부 정책에 따라 / Felcons 사는 개정해야 했고 / 회사 재무제표를 / 명확하게 기록해야 했다 / 회사의 연간 수익 금액을

해설 전치사 어휘 문제로 보기에는 주제 전치사인 (B) 추가 전치사인 (A), 목적 전치사인 (C), 근거 전치사인 (D)가 제시되었다. '정부 정책에 따라 Felcons 사는 개정해야 했다'는 문맥이 자연스러우므로 (D)가 정답이다.

표현 정리 policy 정책 revise 수정하다, 개정하다 clearly 명백하게 state 언급하다, 기록하다 in addition to 게다가 pertaining to ~에 관한 in accordance with ~에 따라

Chapter 03 3개월에 한 번 출제되는 문제

법칙 27 빈칸 앞뒤 단어만 봐도 풀리는 동반, 수단, 수동 전치사

◎ 유형을 파악해 봐
1. (C) 2. (A) 3. (A)

1. 정답 (C)

해석 Mr. Brown은 통보 받았다 / 그의 동료로부터 / 중요한 회의가 있을 예정임을 / 다음 주에

해설 빈칸 앞에 완전한 수동태 문장이 왔고, (C) by가 수동 전치사이므로 먼저 대입해 해석해 본다. '동료에 의해 중요한 미팅이 있을 예정임을 통보 받았다'는 해석이 자연스럽기 때문에 (C)가 정답이다.

표현 정리 inform 통보하다, 알리다 co-worker 동료, 함께 일하는 사람 important 중요한

2. 정답 (A)

해석 Royal Electronics는 보상할 것이다 / 모든 고객들에게 / 전액 환불로 / 그들이 구입한 / 오작동하는 회사 제품들에 대한

해설 compensate 뒤에 with가 오면 보상이 오고, 이어 for 다음에는 보상 이유가 온다. 빈칸 뒤에 a full refund라는 보상이 왔기 때문에 with가 자연스러우므로 (A)가 정답이다.

표현 정리 compensate 보상하다 customer 고객, 손님 full refund 전액 환불 purchase 구매; 구매하다 malfunctioning 오작동하는, 제대로 기능하지 않는 product 제품, 생산품, 상품

3. 정답 (A)

해석 고객들은 / 구입일로부터 3일 이내에 제품을 반품하는 / 교환할 수 있다 / 제품을 / 새것으로 / 어떠한 불이익도 없이

해설 빈칸 앞에 exchange라는 단어가 왔으므로 새것으로 교체한다는 의미가 되고, 빈칸 뒤에 penalties라는 부정적인 명사가 왔으므로 '어떠한 불이익도 없이 새 제품으로 교환할 수 있다'의 뜻이 자연스럽기 때문에 (A)가 정답이다.

표현 정리 return 반품하다 item 물품, 항목 date of purchase 구입일 exchange 교환하다; 교환 penalty 불이익, 형벌, 벌금

◎ 실전에 적용해 봐
1. (A) 2. (B) 3. (C) 4. (A) 5. (B) 6. (A) 7. (B)
8. (C) 9. (B) 10. (B)

1. 정답 (A)

해석 모든 지원서는 / 프로그램을 위한 / 동봉되어 있다 / 프로그램의 혜택들을 설명하는 팸플릿들과 함께 / 봉투 안에

해설 be sealed with는 '~와 함께 동봉되다'의 뜻으로 '팸플릿들과 함께 동봉되어 있다'가 자연스럽기 때문에 (A)가 정답이다.

표현 정리 application form 지원서, 지원 양식 seal 밀봉하다, 봉인

하다 pamphlet 팸플릿 explain 설명하다 benefit 혜택, 이익 envelope 봉투

2. 정답 (B)

해석 최고 관리자는 / 사실상 / 확인했고 / 동의했다 / 프로젝트를 / 요청함으로써 / 프로젝트를 수행하기 위한 예산을

해설 빈칸에 by를 넣어 보면, -ing라는 숙어 표현이 되기 때문에 이를 먼저 대입해 해석해 보면, '예산을 요청함으로써'라는 자연스러운 의미가 되기 때문에 정답이다. (A) with는 '~와 함께,' (C) until은 '~까지,' (D) to는 '~로, ~쪽으로'라는 의미이다.

표현 정리 executive 경영진, 임원 in fact 사실상 ask for 요청하다 carry out 수행하다, 이행하다

3. 정답 (C)

해석 접근할 수 있는 권한이 / SG 코퍼레이션 계정에 / 났다 / 총무부로부터

해설 빈칸 앞에 완전한 수동태 문장이 온 것으로 보아 수동태의 주체를 나타내는 by가 어울릴 것이 예상된다. 해석해 보면 '총무부로부터 승인이 났다'가 자연스럽기 때문에 (C)가 정답이다. (A) on은 정확한 날짜나 위치, (B) to는 방향, (D) in은 위치를 나타내는 전치사이다.

표현 정리 permission 허락, 허가, 승인 access 이용하다, 접근하다 private 사적인, 개인 소유의 account 계좌, 계정 grant 승인하다 General Affairs Department 총무부

4. 정답 (A)

해석 인사부는 검토할 수 없다 / 직원들의 개인 문서들을 / 승인 없이

해설 문장 내용이 '승인 없이는 직원들의 개인 문서들을 검토할 수 없다'는 뜻이므로 (A)가 정답이다. (B) with는 '~로, ~와,' (C) between은 '~사이에'라는 뜻이고, 뒤에 A and B나 복수 명사가 온다. (D) upon이 빈칸에 오면 '승인과 함께'란 뜻이 된다.

표현 정리 Human Resources Department 인사부, 인사과 look through 검토하다 employee 직원, 종업원 personal 개인의, 개인적인 document 서류, 문서 approval 승인, 인가

5. 정답 (B)

해석 당신은 경험할 수 있다 / 새로 나온 Brenda 사의 자동차를 / 신청함으로써 / 7일간의 무료 시승 제안을

해설 빈칸에 by를 넣어 보면, by -ing라는 숙어 표현이 되기 때문에 이를 먼저 대입해 해석해 보면, '시승 제안을 신청함으로써'라는 자연스러운 내용이 되기 때문에 (B)가 정답이다. (A) at은 '~에,' (C) in은 '~안에,' (D) over는 '~보다'라는 뜻의 전치사인데 모두 자연스럽지 않다.

표현 정리 experience 경험하다, 겪다 automobile 자동차 apply 신청하다, 지원하다 free trial offer 무료 체험 제안

6. 정답 (A)

해석 Volca Tech는 허용하지 않는다 / 누구든지 접근하는 것을 / 연구실에 / 직원 ID 카드를 제시하지 않으면 / 근무 중인 직원에게

해설 without 뒤에는 보통 영수증, 통행증, 허가, -ing 등이 오기 때문에 이를 먼저 대입해 해석해 보면, '직원 ID 카드를 제시하지 않으면 접근을 허용하지 않는다'라는 내용이 자연스럽기 때문에 (A)가 정답이다.

표현 정리 access 접근하다, 이용하다; 접근, 이용 laboratory 연구실, 실험 show 보여주다 employee 직원, 종업원 staff member 직원 on duty 근무 중인

7. 정답 (B)

해석 Jazzy Salon은 결정했다 / 더 많은 고객들을 유치하기로 / 온라인 광고를 통해 / 가장 많이 방문하는 웹사이트에 게재된

해설 빈칸 뒤에 online advertisements라는 수단이 왔기 때문에 수단과 매개체를 나타내는 through를 우선 대입해 본다. '온라인 광고를 통해 더 많은 고객들을 유치하기로 했다'는 내용이 자연스럽기 때문에 (B)가 정답이다.

표현 정리 decide 결정하다 attract 끌다, 유치하다 advertisement 광고 place 놓다, 게재하다

8. 정답 (C)

해석 세월이 흘러도 변함없는 고전영화인 / '50 Secrets about Sea'는 / Liam Kidson이 감독한 / 리메이크 됐다 / 다른 감독에 의해 / 그리고 영화와 감독은 / 빠르게 얻었다 / 국제적인 인기를

해설 수동태의 주체가 되는 전치사는 by이다. by는 영화나 소설이 쓰일 때 주로 쓰이는데, 여기서는 앞에 directed 또는 written이 생략되었으며, 따라서 (C)가 정답이다.

표현 정리 timeless 세월이 흘러도 변함없는, 영원한 classic 고전적인, 일류의 remake 고쳐 만들다, 개조하다 quickly 빠르게, 급히 gain 얻다 international 국제적인 popularity 인기

9. 정답 (B)

해석 지금 방금 배송된 물품들은 / 진열돼야 한다 / 선반에 / 점원에 의해 / 매장 문이 열리기 전에

해설 빈칸 앞에 완전한 수동태 문장이 왔고, by가 수동 전치사이므로 먼저 대입해 해석해 보면, '점원에 의해 진열돼야 한다'는 해석이 자연스럽기 때문에 (B)가 정답이다.

표현 정리 item 물품, 항목 deliver 배달하다 place 놓다, 두다 shelf 선반 sales clerk 점원, 판매원

10. 정답 (B)

해석 수입 제품은 / 무게가 10kg 미만인 / 직접 통과할 수 있다 / 검사 절차를 / 지체하지 않고 / 공항에서

해설 빈칸 뒤에 delay가 있으므로, '지체하지 않고 검사 절차를 통과할 수 있다'는 내용이 자연스럽기 때문에 (B)가 정답이다. (A) along은 길이가 긴 사물이나 길, 강 등과 어울리는 전치사이고, (C)는 부사, (D)는 '~를 제외하고'라는 뜻이다.

표현 정리 imported product 수입 제품 directly 즉시, 곧 pass 통과하다, 지나가다 examination 검사, 조사 process 절차, 과정 delay 지체, 지연

법칙 28 조동사, 명령문, 그리고 요구, 주장, 의무, 경령, 제안 뒤는 동사원형

◎ 유형을 파악해 봐
1. (C) 2. (A) 3. (C)

1. 정답 (C)

해설 Chad는 고용해야 한다 / 더 많은 직원을 / 팸플릿을 배포하기 위해 / 매장을 방문하는 고객들에게

해설 should는 '~해야 한다'라는 뜻의 조동사이므로 동사원형인 (C)가 정답이다. (A)는 형용사, (B)는 준동사(동명사나 현재분사), (D)는 단수 동사이다.

표현 정리 hire 고용하다 staff member 직원 distribute 배포하다, 분배하다 pamphlet 팸플릿 customer 고객, 손님

2. 정답 (A)

해설 채널을 고정하세요 / 더 많은 뉴스를 위해 / 곧 이어지는

해설 please 다음에는 동사원형이 와야 하므로 (A)가 정답이다.

표현 정리 stay tuned 채널을 고정하다 come up 다가오다, 이어지다

3. 정답 (C)

해설 Mr. Gratski는 요청했다 / 그의 비서에게 약속을 정할 것을 / 그의 고객과 / 정오에

해설 빈칸 앞에 요구를 나타내는 ask가 왔기 때문에 that 이하에 조동사 should가 생략된 것으로 보아야 한다. 따라서 동사원형인 (C)가 정답이다.

표현 정리 ask 요청하다 secretary 비서 arrange an appointment 약속을 정하다

◎ 실전에 적용해 봐
1. (A) 2. (B) 3. (C) 4. (D) 5. (C) 6. (D) 7. (C)
8. (B) 9. (D) 10. (C)

1. 정답 (A)

해설 변화를 주기 위해서 / 당신의 경력에 / 그저 지원하면 됩니다 / 관리직에 / Alaska 사 / 양식을 작성함으로써

해설 to부터 콤마까지는 to 부정사의 부사적 용법으로 부사 기능을 한다. simply도 부사이므로 빈칸에는 동사원형이 와 '그저 ~하면 됩니다'라는 뜻의 일종의 명령문을 구성하므로 동사원형인 (A)가 정답이다. (B)는 3인칭 단수 동사, (C)는 현재분사, (D)는 과거분사이다.

표현 정리 make a difference 차이를 두다, 의미 있게 만들다 career 경력 simply 그저, 단순히 apply for ~에 지원하다 managerial position 관리직 fill out 작성하다, 기입하다 form 양식

2. 정답 (B)

해설 누구든지 / 예산 보고서가 기준을 만족시키지 않는 사람은 / 요청 받을 것이다 / 수정하도록 / 그리고 다시 제출하도록

해설 빈칸 앞에 온 not은 부사이므로 생략하면, 조동사 do만 남기 때문에 빈칸에는 동사원형인 (B)가 와야 한다.

표현 정리 budget 예산, 비용 report 보고서 standard 기준, 규범 be asked to+동사원형 ~하도록 요청 받다 revise 수정하다, 변경하다 submit 제출하다 meet 충족시키다

3. 정답 (C)

해설 계약서에 서명하기 전에 / 반복하여 확인하시오 / 조건들을 / 계약서 / 잘못된 것이 있는지

해설 please 다음이라서 바로 동사원형인 (A)를 고른다면 함정에 빠지는 문제이다. 밑줄 뒤에 이미 동사원형인 check가 있기 때문에 밑줄은 부사자리이다. (C)가 답.

표현 정리 sign 서명하다, 계약하다 contract 계약, 계약서 check 확인하다, 점검하다 terms and conditions 조건들 repeat 반복하다, 되풀이하다

4. 정답 (D)

해설 비록 당신은 자유로울 수 있지만 / 당신이 원하는 것을 입는데 / 당신이 최종적으로 Venom 사에 입사하면 / 매니저는 요청할지도 모른다 / 당신이 정장을 입을 것을 / 적어도 인터뷰에서는

해설 빈칸 앞에 요구를 나타내는 ask가 왔기 때문에 이어지는 that 문장에서는 should가 생략된 것으로 보아야 한다. 따라서 빈칸에는 동사원형인 (D)가 와야 한다.

표현 정리 free to+동사원형 ~하는데 있어 자유로운 wear 입다, 착용하다 once 일단 ~하면 finally 최종적으로, 마침내, 결국 get accepted 받아들여지다 formal suit 정장 at least 적어도

5. 정답 (C)

해설 건강 보험은 제공한다 / 당신에게 200달러를 / 병원비로 / 하지만 지원해 주지 않는다 / 비용을 / 정기 건강검진을 위한

해설 빈칸 앞에 있는 not은 부사이므로 수식어 처리해 제외하면, 조동사 does만 남기 때문에 빈칸은 동사원형인 (C)가 와야 한다.

표현 정리 health insurance 건강 보험 provide 제공하다 hospital bill 병원비 expense 비용, 돈 regular 규칙적인, 정기적인 health check 건강 검진

6. 정답 (D)

해설 장비를 반납할 때 / 기입해 주세요 / 당신의 서명을 / 당신이 반납한 날짜와 함께 / 종이에 / 책상 위에 놓여진

해설 명령문은 주어 you가 생략된 형태이며, 동사원형으로 시작한다. (A)는 과거동사, (B)는 명사, (C)는 3인칭 단수 동사이다.

표현 정리 when -ing ~할 때 return 반납하다, 돌아오다 equipment 장비, 용품 signature 서명 place 놓다, 두다

7. 정답 (C)

해설 취업 상담가들 중 한 명의 의견은 시사한다 / 대부분의 중견 기업들이 꺼려한다는 것을 / 고용하는 것을 / 더 많은 직원들을

해설 suggest만 보고 동사원형인 (B)를 답으로 고르지 않도록 한다. 여기서 suggest는 '의미하다, 암시하다'의 뜻이므로 '요번주의명지'가 아니며, 따라서 동사원형을 쓸 이유가 없다. 형용사 reluctant는 상태를 나타내는

말이므로 진행시제를 쓰기에는 어색하다.

표현 정리 comment 의견, 논평 suggest 시사하다 mid-sized company 중견 기업 be reluctant to+동사원형 ~하는 것을 꺼리다

8. 정답 (B)

해석 화물이 배달되기 전에 / Mr. Doe에게 / 화물선이 사고를 당했다 / 그리고 화물의 일부분이 분실됐다

해설 빈칸 앞에 조동사가 있는 것으로 보아 빈칸에는 동사원형이 와야 하기 때문에 동사원형인 수동태 (B)가 정답이다. (A)는 현재분사, (C)은 3인칭 단수 동사, (D)는 준동사이다.

표현 정리 shipment 수송 화물, 선적물 transport ship 화물선 accident 사고 lost 분실된, 잃어버린 deliver 배송

9. 정답 (D)

해석 16주년을 기념하기 위해 / Alim 사가 설립된지 / 파트너 회사들의 사장들이 / 참가했다 / 행사에 / 축하 메시지를 전하기 위한

해설 빈칸을 포함한 ,(콤마) 앞 내용은 수식어 부분이기 때문에 to 부정사의 부사적 용법인 (D)가 정답이다. 접속사가 없으면 한 문장에 동사는 하나만 와야 하므로 (B)와 (C)는 탈락하고, 명사 자리가 아니므로 명사인 (A)도 탈락한다.

표현 정리 found 설립하다 several 여럿의, 여러 가지의 attend 참석하다 congratulatory 축하의 commemorate 기념하다

10. 정답 (C)

해석 Alison Motors는 최근에 결정했다 / 판매하기로 / 더 많은 자동차를 / 내년에 / 그리고 요청했다 / 제조 공장이 증가시키기를 / 생산 속도를

해설 빈칸 앞에 요구를 나타내는 request가 있으므로 that 이하에 should가 생략된 것으로 보아야 한다. 따라서 빈칸에는 동사원형인 (C)가 와야 한다. (A)는 과거시제, (B)는 현재완료시제, (D)는 미래시제이다.

표현 정리 recently 최근에 decide 결정하다 automobile 자동차 request 요청하다 manufacturing plant 제조 공장 production 생산 increase 증가시키다

법칙 29 덩어리로 외워야 하는 복합명사 문제

◎ 유형을 파악해 봐
1. (B) 2. (A) 3. (A)

1. 정답 (B)

해석 영업부는 집중했다 / 제품의 품질을 강조하는데 / 향상시키기 위해 / 고객 만족도를

해설 빈칸 앞 customer가 가산명사인데도 a customer나 customers가 아니라면 복합명사의 N1이다. N1과 N2에 명사가 들어가야 하며 '고객 만족도'라는 뜻의 customer satisfaction을 이루는 (B)가 정답이다.

표현 정리 Sales Department 영업부, 판매부 focus on ~에 초점을 맞추다, 집중하다 stress 강조하다 increase 향상시키다, 증가하다 customer satisfaction 고객 만족도

2. 정답 (A)

해석 소지하고 계세요 / 허가증을 / 당신과 함께 / 들어갈 때 / 제한 구역에

해설 (A)가 오면 허가증이라는 복합명사가 되며, (C)가 오면 승인된 카드라는 말이 되어 혼동되기 쉬운 문제이다. 제한 구역에 들어갈 때는 허가를 위한 카드 즉 허가증이 필요하지, 허가가 다 된 카드가 필요한 것은 아니므로 (A)가 답이다.

표현 정리 authorization 허가, 인가 authorization card 허가증 enter 들어가다 restricted area 제한 구역

3. 정답 (A)

해석 McQueen 사 직원들은 가도록 요청 받았다 / 접수대로 / 얻기 위해 / 보안 출입증을 / 공장 안으로 들어가기 위한

해설 security는 불가산명사인데도 앞에 관사 a가 있다는 것은 빈칸에 단수 명사가 와서 security와 복합명사를 이루어야 한다는 것을 의미한다. 이 사실을 몰랐다고 해도, 공장 안으로 들어가기 위해서 필요한 것이 뭘까를 생각해 보면 당연히 보안 출입증을 알 수 있다. 따라서 (A)가 와야 한다. 복합명사의 단수, 복수는 N2에 맞춘다.

표현 정리 employee 직원 be asked to+동사원형 ~하도록 요청 받다 reception desk 접수대 security pass 보안 출입증 get inside 안에 들어가다, 잠입하다 factory 공장

◎ 실전에 적용해 봐
1. (D) 2. (C) 3. (A) 4. (D) 5. (D) 6. (A) 7. (A)
8. (B) 9. (C) 10. (B)

1. 정답 (D)

해석 직원들은 일터를 깨끗하게 해야 하고 / 보고해야 한다 / 모든 문제들을 / 그들이 발견하는 / 공장에서 / 정기적인 보수 점검 동안

해설 빈칸 앞에 관사 the가 있는 것으로 보아 동사 자리는 아니며, 보수 점검이라는 복합명사가 필요한 자리이다. 따라서 (D)가 정답이다.

표현 정리 employee 직원 workplace 직장, 일터 clean up 깨끗이 하다, 청소하다 report 보고하다 regular 정기적인, 규칙적인 maintenance 관리, 유지, 보수

2. 정답 (C)

해석 은퇴 기념 파티를 준비하는 것 대신 / Mr. Tall을 위한 / 공개된 / 모두가 참석할 수 있도록 / Mr. Gallery는 보냈다 / 초대장들을 / 오직 소수의 직원들에게 / Mr. Tall의 요청에 따라

해설 빈칸 앞과 뒤로 관사와 명사가 있기 때문에 동사 (A)는 탈락하고, '은퇴 기념 파티'의 뜻을 이루는 복합명사가 자연스러우므로 (C)가 정답이다.

표현 정리 instead of ~을 대신해 retirement party 퇴직 기념 파티 attend 참석하다 employee 직원 upon request 요청으로

3. 정답 (A)

해석 실시하기 위해 / 안전 검사를 / 제조 시설에 대한 / 모든 기계들의 가동이 중단돼야 한다 / 일시적으로

해설 일단 빈칸에 올 수 있는 것은 안전 검사를 뜻하는 (A)나 형용사인 (C)인데, 검사 자체가 안전한 것이 아니고, 안전성을 검사해야 하므로 (A)가 정답이다.

표현 정리 carry out 실시하다, 이행하다 safety inspection 안전 검사 manufacturing facility 제조 시설 turn off 끄다, 잠그다 temporarily 일시적으로, 임시로

4. 정답 (D)

해설 새 직업을 찾거나 직장을 옮길 사람이라면 / 권장된다 / 오도록 / 취업 설명회로 / Mary Street에서 개최되는 / 이번 주에

해설 명사인 (A)는 job fairness held '개최된 직업 공정성'이란 뜻이 되고, (B)도 명사이지만 '요정'이라는 의미이며, 부사인 (C)는 job fairly held '꽤 개최된 직업'이라는 뜻이 되어 어색하다. 따라서 job fair '취업 설명회'라는 복합명사가 가장 자연스럽기 때문에 (D)가 정답이다.

표현 정리 transfer 전근, 이동 be encouraged to + 동사원형 ~하도록 권장되다 job fair 취업 설명회 hold 개최하다

5. 정답 (D)

해설 모든 신입 직원들은 요구된다 / 제출하도록 / 그들의 고용 확인서를 / 그들의 부서 책임자에게 / 이번 주 말까지

해설 빈칸이 포함되어 있는 'of 전명구'는 to submit의 목적어를 수식하는 목적어이며, 빈칸에는 letter를 수식하는 형용사나 복합명사가 와야 한다. 따라서 '고용 확인서'라는 뜻이 자연스럽기 때문에 (D)가 정답이다.

표현 정리 employee 직원 be required to + 동사원형 ~하도록 요구되다 submit 제출하다 a verification of employment letter 고용 확인서 head 책임자, 장, 우두머리 department 부서

6. 정답 (A)

해설 Innovation Electronics는 예상했다 / 수익률이 30퍼센트를 초과할 것으로 / 이번 년도에

해설 빈칸 앞에 that 접속사가 있고, 빈칸 뒤에는 동사가 있다. 빈칸에는 복합명사의 N2나, 부사가 와야 하는데, 보기 중 복합명사 N2 자리에 올 수 있는 margin이 가장 적절하므로 (A)가 정답이다.

표현 정리 expect 예상하다, 기대하다 profit margin 이익률 exceed 초과하다

7. 정답 (A)

해설 말해 주세요 / 우리에게 / 당신의 저축예금 계좌번호를 / 그러면 보험료는 자동적으로 / 이체될 것입니다 / 매월 말에

해설 빈칸 앞에 소유격 your가 왔고, 뒤에 account number란 명사가 왔다. 해석해 보면 '당신의 저축예금 계좌번호'가 자연스럽기 때문에 (A)가 정답이다.

표현 정리 savings account 보통예금 계좌 insurance fee 보험료 automatically 자동적으로, 기계적으로, 무의식적으로 transfer 이전, 이동, 전근

8. 정답 (B)

해설 당신이 경험하게 될 경우 / 우리 제품의 기능 이상을 / 연락해 / 우리에게 / 설명하세요 / 당신이 안고 있는 문제를 / 당신이 반품하기 전에 / 환불 또는 교환을 위해

해설 빈칸 앞에 an equipment가 왔고, 빈칸 뒤에 전명구가 왔다. equipment는 불가산명사이기 때문에 관사 뒤에 단독으로 쓸 수 없다. 따라서 복합명사를 생각해 봐야 하는데, 관사 an이 있으므로 복수 명사인 (D)는 탈락하고, 단수 명사인 (B)가 답이다.

표현 정리 in case ~할 경우, ~의 경우에 대비해 equipment 장비 explain 설명하다 refund 환불 exchange 교환 malfunction 기능 고장, 오작동

9. 정답 (C)

해설 서류들은 검토되고 제출될 필요가 있다 / 세관 직원으로부터 / 찾을 수 있는 / 이 건물 2층에서

해설 customs라는 복수 명사 앞에 a가 있다는 것은 customs가 N1이고, N2 자리에 단수 명사가 와야 한다는 것을 의미한다. 빈칸 뒤에 who라는 사람을 받는 관계대명사가 왔기 때문에 사람을 나타내는 단수 명사인 (C)가 오면, a customs official이 되므로 정답이다.

표현 정리 document 서류, 문서 review 검토하다 submit 제출하다 customs official 세관 직원 officially 공식적으로

10. 정답 (B)

해설 모든 직원들은 주의 깊게 읽어야 한다 / 서류를 / 작업장 단전 규정을 설명하는 / 오리엔테이션 동안 / 화요일에 있을

해설 오리엔테이션 동안 직원들이 읽어야 할 것은 작업장의 단전 규정에 대해 적힌 서류이므로 (B)가 정답이다. (C)는 '규칙적임, 질서'라는 뜻인데 safety와 복합명사를 이루지 않는다.

표현 정리 employee 직원 carefully 주의 깊게 explain 설명하다 workplace safety 작업장 안전 orientation 오리엔테이션, 예비 교육 regulations 규정

법칙 30 전명구 앞에 잘 오는 부사

◎ 유형을 파악해 봐
1. (C)   2. (C)   3. (D)

1. 정답 (C)

해설 Mr. Wisby는 / 많은 실무 경험을 가진 / 관련 분야에서 / 뛰어난 성과를 보여줬다 / 훈련기간 동안에도 / 새 직장에서

해설 -ly로 끝나지 않았지만 부사 문법 문제이다. 빈칸이 전명구 앞에 있으므로 초점 부사 even을 먼저 대입해 해석해 보면, '훈련기간 동안에도 뛰어난 성과를 보여줬다'는 해석이 자연스럽기 때문에 (C)가 정답이다. (A)는 비교 단서 than이 있어야 사용 가능하고, (B)는 형용사나 부사 앞에 오며, (D)는 부정문에 쓴다.

표현 정리 plenty of 많은 experience 경험 relevant 관련 있는, 적절한 field 분야 outstanding 뛰어난 performance 업무 실적, 성과 workplace 직장, 일터

2. 정답 (C)

해석 모든 자원 봉사자들은 와야 한다 / 장소로 / 버스가 우리 목적지로 향해 출발하는 / 오후 7시 정각에

해설 빈칸 뒤에 전명구가 있다. 보기 중 전명구 앞에 잘 쓰이는 부사는 (C)이다. (B)는 현재시제와 주로 어울리는 부사이며, (D)는 형용사나 p.p. 앞에 와서 그 정도를 강하게 해 줄 때 사용한다.

표현 정리 volunteer 자원 봉사자 venue 장소, 현장 destination 목적지 leave 떠나다 internally 내부적으로, 심적으로 frequently 자주, 빈번하게 promptly 즉시, 지체 없이

3. 정답 (D)

해석 명심하세요 / 당신이 사용하도록 / 이 자가 접착도구를 / 오직 물건에만 / 사람이 아닌 / 어려울 수 있기 때문에 / 떼어내는 것이 / 일단 한번 접착되면

해설 빈칸 뒤에 전명구가 있다. 전명구와 잘 어울리면서 '접착도구를 사람이 아닌 오직 물건에만 사용해야 한다'의 뜻이 자연스럽기 때문에 초점 부사인 (D)가 정답이다.

표현 정리 make sure that that 이하를 확실히 하다 adhesive 들러붙는; 접착제 tool 도구, 수단 object 물건 detach 떼어내다, 분리하다 glue 붙이다; 접착제

◎ 실전에 적용해 봐
1. (A) 2. (D) 3. (B) 4. (A) 5. (A) 6. (A) 7. (C)
8. (B) 9. (A) 10. (A)

1. 정답 (A)

해석 이 헬스 프로그램은 / 전문 트레이너가 집중적으로 관리하는 / 교육받는 사람을 / 3개월 동안 / 제공된다 / 독점적으로 / 개인들에게 / 1년 이상 된 회원들에게

해설 보기 중 전명구와 함께 사용 가능하고, '1년 이상 된 회원들에게 독점적으로 제공된다'는 말이 자연스러운 (A)가 답이다.

표현 정리 fitness 헬스, 신체 단련, 건강 professional 전문적인; 전문가 trainer 트레이너 intensively 집중적으로, 철저하게 manage 관리하다, 다루다 trainee 교육을 받는 사람 offer 제공하다 exclusively 독점적으로 beneficially 유익하게 completely 완전히 mutually 상호간의; 서로

2. 정답 (D)

해석 면접관은 학력을 중요하게 여기는 것으로 보였다 / 지원자들의 / 특히 / 그들의 전공에 관해 / 대학에서

해설 전명구 앞에 와서 전명구를 강조해 주는 부사인 초점 부사 (D)가 오면 '특히 그들의 전공에 관해'라는 말이 되어 자연스럽다. (C) promptly도 전명구와 어울리지만 시각 앞에 와야 한다.

표현 정리 interviewer 면접관 value 중요하게 여기다 educational background 학력 applicant 지원자, 후보자 major 전공 extremely 극도로, 매우 fully 완전히 promptly 즉시, 지체 없이 particularly 특히

3. 정답 (B)

해석 생산 관리자로서 / Mr. Bail의 역할은 확인하는 것이다 / 제품들이 / 항상 최신 유행을 유지하는지 / 현재의

해설 전명구(up to date)와도 잘 어울리면서 '제품들이 항상 최신 유행을 유지하는지 확인하는 것이다'가 자연스럽기 때문에 (B)가 정답이다.

표현 정리 production manager 생산 관리자 make sure that that 이하를 확실히 하다 product 제품, 상품 up to date 최신 유행의, 현대식의 current 현재의 trend 유행, 경향 vaguely 애매하게 consistently 항상 gradually 서서히 consequently 따라서, 그 결과

4. 정답 (A)

해석 우리는 보증한다 / 우리가 판매하는 제품이 / 가장 저렴하다는 것을 / 우리는 제품들을 배달하기 때문에 / 직접 / 제공업체로부터 / 고객들에게

해설 전명구 앞에 사용 가능하면서 가장 저렴한 제품을 직접 고객에게 제공한다는 말이 자연스럽기 때문에 (A)가 정답이다. (B)는 빠짐없이 작성할 때, (D)는 반복, 습관을 나타내는 어울림이 있을 때 사용한다.

표현 정리 ensure 보증하다, 확실하게 하다 goods 상품 provider 제공업자, 제공 업체 customer 고객

5. 정답 (A)

해석 유의하세요 / 배송비가 청구될 것임을 / 별도로 / 주문한 제품 가격과는

해설 주문한 상품 가격과는 별도로 배송비가 청구될 것이라는 내용이 자연스럽기 때문에 (A)가 정답이다. (B)는 '이전에는 ~였던'이란 문맥에서 사용하므로 보통 명사 앞에서 사용되고, (C)는 협력하여 작업할 때 사용하는 부사이며, (D)는 가격이나 매출 등이 급격하게 올라갈 때 사용하는 부사이다.

표현 정리 note 유의하다 shipping fee 배송비 order 주문하다; 주문 separately 별도로, 각각의 formerly 이전에 cooperatively 협력하여 sharply 급격하게

6. 정답 (A)

해석 단지 / 아직 등록비를 지불하지 않은 사람들에 대해서만 / 주로 제한될 것이다 / 특정 시설들을 사용하는 것이 / 체육관에서

해설 those는 '~하는 사람들'이란 뜻의 명사이며, 명사 앞에 올 수 있는 초점 부사 (A)가 정답이다. (B)는 명사 앞에 오는 부사가 아니며, (C)는 접속사, (D)는 대명사나 부사의 기능을 한다.

표현 정리 registration fee 등록비 primarily 주로 restrict 제한하다 specific 특정한, 구체적인, 명확한 gym 체육관 entirely 전적으로

7. 정답 (C)

해석 회사 정책이다 / 오로지 야간 근무 교대 직원들만 사용하도록 허용하는 것이 / 난방장치를 / 일하는 동안

해설 초점 부사인 (C)는 명사 앞에 올 수 있는 기능을 하며, '오직 야간 근무 교대 직원들만'이라는 말이 자연스럽기 때문에 (C)가 정답이다. (B)는 주로 형용사 앞에 와서 정도를 나타내는 정도 부사이고, (D)는 동사를 수식하는다.

표현 정리 night shift worker 야간 근무 교대조 heating equipment

난방장치 widely 널리, 크게

8. 정답 (B)

해설 미팅은 다룰 것이다 / 문제를 / 최근 경기 침체와 관련된 / 특히 그것의 영향에 대해 / 회사 이익에 미치는

해설 (B)가 오면 issue를 구체적으로 말해 주는 초점 부사가 되어 명사 앞에도 쓸 수 있어 정답이다. (A)가 오면 분사구문이 되어 meeting이 its effect를 지정해 말한다는 뜻이 되는데, 미팅은 issue를 다루는 것이지 effect를 지정하는 것은 아니다. 문장에 동사가 있으므로 동사 (C)는 탈락한다.

표현 정리 address 다루다, 대처하다 issue 문제, 이슈 economic downturn 경기 침체 specifically 구체적으로, 명확하게

9. 정답 (A)

해설 전 사장은 / Trent Corporation의 / 시작했다 / 그의 자신의 사업을 / 즉시 / 사임한 후에

해설 immediately는 before나 after를 좋아하는 부사이므로 우선 대입하여 해석해 본다. '사임한 후에 즉시 그의 사업을 시작했다-'가 자연스럽기 때문에 (A)가 정답이다. (B) formerly는 전명구 앞에 사용하는 부사가 아니고, p.p. 앞에 오거나 동사를 수식하고, (C)는 '빠짐없이 기입하다' 등과 어울리다, (D)는 형용사나 부사 앞에 오는 정도 부사이다.

표현 정리 former 이전의 resign 사임하다 immediately 즉시 formerly 이전에 completely 완전히 extremely 극도로, 매우

10. 정답 (A)

해설 Ms. Glow는 연설할 것이다 / 정보기술 발달 / 특히 / 전자상거래 분야에 관해서

해설 빈칸 앞에 완전한 문장이 왔고, 빈칸 뒤에는 전명구 수식어구가 왔기 때문에 전명구를 수식하는 부사가 와야 한다. (A)는 전명구와 잘 어울리는 초점 부사이므로 정답이다.

표현 정리 deliver a speech 연설하다 in the field of ~의 분야에서 e-commerce 전자상거래 particularly 특히 particular (명사 앞에서) 특정한 particularity 독특함, 꼼꼼함, 특이성

법칙 31 문장, 형용사(또는 -ing/p.p.), 부사 앞은 부사 자리

◎ 유형을 파악해 봐
1. (A) 2. (D) 3. (A)

1. 정답 (A)

해설 Innovative Tech는 소개했다 / 휴대폰을 / 완전히 새로운 기술을 갖춘

해설 빈칸 앞에 관사 a가 있고, 빈칸 뒤에는 형용사와 명사가 왔다. 형용사를 꾸며주는 품사는 부사이기 때문에 부사인 (A)가 정답이다. (B)는 현재분사 형태의 형용사, (C)는 동사 및 형용사, (D)는 명사이다.

표현 정리 introduce 소개하다 equipped with ~을 갖춘 completely 완전히

2. 정답 (D)

해설 Anywhere 여행사는 믿는다 / 곧 일류 여행사가 될 것이라고 / 회사가 제공하기 때문에 / 여러 경쟁력 있는 가격의 패키지 여행을

해설 빈칸 앞에 전치사, 빈칸 뒤에 p.p.가 있으므로 빈칸은 priced를 수식하는 부사 자리이다. -ing나 p.p.도 부사의 수식을 받으므로 (D)가 정답이다.

표현 정리 leading 일류의, 뛰어난 competitive 경쟁력 있는 compete 경쟁하다 competition 경쟁 competitively 경쟁적으로

3. 정답 (A)

해설 적극적으로 광고한 결과 / 출시된 최신 자동차 모델을 / Furious Auto는 올렸다 / 지난해의 3배가 되는 수익을

해설 advertising은 동명사이며, 빈칸은 동명사를 수식하는 부사 자리이다. 따라서 (A)가 정답이다.

표현 정리 as a result of ~의 결과 actively 적극적으로, 활동적으로 triple 3배의, 3개로 이루어진

◎ 실전에 적용해 봐
1. (A) 2. (B) 3. (D) 4. (C) 5. (D) 6. (D) 7. (A)
8. (D) 9. (B) 10. (A)

1. 정답 (A)

해설 주차장 수리가 이루어졌다 / 입구를 / 더 쉽게 이용할 수 있도록 하기 위해 / 자동차 소유자들이

해설 빈칸 앞의 make는 5형식 동사로 its entrance가 목적어, accessible이 목적 보어이다. 빈칸은 목적 보어인 형용사를 수식하는 부사 자리이다. more easily는 easily의 비교급 형태로 역시 부사이다. 따라서 (A)가 정답이다.

표현 정리 renovation 수리, 보수 parking lot 주차장 entrance 입구 accessible 이용, 접근 가능한 owner 소유자 easily 쉽게

2. 정답 (B)

해설 처음, Mr. Jacob는 생각했다 / 그의 일이 매우 까다롭다고 / 그러나 2주간의 교육을 받은 후에 / 그는 자신이 생겼다 / 그것을 할 만큼 충분히

해설 동사가 두 개이므로 but이 접속사로 쓰였고, after는 전치사로 쓰였다. 빈칸은 문장 맨 앞에 쓰인 부사 자리이며, 전치사 (A), 접속사 (C)는 올 수 없다. (D)는 문두에 쓰일 경우 앞에 있는 문맥에 대해 '그럼에도 불구하고'라는 의미로 쓰이기 때문에 여기서는 쓸 수 없다. 따라서 '처음에, Mr. Jacob는 일이 매우 까다롭다고 생각했다'라는 의미의 (B)가 정답이다.

표현 정리 demanding 까다로운, 요구가 많은 training 교육, 훈련 confident 자신 있는 at first 처음에

3. 정답 (D)

해설 평가 결과는 / 신입 직원들의 업무 / 통계적으로 일반적인 결과에서 벗어났다

해설 전명구 off the usual results는 '일반적인 결과에서 벗어난'이란 뜻으로 보어의 기능을 하고 있다. 따라서 그 앞에는 부사인 (D)가 와야 한다.

정답 및 해설 47

(A)와 (C)는 명사, (B)는 형용사이다.

표현 정리 result 결과 evaluation 평가 performance 업무 실적, 공연, 수행, 능력 usual 일반적인 statistically 통계상으로

4.　　　　　　　　　　　　　　　　　　　　　　정답 (C)

해석 Central Library는 방문한다 / 많은 지역 주민들이 / 편리한 위치에 있기 때문에 / 아파트 옆

해설 수동태 be와 p.p. 사이에서 p.p.를 수식해 줄 수 있는 품사는 부사이므로 (C)가 정답이다. (A)와 (B)는 명사, (D)는 형용사이다. conveniently located는 '편리하게 위치한'이라는 덩어리 어휘로 알아두면 편리하다.

표현 정리 local 지역의 resident 거주자 located ~에 위치한 conveniently 편리하게

5.　　　　　　　　　　　　　　　　　　　　　　정답 (D)

해석 계약서는 명시해야 한다 / 어떤 제품이 배송되어야 하는지 / 매주 / 그것이 분명하게 이해되도록 하기 위해서

해설 render는 5형식으로 쓰였으며, it이 목적어, understood가 목적 보어이다. 빈칸은 뒤에 있는 p.p.를 수식해 주는 부사 자리이므로 (D)가 정답이다. (A)는 형용사, (B)는 형용사의 비교급, (C)는 과거분사이다.

표현 정리 contract 계약, 계약서 specify 명시하다 ship 배송; 배송하다 render ~하게 하다, (어떤 상태로) 만들다

6.　　　　　　　　　　　　　　　　　　　　　　정답 (D)

해석 Top Cosmetics Shop은 판매한다 / 향수와 화장품들을 / 상당히 높은 가격에 / 그들의 브랜드 가치를 강조해

해설 빈칸 뒤에 higher라는 형용사가 있으므로, 빈칸은 형용사를 수식해 주는 부사 자리이다. 따라서 (D)가 정답이다. (A)는 현재분사 형태의 형용사, (B)는 p.p., (C)는 형용사이다.

표현 정리 fragrance 향수, 향기 beauty product 화장품 emphasize 강조하다 value 가치 significantly 상당히

7.　　　　　　　　　　　　　　　　　　　　　　정답 (A)

해석 Best Tech Electronics는 최근에 소개했고 / 신형 MP3 플레이어를 / 엄청난 성공을 거두었다 / 시장 점유율을 상당히 끌어올리면서

해설 빈칸 뒤에서 its market share라는 목적어를 취하는 increasing은 현재분사이며, 이러한 형태를 분사구문이라고 한다. 현재분사도 부사의 수식을 받으므로 (A)가 정답이다. (B)는 형용사, (C)는 명사, (D)는 동사이다.

표현 정리 recently 최근에 introduce 소개하다 huge 엄청난, 큰 market share 시장 점유율 substantially 상당히

8.　　　　　　　　　　　　　　　　　　　　　　정답 (D)

해석 Formost Electronics는 이끌어왔다 / 컴퓨터 프로그램 산업을 / 혁신적인 기술 개발을 통해 / 특히 / 하드웨어 프로그램 분야에서

해설 소유격과 형용사 사이이므로 명사인 (A)와 동사인 (C)는 우선 탈락이다. 명사 앞에 형용사가 2개도 올 수 있으므로 (D)가 정답이다. '혁신적인 기술 개발'이라는 해석도 자연스럽다. 빈칸 뒤에 형용사가 있다고 해서 부사인 (B)를 고르지 않도록 한다.

표현 정리 lead 이끌다 industry 산업 technical 기술적인 development 개발, 발전 especially 특히 innovative 혁신적인

9.　　　　　　　　　　　　　　　　　　　　　　정답 (B)

해석 Newstar 사는 / 새로 설립된 / 수년 전에 / 확장해 왔다 / 사업을 / 매우 빠르게 / 지난 몇 년 동안

해설 빈칸은 뒤에 있는 rapidly를 수식해 주는 부사가 필요하다. '사업을 매우 빠르게 확장해 왔다'라는 의미가 어울리므로 (B)가 정답이다. (A)는 비교급을 강조할 때 쓰는 부사인데, 수식 받는 부사인 rapidly는 원급이므로 탈락하고, (C)는 전치사, (D)는 주로 의문문 및 부정문에 사용하는 형용사나 대명사이다.

표현 정리 newly 새롭게, 최근에 found 설립하다 a couple of years ago 수년 전에 expand 확장하다 rapidly 빠르게, 급속히

10.　　　　　　　　　　　　　　　　　　　　　　정답 (A)

해석 전문적인 처리 때문에 / 고객은 더 이상 불평하지 않았다 / 서비스에 대해 / 그녀가 받은 / 그리고 오히려 만족해 했다 / 보상과 함께

해설 handling은 동명사가 아니라 -ing로 굳어진 명사이다. 명사는 형용사의 수식을 받기 때문에 형용사인 (A)가 정답이다. 동명사가 부사의 수식을 받는다고 생각해 (B)를 고르는 함정에 빠진 것이다.

표현 정리 due to ~때문에 handling 처리, 조작 no longer 더 이상 ~이 아닌 complain 불평하다 receive 받다, 받아들이다 seem satisfied with ~에 만족하다 compensation 보상

Chapter 04　4개월에 한 번 출제되는 문제

법칙 32 과거시점(yesterday, last, ago, when 과거)이 보이면 과거시제

◎ 유형을 파악해 봐
1. (B)　2. (A)　3. (A)

1.　　　　　　　　　　　　　　　　　　　　　　정답 (B)

해석 만료된 계약은 쓸모 없게 되었다 / 한 달 전에

해설 빈칸은 문장의 정동사 자리이므로 준동사인 (C)는 탈락하고, 주어가 단수이므로 복수 동사인 (A) 역시 탈락한다. 과거 시점인 a month ago(한 달 전)라는 단서가 있으므로 과거시제인 (B)가 답이다.

표현 정리 expired 만료된 contract 계약 obsolete 시대에 뒤진, 쓸모 없게 된 a month ago 한 달 전

2.　　　　　　　　　　　　　　　　　　　　　　정답 (A)

해석 지난 주말에 / JTB 사의 전 직원들은 모였다 / 회사 사장님의 은퇴식을 위한 장소에

해설 빈칸은 문장의 정동사 자리이므로 준동사인 (C)는 탈락하고, 주어가 복수이므로 단수 동사인 (D) 역시 탈락한다. 과거시점인 Last weekend(지난 주말)라는 단서가 있으므로 과거시제인 (A)가 답이다.

표현 정리 employees 직원 venue 장소 retirement 은퇴
president 사장

3. 정답 (A)

해설 인사 배치에 관한 발표가 어제 있을 예정이었다 / 그러나 그것은 게시되지 않았다 / 웹사이트에 / 오늘까지

해설 빈칸은 정동사 자리이며, 주어가 단수이므로 복수 동사인 (B)는 탈락한다. 과거시점인 yesterday(어제)라는 단서가 있으므로 과거시제인 (A)가 정답이다.

표현 정리 announcement 발표 personnel 직원, 인사
arrangements 배치 post 붙이다, 게시하다

◎ 실전에 적용해 봐
1. (C) 2. (D) 3. (C) 4. (A) 5. (D) 6. (C) 7. (B)
8. (B) 9. (A) 10. (C)

1. 정답 (C)

해설 Reborn Corporation은 성장했다 / 주요 회사 중의 하나로 / 국가를 대표하는 / 재정적인 어려움을 극복한 후에 / 작년에

해설 빈칸은 정동사 자리이므로 준동사인 (B)와 (D)는 탈락한다. 과거시점인 last year(작년에)라는 단서가 있으므로 과거시제인 (C)가 정답이다.

표현 정리 major 주요한 corporation 회사 represent 대표하다
overcome 극복하다 financial 재정 difficulty 어려움

2. 정답 (D)

해설 Mr. Pal은 요청 받았다 / 조사를 실시하도록 / 고객에 관한 / 그리고 권고 받았다 / 의견을 반영하도록 / 3주 전에 / 새 모델이 출시되기 전

해설 빈칸은 문장의 정동사 자리이므로 준동사인 (A)와 (C)는 오답이다. 과거 시점인 three weeks ago(3주 전에)라는 단서가 있으므로 과거시제인 (D)가 정답이다.

표현 정리 be asked to+동사원형 ~하도록 요청 받다 conduct a survey 조사를 수행하다 be advised to+동사원형 ~하도록 권고 받다
reflect 반영하다

3. 정답 (C)

해설 Ms. Pill은 환영 받았다 / 그녀의 직장 동료에게 / 그녀가 Hitsby 사로 돌아왔을 때 / 4개월 동안의 출산휴가 후에

해설 빈칸은 문장의 정동사 자리이므로 준동사인 (A)는 탈락한다. 환영 받은 시점은 그녀가 출산 휴가로부터 돌아온 시점과 같으므로, when이 이끄는 부사절과 시제가 같아야 한다. 따라서 (C)가 정답이다.

표현 정리 co-workers 직장동료 maternity leave 출산 휴가

4. 정답 (A)

해설 매니저는 발표했다 / 많은 수의 직원들이 / 승진했다고 / 지난 몇 년 동안

해설 past만 보고 과거시제인 (B)를 답으로 하기 쉬운 함정 문제이다. during부터 years까지는 앞에 있는 have been promoted를 수식한다.

(B)는 수동태이므로 목적어인 that S V가 올 수 없다. 따라서 (A)가 정답이다.

표현 정리 announce 발표하다 employee 직원 promote 승진하다, 승진시키다

5. 정답 (D)

해설 Mr. Cater는 일했다 / 시간제 종사자로 / Joey 레스토랑에서 / Plenty Buffet으로 옮기기 전에 / 하루 9시간 근무를 하기 위해 / 2007년에

해설 빈칸은 문장의 정동사 자리이므로 준동사인 (B)는 탈락한다. 주어가 단수이므로 복수 동사인 (A) 역시 탈락한다. (C)와 (D) 중 'before+과거시제'가 나오면 과거보다 이전에 일어난 일이므로 과거완료시제를 쓰거나 과거시제를 써야 한다. 따라서 (D)가 정답이다.

표현 정리 part-timer 시간제 근로자 move 옮기다 shifts 근무

6. 정답 (C)

해설 지난 달에 / 새 프로젝트를 맡은 엔지니어는 요청했다 / 최고 관리자에게 마감일을 연장할 것을

해설 문두의 Last month만 보고 과거동사인 (D)를 골랐다면 함정에 빠진 것이다. 정동사 requested가 있으므로 빈칸은 준동사 자리이며, 따라서 (C)가 정답이다.

표현 정리 take on ~을 떠맡다 engineer 기술자 request 요청하다
executive manager 최고 관리자

7. 정답 (B)

해설 Fire Investment의 고객 수가 감소했다 / 많은 회사들이 / 파산 했을 때 / 재정적인 어려움 때문에

해설 빈칸은 문장의 정동사 자리이므로 준동사인 (A)는 탈락한다. 'the number of+복수 명사+단수 동사'로 쓰이므로 빈칸에는 단수 동사가 와야 한다. when이 이끄는 부사절의 동사가 과거이므로 주절의 시제는 과거시제인 (B)가 정답이다.

표현 정리 bankrupt 파산된 financial 재정의, 재무의 difficulties 어려움 decrease 감소하다

8. 정답 (B)

해설 Robust Auto는 Mr. Raymond에 의해 설립됐다 / 50년 전에 / 겨우 소수의 유명 자동차 회사만 있을 당시에

해설 빈칸은 문장의 정동사 자리이고, 주어가 단수이므로 복수 동사인 (D)는 탈락한다. found는 '~을 설립하다'는 뜻으로 목적어가 있어야 하는데, 빈칸 뒤에 전명구가 나와 목적어가 없으므로 능동형인 (C) 역시 탈락한다. 과거시점인 50 years ago라는 단서가 있으므로 과거시제인 (B)가 답이다.

표현 정리 renowned 유명한 automobile 자동차 found 설립하다

9. 정답 (A)

해설 Gloria Weddings는 추구해 왔다 / 고객 만족을 / 그들의 첫 번째 목표로 / 10년 전에 회사가 창립된 이래

해설 빈칸은 문장의 정동사 자리이므로 준동사인 (B)는 탈락한다. since가 이끄는 부사절에 과거시제가 왔으므로 주절의 시제는 현재완료시제인 (A)가

정답 및 해설 49

가 정답이다. ten years ago라는 말만 보고 과거시제를 답으로 하면 틀리는 함정 문제이다.

표현정리 satisfaction 만족 primary 주된, 첫째의 found 창립하다, 설립하다 pursue 추구하다

10. 정답 (C)

해석 발표 되었을 때 / 안전 점검이 곧 실시될 것이라고 / Mr. Corazon은 그의 자료들을 치웠다 / 공간을 청소하기 위해

해설 빈칸은 문장의 정동사 자리이므로 준동사인 (B)는 탈락한다. 빈칸 뒤에 목적어가 있으므로 수동형인 (D) 역시 탈락한다. when이 이끄는 부사절에 과거시제가 쓰였으므로 주절의 시제도 과거시제인 (C)가 정답이다. 불규칙 동사인 put의 과거형은 put이며, put이 복수 동사라서 안 된다고 생각했다면 함정에 빠진 것이다.

표현정리 safety 안전 inspection 검사, 점검 announce 발표하다 put away 치우다 clean up 청소하다, 깨끗이 치우다

법칙 33 before[after, when, while]에는 -ing, as[once, unless, if]에는 p.p.

◎ **유형을 파악해 봐**
1. (A) 2. (C) 3. (A)

1. 정답 (A)

해석 전원을 꺼 주세요 / 모든 가전제품의 / 방을 나가기 전에

해설 빈칸 앞에 주어가 없으므로 준동사 자리이며, 정동사인 (C)와 (D)는 탈락한다. 빈칸 뒤에 목적어가 있으므로 -ing 형태인 (A)가 정답이다.

표현정리 make sure 확실히 하다 turn off 전원을 끄다 appliance 가전제품 before -ing ~하기 전에

2. 정답 (C)

해석 Breeze Air의 고객들은 방문할 필요가 있다 / Breeze Air 웹사이트를 / 그리고 먼저 비행 스케줄을 확인할 것을 / 항공편을 예약할 때

해설 빈칸 앞에 주어가 없으므로 준동사 자리이며, 정동사인 (A)와 (D)는 탈락한다. 빈칸 뒤에 목적어가 있으므로 -ing 형태인 (C)가 정답이다. 접속사 when 다음에 to 부정사가 오는 경우는 '언제 ~할지'라는 뜻의 명사절 접속사로 쓰이는 경우이다. when -ing는 분사구문이며, 일종의 부사절 축약 형태이다.

표현정리 customer 고객 visit 방문하다 check 확인하다, 점검하다 reservation 예약

3. 정답 (A)

해석 아침 일찍 언급했듯이 / 우리는 간결한 토론을 할 것이다 / 우리의 프로젝트에 대해 / 오늘 저녁 늦게

해설 빈칸 앞에 주어가 없으므로 준동사 자리이며, 정동사인 (B)와 (D)는 탈락한다. 빈칸 뒤에 목적어가 없고 부사와 전명구가 왔으므로 p.p. 형태인 (A)가 정답이다. (B)와 (D)를 명사로 볼 경우 as는 전치사가 되는데, 이때 as는 '역할, 자격, 기능, 성질' 등을 나타낸다. 즉, '언급의 기능으로서'라는 말이 되어 어색하다.

표현정리 brief 간결한 discussion 토론, 논의 mention 말하다, 언급하다

◎ **실전에 적용해 봐**
1. (B) 2. (A) 3. (D) 4. (B) 5. (C) 6. (C) 7. (D)
8. (A) 9. (A) 10. (B)

1. 정답 (B)

해석 매니저는 결정했다 / 추가 직원을 고용하기로 / 증가된 업무량을 고려한 후에 / 그런데 그 업무량은 너무 많아 다루기 힘들었다 / 현 직원 수로는 / 그의 감독 하에 있는

해설 빈칸 앞에 주어가 없으므로 준동사 자리이며, 정동사인 (A)는 탈락한다. 명사는 연속으로 올 수 없으므로 (C) 역시 탈락한다. 빈칸 뒤에 목적어가 있으므로 -ing 형태인 (B)가 정답이다.

표현정리 hire 고용하다 employee 직원 workload 업무량 handle 다루다 current 현재의 supervision 감독

2. 정답 (A)

해석 이벤트에 참가하는 모든 사람들은 / 가져올 필요가 있다 / 초대장을 / 그들과 함께 / 이벤트에 참석할 때

해설 빈칸 앞에 주어가 없으므로 준동사 자리이며, 정동사인 (B)와 (D)는 탈락한다. 빈칸 뒤에 목적어가 있으므로 -ing 형태인 (A)가 정답이다.

표현정리 participant 참가자 invitation 초대장 attend 참석하다

3. 정답 (D)

해석 피부과 전문의가 추천한 대로 / 이 얼굴 관리 제품은 가장 효과적이다 / 하루에 세 번 사용할 때

해설 빈칸 앞에 주어가 없으므로 준동사 자리이며, 정동사인 (A)는 탈락한다. 빈칸 뒤에 목적어가 없고 전명구가 있으므로 p.p. 형태인 (D)가 정답이다. (C)가 오면 as가 전치사가 되는데, 전치사일 때는 '역할, 자격, 기능, 성질' 등을 나타낸다. 즉, '추천의 기능으로서'라는 말이 되어 어색하다.

표현정리 dermatologist 피부과 의사 facial 얼굴의 care 관리, 돌봄

4. 정답 (B)

해석 시간 부족 때문에 / 사전에 회의를 준비할 / Mr. Lake는 생각했다 / 그가 논의해야 할 것에 대해 / 회의에서 / 운전해 가는 동안 / 지정된 장소로

해설 빈칸 앞에 주어가 없으므로 준동사 자리이며, 정동사인 (A)와 (C)는 탈락한다. 빈칸 뒤에 목적어가 없다고 p.p. 형태를 정답으로 고른다면 함정에 빠진 것이다. 여기서 drive는 1형식 동사이며, 'drive to 장소'는 '~쪽으로 운전하다'라는 뜻이다. 따라서 -ing 형태인 (B)가 정답이다.

표현정리 due to ~때문에 lack 부족, 결핍 prepare 준비하다 beforehand 사전에, 미리 discuss 논의하다, 토론하다 designated 지정된

5. 정답 (C)

해석 온라인으로 신청서를 제출하기 전에 / Mr. Gill은 재차 확인해야 한다 / 이메일 주소를 / 프로그램 매니저의

해설 빈칸 앞에 주어가 없으므로 준동사- 자리이며, 정동사인 (A)와 (D)는 탈락한다. 빈칸 뒤에 목적어가 있으므로 -ng 형태인 (C)가 정답이다.

표현 정리 application form 신청서 double-check 재확인하다 submit 제출하다

6. 정답 (C)

해설 Mr. Nolan의 새 프로젝트는 / 만약 승인된다면 / 더 많은 투자가 수반되어야 할 것 같다

해설 빈칸 앞에 주어가 없으므로 준동사 자리이며, 빈칸 뒤에 목적어가 없으므로 (A)와 (D)는 탈락한다. 따라서 p.p 형태인 (C)가 정답이다. (B)가 오면 주어 'new project가 만약 승인이라면'처럼 동격이 되어 해석이 어색해진다.

표현 정리 be likely to+동사원형 ~ 할 것 같다 investment 투자 carry out 수행하다 approve 승인하다

7. 정답 (D)

해설 알아두세요 / 이 맞춤 제작된 제품들은 / 환불이나 교환될 수 없다는 것을 / 일단 주문하면

해설 빈칸 앞에 주어가 없으므로 준동사 자리이며, (B)와 (C)는 탈락한다. 빈칸 뒤 목적어가 없으므로 (D)가 정답이다.

표현 정리 be aware that ~를 알아두다 customized 맞춤형의 refund 환불하다 order 주문하다; 주문

8. 정답 (A)

해설 그의 행방에 대해 질문 받았을 때 / Mr. Bee는 명확한 답변을 할 수 없었다 / 그가 완전히 새로운 곳에 있었기 때문에 / 그의 출장 동안에

해설 빈칸 앞에 주어가 없으므로 준동사 자리이며, 정동사인 (B)와 (D)는 탈락한다. 빈칸 뒤에 목적어가 있다고 해서 -ing인 (C)를 골랐다면 함정에 빠진 것이다. ask는 4형식 동사이므로 수동태일 때 목적어가 남을 수 있다. 콤마 다음 문장에서 '명확한 답변을 주지 않았다'고 하는 것은 그가 '질문했을 때'가 아닌, '질문 받았을 때'이므로 p.p 인 (A)가 정답이다.

표현 정리 whereabouts 행방, 소재 clear 확실한 completely 완전히 business trip 출장

9. 정답 (A)

해설 Mr. Gibson은 Ms. Stuart에게 요청했다 / 그의 일을 잠깐 맡아달라고 / 출장으로 자리를 비우는 동안

해설 while 다음에는 he is가 생략되었는데, 이러한 형태를 분사구문이라고 하며, while he is away on his business trip이 원래의 문장이다. 전치사가 2개 오는 것이 어색하므로 나머지 보기들은 오답이다.

표현 정리 assume 맡다 temporarily 일시적으로 business trip 출장

10. 정답 (B)

해설 인상적이지는 않았지만 / 한 시간 동안의 / 강의는 / Olsen 교수의 / 꽤 간단하고 명료했다

해설 Though it(= the one-hour lecture) was not impressive에서 it was가 생략된 분사구문이다. 빈칸은 보어 자리이므로 형용사- (B)가 와야 한다.

표현 정리 lecture 강의 rather 꽤 brief and to the point 요점에 딱 들어 맞는, 간단 명료한 impress 깊은 인상을 주다, 감명을 주다

법칙 34 등위접속사(and, but, or, yet)가 답이면 같은 것은 버려라

◎ 유형을 파악해 봐
1. (C) 2. (D) 3. (A)

1. 정답 (C)

해설 당신은 지하철이나 버스를 탈 수 있다 / 센트럴파크 역까지

해설 빈칸 앞에 명사, 뒤에도 명사가 있는 것으로 보아 등위접속사 자리이다. 지하철이나 버스를 탈 수 있다는 말이 자연스러우므로 (C)가 답이다. (B)와 (D)는 부사이다.

표현 정리 subway 지하철 station 역

2. 정답 (D)

해설 Ms. Pratt는 올렸다 / 가장 훌륭한 판매 기록을 / 올해 직원들 중에 / 그리고 보상을 받을 것이다

해설 빈칸 앞에는 완전한 문장이, 빈칸 뒤에는 동사가 왔으므로 접속사- 자리이다. 주어가 같아 생략되었기 때문에 빈칸 뒤에는 주어가 없고, 바로 동사가 나온 경우이다. 빈칸 앞뒤가 순차적인 흐름이므로 (D)가 정답이다.

표현 정리 record 기록하다 among ~중에 employee 직원 receive 받다 award 상

3. 정답 (A)

해설 우리는 철저히 검토하였다 / 당신의 이력서를 / 하지만 당신에게 말해야 한다 / 일자리를 제공 받지 못할 것이라고 / 우리 회사에서

해설 빈칸은 문장과 문장을 이어주는 등위접속사 자리이다. 주어가 같기 때문에, 빈칸 뒤 주어가 생략되고 동사가 바로 나왔다. 이력서를 검토했다는 내용과 일자리가 제공되지 않을 것이라는 내용이 서로 대조를 이루기 때문에 (A)가 정답이다.

표현 정리 thoroughly 철저히 review 검토하다 resume 이력서 offer 제공하다

◎ 실전에 적용해 봐
1. (C) 2. (B) 3. (D) 4. (A) 5. (C) 6. (B) 7. (D)
8. (D) 9. (C) 10. (C)

1. 정답 (C)

해설 'Lost with the Macara' 공연을 위한 티켓들은 / 판매될 것이다 / 정문과 / 건물 2층에서

해설 빈칸 앞뒤로 전명구가 있으므로 등위접속사 자리이다. (B)와 (D)는 부사로 연결기능이 없으므로 탈락한다. 병치 구조가 가능한 (A)와 (C) 중에서 의미가 자연스러운 것을 골라야 하는데, 문맥상 정문과 2층에서라는 말이

정답 및 해설 51

자연스러우므로 (C)가 정답이다.

표현 정리 play 공연 front gate 정문

2. 정답 (B)

해설 행사가 Kensington 가에서 열리든, Bluemerry 가에서 열리든 / 이벤트 계획자는 / 우리에게 반드시 예산 견적서를 제출해야 한다 / 이벤트에 드는

해설 빈칸은 명사와 명사의 병렬구조를 만들어 주는 등위접속사 자리이다. 병렬구조가 가능한 접속사는 문맥상 (B)이다. or는 whether와 함께 쓰여 '~이든, 아니든'이라는 의미를 나타낸다.

표현 정리 whether (or) ~인지 아닌지 budget 예산 estimate 견적서

3. 정답 (D)

해설 KarlBay 의류의 판촉 판매가 / 열릴 것이다 / 본점과 시내 매장에서

해설 빈칸은 전명구와 전명구를 이어주는 등위접속사 자리이다. (A)와 (D) 중 '본점과 시내 매장'이라는 말이 자연스러우므로 (D)가 정답이다. (B)와 (C)는 부사이다.

표현 정리 promotional sales 판촉 판매 downtown 시내

4. 정답 (A)

해설 Ms. Nielson은 / 컴퓨터 프로그래밍 분야에 / 아직 3년 밖에 있지 않지만 / 지명되었다 / 뛰어난 직원 중 한 명으로 / Carper Tech에서

해설 빈칸은 앞 문장과 뒷문장을 이어주는 등위접속사 자리이다. 두 문장의 주어가 Ms. Nielson으로 같아 뒤에서는 주어가 생략돼 동사가 바로 나온 형태이다. 두 문장의 내용이 대조를 이루므로 (A)가 정답이다. (B)는 뒤에 완벽한 문장이 오거나, 콤마 뒤에 쓰여 도치된 문장을 이끈다. (C)는 부사이다.

표현 정리 field 분야 be nominated as ~로 지명되다

5. 정답 (C)

해설 Tabot Oil & Gas는 기업들 중 하나이다 / 몹시 영향을 받은 / 석유가격 폭등에 / 하지만 빠르게 회복했다 / 그리고 사업을 안정시켰다

해설 빈칸은 앞 문장과 뒷문장을 이어주는 등위접속사 자리이다. 주어가 Talbot Oil & Gas로 같기 때문에 뒤에서는 주어가 생략돼 동사가 바로 나온 형태이다. 심각하게 영향을 받았지만 회복했다는 의미가 자연스러우므로, 대조를 이루는 (C)가 정답이다. 연결 기능이 없는 부사인 (B)는 오답이다.

표현 정리 badly 몹시, 심하게 recover 회복되다 stabilize 안정시키다

6. 정답 (B)

해설 Mr. Coy는 끝냈다 / 그의 리포트를 / 조금 전에 / 그리고 그것을 출력했다 / 매니저에게 보여주기 위해

해설 빈칸은 앞 문장과 뒷문장을 연결해 주는 등위접속사 자리이다. 주어가 Mr. Coy로 같아 뒤에서는 생략됐기 때문에 동사가 바로 나온 형태이다. 보기들이 모두 등위접속사이므로 해석이 자연스러운 것으로 결정해야 한다. 빈칸 앞과 뒤가 연속적으로 이어지는 내용이므로 (B)가 정답이다.

표현 정리 a while ago 조금 전에

7. 정답 (D)

해설 Ms. Young은 갖고 있지만 / 많은 근무 경험을 / 회계 분야에서 / 마케팅 분야에 더 많은 관심을 갖고 있었다.

해설 빈칸은 앞 문장과 뒷문장을 연결해 주는 등위접속사 자리이다. 주어가 Ms. Young으로 같기 때문에 뒤에서는 주어가 생략되어 동사가 나온 형태이다. 보기들 중 해석이 가장 자연스러운 것으로 결정해야 한다. 회계 분야에 경험이 있지만 마케팅 분야에 더 관심이 있었다는 내용이므로 대조를 이루는 (D)가 정답이다.

표현 정리 accounting 회계 interest 흥미, 관심

8. 정답 (D)

해설 Hemmington 은행은 / 상당히 낮은 이직률을 갖고 있는 / 기관이다 / 직원 복지가 최우선 사항이었고, 앞으로도 최우선 사항이 될

해설 was 다음에는 the top priority가, will be 앞에는 its employee welfare가 생략된 구조이다. 이러한 구조를 가질 수 있는 (B)와 (D) 중에서 과거에도 그랬고, 미래에도 그럴 것이라는 내용을 이어줄 수 있는 (D)가 정답이다.

표현 정리 significantly 상당히 turnover rate 이직률 institution 기관 welfare 복지 top priority 최우선

9. 정답 (C)

해설 더 많은 고객을 유치하기 위해 / 중요하다 / 고객 만족과 제품의 품질을 높이는 것이

해설 빈칸 앞에 명사, 빈칸 뒤에 명사가 있으므로 등위접속사 자리이다. 등위접속사 (A)와 (C) 중에 해석이 자연스러운 것으로 결정한다. 고객 만족과 제품의 질을 높인다는 말이 자연스럽기 때문에 (C)가 정답이다. (B)는 전치사로 명사 앞에 올 수 있지만, '제품의 질을 제외하고, 고객 만족을 높인다'는 해석이 되기 때문에 틀리고, (D)는 부사이므로 오답이다.

표현 정리 in order to+동사원형 ~하기 위해서 customer satisfaction 고객 만족 quality 품질, 질

10. 정답 (C)

해설 전자상거래 사이트는 권장한다 / 하지만 의무적이지는 않다 / 그들의 고객들이 / 이메일 주소를 확인하도록

해설 빈칸 앞 encourage는 목적어가 생략되어 있고, 빈칸 뒤 does not은 주어가 생략되어 있다. 따라서 동일 요소의 생략이 가능한 등위접속사 자리이다. (B)는 부사절 접속사이므로 완전한 문장이 와야 하므로 탈락하고, (A)와 (C) 중 해석이 더 자연스러운 것으로 결정해야 한다. 권장은 하지만 의무는 아니라는 내용이므로 (C)가 정답이다. (D)는 부사이다.

표현 정리 e-commerce 전자상거래 encourage 권장하다 mandatory 의무적인, 강제의 verify 확인하다, 입증하다

법칙 35 미래 시점 단서(tomorrow, next, future)가 보이면 미래시제 또는 현재진행시제

◎ 유형을 파악해 봐
1. (A)   2. (D)   3. (D)

1. 정답 (A)

해설 소비자 조사 결과가 / 다음 달에 나올 것이다.

해설 빈칸은 문장의 정동사 자리이며, 미래 시점인 next month(다음 달)라는 단서가 있으므로 미래시제인 (A)가 정답이다. 주어가 복수이므로 단수동사인 (B)는 오답이다.

표현 정리 consumer 소비자 survey 조사 come out 나오다, 생산되다

2. 정답 (D)

해설 전시회는 / New Uptown으로 오는 / 다음 주 월요일에 / 개최될 것이다 / 2주 동안

해설 빈칸은 정동사 자리이며, 미래 시점인 next Monday라는 단서가 있으므로 미래시제인 (D)가 정답이다. 준동사인 (A)는 오답이다.

표현 정리 exhibition 전시회 for 2 weeks 2주 동안

3. 정답 (D)

해설 회사는 개최할 것이다 / 공식적인 은퇴 파티를 / 부사장님을 위한 / 내일 아침에

해설 빈칸은 문장의 정동사 자리이며, 미래 시점인 tomorrow morning이라는 단서가 있으므로 미래시제인 (D)가 정답이다.

표현 정리 official 공식적인 retirement 은퇴 vice president 부사장

◎ 실전에 적용해 봐
1. (B)   2. (C)   3. (B)   4. (A)   5. (D)   6. (B)   7. (C)
8. (B)   9. (D)   10. (B)

1. 정답 (B)

해설 Mr. Blonde는 직원들에게 알려줄 것이다 / 수정된 안전 수칙에 대해 / 업무 규정 대신 / 내일

해설 빈칸은 문장의 정동사 자리이며, 미래 시점인 tomorrow라는 단서가 있으므로 미래시제인 (B)가 정답이다.

표현 정리 instruct 알려주다, 지시하다 revised 개정된, 수정된

2. 정답 (C)

해설 증가하는 액체 비누의 수요에 대응하기 위해 / Everyday Needs 사는 개발할 것이다 / 리필 가능한 액체 비누를 / 그리고 소개할 것이다 / 시장에 / 가까운 미래에

해설 빈칸은 문장의 정동사 자리이며, 미래 시점인 in the near future라는 단서가 있으므로 미래시제인 (C)가 정답이다. 준동사인 (B)는 오답이다.

표현 정리 in response to ~에 대한 대응으로 demand 수요 refillable 보충 가능한, 리필 가능한

3. 정답 (B)

해설 Comfy Furniture 사는 계획하고 있다 / 더 많은 모델을 추가할 것을 / 옷장 제품의 / 앞으로 3년 이내에

해설 빈칸은 문장의 정동사 자리이며, 미래 시점인 the next 3 years라는 단서가 있으므로 (B)가 정답이다. 미래적인 어감을 갖는 미래 상당어구인 be planning to는 미래시제처럼 사용 가능하다.

표현 정리 add A to B A를 B에 추가하다 wardrobe 옷장

4. 정답 (A)

해설 본사에서 오는 Mr. Down은 도착할 것이다 / 시내에 / 지사 임원을 만나기 위해 / 늦어도 내일 아침까지

해설 빈칸은 문장의 정동사 자리이며, 미래 시점인 tomorrow morning이라는 단서가 있으므로 미래시제인 (A)가 답이다. 준동사인 (B)와 (C)는 오답이다.

표현 정리 headquarter 본사 official 임원, 공무원 regional office 지사 no later than 늦어도 ~까지

5. 정답 (D)

해설 Trenta Corporation의 대표 이사는 요청했다 / 매니저들이 검토할 것을 / 프로그램 운영상의 문제 원인을 / 미래에

해설 빈칸은 that 절 안의 정동사 자리이다. in the future를 보고 바로 미래시제인 (C)를 고른다면 함정에 빠진 것이다. ask는 '요청하다' 동사 ('법칙 26' 참고)로, that절 안의 동사 앞에는 should가 생략되었으므로 동사원형인 (D)가 와야 한다. 준동사인 (B)는 오답이다.

표현 정리 executive officer 대표 이사 cause 원인 operational problem 운영상의 문제

6. 정답 (B)

해설 Bad Kid 사의 TV 광고는 곧 검토될 것이다 / 적절성에 대해 / 10세 이하의 어린이들에게 괜찮은지의

해설 빈칸은 문장의 정동사 자리이며, 미래시제와 잘 어울리는 부사 soon이 있는 것으로 보아 미래시제인 (B)가 어울린다. 주어가 단수이므로 복수 동사인 (C)는 오답, 빈칸 뒤에 목적어가 없으므로 능동태인 (A) 역시 오답, (D)는 준동사이다.

표현 정리 commercial 광고 appropriateness 타당성 age 나이

7. 정답 (C)

해설 Ms. Rose는 현재 / 필요한 문서들을 복사하고 있다 / 그리고 그것들을 나눠줄 것이다 / 모든 참석자들에게 / 내일 있을 미팅 초반에

해설 and 다음에는 주어인 Ms. Rose가 생략되었다. '내일 있을 미팅 초반' 역시 미래 시점이므로 미래진행시제인 (C)가 정답이다. 복수 동사인 (A)는 오답이다.

표현 정리 currently 현재 distribute 나눠주다, 분배하다 attendee 참석자

8. 정답 (B)

해설 이사회는 / 다음 주 수요일에 개최될 것이다 / 이번 주 목요일 대신에

/ 참가자 중 일부가 / 비즈니스 관계로 도시를 떠나 있기 때문에

해설 빈칸은 정동사 자리이다. 미래 시점을 나타내는 단서 next Wednesday가 있으므로 미래시제를 골라야 하는데, be to는 '~할 것이다'라는 의미의 미래 상당어구이므로 (B)가 정답이다. (A)는 존재하지 않는 말이다.

표현 정리 board meeting 이사회 attendee 참가자

9.   정답 (D)

해설 만약 당신이 내일 열릴 세미나를 예약한다면 / 저에게 확실하게 알려 주세요 / 날짜와 시간을 / 즉시

해설 빈칸은 정동사 자리이다. 미래 시점인 tomorrow가 있다고 해서 (B)를 고른다면 함정에 빠진 것이다. 조건 부사절에서는 현재시제가 미래를 대신하기 때문에 현재시제인 (D)가 정답이다. 준동사인 (C)는 오답이다.

표현 정리 reservation 예약 be sure to+동사원형 ~을 확실하게 하다, 보장하다 right away 즉시

10.   정답 (B)

해설 Sue는 최근에 했다 / 서면 통보를 / 그녀의 부재와 관련해 / 가까운 미래에 계획한 가족 여행으로 인해

해설 빈칸은 정동사 자리이다. recently는 '최근에'라는 뜻으로 현재와 함께 사용될 것 같지만, 과거나 현재완료와 쓰인다. 따라서 정답은 (B)이다. 문장 끝에 for the near future가 있어 미래시제라고 생각할 수 있지만 이는 함정이다. 계획된 여행이 미래임을 말하는 것이지, 통보를 한 시점이 미래가 아니기 때문에 (D)는 오답이다.

표현 정리 written notice 서면 통보 regarding ~에 관하여 absence 부재 planned 계획된

법칙 36 '사람 선행사+_____+동사'는 who

◎ 유형을 파악해 봐
1. (C)   2. (B)   3. (B)

1.   정답 (C)

해설 신입 사원들 / 아직 그들의 이름 카드를 갖고 있지 않은 / 반드시 요청해야 한다 / 그것을 / 이번 주에

해설 빈칸은 앞의 명사를 수식하는 형용사절 접속사 자리이다. 선행사가 사람이고, 빈칸 뒤에 주어가 빠졌으므로 (C)가 정답이다. (A)는 소유격 관계대명사로, 바로 뒤에 명사가 와야 한다. (B)는 명사절 접속사, (D)는 완전한 문장과 쓰인다.

표현 정리 employee 직원 request 요청하다

2.   정답 (B)

해설 제출한 사람은 / 고객 설문조사에 대한 의견을 / 받을 것이다 / 무료 샘플들을 / 우리의 새 미용 제품들의

해설 빈칸 앞에 있는 anyone을 수식하는 형용사절 접속사 자리인데, 형용사절 안의 주어 자리가 비어 있으므로 주격 관계대명사가 와야 한다. 선행사가 사람이므로 (B)가 답이다. (A)는 소유격 관계대명사, (C)는 목적격 관계

대명사, (D)는 형용사절 접속사로 쓰일 경우 선행사가 사물일 때 쓴다.

표현 정리 submit 제출하다 response 응답, 대답 survey 조사

3.   정답 (B)

해설 엔지니어들은 / 공지를 받지 않은 / 할당된 업무에 관한 / 요구된다 / 매니저에게 연락할 것이

해설 정동사가 2개이므로 빈칸은 접속사 자리인데, 빈칸 앞에 있는 Engineers를 수식하는 형용사절 접속사면서, 주격 관계대명사인 (B)가 와야 한다. (C)는 목적격 관계대명사이다.

표현 정리 receive 받다 notice 공지 assigned 할당된 task 업무

◎ 실전에 적용해 봐
1. (D)   2. (A)   3. (A)   4. (D)   5. (C)   6. (B)   7. (A)
8. (C)   9. (D)   10. (D)

1.   정답 (D)

해설 공공 세미나가 / 열렸다 / 사람들을 위한 / 원예에 관심이 있는

해설 문장의 정동사가 2개 왔다. 빈칸 앞의 선행사가 사람이고, 빈칸 뒤에 정동사가 있으므로 주어 역할을 할 수 있는 (D)가 와야 한다. (A)는 목적격, (B)는 소유격 관계대명사이다.

표현 정리 be interested in ~에 관심이 있다 gardening 원예

2.   정답 (A)

해설 직원 매니저는 문서들을 검토해 왔다 / 지원자들이 보낸 / 지사에서 근무할 / 일단 채용되면

해설 문장의 정동사가 2개이므로 접속사가 필요하다. 빈칸부터 끝까지는 빈칸 앞에 있는 applicant를 수식하는 형용사절이다. 주어 자리가 비어있으므로 주격 관계대명사 (A)가 정답이다. (B)는 목적격 관계대명사이다.

표현 정리 regional office 지사

3.   정답 (A)

해설 다수의 여행 프로그램이 제공되었다 / Balloon Tour's의 고객들에게 / 여행을 계획하는 / 휴일 동안

해설 문장의 정동사가 2개 왔다. 빈칸부터 끝까지는 빈칸 앞에 있는 customers를 수식하는 형용사절이며, 빈칸 뒤에 정동사가 있으므로 주격 관계대명사인 (A)가 와야 한다. (B)는 목적격 관계대명사, (D)는 소유격 관계대명사이다.

표현 정리 a number of 다수의 offer 제공하다

4.   정답 (D)

해설 무료 환불과 교환이 허용된다 / 사람들에게 / 다른 사이즈의 옷을 구입한 / 그리고 구매일로부터 3일 이내에 옷을 반품하는

해설 문장의 정동사가 2개 왔다. 빈칸 앞의 선행사가 사람이고, 빈칸 뒤에 정동사가 있으므로 주격 관계대명사인 (D)가 와야 한다. (A)는 소유격 관계대명사이다.

표현 정리 refund 환불 exchange 교환 allow 허용하다 those

who ~하는 사람들 within (특정 기간) 이내에

5. 정답 (C)

해설 증가하는 관광객 수는 / Roam 강을 방문한 / 긍정적인 영향을 끼쳤다 / 지역 경제에

해설 빈칸부터 River까지는 빈칸 앞 tourists를 수식하는 형용사절이다. 주어 자리가 빠져 있으므로 주격 관계대명사 (C)가 와야 한다. (A)는 소유격 관계대명사, (B)와 (D)는 목적격 관계대명사이다.

표현 정리 increasing 증가하는 have an effect on ~에 영향을 미치다 regional 지역의

6. 정답 (B)

해설 고객들만이 / Danny Ferenz의 새로운 앨범을 미리 구매한 / 다음 주 월요일에 배송 받을 것이다 / 출시 하루 전인

해설 문장의 정동사가 2개 왔다. 빈칸 앞의 선행사가 사람이고, 빈칸 뒤에 정동사가 있으므로 주격 관계대명사 (B)가 정답이다. (A)는 소유격 관계대명사, (D)는 목적격 관계대명사이다. preorder를 명사로 착각해 (A)를 답으로 고르지 않도록 하자.

표현 정리 preorder 사전 주문하다 release 출시

7. 정답 (A)

해설 신 모델은 / Vagen Auto 자동차 계열의 / 디자인되었다 / 기술자들에 의해 / 그 분야에서 유명한

해설 문장의 정동사가 2개 왔다. 빈칸 앞의 선행사가 사람이고, 빈칸 뒤에 정동사가 있으므로 주격 관계대명사 (A)가 정답이다. (B)는 소유격 관계대명사이다.

표현 정리 automobile 자동차 renowned 유명한 field 분야

8. 정답 (C)

해설 Mr. Twain은 의학 전문가이다 / Wellbeing 사에서 근무하는 / 직원들의 건강 관리를 담당하기 위해

해설 빈칸 앞의 professional은 '전문가'라는 뜻의 사람 선행사이므로 빈칸은 사람을 선행사로 갖는 형용사절 접속사 자리이다. 빈칸 뒤에 있는 works를 명사로 보고, whose를 답으로 고르기 쉬운 문제이다. 여기서 works는 정동사이므로 주격 관계대명사 (C)가 와야 한다. (B)는 소유격 관계대명사이다.

표현 정리 professional 전문가 handle 다루다, 처리하다

9. 정답 (D)

해설 Mr. Tale은 / 요청 받았다 / Michael Back의 업무를 맡도록 / 잠시 자리를 비운 / 출장을 위해

해설 문장의 정동사가 2개 왔다. 빈칸 앞의 선행사가 사람이고, 빈칸 뒤에 정동사가 있으므로 주격 관계대명사 (D)가 정답이다. (B)는 콤마 다음에 오지 않고, (A)는 소유격 관계대명사이다.

표현 정리 be asked to ~하기를 요구 받다 assume (책임을) 맡다 temporarily 일시적으로

10. 정답 (D)

해설 시설들은 / 작동하는 / 유난히 시끄러운 소리를 내면서 / 고장이 의심된다 / 그리고 교체를 위해 보고돼야 한다

해설 빈칸 앞의 선행사가 사물이고, 빈칸은 형용사절 접속사 자리이다. 빈칸 뒤에 정동사가 있으므로 주격 관계대명사 (D)가 와야 한다. (B)와 (C)는 소유격 관계대명사이다. 빈칸 뒤 function을 명사로 착각해 소유격 관계대명사를 고르지 않도록 하자.

표현 정리 facility 시설 function 가동하다, 기능하다 unusually 유난히 loud 큰, 시끄러운 suspect 의심하다 break down 고장 나다 replacement 대체, 교체

법칙 37 명사를 뒤에서 수식해 주는 분사는 목적어가 있으면 -ing, 없으면 p.p.

◎ 유형을 파악해 봐
1. (D) 2. (B) 3. (A)

1. 정답 (D)

해설 부동산 중개인이 올 것이다 / 가치를 평가하기 위해 / Hale 호수를 둘러싼 지역의

해설 문장에서 정동사는 will come이다. 빈칸 뒤에 관사가 있으므로 빈칸은 앞의 명사를 수식하는 분사 자리이다. 뒤에 목적어가 있으므로 -ing 형태인 (D)가 정답이다.

표현 정리 real estate agent 부동산 중개인 evaluate 평가하다 surround 둘러싸다, 에워싸다

2. 정답 (B)

해설 사고가 발생할 경우 / 비상 조치를 참고하시오 / 게시판에 요약되어 있는

해설 문장에서 정동사는 refer to이다. 빈칸은 앞의 명사를 수식하는 분사 자리이다. 빈칸 뒤에 목적어가 없으므로 p.p. 형태인 (B)가 정답이다.

표현 정리 in case of ~의 경우 refer to+명사 ~을 참고하다 outline 개요를 서술하다, 약술하다 bulletin board 게시판

3. 정답 (A)

해설 Jody 레스토랑의 주인은 / 시간제 여직원을 찾고 있는 / 세 명의 지원자를 인터뷰할 것이다 / 오늘 오후에

해설 문장에서 정동사는 is going이다. 빈칸은 앞의 명사를 수식하는 분사 자리이다. 빈칸 뒤에 목적어가 있으므로 -ing 형태인 (A)가 정답이다.

표현 정리 owner 주인 seek 찾다

◎ 실전에 적용해 봐
1. (D) 2. (B) 3. (C) 4. (D) 5. (B) 6. (C) 7. (C)
8. (B) 9. (A) 10. (D)

1. 정답 (D)

해설 간단한 서류 검사가 있을 것이다 / 출판 일이 우리가 알고 있는 것과 같은지 확인하는

해설 문장에서 정동사는 will be이다. 빈칸 앞의 명사를 수식하는 분사 문제이며, 빈칸 뒤에 목적어인 that절이 있으므로 -ing 형태인 (D)가 정답이다. documents도 명사, verification도 명사라 연속으로 올 수 없으므로 (A)는 오답이다.

표현 정리 brief 간단한 inspection 검사 verify 확인하다, 입증하다 publication 출판

2.　　　　　　　　　　　　　　　　　　정답 (B)

해설 Mr. Marr는 걱정했다 / 그의 프로젝트에 대해 / 필요한 재정적 지원이 부족한 / Rabb 사로부터의

해설 문장에서 정동사는 was concerned이다. 빈칸 앞에 있는 명사를 수식하는 분사 문제이며, 빈칸 뒤에 목적어가 있으므로 -ing 형태인 (B)가 정답이다.

표현 정리 lack ~이 없다, 부족하다 financial support 재정적 지원

3.　　　　　　　　　　　　　　　　　　정답 (C)

해설 진술에 따르면 / 수 시간 전에 발표된 / 관리직에 비워져 있는 / Mr. Joe가 앉을 것이다

해설 문장에서 정동사는 will be filled이다. 빈칸 앞의 명사를 수식하는 분사 문제이며, 목적어가 없으므로 p.p. 형태인 (C)가 정답이다. (B)는 '수 시간 전에 발표될 진술 또는 발표되기 위한 진술'이라는 어색한 해석이 되므로 오답이다.

표현 정리 according to ~에 따르면 statement 진술 issue 발표하다 managerial 관리의, 운영의 remain 남다

4.　　　　　　　　　　　　　　　　　　정답 (D)

해설 Muffler Auto의 엔지니어 자리는 / 이상적이다 / 관심 있는 사람들에게 / 기계학에

해설 문장에서 정동사는 is이며, 빈칸 앞의 명사를 수식하는 분사 문제이다. interest는 감정동사인데, 감정동사로 만든 분사는 수식 받는 명사가 사람일 경우 p.p.를 쓴다. 따라서 (D)가 정답이다. those 뒤에는 who are가 생략된 것으로 봐야 한다.

표현 정리 ideal 이상적인 mechanics 기계학 interested in ~에 관심이 있는

5.　　　　　　　　　　　　　　　　　　정답 (B)

해설 이 팀 프로젝트는 / 꽤 쉬울 것이다 / 직원들에게 / 팀이나 파트너와 함께 일하는 / 정기적으로

해설 문장에서 정동사는 will be이며, 빈칸은 앞의 명사를 수식하는 분사 자리이다. work는 1형식 동사이기 때문에 목적어가 필요 없으며, -ing인 (B)가 정답이다. 목적어가 없다고 해서 p.p.를 정답으로 고르지 않도록 하자. 1형식 동사는 p.p.가 앞의 명사를 수식하지 않는다.

표현 정리 fairly 꽤 employee 직원 on a regular basis 정기적으로

6.　　　　　　　　　　　　　　　　　　정답 (C)

해설 기사는 / 지난주 월요일에 'News Daily'에 실린 / 문제를 다뤘다 / 낮은 고용률에 관한

해설 빈칸은 준동사 자리이다. 빈칸 앞의 명사를 수식하는 분사 문제이며, 빈칸 뒤에 목적어가 없으므로 p.p. 형태인 (C)가 정답이다. 빈칸 뒤에 목적어가 없으므로 (B)와 (D)는 오답이다.

표현 정리 article 기사 publish (신문, 잡지에) 싣다, 게재하다 marketing department 마케팅부

7.　　　　　　　　　　　　　　　　　　정답 (C)

해설 일부 제품들은 / 시내로 배달된 / 보고되었다 / 기술적 결함이 있는 것으로 / 제대로 작동하는 것을 방해하는

해설 빈칸은 준동사 자리이다. 빈칸 앞의 명사를 수식하는 분사 문제이기 때문에 -ing와 p.p. 중 골라야 하는데, 빈칸 뒤에 목적어가 없고 부사가 있으므로 p.p. 형태인 (C)가 정답이다. 빈칸 뒤에 있는 downtown을 목적어로 착각해 -ing로 답을 고르는 함정에 빠지지 않도록 주의하자.

표현 정리 defect 결함 prevent A from B A가 B하는 것을 막다

8.　　　　　　　　　　　　　　　　　　정답 (B)

해설 운송비가 면제될 것이다 / 주문할 경우 / 100달러 이상 / Beauty Cosmetics 숍에서

해설 빈칸은 준동사 자리이다. 빈칸 앞의 명사를 수식하는 분사 문제이며, 빈칸 뒤에 있는 more than $100가 목적어이다. more than을 보고 부사라고 생각해 목적어 없다고 p.p.를 고르면 함정에 빠지는 것이다. 따라서 목적어가 있으므로 -ing인 (B)가 정답이다. (C)와 (D) 모두 뒤에 목적어를 가질 수 없다.

표현 정리 charge 요금 waive 포기하다 order 주문 total 총 ~이 되다

9.　　　　　　　　　　　　　　　　　　정답 (A)

해설 명심하시오 / 당신이 제품 품질 보증서를 받았는지 / 봉투에 동봉된 / 우리가 당신에게 보낸

해설 빈칸은 준동사 자리이다. 빈칸 앞의 명사를 수식하는 분사 문제로 -ing와 p.p. 중에 골라야 하는데, 빈칸 뒤에 목적어가 없으므로 p.p. 형태인 (A)가 정답이다. 명사는 연속으로 올 수 없으므로 (C)는 오답이다.

표현 정리 quality assurance 품질 보증서 envelope 봉투 enclose 동봉하다

10.　　　　　　　　　　　　　　　　　　정답 (D)

해설 제안서는 / 목표를 달성하기 위해서 특정 단계로 구성된 / 받았다 / 긍정적인 피드백 / 중역들로 부터

해설 빈칸은 준동사 자리이다. 빈칸 앞의 명사를 수식하는 분사 문제이며, consist of는 덩어리 어휘로 전치사 of 뒤에 목적어가 있는 형태이다. 따라서 -ing 형태인 (D)가 정답이다. 참고로 consist of는 상태 동사로 be consisted of라는 수동태가 존재하지 않는다.

표현 정리 consist of ~로 이루어지다, 구성되다 accomplish 성취하다 executives 경영진

Chapter 05 5개월에 한 번 출제되는 문제

법칙 38 문장에 정동사 1개는 필수

◎ 유형을 파악해 봐
1. (A) 2. (C) 3. (D)

1. 정답 (A)

해설 점심 식권은 제공될 것이다 / 무료로 / 참석자들에게 / Mr. Brown의 세미나 / 오전 11시부터

해설 한 문장에 정동사 1개는 반드시 필요하므로 빈칸은 정동사 자리이다. 보기 중 정동사는 (A)뿐이다.

표현 정리 luncheon voucher 점심 식권 attendee 참석자

2. 정답 (C)

해설 Mr. Wiley는 보유하고 있었다 / 최고 판매 기록을 / 하지만 그의 기록은 초과되었다 / Ms. Lowe에 의해

해설 접속사 but이 있으므로 정동사는 2개가 있어야 한다. 따라서 빈칸은 정동사 자리이고, 보기 중에 정동사는 (C)뿐이다.

표현 정리 sales record 판매기록 surpass 능가하다, 뛰어넘다

3. 정답 (D)

해설 GK Cloud의 서비스는 가능하게 한다 / 당신이 이용하고 편집할 수 있도록 / 온라인으로 / 당신이 있는 장소와 관계없이

해설 and와 where가 접속사이므로 정동사는 3개가 필요하다. edit, are가 정동사이므로 빈칸은 정동사 자리이며, 보기 중 정동사는 (D)뿐이다.

표현 정리 enable ~을 할 수 있게 하다 access 이용하다, 접근하다 edit 편집하다 no matter where 어디에 있든지

◎ 실전에 적용해 봐
1. (B) 2. (D) 3. (A) 4. (C) 5. (B) 6. (D) 7. (A)
8. (C) 9. (A) 10. (D)

1. 정답 (B)

해설 전시회는 크게 성공적이었다 / 전시된 예술 작품이 / 많은 방문객의 관심을 끌었기 때문에

해설 문장에 접속사 1개(because)가 있으므로 정동사는 2개 필요로 한다. was가 정동사이므로 빈칸은 나머지 정동사 자리이다. 보기 중 (B)가 정답이다. (C)는 명사도 되고, 동사도 되지만 그럴 경우 단수 주어에 맞춰 interests로 써야 한다.

표현 정리 huge success 큰 성공 artwork 예술 작품 displayed 전시된 visitor 방문객

2. 정답 (D)

해설 회의가 / 새 확장 프로젝트에 관한 / 논의될 것이다 / 건물 보수 건과 함께

해설 문장에 정동사 1개(will be)가 있으므로 빈칸에는 정동사가 올 수 없다. 빈칸은 앞의 expansion과 함께 사용될 '확장 프로젝트'라는 말을 이루며, 이를 복합 명사라 한다. 따라서 (D)가 정답이다.

표현 정리 conference 회의 expansion 확장 discuss 논의하다 along with ~와 함께 renovation 개조, 수리, 혁신

3. 정답 (A)

해설 유명한 Deluxe Entertainment는 / 현재 사업을 해외로 확장하고 있는 / 한 때 리투아니아의 작은 회사였다

해설 문장에 정동사가 1개(was) 있고, 접속사는 없으므로 빈칸은 준동사 자리이다. 따라서 (A)가 정답이다.

표현 정리 well-known 잘 알려진, 유명한 expand 확장하다 overseas 해외로

4. 정답 (C)

해설 급행 열차는 / 몇 개의 정거장을 지나치는 / Eastern Terminal로 가는 길에 / 시간을 단축시켰다 / 터미널까지 가는데 걸리는

해설 it 앞에 형용사절 접속사 that(혹은 which)이 생략되어 있다. 문장에 정동사가 2개(has shorten, takes) 있으므로, 빈칸은 준동사 자리이다. 보기 중 준동사는 (C)뿐이다.

표현 정리 express train 급행 열차 skip 건너뛰다, 지나치다 on the way ~하는 중에, 가는 중인 shorten 단축시키다

5. 정답 (B)

해설 K-Watts Lights는 최근에 소개했다 / 램프를 / 사용자들에게 밝기 조절을 가능하게 하는 / 다양한 목적으로 다른 양의 조명을 선호하는 사람들을 위해

해설 who부터 purposes까지는 앞의 those를 꾸며주는 형용사절이며, 빈칸은 형용사절 속 정동사 자리이다. 보기 중 정동사인 (B)가 정답이다.

표현 정리 introduce 소개하다 allow 가능하게 하다, 허용하다 brightness 밝기 lighting 조명 various 다양한 prefer 선호하다 preference 선호 preferential 우선권을 주는

6. 정답 (D)

해설 우리 매장 관리자는 진정으로 받을 만하다 / 승진과 임금 인상을 / Everyday Low Store에 대한 그의 헌신으로

해설 접속사 and 앞에 있는 문장에 정동사가 없으므로 빈칸은 정동사 자리이며, 보기 중 정동사는 (D)뿐이다.

표현 정리 truly 진정으로, 정말로 deserve 자격이 있다 promotion 승진 dedication 헌신

7. 정답 (A)

해설 본점에서 판매될 상품의 수는 이번 달에도 계속 같을 것이다 / 시장 상황과 관계없이

해설 빈칸 앞에 조동사가 있으므로 빈칸은 동사원형 자리이며 보기 중 동사원형인 (A)가 정답이다.

표현 정리 remain ~인 상태이다, 남아 있다 regardless of ~에

상관없이

8. 정답 (C)

해설 전 직원들이 / 판매 직원들을 포함해 / 모일 것이다 / Brookade Building에서 / 은퇴식을 위해

해설 문장에 정동사가 이미 있으므로 정동사인 (A), (D)는 오답이다. 전치사 including 뒤의 표현이 사람을 뜻하는 말이 와서 앞의 All employees 를 수식해야 하며, sales representatives는 '판매 직원들'이란 뜻의 복수 명사이므로 (C)가 정답이다.

표현 정리 sales representative 판매 직원 convene 모이다, 소집하다 retirement 은퇴 retirement party 은퇴식

9. 정답 (A)

해설 끊임없이 발전하는 기술과 함께 / 디지털 장비들은 빠르게 구식이 된다 / 그것들이 시장에 출시되자마자

해설 the moment는 the moment when의 줄임말로 접속사처럼 보이지 않지만 접속사이다. are가 정동사이므로 빈칸도 정동사 자리이며, (A)가 정답이다. become은 자동사이므로 수동태로 쓸 수 없어 (D)는 오답이다.

표현 정리 constantly 끊임없이 advance 진전을 보다, 발전하다 obsolete 구식의, 더 이상 쓸모가 없는 the moment ~하자마자 release 출시하다

10. 정답 (D)

해설 Mr. Weld를 돕는 직원들이 / 작은 운영상의 문제들을 안고 있는 / 더 많은 일들을 처리하기 시작했기 때문에 / Mr. Weld는 집중할 수 있었다 / 그의 사업에 더

해설 문장에 접속사가 1개(Because), 정동사가 2개(began, was) 있으므로 빈칸은 준동사 자리이며, 명사와 명사를 연결해 줄 수 있는 것은 (D)뿐이다.

표현 정리 staff member 직원 assist 돕다 minor 작은, 가벼운 managerial 경영의, 관리의, 운영의 handle 다루다 concentrate 집중하다

법칙 39 '전치사와 a, the, 소유격+명사' 사이에는 동명사

◎ 유형을 파악해 봐
1. (A) 2. (D) 3. (C)

1. 정답 (A)

해설 MP3는 인기를 얻었다 / 균형을 잘 유지해 / 가격과 성능 사이에서의

해설 빈칸 앞 전치사, 빈칸 뒤는 관사와 명사가 왔으므로 빈칸에는 동명사 (A)가 와야 한다. (B)는 문장에 정동사(has gained)가 있으므로 오답이고, to 부정사 (C)는 전치사의 목적어 자리에 올 수 없다. (D)는 관사를 건너뛰어 명사를 수식 할 수 없다.

표현 정리 gain 얻다 popularity 인기 keep a good balance 균형을 잘 유지하다 price and performance 가격과 성능

2. 정답 (D)

해설 위원회 멤버들은 검토할 것을 요청 받았다 / 제안을 / 본사를 이전하는 것에 대한

해설 문장에는 정동사가 1개(were) 있으므로 정동사인 (A)는 오답이다. 빈칸 앞 전치사, 빈칸 뒤는 관사와 명사가 왔으므로 빈칸에는 동명사인 (D)가 와야 한다. 명사인 (B)는 뒤의 명사와 연속으로 올 수 없고, (C)는 전치사 뒤에 사용할 수 없다.

표현 정리 committee 위원회 review 검토하다 proposal 제안 relocate 이동하다 main office 본사

3. 정답 (C)

해설 단골 고객들의 숫자를 증가시키기 위한 목적으로 / Ellusion Cosmetics는 개최했다 / 판촉 행사를 / 지난주에

해설 빈칸 앞 전치사, 빈칸 뒤는 관사와 명사가 왔으므로 빈칸에는 동명사인 (C)가 와야 한다. 문장에 정동사 1개(held)가 이미 있으므로 정동사인 (A)는 오답, 전치사 뒤에 (B)는 올 수 없고, (D)는 관사를 건너뛰어 명사를 수식 할 수 없다.

표현 정리 for the purpose of ~를 위한 목적으로 loyal customers 단골 고객 promotional event 판촉 행사

◎ 실전에 적용해 봐
1. (B) 2. (B) 3. (C) 4. (D) 5. (A) 6. (C) 7. (B)
8. (B) 9. (A) 10. (A)

1. 정답 (B)

해설 문제가 / 시설들의 자동 정지를 예방하고자 하는 것에 대한 / 반복적으로 지적되었다

해설 전치사 뒤에는 명사나 동명사가 올 수 있는데, 빈칸 뒤에 목적어가 있으므로 빈칸은 동명사인 (B)가 와야 한다. (A)는 정동사이고, (D)는 관사를 건너뛰어 명사를 수식할 수 없다.

표현 정리 prevent 막다, 예방하다 shutdown 정지, 멈춤, 폐쇄 facility 시설, 설비, 공장 repeatedly 반복적으로 point out 지적하다

2. 정답 (B)

해설 많은 인사부 직원들 중에 / Ms. Tomoya는 재능이 있었다 / 동기를 유발하는 것에 / 직원들이 일을 열심히 하도록

해설 전치사 뒤에는 명사나 동명사가 올 수 있는데, 빈칸 뒤에 목적어가 있으므로 빈칸은 동명사인 (B)가 와야 한다. (A)는 정동사이고, (C)는 관사를 건너뛰어 명사를 수식할 수 없다.

표현 정리 among ~중에 Human Resources Department 인사부 talented at ~에 재능이 있는 motivate 동기를 유발하다 motivation 동기

3. 정답 (C)

해설 Mr. Cooper는 스카우트되었다 / Exton Technologies에 의해 / 그가 차량들을 조종하는데 고도로 숙련되어 있었기 때문에

해설 전치사 뒤에는 명사나 동명사가 올 수 있는데, 빈칸 뒤에 목적어가 있

으므로 빈칸은 동명사인 (C)가 정답이다. (A)는 정동사이고, (B)는 관사를 건너뛰어 명사를 수식할 수 없고, (D)는 전치사 뒤에 쓸 수 없다.

표현 정리 headhunt 스카우트하다 skilled 숙련된 maneuver 조종하다, 기동하다

4.   정답 (D)

해석 첫 단계는 / 적절한 작업 규칙을 정하는데 있어서의 / 분석하는 것이다 / 직원들이 현재 그들 감독관의 조언을 지켜가며 일하는지를 / 항상

해설 만약 proper working rules 앞에 관사나 소유격이 있다면 동명사를 쉽게 고를 수 있는 문제지만, 관사가 없으므로 혼동될 수 있는 문제이다. '적절한 작업 규칙을 정하는데 있어서의 첫 단계'라는 말이 자연스러우므로 전치사 in 다음에는 동명사 (D)가 오는 것이 적절하다.

표현 정리 proper 적절한 working rules 작업 규칙 analyze 분석하다 in compliance with ~에 따라 supervisor 감독관, 관리자 at all times 항상, 언제나 establish 설정하다

5.   정답 (A)

해석 우리 생산 관리자는 책임이 있다 / 감독하는 일에 / 직원들과 각각의 제조 과정을

해설 전치사 뒤에는 명사나 동명사가 올 수 있는데, 빈칸 뒤에 목적어가 있으므로 빈칸은 동명사인 (A)가 와야 한다. (B)와 (C)는 정동사이고, (D)는 관사를 건너뛰어 명사를 수식할 수 없다.

표현 정리 production manager 생산 관리자 be responsible for ~에 책임이 있다 staff 직원 manufacturing process 제조 과정 supervise 감독하다

6.   정답 (C)

해석 고객의 의견을 분석하는 것이 강력히 추천된다 / 하나의 방법으로 / 서비스 질을 향상시키는

해설 전치사 뒤에는 명사나 동명사가 올 수 있는데, 빈칸 뒤에 목적어가 있으므로 빈칸은 동명사인 (C)가 와야 한다. (A)와 (B)는 정동사이다.

표현 정리 recommend 추천하다 means 방법, 수단 improve 향상시키다, 향상하다

7.   정답 (B)

해석 Mr. Poll은 분명히 능력 있는 사람이었다 / 하지만 영업부는 Mr. Back을 원했다 / 고객 불만을 처리하는데 더 나은 / 사주실에서

해설 전치사 뒤에는 명사나 동명사가 올 수 있는데, 빈칸 뒤에 목적어가 있으므로 빈칸은 동명사인 (B)가 와야 한다. (A)는 정동사이고, (C)와 (D)는 명사이다.

표현 정리 surely 분명히, 확실히 Sales Department 영업부 customer complaint 고객 불만 manage 처리하다

8.   정답 (B)

해석 그의 파트너의 조언에 따라, Mr. Chev는 준비하기로 했다 / 그의 정년을 Forrester 사에서 하는 것으로

해설 전치사와 전치사 사이에는 명사가 와야 한다고 생각해서 (D)

investment를 고르지 않도록 한다. 함정 문제이다. 전치사 다음에 동명사 investing이 오면 '~함으로써'라는 뜻이 되면서 자연스럽다. 따라서 (B)가 정답이다. investment는 주로 가산명사로 사용되므로 investments라고 해야 어울린다.

표현 정리 prepare 준비하다 retirement age 정년 by -ing ~함으로써 invest in ~에 투자하다

9.   정답 (A)

해석 당신은 미리 고려해야 한다 / 얼마를 지불할 것인지 / 비슷한 주택에 대해 / 만약 당신이 그것을 빌려야 한다면

해설 housing은 '집, 주택'이란 뜻의 불가산명사이며, '비슷한 주택'에 대해 얼마를 지불할 것인지를 고려해야 한다는 문맥이므로 (A)가 답이다. (D)는 '비교하는 것에 대해 얼마를 지불할 것인지'라는 말이 되어 어색하다. (B)와 (C)는 전치사 뒤에 올 수 없다.

표현 정리 beforehand 이전에 housing 주택, 주택 공급 compare 비교하다

10.   정답 (A)

해석 'Queen Newspapers'는 날짜를 확인했다 / 유적이 발견된 / 새로운 발견을 대중에게 알리기 전에

해설 전치사 뒤에는 명사나 동명사가 올 수 있는데, 빈칸 뒤에 목적어가 있으므로 빈칸은 동명사인 (A)가 와야 한다. (B)는 명사, (C)는 정동사이고 (D)는 관사를 건너뛰어 명사를 수식 할 수 없다.

표현 정리 verify 확인하다, 입증하다 ruins 유적, 폐허 prior to ~이전에 discovery 발견 notify 알리다

법칙 4C 명사절이 완전하면 that, 불완전하면 what, 선택은 whether

◎ **유형을 파악해 봐**
1. (D)   2. (C)   3. (D)

1.   정답 (D)

해석 전시회장 직원은 요청했다 / 방문자들이 / 조용히 해 줄 것을

해설 문장에 정동사 2개가 있으므로, 빈칸에는 문장과 문장을 이어줄 접속사 (D)가 와야 한다. (A)는 뒤의 문장이 불완전할 때 사용하고, (B)는 빈칸 앞 주절에 ask나 wonder 등 불확정적인 말이 올 때 사용한다. request와 같은 동사를 '생말예제' 동사라고 하며, 주로 뒤에 that 문장을 목적어로 취한다.

표현 정리 exhibition 전시회 request 요청하다 silent 침묵하는, 말을 안 하는

2.   정답 (C)

해석 팜플렛들은 설명해 준다 / 당신이 무엇을 가져올 필요가 있는지 / 멤버십을 신청하는데

해설 빈칸 이하가 explain의 목적어이므로 빈칸은 명사절 접속사 자리이며, 빈칸 뒤 문장에는 bring의 목적어가 빠져 있으므로 (C)가 정답이다. (A)는 주어가 빠졌을 때, (B)는 완전한 문장이 따라올 때 사용하고, (D)는 앞의

동사가 choose 등과 같이 선택의 어울림이 있을 때 사용한다.

표현 정리 pamphlet 팜플렛 apply for ~를 신청하다

3. 정답 (D)

해석 Mr. Neil은 결정해야 한다 / 더 많은 직원을 고용해야 할지를 / 그의 회사에

해설 빈칸은 decide의 목적어가 와야 하는 자리이며, 빈칸 뒤에 있는 or not과 어울리는 명사절 접속사 (D)가 정답이다. (B)와 (C)는 접속사가 아니다.

표현 정리 decide 결정하다 hire 고용하다 employee 직원

◎ 실전에 적용해 봐
1. (A)   2. (A)   3. (B)   4. (C)   5. (B)   6. (B)   7. (C)
8. (A)   9. (B)   10. (C)

1. 정답 (A)

해석 Ms. Sun은 요청한다 / 당신이 보고서들을 제출할 것을 / 마감일인 오늘까지 / 가능한 한 빨리

해설 requests의 목적어 자리에 문장이 왔으므로 빈칸은 명사절 접속사 (A) 자리이다. '생떼예제' 동사인 request가 올 경우 that 이하의 문장은 원형동사가 온다.

표현 정리 request 요청하다 submit 제출하다 report 보고서 due ~하기로 되어 있는, 예정된 as soon as possible 가능한 한 빨리

2. 정답 (A)

해석 Glad 사에 관한 흥미로운 점은 / 모든 직원들이 그곳에서 일했다는 것이다 / 적어도 5년 이상

해설 문장에 정동사 3개(is, is, has worked), 접속사가 1개(that) 있으므로 빈칸에는 접속사가 한 개 더 와야 한다. 빈칸 뒤에 주어가 빠져 있으므로 (A)가 정답이다. (B)와 (D)는 완전한 문장과 쓰이고, (C)가 명사절 접속사로 사용될 경우에는 선택적 어울림이 있어야 한다.

표현 정리 interesting 흥미로운 employee 직원 work 일하다 at least 적어도, 최소한

3. 정답 (B)

해석 중요하다 / 모든 직원들이 즉시 매니저에게 알리는 것이 / 가동상의 문제가 있을 경우 / 시설들에

해설 가주어와 진주어 구문으로, 진주어에는 to 부정사나 명사절이 온다. 빈칸 뒤에 주어와 동사가 왔으므로 빈칸은 명사절 접속사 자리이다. 명사절 접속사 that과 what 중에서 빈칸 뒤 문장이 완전하므로 (B)가 정답이다.

표현 정리 crucial 중대한 immediately 즉시 notify 알리다 operational 운영상의, 가동상의

4. 정답 (C)

해석 위원회 회원들은 결정할 것이다 / 계약을 연장하는 것이 Voltax Corporation에 유익할 것인지를

해설 determine의 목적어 자리에 문장이 왔으므로 빈칸은 명사절 접속사 자리이다. 명사절 접속사 기능이 있는 (B)와 (C) 중에서 (B)는 불완전한 문장이, (C)는 완전한 문장이 온다. 여기서는 빈칸 뒤에 2형식의 완전한 문장이 왔으므로 (C)가 정답이다.

표현 정리 committee 위원회 determine 결정하다, 밝히다 extend 연장하다 contract 계약 beneficial 유익한

5. 정답 (B)

해석 연구는 보여준다 / 매 시간 마다 5분의 휴식을 취하는 것이 / 일할 때 / 개인의 업무 효율을 증대시킨다는 것을

해설 빈칸 이하의 내용이 shows의 목적어 자리이며, 빈칸 뒤에는 문장이 왔으므로 명사절 접속사가 와야 한다. 빈칸 뒤 문장이 완전한 문장으로 왔으므로 (B)가 정답이다. (A)와 (D)는 주어나 목적어가 빠진 불완전한 문장과 쓰인다.

표현 정리 study 연구 take a break 휴식을 취하다 at work 직장에서, 일터에서 work efficiency 업무 효율

6. 정답 (B)

해석 팀 리더십에 관한 워크숍은 / Mr. Tsubasi의 강의를 포함한다 / 구체적인 노하우를 제공하는 / 팀 성과를 향상시킬 수 있는

해설 문장에 정동사가 2개 있으므로, 빈칸은 접속사 자리이다. 빈칸 뒤에 주어가 빠진 불완전한 문장이 왔다고 해서 (A)를 답으로 고르지 않도록 한다. (A)는 명사절 접속사로서 앞에 선행사를 가질 수 없다. 빈칸 앞에 선행사가 있고, 빈칸 뒤에 동사가 바로 나오므로 형용사절 접속사 (B)가 와야 한다. 형용사절 that 다음에는 주어나 목적어가 빠진 불완전한 문장이 온다.

표현 정리 include 포함하다 lecture 강의 provide 제공하다 specific 구체적인, 명확한 improve 향상시키다, 개선하다 performance 성과, 실적

7. 정답 (C)

해석 Mr. Wiley는 지시했다 / 직원들에게 적으라고 / 박스들이 무엇을 포함하고 있는지 / 그것들의 겉면에

해설 빈칸은 write의 목적어 자리이며, 빈칸 뒤에는 문장이 왔으므로 빈칸은 명사절 접속사 자리이다. 빈칸 뒤 문장은 contain의 목적어가 없으므로 불완전한 문장이다. 따라서 (A)와 (C)가 가능한데, (A)가 명사절 접속사로 사용될 때는 선택적 어울림이 있어야 하는데, 여기서는 그렇지 못하다. 따라서 (C)가 정답이다. (B)와 (D)는 뒤의 문장이 완전할 때 사용한다.

표현 정리 order 지시하다, 명령하다 cover 표지, 겉면

8. 정답 (A)

해석 설문 조사는 / National Research Institue가 실시한 / 보여준다 / 점점 많은 수의 신입 직원들이 / 1년이 안 돼 그만둔다는 것을

해설 shows의 목적어 자리에 문장이 왔으므로 빈칸은 명사절 접속사 자리이다. 빈칸 뒤 문장이 완전하므로 (A)가 정답이다. (B)와 (C)는 빈칸 뒤 문장이 불완전할 때 사용한다.

표현 정리 survey 설문 조사 conduct 실시하다 new hire 새로 고용된 사람, 신입 직원

9.　　　　　　　　　　　　　　　　　정답 (B)

해석 두고 봐야 한다 / 올해의 연례 자선행사가 열릴 것인지는 / 12월에 / 작년과 같이

해설 가주어와 진주어 구문이며, 진주어에는 to 부정사나 명사절이 온다. 빈칸 뒤에 문장이 왔으므로 빈칸은 명사절 접속사 자리이다. to be seen은 remain의 보어인데, 이것을 진주어라고 생각하고 부사절 접속사 (C)를 고르면 오답이다. 명사절 접속사인 (B)와 (D) 중 빈칸 뒤기 완전한 문장이 왔으므로 (B)가 정답이다. 'It remain to be seen ~.'은 '두고 봐야 한다'라는 관용어구로 알아두자.

표현 정리 annual 연례의, 매년의　charitable event 자선행사

10.　　　　　　　　　　　　　　　　　정답 (C)

해석 Cameron 사에 근무하는 모든 직원들은 / 그들의 감독관들이 알도록 해야 한다 / 그들이 임금 인상을 원하는지, 아니면 주식인수권을 원하는지 / 회계연도 전까지

해설 빈칸은 know의 목적어 자리이며, 빈칸 뒤에는 문장이 왔으므로 명사절 접속사 자리이다. 뒤에 or가 언급되어 있으므로 (C)가 정답이다. (B)는 뒤에 주어나 목적어가 빠진 문장과 쓰이고, know를 보고 바로 (D)를 답으로 고르지 않도록 한다.

표현 정리 supervisor 감독관, 관리자　pay raise 임금 인상　stock options 주식인수권　fiscal year 회계연도

법칙 41 숫자 앞에는 숫자 수식 부사

◎ **유형을 파악해 봐**
1. (B)　2. (D)　3. (A)

1.　　　　　　　　　　　　　　　　　정답 (B)

해석 거의 두 달 정도 걸릴 것이다 / 화물들이 도착하기까지 / 이곳에

해설 숫자 앞에 빈칸이 존재하므로 숫자 수식 부사인 (3)가 답일 확률이 높지만 실수를 막기 위해 문장 구조를 살펴보면 문장이 완전하므로 빈칸은 (B) 부사 자리가 맞다.

표현 정리 approximately 거의, 가까이　shipment 수송품, 화물　arrive 도착하다

2.　　　　　　　　　　　　　　　　　정답 (D)

해석 가전제품의 매출이 거의 20퍼센트 하락했다 / 올해

해설 숫자 앞에 빈칸이 존재하므로 숫자 수식 부사인 (D)가 답일 확률이 높지만 실수를 막기 위해 문장 구조를 살펴보면 문장이 완전하므로 빈칸은 부사 자리가 맞다. near는 거리상 '가까이'라는 뜻이다.

표현 정리 sales 매출　home appliances 가전제품　drop 떨어지다　nearly 거의

3.　　　　　　　　　　　　　　　　　정답 (A)

해석 McCoy Corporation의 직원 70퍼센트 이상은 / 말한다 / 그들은 만족한다고 / 그들의 급료에 대해

해설 숫자 앞에는 숫자 수식 부사가 필요하다. (A)는 more than과 같은 의미의 숫자 수식 부사이므로 정답이다. (B)는 전치사로 완전한 문장 앞에 올 수 없다. (C)는 보통 비교급의 than이 있어야 사용 가능하다. (D)는 숫자 수식 부사지만, 대명사 혹은 형용사로서 '대부분, 대부분의'라는 뜻으로 사용된다.

표현 정리 over ~이상, ~이 넘는　employee 직원　be satisfied with ~에 만족하다　salaries 급료　beyond ~너머, 저편에

◎ **실전에 적용해 봐**
1. (C)　2. (D)　3. (B)　4. (A)　5. (C)　6. (D)　7. (E)
8. (D)　9. (A)　10. (C)

1.　　　　　　　　　　　　　　　　　정답 (C)

해석 가입하고 / 우리의 연간 회원으로 / 지금 / 할인 받으세요 / 40퍼센트까지 / 구입한 모든 제품에 대해

해설 숫자 앞에 빈칸이 존재하므로 숫자 수식 부사인 (C)가 정답이다. (A)는 비교급이나 최상급을 수식하는 부사이고, (B)와 (D)는 전치사로 사용된다.

표현 정리 annual 연례의, 매년의　receive 받다　discounts 할인　up to ~까지

2.　　　　　　　　　　　　　　　　　정답 (D)

해석 공항에 나와 주세요 / 적어도 도착 시간 30분 전에 / 당신이 그를 태워갈 수 있도록 / 즉시

해설 빈칸 뒤에 있는 half를 명사로 생각하고 형용사를 고르지 않도록 한다. half는 모양은 숫자가 아니지만 '절반, 50%'라는 뜻의 숫자이다. 숫자 앞에 빈칸이 존재하므로 숫자 수식 부사인 (D)가 정답이다. 나머지 보기들은 모두 형용사이다.

표현 정리 present 있는, 출석한　half an hour 30분　arrival time 도착 시간　pick somebody up ~를 태우다

3.　　　　　　　　　　　　　　　　　정답 (B)

해석 다양한 홍보 활동 때문에 / 올해의 모금액은 / 거의 두 배가 되었다 / 이전 년도와 비교해

해설 숫자의 모양새가 아니지만 의미상 숫자인 doubled 앞에 빈칸이 존재하므로 숫자 수식 부사인 (B)가 정답이다.

표현 정리 due to ~때문에　various 다양한　promotional 홍보의　fund 기금, 자금　double 두 배로 되다, 두 배로 만들다　compared to ~와 비교하여

4.　　　　　　　　　　　　　　　　　정답 (A)

해석 회의에서 / 직원들 교육에 관한 논의가 / 지속되었다 / 대략 2시간 동안

해설 숫자 앞에 빈칸이 있으므로 숫자 수식 부사인 (A)가 와야 한다. (B)는 '크게, 몹시'의 뜻이며, 보통 좋은 의미를 가지는 동사, 분사, 형용사들을 수식할 때 사용한다. (C)는 준부정어로 주로 동사 앞에 사용한다.

표현 정리 discussion 논의　training session 교육　roughly 대략　hardly 거의 ~아니다　openly 터놓고, 드러내 놓고

5. 정답 (C)

해설 구할 수 있는 관리직은 / Reb Auto에서 / 요구한다 / 3년 이상의 경험을 / 관련 분야에서

해설 숫자 앞에 빈칸이 있으므로 숫자 수식 부사인 (C)가 정답이다. 나머지 보기들은 부사가 아니다.

표현 정리 managerial position 관리직 available 구할 수 있는, 이용할 수 있는 relevant 관련 있는 field 분야

6. 정답 (D)

해설 손님들은 / 그들의 차를 가져왔고 / Best Hotel에 머물고 있는 / 2일 이상 / 반드시 요청해야 한다 / 주차증을 / 안내 데스크에서

해설 숫자 앞에 빈칸이 존재하므로 숫자 수식 부사인 (D)가 정답이며, 다른 보기들은 부사가 아니다.

표현 정리 guest 손님, 고객 parking permit 주차증 front desk 안내 데스크

7. 정답 (B)

해설 지난주에 실시한 설문조사에서 / 세미나 참가자의 절반 가까이가 대답했다 / 그들은 기꺼이 하겠다고 / 다시 세미나에 참석 / 만약 세미나가 같은 주제로 열린다면

해설 빈칸 뒤 half를 명사라고 생각해 형용사를 고르지 않도록 한다. half는 숫자의 모양새는 아니지만 '절반, 50%'라는 뜻의 숫자이다. 숫자 앞에 빈칸이 존재하므로 숫자 수식 부사인 (B)가 정답이다.

표현 정리 conduct 실시하다 attendee 참석자 be willing to+동사원형 기꺼이 ~하다 approximately 거의

8. 정답 (D)

해설 약 7개월간의 지연 후에 / Harley Bridge 공사가 / 마침내 재개될 것이다 / 다음 주에

해설 숫자 앞에 빈칸이 존재하므로 숫자 수식 부사인 (D)가 정답이며, 나머지 보기들은 숫자 수식 부사가 아니다. (C)는 준부정어로서 주로 동사 앞에 위치한다.

표현 정리 delay 지연 construction 공사 finally 마침내 resume 재개하다 around 약, ~쯤

9. 정답 (A)

해설 약 13년 동안 / Veronica Jewel 사는 제공해 왔다 / 우리 고객들에게 최고급 보석을 / 가장 합리적인 가격으로

해설 숫자 앞에 빈칸이 존재하므로 숫자 수식 부사인 (A)가 정답이다. (A)를 전치사뿐 아니라 숫자 수식 부사 기능도 한다.

표현 정리 offer 제공하다 finest 최고급의, 최상의 jewelry 보석, 보석류 reasonable 합리적인

10. 정답 (C)

해설 증가시키기 위한 노력으로 / 미용 제품의 판매를 / Everlast Cosmetics Shop은 제공했다 / 30퍼센트에 해당하는 할인을 / 일반 가격의

해설 숫자 앞에 빈칸이 존재하므로 숫자 수식 부사인 (C)가 정답이다.

표현 정리 in an effort to+동사원형 ~할 노력으로 increase 증가시키다 offer 제공하다 as much as ~만큼의

법칙 42 '사물 선행사+_____+주어, 목적어가 없는 문장'은 which 혹은 that

◎ 유형을 파악해 봐
1. (B)   2. (A)   3. (C)

1. 정답 (B)

해설 Ms. Pale은 최근에 차를 구입했다 / 잘 작동하지 않는 / 때문에 그는 그것을 팔기를 원한다

해설 보기에 접속사와 그렇지 않은 것이 섞여 있을 때는 동사의 개수를 확인한다. so는 접속사이며, 이어 문장이 나왔다. 앞의 문장을 확인해 보면, 동사의 개수가 bought와 work 2개이므로 빈칸에는 접속사가 필요하다. 빈칸 앞에 선행사 a car가 있고, 빈칸 뒤에는 동사가 바로 나왔으므로 형용사절 접속사로 쓰인 (B)가 정답이다. (A)는 선행사를 갖지 않으며, (C) 뒤에는 완전한 문장이 와야 한다.

표현 정리 recently 최근에 work 작동하다

2. 정답 (A)

해설 새 Lob Home Furnishings 매장은 / Seventh Street Station 근처에 오픈한 / 접근이 매우 쉽다

해설 문장에 정동사가 2개 있으므로 빈칸은 접속사 자리이다. 빈칸 앞에 선행사 Furnishings가 있고, 빈칸 뒤에는 주어가 빠진 문장이 나오므로 주격 관계대명사 (A)가 정답이다. (B)는 뒤에 완전한 문장이 올 때 사용하고, (D)는 선행사를 갖지 않는다.

표현 정리 furnishing 가구, 비품 accessible 접근 가능한, 이용 가능한

3. 정답 (C)

해설 동봉된 것은 / 당신이 요청한 일정표이다 / 당신의 여행을 위해 / 전에

해설 문장에 정동사가 2개 있으므로 빈칸은 접속사 자리이다. 빈칸 앞에 선행사 itinerary가 있고, 빈칸 뒤에는 requested의 목적어가 없으므로 목적격 관계대명사로 쓰인 (C)가 정답이다. (B)는 선행사를 갖지 않으며, (D)는 부사절 접속사로 쓰인다.

표현 정리 attached 첨부된 itinerary 일정표 request 요청하다 earlier 이전에, 더 일찍

◎ 실전에 적용해 봐
1. (D)   2. (C)   3. (C)   4. (B)   5. (D)   6. (D)   7. (C)
8. (A)   9. (B)   10. (D)

1. 정답 (D)

해설 만약 이번이 처음이라면 / 당신이 Memorial Hall을 방문하는 것이 / 제시해 주세요 / 당신의 신분증을 / 직원에게 / 허가증을 받기 위해 / 당신에게 자유로운 출입을 허락하는 / 일주일 동안

해설 빈칸 앞에 있는 present도 동사이고, 빈칸 뒤에 있는 grants도 동사이므로 빈칸은 접속사 자리이다. 빈칸 앞에 선행사 permit이 있고, 빈칸 뒤에는 동사가 바로 왔으므로 주격 관계대명사인 (D)가 정답이다. (A)는 명사절 접속사, (B)는 등위접속사 혹은 부사, (C)는 등위접속사 혹은 전치사이다.

표현 정리 present 제시하다, 제출하다 ID card 신분증 receive 받다 permit 허가증 grant 부여하다, 승인하다 free access 자유로운 출입, 무상 출입

2. 정답 (C)

해설 Safe Pharmaceuticals는 인정 받았다 / 약을 개발한 것으로 / 효과적인 것으로 입증된 / 졸음을 유발하지 않고

해설 문장에 정동사가 2개(has been, have been) 있으므로 빈칸은 접속사 자리이다. 빈칸 앞에 있는 선행사가 사물이므로 (C)가 정답이다. (D)는 선행사가 사람일 때 쓴다.

표현 정리 acknowledged 인정 받은 develop 개발하다 pill 약, 정제 proven 입증된, 증명된 effective 효과적인 cause 야기하다, 일으키다 drowsiness 졸음, 졸림

3. 정답 (C)

해설 환불이나 교환은 가능하다 / 당신이 영수증을 가져올 때만 / 당신이 받은 / 구입한 물건들과 함께

해설 문장에 정동사가 3개(are, bring, receive) 있고, 접속사가 1개(when) 있으므로 빈칸은 접속사 자리이다. 빈칸 앞에 선행사 receipts가 있고, 빈칸 뒤에는 received의 목적어가 없으므로 목적격 관계대명사 (C)가 답이다. (A)는 명사절 접속사이다.

표현 정리 refund 환불 exchange 교환 available 가능한 bring 가져오다 receipt 영수증 receive 받다 along with ~와 함께 purchased 구입한

4. 정답 (B)

해설 Mr. Vogel를 위한 은퇴식은 / 열릴 것이다 / Ronn Tower에서 / 출입구는 찾을 수 있다 / 분수 옆에서

해설 문장에 정동사가 2개(will be, can be) 있으므로 빈칸은 접속사 자리이다. 빈칸 앞에 있는 entrance는 타워 출입구를 의미하며, 선행사가 바로 앞에 나오지 않았고, of의 목적어가 없으므로 목적격 관계대명사인 (B)가 정답이다. (D)는 명사절 접속사이므로 선행사도 가질 수 없고, 뒤의 문장도 불완전해야 한다.

표현 정리 retirement party 은퇴식, 은퇴 기념 파티 hold 열다, 개최하다 entrance 입구, 출입구 next to ~옆에, ~다음에 fountain 분수

5. 정답 (D)

해설 SecretX Security는 / 보안 서비스를 전문으로 하는 / 대기업들의 의한 / 위탁 받았다 / BK Tech 계정의 보호를

해설 문장에 정동사가 2개(specializes, is) 있으므로 빈칸은 접속사 자리이다. 빈칸 앞에 선행사 Security가 있고, 빈칸 뒤에는 동사가 바로 나왔으므로 주격 관계대명사인 (D)가 정답이다. (A)는 부사절 접속사이고, (B)는 콤마 뒤에 쓰지 않으며, (C)는 선행사를 갖지 않는다.

표현 정리 specialize in ~을 전문으로 하다 security 보안 large company 대기업 be entrusted with+명사 ~를 위탁 받다, 위임 받다 protection 보호 account 계정, 계좌

6. 정답 (D)

해설 Ms. Cole은 요청 받았다 / 상품들의 수를 기록하도록 / 반품된 / 잘못된 주소 때문에

해설 문장에 정동사가 2개(was, have been) 있으므로 빈칸은 접속사 자리이다. 빈칸 앞에 선행사 items가 있고, 빈칸 뒤에는 동사가 바로 나왔으므로 주격 관계대명사인 (D)가 정답이다. (A)는 등위접속사이며, (C)는 뒤에 완전한 문장이 올 때 사용한다.

표현 정리 record 기록하다 return 돌려주다, 반품하다

7. 정답 (C)

해설 신청서를 찾아 작성해 주세요 / 소책자 안에 동봉되어 있는 / 그리고 우리에게 돌려 보내 주세요 / 우편으로

해설 빈칸 앞과 뒤로 동사가 왔으므로 빈칸은 접속사 자리이다. 빈칸 앞에 선행사 form이 왔고, 빈칸 뒤에는 동사가 바로 왔으므로 주격 관계대명사 (C)가 정답이다. (A)는 뒤에 완전한 문장이 올 때 사용하고, (B)는 명사절 접속사이다.

표현 정리 complete 작성하다, 기입하다 application form 신청서 enclose 동봉하다 booklets 소책자, 작은 책자

8. 정답 (A)

해설 당신의 위치 근처에 있는 매장들은 / 상품을 갖추고 있지 않은 것 같다 / 당신이 지금 주문한

해설 빈칸 앞과 뒤로 동사가 있으므로 빈칸은 접속사 자리이다. 빈칸 앞에 선행사 item이 있고, 빈칸 뒤에는 ordered의 목적어가 없으므로 목적격 관계대명사인 (A)가 정답이다. (C)는 명사절 접속사이고, (D)는 완전한 문장이 올 때 사용한다.

표현 정리 none of ~중 아무(것)도 ~않다 item 상품 order 주문하다

9. 정답 (B)

해설 Harbor Burger는 발표했다 / 곧 다음 매장을 열 것이라고 / 회사의 100번째 가맹점을 기념할

해설 빈칸 앞과 뒤로 동사가 있으므로 빈칸은 접속사 자리이다. 빈칸 앞에 선행사 store가 있고, 빈칸 뒤에는 동사가 바로 왔으므로 빈칸은 주격 관계대명사인 (B)가 정답이다. (A)는 뒤에 완전한 문장이 와야 하고, (C)는 부사, (D)는 대명사나 형용사이다.

표현 정리 announce 발표하다 open 열다, 개업하다 mark 기념하다, 특징 짓다 franchise 가맹점

10. 정답 (D)

해설 영업부 직원들은 추천했다 / Exia Station을 아주 좋은 장소로 / 그들의 신제품에 대한 설문조사를 하기에 / 많은 수의 역 방문객들이 있어

해설 빈칸 뒤에 있는 to는 주어와 조동사를 줄여 쓴 것이다. 따라서 문장이 온 것이므로 빈칸은 접속사 자리이다. 여기서 선행사는 place이며, in을 문장의 가장 뒤로 보내면 선행사는 사물이고, 전치사 in의 목적어가 빠져

있으므로 which가 답이 된다. 이때 in을 앞으로 보내면 in which가 되며, where와 같은 의미가 된다. 결국 (A)를 답으로 하려면 빈칸 앞에 in이 없어야 한다. 따라서 (D)가 답이 된다.

표현 정리 Sales Department 영업부 suggest 추천하다 conduct 실시하다 survey 설문조사, 조사 daily visitor 하루 방문객

Chapter 06 6개월에 한 번 출제되는 문제

법칙 43 '(in order) to+동사원형'은 문장 전체를 수식

◎ 유형을 파악해 봐
1. (B)   2. (C)   3. (C)

1. 　　　　　　　　　　　　　　　　정답 (B)

해석 당신의 멤버십을 갱신하기 위해서 / 당신은 필요할 것이다 / 전화하는 것이 / 사무실에 / 그리고 요청하는 것이 / 갱신을

해설 빈칸이 전체 문장의 맨 앞에 오고, 주어 앞에 콤마가 있는 경우에는 빈칸이 속한 구가 문장 전체를 수식하는 부사 기능을 한다. 빈칸 뒤에 동사원형이 왔으므로 (B)는 to 부정사의 부사적 용법으로 쓰인다. (C)는 전치사/접속사이기 때문에 전치사라면 뒤에 명사, 접속사라면 문장이 와야 한다. (A)와 (D)는 자체가 부사이다.

표현 정리 renew 갱신하다, 연장하다 need to+동사원형 ~할 필요가 있다 renewal 갱신 instead 그 대신에 in order to+동사원형 ~하기 위해서 since ~이래로, ~때문에 otherwise 그렇지 않으면, 그 이외의

2. 　　　　　　　　　　　　　　　　정답 (C)

해석 사고 발생을 막기 위해 / 안전 검사는 정기적으로 실시되어야 한다

해설 빈칸이 전체 문장의 맨 앞에 오고, 주어 앞에 콤마가 있는 경우에는 빈칸이 속한 구가 문장 전체를 수식하는 부사 기능을 한다. 빈칸 뒤에 동사원형이 왔으므로 (C)는 to 부정사의 부사적 용법으로 쓰인다. (A)와 (B)는 접속사이므로 뒤에 문장이 와야 하고, (D)는 전치사로 뒤에 명사가 와야 한다.

표현 정리 prevent A from -ing A가 ~하는 것을 막다, 예방하다 accident 사고 safety 안전 inspection 검사, 조사 regularly 정기적으로 carry out 수행하다, 이행하다 unless ~하지 않는다면 whereas 반면에 in regards to ~에 관해서

3. 　　　　　　　　　　　　　　　　정답 (C)

해석 모든 전단지를 나눠주기 위해 / 다음 주까지 / 우리는 제작하는 것을 마쳐야 한다 / 그것들을 / 늦어도 화요일까지

해설 빈칸이 전체 문장의 맨 앞에 오고, 주어 앞에 콤마가 있는 경우에는 빈칸이 속한 구가 문장 전체를 수식하는 부사 기능을 한다. 빈칸 뒤에 동사원형이 왔으므로 (C)는 to 부정사의 부사적 용법으로 쓰인다. (A)는 전치사/접속사/부사이며, 전치사라면 뒤에 명사가, 접속사라면 문장이, 부사라면 구가 문장 전체를 수식하는 부사 역할을 할 수 없다. (B)는 부사/접속사이며, 접속사로 쓰이는 경우는 바로 뒤에 형용사나 부사가 온다. (D)는 전치사로 뒤에 명사가 와야 한다.

표현 정리 hand out 나누어주다, 배포하다 flyer 전단지 no later than 늦어도 ~까지 since ~이래로, ~때문에 however 그러나 prior to ~전에

◎ 실전에 적용해 봐
1. (D)   2. (D)   3. (A)   4. (A)   5. (D)   6. (B)   7. (C)
8. (B)   9. (D)   10. (D)

1. 　　　　　　　　　　　　　　　　정답 (D)

해석 신문이 배달되게 하기 위해서는 / 당신의 집으로 매일 / 당신은 지불해야 한다 / 10달러의 연간 구독료를

해설 빈칸 뒤에 동사원형이 왔으므로 (D)는 to 부정사의 부사적 용법으로 문장 전체를 수식하는 부사 기능을 한다. 전치사인 (A), (B), (C)는 뒤에 명사가 와야 한다.

표현 정리 deliver 배달하다 every day 매일 annual subscription 연간 구독 prior to ~전에 instead of ~대신에 by means of ~에 의하여, 수단으로 하여 in order to+동사원형 ~을 위해서

2. 　　　　　　　　　　　　　　　　정답 (D)

해석 당신에게 더 좋은 서비스를 하기 위해 / 우리는 원한다 / 당신이 작성하기를 간단한 설문지를 / 우리의 서비스 품질에 관한

해설 빈칸 뒤에 동사원형이 왔으므로 (D)는 to 부정사의 부사적 용법으로 문장 전체를 수식하는 부사 기능을 한다. (A)와 (B)는 접속사로 뒤에 문장이 와야 하고, (C)는 전치사로 명사가 와야 한다.

표현 정리 serve (상품, 서비스) 제공하다 fill out 작성하다, 기입하다 brief 간단한, 짧은 questionnaire 질문사항, 설문지 regarding ~에 관한 quality 품질 whether ~인지 아닌지 because ~때문에

3. 　　　　　　　　　　　　　　　　정답 (A)

해석 알리기 위해서 / Jacob Nelson의 임명을 / 임원으로의 / 사장은 조용히 하도록 했다 / 모든 직원들이 / 장소에 있던

해설 (A)는 to 부정사의 부사적 용법으로 문장 전체를 수식하는 부사 기능을 한다. (B)는 명사로 명사 앞에 명사가 올 수 없고, (C)는 동사이고, (D)는 p.p. 형태이므로 목적어를 이끌 수 없다.

표현 정리 appointment 약속, 임명 president 사장, 회장 silence 조용하게 만들다, 침묵시키다 announce 알리다, 발표하다

4. 　　　　　　　　　　　　　　　　정답 (A)

해석 기념하기 위해 / 리조트의 개업을 / 리조트에 머무르고 있는 모든 손님들은 받았다 / 하루 / 무료 숙박을

해설 (A)는 to 부정사의 부사적 용법으로 문장 전체를 수식하는 부사 기능을 한다. (B)는 전명구를 제외하면 콤마 앞에 명사만 남기 때문에 탈락, (C)는 p.p. 형태이므로 목적어를 이끌 수 없고, (D)는 동사이다.

표현 정리 grand opening 개업식 stay 머무르다 celebrate 기념하다, 축하하다

5. 정답 (D)

해설 프로젝트를 진행하기 위해 / 보여주세요 / 프로젝트의 개요를 / 지도자에게 / 당신 부서의 / 그리고 받으세요 / 그의 승인을 / 먼저

해설 빈칸 뒤에 동사원형이 왔으므로 (D)는 to 부정사의 부사적 용법으로 문장 전체를 수식하는 부사 기능을 한다. (A)는 전치사, (B)와 (C)는 접속사로 뒤에 완전한 문장이 와야 한다.

표현 정리 proceed with ~을 진행하다 outline 윤곽, 개요 approval 승인, 동의 first 우선, 먼저 prior to ~전에 because ~때문에 unless ~하지 않는다면

6. 정답 (B)

해설 건강한 이미지를 홍보하기 위해 / 새롭게 출시된 음료의 / Drizzle Beverage Company는 주력했다 / 광고에 / 음료의 긍정적인 영향을 / 신체에 대한

해설 (B)는 to 부정사의 부사적 용법으로 문장 전체를 수식하는 부사 기능을 한다. (A)와 (D)를 넣으면 뒤에 명사가 연달아 나올 수 없으므로 탈락. (C)가 올 경우 뒤에 전명구를 제외하면 문장의 앞에 명사만 남기 때문에 오답이다.

표현 정리 healthy 건강한 newly 새롭게 launch 출시하다, 개시하다 beverage 음료 focus on ~에 주력하다, 집중하다 advertise 광고하다, 홍보하다 effect 영향, 효과 promote 홍보하다, 촉진하다

7. 정답 (C)

해설 Ms. Stewart의 개인 상담가는 조언했다 / 그녀에게 / 휴식을 취하라고 / 직장 일로부터 / 그녀가 / 스트레스를 해소하기 위해

해설 in order와 to 사이에 to 부정사의 의미상의 주어로 'for+목적격'이 쓰였다. 빈칸 앞만 보고 to를 고르면 틀리는 함정 문제이다. 따라서 (C)가 정답이다.

표현 정리 personal 개인의, 개인적인 counselor 상담가 advise 조언하다, 권하다 take a break 휴식을 취하다 relieve 완화시키다, 경감하다

8. 정답 (B)

해설 우리는 아직 결정하지 못했다 / 박물관으로 곧장 갈지 / 식당에 잠시 들를지 / 점심을 먹기 위해

해설 빈칸 이후가 decide의 목적어이다. 'whether+to 동사 or 동사'는 주어와 조동사 will이 to로 줄여진 형태다. 따라서 목적어의 기능이 될 수 있으므로 (B)가 정답이다. (A)는 부사의 기능, (C)는 빈칸 뒤 to와 함께 전치사로 쓰이므로 목적어가 될 수 없고, (D)도 '~하는 방법으로' 명사절을 이끌 수는 있으나 선택적 의미가 있을 때는 쓰이지 않는다. to 동사원형만을 보고 in order to를 답으로 고르지 않도록 하자.

표현 정리 directly 곧장, 즉시 head 나아가다 stop by 잠시 들르다 depend on ~에 달렸다, ~에 의존하다

9. 정답 (D)

해설 논리적으로 보이게 하느냐는 / 글이 / 특히 논문이나 보고서에서 / 많은 직원들이 갖고 있는 주제이다

해설 is가 동사이며, 그 앞은 주어가 와야 한다. 따라서 빈칸부터 is 앞까지 주어의 기능, 즉 명사가 될 수 있도록 해야 한다. (D)는 주어 자리에 있는 문장을 이끄는 접속사로 명사절을 이끈다. (A)와 (C)는 to와 함께 전치사로 쓰이므로 탈락. (B)는 to 부정사의 부사적 용법으로 문장 전체를 수식하는 부사 기능을 하므로 탈락.

표현 정리 sound ~인 것 같다, ~처럼 들리다 logical 논리적인, 타당한 especially 특히, 두드러지게 owing to ~때문에, ~덕분에 in addition to 게다가, ~에 더해

10. 정답 (C)

해설 긍정적인 결과를 예상하기 위해 / 그의 사업 계획으로부터 / Mr. Ken은 우선 고려해야 한다 / 가능성을 / 효과적으로 수행할 수 있는지를

해설 빈칸 뒤에 동사원형이 왔으므로 (D)는 to 부정사의 부사적 용법으로 문장 전체를 수식하는 부사 기능을 한다. (A)와 (C)는 접속사로 탈락, (B)는 자체가 부사이므로 문장 전체를 수식하는 부사 역할을 할 수 없다.

표현 정리 expect 예상하다, 기대하다 positive 긍정적인 outcome 결과, 성과 first 우선, 먼저 consider 고려하다, 생각하다 possibility 가능성, 기회 carry out 성취하다, 수행하다, 이행하다 although 비록 ~이지만 therefore 그러므로 whether ~인지 아닌지

법칙 44 빈칸 앞에 한정사가 없고, 보기에 단수 명사가 있으면 불가산명사가 답

◎ 유형을 파악해 봐
1. (A) 2. (D) 3. (B)

1. 정답 (A)

해설 고객들은 / 도움이 필요한 / 고객들이 구매한 제품에 대해 / 연락할 수 있다 / 우리에게 / 전화함으로써 / 수신자 부담 전화로

해설 보기가 한 단어의 변형 형태이며, 빈칸 앞은 타동사, 빈칸 뒤는 전명구이므로 빈칸은 명사 자리이다. 따라서 불가산명사인 (A)가 정답이다. (B)는 동사, (C)는 동사의 과거형 또는 p.p. 형태이므로 탈락, (D)는 형용사/명사로 쓰이지만, 명사로 쓰일 경우 가산명사이므로 앞에 한정사가 필요하다.

표현 정리 purchase 구입하다, 구매하다 reach 연락하다, 드달하다 toll-free number 수신자 부담 전화 assistance 지원, 도움 assist 돕다, 지원하다 assistant 조수, 보조, 도움이 되는

2. 정답 (D)

해설 Ms. Lake는 찾고 있었다 / 임시직을 / Gohl Corportaiton에서 / 그녀가 일하고 있는

해설 보기가 한 단어의 변형 형태이며, 빈칸 앞은 형용사, 빈칸 뒤는 전명구이므로 빈칸은 명사 자리이다. 따라서 불가산명사로 한정사를 필요로 하지 않는 (D)가 정답이다. (B)는 동명사라서 뒤에 목적어도 필요하고 형용사의 수식을 받지 않으며, (A)와 (C)는 가산명사이므로 단수로 쓸 경우 앞에 한정사가 필요하다.

표현 정리 part-time employment 임시직 employee 직원, 고용인 employer 고용주, 경영자 employment 고용, 일자리, 업무

3. 정답 (B)

해설 시험에 합격한 후에 / Ms. Earnings는 받았다 / 자격증을 / 전문 □

정답 및 해설 65

용사

해설 보기가 한 단어의 변형 형태이고, 빈칸 앞 타동사, 빈칸 뒤는 전명구이므로 빈칸은 명사 자리이다. 따라서 불가산명사인 (B)가 정답이다. (A)는 형용사, (C)는 동사, (D)는 가산명사이므로 빈칸 앞에 관사가 오거나 복수형으로 써야 한다.

표현 정리 pass 통과하다, 합격하다 examination 시험, 검사, 조사 receive 받다, 수상하다 certificated 면허를 취득한 certification 증명, 자격 certify 증명하다, 보증하다 certificate 증서, 자격증

◎ 실전에 적용해 봐
1. (A) 2. (C) 3. (B) 4. (D) 5. (C) 6. (B) 7. (D)
8. (A) 9. (A) 10. (C)

1. 정답 (A)

해설 프로젝트는 보이고 있다 / 꾸준한 진척을 / 관리자의 엄격한 진행 하에 / 맞추기 위해 / 프로젝트의 마감일을

해설 빈칸 앞은 형용사, 빈칸 뒤는 전명구이므로 빈칸은 명사 자리이다. '관리자의 엄격한 진행 하에'라는 말이 자연스럽기 때문에 (A)가 정답이다. (B)와 (D)는 동사/명사로 쓰이지만 '관리자의 엄격한 좌표 하에'라는 말은 어색하므로 적절하지 않다. under 다음에 사람이 오는 것도 어색하다.

표현 정리 steady 꾸준한, 지속적인, 확고한 progress 진전, 성과 supervisor 관리자, 감독 tight 빠듯한, 엄격한 meet deadline 마감일을 맞추다 coordination 조정, 협동 coordinate 조정하다, 협력하다 coordinator 조정자, 코디네이터

2. 정답 (C)

해설 주의 깊은 기획 때문에 / 정기 회의가 개최되는 것을 피할 수 있었다 / 연례 직원 감사 식사와 같은 날에

해설 빈칸 앞은 형용사이고, 그 앞은 전치사이므로 빈칸은 명사 자리이다. 명사인 (A), (B), (C) 중에서 (A)는 가산명사로 한정사가 필요하며, (B)는 동사/명사로 쓰이지만 명사일 경우 가산명사이므로 탈락하고, (C)는 불가산명사로 정답이다.

표현 정리 careful 주의 깊은, 철저한 regular 정기적인, 규칙적인 avoid ~을 피하다 on the same day 같은 날에 annual employee appreciation dinner 연례 직원 감사 식사 planner 계획자 plan 계획하다; 계획 planning 계획, 예정

3. 정답 (B)

해설 정리하기와 일정 잡기에 대한 세부적 관심이 / 결과를 가져온 부분이다 / 아마도 가장 유용한 기능이라는 / GX 소프트웨어의

해설 빈칸은 전치사 뒤이므로 명사 자리이다. (A)는 동사의 과거/p.p. 형태이므로 탈락, (C)는 가산명사로 한정사가 필요하며, (D)는 동사이다. (B)는 불가산명사로 사용되어 '정리하기'의 뜻으로 쓰였다.

표현 정리 attention to ~에 대한 관심 scheduling 일정 잡기 probably 아마도 lead to ~한 결과를 낳다 useful 유용한 feature 기능 organized 정리된, 정돈된 organization 단체, 기구, 조직, 준비 organizer 조직자, 주최자 organize 조직하다, 개최하다, 정리하다

4. 정답 (D)

해설 Ms. Wang은 참석했다 / Mr. Khan의 세미나에 / 수요일에 개최된 / 그의 초청에 따라

해설 전치사와 소유격대명사 뒤 명사 자리이다. (A)는 동사이고, (B)가 오면 동명사로 쓰이지만 목적어를 이끌어야 하므로 탈락, (C)는 형용사이다. 따라서 불가산명사로 사용 가능한 (D)가 정답이다.

표현 정리 attend 참석하다 hold 개최하다 upon invitation 초대에 따라, 초대로

5. 정답 (C)

해설 더 많은 돈을 모으기 위해 / 이번 달에 / Ms. Yale은 줄이기로 했다 / 그녀의 지출을 / 특히 식비에서

해설 소유격 뒤 명사 자리이다. (C)를 동명사라고 생각하고 뒤에 목적어가 없어 오답이라고 생각하면 안 된다. spending은 가산, 불가산명사가 다 되는 '지출, 소비'라는 뜻의 명사로 사용되기 때문에 뒤에 목적어가 필요 없어 정답이다. (B)는 사람을 뜻하는 말로 소유격 뒤에는 올 수 있으나 사람을 최소화시킨다는 말이 어울리지 않는다.

표현 정리 save money 돈을 모으다 minimize 줄이다, 최소 한도로 하다 especially 특히, 두드러지게 dining 식사, 정찬 spend 지출하다, 보내다 spender 낭비자, 소비자 spending 지출, 소비

6. 정답 (B)

해설 빌딩 출입은 / 제한된다 / 허가 없이는 / 사무장의

해설 빈칸은 전치사 뒤에 있고, 빈칸 뒤에 있는 p.p. 형태의 수식을 받는 명사 자리이다. (A)는 동사/명사로 쓰이지만 명사일 때는 가산명사이므로 앞에 관사나 소유격이 있거나 복수형으로 써야 한다. (C)는 동사의 과거/p.p. 형태이므로 탈락, (D)는 -ing 형태로 뒤에 목적어가 필요하다. (B)는 불가산명사로 관사 없이 올 수 있어 정답이다. without permission은 '허가 없이'라는 뜻이다.

표현 정리 be restricted to+명사 ~에게 제한되다 grant 부여하다, 허가하다 permit 허용하다, 허가하다; 허가증 permission 허가, 허락, 허용 permitted 허가된, 허락된

7. 정답 (D)

해설 우리는 당신에게 요청한다 / 답변하도록 / 다음과 같은 질문에 / 솔직하게 / 그리고 우리는 보장한다 / 당신과 우리와의 서신 왕래가 / 유지될 것을 / 비밀로

해설 빈칸 앞은 소유격, 빈칸 뒤는 동사이므로 빈칸은 명사 자리이다. 소유격 다음에는 단수 명사, 복수 명사, 불가산명사 모두 올 수 있다. 따라서 문맥으로 풀어야 하는 문제이다. (C) correspondent(특파원)보다는 (D) correspondence(서신 왕래)가 문맥상 어울린다.

표현 정리 following 다음의, ~후에 honestly 솔직하게, 정직하게 guarantee 보장하다; 보증 confidential 기밀의, 비밀의 corresponding 상응하는, 일치하는; 연락 correspond 해당하다, 일치하다 correspondent 특파원, 기자 correspondence 서신, 편지

8. 정답 (A)

해설 물품들은 / 당신이 주문한 / 배송될 것이다 / 곧바로 / 대금을 받는

대로

해설 빈칸 앞은 전치사, 빈칸 뒤는 전명구이므로 빈칸은 명사 자리이다. (A)와 (C)는 가산명사로 쓰일 경우 '영수증'이라는 뜻인데, '지불의 영수증이 되자마자'라는 의미는 어색하므로 탈락하고, 불가산명사로 쓰일 경우 '지불이 되자마자'라는 의미로 문맥상 적절하다. (B)는 수령인을 뜻하는 가산명사이고, (D)는 동사의 과거/p.p. 형태이다.

표현 정리 ship 보내다, 선적하다 right away 곧바로, 즉시 on receipt of ~을 받는 대로 payment 지불(금), 지급 recipient 수령인, 수취인

9. 정답 (A)

해석 자전거 수리 도구들은 / 값이 비싸지만 / Mr. Herrington은 구입했다 / 그것들을 / 그는 다른 대안이 없기 때문에.

해설 빈칸은 동사의 목적어 자리이고, 빈칸 앞에 형용사가 있으므로 명사 자리이다. no other 다음에는 복수 명사가 오거나 불가산명사가 와야 한다. 따라서 (A), (B)가 올 수 있는데, '다른 대안이 없었기 때문에 비싼 자전거 수리 도구들을 구입했다'는 말이 자연스러워 (A)가 답이다. (B)는 '교대, 교체'라는 뜻이다.

표현 정리 tool 도구, 수단 repair 고치다 costly 값비싼, 사치스러운 alternatives 대체 alternation 교대, 교체 alternative 대안, 대체 alternate 대체하다, 번갈아 하다

10. 정답 (C)

해석 넣어 주세요 / 모든 당신의 소지품을 / 당신의 수화물을 포함해 / 컨베이어 벨트에 / 검사를 통과하기 위해 / 불법적인 물품에 대한

해설 빈칸 앞에 소유격이 있으므로 빈칸은 명사 자리이다. luggage는 불가산명사이므로 (A)처럼 복수형으로 쓸 수 없어 (C)가 정답이다. (B)와 (D) 같은 형태 존재하지 않는다.

표현 정리 belonging 소지품 including ~을 포함한 through ~을 통하여, 지나서 inspection 검사, 조사 illegal 불법적인, 위법인 luggage 짐, 수화물, 가방

법칙 45 원급, 비교급, 최상급을 수식해 주거나 비교급, 최상급을 만들어 주는 부사

◎ 유형을 파악해 봐
1. (B) 2. (D) 3. (B)

1. 정답 (B)

해석 부장은 매우 엄격했다 / 맞추는 것에 / 보고서 마감일을

해설 빈칸은 be 동사 뒤, 형용사 앞이므로 빈칸은 형용사를 수식하는 부사 자리이다. 따라서 원급 수식 부사 (B)가 자연스럽다. (A)는 주로 숫자를 수식하는 부사, (C)는 전치사, (D)는 형용사이다.

표현 정리 strict 엄격한, 강력한 meet deadline 마감일을 맞추다 nearly 거의, 가까이 very 매우, 아주 among ~중에, ~사이에 single 하나의, 단일의

2. 정답 (D)

해석 직장에 출근하는 것은 / 매일 오전 8시에 / 훨씬 더 어렵다 / 예상했던 것보다

해설 빈칸은 be 동사 뒤, 형용사 앞이므로 빈칸은 형용사를 수식하는 부사 자리이다. 빈칸 뒤의 비교급을 수식해 주는 부사인 (D)가 정답이다. (A)는 주로 전치사로 쓰이지만, 부사로 쓰일 경우에는 숫자 앞에 쓰인다. (B)도 부사로 쓰일 경우 숫자 앞에 주로 쓰인다. (C)는 접속사이다.

표현 정리 commute 통근하다 every day 매일, 일상에서 hard 어려운, 힘든 expect 예상하다, 기대하다, 생각하다 because ~때문에 much 많은, 매우, 훨씬

3. 정답 (B)

해석 단일 규모로 가장 큰 고용주는 / 유럽에서 / 소매업체 Mcres Superstore이다

해설 빈칸은 최상급을 수식하는 부사 자리이다. (A)와 (C)는 비교급 수식 부사이고, (D)는 원급 수식 부사이다. 따라서 최상급 수식 부사인 (B)가 정답이다.

표현 정리 employer 고용주, 사업주 retailer 소매 상인, 소매점 single 하나의, 단일의

◎ 실전에 적용해 봐
1. (B) 2. (C) 3. (A) 4. (D) 5. (A) 6. (C) 7. (B)
8. (A) 9. (C) 10. (D)

1. 정답 (B)

해석 Mr. Dunken는 반납했다 / 그가 구매했던 테이블을 / 며칠 전에 / 훨씬 더 작았기 때문에 / 그가 생각했던 것보다

해설 빈칸 뒤의 비교급을 수식해 주는 부사인 (B)가 정답이다. (A)와 (D)는 최상급 수식 부사이고, (C)는 부사일 때는 비교급을 수식하지 않는다.

표현 정리 return 반납하다, 돌려주다 purchase 구입하다, 구매하다 few days 며칠 small 작은, 적은, 소규모의 single 하나의, 단일의

2. 정답 (C)

해석 고객들의 개인정보 유출은 더 문제가 많았다 / Joan Holdings가 예상했던 것보다 / 소송이 진행 중이기 때문에 / 그것에 대해

해설 than이 있는 것으로 보아 형용사 비교급이 와야 한다. problematic 같은 3음절 이상의 단어는 앞에 more를 붙여 비교급을 만들기 때문에 (C)가 정답이다. 어차피 than이 있으므로 반드시 비교급 표현이 앞에 등장해야 한다. (A)는 동사를 수식하거나, 형용사나 부사의 비교급을 수식하는 강조 부사이고, (B)는 부사절 접속사이다.

표현 정리 leakage 누출, 누설 problematic 문제가 있는 expect 예상하다, 기대하다 sue 고소하다 a lot 훨씬, 많이 because ~때문에, 왜냐하면

3. 정답 (A)

해석 2가의 프로젝트 진행은 / 굉장히 어려웠다 / 그리고 Ms. Fray는 겨우 4시간의 수면을 취하고 있었다 / 매일

해설 빈칸 뒤에 형용사 원급이 왔으므로 빈칸은 원급 수식 부사인 (A)가 적절하다. (B)는 비교급/최상급 수식 부사이고, (C)는 주로 비교급 뒤에 사용하며, (D)는 부사로 쓰일 경우 숫자 앞에 주로 쓰인다.

표현 정리 more than ~이상 at the same time 동시에, 한번에 difficult 어려운, 힘든 every day 매일, 날마다 extremely 매우, 극도로, 굉장히

4. 정답 (D)

해설 World's Best Noodles인 / 우리는 약속한다 / 제공할 것을 / 우리 고객들에게 / 오직 최고의 요리를 / Michelin 선정 요리사들이 만드는

해설 빈칸 뒤에 온 최상급을 수식할 수 있는 부사인 (D)가 정답이다. (A)는 부사의 기능이 있기는 하나 최상급을 수식하지는 않고, (B)는 부사로 쓰일 경우 숫자 앞에 주로 쓰이며, (C)는 형용사나 부사의 원급 수식 부사이다.

표현 정리 promise 약속하다, 공약하다 fine 좋은, 고급의 cuisine 요리, 요리법 chef 요리사, 주방장 extremely 매우, 굉장히

5. 정답 (A)

해설 Ms. Koy는 부여 받았다 / 새로운 업무를 / 훨씬 더 복잡해 보이는

해설 빈칸 뒤에 온 비교급이나 최상급을 수식하는 부사 (A)가 정답이다. (B)는 부사의 기능이 있으나 비교급을 수식하지는 않고, (C)는 접속사나 부사이며, 부사로 쓰일 경우 원급을 수식한다. (D)는 주로 비교급 뒤에 쓰인다.

표현 정리 assign 할당하다, 부여하다 task 업무, 일 confusing 혼란스러운

6. 정답 (C)

해설 Fluto Photo Exhibition은 / Ms. Knowles에게 많은 감명을 줘서 / 그녀는 조금도 의심이 없었다 / 그것이 가장 위대한 전시회라는 것에 / 그녀가 지금까지 봤던 것 중

해설 전치사 by와 'the+명사' 사이에 부사나 접속사는 올 수 없다. 빈칸 앞 by와 함께 뒤에 있는 최상급 표현을 강조해 줄 수 있는 부사를 이룰 수 있는 것은 (C)뿐이다. (A)는 접속사나 부사, (B)는 형용사나 부사의 원급을 수식하는 부사, (D)는 부사의 기능이 있으나 최상급을 수식하지는 않는다.

표현 정리 impress 감동시키다, 감명을 주다 doubt 의심, 의혹 exhibition 전시회 extremely 매우, 굉장히

7. 정답 (B)

해설 매니저는 노력했다 / 격려하려고 / 신입 직원들이 / 토론에 참가하도록 / 더 적극적으로 / 서로를 알 수 있는 시간을 가짐으로써

해설 빈칸 뒤에 온 원급 부사를 수식할 수 있는 (B)가 정답이다. more actively도 덩어리로 부사가 된다. (A)와 (C)는 접속사, (D)는 주로 비교급과 함께 쓰인다.

표현 정리 try to+동사원형 ~하기를 노력하다, 시도하다 encourage 격려하다, 장려하다 participate in ~에 참여하다, ~에 관여하다 actively 적극적으로, 활발하게 ice-breaking 서먹한 분위기를 없애는

8. 정답 (A)

해설 Mr. West가 요청했음에도 불구하고 / 제품의 배달이 가능한 한 빨리 이루어지도록 / 제품들은 배송되었다 / 평소보다 훨씬 늦게

해설 빈칸 뒤 비교급을 수식할 수 있는 부사인 (A)가 정답이다. (B)는 형용사나 부사의 원급을 수식하는 부사이고, (C)는 주로 숫자를 수식하는 부사이며, (D)는 전치사이다.

표현 정리 although 비록 ~일지라도 delivery 배달, 배송 product 제품, 상품 as soon as possible 가능한 한 빨리 deliver 전달하다, 배달하다 late 늦게 usual 평소의, 보통의

9. 정답 (C)

해설 가능한 자리가 없었기 때문에 / A Taste of India에 / Mr. Brown은 전화했다 / Eddy's에 / 두 번째로 가장 큰 레스토랑인 / 시내에서

해설 최상급 앞에 부사가 아닌 형용사가 오는 경우로, 이때 빈칸은 최상급을 강조해 주며, (C)가 정답이다. the second largest는 '두 번째로 큰'이라는 의미이다. (B)는 형용사나 부사의 원급을 수식하는 부사, (D)는 주로 비교급 뒤에 쓰인다.

표현 정리 available 이용할 수 있는 secondly 두 번째로, 둘째로

10. 정답 (D)

해설 사진사 Naomi Jerome는 초대했다 / 심지어 가장 가혹한 예술 비평가들까지도 / 그녀의 개인 전시회에 / 그녀는 자신감을 갖고 있었기 때문에 / 그녀의 작품에 대해

해설 빈칸 뒤에 온 the로 시작하는 명사구만 보고, 명사 앞이라고 착각해 전치사를 고르지 않도록 한다. 명사 앞에서 명사를 강조할 수 있는 초점 부사 (D)가 정답이다. (A)는 형용사나 부사의 원급을 수식하는 부사이므로 최상급 앞에 쓸 수 없고, (B)는 부사, (C)는 전치사이다.

표현 정리 photographer 사진사 harsh 냉엄한, 가혹한, 거친 critic 비평가, 비판가 private exhibition 개인 전시회 confidence 자신감, 신뢰 work 작품

법칙 46 앞뒤 내용이 상반되면 but, 순차적이면 and나 or, 인과관계면 so

◎ 유형을 파악해 봐
1. (A) 2. (B) 3. (C)

1. 정답 (A)

해설 설치 설명서와 품질 보증 정보가 포함되어 있다 / 제품 패키지에 / 그러나 배터리는 아니다

해설 빈칸 앞에도 문장, 콤마 다음에도 문장이 있으므로 접속사 자리이다. (A)를 먼저 대입해 해석해 보면, '설치 설명서와 품질 보증 정보가 포함되어 있다. 그러나 배터리는 아니다'라는 해석이 자연스러우므로 (A)가 정답이다. (C)는 전치사이고, (D)는 대명사나 형용사로 쓰인다.

표현 정리 installation 설치 instruction 설명서 warranty 보증, 보증서

2. 정답 (B)

해설 구독하세요 / 'Region Businessweek'를 / 그리고 받으세요 / 소식지 / 천만 명 이상이 구독 중인

해설 빈칸 앞과 뒤에 동일한 구조의 문장이 왔으므로 빈칸은 등위접속사 자리이다. 우선 순위인 (D)를 먼저 대입해 해석해 보면, '구독하세요, 그러나 받으세요'라는 말은 어색하다. '구독하세요, 그리고 받으세요'라는 말이 어울리므로 (B)가 정답이다. (C)는 관계대명사로 사용되는 경우 앞에 사물 명사를 선행사로 받을 수 있으나, 그럴 경우 선행사에 수일치 시켜 빈칸 다음에 단수 동사가 와야 한다.

표현 정리 subscribe to+명사 ~을 구독하다 receive 받다, 수상하다 newsletter 소식지, 시사 통신 read 읽다, 독서하다

3. 정답 (C)

해설 정문 보수는 / 곧 시작될 것이다 / 그래서 방문자들은 사용하도록 요청 받는다 / 후문을

해설 빈칸 앞에도 문장, 콤마 다음에도 문장이 있으므로 접속사 자리이다. because와 so는 뜻이 비슷하여 자칫 혼동하기 쉬운 접속사이다. 앞 문장인 '정문 보수는 시작될 것이다'가 원인, 뒷문장 '방문자들은 후문을 사용하도록 요청 받는다'가 결과이므로 (C) so(그래서)가 정답이다. (A)는 뒤에 도치된 문장이 오거나, 주로 neither A nor B 형태로 쓰인다. (B) because 뒤에는 원인이 와야 하고, (D)는 전치사이다.

표현 정리 renovation 수리, 혁신 be advised to+동사원형 ~하도록 요청 받다 rear 뒤의 except for ~을 제외하고

◎ 실전에 적용해 봐
1. (D) 2. (D) 3. (B) 4. (C) 5. (C) 6. (A) 7. (A)
8. (D) 9. (D) 10. (C)

1. 정답 (D)

해설 10달러 보증금을 지불해야 한다 / 객실 예약 시 / 그리고 돌려 받을 수 있다 / 당신이 체크아웃할 때

해설 정동사가 2개(must be, can have)이므로 접속사가 필요하다. '보증금을 지불해야 한다. 그리고 체크아웃할 때 돌려받을 수 있다'라는 해석이 자연스럽기 때문에 (D)가 정답이다.

표현 정리 deposit 보증금, 입금 submit 제출하다, 제시하다 reservation 예약 return 돌아오다, 돌려주다

2. 정답 (D)

해설 빌딩 수리가 끝날 예정이었다 / 수요일에 / 그러나 그것들은 끝나지 않을 것이다 / 다음 주 금요일까지

해설 정동사가 2개(was, will not be)이므로 접속사 자리이다. 빈칸 앞에서 '수리가 수요일에 끝날 예정이라고' 했는데, 빈칸 뒤에서는 '금요일까지 끝나지 않을 것'이라고 반대되는 내용이 이어졌으므로 (D)가 정답이다.

표현 정리 renovation 수리, 혁신 be scheduled to+동사원형 ~하기로 예정되어 있다 finish 끝나다, 마치다 until ~할 때까지, ~까지

3. 정답 (B)

해설 시장 상황은 다소 불리한 상태였다 / 그러나 Sweet Home Furnishings의 수익은 올해 실제로 증가했다

해설 정동사가 2개(were, increased)이므로 접속사인 (B)가 정답이다. (A), (C), (D)는 모두 부사이다.

표현 정리 condition 조건, 상황 rather 오히려, 차라리, 다소 unfavorable 불리한, 비호의적인 profit 이익, 수익

4. 정답 (C)

해설 Mr. Hague의 이력서가 검토되었고 / 그의 근무 경험이 인정되었기 때문에 / 그는 참석하라고 요청 받았다 / Jennings Company의 면접에

해설 As 다음에 완전한 문장이 왔고, 그 안에서 '주어+동사'와 '주어+동사'가 연결되는 구조이므로 등위접속사가 필요하다. (A)와 (B)는 뜻이 같아서 둘 다 탈락시키고, that은 주로 명사절이나 형용사절 접속사로 사용되므로 (C)가 정답이 된다.

표현 정리 resume 이력서; 다시 시작하다 working experience 근무 경험 recognize ~을 인정하다

5. 정답 (C)

해설 당신의 티켓을 / 미리 준비하고 계세요 / 그것들을 보여주기 위해 / 입구에서 직원에게 / 그러면 당신은 내부로 들어갈 수 있습니다 / 지체되지 않고

해설 (A)와 (B) 모두 부사절 접속사로 빈칸에 올 수 있으나, (A) 뒤에는 원인이 나와야 하고, (B)가 '들어간다면 티켓을 준비하라'라는 어색한 내용이 된다. 빈칸 앞에는 '티켓을 가지고 있으세요', 빈칸 뒤에는 '지체되지 않고 들어갈 수 있습니다'라는 의미를 나타내는 (C)가 정답이다. so that에서 that은 생략이 가능하다.

표현 정리 prepare 준비하다, 대비하다 in advance 미리, 사전에 present 보여주다, 제시하다 staff 직원, 스태프 entrance 입구, 현관

6. 정답 (A)

해설 애널리스트들은 말한다 / 지역 경제성장이 침체되어 왔다고 / 지난 수 년에 걸쳐 / 그러나 실제 공공 지출은 증가했다 / 5퍼센트

해설 빈칸 앞에는 '경제성장이 침체되었다'는 내용이, 빈칸 뒤에는 '지출은 증가했다'라는 상반되는 내용이 왔으므로 (A)가 정답이다.

표현 정리 analyst 분석가, 전문가 growth 성장, 증가, 상승 stagnant 정체된, 불경기의, 침체한 in fact 사실상, 실제로 spending 지출, 소비 if 만약 ~라면

7. 정답 (A)

해설 Dr. Jones는 권했다 / Ms. Riley에게 약을 복용할 것을 / 그녀가 경험할 때 / 메스꺼나 현기증을

해설 빈칸의 앞 뒤에 같은 품사인 명사가 왔으므로 이것을 이어줄 수 있는 등위접속사가 와야 한다. 그녀가 메스꺼움 '또는' 어지러움을 느낄 때 약을 복용하도록 권했다는 의미가 되므로 (A)가 정답이다. 빈칸과 dizziness 사이에는 주어와 동사(she experiences)가 생략된 병치구조이다. (C)는 병치가 될 수 없고, 이어지는 문장이 완전해야 하므로 탈락. (B)는 대명사의 혼용으로 쓰이고, (D)는 앞뒤 문맥이 상반될 때 쓴다.

표현 정리 advise 조언하다, 권하다, 알리다 nausea 구역질, 메스꺼움 dizziness 현기증

8. 정답 (D)

해설 Ms. Kerr는 가져오지 않았다 / 자료를 / 보통 필요한 / 경기 세미나

를 위해 / 그는 인쇄하는 것도 역시 기억하지 못했다 / 문서의 추가본을 / Mr. Shin이 요청한

해설 빈칸 뒤에 주어(he)와 동사(did)가 도치되어 있다. 이러한 구조가 가능하도록 하는 것은 보기 중 (D)밖에 없다. 부정어가 문두에 올 때는 주어와 동사가 도치된다. 접속사인 (A), (B), (C) 뒤에 문장이 올 때는 도치가 발생하지 않는다.

표현 정리 bring 가져오다 material 자료, 재료 print 인쇄하다, 인쇄물 extra 추가의, 임시의

9. 정답 (D)

해석 Mr. Gilbert는 떠났다 / 사무실을 / 오늘은 평소보다 일찍 / 그는 저녁 약속이 있었기 때문에 / 고객과

해설 (A)와 (D)가 모두 인과관계를 나타내는 접속사이므로 쓰임이 혼동되기 쉬운 함정 문제이다. 빈칸 앞의 내용 '평소보다 일찍 떠났다'가 결과, 빈칸 뒤의 내용 '그는 약속이 있다'가 원인이므로 (D)가 정답이다. (A)가 답이 되려면 앞쪽에 원인, 뒤쪽에 결과가 나와야 한다.

표현 정리 leave 떠나다, 나가다 have an appointment with ~와 약속이 있다 if 만약 ~라면 because ~때문에, 왜냐하면

10. 정답 (C)

해석 당신이 알았을 때 / 제품의 재고가 바닥나고 있다는 것을 / 창고에 보고하세요 / 인근에 있는 / 우리가 확인할 수 있도록 / 제품들이 이용 가능한지 / 항상

해설 빈칸은 앞 문장과 뒷문장을 연결해 주는 접속사 자리이다. '보고하세요. 그래서 우리 제품들이 이용 가능한지 확인할 수 있도록 ~'이라는 뜻이 자연스러우므로 (C)가 정답이다. 여기서 so는 so that과 같은 기능이며, '그래야 ~하니까'의 뜻이다. (B)는 부사 또는 형용사로 쓰인다.

표현 정리 out of stock 재고가 없는, 품절이 된 warehouse 창고 nearby 근처에, 바로 옆에 available 가능한, 이용할 수 있는, 유용한

법칙 47 of가 답이 되는 주격, 목적격, 소유격, 동격

◎ 유형을 파악해 봐
1. (C) 2. (D) 3. (C)

1. 정답 (C)

해석 프로젝트의 성공은 / 여부에 달려 있다 / 헌신 / 관련된 팀원들의

해설 전치사 어휘 문제로 빈칸 앞뒤만 보고 풀 수 있는 문제이다. (A)는 팀원에 대한 헌신을 의미하고, (C)는 주격의 of가 되어 '팀원들이 헌신'하는 것을 의미한다. 앞부분을 확인해 보면 '팀원들의 헌신에 프로젝트 성공 여부가 달려 있다'는 말이므로 (C)가 정답이다. 빈칸 뒤에 '팀원들'이 왔으므로 기간 명사와 사용하는 (D)는 오답이다.

표현 정리 success 성공, 성과 attributable 기인하는, 원인을 돌릴 수 있는 commitment 약속, 헌신, 공약

2. 정답 (D)

해석 위험에 대한 평가는 / 사업 확장과 관련된 / 부정적이다

해설 전치사 어휘 문제로 빈칸 앞뒤를 확인하여 푼다. (D)가 오면 '위험을 평가하다'로 해석되는 목적격 of가 되어 자연스럽다. (A)는 주로 수동태에서 행위자 앞에 쓰이고, (B)는 장소나 시각 앞에 쓰이고, (C)는 방향이나 출발 시점의 앞에 사용한다

표현 정리 assessment 평가, 사정 risk 위험, 위기, 우려 expansion 확장, 확대 negative 부정적인, 부정의

3. 정답 (C)

해석 당신은 보상을 받을 자격이 있다 / 2주의 휴가 / 당신의 최근 공헌에 대한 / Jamison 사에서

해설 전치사 어휘 문제로 빈칸 앞뒤를 해석하여 확인한다. 보상과 2주의 휴가가 동격의 관계로, 동격의 of 자리이다. (A)는 주로 수동태에서 행위자 앞에, (B)는 방향 전치사, (D)는 주제를 나타낼 때 사용한다.

표현 정리 deserve ~할 만하다, ~할 가치가 있다 compensation 보상 vacation 휴가 contribution 기여, 공헌, 기부

◎ 실전에 적용해 봐
1. (B) 2. (A) 3. (C) 4. (D) 5. (C) 6. (A) 7. (B)
8. (D) 9. (C) 10. (D)

1. 정답 (B)

해석 Mr. Fray는 / Elaska 사의 설립자인 / 곧 임명할 것이다 / 새로운 CEO를 / 그의 자리를 맡을 / 그가 은퇴한 후에

해설 전치사 어휘 문제로 빈칸 앞뒤를 해석하여 확인한다. 빈칸은 '회사의 설립자'의 뜻으로 '회사를 설립한 사람'이 되어 일종의 목적격 of로 볼 수 있다. 혹은 설립자도 회사에 속한다고 보면 일종의 '소유격 of'로 봐도 좋다. 따라서 (B)가 자연스럽다. (A)는 주제를 나타낼 때, (C)는 방향의 전치사, (D)는 동반, 수단의 전치사이다.

표현 정리 founder 창설자 appoint 임명하다, 지명하다 retire 은퇴하다, 퇴직하다

2. 정답 (A)

해석 모든 지원자 중에서 / Ms. Wozniak는 가장 포괄적인 이해력을 갖고 있는 것 같다 / 우리 회사 그리고 그녀의 직업에 대해

해설 빈칸 뒤에 명사가 나왔으므로 접속사인 (B)와 (D)는 탈락한다. (B)를 전치사로 본다면 뒤에 과거시점이 나와야 한다. (C)는 초점 부사라고 하며, 명사 앞에 올 수는 있으나 이어서 문장이 오고 있으므로 빈칸부터 콤마까지 부사 기능이 되어야 한다. 따라서 (C)가 오게 되면 명사만 남는 꼴이 되어 탈락한다. (A)가 오면 소유격의 of가 되는데 해석은 '~중에서'가 되며 최상급 표현과도 잘 어울린다.

표현 정리 comprehensive 종합적인, 포괄적인 understanding 이해력, 이해, 지식

3. 정답 (C)

해석 많은 분석가들은 예측했다 / Mr. Jobs의 은퇴는 큰 손실이 될 것이라고 / Innovation Corporation에 / 그런데 회사는 보유하고 있지 않다 /

그와 같이 재능 있는 임원을

해설 전치사 어휘 문제로 빈칸의 앞뒤를 확인해야 한다. 'Mr. Jobs의 은퇴'라는 의미로 (C)가 정답이다. 'Mr. Jobs가 은퇴하다'라는 의미로 주격의 of라고도 한다. (A)는 수동태에서 행위자 앞에 주로 쓰이며, (B)은 출처나 시점과 사용하고, (D)는 동반되는 것이나 수단이 뒤에 따라온다.

표현 정리 predict 예상하다, 예측하다 retirement 은퇴 loss 손실, 감소 executive 임원, 경영자 talented 재능 있는, 뛰어난, 유능한

4. 정답 (D)

해설 최종 목표는 / 프로젝트의 / 고취시키기 위한 것이다 / 과자점의 인식을 세계적으로 / 인도네시아에 있는

해설 전치사 어휘 문제로 빈칸의 앞뒤를 확인해야 한다. '프로젝트의 목표'라는 해석이 자연스러우므로 (D)가 정답이다. '프로젝트가 목표다'라는 것으로 보면 일종의 주격의 of가 된다. (A)는 시간이나 장소 앞, (B)는 방향 앞, (C)는 '~내에'라는 뜻으로 범위, 거리, 기간 앞에 오는 전치사이므로 자연스럽지 못하다.

표현 정리 ultimate 궁극적인, 최종의 global 세계적인, 글로벌 awareness 인식, 지각, 의식 sweatshop 과자점

5. 정답 (C)

해설 비록 수리는 / 장소의 / 내일 끝날 예정이지만 / 그것은 개방되지 않을 것이다 / 다음 주까지

해설 전치사 어휘 문제로 빈칸의 앞뒤를 확인해야 한다. '장소의 수리'라는 해석이 자연스러우므로 (C)가 정답이다. (A)는 주제를 나타내는 말, (B)는 동반이나 수단, (D)는 방향을 나타내는 말과 사용한다.

표현 정리 although 비록 ~이지만 venue (행사의) 장소 done 다 같은, 완성된 until ~할 때까지, ~까지

6. 정답 (A)

해설 회사 정책은 요구한다 / 적어도 2번의 테스트 실행을 / 자동차들의 / 그것들이 공식적으로 출시되기 전에

해설 빈칸은 전치사 어휘 문제로 빈칸 앞뒤의 관계를 확인해야 한다. '자동차의 테스트 실행'이라는 뜻이므로 (A)가 정답이다. '자동차들을 테스트 하다'는 관계이므로 일종의 주격의 of가 된다. (B)는 장소나 기간이, (C)는 기간 명사가, (D)는 주제를 나타내는 명사가 온다.

표현 정리 require 필요하다, 요구하다 at least 적어도, 최소한 officially 공식적으로 release 출시하다, 개시하다 within ~안에, ~이내에

7. 정답 (B)

해설 도와주세요 / 사람들을 / 줄을 서서 기다리는 / 질문이 있어 / 티켓 가격에 대해

해설 전치사 어휘 문제로 빈칸의 앞뒤의 관계를 확인해야 한다. '티켓들의 가격'이라는 의미가 되어야 하므로 of가 자연스럽다. 이러한 of를 관련, 한정의 of라고 한다. (A)는 주로 장소, 속도, 가격, 비율을 나타내는 말과 함께, (C)는 기간 명사 앞에, (D)는 방향을 나타내는 말과 사용한다.

표현 정리 assist 돕다, 지원하다 those 사람들 wait in line 줄을 서서 기다리다 inquiry 문의

8. 정답 (C)

해설 강의는 / 기업가 정신에 관한 / 그리고 그 강의는 의무적인 과정인데 / 판매부의 직원을 위한 / 열릴 예정이다 / 780 룸에서 / 매주 토요일에

해설 빈칸은 전치사 어휘 문제로 빈칸 앞뒤 관계를 해석을 통해 확인해야 한다. 빈칸 앞은 강의, 뒤는 강의 내용이므로 주제와 분야에 관한 전치사인 (D)가 정답이다. (A)가 오려면 뒤에 사람이 와서 '사람이 하는 강의'라는 답이 된다. 명사와 명사 사이에 of가 온다고만 알고 있으면 틀리는 함정 문제이다.

표현 정리 lecture 강의, 강연 entrepreneurship 기업가 정신 mandatory 의무적인, 필수적인 be scheduled to+동사원형 ~할 예정이다

9. 정답 (C)

해설 모든 가능한 직업 중에서 / 회계사가 가장 적합한 직업인 것 같다 / Mr. Benford을 위한 / 큰 흥미를 가진 / 회계학에

해설 빈칸은 전치사 어휘 문제로 빈칸 앞뒤의 관계를 확인해야 한다. (C)가 오면 소유격 of가 되는데 해석은 '~중에서'가 되며 최상급 표현과도 잘 어울린다. (A)는 수동태에서 행위자 앞에 쓰이고, (B)는 목적, 용도, 대상의 전치사, (D)는 길이가 긴 사물하고 쓰인다.

표현 정리 career 경력, 직업, 활동, 커리어 path 길, 방향, 경로 accounting 회계, 회계학 suitable 적합한, 적절한 interest 흥미, 관심

10. 정답 (D)

해설 R&M 연구소는 수행해 왔다 / 연구를 / 방법에 대한 / 동기를 주기 위한 / 직원들에게 / 강화하는 것을 목표로 / 일반적인 근무 조건을 / 지역 회사들에서

해설 빈칸은 전치사 어휘 문제로 빈칸 앞뒤의 관계를 확인해야 한다. aim은 동사일 때는 at을 좋아하지만 at을 답으로 하면 틀리는 함정 문제이다. with the aim of는 '~할 목적으로'라는 표현이므로 알아두는 것이 좋다. 이 때 of는 동격의 of라고 한다.

표현 정리 Research Institute 연구소 conduct 수행하다, 시행하다 motivate 동기를 주다, 자극하다 with the aim of ~할 목적으로 enhance 강화하다, 높이다 general 일반적인

Chapter 07 7~8개월에 한 번 출제되는 문제

법칙 46 희망, 요청, 설득, 허락 동사가 오면 to 부정사

◎ 유형을 파악해 봐
1. (A)   2. (C)   3. (A)

1. 정답 (A)

해설 최고 관리자는 요청했다 / 영업 부장에게 / 보고하도록 / 판매 기록을

/ 지난 분기

해설 문장에서 asked가 정동사이므로 빈칸은 준동사 자리이다. 빈칸은 '결혼승낙' 동사 ask의 목적 보어 자리이다. '결혼승낙' 동사는 to 부정사를 목적 보어로 취하므로 정답은 (A)이다. (B)는 과거분사로 뒤에 목적어 the sales record가 있으므로 역시 부적합하다.

표현 정리 executive manager 최고 관리자, 경영 책임자 head 책임자 Sales Department 영업부 quarter 분기

2. 정답 (C)

해설 Blooming Audio 사장은 예상한다 / 회사 이익률이 / 이번 년도 / 초과할 것이라고 / 예측한 이익률을 / 작년에

해설 문장에서 expect가 정동사이므로 빈칸은 준동사 자리이다. 빈칸은 '결혼승낙' 동사 expect의 목적 보어 자리라 to 부정사가 필요하므로 정답은 (C)이다. (D)는 과거분사로 뒤에 목적어 the rate predicted가 있으므로 역시 부적합하다.

표현 정리 expect 예상하다 profit margin 이익률 rate 비율 exceed 넘어서다 predict 예측하다

3. 정답 (A)

해설 이 약들은 권고된다 / 복용하도록 / 적어도 식후 30분에 / 하루에 3번

해설 문장에서 are advised가 정동사이므로 빈칸은 준동사 자리이다. advise는 '결혼승낙' 동사이므로 수동태로 쓰일 때는 목적 보어가 남는다. 따라서 빈칸은 '결혼승낙' 동사의 목적 보어 자리인 to 부정사가 필요하며, 따라서 정답은 (A)이다. '결혼승낙' 동사의 수동태는 'be p.p. to 동사원형'의 숙어 형태로 외워두면 편리하다.

표현 정리 pill 약, 알약 be advised to+동사원형 ~하도록 권고 받다 at least 적어도 half an hour 30분 meal 식사

◎ 실전에 적용해 봐
1. (D) 2. (D) 3. (B) 4. (A) 5. (B) 6. (C) 7. (D)
8. (C) 9. (C) 10. (D)

1. 정답 (D)

해설 Dailywear Outfitters는 허용한다 / 매장 직원이 받는 것을 / 20%를 할인 / 모든 구입품의 / 그들이 상품들을 구입할 때 / 매장에서

해설 문장에 접속사가 1개(when), 정동사가 2개(allows, purchase) 있으므로 또 정동사가 올 수 없다. 빈칸은 '결혼승낙' 동사인 allow의 목적 보어인 to 부정사가 필요하므로 정답은 (D)이다. (B)는 명사 뒤엔 명사가 또 올 수 없으므로 오답이다.

표현 정리 allow 허락하다 staff 직원 discount 할인 purchase 구매; 구매하다

2. 정답 (D)

해설 직원 교육 전문가로서 / Mr. Hills는 요청 받았다 / 설명하도록 / 기본적인 에티켓을 / 직장에서의 / 신입 사원들에게

해설 문장에서 was asked가 정동사이므로 빈칸은 준동사 자리이다. ask는 '결혼승낙' 동사이므로 수동태로 쓰일 때 목적 보어가 남는다. 따라서 to 부정사가 필요한데, 뒤에 basic etiquette라는 목적어가 왔으므로 (B)와 (D) 중에 능동태인 (D)가 정답이다. (C)는 '결혼승낙' 동사의 목적 보어로 쓰일 수 없다. '결혼승낙' 동사의 수동태는 'be p.p. to 동사원형'의 숙어 형태로 외워두면 편리하다.

표현 정리 employee training specialist 직원 교육 전문가 be asked to+동사원형 ~하도록 요청 받다 basic 기본적인 etiquette 에티켓 workplace 직장 newcomer 신입 사원 explain 설명하다

3. 정답 (B)

해설 직원들은 장려된다 / 온라인 강의를 듣도록 / 내부고발에 대한 / 제공된 / 무료로 / 모든 직원들을 위해

해설 문장에 접속사가 1개(that), 정동사가 2개(are encouraged, are provided) 있으므로 빈칸에 또 정동사가 올 수 없다. encourage는 '결혼승낙' 동사이므로 수동태로 쓰일 때 목적 보어가 남는다. 따라서 to 부정사가 필요하므로 정답은 (B)이다. (A)와 (C)는 '결혼승낙' 동사의 목적 보어로 쓰일 수 없다.

표현 정리 be encouraged to+동사원형 ~하도록 장려되다 online lesson 온라인 강의 whistleblowing 내부고발 provide 제공하다 for free 무료로

4. 정답 (A)

해설 매니저는 원한다 / Mr. Doe가 Mr. Browne와 짝을 이루기를 / 회계부에서 온 / 새 프로젝트에 관여하기 위해

해설 문장에서 wants가 정동사이므로 빈칸은 준동사 자리이다. 빈칸은 '결혼승낙' 동사 want의 목적 보어 자리이며, 따라서 to 부정사가 필요하므로 정답은 (A)가 된다.

표현 정리 manager 관리자 pair up with ~와 짝을 이루다 Accounting Department 회계부

5. 정답 (B)

해설 모든 지원자들은 요구된다 / 온라인 또는 오프라인 결제 중 하나를 하도록 / 이번 주말 전에 / 그렇지 않으면, 그들의 등록은 취소될 것이다

해설 문장에서 are required가 정동사이므로 빈칸은 준동사 자리이다. require는 '결혼승낙' 동사이므로 수동태로 쓰일 때 목적 보어가 남는다. 따라서 빈칸은 '결혼승낙' 동사의 목적 보어 자리인 to 부정사가 필요하므로 정답은 (B)이다.

표현 정리 applicant 지원자 be required to+동사원형 ~하도록 요구되다 otherwise 그렇지 않으면, 달리 registration 등록 cancel 취소하다

6. 정답 (C)

해설 감독관은 상기시켰다 / 직원들에게 / 공사 현장에서 일하는 / 안전 지침을 준수하도록 / 항상 / 그가 주위에 없는 경우에도

해설 문장에서 접속사가 1개(when), 정동사가 2개(reminded, is)이므로 빈칸은 정동사가 또 올 수 없다. 빈칸은 '결혼승낙' 동사 remind의 목적 보어 자리이므로 to 부정사가 필요하며, 따라서 정답은 (C)이다. (A), (D)는 '결혼승낙' 동사의 목적 보어 자리에 쓰일 수 없다.

표현 정리 supervisor 감독관 remind 상기시키다 construction

site 공사 현장 safety guideline 안전 지침 at all times 항상, 언제나

7. 정답 (D)

해설 JR Holdings는 직원들이 사용할 수 있도록 한다 / 회사 자동차들을 / 무료로 / 최대 3주 동안

해설 문장에서 let이 정동사이다. let은 사역동사이므로 목적 보어로 동사원형이나 p.p.를 취한다. (C)는 뒤에 목적어가 있기 때문에 탈락하고, 정답은 동사원형인 (D)이다.

표현 정리 automobile 자동차 for free 무료로 maximum 최대의 use 사용하다

8. 정답 (C)

해설 대부분의 그녀의 친구들은 / 다른 회사에서 / 일하고 있었기 때문에 / 더 좋은 근로 조건에서 / Ms. Stephen은 설득되었다 / 옮기도록 / 그녀의 직장을

해설 문장에서 접속사가 1개(Since), 정동사가 2개(were working, was convinced)이므로 빈칸은 또 정동사가 올 수 없다. convince는 '결혼승낙' 동사이므로 수동태로 쓰일 때 목적 보어가 남는다. 따라서 빈칸은 '결혼승낙' 동사의 목적 보어 자리에 to 부정사가 필요하며, 정답은 (C)가 된다.

표현 정리 favorable 좋은, 호의적인 working condition 근로 조건 be convinced to+동사원형 ~하도록 설득 당하다

9. 정답 (C)

해설 관리자는 시켰다 / Ms. Dawson으로 하여금 소집하도록 / 모든 직원들을 / 전달하기 위해 / 소식을 / 최근 정책 변화에 대해

해설 문장에서 got이 정동사이므로 빈칸은 준동사 자리이다. get이 5형식으로 쓰일 때에는 준사역동사라고 하며, 목적 보어로 to 부정사나 p.p.를 취한다. 따라서 (C)가 정답이다.

표현 정리 manager 관리자 deliver 전달하다 announcement 소식, 발표 recent 최근의 gather 모으다

10. 정답 (D)

해설 Mr. Gohr는 보냈다 / 최고 관리자에게 이메일을 / 그가 희망한다고 / 그에게 주어진 시간을 연장하기를 / 그의 발표를 위해

해설 빈칸은 that 절의 정동사 자리이다. 빈칸 뒤 to와의 어울림이 좋다고 생각해 allow를 답으로 고르지 않도록 한다. allow는 to 부정사를 목적 보어로 취하는 동사('결혼승낙' 동사)이지, 목적어로 취하는 동사'응큼쟁이' 동사, '법칙 58' 참고)가 아니다. 빈칸은 빈칸 뒤 to extend를 목적어로 취하는 '응큼쟁이' 동사 자리이므로 (D)가 정답이다. (A)와 (B)는 3형식으로 쓰일 경우, -ing를 목적어로 취하는 동사이다.

표현 정리 executive manager 최고 관리자 extend 연장하다 presentation 발표 consider 고려하다

법칙 49 감정분사는 '사물잉, 사람을 패?'

◎ 유형을 파악해 봐
1. (C) 2. (B) 3. (C)

1. 정답 (C)

해설 우리는 알리게 되어 기쁘다 / Shop n' More's의 76번째 매장 개점을 / Maryland에 있는

해설 be 동사 뒤에는 형용사의 기능을 하는 분사가 필요하다. 따라서 동사인 (D)는 탈락한다. 명사인 (B)가 보어 자리에 오려면 주어와 동격이어야 하는데 '우리 = 기쁨'의 관계는 성립되지 않으므로 탈락. (A)와 (C) 중에서 주어(We)가 사람이므로 p.p.인 (C)를 써야 한다.

표현 정리 be pleased to+동사원형 ~하게 되어 기쁘다 announce 알리다, 발표하다 grand opening 개점, 개장

2. 정답 (B)

해설 전시회를 준비하는데 1년이나 걸렸음에도 불구하고 / 방문자들의 과반수는 말했다 / 그것은 실망스러웠다고

해설 be 동사 뒤에는 형용사의 기능을 하는 분사가 필요하다. 따라서 동사인 (D)는 탈락한다. 명사인 (A)가 보어 자리에 오려면 주어와 동격이 되어야 하는데 '그것(전시회) = 실망'의 관계는 성립하지 않으므로 탈락. (B)와 (C) 중에서, 주어(it)가 사물이므로 -ing인 (B)가 정답이다.

표현 정리 exhibition 전시회 a whole year 꼬박 1년 prepare 준비하다 majority 과반수 disappointing 실망스러운 disappoint 실망시키다

3. 정답 (C)

해설 Ms. Grin은 참석하기를 기대한다 / 개최될 행사에 / 다음 주에 / 그녀는 들었기 때문에 / 행사의 규모가 압도적이라고

해설 be 동사 뒤에는 형용사의 기능을 하는 분사가 필요하다. 따라서 동사인 (D)는 탈락한다. 부사는 보어 자리에 올 수 없으므로 부사인 (B) 역시 탈락. (A)와 (C) 중에서 주어(the show)가 사물이므로 -ing인 (C)가 정답이다.

표현 정리 look forward to -ing ~하는 것을 기대하다 attend 참석하다 hold 개최하다 overwhelming 압도적인

◎ 실전에 적용해 봐
1. (B) 2. (D) 3. (A) 4. (D) 5. (A) 6. (A) 7. (B)
8. (D) 9. (B) 10. (C)

1. 정답 (B)

해설 인증해 주세요 / 당신의 이메일 주소를 / 받기 위해 / 우리의 흥미로운 관광 프로그램 제의들을 / 무료로

해설 소유격과 명사 사이이므로 명사를 수식하는 기능을 하는 분사가 필요하다. 따라서 동사인 (C)는 탈락한다. (A)와 (B) 중에서 빈칸 뒤 수식 받는 명사(tour program)가 사물이므로 -ing인 (B)가 정답이다.

표현 정리 validate 인증하다 e-mail address 이메일 주소 receive 받다 offer 제의, 제안 for free 무료로

2. 정답 (D)

해설 책은 / Ms. Brookyln가 쓴 / 포함하고 있다 / 대단히 흥미로운 이야기를 / 삶에 관한 / 가방 디자이너로서의 / 뉴욕에서 / 그녀 자신의 경험을 바탕으로 한

해설 관사와 명사 사이이므로 명사를 수식하는 기능을 하는 분사가 필요하다. (B), (C)는 명사이므로 탈락. (A)와 (D) 중에서 빈칸 뒤 수식 받는 명사(story)가 사물이므로 -ing인 (D)가 정답이다.

표현 정리 contain 포함하다 based on ~에 근거하여, ~에 기반을 둔 fascinating 대단히 흥미로운

3. 정답 (A)

해설 최고 관리자는 깜짝 놀랐다 / 경쟁사가 유명인사와 계약해 광고하도록 했을 때 / 회사 제품을 / 그의 회사와 똑같은

해설 be 동사 뒤에는 형용사의 기능을 하는 분사가 필요하다. 따라서 동사인 (C), (D)는 탈락한다. 주어(The executive manager)가 사람이므로 p.p.인 (A)가 정답이다.

표현 정리 rival firm 경쟁 회사 celebrity 유명인사 advertise 광고하다 startle 깜짝 놀라게 하다

4. 정답 (D)

해설 당신은 이 약을 먹을 수 있습니다 / 안심하고 / 그것은 어떠한 부작용이 없기 때문에 / 당신의 건강에

해설 빈칸 뒤 명사를 수식할 수 있는 분사가 필요하기 때문에 동사인 (A)와 (C)는 탈락한다. 수식 받는 명사(effects)가 사물이므로 -ing인 (D)가 정답이다.

표현 정리 medicine 약 relief 안심, 안도 effect 영향 health 건강 worry 걱정하다

5. 정답 (A)

해설 워크숍은 / 전자 상거래 웹사이트를 관리하는 것에 대한 / 개최될 것이다 / 무료로 / 관심 있는 사람들을 위해

해설 anyone을 수식하는 형용사의 기능을 하는 분사가 필요하므로, 부사인 (C)와 to 부정사인 (D)는 탈락한다. anyone은 사람을 가리키는 대명사이므로 p.p.인 (A)가 정답이다.

표현 정리 workshop 워크숍 manage 관리하다 e-commerce 전자 상거래 hold 개최하다 interest ~의 관심을 끌다

6. 정답 (A)

해설 Mr. Bean은 당황했다 / 그가 입장했을 때 / 교실에 / 20분 후에 / 강의가 이미 시작한지

해설 be 동사 뒤에는 형용사의 기능을 하는 분사가 필요하므로 동사인 (B), (D)는 탈락한다. 주어인 Mr. Bean이 사람이므로 p.p.인 (A)가 정답이다.

표현 정리 enter 입장하다 classroom 교실 lecture 강의 arrive 도착하다 embarrass 당황스럽게 하다

7. 정답 (B)

해설 Power Auto Parts는 영광스럽다 / 알리게 되어 / 마침내 된 것을 / Kansas City 지역 사업 협회의 일원이

해설 be 동사 뒤에 형용사의 기능을 하는 분사가 필요하므로 동사인 (A), (D)는 탈락한다. 주어인 Power Auto Parts가 사람이 아니라고 생각해 -ing인 (C)를 고르지 않도록 한다. 회사는 사람으로 취급하므로 p.p.인 (B)가 정답이다.

표현 정리 be honored to+동사원형 ~하게 돼 영광이다 announce 알리다, 발표하다 finally 마침내 local business 지역 사업 association 협회

8. 정답 (D)

해설 단편 연극인 'Dancing with Aria'는 / 받지 못했다 / 많은 긍정적인 피드백을 / 청중으로부터 / 그것이 지루하다고 생각했던

해설 be 동사 뒤에는 형용사의 기능을 하는 분사가 필요하므로 동사인 (C)는 탈락한다. 부사는 주격 보어가 될 수 없으므로 (B) 역시 탈락. 주어인 it은 The short play 'Dancing with Aria'를 가리킨다. play(연극)는 사물이므로 -ing인 (D)가 정답이다.

표현 정리 play 연극 receive 받다 feedback 피드백, 반응 audience 청중 boring 지루한

9. 정답 (B)

해설 Ms. Plain은 좌절했다 / 그녀의 제안이 / 공을 들인 / 한 달 내내 / 거절되었기 때문에 / 최고 관리자로부터

해설 be 동사 뒤에는 형용사의 기능을 하는 분사가 필요하므로 동사인 (C)는 탈락한다. 명사인 (A)는 Ms. Plain과 동격이 될 수 없어 역시 탈락. 주어인 Ms. Plain이 사람이므로 p.p.인 (B)가 정답이다.

표현 정리 proposal 제안 work on ~에 공을 들이다, 애쓰다 entire 전체의 reject 거절하다 executive manager 최고 관리자

10. 정답 (C)

해설 최근 소식은 / 비극적인 사고에 대한 / Northeast Town에서 일어난 / 모든 주민들이 걱정하게 만들었다 / 마을 안전에 대해

해설 빈칸은 5형식 동사 leave의 목적어 다음 목적 보어 자리로 형용사나 분사가 와야 한다. residents는 사람이므로 p.p.인 (C)가 정답이다. news가 사물이라고 -ing을 답으로 하면 함정에 빠지는 문제이다. 5형식 문장의 목적 보어 자리는 목적어와의 어울림을 따져야지 주어와의 어울림을 따져서는 안 된다.

표현 정리 recent 최근의 tragic 비극적인 accident 사고 resident 주민, 거주자 security 안전, 보안

법칙 50 완전한 문장 뒤에서는 '(in order) to 동사원형'이 동사를 수식

◎ 유형을 파악해 봐
1. (B) 2. (A) 3. (D)

1. 정답 (B)

해설 무료 오찬이 열릴 것이다 / 구내 식당에서 / 기념하기 위해 / Mr. Guru의 은퇴를

해설 문장에서 정동사는 will be held이므로 빈칸은 준동사 자리이다. 빈칸 뒤에 있는 the retirement를 목적어로 취할 수 있는 (B)가 정답이다. (C)는 분사로 볼 경우, 뒤에서 앞의 명사 cafeteria를 수식할 수는 있으나, 뒤

에 목적어를 가질 수 없다.

표현 정리 luncheon 오찬 hold 열다, 개최하다 cafeteria 구내 식당 retirement 은퇴 celebrate 기념하다

2. 정답 (A)

해석 지원자들은 소지하고 있어야 한다 / 운전 면허증을 / 지원하기 위해 / 시간제 버스 운전직에

해설 문장에서 정동사는 have이므로 빈칸은 준동사 자리이다. 빈칸 뒤에 목적어가 없다고 해서 p.p.인 (B)를 찍는 함정에 빠지지 않도록 하자. apply for는 덩어리로 쓰이는 동사로 a ~ position이 목적어이다. 따라서 (A)가 정답이다.

표현 정리 applicant 지원자 driver's license 운전 면허증 apply for 명사 ~에 지원하다 part-time 시간제

3. 정답 (D)

해석 주민들은 보여줘야 한다 / 그들의 거주자 등록증을 / 경비원에게 / 주차하기 위해 / 그들의 차를 / 주차장에 / 무료로

해설 빈칸 앞까지 3형식 완전한 문장이 왔고, 뒤에는 동사원형 park가 있으므로 동사원형 앞에 쓸 수 있는 것은 to 부정사인 (D) 뿐이다. 'in order to+동사원형'은 'to+동사원형' 형태의 to 부정사와 마찬가지로 '~하기 위해서'라는 의미의 부사적 용법이다. 따라서 정답은 (D)이다. 전치사인 (A), (C) 뒤에는 명사가 와야 하며, 부사절 접속사인 (B)는 완전한 문장 앞에 쓰여야 한다.

표현 정리 resident 주민 show 보여주다 identity card 등록증, 신분증 security guard 경비원 park 주차하다 the lot 주차장, 터

◎ *실전에 적용해 봐*

1. (B) 2. (D) 3. (C) 4. (C) 5. (B) 6. (A) 7. (B)
8. (A) 9. (C) 10. (D)

1. 정답 (B)

해석 화장품 무료 샘플들이 제공되었다 / 고객들에게 / 50달러 또는 그 이상 구입한 / 그들을 장려하기 위해 / 더 많은 제품을 사도록

해설 문장에서 정동사는 were given이므로 빈칸은 준동사 자리이다. 따라서 준동사인 (B)가 정답이다.

표현 정리 free sample 무료 샘플 beauty product 화장품 purchase 구매, 구입 encourage 격려하다

2. 정답 (D)

해석 우리는 배송한다 / 모든 주문된 물품들을 / 2일 이내에 / 지불이 확인되고 / 보장하기 위해 / 우리의 고객들에게 / 신속한 배달을

해설 빈칸 앞에 3형식 완전한 문장이 왔고, 뒤에는 동사원형 guarantee가 왔다. 동사원형 앞에 올 수 있는 경우는 to 부정사뿐이다. 'in order to+동사원형'은 'to+동사원형' 형태의 to 부정사와 마찬가지로 '~하기 위해서'라는 의미의 부사적 용법이다. 따라서 정답은 (D)이다. 두사인 (C)가 오면 한 문장에 정동사가 두 개가 되므로 탈락하고, 부사절 접속사인 (A)와 (B)는 주어가 없으므로 오답이다.

표현 정리 ship 배송하다, 배달하다 payment 지불 confirm 확인하다 guarantee 보장하다 prompt 신속한

3. 정답 (C)

해석 당신의 응답은 / 우리의 고객 여론조사 문항에 대한 / 신중하게 검토될 것이다 / 그리고 숙고될 것이다 / 개선하기 위해 / 우리의 서비스 품질을

해설 이 문제는 reflect upon이 '~를 숙고하다'는 뜻의 동사이며, 밑줄 앞에는 be동사가 생략되어 be reflected upon까지가 이미 완전한 문장임을 알아야 함정에 빠지지 않는 문제이다. 이어서 '향상시키기 위해서'라는 부사의 기능인 (C)가 정답이며, 이어서 오는 improve는 앞에 to가 생략되어 help의 목적어가 된다. 전치사 뒤에 명사나 동명사가 온다고 생각하여 (D)를 쓰게 되는 함정에 빠지게 된다.

표현 정리 response 응답 customer survey 고객 여론 조사 carefully 신중하게 review 검토하다 reflect upon ~를 숙고하다 improve 개선하다 quality 품질

4. 정답 (C)

해석 당신은 전화해야 한다 / Friday Night 식당에 / 적어도 기를 먼저 / 테이블을 예약하기 위해 / 15명을 위한

해설 빈칸 앞의 문장이 3형식 완전한 문장이 왔다. 명사 앞에 또 명사가 올 수 없으므로 (D)는 탈락. 과거분사인 (B)는 앞의 advance라는 부사와 뒤의 a table이라는 명사를 연결해 줄 수 없다. (A)와 (C) 중 '예약하기 위해서'라는 해석이 자연스러운 (C)가 답이다. (A)는 '예약하고 있는'이란 뜻이 되어 어색하다.

표현 정리 at least 적어도 in advance 미리, 이전에 reserve 예약하다

5. 정답 (B)

해석 Ms. Clarkson는 사용한다 / 그녀의 회사 차량을 / 태우러 가기 위해서만 / 중요한 고객들을 / 공항에서 / 그리고 그것을 절대 사용하지 않았다 / 다른 목적을 위해서는

해설 pick up이 동사이다. (C)와 (D)는 뒤에 주어와 동사가 모두 있기에 하기 때문에 오답이며, 따라서 (B)가 정답이다. to 부정사 앞에 only가 올 때 '단지 ~를 위해서만'이라는 뜻으로 사용한다.

표현 정리 vehicle 차량 pick up ~를 태우러 가다 client 고객 purpose 목적

6. 정답 (A)

해석 Mr. Toffler는 요청 받았다 / 옮기도록 / 모든 물건을 / 비품실에 있는 / 다른 곳으로 / 공간을 만들기 위해 / 새로운 프린터를 위한

해설 빈칸 앞에 완전한 문장이 왔으므로 준동사인 to 부정사가 와야 한다. 빈칸 뒤에 목적어가 있으므로 답은 (A)이다. 해석도 '~를 하기 위해서'로 더 어울린다. to -ing는 'look forward to -ing' 등 동명사 관용어구인 경우에만 가능하다.

표현 정리 be asked to+동사원형 ~하도록 요청 받다 move 옮기다, 움직이다 stuff 물건, 것, 것들 supply room 비품실 make room 공간을 만들다

7. 정답 (B)

해설 사용 설명서는 / 오디오 플레이어를 위한 / 설명한다 / 처리하는 방법을 / 일시적인 기술적 문제들을 / 갑작스런 전원 꺼짐과 같은 / 상세하게

해설 빈칸 뒤 to 부정사가 있다고 해서 (C)를 바로 답으로 고르지 않도록 하자. 문장의 동사인 explains의 목적어 자리에 빈칸부터 문장 끝까지의 부분이 들어간다. 빈칸은 명사절 접속사 자리이므로 (C)는 탈락. 빈칸 뒤 to는 '주어 + 조동사'를 줄인 to로써 (145페이지 참고) 이러한 구조를 취할 수 있는 것은 (A) 또는 (B)이다.

표현 정리 user guide 사용 설명서 explain 설명하다 deal with ~를 처리하다 temporary 일시적인 technical 기술적인 such as ~와 같은

8. 정답 (A)

해설 Deli Foods의 모든 판매 직원은 / 요구된다 / 매장에 오도록 / 정오까지 / 시설을 청소하기 위해 / 위생검사에 앞서

해설 빈칸 앞에 완전한 문장이 왔고, to 다음에 올 수 있는 것은 to 동사원형 아니면 to -ing인데, to -ing는 주로 동명사 관용어구일 때 사용한다 ('법칙 63' 참고). 해석해 보면 '설비를 청소하기 위해서'로 해석되므로 to 부정사를 만들어 주는 (A)가 정답이다.

표현 정리 sales staff 판매 직원 be required to+동사원형 ~하도록 요구되다 prior to ~이전에 sanitary inspection 위생 검사 clean up ~을 치우다

9. 정답 (C)

해설 도와주세요 / 고객들을 / 줄 서서 기다리는 / 받기 위해 / 그들이 원하는 서비스를 / 그들이 기다리지 않게 하기 위해 / 담당자가 도착할 때까지

해설 빈칸 앞에 in order가 있다고 해서 to를 답으로 고르지 않도록 하자. in order to의 to는 이미 뒤에 있는 have 앞에 쓰였고, 그 사이에 to 부정사의 의미상 주어가 들어간 구조이다. to 부정사의 의미상 주어는 'for+목적격'으로 쓰이므로 (C)가 정답이다.

표현 정리 assist 돕다, 도움이 되다 waiting 기다리고 있는 receptionist 접수 담당자

10. 정답 (D)

해설 Ms. Lam은 결정해야 한다 / 등록할지 말지를 / 초보자 또는 중간 과정의 수영 수업을 / 마감일 전에

해설 빈칸 뒤에 to 동사원형이 있다고 해서 바로 in order를 고르지 않도록 하자. in order to는 앞의 문장이 완전해야 쓸 수 있는데, 빈칸 앞 decide의 목적어가 빠진 불완전한 문장이므로 쓸 수 없다. 빈칸부터 끝까지 decide의 목적어가 되어야 한다. 빈칸 앞 needs to decide가 불확정적인 상황을 나타내고, 뒤에 or로 선택 사항이 나오므로 '~인지 아닌지'의 의미를 가진 (D)가 정답이다.

표현 정리 register 등록하다 entry level 입문의 intermediate level 중간 수준의 deadline 마감일

법칙 51 과거 시점보다 이전은 과거완료

◎ 유형을 파악해 봐
1. (C)   2. (A)   3. (C)

1. 정답 (C)

해설 Mrs. McQuire가 승진하기 전에 / 매장 관리자로 / 그녀는 시간제로 일했다 / 매장에서 / 평일에

해설 빈칸은 정동사 자리이므로 준동사인 (D)는 탈락한다. 승진된 시점이 과거이기 때문에 일했던 시점은 과거보다 이전이 되어야 한다. 그러므로 과거완료시제인 (C)가 정답이다. (A)는 미래, (B)는 현재시제이다.

표현 정리 be promoted to ~로 승진되다 manager 관리자 part-time 시간제

2. 정답 (A)

해설 Mr. Krowski는 받았다 / 이메일을 / 그의 질문에 대해 회신하는 / Anywhere Travel로부터 / 그가 요청한 후 / 세부사항을 / 그의 여행 일정에 대해

해설 빈칸은 정동사 자리이므로 준동사인 (D)는 탈락한다. 먼저 세부사항을 요청한 후에 이메일을 받았고, 이메일을 받은 시점이 과거이기 때문에 과거보다 이전의 상황을 묘사해야 하므로 과거완료시제인 (A)가 정답이다. (B)는 미래, (C)는 현재시제이다.

표현 정리 receive 받다 reply to+명사 ~에 회신하다, 답하다 inquiry 문의 details 세부사항 itinerary 여행 일정표

3. 정답 (C)

해설 Yum Bakery가 계획하기 시작했을 때 쯤 / 사업 확장을 / 해외로 / 10억개 이상의 회사 도너츠가 팔렸다 / 중국 시장에서

해설 빈칸은 정동사 자리인데, 보기가 모두 정동사로 왔다. 사업 확장을 계획할 때가 과거이기 때문에 도너츠가 팔린 시점은 과거보다 이전의 상황을 묘사해야 하므로 과거완료시제인 (C)가 정답이다. (A)는 미래, (B)는 현재시제이고, (D)는 수일치가 맞지 않는다.

표현 정리 by the time ~할 때까지, 그때까지 expansion 확장 overseas 해외로 billion 10억 doughnut 도너츠

◎ 실전에 적용해 봐
1. (B)   2. (A)   3. (D)   4. (D)   5. (B)   6. (A)   7. (B)
8. (D)   9. (C)   10. (D)

1. 정답 (B)

해설 Ms. Bourne가 숙달한 후에 / 옷을 만들기 위한 기술을 / 그녀는 허락되었다 / 남은 교육을 건너뛰도록 / 그리고 일하도록 / 정식 사원으로 / Clothes 4 All에서

해설 빈칸은 정동사 자리인데, 보기가 모두 정동사로 왔다. 기술을 숙달한 이후에 남은 교육을 건너 뛰도록 허락되었고, 허락된 시점이 과거이기 때문에 과거보다 이전의 상황을 묘사해야 하므로 과거완료시제인 (B)가 정답이다. (A)는 현재완료, (D)는 현재시제이다.

표현 정리 master 숙달하다 skill 기술, 능력 garment 옷, 의복 be allowed to+동사원형 ~하도록 허락되다 training session 교육 regular employee 정식 사원

2. 정답 (A)

해석 무료 배송 쿠폰이 제공됐다 / Mr. Titus에게 / 그의 다음 상품 구매를 위한 / SellForLess.com에서 / 상품들의 지연된 배송 때문에 / 그가 예상했던 것보다 늦게 도착한

해설 빈칸은 정동사 자리이므로 준동사인 (C)는 탈락한다. 상품들의 배송을 예상한 것이 배송이 완료된 과거 시점보다 이전의 상황이므로 과거완료시제인 (A)가 정답이다. (B)는 현재진행, (D)는 과거시제이다.

표현 정리 delivery 배송 be provided to ~로(에게) 제공되다 due to ~때문에 delayed 지연된 anticipate 예상하다

3. 정답 (D)

해석 Kolk Mobile의 합병이 / 주 기업인 Everywhere Network와 / 발표될 때쯤 / Kolk Mobile의 주가는 / 최고치에 달했다

해설 발표가 된 시점이 과거이기 때문에 주가가 절정에 도달한 시점은 과거보다 이전의 상황을 묘사해야 하므로 과거완료시제인 (D)가 정답이다. (A)는 현재, (B)는 미래, (C)는 현재진행시제이다.

표현 정리 by the time ~할 즈음, ~할 때까지 merger 합병 corporation 기업 announce 발표하다, 알리다 stock price 주가

4. 정답 (D)

해석 프로젝트 감독은 시작했다 / 세미나 참석자들의 수를 예측하는 것을 / 세미나 날짜와 장소가 발표되기도 전에

해설 발표하기 전의 상황이 과거이기 때문에 참가자의 수를 추정하는 것은 과거보다 이전이 되어야 한다. 그러므로 과거완료시제인 (D)가 정답이다. (A)는 현재진행, (B)는 현재완료, (C)는 현재시제이다.

표현 정리 project director 프로젝트 감독 estimate 추정하다 the number of ~의 수 attendee 참석자 announce 발표하다, 알리다

5. 정답 (B)

해석 Ms. Kinsey는 표들을 구입했다 / 오페라 'Haunted House'의 / 팬들이 표들을 모두 구입하기 전에 / 온라인과 오프라인으로

해설 빈칸은 정동사 자리이므로 준동사인 (D)는 탈락한다. 팬들이 표를 모두 구입하기 전의 상황이 과거이기 때문에 표를 구입했을 때는 과거보다 이전이 되어야 한다. 그러므로 과거완료시제인 (B)가 정답이다. (A)는 미래완료, (C)는 미래진행시제이다.

표현 정리 purchase 구매하다; 구매 both A and B A와 B 둘 다

6. 정답 (A)

해석 대중 매체가 보도한 후에 / 애니메이션 시장의 잠재력에 대해 / 점점 더 많은 수의 구직자들이 지원했다 / Joy Pictures의 일자리에

해설 보도한 이후에 일자리에 지원했고, 일자리에 지원했던 시점이 과거이기 때문에 과거보다 이전이 되어야 한다. 그러므로 과거완료시제인 (A)가 정답이다. (C)는 현재진행, (D) 미래시제이다.

표현 정리 media 대중 매체 potential 잠재력 increasing number of+명사 점점 더 많은 수의 apply for ~에 지원하다

7. 정답 (B)

해석 Mr. Martin은 지원했다 / 일자리에 / 50개 이상의 중간 규모 회사들의 / 프랑스에 있는 / 그가 마침내 취직할 때까지 / Branson Resources에

해설 빈칸은 정동사 자리이며, 보기가 모두 정동사로 왔다. 취직할 때까지 일자리에 지원해 왔고, 취직된 시점이 과거이기 때문에 일자리에 지원해 온 시점은 과거보다 이전이 되어야 한다. 그러므로 과거완료시제인 (B)가 정답이다. (A)는 현재, (C)는 현재진행, (D) 미래시제이다.

표현 정리 apply for ~에 지원하다 job 일자리, 일 mid-sized 중간 크기의, 보통 크기의 hire 고용하다

8. 정답 (D)

해석 Ms. Packer는 도왔다 / 마케팅 팀의 프로젝트를 / 분석하는 / 지역 소비자들의 수요를 / 그녀가 전근되기 전에 / 국제 사업부로

해설 빈칸은 정동사 자리이며, 보기는 모두 정동사이다. 국제 사업부로 전근되기 전에 보조를 했고, 전근한 시점이 과거이기 때문에 과거보다 이전이 되어야 한다. 그러므로 과거완료시제인 (D)가 정답이다. (A)는 미래, (B)현재진행, (C)는 현재시제이다.

표현 정리 assist 보조하다, 도와주다 analyze 분석하다 needs 수요, 요구 local 지역의 consumer 소비자 transfer 전근하다, 전근시키다 international division 국제 사업부

9. 정답 (C)

해석 다행이었다 / Mr. Harrison이 저장한 것이 / 모든 문서들을 / 그의 컴퓨터에 / 전원이 나가기 전에

해설 빈칸은 정동사 자리이며, 보기가 모두 정동사로 왔다. 전원이 나가기 전에 저장을 했고, 전원이 나간 시점이 과거이기 때문에 과거보다 이전이 되어야 한다. 그러므로 과거완료시제인 (C)가 정답이다. (A)는 현재, (B)는 과거진행, (D)는 미래시제이다.

표현 정리 fortunate 다행한, 운 좋은 document 문서, 서류 go out (전기 등이) 나가다, 꺼지다 save 저장하다

10. 정답 (D)

해석 Acvanced Technologies는 일했다 / 협력 관계로 / Bayfold Production과 / 다른 제조회사가 제안할 때까지 / 거래를 / 더 많은 이익을 갖는 / 같은 조건에 대해

해설 빈칸은 정동사 자리이며, 보기가 모두 정동사로 왔다. 다른 회사가 제안할 때까지 협력 관계로 일했던 시점이 과거완료이기 때문에 제안한 시점은 과거완료보다 이후가 되어야 한다. 그러므로 과거시제인 (D)가 정답이다. 과거완료시제는 과거시제를 뛰어넘을 수 없으므로 과거시제가 있어야 쓸 수가 있다. (A)는 과거완료, (B)는 미래, (C)는 현재시제이다.

표현 정리 in a partnership 협력 관계로 manufacturing company 제조 회사 deal 거래 benefit 이익

법칙 52 시간[조건] 부사절 또는 반복[습관]적 사실의 단서가 보이면 현재시제

◎ 유형을 파악해 봐
1. (B) 2. (C) 3. (A)

1. 정답 (B)

해설 Mr. Talbot가 방문할 때 / North Cape을 / 그는 참석할 것이다 / 지역 학회에

해설 빈칸은 정동사 자리이므로 준동사인 (D)는 탈락한다. 주절의 시제는 미래이고, when은 시간 부사절이므로 현재시제가 미래를 대신해 정답은 (B)이다. (A)는 과거진행, (C)는 과거시제이다.

표현 정리 visit 방문하다 attend 참석하다 regional 지역의 conference 학회, 회의

2. 정답 (C)

해설 그녀의 아이들 때문에 / Ms. Chad는 피자를 주문한다 / 저녁 식사로 / 매주 금요일 밤에

해설 빈칸은 정동사 자리이므로 준동사인 (A)와 (D)는 탈락한다. every Friday night이라는 반복 습관적 사실의 단서가 있으므로 정답은 현재시제인 (C)가 답이다. (B)는 과거시제이다.

표현 정리 because of ~때문에 order 주문하다

3. 정답 (A)

해설 당신은 퇴장할 수 있고 / 그리고 다시 입장할 수 있습니다 / 극장에 / 연극 시작하기 10분 전에

해설 빈칸은 정동사 자리이므로 준동사인 (D)는 탈락한다. 주절의 시제는 미래이고, before는 시간 부사절이다. 시간 부사절에서는 현재시제가 미래를 대신하므로 정답은 (A)이다. (B)는 과거시제이다.

표현 정리 exit 퇴장하다 reenter 재입장하다

◎ 실전에 적용해 봐
1. (D) 2. (A) 3. (D) 4. (B) 5. (C) 6. (A) 7. (C)
8. (D) 9. (B) 10. (B)

1. 정답 (D)

해설 Mr. Kernings는 읽는다 / 주간 신문을 / 그의 집에 배달된 / 매주 일요일 아침에

해설 빈칸은 정동사 자리이므로 준동사인 (B)는 탈락한다. 주어(Mr. Kernings)는 단수인데 (A)는 복수 동사이므로 탈락하고, every Sunday morning이라는 반복 습관적 사실의 단서가 있으므로 답은 현재시제인 (D)이다. (C)는 과거진행시제이다.

표현 정리 weekly 주간의, 매주의 newspaper 신문 be delivered to+명사 ~에 배달되다

2. 정답 (A)

해설 방문객들은 / 허용되지 않는다 / 사진 촬영이 / 전시된 그림들의 / 박물관에 / 항상

해설 빈칸 뒤 allowed는 바로 뒤에 목적어가 없기 때문에 동사가 아니라 과거분사이다. 따라서 빈칸은 정동사가 와야 한다. 박물관에서는 사진 촬영이 허용되지 않는다는 일반적인 사실이나 규칙 등이 언급되고 있으므로 현재시제가 와야 한다. (A)가 정답이다.

표현 정리 allow 허락하다 take photograph 사진을 찍다 displayed 전시된 painting 그림 at any time 항상, 언제라도

3. 정답 (D)

해설 만약 설치된 소프트웨어 프로그램이 계속해서 멈춘다면 / 삭제하세요 / 프로그램을 / 그리고 그것을 다시 설치하세요

해설 빈칸은 정동사 자리이다. 주절은 명령문이므로 미래시제이고, if가 이끄는 조건 부사절에서는 현재시제가 미래를 대신하므로 답은 (D)이다. 주어(the ~ program)는 단수인데 (A)는 복수 동사이므로 탈락하고, (B)는 미래, (C)는 과거진행시제이다.

표현 정리 installed 설치된 continue 계속하다, 계속되다 shut down 정지되다 randomly 아무렇게나, 닥치는 대로 delete 삭제하다 reinstall 재설치하다

4. 정답 (B)

해설 바람직하다 / 당신이 약을 복용하는 것이 / 매일 적어도 두 번 / 완화시키기 위해 / 당신의 만성 편두통을

해설 빈칸은 정동사 자리이므로 준동사인 (A)와 (C)는 탈락한다. advisable은 '요번주의 명제'에 해당된다('법칙 28' 참고). 따라서 you 다음에는 동사원형이 온다. 이것을 몰랐다고 해도 뒤에 나오는 every day로 보아 빈칸은 반복 습관적인 사실을 묘사하는 현재시제가 잘 어울린다. 따라서 정답은 (B)이다.

표현 정리 advisable 바람직한, 권할 만한 pill 약, 알약 at least 적어도, 최소한 relieve 완화하다, 없애주다 chronic 만성적인 migraine 편두통

5. 정답 (C)

해설 Ms. Murray는 시작할 것이다 / 할당된 서류 작업을 / 모두 완료돼야 하는 / 다음 주 수요일까지 / 그녀가 돌아오면 / 파리에서 / 이번 주

해설 빈칸은 정동사 자리이므로 준동사인 (D)는 탈락한다. 주절의 시제는 미래이고, once는 조건 부사절이다. 조건 부사절에서는 현재시제가 미래를 대신하므로 정답은 (C)이다. (A)는 미래, (B)는 과거시제이다.

표현 정리 assigned 할당된 paperwork 서류 작업 once ~할 때 return 돌아오다

6. 정답 (A)

해설 Erox Steel이 계속 있는 한 / 협력 관계로 / Camp Quest 사와 / 세계적 철강회사인 / Camp Quest는 유지할 것이다 / 선두를 / 해당 산업에서

해설 빈칸은 정동사 자리이므로 준동사인 (C)는 탈락한다. 주절의 시제는 미래이고, as long as는 조건 부사절이므로 현재시제가 미래를 대신한다. 따라서 (A)가 정답이다. (B)는 과거, (D)는 과거진행시제이다.

표현 정리 as long as ~하는 한, ~하는 동안 partner with ~와 협력하다 global 세계적인 steel 철강, 강철 lead 선두 remain 계속

~이다, 남아 있다

7. 정답 (C)

해석 당신은 승인되지 않는다 / 데이터베이스에 대한 접근이 / 사용자가 열람할 수 있는 / 직원들의 개인 프로필을 / Gohr Corporation의

해설 빈칸은 주격 관계대명사 that 절 안의 정동사 자리이므로 준동사인 (E)는 탈락한다. 데이터베이스에 접근하는 것이 허락되지 않는다는 규정이 언급되고 있으므로 현재시제인 (C)가 정답이다.

표현 정리 authorize 승인하다 access 접근하다, 이용하다 browse 열람하다, 대강 훑어보다 allow 허용하다, 가능하게 하다

8. 정답 (D)

해석 연례회의는 모인다 / 지역 회의장에서 / 첫째 주에 / 매년 7월

해설 빈칸은 정동사 자리이므로 준동사인 (C)는 탈락한다. every year라는 반복 습관적 사실의 단서가 있으므로 정답은 현재시제인 (D)이다. (A)는 과거, (B)는 미래시제이다.

표현 정리 annual 연례의 council 의회, 협의회 local 지역의 conference hall 회의장 convene 회합하다, 소집하다

9. 정답 (B)

해석 나는 회신합니다 / 당신의 문의에 / 예약 날짜를 바꾸고자 하는 / 당신이 정한 / 이번 주 토요일로

해설 빈칸은 정동사 자리이므로 준동사인 (C)는 탈락한다. 현재완료시제는 구체적인 단서가 있어야 쓸 수 있고, 현재시제는 반복 습관적 사실과 함께 쓰는데, 문의를 반복 습관적으로 한다는 것은 어색하므로 진행형인 (B)가 정답이다.

표현 정리 reply to+명사 ~에 답하다 inquiry 문의, 질의 regarding ~에 관하여 reservation 예약

10. 정답 (B)

해석 당신의 'Evon Magazine' 구독은 / 만료됩니다 / 다음 주 금요일에 / 그래서 만약 당신이 원한다면 / 잡지를 더 받아 보기를 / 우리에게 보내주세요 / 20달러의 갱신 요금을

해설 빈칸은 정동사 자리이므로 준동사인 (C)는 탈락한다. next Friday를 보고 미래시제로 착각하지 않도록 한다. expire라는 동사 자체에 미래적인 어감이 있으므로 미래시제 대신 현재시제를 쓰기도 한다. 따라서 정답은 (B)이다. (A)는 과거, (D)는 과거진행시제이다.

표현 정리 subscription 구독 receive 받다 issue 잡지, 신문 같은 정기 간행물의 호 send 보내다 renewal fee 갱신 요금 expire 만료되다

법칙 53 'since+과거 시점, over/for+기간'이 보이면 현재완료시제

◎ 유형을 파악해 봐
1. (C) 2. (A) 3. (D)

1. 정답 (C)

해석 Montana Food의 Meals-to-Go는 판매되었다 / 독점적으로 / Max Superstore에서 / 지난 5년 동안

해설 빈칸은 정동사 자리이다. 시제 문제에는 단서가 제시되기 마련인데, for the last five years(지난 5년 동안)이라는 단서가 있으므로 정답은 현재완료인 (C)이다.

표현 정리 sell 판매하다 exclusively 독점적으로, 전적으로

2. 정답 (A)

해석 Ms. Ford는 도와 왔다 / Mr. Jones를 / 그의 비서로서 / 거의 10년 동안

해설 빈칸은 정동사 자리이다. 보기는 모두 주어인 Ms. Ford 뒤에 올 수 있는 동사이므로 시제를 따져야 한다. 여기서는 for almost ten years(거의 10년 동안)라는 단서가 있으므로 정답은 현재완료인 (A)이다.

표현 정리 assist 돕다, 지원하다 as ~로서 secretary 비서 almost 거의, 약

3. 정답 (D)

해석 Wegner Tech와 합병한 이후 / 10년 전에 / Reality Games는 향상시켰다 / 그래픽 디자인 품질을 / 회사 모바일 게임의

해설 빈칸은 정동사 자리이므로 준동사인 (A)는 탈락한다. Since ~ ten years ago 부분을 보면, 주절의 시제를 파악할 수 있다. 따라서 현재완료인 (D)가 정답이다.

표현 정리 merger 합병 quality 품질, 질 improve 개선하다

◎ 실전에 적용해 봐
1. (B) 2. (D) 3. (D) 4. (A) 5. (D) 6. (C) 7. (D)
8. (A) 9. (C) 10. (C)

1. 정답 (B)

해석 BestGear Auto 수리 서비스는 제공되었다 / 무료로 / 모든 고객에게 / 2010년 설립 이래

해설 빈칸은 정동사 자리이다. 시제 문제에는 단서가 제시되기 마련이며, since ~ 2010 부분에 'Since+과거시점'이라는 단서가 있으므로 현재완료인 (B)가 정답이다.

표현 정리 repair service 수리 서비스 provide 제공하다, 공급하다 for free 무료로 since ~이래로 foundation 설립, 창립

2. 정답 (D)

해석 5년이 흘렀다 / Ms. Bell이 제의 받은 지 / 판매 관리직을 / YM Company에서 / 그리고 그녀는 여전히 즐긴다 / 그녀의 직업을

해설 부사절의 since가 과거 시점일 때, 주절은 현재완료가 된다. 따라서 (D)가 정답이다.

표현 정리 pass 지나가다 since ~이래로 offer 제의하다, 제안하다 sales manager 판매 관리자

3. 정답 (D)

해설 Jennings Restaurant은 서비스해 왔다 / 우리 고객들에게 / 100개 이상의 매장에서 / 해외에 있는 / 지난 17년에 걸쳐

해설 빈칸은 정동사 자리이므로 준동사인 (B)는 탈락한다. over the last 17 years(지난 17년에 걸쳐)라는 단서가 있으므로 현재완료인 (D)가 정답이다.

표현 정리 store 매장, 점포 overseas 해외에, 외국에 over ~에 걸쳐서 serve 응대하다, 제공하다

4. 정답 (A)

해설 Mr. Bloom이 회사를 떠난 이래 / 3년 전 / 작업량은 증가했다 / 남은 직원들의

해설 빈칸은 정동사 자리이므로 준동사인 (D)는 탈락한다. 부사절의 Since가 과거 시점일 때, 주절은 현재완료가 오므로 (A)가 정답이다.

표현 정리 since ~이래로 workload 작업량 rest 나머지 increase 증가하다, 인상되다 employee 직원

5. 정답 (D)

해설 요가 수업을 등록한 사람은 / Wellness Fitness Center에서 / 지난주에 / 참가하도록 권장된다 / 오리엔테이션 수업에 / 무료로 열리는 / 다음 주 수요일에

해설 during the last week(지난주 동안)이라는 단서만 보고 현재완료인 (B)를 답으로 고르지 않도록 한다. during과 현재완료가 함께 사용되면 '지난주 동안 계속 등록을 해 왔었다'이라고 해석돼 어색하다. during the last week는 과거 시점도 되므로 과거시제와 함께 사용할 수 있는데, 이 경우 '지난주에 등록한'이라고 해석돼 자연스럽다. 따라서 (D)가 답이다.

표현 정리 register for 등록하다 be encouraged to+동사원형 ~하도록 권장되다, 장려되다 for free 무료로

6. 정답 (C)

해설 Mr. Hawk는 / 명성 있는 연구원인 / 생물학 분야에서 / 헌신했다 / 그의 일생을 / 연구하는데 / 늘리는 방법들을 / 인간의 수명을 / 지난 50년에 걸쳐

해설 빈칸은 정동사 자리이다. over the past 50 years(지난 50년에 걸쳐)라는 단서가 있으므로 답은 현재완료인 (C)가 된다.

표현 정리 renowned 명성 있는, 유명한 researcher 연구원 field 분야 biology 생물학 entire life 일생, 평생 life expectancy 수명

7. 정답 (D)

해설 우리 생산 매니저는 / 감독하는 책임을 맡은 / 제품의 제조 과정 / 지난해부터 / 승진할 것이다 / 생산부 부장으로

해설 빈칸은 정동사 자리이므로 준동사인 (A)는 탈락한다. since last year(지난해부터)라는 단서가 있으므로 현재완료인 (D)가 정답이다.

표현 정리 be responsible for ~에 대한 책임이 있다, ~을 담당하다 supervise 감독하다, 관리하다 manufacturing process 제조 과정 be promoted to ~의 자리로 승진되다

8. 정답 (A)

해설 최근 회계 감사 이후 / 지역 회사들에 대한 / Plaque 사는 모집했다 / 많은 주주들을 / 회사에 가까이 투자하려는 / 꾸준히 성장을 하는

해설 빈칸은 정동사 자리이다. 'Since+과거시점'이라는 단서로 보아 현재완료인 (A)가 정답이다.

표현 정리 since ~이래로 financial audit 회계 감사 be willing to+동사원형 기꺼이 ~하다 invest 투자하다 steadily 꾸준히

9. 정답 (C)

해설 연례 세미나는 받을 것이기 때문에 / 제한된 예산을 / 올해 / 적은 수의 초청 연사들이 올 것이다 / 세미나에

해설 주어인 a smaller ~ speakers 다음에 복수 동사가 와야 하므로 단수 동사인 (A)는 오답이다. 여기서 since는 '~이래로'라는 뜻이 아닌, '~때문에'라는 의미로 쓰였으며, 세미나가 아직 열린 것이 아니기 때문에 빈칸의 시제 또한 (C) 미래시제가 되어야 한다. 문두의 Since만 보고 현재완료시제인 (A)를 고르지 않도록 한다.

표현 정리 annual 연례의 limited 제한된, 한정된 budget 예산 guest speaker 초청 연사

10. 정답 (C)

해설 최근 조사에 따르면, 대부분의 직원들은 믿는다 / 그들이 받는 급여의 실제 가치가 / 하락했다고 / 최근 몇 년 동안 / 물가 인상을 고려할 때

해설 빈칸은 정동사 자리이므로 준동사인 (B)는 오답이다. in recent years(최근 몇 년 동안)라는 단서가 있으므로 현재완료인 (C)가 정답이다. 과거완료인 (D)가 오려면 과거시점이 있어야 한다.

표현 정리 according to ~에 따르면 survey 조사 value 가치 inflation 인플레이션, 물가 인상 take A into consideration A를 고려[참작]하다 drop 떨어지다

법칙 54 '선행사+_____+명사+동사'는 whose

◎ 유형을 파악해 봐
1. (A)   2. (C)   3. (D)

1. 정답 (A)

해설 지원자는 / 이력서가 검토된 / 판매부 관리자에 의해 / 연락이 갔다 / 입사 면접을 위해

해설 정동사의 개수가 2개(was, was)이므로 빈칸은 접속사 자리이다. resume가 명사이므로 이 명사를 수식하는 소유격이 필요하다. 따라서 소유격 관계대명사인 (A)가 정답이다. (C), (D)는 형용사절 접속사로 쓰일 경우 뒤에 주어나 목적어가 빠진 불완전한 문장이 와야 한다.

표현 정리 applicant 지원자 resume 이력서 review 검토하다, 재검토하다 contact 연락하다 job interview 입사 면접

2. 정답 (C)

해설 기록해 놓으세요 / 회사들을 / 그들의 제품이 영향을 미칠지 모르는 /

우리 회사 제품 판매에

해설 정동사의 개수가 2개(make, may affect)이므로 빈칸은 접속사 자리이다. 빈칸 뒤 products가 명사이므로 소유격이 필요하다. 따라서 소유격 관계대명사인 (C)가 정답이다. (A), (B)는 형용사절 접속사로 쓰일 때 뒤에 주어나 목적어가 빠진 불완전한 문장이 와야 한다. (D)는 선행사가 사람일 때 사용한다.

표현 정리 make a note of+명사 ~를 기록하다, 메모하다 affect ~에 영향을 미치다

3. 정답 (D)

해설 Brian O'neil은 소설가이다 / 최근 작품이 큰 히트를 친 / 전 세계에서

해설 정동사의 개수가 2개(is, has been)이므로 빈칸은 접속사 자리이다. 빈칸 뒤 latest book이 명사이므로 소유격이 필요하다. 따라서 소유격 관계대명사인 (D)가 정답이다. (A), (B)가 형용사절 접속사로 쓰이면 주어나 목적어가 빠진 불완전한 문장이 와야 한다. (C)는 바로 뒤에 동사가 와야 한다.

표현 정리 fiction 소설 novelist 소설가 latest 최근의, 최신의 mega 매우 큰 around the world 전 세계에서

◎ 실전에 적용해 봐
1. (C) 2. (A) 3. (A) 4. (C) 5. (B) 6. (D) 7. (B)
8. (D) 9. (B) 10. (A)

1. 정답 (C)

해설 전시회는 보여준다 / Riley Jones의 삶을 / 그림들이 평가된 / 많은 이들에 의해 / 걸작으로

해설 정동사의 개수가 2개(presents, have been)이므로 빈칸은 접속사 자리이다. paintings가 명사이므로 소유격이 필요하다. 따라서 소유격 관계대명사인 (C)가 정답이다.

표현 정리 exhibition 전시회 present 보여주다, 제시하다 painting 그림 appraise 평가하다, 값을 매기다 masterpiece 걸작, 명작

2. 정답 (A)

해설 Ms. Keys는 / 인사 부장인 / 직원들을 기억한다 / 그녀가 이력서를 검토했던 / 그들이 지원했을 때 / Nikka Corporation의 일자리에

해설 정동사의 개수가 2개(remembers, reviewed)이므로 빈칸은 접속사 자리이다. resume가 명사이므로 소유격이 필요하다. 따라서 소유격 관계대명사인 (A)가 정답이다.

표현 정리 Human Resources Department 인사부 remember 기억하다, 기억나다 review 검토하다, 재검토하다 apply to+명사 ~에 지원하다

3. 정답 (A)

해설 BTB Design은 약속했다 / 직원들에게 더 많은 혜택을 주기로 / 올해 / 성과가 회사 수익에 기여하면

해설 정동사의 개수가 2개(promised, contribute)이므로 빈칸은 접속사 자리이다. performances가 명사이므로 소유격이 필요하다. 따라서 소유격 관계대명사인 (A)가 정답이다.

표현 정리 promise 약속하다, 공약하다 incentive 보너스, 인센티브 performance 실적, 성과 contribute to+명사 ~에 기여하다 profit 수익, 이익

4. 정답 (C)

해설 권한다 / 계획하는 사람들은 / 인도를 방문하려고 / 향후 2개월 동안 / 홍역 예방 접종을 받을 것을 / 떠나기 전에

해설 문장에서 정동사의 개수가 3개(is, plan, be), 접속사가 1개(that)이므로 빈칸은 접속사 자리이다. 빈칸 뒤 plan을 명사로 생각해 소유격 관계대명사인 (D)를 고르지 않도록 하자. 여기서 plan은 동사로 쓰였고, 빈칸은 선행사인 any individuals를 수식하는 주격 관계대명사 자리이다. 선행사가 사람이므로 (C)가 정답이다.

표현 정리 advisable 권할 만한 plan to+동사원형 ~할 계획이다 vaccinate against+명사 ~의 예방 접종을 하다 measles 홍역

5. 정답 (B)

해설 어제 공표된 발표문에 의하면 / Cloud 사는 찾고 있는 중이다 / 신임 CFO를, / 연봉이 150,000달러부터 234,000달러 사이인 / 매년

해설 정동사의 개수가 2개(is searching, could range)이므로 빈칸은 접속사 자리이다. pay가 명사이므로 소유격이 필요하다. 따라서 소유격 관계대명사인 (B)가 정답이다.

표현 정리 according to ~에 의하면 issued 공표된 CFC 최고 재무 담당 책임자(= Chief Financial Officer) range between A and B 범위가 A에서 B 사이이다

6. 정답 (D)

해설 Arson Holdings는 / 고객들이 한 때 불평했던 / 회사 서비스에 대해 / 최근에 지명되었다 / 최고 등급의 회사로 / 고객 만족도에 있어서

해설 정동사의 개수가 2개(used, was)이므로 빈칸은 접속사 자리이다. 빈칸 뒤 customers가 명사이므로 소유격이 필요하다. 따라서 소유격 관계대명사인 (D)가 정답이다. (C)는 명사절/부사절 접속사라 앞에 선행사를 갖지 못한다.

표현 정리 customer 고객 used to+동사원형 한 때는 ~했다 recently 최근에 name 지명하다, 명명하다 rating 등급, 평가, 순위 customer satisfaction measurement 고객 만족도

7. 정답 (B)

해설 이메일에 첨부된 것은 / 연구원들의 명단이다 / 내가 보기에 그들이 보고서에 도움이 될 만한 / 더 많은 참고 문헌이 필요할 경우 / 당신의 프로젝트를 위해

해설 정동사의 개수가 3개(is, found, need)이고, 접속사가 1개(in case)이므로 빈칸은 접속사가 와야 한다. 빈칸 뒤 reports가 명사이므로 소유격이 필요하다. 따라서 소유격 관계대명사인 (B)가 정답이다.

표현 정리 attached 첨부된, 덧붙여진 researcher 연구원 helpful 도움이 되는, 유용한 in case ~에 대비해, ~의 경우 reference 참고 문헌

8. 정답 (D)

해설 임원 회의가 소집될 것이다 / Ms. Ford 없이 / 보고서를 읽을 예정이던 / 회의에서 있었던 토론 내용이 수록된 / 그녀가 그녀의 출장에서 돌아오면

해설 정동사의 개수가 2개(will convene, plans)이므로 빈칸은 접속사 자리이다. 빈칸 뒤 plans를 명사로 생각해 소유격 관계대명사인 (A)를 고르지 않도록 하자. 이 문장에서 plan은 동사로 쓰였다. 따라서 앞의 사람을 수식하는 주격 관계대명사인 (D)가 정답이다. (B)는 목적어가 빠진 문장이 오고, (C)는 명사절/부사절 접속사이므로 선행사를 갖지 않는다.

표현 정리 executive 임원, 대표 convene 회합하다, 소집하다 plan to+동사원형 ~할 계획이다 business trip 출장

9. 정답 (B)

해설 회의실 입장이 / 거부되었다 / Mr. Collins의 / 회의실 참석을 위한 출입증이 / 유효하지 않은 것으로 밝혀진

해설 정동사의 개수가 2개(was, turned out)이므로 빈칸은 접속사 자리이다. 빈칸 뒤 pass가 명사이므로 소유격이 필요하다. 따라서 소유격 관계대명사인 (B)가 정답이다.

표현 정리 access to+명사 ~로의 입장, 접근 deny 거부하다 pass 출입증, 허가증 attend 참석하다 turn out to be 밝혀지다 invalid 유효하지 않은

10. 정답 (A)

해설 사장은 요청했다 / 프로젝트가 관리되기를 / Mr. Edward에 의해 / 전공이 경제학인

해설 정동사의 개수가 3개(requested, be, was), 접속사가 1개(that)이므로 빈칸은 접속사 자리이다. 빈칸 뒤 major가 명사이므로 소유격이 필요하다. 따라서 소유격 관계대명사인 (A)가 정답이다.

표현 정리 request 요청하다 supervise 감독하다, 관리하다 major 전공 economics 경제학

법칙 55 recent, past는 과거, current는 현재, upcoming, near, next는 미래

◎ 유형을 파악해 봐
1. (A)   2. (C)   3. (A)

1. 정답 (A)

해설 Yoyo Gym은 이전될 예정이다 / 6번 가로 / 내년에

해설 빈칸은 year를 수식하는 형용사 자리이다. 보기가 모두 형용사지만 빈칸 앞 문장이 완전하므로 빈칸은 year와 함께 부사 기능을 해야 한다. (C), (D)는 year와 함께 부사 기능을 하는 것은 아니므로 탈락한다. 시제가 미래이므로 (A)가 정답이다.

표현 정리 relocate 이전하다, 이동하다 recent 최근의, 최신의

2. 정답 (C)

해설 Ms. Sick은 디자인할 것이다 / 우리의 운동복 제품들을 / 그것들이 따르도록 / 최신 유행을

해설 빈칸은 trend를 수식하는 형용사 자리인데, 보기가 모두 형용사로 왔다. 문맥상 '현재의 유행을 따르도록'이 자연스러우므로 (C)가 정답이다.

표현 정리 design 디자인하다, 설계하다 sportswear 운동복 trend 유행, 추세, 경향 former 이전의 late 늦은, 말기의 current 현재의

3. 정답 (A)

해설 지난 수 년 동안 / Goodwill Charity는 명성을 상당히 높였다

해설 빈칸은 few years를 수식하는 형용사 자리이다. has improved는 현재완료시제이므로 과거를 나타내는 (A)가 정답이다. (B)는 year 보다는 주로 future를 수식하고, (C)는 보통 미래시제와 어울린다.

표현 정리 substantially 상당히 reputation 명성, 평판 past 지난 following 다음의

◎ 실전에 적용해 봐
1. (D)   2. (C)   3. (B)   4. (B)   5. (C)   6. (A)   7. (B)
8. (C)   9. (A)   10. (D)

1. 정답 (D)

해설 개발 이전에 / 신제품의 / 생산 관리자는 제안했다 / 팀이 참조할 것을 / 최근 소비자 조사 내용을 / 분석하기 위해 / 소비자 수요를

해설 빈칸은 관사 뒤, 명사 앞이므로 명사를 수식하는 형용사가 와야 한다. (B)를 대입해 해석해 보면, '늦은 소비자 조사'라는 어색한 의미가 되지만, (D)는 '최근 소비자 조사 내용'이라는 자연스러운 의미가 되어 정답이다.

표현 정리 prior to ~이전에 development 개발, 발전 refer to+명사 ~를 참조하다 analyze 분석하다, 조사하다 need 수요, 요구 recent 최근의, 최신의

2. 정답 (C)

해설 회의 후에 / 이사들과 대표이사는 / 합작회사의 / 만나기로 약속했다 / 다음 회의에서 / 가까운 시일 내에

해설 빈칸은 관사 뒤, 명사 앞이므로 빈칸 뒤 명사를 수식하는 형용사가 와야 한다. (A)와 (D)는 과거나 현재완료시제와 주로 어울리는데, 빈칸에 쓸 경우 의미가 어색하다. (B)는 형용사 기능이 없다. in the near future(가까운 미래에)라는 표현의 (C)가 정답이다.

표현 정리 board member 이사 CEO 대표이사, 사장(= Chief Executive Officer) promise 약속하다 in the near future 가까운 시일 내에 past 지난

3. 정답 (B)

해설 Ms. Bufford는 마침내 반납했다 / 사무용품들을 / 그녀가 빌린 / 1주일 전에 / 비품실이 잠겨 있었기 때문에 / 지난 번에 그녀가 왔을 때 / 그것들을 반납하려고

해설 빈칸은 관사 뒤, 명사 앞이므로 명사를 수식하는 형용사가 와야 한다. 빈칸 앞 동사의 시제가 과거이고, '지난 번(the last time)에 왔을 때는 문이 잠겨 있었지만 마침내 반납했다'는 의미가 자연스러우므로 (B)가 정답이다.

표현 정리 finally 마침내, 드디어 return 반납하다, 돌려주다 office supplies 사무용품 last time 지난 번에, 일전에

4. 정답 (B)

해설 뮤지컬 'Call of the Wind'은 공연될 것이다 / 최소한 앞으로 5개월 동안 / Northwest Arts Plaza에서

해설 문장 시제가 미래이므로 미래와 잘 어울리는 (B)를 먼저 대입해 해석해 본다. '앞으로 5개월 동안 공연될 것이다'라는 말이 자연스러워 정답이다. (A)는 주로 과거, (C)는 과거나 현재완료, (D)는 현재시제와 어울린다.

표현 정리 musical 뮤지컬 perform 공연하다 at east 적어도, 최소한 past 지난 current 현재의

5. 정답 (C)

해설 모든 필요한 자료들은 / 유인물을 포함해 / 복사되고, 준비되었다 / 다가오는 세미나를 위해

해설 빈칸은 관사 뒤, 명사 앞이므로 빈칸 뒤 명사를 수식하는 형용사가 와야 한다. '다가오는 세미나를 위해 유인물이 복사되고, 준비되었다'는 내용이 자연스러우므로 (C)가 정답이다. (A)는 '최근 세미나'라고 하면 시제가 과거가 되고, 그에 대한 준비는 그보다 더 먼저 일어난 일이므로 과거완료시제를 쓰는 것이 더 적합하다. (B)는 주로 복수 명사 앞에 사용한다.

표현 정리 required 필요한, 요구된 handout 유인물, 인쇄물 prepare 준비하다 frequent 빈번한 upcoming 다가오는

6. 정답 (A)

해설 예상된다 / Tranquil Medic이 관리직 직원들을 더 고용할 것으로 / 시설들을 유지하는 것이 어렵기 때문에 / 현 직원 수로는

해설 빈칸은 관사 뒤, 명사 앞이므로 빈칸 뒤 명사를 수식하는 형용사가 와야 한다. '현 직원 수로는 시설을 유지하는 것이 어렵다'는 내용이 자연스러우므로 (A)가 정답이다. '가까운'이라는 의미의 (B)와 '지나간'이라는 의미의 (C)는 빈칸 뒤 number를 수식하기에 적절하지 않다.

표현 정리 expect 예상하다 hire 고용하다, 채용하다 managerial staff 관리직 직원 maintain 유지하다 past 지난, 과거의

7. 정답 (B)

해설 돼지고기 가격이 / 상당히 하락했다 / 최근 뉴스 때문에 / 돼지 콜레라 발생에 관한

해설 문장의 동사가 과거시제이다. '콜레라 발생에 관한 최근 뉴스 때문에 가격이 하락했다'는 의미가 자연스러우므로 (B)가 정답이다. (A)나 (C) 때문에 가격이 떨어졌다는 것은 무엇을 가리키는지 불분명해서 어색하다. '가능한 뉴스'도 무엇이 가능한 것인지 불분명하다.

표현 정리 significantly 상당히 drop 떨어지다 due to ~때문에 outbreak 발생 swine fever 돼지 콜레라 upcoming 다가오는

8. 정답 (C)

해설 Borders 사의 연 수익은 / 올해에 크게 달려 있다 / 현재의 경제 상황에

해설 문장의 동사가 현재시제이므로 현재시제와 잘 어울리는 (C)가 정답이다. 의미를 봐도 '올해의 수익이 현재의 경제 상황에 달려 있다'는 것이 가장 적절한 내용이다.

표현 정리 annual revenue 연 수익 heavily 대단히, 심하게 depend on+명사 ~에 의존하다, ~에 달려 있다 economic conditions 경제 상황, 경제 조건

9. 정답 (A)

해설 당신의 답변은 / 다음의 설문조사 문항들에 대한 / 반영될 것이다 / 다음 호의 주요 기사에

해설 문장의 동사가 미래시제이므로 이와 어울리는 (A)가 정답이다.

표현 정리 response 응답, 반응 following 다음의 reflect 반영하다 article 기사 issue (잡지와 신문 같은 정기 간행물의) 호

10. 정답 (D)

해설 Mr. Czar의 과거 경력들은 / 면접 담당자들을 놀라게 했다 / 그것들이 관련이 없었기 때문에 / 웹 페이지 디자인 자리와 / 그가 현재 지원한

해설 빈칸은 소유격 뒤, 명사 앞이므로 빈칸 뒤 명사를 수식하는 형용사 자리이다. 문장의 동사(surprised)가 과거시제이므로 과거와 잘 어울리는 (D)가 정답이다. 'Mr. Czar의 과거 경력이 면접관들을 놀라게 했다'는 의미가 자연스럽다.

표현 정리 career 경력, 직업 surprise 놀라게 하다 position 직책, 자리, 직위 apply for ~에 지원하다

Chapter 03 평균 2년에 한 번 출제되는 문제

법칙 56 복합관계사절은 형용사절이 아니다

◎ 유형을 파악해 봐
1. (A) 2. (B) 3. (B)

1. 정답 (A)

해설 주말에 일할 수 있는 사람은 / 더 많은 기회를 가질 것이다 / 고용될 수 있는 / 다른 지원자들보다

해설 문장에 정동사가 2개 있으므로, 빈칸은 접속사 자리이다 (B)와 (D)는 접속사가 아니므로 오답이다. 빈칸부터 weekend까지는 will have의 주어가 될 수 있는 명사절 접속사가 필요하다. 또한 빈칸 다음에 바로 동사가 나오므로 빈칸은 접속사 기능과 주어의 기능도 하는 (A)가 정답이다. (C)는 형용사절 접속사로 쓰일 경우 완전한 문장이 와야 한다.

표현 정리 weekend 주말 higher 높은 chance 기회 hire 고용하다 applicant 지원자

2. 정답 (B)

해설 Ms. Cook은 항상 최선을 다한다 / 어떤 일이든 / 그녀가 부여 받은

해설 빈칸은 접속사 자리이다. 빈칸 뒤 문장은 필수요소가 모두 있으나 그 어순이 틀어져 있으므로 복합관계형용사인 (B)가 정답이다. (C)도 (B)와 같은 성격이 있으나 '~것' 하나만을 가리키는 말이라 자연스럽지 않다. (A)와 (D) 다음에는 정상적인 어순의 완전한 문장이 온다.

표현 정리 do one's best 최선을 다하다 job 일

3. 정답 (B)

해설 Mr. Morrison은 전화한다 / 엔지니어에게 / 그의 컴퓨터가 작동하지 않을 때마다

해설 빈칸은 접속사 자리이다. 빈칸 뒤 문장은 완전하므로 복합관계부사인 (B)가 정답이다. (C)와 (D)는 불완전한 문장과 쓰이므로 오답이다. (A)는 형용사나 부사가 바로 따라오는 완전한 문장과 쓰인다.

표현 정리 technical engineer 기능공 work 작동하다 whenever ~할 때마다

◎ 실전에 적용해 봐

1. (A) 2. (D) 3. (D) 4. (C) 5. (D) 6. (A) 7. (B)
8. (C) 9. (D) 10. (C)

1. 정답 (A)

해설 물품의 특허를 처음 출원하는 사람이 / 권리를 가질 것이다 / 새 기술을 사용할

해설 동사의 개수가 2개(patents, will have)이므로 빈칸은 접속사 자리이다. (A)는 접속사이자, 명사절 안에서 주어의 기능을 하므로 정답이다. (B), (C)와 (D)는 접속사가 아니다.

표현 정리 patent 특허를 받다 right 권리

2. 정답 (D)

해설 Ms. Dawson은 기꺼이 받아들일 것이다 / M&E 사에서 그녀의 상사가 지시하는 일은 무엇이든지 / 그녀가 몹시 원하기 때문에 / 승진을

해설 빈칸은 3형식 동사의 목적어가 되는 명사절이 와야 한다. to do의 목적어가 빠진 상태이므로 명사절이 불완전할 때 쓰는 (A), (D) 중에서 '승진을 원하기 때문에 지시하는 일이라면 무엇이든지'라는 뜻과 어울리는 (D)가 답이다. (A)는 '둘 중에 어떤 것'의 어울림이 있을 때 사용한다.

표현 정리 be willing to 기꺼이 ~하다 accept 받아들이다 order 명령하다 desperately 몹시

3. 정답 (D)

해설 우리 신제품을 구매하는 사람은 / 30퍼센트 할인 받을 것이다 / 상품이 출시되면 / 다음 주 수요일

해설 빈칸부터 product까지를 will receive의 주어로 쓸 수 있는 명사절 접속사 (D)가 정답이다. (A)와 (B), 그리고 (C)는 접속사가 아니다.

표현 정리 purchase 구매하다 receive 받다 introduce (상품을) 출시하다, 소개하다

4. 정답 (C)

해설 Ms. Penning은 좋아한다 / 그녀의 새 직장을 / 신입 사원들조차 말하도록 격려하기 때문에 / 생각나는 것은 무엇이든지 / 회의에서

해설 빈칸은 접속사 자리이다. 빈칸부터 meetings까지는 say의 목적어가 되는 동시에 주어의 기능도 갖고 있어야 하므로 (C)가 정답이다. (A)와 (B)는 부사절 접속사이며, 뒤에 완전한 문장이 온다. (D)는 접속사가 아니다.

표현 정리 workplace 직장 new employee 신입 사원 encourage 장려하다

5. 정답 (D)

해설 안전모들과 자켓들이 / 놓여져 있다 / 직원들이 그것들을 어디서든 쉽게 찾을 수 있도록 / 건설 현장에서

해설 문장에 정동사가 2개이므로 빈칸은 접속사 자리이며, 완전한 문장과 쓰이는 (D)가 정답이다. (A)는 불완전한 문장과 쓰이고, (B)가 접속사로 쓰일 경우 형용사나 부사가 바로 따라오는 완전한 문장과 쓰이며, (C)는 접속사가 아니다.

표현 정리 safety helmet 안전모 place 놓다, 배치하다 locate (물건의 위치 등을) 발견하다 construction 건설

6. 정답 (A)

해설 Elvis Record 사는 팔 것이다 / 곡들의 저작권을 / 음반 회사들에게 / 가장 높은 액수를 제시하는

해설 빈칸은 접속사 자리이다. 빈칸 뒤 문장은 필수요소가 다 있으나 관사가 빠져 있으므로 복합관계형용사인 (A)가 정답이다. whichever ~ offer는 any ~ that offer로 바꿀 수 있다. (B)는 접속사가 아니고, (C)와 (D)는 주어나 목적어가 빠진 불완전한 문장과 쓰인다.

표현 정리 sell 팔다 copyright 저작권 record 음반 offer 제안하다 amount 액수

7. 정답 (B)

해설 Shoes 'n More의 멤버가 되는 사람은 누구든 / 30퍼센트 할인 받을 것이다 / 그 또는 그녀의 첫 신발 구매에 대해 / 매장에서

해설 빈칸부터 More까지는 will receive의 주어가 될 수 있는 명사절이 필요하며, 동시에 주어의 기능도 가지고 있어야 한다. (A), (B)와 (C)에서 ever가 없다고 생각하면 멤버가 되는 것은 사람이 하는 것이므로 who가 어울리며, 따라서 (B)가 정답이다. (C)는 선택사항이 문맥에 제시될 때 사용 가능하고, (D)는 완전한 문장과 쓰인다.

표현 정리 receive 받다 discount 할인 purchase 구매

8. 정답 (C)

해설 Mr. Browne은 휴대폰을 구매할 것이다 / Alan Electronics나 Pabo 사의 / 휴대하기에 보다 편리한 것을 파는

해설 빈칸은 접속사 자리이다. 빈칸 앞의 문장이 완전하므로 부사절 접속사인 (C)가 답이다. (A)는 명사절 접속사이고, (B)와 (D)는 접속사가 아니다.

표현 정리 buy 구매하다 mobile phone 휴대폰 portable 휴대하기 쉬운

9. 정답 (D)

해설 새 카메라의 구입 비용이 아무리 많이 들어도 / Ms. Jennings는 구입할 것이다 / 새것을 / 그녀의 카메라가 작동하지 않기 때문에

해설 빈칸은 접속사 자리이다. 빈칸 뒤에 형용사가 앞으로 도치되어 있는 완전한 문장을 이끄는 접속사인 (D)가 정답이다. however는 'However+형/부+주어+동사' 구조로 쓰일 때만 접속사의 기능을 한다. (B)는 접속사가 아니다.

표현 정리 costly 많은 돈이 드는 purchase 구매하다 work (기계 등이) 작동되다, 기능하다

10. 　　　　　　　　　　　　　　　　　　　　　　정답 (C)

해석 Mr. Fowler가 Mega Sale Store에서 구입하고자 했던 것이 무엇이든 / 또한 구할 수 있었다 / 새로운 매장에서도 / 그의 집 근처에 오픈한

해설 빈칸은 접속사 자리이다. purchase의 목적어 기능을 가진 접속사인 (C)가 정답이다. (A)가 접속사로 쓰일 경우 형용사나 부사가 바로 따라오며, (B)와 (D)는 접속사가 아니다.

표현 정리 purchase 구매하다 available 구할 수 있는, 이용할 수 있는

법칙 57 plan[opportunity, way, effort, right]+to 부정사

◎ 유형을 파악해 봐
1. (B)　2. (A)　3. (B)

1. 　　　　　　　　　　　　　　　　　　　　　　정답 (B)

해석 MIC Media 인턴십 프로그램은 / 지원자들에게 기회를 제공한다 / 실습생 리포터로 일할 수 있는

해설 문장에 정동사가 있으므로 빈칸은 준동사 자리이다. 빈칸 앞에 완전한 문장이 있고, 빈칸은 뒤에서 앞으로 opportunity라는 명사를 수식해야 하는 자리이다. 뒤에서 앞의 명사를 수식할 수 있는 (A)와 (B) 중 opportunity는 to 부정사의 수식을 잘 받는 'POWER'이므로 먼저 대입해 해석하면 '지원자들에게 일할 기회를 제공한다'는 말이 자연스러우므로 (B)가 정답이다.

표현 정리 applicant 지원자 opportunity 기회 apprentice 실습생, 견습생

2. 　　　　　　　　　　　　　　　　　　　　　　정답 (A)

해석 Mr. Blanski에게 말하시오 / 컴퓨터 프로그래밍을 배우는 가장 좋은 방법은 / 참가하는 것이라고 / 워크숍에 / 매달 개최되는

해설 문장에는 정동사가 2개 있고, 접속사가 1개 있으므로 빈칸은 준동사 자리이다. 빈칸 앞 way는 to 부정사의 수식을 잘 받는 'POWER'이므로 먼저 대입해 해석하면 '컴퓨터 프로그래밍을 배우는 가장 좋은 방법'이 자연스러우므로 (A)가 정답이다.

표현 정리 way 방법 participate 참가하다 hold 개최하다

3. 　　　　　　　　　　　　　　　　　　　　　　정답 (B)

해석 더 많은 관광객을 / 유치하기 위한 시도로 / Anywhere Travel 사는 결정했다 / 연장하기로 / 홍보 이벤트 기간을

해설 빈칸 앞 attempt는 to 부정사의 수식을 잘 받는 'POWER'이므로 먼저 대입해 해석하면 '유치하기 위한 시도'가 자연스러우므로 (B)가 정답이다.

표현 정리 attempt 시도 extend 연장하다 period 기간 promotional 홍보의

◎ 실전에 적용해 봐

1. (B)　2. (D)　3. (A)　4. (C)　5. (C)　6. (C)　7. (C)
8. (D)　9. (B)　10. (A)

1. 　　　　　　　　　　　　　　　　　　　　　　정답 (B)

해석 공항 픽업 서비스는 제공한다 / 편리한 방법을 / 인천국제공항을 방문하는 고객들이 / 그들의 호텔로 이동하는

해설 문장에 정동사가 1개 있으므로 빈칸은 준동사 자리이다. 빈칸 앞에 완전한 문장이 있고, 빈칸은 뒤에서 앞의 way라는 명사를 수식하는 자리이다. way는 to 부정사의 수식을 잘 받는 'POWER'이므로 먼저 대입해 해석하면 '그들의 호텔로 이동하는 편리한 방법'이 자연스러우므로 (B)가 정답이다. for부터 Airport까지는 to 부정사의 의미상 주어이다.

표현 정리 provide 제공하다 convenient 편리한 customer 고객 proceed 이동하다

2. 　　　　　　　　　　　　　　　　　　　　　　정답 (D)

해석 공과금을 줄이려는 노력으로 / Ms. Lesborne는 충고한다 / 직원들이 불을 끄도록 / 그것들을 사용하지 않을 때

해설 빈칸은 앞에 to와 함께 effort라는 명사를 수식하는 자리이다. effort는 to 부정사의 수식을 잘 받는 'POWER'이므로 먼저 대입해 해석하면 '공과금을 줄이려는 노력'이 자연스러우므로 (D)가 정답이다.

표현 정리 in an effort to ~하려는 노력으로 utility bill 공과금 urge (~하도록) 충고하다 turn off 끄다

3. 　　　　　　　　　　　　　　　　　　　　　　정답 (A)

해석 Mr. Gibert가 들었을 때 / 그가 팀에 배정되었다는 것을 / Ms. Lowe와 함께 / 그는 믿었다 / 이것이 좋은 기회라고 / 그녀에 대해 알게 될

해설 빈칸 앞에 완전한 문장이 있으므로 빈칸은 뒤에서 앞의 chance를 수식하는 자리이다. chance는 to 부정사의 수식을 잘 받는 'POWER'이므로 (A)가 정답이다. get to know 알게 되다

표현 정리 assign 배정하다 chance 기회

4. 　　　　　　　　　　　　　　　　　　　　　　정답 (C)

해석 매니저는 설명했다 / 몇 가지 방법들을 / 고객 불만들을 다루는 / 매장의 새 아르바이트생들에게

해설 빈칸 앞에 완전한 문장이 있으므로 빈칸은 뒤에서 앞의 ways를 수식하는 자리이다. way는 to 부정사의 수식을 잘 받는 'POWER'이므로 (C)가 정답이다.

표현 정리 customer 고객 complaint 불만 part-timer 시간제 근무 직원 handle 다루다

5. 　　　　　　　　　　　　　　　　　　　　　　정답 (C)

해석 법률 팀이 담당하고 있는 일들은 포함한다 / 확실히 하는 것을 / 모든 직원들에 보장받는 것을 / 안전한 환경에서 근무할 권리를

해설 빈칸 앞에 완전한 문장이 있으므로 빈칸은 뒤에서 앞의 right를 수식하는 자리이다. right는 to 부정사의 수식을 잘 받는 'POWER'이므로 (C)가 정답이다.

표현 정리 assume 맡다 include 포함하다 make sure 반드시

~하도록 하다 employee 직원 guarantee 보장하다 right 권리

6. 정답 **(C)**

해설 미팅이 한 시간 연기되었기 때문에 / Mr. Phillips는 안도했다 / 그가 기회를 가져서 / 그의 제안을 수정할 / 나중에 회의에서 설명할

해설 빈칸 앞에 완전한 문장이 있으므로 빈칸은 뒤에서 앞의 opportunity를 수식하는 자리이다. opportunity는 to 부정사의 수식을 잘 받는 'POWER'이므로 (B)와 (C) 중 하나가 와야 하며, 빈칸 뒤로는 목적어를 이끌고 있으므로 능동 형태인 (C)가 정답이다.

표현 정리 postpone 연기하다 relieved 안도하는 proposal 제안 revise 수정하다

7. 정답 **(C)**

해설 새 컴퓨터는 / 작동시킬 능력을 갖추고 있었다 / 두 개 이상의 컴퓨터 설계 도구들을 / 동시에

해설 빈칸 앞에 완전한 문장이 있으므로 빈칸은 뒤에서 앞의 ability를 수식하는 자리이다. ability는 to 부정사의 수식을 잘 받는 'POWER'이므로 (C)가 정답이다.

표현 정리 ability 능력 operate 운용하다, 가동시키다 tool 도구 at the same time 동시에

8. 정답 **(D)**

해설 회사 정책으로써 / 설치할 계획이 있는 사람은 누구든지 / 새로운 바이러스 백신 프로그램을 / 그들의 컴퓨터에 / 이번 주에 / 반드시 매니저에게 보고해야 한다 / 설치가 완료되면

해설 빈칸 앞에 완전한 문장이 있으므로 빈칸은 뒤에서 앞의 plan을 수식하는 자리이다. plan은 to 부정사의 수식을 잘 받는 'POWER'이므로 (D)가 정답이다.

표현 정리 policy 정책, 방침 antivirus 바이러스 퇴치용인 installation 설치 install 설치하다

9. 정답 **(B)**

해설 당신은 곧 듣게 될 것이다 / 우리의 고객 서비스 팀으로부터 / 답변을 제공할 책임이 있는 / 우리 웹사이트에서의 질문에 대해 / 배송에 관해

해설 answer는 'to 명사'가 오면 '~에 대한 답변'으로 해석된다. 여기서도 '질문에 대한 답변'이라고 해야 하므로 빈칸은 명사 자리이고, 따라서 명사인 (B)가 답이다. to가 있다고 동사원형을 골랐다면 함정에 빠진 것이다.

표현 정리 customer service 고객 서비스 responsible 책임이 있는 provide 제공하다 regarding ~에 관하여 shipment 배송 inquire 묻다 inquiry 질문, 문의

10. 정답 **(A)**

해설 확실히 해 주세요 / 당신이 모든 작업 내용을 저장하는 것을 / 컴퓨터에 / 그것을 분실하는 것을 막기 위해 / 갑작스런 정전으로 인해

해설 '갑작스런 정전으로 인해'라는 복합명사가 자연스러우므로 (A)가 정답이다. 'due to+명사'로 알아두자.

표현 정리 work 작업 avoid 방지하다, 막다 lose 잃어버리다 due to ~에 기인하는, ~때문에 sudden 갑작스러운 power failure 정전

법칙 58 to 부정사만 목적어로 취하는 동사

◎ 유형을 파악해 봐
1. (C)   2. (A)   3. (B)

1. 정답 **(C)**

해설 Mr. Pope은 / 계획이다 / 그의 보고서를 수정하는 것을 끝내기로 / 수요일까지

해설 문장에 정동사가 있으므로 빈칸은 plans의 목적어인 준동사 자리이다. plans은 to 부정사를 목적어로 취하는 '응큼쟁이' 동사이므로 (C)가 정답이다. 빈칸 뒤 revising은 to 부정사의 목적어이다.

표현 정리 plan 계획하다 revise 수정하다 report 보고서 finish 끝내다

2. 정답 **(A)**

해설 프로젝트 매니저는 원한다 / 워크숍에 참가하기를 / 수요일에

해설 문장에 정동사가 있으므로 빈칸은 wants의 목적어인 준동사 자리이다. wants는 to 부정사를 목적어로 취하는 '응큼쟁이' 동사이므로 (A)가 정답이다.

표현 정리 attend 참여하다 workshop 워크숍, 연수회

3. 정답 **(B)**

해설 Golden Holdings는 만회하려고 애쓴다 / 손실을 / 서브프라임 모기지 위기로 인한 / 2008년

해설 문장에 정동사가 있으므로 빈칸은 준동사 자리이다. 빈칸 앞 자동사 strives는 to 부정사와 어울리는 동사이다. 빈칸 뒤에는 to 부정사의 목적어로 losses가 왔으므로 능동 형태의 (B)가 정답이다. (D)는 수동형이므로 오답이다.

표현 정리 strive 분투하다, 애쓰다 loss 손실 subprime mortgage 서브프라임 모기지 crisis 위기 recover 되찾다, 만회하다

◎ 실전에 적용해 봐
1. (A)   2. (D)   3. (C)   4. (D)   5. (C)   6. (B)   7. (B)
8. (B)   9. (A)   10. (A)

1. 정답 **(A)**

해설 오작동하는 제품을 구입한 고객들은 / 선택할 수 있다 / 현금 환불이나 할인 쿠폰을 받는 것을 / 그들이 다음에 구매할 때

해설 문장에 정동사가 2개 있고, 접속사가 1개 있으므로 빈칸은 준동사 자리이다. 빈칸 앞 choose는 to 부정사를 목적어로 취하는 동사이므로 (A)가 정답이다.

표현 정리 malfunction 제대로 작동하지 않다 product 제품 choose 선택하다 cash 현금 refund 환불

2. 정답 (D)

해설 Newhope Charity Organization은 / 감사를 표현하기를 원한다 / 모든 기부자들과 다른 모든 사람들에게 / 그들의 시간·돈을 기여한 / 이 행사를 가능하게 만들기 위해

해설 문장에 정동사가 2개 있고, 접속사가 1개 있으므로 빈칸은 준동사 자리이다. 빈칸 앞 would like은 want와 같은 의미로 to 부정사를 목적어로 취한다. 따라서 (D)가 정답이다.

표현 정리 charity 자선 organization 조직, 단체 donor 기부자 contribute 기여하다 event 행사 possible 가능한

3. 정답 (C)

해설 Kimko Audio Technologies는 희망한다 / 새로운 오디오 플레이어를 출시하기를 / 올해

해설 문장에 정동사가 있으므로 빈칸은 준동사 자리이다. 빈칸 앞 hope는 to 부정사를 목적어로 취하는 '응큼쟁이' 동사이다. 따라서 to 부정사가 되려면 동사원형이 와야 하므로 (C)가 정답이다.

표현 정리 hope 소망하다, 희망하다 launch 출시하다

4. 정답 (D)

해설 Megatech 사는 인수할 예정이다 / 더 많은 신규 업체들을 / 휴대폰 액세서리 제조를 전문으로 하는 / 확장하기 위해 / 모바일 시장으로

해설 문장에 정동사가 2개 있고, 접속사가 1개 있으므로 빈칸은 준동사 자리이다. 빈칸 앞 intends는 to 부정사를 목적어로 취하는 '응큼쟁이' 동사이다. 빈칸 뒤 to 부정사의 목적어가 있으므로 능동형으로 쓰인 (D)가 정답이다.

표현 정리 intend 작정하다, ~하려고 생각하다 start-up 신규 업체 specialize in ~을 전문으로 하다 manufacture 제조하다, 생산하다 expand 확장시키다 mobile 휴대폰 acquire 인수하다

5. 정답 (C)

해설 배송에 관한 정보를 얻기 위해서는 / 당신이 주문한 상품들의 / 저희에게 연락해 주세요 / 저희의 무료 전화번호로 / 그리고 대화를 요청하세요 / 고객 서비스 사무실 직원과의

해설 문장에 정동사가 2개 있고, 접속사가 1개 있으므로 빈칸은 준동사 자리이다. 빈칸 앞 ask는 to 부정사를 목적어나 목적 보어로 취하는 동사이므로 (C)가 정답이다.

표현 정리 in order to ~하기 위해서 get 얻다 item 물품, 품목 order 주문하다 contact 연락하다, 접촉하다 toll-free number 무료 전화번호

6. 정답 (B)

해설 Mr. Gore는 결정했다 / 스케줄을 재조정하기로 / 그의 교육을 위한 / 그가 알고는 / 출장을 가야 한다는 것을 / 한 주 동안

해설 빈칸 앞 decided는 to 부정사를 목적어로 취하는 '응큼쟁이' 동사이다. 따라서 'to 동사원형'으로 (B)와 (D) 중 하나가 쓰일 수 있는데, 빈칸 뒤에 목적어가 있으므로 능동형인 (B)가 정답이다. (D)는 수동형으로 목적어를 이끌지 못한다.

표현 정리 training session 교육 (과정) realize 깨닫다 business trip 출장 rearrange 재조정하다

7. 정답 (E)

해설 그것이 성공적으로 설치되었으므로 / 프로그램은 제대로 작동해야 한다 / 하지만 그것은 끊임없이 오류를 일으킨다.

해설 빈칸 앞 자동사 fail은 to 부정사와 어울리는 동사이므로 (3)가 정답이다.

표현 정리 successfully 성공적으로 install 설치하다 run 작동하다, 기능하다 properly 제대로 consistently 끊임없이 fail 실패하다, ~하지 못하다 operate 작동되다

8. 정답 (E)

해설 우리 사장은 반대한다 / Gwen Industries와의 합병을 / 많은 분석가들이 주장하기 때문에 / 그 합병이 큰 효과를 주지 않는다고 / 회사 이익에

해설 빈칸 앞 object to 다음에는 명사나 동명사가 온다. 따라서 명사인 (B)가 정답이다. object를 '응큼쟁이' 동사로 착각하여 동사원형을 썼다는 함정에 빠진 것이다.

표현 정리 object to ~에 반대하다 analyst 분석가 claim 주장하다 substantial 상당한 effect 효과 profit 이익 merge 합병하다 merger 합병

9. 정답 (A)

해설 구입을 취소하기를 원하는 사람들은 / 제시해야 한다 / 영수증과 신용카드를 / 그들이 제품들을 구입할 때 사용한

해설 빈칸 앞 wish는 to 부정사를 목적어로 취하는 '응큼쟁이' 동사이다. 따라서 (A)가 정답이다.

표현 정리 purchase 구매하다 present 제시하다 receipt 영수증 credit card 신용 카드 cancel 취소하다

10. 정답 (A)

해설 지침을 읽어 주십시오 / 기계를 처음 사용하는 것에 관한 / 부적절한 기계 사용이, 궁극적으로 생산 중단을 초래할 수도 있으므로

해설 문장에 정동사가 있으므로 빈칸은 준동사 자리이다. lead가 to 부정사를 목적어로 취하는 동사라고 생각하여 (C)를 답으로 고르면 함정에 빠지는 문제이다. lead to는 '~한 결과를 낳다, 초래하다'라는 의미의 덩어리 동사이므로 to 다음은 명사가 와야 한다. 따라서 (A)가 답.

표현 정리 guideline 지침 improper 부적절한 ultimately 궁극적으로, 결국 lead (결과적으로) ~에 이르다, ~하게 되다 interruption 중단 interrupt 중단시키다, 방해하다

법칙 59 동명사만 목적어로 취하는 동사

◎ 유형을 파악해 봐
1. (B)   2. (A)   3. (D)

1. 정답 (B)

해설 피하십시오 / 기계를 작동하는 것을 / 물이나 액체 가까이에서 / 그렇게 하면 야기할 수 있으므로 / 오작동을

해설 문장에 정동사가 2개 있고, 접속사가 1개 있으므로 빈칸은 준동사 자리이자 '회장아들' 동사 avoid의 목적어 자리이다. '회장아들' 동사는 동명사를 목적어로 취하므로 (B)가 정답이다. (D)는 명사이므로 또 명사가 올 수 없다.

표현 정리 avoid 피하다 fluid 액체 malfunction 제대로 작동하지 않다 operate 가동하다

2. 정답 (A)

해설 Ms. Camora는 즐긴다 / 그녀의 가족과 캠핑 가는 것을 / 그녀의 집 근처에 있는 공원으로 / 여가 시간에

해설 문장에 정동사가 1개 있으므로 빈칸은 준동사 자리이자 '회장아들' 동사 enjoys의 목적어 자리이다. '회장아들' 동사는 동명사를 목적어로 취하므로 (A)가 정답이다.

표현 정리 enjoy 즐기다 spare 여분의, 남는

3. 정답 (D)

해설 소문에 의하면 / CEO는 사실상 고려 중이다 / 지사를 옮기는 것을 / Newtown으로

해설 문장에 정동사가 1개 있으므로 빈칸은 준동사 자리이자 '회장아들' 동사 considering의 목적어 자리이다. '회장아들' 동사는 동명사를 목적어로 취하므로 (D)가 정답이다. (A)는 명사이므로 또 명사가 올 수 없다.

표현 정리 according to ~에 따르면 CEO 최고 경영자(= Chief Executive Officer) in fact 사실상 consider 고려하다 regional office 지사 relocate 이전하다

◎ 실전에 적용해 봐

1. (C) 2. (D) 3. (C) 4. (B) 5. (B) 6. (A) 7. (D)
8. (B) 9. (B) 10. (D)

1. 정답 (C)

해설 매장 전체 매출의 70%가 토요일에 이루어지기 때문에 / 매니저는 제안했다 / 평상시보다 늦게 닫을 것을 / 주말에

해설 문장에 정동사 2개가 있고, 접속사가 1개 있으므로 빈칸은 준동사 자리이다. 또한 빈칸은 '회장아들' 동사 suggested의 목적어 자리이기도 하다. '회장아들' 동사는 동명사를 목적어로 취하므로 (C)가 정답이다.

표현 정리 total 전체의 sale 판매, 매출 suggest 제안하다 usual 평상시의

2. 정답 (D)

해설 신규 건설 프로젝트에 관해 발표하는 것은 / 도전적인 것임에 틀림없다 / 신입 직원에게는 / 하지만 절대 포기할 생각하지 마라 / 너의 선택 중 하나로서

해설 빈칸은 준동사 자리이자 '회장아들' 동사 consider의 목적어 자리이기도 하다. '회장아들' 동사는 동명사를 목적어로 취하므로 (D)가 정답이다.

표현 정리 deliver a presentation 발표하다 construction 건설 challenging 도전적인 option 선택권 give up 포기하다

3. 정답 (C)

해설 Ms. Edmond는 기술자를 불렀다 / 자신의 컴퓨터를 봐 달라고 / 그런데 컴퓨터는 자주 작동을 멈췄다.

해설 빈칸은 준동사 자리이자 stopped의 목적어 자리이다. stop은 to 부정사와 동명사를 목적어로 취하므로 해석해 보면 '작동을 멈추는'이 자연스럽다. 따라서 (C)가 답이다. 반면에 'stop+to 부정사'는 '~하기 위해서 멈추다'로 (A)는 오답이다.

표현 정리 look at ~을 (자세히) 살피다 frequently 자주 freeze (시스템이) 정지하다 run 작동하다

4. 정답 (B)

해설 휴대용 전화의 수요가 빠르게 증가했기 때문에 / Revo Tech는 개발을 시작했다 / 시장에서 가장 가벼운 전화기

해설 빈칸은 준동사 자리이자 동시에 began의 목적어 자리이다. 또한 빈칸 뒤에 목적어를 가지므로 동명사인 (B)가 정답이다. (A)는 명사이므로 또 명사가 올 수 없다.

표현 정리 since ~때문에 demand 수요 portable 이동하기 쉬운 cell phone 휴대폰 quickly 빠르게 develop 개발하다

5. 정답 (B)

해설 Mr. Kim에게 물어봐라 / 그가 기꺼이 너를 데리러 갈 것인지 / 회의가 끝나고 / 왜냐하면 그는 아마 꺼려하지 않을 것이다 / 그곳까지 운전하는 것을 / 그의 집이 바로 가까이에 있기 때문에

해설 빈칸은 준동사 자리이면서 '회장아들' 동사 mind의 목적어 자리이기도 하다. '회장아들' 동사는 동명사를 목적어로 취하므로 (B)가 정답이다.

표현 정리 be willing to 기꺼이 ~하다 conference 회의 probably 아마도 nearby 바로 가까이에

6. 정답 (A)

해설 Mr. Gallos가 곧 처벌받을 것임은 명백하다 / 그가 부정행위를 했음을 인정했기 때문에 / 그의 승진 시험에서

해설 빈칸은 준동사 자리이기 때문에 정동사인 (C)는 오답이다. 또한 빈칸은 '회장아들' 동사 admit의 목적어 자리이다. '회장아들' 동사는 동명사를 목적어로 취하므로 (A)가 정답이다.

표현 정리 obvious 명백하다 penalize 처벌하다 admit 인정하다 promotion 승진, 진급 cheat 부정행위를 하다

7. 정답 (D)

해설 그가 집으로 돌아가는 동안 / Mr. Daniels는 들렀다 / 주간 신문을 사려고 / 신문판매대에

해설 빈칸은 준동사 자리이자 stopped의 목적어 자리이다. stop은 to 부정사와 동명사를 동시에 목적어로 취하는 동사이다. 해석해 보면 '사기 위해 멈추다'가 자연스러우므로 (D)가 정답이다. 반면에 'stop+동명사'는 '~하는 것을 멈추다'로 (A)는 오답이다.

표현 정리 while ~하는 동안 weekly newspaper 주간 신문
newsstand 신문판매대

8. 정답 (B)

해설 발표되었다 / 본사가 연기할 것이라고 / 회사의 전 신입 사원들의 교육을 / 추후 통지가 있을 때까지

해설 빈칸은 준동사 자리이자 동시에 '회장하다' 동사 put off의 목적어 자리이다. '회장하다' 동사는 동명사를 목적어로 취하므로 (B)가 정답이다.

표현 정리 announcement 발표 headquarters 본사 put off 연기하다 until further notice 추후 통고가 있을 때까지

9. 정답 (B)

해설 Ms. Hawkins는 잊었다 / 두꺼운 코트를 가져가는 것을 / 러시아로 출장을 떠나기 전에 / 그래서 감기에 걸렸다 / 그곳에서

해설 빈칸은 준동사 자리이자 forgot의 목적어 자리이다. forgot은 to 부정사와 동명사를 동시에 목적어로 취한다. 해석해 보면 '두꺼운 코트를 가져가는 것을 잊다'가 자연스러우므로 (B)가 정답이다. 반면에 'forget+동명사'는 '~한 것을 잊다'의 의미로 (A)는 오답이다.

표현 정리 heavy 두꺼운 business trip 출장 catch a cold 감기에 걸리다

10. 정답 (D)

해설 인사부 직원의 주요 임무 중 하나는 포함한다 / 직원 만족에 대한 설문 조사 결과를 보고하는 것을 / CEO에게

해설 빈칸은 준동사 자리이자 '회장하다' 동사 included의 목적어 자리이다. '회장하다' 동사는 목적어로 동명사를 취하므로 (D)가 정답이다.

표현 정리 main 주요한 Human Resources 인사부 staff 직원 survey (설문) 조사 employee 직원 satisfaction 만족 CEO 최고 경영자(= Chief Executive Officer)

법칙 60 완전한 문장 뒤에 온 콤마는 -ing(분사구문)

◎ 유형을 파악해 봐
1. (D) 2. (B) 3. (C)

1. 정답 (D)

해설 최근의 홍수는 불리한 영향을 끼쳤다 / 식당에 / 벽에 금이 가기 시작했기 때문에 / 따라서 보수를 필요로 했다

해설 문장에 정동사가 있으므로 빈칸은 준동사 자리이며, 빈칸 뒤에 목적어가 있으므로 현재분사인 (D)가 정답이다. 부사인 (A)는 명사를 수식하지 않고, (B)는 과거분사로 목적어를 갖지 않으며, (C)는 명사이다.

표현 정리 flood 홍수 adversely 불리하게 affect ~에 영향을 미치다 crack 갈라지다, 금이 가다 renovation 수리, 보수 necessarily 어쩔 수 없이 necessitate ~을 필요로 하다 necessaries 필수품들

2. 정답 (B)

해설 Mr. Chez는 옮겼다 / 모든 사무용품들을 / 또 다른 공간으로 / 공간을 확보하기 위해 / 허용하도록 / 새 테이블이 사무실에 놓일 수 있게

해설 문장에 정동사가 있으므로 빈칸은 준동사 자리이며, 빈칸 뒤에 목적어가 있으므로 현재분사인 (B)가 정답이다. (A)는 과거분사로 목적어를 갖지 않고, 부사인 (D)는 명사를 수식하지 않는다.

표현 정리 move 옮기다 office supplies 사무용품 set 놓다 allow 허용하다 allowably 허용 범위 내에서

3. 정답 (C)

해설 Ms. Horton의 여행 가이드는 / 그녀에게 일정표를 보냈다 / 스페인 여행을 위한 / 수정된 스케줄을 재확인했다

해설 문장에 정동사가 있으므로 빈칸은 준동사 자리이며, 빈칸 뒤에 목적어가 있으므로 현재분사인 (C)가 정답이다. (B)와 (D)는 과거분사로 목적어를 갖지 않는다.

표현 정리 tour guide 여행 가이드 itinerary 일정표 revise 수정하다, 변경하다 reconfirm 재확인하다

◎ 실전에 적용해 봐
1. (D) 2. (B) 3. (C) 4. (A) 5. (A) 6. (D) 7. (D)
8. (B) 9. (C) 10. (A)

1. 정답 (D)

해설 Euros Air로부터 온 이메일은 언급했다 / 지불이 성공적으로 되었다고 / 그래서 항공편 예약을 확인해 주었다

해설 빈칸은 준동사 자리이며, 빈칸 뒤에 목적어가 있으므로 현재분사인 (D)가 정답이다. (B)는 과거분사로 목적어를 갖지 않으며, (C)는 명사이므로 또 명사가 올 수 없다.

표현 정리 state 언급하다, 명시하다 payment 지불 successfully 성공적으로 reservation 예약 confirm 확인해 주다

2. 정답 (B)

해설 Lyson Electronics는 최근에 소개했다 / 신형 컴퓨터 모델을 / 고도의 기능을 갖춘 / 그렇게 함으로써 만들었다 / 새로 출시된 경쟁사 모델을 / 경쟁력이 없도록

해설 빈칸은 준동사 자리이며, 빈칸 뒤에 목적어가 있으므로 현재분사인 (B)가 정답이다. (A)는 수동형으로 목적어를 갖지 않고, (C)는 과거분사로 목적어를 갖지 않는다.

표현 정리 equip 갖추다 highly advanced 고도로 발전된 function 기능 thereby 그렇게 함으로써, 그것 때문에 launch 출시하다 uncompetitive 경쟁력이 없는 render (어떤 상태가 되게) 만들다

3. 정답 (C)

해설 CEO는 Mr. Harlen을 임명했다 / 올해의 우수 직원으로 / 그의 공헌을 인정하며 / 계약을 성공적으로 맺은 / Regina Pipelines와의

해설 빈칸은 준동사 자리이며, 빈칸 뒤에 목적어가 있으므로 현재분사인 (C)가 정답이다. (D)는 과거분사로 목적어를 갖지 않는다.

표현 정리 CEO 최고 경영자(= Chief Executive Officer) name 임명

하다 outstanding 뛰어난 contribution 기여, 공헌 conclude 끝내다 contract 계약 acknowledge 인정하다

4.　　　　　　　　　　　　　　　　　　　　　　정답 (A)

해설 Mount National Monument의 보수가 시작되었다 / 부분들을 복원하며 / 녹으로 부식된

해설 빈칸은 준동사 자리이며, 빈칸 뒤에 목적어가 있으므로 현재분사인 (A)가 정답이다. (B)는 과거분사로 목적어를 갖지 않으며, (C)는 형용사이다.

표현 정리 renovation 보수 corrode 부식시키다 rust 녹 restore 복구하다

5.　　　　　　　　　　　　　　　　　　　　　　정답 (A)

해설 퇴실할 시간이 되었을 때 / Mr. Ming은 그의 짐을 챙겼다 / 그리고 열쇠를 반납했다 / 프런트에 / 방을 떠나면서

해설 빈칸은 준동사 자리이며, 빈칸 뒤에 목적어가 있으므로 현재분사인 (A)가 정답이다. (C)는 과거분사로 목적어를 갖지 않으며, (D)는 명사이다.

표현 정리 check out 퇴실하다 pack 꾸리다, 챙기다 luggage 짐 vacate 비우다

6.　　　　　　　　　　　　　　　　　　　　　　정답 (D)

해설 ABC Tech는 / 단지 2달 전에 설립된 / 이미 고용하고 있다 / 50명의 직원을

해설 established는 준동사이므로 빈칸에는 정동사가 와야 한다. 따라서 (C)와 (D) 중에서 주어가 단수이므로 단수 동사인 (D)가 답이 된다. 앞에 문장이 왔다고 생각해 -ing를 답으로 고르면 틀리는 함정 문제이다.

표현 정리 already 이미 employ 고용하다 employee 직원

7.　　　　　　　　　　　　　　　　　　　　　　정답 (D)

해설 Bodywell Fitness Center는 제공해 왔다 / 특별 가격을 / 핫 요가 수업을 위한 / 제한된 시간 동안 / 더 많은 사람들이 등록하도록 장려하며 / 수업을

해설 빈칸은 준동사 자리이며, 빈칸 뒤에 목적어가 있으므로 현재분사인 (D)가 정답이다. (A)는 과거분사로 목적어를 갖지 않는다.

표현 정리 offer 제공하다 limited 제한된 register 등록하다 encourage 장려하다

8.　　　　　　　　　　　　　　　　　　　　　　정답 (B)

해설 당신은 우리 사무실을 찾을 수 있다 / Bright Bridge 가에 위치한 / Stars Building에 바로 인접한

해설 'Stars Building에 바로 인접한'이라는 말이 어울리므로 (B)가 정답이다. 앞에 완전한 문장이 왔다고 해서 -ing를 답으로 고민할 수 있지만 빈칸 뒤에 목적어가 없으므로 현재분사인 (C)는 오답이다. '유도된'의 뜻을 가진 (A)는 어색하다.

표현 정리 locate 위치하다 adjacent to ~에 인접한, 가까운 directed 유도된 directly 바로 direct ~로 향하다, 안내하다

9.　　　　　　　　　　　　　　　　　　　　　　정답 (C)

해설 생산부 매니저는 요청했다 / 팀들이 주로 페인팅 작업에 집중할 것을 / 일부 불필요한 생산 과정들을 없애는

해설 빈칸은 준동사 자리이며, 빈칸 뒤에 목적어가 있으므로 현재분사인 (C)가 정답이다. (A)는 과거분사로 목적어를 갖지 않으며, (B)는 명사이므로 또 명사가 올 수 없다.

표현 정리 request 요청하다 primarily 주로 focus on ~에 주력하다, 집중하다 redundant 불필요한, 쓸모 없는 production 생산 eliminate 없애다, 제거하다

10.　　　　　　　　　　　　　　　　　　　　　정답 (A)

해설 홍보 행사는 / 새로운 쇼인 'Rain in Seattle'의 / 소문이 났다 / 인터넷에 / 결과적으로 티켓 판매의 증가를 가져왔다

해설 빈칸은 준동사 자리이다. result는 자동사이므로 과거분사 형태로 쓸 수 없고, 전치사 in과 덩어리로 쓰이므로 (A)가 정답이다. (D)는 완전한 문장 뒤에 명사만 쓰일 수 없으므로 오답이다.

표현 정리 promotional 홍보의 go viral 입소문이 나다 boost 증가, 상승 result in ~을 낳다, 야기하다

법칙 61 완료시제에 have만 있다면 p.p.

◎ 유형을 파악해 봐
1. (C)　2. (B)　3. (D)

1.　　　　　　　　　　　　　　　　　　　　　　정답 (C)

해설 Ms. Evans는 / Mr. Holmes를 알고 지냈다 / 7년 이상

해설 빈칸은 준동사 자리이며, 빈칸 앞에 있는 has가 '가지고 있다'는 뜻의 본동사인지, 현재완료시제를 만드는 조동사인지를 구분해야 한다. 여기서 본동사는 뒤에 동명사를 목적어로 취하지 않으므로 (A)는 오답이다. 따라서 has는 조동사이며, 뒤에 p.p.가 오는 현재완료시제가 되어 '7년 동안 알아왔다'는 의미를 이루는 (C)가 정답이다.

2.　　　　　　　　　　　　　　　　　　　　　　정답 (B)

해설 매니저는 계획을 세웠다 / 후속 검토를 끝내기로 / 이번 주까지

해설 빈칸은 준동사 자리이며, 빈칸 뒤 to 부정사가 왔으므로 이를 목적어로 취하는 3형식 동사가 필요하다. 따라서 빈칸은 앞의 has와 함께 현재완료시제를 이루는 p.p.가 와야 하므로 (B)가 정답이다. (A)를 명사로 보면 앞에 관사가 있어야 한다.

표현 정리 follow-up 후속 조치, 후속편 review 검토

3.　　　　　　　　　　　　　　　　　　　　　　정답 (D)

해설 연구원들은 확인했다 / 8시간의 수면이 보장된다는 사실을 / 사람들이 좋은 컨디션을 유지하는 것을

해설 빈칸은 준동사 자리이다. (B)는 명사이며, (C)는 형용사로 관사를 뛰어넘어 명사를 수식할 수 없다. 따라서 have는 조동사이며, 뒤에 p.p.가 와서 '확인했다'는 의미를 이루는 (D)가 정답이다.

표현 정리 researcher 연구원 ensure 보장하다 verify 입증하다,

확인하다 verification 확인, 입증 verifiable 증명할 수 있는

◎ 실전에 적용해 봐
1. (B) 2. (B) 3. (C) 4. (A) 5. (D) 6. (B) 7. (D)
8. (C) 9. (C) 10. (A)

1. 정답 (B)

해설 Mr. Kimberly는 이미 끝낸 뒤였다 / 그의 서류 작업을 / Ms. Gray가 도움을 주러 왔을 때

해설 빈칸은 준동사 자리이며, 빈칸 앞에 있는 had가 본동사라면 명사를 목적어로 취하지 않으므로 (C)는 오답이다. 따라서 had는 조동사이며, 뒤에 p.p.가 오면 과거완료시제가 되어 '이미 끝냈다'는 의미를 이루게 되어 (B)가 정답이다.

표현 정리 already 이미 paperwork 서류 작업 offer 제공하다

2. 정답 (B)

해설 Ms. Simmons은 허락했다 / 그녀의 동료들이 머무르도록 / 그녀의 집에 / 그들이 찾을 때까지 / 이사가 가능한 집을

해설 빈칸은 준동사 자리이며, 빈칸 앞에 온 has가 본동사라면 명사를 목적어로 취하지 않으므로 (D)는 오답이다. 따라서 has는 조동사이며, 뒤에 p.p.가 와서 '머무르도록 허락했다'는 의미를 이루는 (B)가 정답이다.

표현 정리 co-worker 동료 afford ~할 여유가 되다 allow 허락하다

3. 정답 (C)

해설 대부분의 시민들은 동의한다 / 시가 늘려야 한다는 것에 / 보조금을 / 저소득층 가정을 위해 / 내년에.

해설 has 만 보고 pp인 (A)를 답으로 하였다면 함정에 빠진 것이다. in the coming year는 미래시제부사로서 현재완료시제와 어울리지 않는다. '~해야 한다'라는 뜻을 가진 (C)는 미래시제부사와도 사용될 수 있다.

표현 정리 amount 양 subsidy 보조금 low-income 저소득의 households 가계, 가구 increase 증가시키다

4. 정답 (A)

해설 우리가 조사하게 될 것이기 때문에 / 500명이 넘는 고객을 / 다음 주까지는 / 우리는 분석해야 한다 / 고객 설문조사 결과를 / 그 후에

해설 빈칸은 준동사 자리이므로 정동사인 (B)와 (D)는 오답이다. 빈칸 앞에 온 have가 본동사라면 명사를 목적어로 취하지 않으므로 (C)는 오답이다. 따라서 have는 조동사이며, 뒤에 p.p.가 오면 미래완료시제가 되어 '조사하게 될 것이다'라는 의미를 이루는 (A)가 정답이다.

표현 정리 customer 고객 analyze 분석하다 result 결과 survey 조사하다

5. 정답 (D)

해설 불행한 일이었다 / Mr. Butler가 돈이 전혀 없다는 것 / 그가 투자했기 때문에 / 급여의 대부분을 / 주식 시장에

해설 빈칸은 준동사 자리이므로 정동사인 (C)는 오답이다. 빈칸 앞에 온 had가 본동사라면 명사를 목적어로 취하지 않으므로 (A)는 오답이다. 따라서 had는 조동사이며, 뒤에 p.p.가 오면 과거완료시제가 되어 '수입의 대부분을 투자했기 때문에'라는 자연스러운 의미를 이루므로 (D)가 정답이다.

표현 정리 unfortunate 불행한 stock market 주식 시장 invest 투자하다

6. 정답 (B)

해설 사람들은 최근에서야 선호했다 / 장치들을 사용하는 것을 / 휴대폰에 있는 / 휴대가 용이하기 때문에

해설 빈칸은 준동사 자리이며, 부정어나 only가 문두에 오면서 조동사 have가 앞으로 나간 도치구문이다. 따라서 빈칸은 have와 함께 현재완료를 이루는 p.p. 자리로 '장치들을 사용하는 것을 선호했다'는 자연스러운 의미가 되므로 (B)가 정답이다.

표현 정리 recently 최근에 wearable 착용 가능한 device 장치 portability 휴대성 prefer 선호하다

7. 정답 (D)

해설 최고 관리자는 고려 중이었다 / Mr. Hudson이 다음 프로젝트를 이끌게 하려고 / 그녀가 기대 이상으로 수행했기 때문에 / 지난 번 프로젝트를

해설 빈칸은 준동사 자리이다. 빈칸 앞에 온 had가 본동사라면 명사를 목적어로 취하지 않으므로 (A)는 오답이다. 본동사라면 뒤에 목적어가 와야 하므로 (C) 역시 오답이다. 따라서 had는 조동사이며, 뒤에 p.p.가 오면 과거완료시제가 되어 '그녀가 수행했기 때문에'라는 자연스러운 의미를 이루므로 (D)가 정답이다.

표현 정리 executive 경영의, 최고의 consider 고려하다 lead 이끌다 upcoming 다가오는 above and beyond ~에 더하여 expectation 기대 perform 수행하다

8. 정답 (C)

해설 Mr. Dunn은 일했다 / Jinko 사에서 / 3년 이상 / Revolution Tech로 이직하기 전에

해설 빈칸 뒤에 완료시제와 어울리는 for over 3 years가 있는 것으로 보아 had는 조동사이며, 빈칸은 p.p.가 와야 한다. 따라서 (C)가 답이다.

9. 정답 (C)

해설 Ms. Bailey는 보낸 적이 없다 / 하루 이상을 / 그녀의 컴퓨터를 고치는데 / 치명적인 바이러스에 감염된

해설 빈칸은 준동사 자리이다. 부정어나 only가 문두에 오면서 조동사 has가 앞으로 나간 도치 구문이다. 따라서 빈칸은 has와 함께 현재완료를 이루는 p.p.가 와야 하며, '하루 이상을 보낸 적이 없다'는 자연스러운 내용을 이루므로 (C)가 정답이다.

표현 정리 fix 고치다 affect 영향을 미치다 serious 심각한 spend (시간을) 보내다

10. 정답 (A)

해설 그의 고객은 그의 사무실 밖으로 막 나간 상태였다 / Mr. Walker가 그녀를 다시 불렀을 때 / 그녀의 전화기를 주려고 / 그녀가 두고 간 / 사무실에

해설 빈칸은 준동사 자리이다. 부정어나 only가 문두에 오면서 조동사

had가 앞으로 나간 도치 구문이다. 따라서 빈칸은 had와 함께 과거완료를 이루는 p.p. 자리로 '밖으로 막 나간 상태였다'는 자연스러운 내용이 되므로 (A)가 정답이다.

표현 정리 hardly 거의 ~하지 않은 client 고객, 의뢰인

법칙 62 'Those+형용사' 류는 '~하는 사람들'

◎ 유형을 파악해 봐
1. (B)   2. (C)   3. (C)

1.   정답 (B)

해설 더 많은 정보를 얻고 싶은 사람들은 / 다음 주에 열리는 직업 박람회에 관한 / 사무실에 전화해야 한다

해설 빈칸은 주어 자리이다. who부터 next week까지가 주어를 수식하는 형용사절이다. 대명사 중에 형용사절의 수식을 받아 '~하는 사람들'이란 뜻을 가진 (B)가 정답이다. (A)와 (C)는 형용사절의 수식을 받지 못하고, (D)는 주어의 기능이 없다.

표현 정리 get 얻다 information 정보 job fair 직업박람회 hold 열다, 개최하다

2.   정답 (C)

해설 The Inka Corporation은 제공한다 / 무료 정기 건강검진을 / 35세 이상의 정규직 직원에게 / 회사

해설 빈칸은 to의 목적어 자리이다. (A)와 (B)는 접속사이므로 오답이고, (D)는 전명구의 수식을 받을 수 없다. 따라서 정기 건강검진을 받는 것은 사람이므로 (C)가 정답이다.

표현 정리 provide 제공하다 free 무료의 regular 정기적인 checkups 건강검진

3.   정답 (C)

해설 고객 설문조사를 참조하세요 / 브랜드 선호도에 관한 / 실시된 것들을 제외하고 / 작년에

해설 빈칸은 for의 목적어 자리이며, 따라서 surveys를 의미하는 지시대명사 those가 와야 한다. (C)가 정답이다. (B)는 단수 명사를 받고, (D)는 형용사류의 수식을 받지 않는다.

표현 정리 refer 참조하다 survey (설문) 조사 regarding ~에 관하여 preference 선호 except for ~을 제외하고 conduct 수행하다

◎ 실전에 적용해 봐
1. (D)   2. (A)   3. (B)   4. (B)   5. (D)   6. (D)   7. (C)
8. (B)   9. (D)   10. (D)

1.   정답 (D)

해설 상품을 주문한 사람들은 / 화요일 전에 / 가능할 것이다 / 상품이 배송되는 것이 / 휴일 전에 / 하지만 화요일 이후에 주문하는 상품들은 / 배송될 것이다 / 휴일 이후에

해설 빈칸은 주어 자리이다. who부터 Tuesday까지가 주어를 수식하는 형용사절이다. 따라서 '~하는 사람들'이란 뜻을 가진 (D)가 정답이다. 주어의 기능이 없는 (B)와 (C)는 오답, (A)는 형용사절의 수식을 받지 못한다.

표현 정리 place an order 주문하다 item 물품, 품목 deliver 배송하다 order 주문하다

2.   정답 (A)

해설 Mr. Wagner은 여행할 수 있을 것이다 / 리비아와 이집트로 / 최근에 이 국가들이 제한을 풀었기 때문에 / 방문객들의 출입

해설 빈칸 앞에 접속사 as가 있으므로 접속사인 (C)와 (D)는 오답이다. 따라서 지시형용사인 (A)가 정답이며, these는 지시대명사/지시형용사의 일반 기능을 한다. 소유대명사인 (B)는 명사 앞에 쓸 수 없다. (D)도 지시형용사가 가능하나 단수 명사 앞에 써야 한다.

표현 정리 recently 최근에 lift (제재를) 풀다, 해제하다 restriction 제한, 규제 enter 들어가다

3.   정답 (B)

해설 토론 주제는 언급된 것이었다 / 지난 번 회의에서

해설 빈칸은 was의 보어가 되는 단수 명사 자리이면서, which ~ meeting까지의 수식을 받아야 한다. 보기 중 topic을 가리키면서 단수가 되는 (B)가 답이다. (A) those는 복수 명사를 받을 때 사용하며, (C) it은 형용사절의 수식을 받지 않고, (D) either는 둘 중 아무거나 하나를 뜻하는 말로 2개라는 어울림이 없는 상태의 문장에 들어오는 것도 어색하다.

표현 정리 discussion 토론 raise 언급하다

4.   정답 (B)

해설 유효한 주차증을 가진 사람들만이 / 허용될 것이다 / 그들의 차량들을 주차하도록 / 그 지역에 / 무료로

해설 빈칸은 주어 자리이다. 전명구의 수식을 받아 '~하는 사람들'이란 뜻을 가진 (B)가 정답이다. 주어의 기능이 없는 (A)와 (C)와 (D)는 오답이다. 특히 (C)와 (D)는 접속사인데, 동사의 개수가 1개라 탈락이다.

표현 정리 valid 유효한 parking permit 주차증 allow 허용하다 vehicle 차량 lot (특정 용도용) 지역 for free 무료로

5.   정답 (D)

해설 세미나는 준비되었다 / 내일 열리도록 / 도움 덕분에 / 그들의 시간을 자발적으로 제공한 사람들의

해설 빈칸은 of의 목적어 자리이다. 형용사절의 수식을 받으며 '~하는 사람들'의 뜻을 가진 (D)가 정답이다. (A)는 목적어의 기능이 없고, (B)와 (C)는 접속사이다.

표현 정리 hold 개최하다 thanks to ~덕분에 volunteer 자발적으로 나서다

6.   정답 (D)

해설 2015년 모금활동은 / 더 많은 자금을 모았다 / 전 세계적으로 / 지난해보다

해설 빈칸 앞에 접속사가 있으므로 접속사인 (B)와 (C)는 오답이다. 빈칸은 복수 명사인 fundraising campaigns를 받는 지시대명사가 필요하며, 따

라서 복수 명사를 받는 (D)가 답이다. (A)는 전명구의 수식을 받지 못하며, (B)도 대명사 기능이 있으나 단수 명사를 받을 때 사용한다.

표현 정리 fundraising 모금활동 collect 모으다 fund 자금 globally 전 세계적으로

7. 　　　　　　　　　　　　　　　　　　　　　　　**정답 (C)**

해석 즉시 도와 안내하세요 / 자리를 기다리는 사람들을 / 빈 테이블로

해설 빈칸은 목적어 자리이며, 기다리는 건 사람이므로 '~하는 사람들'이란 (C)가 정답이다. 접속사인 (D)와 목적어 기능이 없는 (A)는 오답이다.

표현 정리 immediately 즉시 assist 돕다 escort 안내하다 seat 앉히다, 앉다

8. 　　　　　　　　　　　　　　　　　　　　　　　**정답 (B)**

해석 R&S Research Institute가 주최한 연례 세미나는 / 허용했다 / 모든 방문객들을 / 포함하여 / 지난 해에 세미나에 참석하지 않은 사람들을 / 연설을 듣기 위해

해설 who부터 last year까지 빈칸을 수식하는 형용사절이며, '사람들'이란 뜻을 가지는 (B)가 답이다. (A)는 주어의 기능이 없고, (C)와 (D)는 형용사절 수식을 받지 못한다.

표현 정리 annual 연례 host 주최하다 allow 허용하다 attend 참석하다

9. 　　　　　　　　　　　　　　　　　　　　　　　**정답 (D)**

해석 자유롭게 제공해라 / 화장품 샘플들을 / 우리 매장을 방문하는 손님들에게 / 창고에 충분한 양이 있으므로

해설 빈칸은 cosmetic samples를 가리키는 대명사 자리이며, 복수를 받는 (D)가 올 수 있다. 따라서 정답은 (D)이다. (A)는 주어 자리에 와야 하고, (B)는 그들의 것이 무엇을 가리키는지 분명하지 않고, (C)는 부사이다.

표현 정리 feel free 마음 놓고 ~하다 cosmetic 화장품 customer 손님 store 매장 plenty of 많은 storage 창고

10. 　　　　　　　　　　　　　　　　　　　　　　　**정답 (D)**

해석 우리 최신 모델 차에 관심이 있는 사람들은 / 사전에 주문하도록 권장된다 / 받기 위해 / 무료 시승과 10퍼센트 할인 구매를

해설 interested는 동사가 아니고, p.p.이므로 빈칸에는 대명사 주어가 와야 한다. 형용사류의 수식을 받으며 '사람들'의 뜻을 갖는 (A), (D) 중에서 뒤에 단수 동사 is가 있는 것으로 보아 단수 취급하는 (D)가 정답이다. (B)는 접속사이고, (C)는 형용사류의 수식을 받지 않는다.

표현 정리 latest (가장) 최근의 encourage 권장하다 장려하다 place a preorder 사전 주문하다 free-trial offer 사전 시험 사용 purchase 구매

법칙 63 무조건 동명사

◎ 유형을 파악해 봐
1. (B)　2. (D)　3. (C)

1. 　　　　　　　　　　　　　　　　　　　　　　　**정답 (B)**

해석 Ms. Laymore는 기대한다 / 가족 모임을 갖기를 / 다가오는 연휴 동안

해설 문장에 정동사가 1개 있으므로 빈칸과 to가 결합하여 준동사가 되어야 한다. 빈칸 앞에 동명사 관용어구 looks forward to -ing가 있으므로 빈칸은 동명사인 (B)가 정답이다.

표현 정리 look forward to -ing ~을 기대하다 reunion 모임 upcoming 다가오는

2. 　　　　　　　　　　　　　　　　　　　　　　　**정답 (D)**

해석 최고 관리자는 / 어려움을 겪었다 / 할당하는데 / 필요한 자료를 / 경업부가 요청한

해설 문장에 정동사가 1개 있으므로 빈칸은 준동사 자리이다. 빈칸 앞에 동명사 관용어구 had difficulty (in) -ing가 있으므로 빈칸은 동명사인 (D)가 정답이다.

표현 정리 difficulty 어려움 allocate 할당하다 necessary 필요한 resource 재료 request 요청하다

3. 　　　　　　　　　　　　　　　　　　　　　　　**정답 (C)**

해석 Mr. Hall은 회의에 참석했다 / 초청 연설자로 / Ms. Gale's의 시간에 / 그녀가 프로젝트를 감독하느라 바빴기 때문에

해설 문장에 정동사가 1개 있으므로 빈칸은 준동사 자리이다. 빈칸 앞에 동명사 관용어구 be busy (in) -ing가 있으므로 빈칸은 동명사인 (C)가 정답이다.

표현 정리 attend 참석하다 guest speaker 초청 연사 supervise 감독하다

◎ 실전에 적용해 봐
1. (C)　2. (A)　3. (B)　4. (C)　5. (D)　6. (A)　7. (A)
8. (D)　9. (B)　10. (B)

1. 　　　　　　　　　　　　　　　　　　　　　　　**정답 (C)**

해석 Sharing Society는 자선 단체이다 / 공공복지에 기여하는 / 자금을 지원함으로써 / 저소득층 가족의 아이들에게 / 교육받도록 / 무료로

해설 be committed to 다음에는 명사 또는 -ing 형이 와야 하므로 (C)가 정답이다. 동명사의 목적어가 없다고 (A)를 답으로 하면 함정에 빠진 것이다. contribute는 1형식 동사일 때는 바로 to가 와서 '~에 기여하다'는 뜻으로 사용한다.

표현 정리 charity 자선, 자선단체 organization 단체, 조직 be committed to ~에 전념하다 public welfare 공공복지 fund 자금을 제공하다 low-income 저소득의 contribute 기여하다, 이바지하다

2. 　　　　　　　　　　　　　　　　　　　　　　　**정답 (A)**

해석 Arts Design에 입사하고 3년이 지난 후에 / Ms. Cha는 완벽하게 익숙해졌다 / 디자이너로 일하는 것에 / 회사에서

해설 빈칸은 to와 함께 쓰이는 준동사 자리이다. to와 함께 준동사가 될 수 없는 (B)는 오답이다. 앞에 동명사 관용어구 became accustomed to

-ing가 있으므로 빈칸은 동명사인 (A)가 정답이다.

표현 정리 join 입사하다 fully 완전히 become accustomed to ~에 익숙해지다

3. 정답 (B)

해석 Glorious Wedding Shop은 헌신한다 / 당신에게 최상의 서비스를 제공하는데 / 당신의 특별한 날을 위해

해설 빈칸은 to와 함께 쓰이는 준동사 자리이다. to와 함께 준동사가 될 수 없는 (C)는 오답이다. 뒤에 목적어가 있으므로 (D)도 오답이다. 빈칸 앞에 동명사 관용어구 be dedicated to -ing가 있으므로 빈칸은 동명사인 (B)가 정답이다.

표현 정리 be dedicated to ~에 헌신하다 quality 질 occasion 경우

4. 정답 (C)

해석 Dr. Bryant은 당신에게 충고했다 / 약을 복용하도록 / 만성 편두통을 치료하는데 사용되는 / 규칙적으로

해설 'be used to+-ing'는 '~하는 것에 익숙하다'는 의미이고, 'be used to+동사원형'은 '~하기 위해서 사용되다'는 의미로 이 문장에서는 '편두통을 치료하기 위해 사용하는 약'이 자연스러우므로 (C)가 정답이다.

표현 정리 advise 충고하다 take medicine 약을 먹다 chronic 만성의 migraine 편두통 regularly 정기적으로 treat 치료하다

5. 정답 (D)

해석 Mountain Outdoors는 / 야외 스포츠 장비 소매상이다 / 사람들을 장려하는 / 그들의 여가 시간을 야외 활동에 보내도록

해설 빈칸은 준동사 자리이다. 빈칸 앞에 on이 생략되어 있는 동명사 관용어구 spend time (on/in) -ing가 있으므로 빈칸은 동명사인 (D)가 정답이다.

표현 정리 outdoor 야외의 equipment 장비 retailer 소매상 encourage 장려하다 spend 소비하다

6. 정답 (A)

해석 그녀의 동료들이 아무리 열심히 그녀를 설득하려고 노력해도 / 휴식을 취하라고 / Ms. Rose는 계속해서 계획을 추진했다 / 신제품을 출시하는

해설 빈칸은 준동사 자리이다. 빈칸 앞에 동명사 관용어구 keep (on) -ing가 있으므로 빈칸은 동명사인 (A)가 정답이다.

표현 정리 no matter how 아무리 ~해도 co-worker 동료 convince 설득하다 take a break 휴식을 취하다 pursue a plan 계획을 실행하다 launch 출시하다 pursuit 추구

7. 정답 (A)

해석 그녀의 집이 두 시간 거리이기 때문에 / 그녀의 직장에서 / 차로 / Rhonda는 항상 어려움을 겪었다 / 사무실까지 통근하는데

해설 빈칸은 준동사 자리이다. 빈칸 앞에 동명사 관용어구 had a hard time (in) -ing가 있으므로 빈칸은 동명사인 (A)가 정답이다.

표현 정리 away 떨어져 work 직장 commute 통근하다 commutable 통근 가능한

8. 정답 (D)

해석 저명한 저널리스트인 Mr. Gratski는 / 세계를 여행하는데 전념했다 / 기사를 쓰기 위해 / 각기 다른 문화에 대한

해설 빈칸은 준동사 자리이다. 빈칸 앞에 동명사 관용어구 devoted oneself to -ing가 있으므로 빈칸은 동명사인 (D)가 정답이다.

표현 정리 renowned 유명한 journalist 기자 devote oneself to ~에 전념하다 article 기사

9. 정답 (B)

해석 접착 고리들은 사용된다 / 도구들을 거는데 / 보통 너무 무겁지 않은 / 벽에

해설 'be used to+동사원형'은 '~하기 위해 사용되다'라는 의미로, 이 문장에서는 '물건을 걸기 위해 사용된다'는 내용이 자연스러우므로 (B)가 정답이다.

표현 정리 self-adhesive 자기 접착성의, 풀이 묻은 hook 고리 hang 걸다 material 도구 heavy 무거운

10. 정답 (B)

해석 회사 차가 고장 났기 때문에 / 그가 가는 도중에 / 회의 장소로 / Mr. Nielson은 그가 가진 돈을 써야 했다 / 차를 수리하는데

해설 빈칸은 준동사 자리이다. 빈칸 앞에 동명사 관용어구 spend money on -ing가 있으므로 빈칸은 동명사인 (B)가 정답이다.

표현 정리 break down 고장 나다 in the middle of ~의 도중에 head 가다, 향하다 spend 소비하다

법칙 64 '번지점프' to 동사원형

◎ 유형을 파악해 봐
1. (B)   2. (C)   3. (A)

1. 정답 (B)

해석 매니저는 수정할 수 있었다 / 서류들을 / 그의 비서의 도움으로

해설 문장에 정동사가 1개 있으므로 빈칸은 준동사 자리이다. 빈칸 앞에 able이 있으므로 able과 잘 어울리는 '번지점프 to 부정사'가 필요하므로 (B)가 정답이다.

표현 정리 document 서류 secretary 비서 revise 수정하다

2. 정답 (C)

해석 10개월 간의 준비 후에 / 연출자 John Hibbert는 / 공개할 준비가 되었다 / 쇼를 / 대중에게

해설 빈칸 앞에 'be ready to 부정사'가 왔으므로 빈칸은 동사원형이 온다. (C)와 (D) 중 뒤에 목적어가 왔으므로 능동태인 (C)가 정답이다.

표현 정리 preparation 준비 director 연출자 public 대중 reveal

드러내다, 밝히다

3. 정답 (A)

해석 꼭 명심해 주세요 / 보고서들을 언급하는 것을 / Mr. Shin이 당신에게 준 / 서류 작업을 할 때

해설 빈칸 앞에 'make sure to 부정사'가 왔으므로 빈 칸에는 동사원형이 온다. refer는 보통 to와 함께 쓰여 '~를 참고하다'라는 뜻으로 사용한다. 따라서 (A)가 정답이다.

표현 정리 make sure to ~을 확실히 하다 report 보고서 paper 과제, 논문, 서류 refer 언급하다

◎ 실전에 적용해 봐

1. (A) 2. (A) 3. (D) 4. (B) 5. (B) 6 (B) 7. (B)
8. (D) 9. (D) 10. (C)

1. 정답 (A)

해석 다음 주 목요일에 비가 올 예정이기 때문에 / 오찬 회의를 위한 장소는 / 변경될 것 같다 / 건물 안 어딘가로

해설 빈칸 앞에 'be likely to 부정사'가 왔으므로 빈칸더는 동사원형 (A)가 온다. to를 전치사로 생각해 뒤에 명사나 동명사를 답으로 한다면 함정에 빠지는 것이다.

표현 정리 luncheon 오찬

2. 정답 (A)

해석 비록 그렇게 하는 것이 불가피하기는 했지만 / Mr. Cruz는 망설였다 / 개인적인 질문들을 하는 것을 / 그의 고객에게 / 그녀가 불쾌하다고 생각할 수도 있기 때문에

해설 빈칸 앞에 'be hesitant to 부정사'가 왔으므로 빈칸에는 동사원형 (A)가 와야 한다.

표현 정리 although 비록 ~이긴 하지만 necessary 필연적인, 불가피한 be hesitant to ~하는 것을 주저하다 personal 개인적인 offensive 모욕적인, 불쾌한

3. 정답 (D)

해석 직사광선으로부터 피해라 / 이 상품의 상태가 변하는 경향이 있으므로 / 기온에 따라

해설 'be apt to 동사원형'도 '번지점프 to 부정사'이다 따라서 동사원형인 (D)가 답이다. alter는 여기서 1형식 동사로 사용되었다.

표현 정리 out of ~바깥에, 범위 밖에 direct sunlight 직사광선 be apt to ~하는 경향이 있다 depending on ~에 따라 alter 변하다, 달라지다

4. 정답 (B)

해석 65살 이상인 사람들은 / 혜택을 받을 권리가 있다 / 국민연금에 의해 보장을 받음으로써

해설 entitled는 뒤에 'to 부정사'와 'to 명사' 모두 올 수 있다. 여기서는 'to 명사'가 와야 하므로 (B)가 답이며, 이때 benefits는 복수 명사이다.

표현 정리 age 나이 be entitled to ~할 권리가 있다 cover 보장하다 national pension 국민연금 benefits 혜택

5. 정답 (B)

해석 만약 Ms. Hail이 받을 수 있다면 / 지난 번과 같은 서비스를 / 그녀는 기꺼이 지불할 것이다 / 더 많은 돈을

해설 빈칸 앞에 'be willing to 부정사'가 왔으므로 빈칸에는 동사원형이 와야 하며, 뒤에 목적어가 있으므로 능동태인 (B)가 정답이다. 수동태인 (C)는 뒤에 목적어를 취하지 않으므로 오답이다.

표현 정리 be willing to 기꺼이 ~하다 pay 지불하다

6. 정답 (B)

해석 Postop Software의 매니저 일은 알려져 있기 때문에 / 대우 힘들다고 / Ms. Moon은 망설였다 / 그녀의 이력서를 제출하는 것을

해설 빈칸 앞에 'be reluctant to 부정사'가 왔으므로 빈칸에는 동사원형이 와야 하며, 뒤에 목적어가 있으므로 능동태인 (B)가 정답이다. 수동태인 (C)는 뒤에 목적어를 취하지 않으므로 오답이다.

표현 정리 demanding 힘든 be reluctant to ~을 주저하다, 망설이다 submit 제출하다 submission 제출

7. 정답 (B)

해석 꼭 유의하시오 / 관세법에 따라 / 부가세가 추가될 것이라는 것을 / 주문에 / 500달러 이상의

해설 be added to 다음에 동사원형을 답으로 고르면 틀리는 함정 문제이다. 빈칸은 명사 자리이며, order는 가산명사이므로 복수형으로 써야 한다. 따라서 (B)가 정답이다.

표현 정리 note ~에 주목하다, 주의하다 in compliance with ~에 따라 customs law 관세법 additional 추가의 tax 세금 add 더하다

8. 정답 (D)

해석 Mr. Chad의 성과가 영업부 직원들 중 최고였기 때문에 / 그는 승진할 것을 확신했다 / 이번에

해설 be certain to는 '번지점프 to 부정사' 형태이며, 'be sure to 부정사'와 같은 의미로 사용된다. 따라서 빈칸에는 동사원형 (D)가 와야 한다.

표현 정리 performance 실적, 성과 employee 직원 promotion 승진, 진급 receipt 영수증 receive 받다

9. 정답 (C)

해석 무료 셔틀 버스가 이용 가능하다 / 방문객들에게 / 신청함으로써 / 늦어도 공항 도착 1주일 전에 예약을

해설 'A is available to 사람'은 'A가 사람에게 이용 가능하다' 즉 '사람이 A를 이용할 수 있다'는 뜻이다. 따라서 사람을 뜻하는 (D)가 정답이다. to를 to 부정사의 to나 to -ing의 to로 보면 (B)와 (C)를 대입해 볼 수는 있으나, 그럴 경우 visit의 목적어가 필요한 상태가 되므로 오답이다.

표현 정리 shuttle bus 셔틀버스 available 이용 가능한 upon request 신청에 의해 make a request ~을 요청하다 at least 적어도, 최소한

10. 정답 (C)

해설 Mr. Vonin이 Kamore 사의 일에 익숙해졌기 때문에 / 그는 수락할 것 같지 않았다 / 일자리 제안을 / 그가 전에 지원했던 회사로부터의

해설 빈칸 앞에 'be likely to 부정사'가 왔으므로 빈칸은 동사원형 (C)가 정답이다.

표현 정리 get accustomed to ~에 익숙해지다 be likely to ~할 것 같다 job offer 일자리 제안 previously 이전에 apply 지원하다 accept 수락하다, 받아들이다

법칙 65 무엇을 가리키는지 알 수 있을 때는 소유대명사

◎ 유형을 파악해 봐
1. (C) 2. (D) 3. (B)

1. 정답 (C)

해설 대부분의 직원들이 이미 받았기 때문에 / 직원 ID 카드를 / Ms. Eve는 요청했다 / 그녀의 것을

해설 빈칸 앞에 타동사가 있으므로 빈칸은 목적격 자리이다. '대부분의 직원들이 직원 ID 카드를 받았으므로, Ms. Eve도 그녀 자신의 카드를 요청했다'는 해석이 자연스러우므로 빈칸에는 '그녀 자신의 카드'를 가리키는 말, 즉 '그녀의 것'이라는 소유대명사 (C)가 적절하다.

표현 정리 employee 직원 already 이미 receive 받다 request 요청하다

2. 정답 (D)

해설 Ms. Blue가 들어올리려고 했을 때 / 테이블 위의 가방을 / Mr. Browning이 그녀에게 말했다 / 그 가방이 자신의 것이라고

해설 빈칸 앞에 be 동사가 있으므로 빈칸은 보어 자리이다. 주어와 보어는 동격이 되어야 한다. the bag은 사물이고, 보기 중 사물을 가리킬 수 있는 말은 소유대명사 (D)뿐이다.

표현 정리 try to ~하려고 하다 pick up ~을 들어 올리다

3. 정답 (B)

해설 내가 지갑을 찾을 수 없기 때문에 / 어디에서도 / 누군가 분명 내 것을 잘못 알았을 것이다 / 자신의 것으로

해설 빈칸 앞에 타동사가 있으므로 빈칸은 목적격 자리이다. '내 것을 그의 것으로 오해했음이 분명하다'는 뜻이 자연스러우므로 빈칸은 소유대명사 (B)가 적절하다. (A)는 뒤에 명사가 와야 하며, '나 자신'과 '누군가'가 같은 사람일 수 없으므로 (C)는 오답이다.

표현 정리 purse 지갑 anywhere 어디에서도 must have p.p. ~했음에 틀림없다

◎ 실전에 적용해 봐
1. (B) 2. (D) 3. (C) 4. (C) 5. (D) 6. (A) 7. (A)
8. (A) 9. (A) 10. (B)

1. 정답 (B)

해설 다른 모든 사람들이 제출했다 / 그들의 제안서들을 / 프로젝트에 관한 / 내일까지인 / 하지만 Mr. Will은 제출하지 않았다 / 아직 그의 것을

해설 빈칸 앞에 타동사가 있으므로 빈칸은 목적격 자리이다. '다른 사람들은 제안서를 제출했지만 Mr. Will은 그의 것을 아직 제출하지 않았다'는 뜻이 자연스러우므로 빈칸은 소유대명사 (B)가 적절하다. '그'나 '그 자신'을 제출할 리가 없으므로 (A)와 (C)는 오답이다.

표현 정리 submit 제출하다 proposal 제안서 due ~하기로 되어 있는 yet 아직

2. 정답 (D)

해설 Ms. Stoney는 반납했다 / 보관함 키를 / 탈의실에서 가져온 / 그것들이 자신의 것이라 생각하고 / 프런트에

해설 빈칸 앞에 be 동사가 있으므로 빈칸은 보어 자리이다. they는 the locker keys를 가리킨다. 따라서 빈칸은 the locker key와 동격이 되어야 하므로 사물을 뜻하는 소유대명사 (D)가 답이다. 나머지 보기는 모두 사람을 가리키는 말이다.

표현 정리 return 반납하다 locker 개인 물품 보관함 changing room 탈의실 front desk 프런트, 안내 데스크

3. 정답 (C)

해설 대부분의 차들은 / 직원들이 모는 / 그들의 것이 아니고 / Gear Auto의 재산이다

해설 빈칸 앞에 be 동사가 있으므로 빈칸은 보어 자리이다. 주어는 'Most of the vehicles'다. 빈칸은 주어와 동격이 되어야 하므로 사물을 가리키는 말이 필요하다. 따라서 소유대명사인 (C)가 정답이다.

표현 정리 vehicle 탈 것 not A but B A가 아니고 B이다 property 재산, 소유물

4. 정답 (C)

해설 Ms. Earning은 놀랐다 / 들어서 / 신임 CEO의 집이 위치해 있다는 것을 / 그녀의 집 바로 옆에

해설 빈칸 앞에 전치사가 있으므로 빈칸은 명사 자리이다. '그녀의 집 옆에 위치해 있다'는 말이 자연스러우므로 소유대명사인 (C)가 정답이다. '그녀'와 '그녀 자체'의 옆이 아니므로 (A), (B)는 오답이다.

표현 정리 CEO 최고 경영자(= Chief Executive Officer) located ~에 위치한

5. 정답 (D)

해설 최고 관리자는 제한시켰다 / 회사 신용카드 사용을 / 그리고 직원들에게 요청했다 / 일과 직접 관련이 없는 비용은 지불하라고 / 그들 자신의 것으로

해설 빈칸 앞에 전치사가 있으므로 빈칸 뒤는 명사이고, 빈칸은 이 명사를 수식하는 소유격 자리이다. 따라서 (D)가 정답이다.

표현 정리 limit 제한하다 expense 돈, 비용 directly 직접적으로 related to ~와 관련 있는

6. 정답 (A)

해설 Mr. Gail은 혐의를 받고 있다 / 그의 박사 학위 논문을 표절한 / 다수의 연구자들이 주장함에 따라 / 그것이 많은 항목들과 구절들을 갖고 있다고 / 그들의 것에서 베낀

해설 빈칸 앞에 전치사가 있으므로 빈칸은 명사 자리이다. '그들의 것에서 베낀'으로 해석하는 것이 자연스러우므로 소유대명사인 (A)가 정답이다. 빈칸 뒤에 아무것도 없으므로 소유격 (C)는 오답이며, 그것들 자신으로부터 복사한 것이 아니므로 재귀대명사 (D)도 오답이다.

표현 정리 be suspected of ~의 혐의를 받다 plagiarize 표절하다 doctoral thesis 박사 학위 논문 claim 주장하다 clause 절, 조항, 항목 phrase 구, 구절

7. 정답 (A)

해설 대부분의 다른 제안서들이 / 계약에 관한 / 채굴 사업을 위한 / 오직 그것의 이득에만 초점을 둔 반면에 / 나의 것은 언급한다 / 불리한 점 또한

해설 빈칸은 주어 자리이므로 소유격인 (C)는 오답이다. 빈칸 뒤 동사 mention에 s가 붙어 있으므로 1인칭인 (D)도 오답이다. '다른 제안서들이 이득에만 초점을 둔 반면 나의 것은 불리한 점까지 언급하고 있다'는 해석이 자연스러우므로 소유대명사 (A)가 정답이다. 재귀대명사 (B)는 단독으로 주어 자리에 오지 않는다.

표현 정리 proposal 제안서 contract 계약 regarding ~에 관하여 mining 채굴, 광업 focus on ~에 초점을 맞추다 benefit 혜택, 이득 disadvantage 불리한 점, 난점 as well ~도, 또한

8. 정답 (A)

해설 Joan의 팀은 자랑스러웠다 / 최고 관리자가 거절하고 / 모든 다른 제안서들을 / 진행하기로 결정해서 / 그들의 것을

해설 빈칸 앞에 전치사가 있으므로 빈칸은 명사 자리이다. 빈칸 뒤에 아무것도 없으므로 소유격 (B)는 오답이다. '다른 모든 제안서들을 거절하고, 그들의 것을 진행하기로 했다'는 해석이 자연스러우므로 소유대명사 (A)가 정답이다.

표현 정리 proud 자랑스러워하는 reject 거부하다, 거절하다 proposal 제안서 proceed 진행하다

9. 정답 (A)

해설 어떤 지갑도 / 분실물 보관소에 있는 / Mr. Penning의 것이 아니다 / 하지만 그는 찾았다 / 그의 것을 / 사무실 근처 건물에서

해설 빈칸 앞에 타동사가 있으므로 빈칸은 목적어 자리이다. '그의 지갑을 찾았다'는 해석이 자연스러우므로 소유대명사 (A)가 정답이다. 다른 누군가의 것을 찾은 것이 아니므로 (B)는 오답이며, 그 자신을 찾은 것도 아니므로 (C)도 역시 오답이다.

표현 정리 wallet 지갑 Lost and Found Office 분실물 보관소 belong to ~소유이다, ~에 속하다

10. 정답 (B)

해설 Ms. Wells는 항상 자신의 동료들이 자신을 태워주게 한다 / 직장까지 / 왜냐하면 너무 비쌌기 때문에 / 그녀 자신의 차를 구입하기에는

해설 빈칸 앞에 전치사가 있으므로 빈칸은 명사 자리이다. 빈칸 뒤에 아무것도 없으므로 소유격 (A)는 오답이고, of one's own은 '자기 자신의'라는 뜻이므로 (B)가 정답이다. (C)는 '그녀의 차들 중 하나의 차를 사는' 것에 다소 어색하다.

표현 정리 co-worker 동료 drive 태워주다 workplace 직장 costly 많은 돈이 드는

법칙 6E 보기에 미래완료시제나 would have pp가 오면 주로 오답

◎ 유형을 파악해 봐
1. (D) 2. (D) 3. (D)

1. 정답 (D)

해설 만약 방문객들이 허용된다면 / 그들은 사진을 찍는 것이 가능할 텐데 / 고대 유적들의

해설 보기가 모두 정동사이며, 수일치가 되어 있고, 능동태이므로 시제 문제이다. 시제 문제는 반드시 단서가 있다. 'If S were ~'의 형태가 등장하면 가정법 과거이며, 주절에는 would[should, could, might] 동사원형이 온다. 따라서 (D)가 정답이다.

표현 정리 take photographs 사진을 찍다 ancient 고대의 monument 기념물

2. 정답 (D)

해설 만약 Ms. Hudson이 알았더라면 / 오늘 회의가 있었다는 것을 / 그녀는 회의실을 예약했었을 텐데 / 사전에

해설 보기가 모두 정동사이며, 수일치가 되어 있고, 능동태이므로 시제 문제이다. 'If S had p.p. ~' 형태가 등장하면 가정법 과거완료이며, 주절에는 would[should, could, might] have p.p.가 와야 한다. 따라서 (D)가 정답이다.

표현 정리 meeting room 회의실 in advance 사전에, 미리 reserve 예약하다

3. 정답 (D)

해설 Mr. Wilson이 공항에 도착할 때쯤 / 리무진은 도착했을 것이다 / 그를 픽업하기 위해

해설 보기가 모두 정동사이며, 수일치가 되어 있고, 능동태이므로 시제 문제이다. 'by the time S+V(현재시제)'의 형태가 등장하면 주절에는 미래완료시제를 쓰므로 (D)가 정답이다.

표현 정리 arrive 도착하다 airport 공항 limousine 리무진, 대형 승용차

◎ 실전에 적용해 봐
1. (B) 2. (C) 3. (A) 4. (C) 5. (A) 6. (C) 7. (B)
8. (B) 9. (D) 10. (A)

1. 정답 (E)

해설 만약 Ms. Halland가 끝냈더라면 / 그녀의 프로젝트를 / Mr. Raymond가 출장을 떠나기 전에 / 그녀는 받을 수 있었을 텐데 / 그의 디

드백을 / 프로젝트에 관한

해설 보기가 모두 정동사이며, 수일치가 되어 있고, 능동태이므로 시제 문제이다. 'If S had p.p. ~' 형태가 등장하면 가정법 과거완료이며, 주절에는 would[should, could, might] have p.p.가 와야 하므로 (B)가 정답이다.

표현 정리 business trip 출장 receive 받다 feedback 피드백

2. 정답 (C)

해설 그녀의 매니저가 비행기를 탈 수 없었기 때문에 / 제시간에 / Ms. Lee는 매니저에게 말했다 / 세미나에 참석할 것이라고 / 그녀 혼자 / 내일

해설 시제 문제 같지만 그 전에 능동태 자리인지, 수동태 자리인지부터 확인한다. 목적어가 있으므로 능동태인 (C)가 답이다. 나머지 보기들은 모두 수동태이다. 잘 모르겠다면 가정법이나 미래완료형은 정답으로 잘 출제되지 않는다는 것을 기억하자.

표현 정리 on time 제 시간에 seminar 세미나 by oneself 혼자 attend 참석하다

3. 정답 (A)

해설 최고 관리자가 그의 출장에서 돌아왔을 때쯤 / 마케팅부는 끝냈을 것이다 / 고객 설문조사를 / 그에게 제출할

해설 보기가 모두 정동사이며, 수일치가 되어 있고, 능동태이므로 시제 문제이다. 'by the time S+V(현재시제)' 형태가 등장하면 주절에는 미래완료 시제를 쓰므로 (A)가 정답이다.

표현 정리 return 돌아오다 business trip 출장 customer survey 고객 여론조사 submit 제출하다 complete 끝내다

4. 정답 (C)

해설 만약 Pioneer Bank가 / 성공적으로 유지한다면 / 현재의 이윤 폭을 / 은행은 열 것이다 / 다른 지점을 / 다른 도시에

해설 보기가 모두 정동사이며, 수일치가 되어 있고, 능동태이므로 시제 문제이다. 'If S+동사원형 ~' 형태가 등장하면 가정법 현재이며, 주절에는 미래시제가 와야 하므로 (C)가 정답이다.

표현 정리 successfully 성공적으로 maintain 유지하다 current 현재의 profit margins 이윤 폭 branch 지점

5. 정답 (A)

해설 만약 판매원들이 알았더라면 / 몇 개의 상품들이 떨어져 가고 있다는 것을 / 그들은 매니저들에게 알렸을 것이다.

해설 보기가 모두 정동사이며, 수일치가 되어 있고, 능동태이므로 시제 문제이다. 주절에는 'S would[should, could, might] have p.p. ~' 형태가 왔으므로, 부사절에는 'If S had p.p. ~' 형태의 가정법 과거완료가 오므로 (A)가 정답이다.

표현 정리 sales clerk 판매원 run low on ~이 적어지다 item 물품 notify 알리다

6. 정답 (C)

해설 최근 변동은 / 휘발유 가격의 / 영향을 미쳤다 / 모든 상품들 가격에 / 항구로부터 운송되는 / 각 지역 매장으로

해설 보기는 모두 정동사이며, 수일치가 되어 있다. 빈칸 뒤에 목적어를 취하므로 수동태인 (A)와 (D)는 오답이다. 미래 시점이 딱히 제시되지 않았으므로 (C)가 정답이다. 미래완료시제는 거의 정답이 되지 않으므로 오답이라고 생각해도 좋다.

표현 정리 recent 최근의 fluctuation 변동 affect 영향을 미치다 transport 수송하다, 이동시키다 port 항구 region 지역

7. 정답 (B)

해설 Ms. Hall은 절약했을 것이다 / 4,000달러 이상을 혼자 / 예약할 때쯤에는 / 괌으로 가는 패키지 투어를

해설 보기가 모두 정동사이며, 수일치가 되어 있고, 능동태이므로 시제 문제이다. 'by the time S+V(현재시제)' 형태가 등장하면 주절에는 미래완료 시제를 쓰므로 (B)가 정답이다.

표현 정리 by oneself 혼자 book 예약하다 package tour 패키지 여행

8. 정답 (B)

해설 만약 Mr. Campbell이 통보 받았다면 / 늘어난 보험 혜택에 대해 / 그가 관심 있어했던 / 그는 아마 구입했을 텐데 / 망설임 없이

해설 보기가 모두 정동사이며, 수일치가 되어 있다. 목적어가 있으므로 수동태인 (C)와 (D)는 오답이다. 'If S had p.p. ~' 형태가 등장하면, 가정법 과거완료이며, 주절에는 would[should, could, might] have p.p.가 와야 하므로 (B)가 정답이다.

표현 정리 inform 알리다 increased 증가한 benefit 이익, 혜택 insurance 보험 hesitation 망설임, 주저

9. 정답 (D)

해설 그가 알고 있었더라면 / 그의 직업이 수반한다는 것을 / 상당수의 출장을 / 매년 / 그는 지원하지 않았을 텐데 / 그 일에

해설 가정법 과거완료 도치구문이다. 따라서 빈칸은 p.p. 자리이므로 (D)가 정답이다. 나머지는 had와 함께 쓰지 않으므로 오답이다.

표현 정리 involve 포함하다 quite a few 상당수의 business trip 출장 apply for ~에 지원하다

10. 정답 (A)

해설 안전 검사관은 상품들을 신고했다 / 생산 날짜가 위조된

해설 시제 문제이다. 위조된 것이 신고한 것보다 먼저 일어난 일이므로 과거보다 더 먼저 일어난 일을 묘사할 때 쓰는 과거완료시제 (A)가 답이다.

표현 정리 inspector 조사관 report 보고하다, 신고하다 product 상품 manufacture 제조, 생산 forge 위조하다

법칙 67 고득점을 위한 기타 명사절 접속사

◎ 유형을 파악해 봐
1. (B)   2. (C)   3. (C)

1. 정답 (B)

해설 인센티브의 양은 달려 있다 / 당신의 부서 성과가 얼마나 좋으냐에 / 한 해 동안

해설 문장에 정동사가 2개 있으므로 빈칸은 접속사 자리이다. 빈칸 앞에 전치사가 있으므로 뒤에 오는 절은 명사절이며, 명사절 종속사가 아닌 (D)는 오답이다. (D)는 3형식 동사 뒤에 올 때에만 명사절로 쓰인다. 빈칸 뒤에 비정상적인 어순의 문장이 왔으므로 (B)가 정답이다. 〈how+형/부 S+V〉

표현 정리 incentive 장려금 depends on ~에 달려 있다 department 부서 perform 수행하다

2. 정답 (C)

해설 프로그램 매니저는 결정해야 한다 / 어떤 프로젝트에 / 더 많은 자금을 배정할지 / 이번 주에

주에

해설 문장에 정동사가 2개 있으므로 빈칸은 접속사 자리이다. 빈칸 앞에 타동사가 있으므로 뒤에 오는 절은 명사절이다. 빈칸 뒤 to는 '주어+조동사'를 줄여 쓴 말로, project가 주어보다 앞으로 도치되어 있는 비정상적인 어순이 왔다. 이렇게 자신이 수식하는 목적어를 앞으로 당겨 사용하는 의문형용사 (C)가 정답이다. (A)와 (D)는 완전한 문장과 쓰이는 명사절 접속사이고, (B)는 뒤에 동사가 바로 와야 한다.

표현 정리 decide 결정하다 give 주다 fund 자금

3. 정답 (C)

해설 매니저는 결정할 것이다 / 누구의 제안이 채택될 것인지 / 다음 마케팅 계획을 위해

해설 문장에 정동사가 2개 있으므로 빈칸은 접속사 자리이고, 빈칸 앞에 타동사가 있으므로 뒤에 오는 절은 명사절이다. 빈칸 뒤 명사를 수식해 주는 의문형용사 (C)가 정답이다. (B)는 뒤에 바로 동사가 오므로 오답이다.

표현 정리 decide 결정하다 suggestion 제안 adopt 채택하다 plan 계획

◎ 실전에 적용해 봐
1. (B) 2. (D) 3. (D) 4. (D) 5. (B) 6. (A) 7. (A)
8. (D) 9. (D) 10. (C)

1. 정답 (B)

해설 계약서는 명확하게 해야 한다 / 어떤 방식으로 비용이 충당될지 / 상품 배송에 지연이 있을 경우에

해설 빈칸은 접속사 자리이며, 빈칸 앞에 타동사가 있으므로 뒤에 오는 절은 명사절이다. 빈칸 뒤에 완전한 문장이 왔으므로 (B)가 정답이다. (A)와 (D)는 불완전한 문장이 오므로 오답이다.

표현 정리 contract 계약서, 계약 clarify 명확하게 하다 cost 비용 case 사건

2. 정답 (D)

해설 Trust Investments는 당신이 결정하는 것을 도와 줄 수 있다 / 어떤 투자 프로그램을 선택해야 하는 / 당신이 최고의 이익을 올리기 위해

해설 빈칸은 접속사 자리이며, 빈칸 앞에 타동사가 있으므로 뒤에 오는 절은 명사절이다. 빈칸 뒤에 to choose의 to는 '주어+조동사'를 줄여 쓴 말로 investment program이 주어보다 앞으로 도치되어 있는 비정상적인 어순이 왔다. 이렇게 자신이 수식하는 목적어를 앞으로 당겨 사용하는 의문형용사 (D)가 정답이다. (A)와 (C)는 뒤에 정상적인 어순의 완전한 문장이 오므로 오답이다.

표현 정리 determine 알아내다, 밝히다 investment 투자 interests 이익

3. 정답 (C)

해설 Gam 사의 관리직은 오랫동안 채워지지 않은 상태로 남아 있다 / 왜냐하면 CEO가 여전히 확신하지 못하기 때문에 / 누가 그 일을 가장 잘 다룰 것인지

해설 빈칸은 접속사 자리이며, unsure 뒤에는 전치사가 생략되었다. (A), (C), (D) 모두 빈칸인 주어 자리에 올 수 있으나, 일을 가장 잘 다루는 것은 사람이므로 (D)가 정답이다.

표현 정리 position 자리, 위치 unfilled 비어 있는 unsure 확신하지 못하는 handle 다루다

4. 정답 (D)

해설 우리 판매 팀의 정책의 일부는 설명한다 / 고객 불만을 어떻게 다루어야 하는지를 / 고객들에게 어떠한 불편함도 끼치지 않기 위해

해설 빈칸은 접속사 자리이다. 빈칸 앞에 타동사가 있으므로 뒤에 오는 절은 명사절이다. 빈칸 뒤에 있는 문장이 완전하므로 (D)가 정답이다. (A)는 뒤에 불완전한 문장이 와야 하므로 오답이다.

표현 정리 policy 정책 describe 묘사하다 complaint 불만 inconvenience 불편

5. 정답 (B)

해설 마지막 팀이 그들의 발표를 끝냈을 때 / 최고 관리자들은 결정해야 한다 / 어느 팀이 상을 받을 것인지 / 그들의 평가를 기초로

해설 빈칸은 접속사 자리이다. 빈칸 앞에 타동사가 있으므로 뒤에 오는 절은 명사절이다. 빈칸 뒤에 온 team은 가산명사이므로 단수로 쓰일 경우에 관사를 필요로 한다. 그러나 오직 명사만 온 것으로 보아 의문형용사로 쓰인 (B)가 정답이다.

표현 정리 presentation 발표 decide 결정하다 receive 받다 evaluation 평가

6. 정답 (A)

해설 Mr. Wilson은 조언을 구했다 / 적절한 팀 전략을 짜는 방법에 대한 / 협동 작업을 위한 / 워크숍 강사로부터

해설 일단 software는 불가산 명사이므로, 복수명사와 사용하는 these나 among은 소거한다. 의문사 뒤 주어와 조동사는 to로 줄여쓸 수 있으므로 which software we will install next가 어울릴 지, how software we will install next가 어울릴 지를 생각해본다. choose는 선택사항과 어울리는 동사이므로 '어떤 소프트웨어를 설치할 지'라는 말이 자연스럽다.

표현 정리 formulate 표현하다, 만들어 내다 appropriate 적절한 strategy 전략 collaborative 협동적인

7. 정답 (A)

해설 운영시스템 제공자인 Ubiquitous 사와의 계약이 만료되었을 때 / 우리 회사는 선택해야 했다 / 다음에 어떤 소프트웨어를 설치할지

해설 문장에 정동사가 2개 있으므로 빈칸은 접속사 자리이며, 빈칸 뒤에 온 to는 '주어+조동사'를 줄여 쓴 말로 software가 주어보다 앞으로 도치되어 있는 비정상적인 어순이다. 이렇게 자신이 수식하는 목적어를 앞으로 당겨 사용하는 의문형용사 (A)가 정답이다. (C)는 정상적 어순의 완전한 문장이 오므로 오답이다.

표현 정리 contract 계약 operating 운영의 provider 제공자 expire 만료되다

8. 정답 (D)

해설 회의에 초청된 연설자는 이야기했다 / 휴대폰 시장이 어떻게 바뀔지 / 미래에

해설 문장에 정동사가 2개 있으므로 빈칸은 접속사 자리이며, 빈칸 앞에 전치사가 있으므로 뒤에 오는 절은 명사절이다. '휴대폰 시장이 어떻게 바뀔지'가 자연스러우므로 완전한 문장과 같이 쓰이는 접속사 (D)가 정답이다.

9. 정답 (D)

해설 최고 관리자는 요청했다 / Ms. Carr에게 사무용품을 주문하도록 / 온라인에서 모두 팔린 / 하지만 명시하지 않았다 / 어떤 매장에서 주문해야 하는지

해설 문장에 정동사가 2개 있으므로 빈칸은 접속사 자리이며, 빈칸 뒤에 온 to는 '주어+조동사'를 줄여 쓴 말로 store가 주어보다 앞으로 도치되어 있는 비정상적인 어순이다. 이렇게 자신이 수식하는 목적어를 앞으로 당겨 사용하는 의문형용사 (D)가 정답이다. specify를 보고 바로 that을 골랐다면 함정에 빠진 것이다. 전치사 from의 목적어가 빠진 것에 주의하자.

표현 정리 office supply 사무용품 run out 다 떨어지다 specify 명시하다

10. 정답 (C)

해설 마케팅 부장은 / 곧 결정할 것이다 / 누구의 보고서가 제출될 것인지를 / CEO가 검토하도록

해설 문장에 정동사가 2개 있으므로 빈칸은 접속사 자리이며, 빈칸 앞에 타동사가 있으므로 뒤에 오는 절은 명사절이다. (A), (B), (D)는 주어나 목적어가 없는 불완전한 문장과 쓰이므로 오답이다. '누구의 보고서가 제출될 것인지를 결정할 것이다'가 자연스러우므로 의문형용사 (C)가 정답이다.

표현 정리 Marketing Department 마케팅 부서 determine 결정하다 report 보고서

법칙 68 고득점을 위한 기타 형용사절 접속사

◎ 유형을 파악해 봐
1. (B) 2. (C) 3. (A)

1. 정답 (B)

해설 공무원이 / 건축 허가증을 살펴 볼 / 공사장을 방문할 것이다 / 오늘

해설 빈칸 앞에 온 official은 to를 뒤에 데리고 다니는 명사가 아니므로, 이 to는 shown 다음에 와야 하는 to이며, official이 선행사이고 빈칸부터 shown to까지가 형용사절이다. 전치사 to의 목적어가 빠져 있으므로 (B)가 정답이다.

표현 정리 government official 공무원 permit 허가증 conduction 수행 site 장소

2. 정답 (C)

해설 Ms. Clark은 Mr. Shaw에게 전화했다 / 일요일 오후에 / 보통 그가 집에 있는 때인

해설 빈칸 뒤에 완전한 문장이 왔으므로 관계부사 자리이다. 선행사가 시간을 나타내므로 시간을 수식하는 관계부사인 (C)가 정답이다. (D)가 오면 부사절이 되는데 주절과 시제가 맞지 않는다.

3. 정답 (A)

해설 Orlando는 / 세계에서 가장 유명 관광지 중 한 곳이 위치한 / 방문한다 / 많은 여행객들이

해설 선행사가 장소이고, 빈칸 뒤에 완전한 문장이 왔으므로 관계부사 where가 필요하며, 따라서 (A)가 정답이다.

◎ 실전에 적용해 봐
1. (D) 2. (D) 3. (A) 4. (A) 5. (C) 6. (C) 7. (A)
8. (D) 9. (B) 10. (A)

1. 정답 (D)

해설 요리책은 받았다 / 독자들로부터 매우 긍정적인 피드백을 / 그 중 몇몇은 심지어 전문 요리사였다

해설 빈칸은 접속사 중에서도 전치사 뒤에 올 수 있는 형용사절 접속사 자리이다. 선행사인 readers를 받는 관계대명사 중 전치사의 목적격 자리이므로 (D)가 답이다. (A)는 전치사 뒤에 쓸 수 없고, (B)는 부사절 접속사이며, (C)는 명사절 접속사이다.

표현 정리 recipe book 요리책 receive 받았다 positive 긍정적인

2. 정답 (D)

해설 Mr. McKnight의 새 발명품에 관한 발표에서 / 이유를 설명했다 / 왜 이것이 많은 젊은 고객들을 불러 모을지에 대한

해설 빈칸 뒤에 완전한 문장이 왔고, 선행사가 이유를 나타내므로 이유를 수식하는 관계부사인 (D)가 정답이다.

표현 정리 presentation 발표 invention 발명품 explain 설명하다 attract 마음을 끌다

3. 정답 (A)

해설 홍보용 증정 행사는 / 토요일 오후에 Max Superstore에서 정기적으로 열린다 / 고객들이 매장에 가장 많이 방문할 때인

해설 빈칸 뒤에 완전한 문장이 왔고, 선행사가 시간을 나타내므로 시간을 수식하는 관계부사인 (A)가 정답이다. (B)와 (D)는 접속사가 아니며, (C)는 접속사의 기능이 있어 쓸 수 있으나 의미상 적절하지 않다.

표현 정리 promotional 홍보의 giveaways 증정품, 경품 regularly 정기적으로 hold 개최하다

4. 정답 (A)

해설 우리의 오프라인 매장을 방문하시오 / 당신이 관심 있어하는 상품들을 20퍼센트 낮은 가격으로 구매할 수 있는 / 온라인 매장에 비해

해설 the items와 you 사이에는 목적격 관계대명사가 생략되어 있다. 따라서 you are interested in은 형용사절이므로 빼낸다. 빈칸 앞은 선행사가 장소이고, 빈칸 뒤는 the items가 주어, can be purchased가 동사인 완전한 문장으로 빈칸에는 관계부사 where가 필요하다.

5. 정답 (C)

해설 Mr. Morrison은 사무용품 구매를 담당했다 / 그런데 그것들 모두 구매될 수 있다 / 회사 근처 매장에서

해설 빈칸은 접속사 역할을 하면서 대명사 역할을 할 수 있는 관계대명사 자리이므로 (C)가 정답이다. (B)는 전치사 뒤에 쓰지 않는다.

표현 정리 in charge of ~를 담당하는 office supplies 사무용품

6. 정답 (C)

해설 영화 감독 Derick Brown은 결정했다 / 오늘 자정에 Star Avenue 에서 영화를 찍기로 / 거리에 사람이 많이 없을 때인

해설 빈칸 뒤에 완전한 문장이 왔고, 선행사가 시간을 나타내므로 시간을 수식하는 관계부사인 (C)가 정답이다. (A)와 (D)는 명사절 접속사이므로 앞에 3형식 동사가 있어야 하고, (B)는 명사절, 형용사절이 가능하나 뒤의 문장이 불완전할 때 사용한다.

표현 정리 movie director 영화감독 shoot 촬영하다 film 영화 midnight 자정

7. 정답 (A)

해설 공지가 참석자들에게 보내졌다 / 그런데 그들 모두 제시간에 올 것을 요청 받았다 / 세미나를 위해 / 늦은 입장이 허락되지 않기 때문에

해설 빈칸은 접속사 역할을 하면서 대명사 역할을 동시에 하는 관계대명사가 와야 한다. 또한 전치사의 목적격 자리이기도 하므로 (A)가 답이다. (B)는 전치사 뒤에 쓸 수 없으므로 오답이다.

표현 정리 notice 공지 entrance 입장 permit 허락하다

8. 정답 (D)

해설 Alkemi Manufacturing은 계획이다 / 생산 공장이 광산 주변에 위치하도록 할 / 지하자원이 풍부한

해설 빈칸 뒤에 완전한 문장이 있고, 선행사가 장소를 나타내므로 장소를 수식하는 관계부사인 (D)가 정답이다.

표현 정리 locate 위치시키다 production plants 생산 공장 mine 광산 underground resources 지하자원 abundant 풍부한

9. 정답 (B)

해설 누구도 완전히 알지 못했다 / Mr. Hunt가 어떻게 새 CEO가 되었는지 / Murray 사에 입사한지 5년 만에 / 하지만 그의 업적은 인상적이었다

해설 빈칸 앞이 3형식 동사, 빈칸 뒤가 완전한 문장이 왔으므로 명사절 접속사 자리이다. (B)는 접속사는 아니지만 the way 다음에는 관계부사 how가 생략되었으므로 (B)가 정답이다.

표현 정리 accomplishment 업적 impressive 인상적인

10. 정답 (A)

해설 IT 벤처 기업들에게 / Central Valley는 이상적인 장소이다 / 다양한 기술 장치를 개발하기 위한

해설 빈칸 앞에 있는 place는 in을 뒤에 데리고 다니는 명사가 아니고, devices 다음에 와야 하는 in이다. place가 선행사이고, 빈칸부터 devices in까지가 형용사 절이다. 전치사 in의 목적어가 빠져있으므로 (A)가 정답이다. where는 in which와 같은 뜻이다. how는 장소 선행사와 상관이 없고, any는 접속사가 아니다.

표현 정리 ideal 이상적인 develop 개발하다 various 다양한 device 장치

법칙 69 고득점을 위한 기타 전치사

◎ 유형을 파악해 봐
1. (B)   2. (C)   3. (D)

1. 정답 (B)

해설 날씨가 나쁠 경우에 / 야외 콘서트는 쉽게 옮겨질 수 있다 / 실내 홀로

해설 문장에 정동사가 한 개 있으므로 빈칸은 전치사 자리이다. (C)는 접속사, (D)는 부사이므로 오답이다. (A)는 '~와는 반대로', (B)는 '~인 경우에' 이므로 대입해 해석해 보면 '날씨가 나쁠 경우에'가 자연스러우므로 (B)가 정답이다.

표현 정리 outdoor 야외의 easily 쉽게 indoor 실내의 in the event of ~인 경우에

2. 정답 (C)

해설 Sound Electronics는 / 고품질 오디오를 생산하는 회사이다 / 경쟁력 있는 가격에

해설 빈칸 뒤에 competitive prices가 왔다. (A)는 주로 시점이나 기간과 함께 쓰이고, (B)와 (D) 역시 시간이나 장소와 주로 어울리므로 제외한다. (C)도 시간이나 장소와 함께 사용하지만 가격 앞에도 쓰이므로 (C)가 정답이다.

표현 정리 company 회사 quality 양 competitive 경쟁력 있는

3. 정답 (D)

해설 사무용품이 종종 다 떨어지기 때문에 / 짧은 시간에 / 유의하시오 / 당신이 그것들을 주문하도록 / 미리

해설 전치사 어휘 문제로 뒤에 advance와 잘 어울리는 전치사가 와야 한다. in advance는 '사전에, 미리'라는 뜻으로 외워두면 좋다. '미리 사무용품을 주문하라'는 해석이 자연스러우므로 (D)가 정답이다. (A)는 시간이나 장소 앞에 오며, (B)는 이유, 용도, 대상, 목적의 전치사이다.

표현 정리 office supply 사무용품 run out 떨어지다 order 주문하다 in advance 미리

◎ 실전에 적용해 봐
1. (D)   2. (A)   3. (C)   4. (D)   5. (B)   6. (A)   7. (B)
8. (D)   9. (A)   10. (A)

1.   정답 (D)

해설 그의 표정으로 판단할 때 / 매니저는 만족했음에 틀림없다 / 직원들의 업무성과에

해설 전치사 어휘 문제로 해석을 통해 가장 자연스러운 전치사를 정답으로 골라야 한다. (A)는 '표정 때문에,' (B)는 '표정과 반대로,' (C)는 '표정에도 불구하고'라는 뜻으로 모두 문맥에 어울리지 않는다. '표정으로 판단컨대, 매니저는 만족했음에 틀림없다'라는 뜻이 자연스러우므로 (D)가 정답이다.

표현 정리 satisfy 만족시키다 performance 업무, 성과 judging from ~으로 판단하건대

2.   정답 (A)

해설 갑작스러운 정전이 발생할 경우 / 모든 전원을 뽑고 / 다시 꽂으시오 / 적어도 10초 기다린 후에

해설 빈칸 뒤에 명사구가 왔으므로 접속사인 (B), (C)와 전명구인 (D)는 오답이다. '갑작스러운 정전이 발생할 경우'라는 해석이 자연스러우므로 (A)가 정답이다.

표현 정리 blackout 정전 unplug 플러그를 뽑다 at least 적어도 in the event of ~인 경우에

3.   정답 (C)

해설 ABT Air는 제공한다 / 다양한 종류의 채널을 / 하지만 다른 방송업계와 다르게 / 그것은 프로그램을 방송한다 / 다른 언어들로

해설 전치사 어휘 문제로 문맥에서 가장 자연스러운 전치사를 정답으로 고른다. (A)는 '다른 방송사를 제외하고,' (B)는 '다른 방송사를 따라,' (D)는 '다른 방송사 없이'라는 어색한 해석이 되므로 오답이다. '다른 방송사와 다르게 다양한 채널을 제공한다'라는 해석이 자연스러우므로 (C)가 정답이다.

표현 정리 air 방송하다 a wide selection of 매우 다양한 broadcasting 방송 업계

4.   정답 (D)

해설 Bleam 사를 방문기 위해서는 / 지하철을 타고 Bowrail 역에서 내리시오 / Bleam 사 건물 바로 맞은 편에 있는

해설 전치사 어휘 문제로 get과 어울리는 동시에 뒤에 있는 장소와도 어울리는 전치사를 골라야 한다. (A)와 (C)는 전치사이며, 뒤에 at이라는 전치사가 있어 또 나올 수 없다. (B)와 (D)는 부사로 get과 덩어리로 사용될 수 있고, 자동사로의 기능도 있어 뒤에 전명구 at Bowrail Station이 올 수 있다. 전철을 타고 내린다는 어울림이 있으므로 (D)가 정답이다. (B)는 침대 등에서 일어난다는 뜻이다.

5.   정답 (B)

해설 고객들이 선호하는 것을 고려할 때 / 작은 패키지로 되어 있는 상품들을 / 휴대하기 쉬운 / 우리는 패키지 디자인을 바꿔야 할 것이다

해설 that과 잘 어울리는 것은 (B)와 (C)인데, '고객들이 선호하기 위해서, 우리는 바꿔야 한다'라는 해석보다는 '고객들이 선호한다는 것을 고려할 때, 우리는 바꿔야 한다'는 말이 자연스럽다. 따라서 (B)가 정답이다. 나머지는 that과 함께 쓰지 않으며, given that은 접속사로 본다.

표현 정리 prefer 선호한다

6.   정답 (A)

해설 당신은 또한 상품의 다른 색상도 확인하고 싶을지 모른다 / 왜냐하면 현재 이용 가능하기 때문에 / 파랑, 오렌지, 그리고 핑크색으로도

해설 전치사 in은 색깔이나 맛, 치수 등과 잘 어울리므로 (A)가 답이다.

표현 정리 item 상품 currently 현재 available 가능한

7.   정답 (B)

해설 우리는 Ms. Admas 당신에게 진심으로 사과한다 / HK Corps의 CEO를 대표해 / 현재 당신의 전화를 받을 수 없는

해설 빈칸은 전치사 자리이다. 'CEO를 대표해 사과한다'는 해석이 자연스러우므로 (B)가 정답이다.

표현 정리 sincere 진실된 currently 현재 due to ~때문에

8.   정답 (D)

해설 최근 조사에 따르면 / 고객들은 중요시하는 것 같다 / 저렴한 가격보다 질을 / 상품을 구매할 때

해설 빈칸은 명사와 명사를 이어주는 전치사 자리로 접속사인 (B)는 오답이다. '저렴한 가격 때문에 질을 중요시한다'라기 보다는 '저렴한 가격보다 질을 중요시한다'라는 내용이 자연스러우므로 (D)가 정답이다. (A)는 '~를 제외하고 다른'이란 뜻이므로 역시 자연스럽지 못하다.

표현 정리 according ~에 따르면 survey 조사 customer 고객 quality 품질

9.   정답 (A)

해설 업무 조건 면에서 / Goodwill 사는 보장한다 / 직원들이 복지 혜택을 받을 것을 / 경쟁사가 제공하는 복지보다 나은

해설 빈칸은 전치사 자리이다. '업무 조건 면에서 Goodwill 사는 나은 복지를 보장한다'라는 의미이므로 (A)가 정답이다. (C)는 부사이다.

표현 정리 condition 조건 ensure 보장하다 benefit 복지혜택 in terms of ~면에서

10.   정답 (A)

해설 증가하는 수요에 대비해 / 혁신적인 자동차 디자인에 대한 / Wheel Auto는 고용했다 / 더 많은 자동차 디자이너를

해설 빈칸은 전치사 자리로 전체적인 내용이 원인과 결과의 흐름이다. '늘어나는 수요에 대비해, Wheel Auto는 디자이너를 고용했다'라는 해석이 자연스러우므로 (A)가 정답이다. (B)는 전치사로 쓰일 때 뒤에 과거 시점이 나와야 한다.

표현 정리 innovative 혁신적인 hire 고용하다 in response to ~에

대응해

법칙 70 목표[계획] is to 부정사

◎ 유형을 파악해 봐
1. (A)   2. (D)   3. (C)

1. 정답 (A)

해석 Raymond Holdings의 목표는 / 고객들의 필요를 충족시키는 것이다 / 완벽히

해설 문장에 정동사가 없으므로 빈칸은 정동사 자리이다. 주어 자리에 '목표, 목적, 계획'을 나타내는 단어가 있을 때 동격으로 to 부정사를 필요로 하는 경우로, 여기서는 (A)가 정답이다. (B)는 수동태이므로 뒤에 목적어를 가질 수 없고, (C)는 수일치가 되지 않았으므로 오답이다.

표현 정리 goal 목표 need 욕구 to the fullest 완벽하게 meet 충족시키다

2. 정답 (D)

해석 주지하시오 / 이 조사의 목적은 / 오직 고객들의 만족도를 분석하는 것임을

해설 문장에 접속사가 1개 있으므로 빈칸은 정동사 자리이다. 주어 자리에 '목적'을 나타내는 단어가 있을 때 동격으로 to 부정사를 필요로 하는 경우로 (D)가 정답이다. (B)는 수일치가 되지 않았다.

표현 정리 note 주지하다, 주목하다 purpose 목적 survey 조사 analyze 분석하다

3. 정답 (C)

해석 우리 팀의 계획은 / 다가오는 프로젝트에 관한 / 윤곽을 논의하는 것이다 / 수요일에 / 그리고 / 다음 주까지 초안을 완성하는 것이다

해설 문장에 정동사가 없으므로 빈칸은 정동사 자리이다. 주어 자리에 '계획'을 나타내는 단어가 있을 때 동격으로 to 부정사를 필요로 하는 경우로 (C)가 정답이다.

표현 정리 upcoming 다가오는 outline 윤곽 draft 초안 discuss 논의하다

◎ 실전에 적용해 봐
1. (A)   2. (D)   3. (A)   4. (B)   5. (C)   6. (B)   7. (B)
8. (C)   9. (D)   10. (A)

1. 정답 (A)

해석 자선 기금모금의 임무는 모으는 것이다 / 적어도 백만 달러 이상을 / 자선단체 Hope Society에 기부하기 위한

해설 문장에 정동사가 없으므로 빈칸은 정동사 자리이다. 주어 자리에 '계획'을 나타내는 단어가 있을 때 동격으로 to 부정사를 필요로 하는 경우로 (A)가 정답이다. (C)는 수동태이므로 뒤에 목적어를 가질 수 없으므로 탈락, (D)는 수일치가 되지 않았다.

표현 정리 mission 임무 fundraising campaign 기금모금 행사 at least 적어도 donate 기부하다 raise 모으다

2. 정답 (D)

해석 Carsons Technology Solutions는 / 목표에 도달하기 위해 헌신한다 / 그런데 그것은 IT 산업에서 선두적인 회사가 되는 것이다

해설 문장에 접속사가 1개 있으므로 빈칸은 정동사 자리이다. 주어 자리에 '목표'를 나타내는 단어가 있을 때 동격으로 to 부정사를 필요로 하는 경우로 (D)가 정답이다. (B)는 수일치가 되지 않았고, (C)는 수동태인데 2형식 동사는 수동태가 존재하지 않는다.

표현 정리 be committed to ~에 헌신하다 objective 목적 leading 선두적인

3. 정답 (A)

해석 이 프로젝트를 위한 우리의 목적은 / 방법들을 분석하는 것이다 / 서비스의 고객만족을 극대화하는 / 그들에게 제공되는

해설 문장에 정동사가 없으므로 빈칸은 정동사 자리이다. 주어 자리에 '목표'를 나타내는 단어가 있을 때 동격으로 to 부정사를 필요로 하는 경우로 (A)가 정답이다. (B)와 (C)는 목표가 직접 분석할 수 없으므로 오답이다.

표현 정리 goal 목적 maximize 최대화 analyze 분석하다

4. 정답 (B)

해석 Ms. Moreno가 May Town으로 이사하기로 한 이유는 / 돈을 절약하기 위해서였다 / 회사로 매일 출근하는 비용을 저렴하게 함으로써

해설 문장에 정동사가 없으므로 빈칸은 정동사 자리이다. 주어 자리에 '이유'를 나타내는 단어가 있을 때 동격으로 to 부정사를 필요로 하는 경우로, 'May Town으로 이사하기로 한 이유는 돈을 절약하기 위해서'긴 (B)가 정답이다. (C)와 (D)가 오면 이유가 옮기는 동작의 주체가 되어 어색하다.

표현 정리 reason 이유 move 이사하다, 옮기다 commute 통근하다

5. 정답 (C)

해석 전국적인 운동의 목적은 / 필요에 대한 인식을 높이는 것이다 / 자연과 야생동물을 보존하는 것의

해설 be 동사 뒤에 동격으로 to 부정사가 온 경우에 주어 자리에는 '목표, 목적, 계획'을 나타내는 단어가 오므로 (C)가 정답이다.

표현 정리 awareness 인식 preserve 보존하다 wildlife 야생동물 inquiry 연구, 조사

6. 정답 (B)

해석 이 편지는 / 당신에게 알리기 위함이다 / 당신의 자동차 보험이 다음 주에 만료된다는 것을 / 그리고 갱신을 필요로 하는 것을

해설 문장에 정동사가 2개 있고, 접속사 1개가 있으므로 빈칸은 준동사 자리이다. '이 편지는 알리기 위한 것'이 자연스러우므로 (B)가 정답이다. (C)가 오면 수동태가 되어 바로 'that S+V'가 와야 한다.

표현 정리 insurance 보험 expire 만료하다 renewal 갱신하다 inform 알리다

7. 정답 (B)

해설 National Health Organization의 역할은 / 다양한 규범과 기준을 수립하는 것이다 / 건강과 관련된 이슈에 대해 / 대중의 건강을 증진시키기 위해

해설 be 동사 뒤에 동격으로 to 부정사가 온 경우이다. 주어인 'National Health Organization의 역할'이 곧 '다양한 규범과 기준을 수립하는 것'이므로 동격을 이룬 (B)가 정답이다. 문맥상으로 파악하는 것도 한 가지 방법이 될 수 있다.

표현 정리 establish 설립하다, 수립하다 various 다양한 norms 규범 standard 기준

8. 정답 (C)

해설 교육의 목표는 / 보장하는 것이다 / 모든 직원들이 CAD 프로그램으로 작업하는 것이 편안하도록

해설 문장에 접속사가 1개, 정동사가 2개 필요하므로 정동사 자리이다. 주어 자리에 '목표'를 나타내는 단어가 있을 때 동격으로 to 부정사를 필요로 하는 경우로 (C)가 정답이다. (B)와 (D)가 답이 되면 목표가 주체가 되어 보장한다는 어색한 말이 된다.

표현 정리 training 교육 employee 직원 comfortable 편안한

9. 정답 (D)

해설 Delton Airlines에서 / Mr. Nielson 업무는 / 승객들을 돕는 것이다 / 승강장에 대해 묻는 / 어떤 문으로 나가야 하는지

해설 be 동사 뒤에 동격으로 to 부정사가 온 경우이다. '승객을 돕는 것'이 'Mr. Nielson의 업무'라고 볼 수 있으므로 (D)가 정답이다.

표현 정리 assist 돕다 inquiry 문의, 질문 asset 자산 consideration 사려, 숙고, 고려사항

10. 정답 (A)

해설 바이러스성 마케팅의 목표는 / 고객들을 확인하는 것이다 / 소셜 네트워크 서비스에 매우 의존하는 / 그리고 그들을 노출시키는 것이다 / 온라인 상품 광고에

해설 문장에 정동사가 없으므로 빈칸은 정동사 자리이다. 주어 자리에 '목표'를 나타내는 단어가 있을 때 동격으로 to 부정사를 필요로 하는 경우로 (A)가 정답이다.

표현 정리 aim 목표 viral marketing 바이러스성 마케팅, 이메일을 통한 홍보 expose 드러내다 advertisements 광고

Chapter 09 동사 어휘 문제(매월 4문제)

법칙 71 특정 명사를 목적어로 쓰는 3형식 동사

◎ 유형을 파악해 봐
1. (C) 2. (C) 3. (D)

1. 정답 (C)

해설 Ms. Elmore는 예약했다 / 참석하기 위해 / 영화 시사회에

해설 빈칸의 to 부정사는 뒤에 목적어가 왔기 때문에 목적어를 필요로 하는 3형식 동사가 와야 한다. (A) apply는 주로 for와 함께 쓰이는 덩어리 동사로 쓰거나 apply A to B의 형태로 사용한다. (B) forward는 목적어로 A to B 형식을 취하며, (D) allow는 주로 목적어와 to 부정사를 목적 보어로 취하는 5형식 동사이다. (C)는 뒤에 행사 명을 목적어로 취하는 3형식 동사이므로 정답이다.

표현 정리 make a reservation 예약하다 preview 시사회 apply 지원하다, 적용하다 forward 나아가게 하다, 진행시키다 attend 참석하다 allow ~을 허락하다

2. 정답 (C)

해설 매니저는 검토하고 있을 것이다 / 이력서를 / 면접 전에

해설 (A)는 자동사로 '작동되다, 수술하다'라는 뜻으로 쓰이고, 타동사일 때는 기계 따위를 '가동하다'는 뜻이므로 오답이다. (B) direct는 목적어로 A to B 형식을 주로 취한다. (D) offer는 주로 뒤에 간접목적어, 직접목적어를 갖는 4형식 동사이므로 오답이다. (C) review는 뒤에 '예산안, 제안서' 등과 같은 목적어를 취하는 3형식 동사이므로 정답이다.

표현 정리 resume 이력서 job interview 면접 operate 운영되다, 작동되다 direct 감독하다, 지시하다 review 검토하다

3. 정답 (D)

해설 보여 주세요 / 당신의 멤버십 카드를 / 할인을 받기 위해 / 당신의 구입품에 대한

해설 신분증, 출입증 등과 자연스럽게 어울리는 (D)가 정답이다. (B)는 주로 5형식 동사로 사용된다.

표현 정리 purchase 구매 enter 들어가다, 입장하다 allow 허락하다 observe 준수하다, 관찰하다

◎ 실전에 적용해 봐
1. (D) 2. (A) 3. (A) 4. (D) 5. (C) 6. (A) 7. (A)
8. (B) 9. (C) 10. (C)

1. 정답 (D)

해설 시 의회는 결정했다 / 광고를 내기로 / 금연 캠페인을 홍보하기 위해

해설 promote는 '승진시키다'란 뜻도 있지만, '홍보하다'라는 광고나 캠페인 앞에 주로 쓰인다. '금연 캠페인을 홍보하기 위해서 광고를 하는 것'이 가장 자연스럽기 때문에 (D)가 정답이다.

표현 정리 decide to ~하기로 결정하다 advertising 광고 nonsmoking 금연 impose 부과하다, 제한하다 admit 인정하다, 허가하다 intervene 개입하다, 끼어들다 promote 홍보하다, 촉진하다

2. 정답 (A)

해설 Alpa Productions는 고용할 계획이다 / 경험 있는 작업 팀장을 / 생산성을 증가시키기 위해

해설 hire란 단어는 '고용하다'라는 뜻으로 사용해, 뒤에 주로 직책 명이나

사람이 온다. '경력 있는 작업 팀장을 고용할 계획이다'가 자연스럽기 때문에 (A)가 정답이다. (B)는 뒤에 장소나 데이터, (C)는 신원을 목적어로 취하며, (D)는 전치사 in과 주로 함께 '등록하다'라는 뜻으로 쓰인다.

표현 정리 plan to ~할 계획이다 experienced 경험 있는 increase 향상시키다 productivity 생산성, 생산력

3.   정답 (A)

해설 승강장으로 가기 위해서는 / 당신은 제시해야 한다 / 당신의 여권과 티켓을 / 출입문 근처 직원에게

해설 present는 티켓이나 표를 누구에게 보여주거나 발표를 할 때 쓰이는 단어이다. '당신의 여권과 티켓을 직원에게 제시해야 한다'가 자연스럽기 때문에 (A)가 정답이다. (B)는 '확인하다,' (C)는 '분석하다,' (D)는 '놓다, 두다'라는 뜻으로 '여권과 티켓'이라는 목적어와 쓰기에는 모두 어색하다.

표현 정리 proceed to ~으로 나아가다, ~에 이르다 platform 플랫폼, 승강장 passport 여권 present 제시하다, 보여주다 confirm 확인하다, 공식화하다 analyze 분석하다 place ~을 놓다

4.   정답 (D)

해설 컴퓨터 기술자는 설치했다 / 소프트웨어 프로그램을 / 보안 수준을 높인 / 바이러스에 대한 / 회사 컴퓨터

해설 install은 '설치하다'는 뜻으로 목적어로는 주로 프로그램을 가지는 동사이다. '소프트웨어 프로그램을 설치했다'가 가장 자연스럽기 때문에 (D)가 정답이다. (A)는 주로 5형식 동사로 사용되며, (C)는 사람을 목적어로 취하는 동사이다.

표현 정리 engineer 기술자, 엔지니어 increase ~을 높이다, 개선하다 permit 허용하다, 허가하다 sustain 지속하다 install 설치하다, 장착하다

5.   정답 (C)

해설 Shoppin' Spree가 공지했기 때문에 / 점포 정리 세일을 한다고 / 그곳은 고객들로 가득했다 / 물품들을 구매하기 위해 온 / 할인된 가격에 파는

해설 purchase는 동사로 쓰일 때 '물건을 구입하다'는 뜻으로 쓰이므로 목적어로 물건을 가지는 동사이다 '물품들을 구매하기 위해서'가 가장 자연스럽기 때문에 (C)가 정답이다. (A)는 주문, 약속 등을 이행할 때, (B)는 일정을 지연시킬 때 사용하며, (D)는 A with B의 어울림을 가진다.

표현 정리 clearance sale 점포 정리 세일 announce 공지하다, 발표하다 pack 채우다 discounted price 할인된 가격 fulfill 성취하다, 실행하다 purchase 구입하다, 구매하다 replace 대체하다, 교체하다

6.   정답 (A)

해설 Mr. Lim의 송별회는 / Lean 씨를 은퇴하는 / 개최될 것이다 / 다음 주 토요일에 / 회사 건물 근처 레스토랑에서

해설 held는 앞에 be가 있기 때문에 hold의 p.p. 형이다. hold는 주로 '연회를 개최하다, 파티를 개최하다'라는 뜻으로 쓰이며, 목적어로 주로 행사명이 온다. '송별회는 다음 주 토요일에 열릴 것이다'가 가장 자연스럽기 때문에 (A)가 정답이다. (B)는 이미 미래적인 어감을 포함하고 있어 will과 어울리지 않고, (C)는 누구에 의해 지지되는지 불분명하다.

표현 정리 farewell party 송별회, 환송회 retire 은퇴하다, 퇴직하다 hold 열다, 개최하다 expect 예상하다, 기대하다 support 지지하다, 지원하다 maintain 유지하다, 주장하다

7.   정답 (A)

해설 자선단체인 National Support Foundation은 / 고마움을 표했다 / 기증자에게 / 원하는 자금을 모금하는데 도움을 준 / 올해

해설 express는 주로 감정이나 견해를 목적어로 취한다. '기증자에게 그 마음을 표했다'가 가장 자연스럽기 때문에 (A)가 정답이다. (B)와 (C)는 목적어 뒤에 to 부정사를 목적 보어로 취하는 5형식 동사이다.

표현 정리 charity 자선 (단체), 구호 gratitude 감사, 고마움 donor 기부자, 기증자 raise 모으다, 올리다 fund 자금; 투자하다 express 표현하다, 나타내다 encourage 격려하다, 장려하다 acknowledge 인정하다, 확인하다

8.   정답 (B)

해설 다음 연주회 준비를 위해 / New York Orchestra Club은 채용할 계획이다 / 추가 무대 관리자들을

해설 recruit는 '채용하다'라는 뜻으로 쓰였으며, 목적어로 주로 사람이 온다. '추가 무대 관리자들을 채용할 계획이다'가 가장 자연스럽기 때문에 (B)가 정답이다. (A)는 주로 5형식 동사로 사용되고, (C)는 A to B의 어울림을 갖는다.

표현 정리 in preparation for ~을 준비하기 위해 plan to ~할 계획이다 recruit 채용하다, 모집하다 submit 제출하다, 제시하다 enlarge 확대하다, 확장하다

9.   정답 (C)

해설 현재 이익을 유지하기 위해 / 대부분의 소매 상점들은 인상해야 했다 / 식료품 가격을 / 생산이 주로 영향을 받은 / 최근 홍수에 의해

해설 increase는 목적어로 주로 '매출, 가격, 비용'을 받는다. '식료품 가격을 인상해야 했다'가 가장 자연스럽기 때문에 (C)가 정답이다. (A)는 건물을 건축할 때, (D)는 예산안, 계획 등을 목적어로 갖는다.

표현 정리 maintain 유지하다, 주장하다 retail store 소매점 grocery 식료품 affect 영향을 주다, 작용하다 sustain 지속하다, 지탱하게 하다 propose 제안하다, 제의하다

10.   정답 (C)

해설 인사 부장은 이끌게 될 것이다 / 오리엔테이션을 / 신입 직원들을 위한 / 회사 방침과 규칙에 대한 / 다음 주

해설 lead는 목적어로 주로 '토론회, 점검, 계획' 등을 받는다. '신입 사원들을 위한 오리엔테이션을 이끌게 될 것이다'가 가장 자연스럽기 때문에 (C)가 정답이다. (A)는 주로 with와 함께 쓰여 '상호 작용을 하다'라는 뜻으로 쓰이고, (B)는 A(from B)의 형태로 'B로부터 A를 배우다'는 뜻이다.

표현 정리 interact 상호 작용하다, 대화하다 lead 이끌다, 선도하다 reject 거부하다, 거절하다

법칙 72 특정 전치사와 잘 어울리는 3형식 동사

◎ 유형을 파악해 봐
1. (A)　2. (C)　3. (D)

1.　　　　　　　　　　　　　　　　　　　　　　정답 (A)

해석　더 많은 자금을 필요로 할 것이다 / 전환하기 위해 / 비포장 도로를 포장 도로로 / 도시의

해설　빈칸 뒤에 목적어가 있으므로 3형식 동사를 골라야 한다. 보기가 모두 3형식 동사이지만 목적어인 a dirt road 뒤에 into가 보인다. A into B로 쓸 수 있는 'A를 B로 전환시키다'의 뜻인 (A) convert가 정답이다. (B)는 A to B의 어울림이 있고, (C)는 제품을 목적어로, (D)는 건물을 목적어로 취한다.

표현 정리　require 필요하다, 요구하다　dirt road 비포장 도로　paved 포장된　convert 전환하다, 바꾸다　relocate 재배치하다, 새 장소에 두다　produce ~을 생산하다, 만들다　construct 건설하다, 만들다

2.　　　　　　　　　　　　　　　　　　　　　　정답 (C)

해석　교통 혼잡이 방해하면 안 된다 / 물건이 / 제때 배달되는 것을

해설　빈칸 뒤에 the items만 남으므로 목적어를 가지는 3형식 동사가 정답이다. 전치사 from과 잘 어울리는 동사인 (C) prevent를 우선 대입해 본다. '물건이 정시에 배달되는 것을 방해하면 안 된다'가 가장 자연스럽기 때문에 (C)가 정답이다. 여기서 prevent A from B는 'A가 B하지 못하도록 하다'라는 뜻이다.

표현 정리　heavy traffic 교통 혼잡　commence 시작하다　rush 서두르다, 돌진하다　prevent 막다, 방지하다, 예방하다　achieve 달성하다, 성취하다

3.　　　　　　　　　　　　　　　　　　　　　　정답 (D)

해석　전시회 개막식은 / 연기될 것이다 / 추후 통지가 있을 때까지

해설　전치사 until과 어울리는 동사는 postpone이므로 우선 대입해 본다. '추후 통지가 있을 때까지 연기될 것이다'가 가장 자연스럽기 때문에 (D)가 정답이다. 여기서 'postpone A until B'는 'A를 B까지 연기하다'라는 뜻이다.

표현 정리　exhibition 전시회, 박람회　until further notice 추후 통지가 있을 때까지　propose 제안하다, 제의하다, 제시하다　define 한정하다, 정의하다　postpone 연기하다, 미루다

◎ 실전에 적용해 봐
1. (D)　2. (C)　3. (A)　4. (A)　5. (D)　6. (C)　7. (B)
8. (C)　9. (A)　10. (D)

1.　　　　　　　　　　　　　　　　　　　　　　정답 (D)

해석　Best Flight Air 승무원들은 / 칭찬 받았다 / 적절한 조치를 취한 것에 대해 / 긴급 상황에 / 최근 비행 중에 있었던 /

해설　전치사 for와 어울리는 동사는 commend이므로 우선 대입해 본다. '승무원들은 적절한 조치를 취한 것에 대해 칭찬 받았다'가 가장 자연스럽기 때문에 (D)가 정답이다. 여기서 commend A for B는 'A를 B로 칭찬하다'라는 뜻이다. (B)도 가능하긴 하나 ask A for B는 'A에게 B에 대해 요청하다'는 뜻이다. entitle은 A to B와 어울리므로 이것이 수동태가 되면 A is entitled to B의 모양이 된다.

표현 정리　flight attendant 비행기 승무원　take measures 조치를 취하다　emergency situation 긴급 상황, 비상 사태　claim 주장하다, 요구하다　entitle 자격을 주다　commend 칭찬하다, 추천하다

2.　　　　　　　　　　　　　　　　　　　　　　정답 (C)

해석　모든 고객 문의들은 / 제품 사용 법에 대한 / 보내져야 한다 / 고객 서비스 사무실로

해설　전치사 to와 어울리는 동사는 directed이므로 우선 대입해 본다. '모든 고객 문의들은 고객 서비스 사무실로 보내져야 한다'가 가장 자연스럽기 때문에 (C)가 정답이다. 여기서 direct A to B는 'A를 B로 보내다'라는 뜻이고, 주로 be directed to로 사용된다.

표현 정리　inquiry 조사, 문의　be directed to ~에게 보내지다　indicate 나타내다, 가리키다　refer 말하다, 언급하다　direct 감독하다, 지시하다

3.　　　　　　　　　　　　　　　　　　　　　　정답 (A)

해석　Mr. Daniels는 편지를 계속 받았기 때문에 / 그의 이전 집 주인에게 온 / 그는 그들에게 전화했다 / 예전 주소가 삭제되도록 하기 위해 / 다양한 수신 리스트에서

해설　전치사 from과 어울리는 동사는 remove이므로 우선 대입해 본다. '메일 리스트로부터 그의 주소를 삭제하다'가 가장 자연스럽기 때문에 (A)가 정답이다.

표현 정리　keep -ing 계속해서 ~하다　remove 제거하다, 삭제하다　forward 나아가게 하다, 진행시키다　alternate 번갈아 하다, 대체하다

4.　　　　　　　　　　　　　　　　　　　　　　정답 (A)

해석　즉시 반납하세요 / 물품들을 / 공급실로 / 물품 사용이 끝나면

해설　A to B의 형태로 쓰는 동사는 return이므로 우선 대입해 본다. '공급실로 물품들을 즉시 반납하세요'가 자연스럽기 때문에 (A)가 정답이다. (C)는 주로 전치사 to와 덩어리로 쓰여 '~를 참고하다'의 뜻이 되며, (D)는 사람 명사를 목적어로 취한다.

표현 정리　supplies 저장품, 물품　supply room 비품실, 공급실　return 반납하다, 돌려주다　abandon 버리다, 포기하다　refer 말하다, 언급하다　inform 알리다, 통보하다

5.　　　　　　　　　　　　　　　　　　　　　　정답 (D)

해석　Jerome 사의 CEO는 / 10억 달러 이상의 순이익을 가진 벤처 기업인데 / 회사의 성공을 현재 IT 시대 덕분으로 돌린다

해설　A to B 형태로 사용 가능한 attributes이므로 우선 대입해 본다. '그것의 성공을 현재 IT 시대 덕으로 돌린다'가 자연스럽기 때문에 (D)가 정답이다. 여기서 attribute A to B는 'A를 B의 탓/덕분으로 돌리다'라는 뜻이다. (A), (B), (C)는 모두 'that S+V'를 목적어로 취하는 동사들이다.

표현 정리　net profit 순이익　current 현재의　era 시대　expect 예상하다, 기대하다　predict 예측하다, 전망하다　attribute A to B A를 B의 탓으로 돌리다

6. 정답 (C)

해설 Ms. Harrington이 Mr. Skully를 대신하게 될 것이다 / 그가 위원회 회의에 참석하느라 떠나 있는 2주 동안

해설 뒤에 목적어가 오지 않고 전치사가 왔으므로 타동사인 (A), (D)는 탈락이다. (B), (C)는 타동사뿐 아니라 자동사도 가능하다. (B)의 경우는 A to B에서 A가 생략되어 to B로 쓰는데 (C)의 경우는 A for B에서 A가 생략된 for B의 형태로 쓸 수 있다. 이 경우 '~를 대체하다'는 뜻이 되므로 (C)가 정답이다.

표현 정리 be away 떨어져 있다, 부재 중이다 manage 관리하다, 운영하다 substitute 대체하다, 대신하다 appoint 임명하다, 지명하다

7. 정답 (B)

해설 모든 참석자들은 / 다가오는 엑셀 교육 / 가져오도록 요청 받을 것이다 / 그들 자신의 기기들을 / 수업에 / 프로그램을 사용하기 위해

해설 A to B의 형태로 사용 가능한 (B)를 우선 대입해 본다. '그들 자신의 기기들을 수업에 가져오도록 요청 받을 것이다'가 자연스럽다. 따라서 (B)가 정답이다. (A)는 행사 명, (C)는 소프트웨어 등을 목적어로 갖는다.

표현 정리 attendant 참석자 be required to ~하도록 요구되다 device 기기, 장치 run 운영하다, 작동하다 install 설치하다, 임명하다 develop 개발하다, 발전하다

8. 정답 (C)

해설 Jane Beauty Parlor는 가졌다 / 부러진 의자를 / 그 의자는 교체되어야만 했다 / 새것으로

해설 A with B의 어울림을 갖는 동사의 수동태 모양이다. 어울리는 동사는 replace이므로 우선 대입해 본다. '새것으로 교체되야 했던 부러진 의자'가 자연스럽기 때문에 (C)가 정답이다. (D)는 1형식 동사이므로 수동태를 쓰지 않는다.

표현 정리 stool 등받이 의자 gather 모이다, 수집하다 replace 대체하다, 교체하다 proceed 진행하다, 추진하다

9. 정답 (A)

해설 모든 직원들은 요구 받는다 / 제출할 것을 / 그들의 보고서를 / 판매 실적에 관한 / 직속 상관에게 / 매 분기마다

해설 뒤에 their reports라는 목적어가 있으므로 사람 목적어를 취하는 (B)는 오답이다. 목적어 뒤 전명구 on ~ performance를 수식어 처리하여 빼내면 전치사 to와 어울리는 동사가 정답이다. 여기서 submit A to B는 'A를 B로 제출하다'라는 자연스러운 해석이 되므로 (A)가 정답이다.

표현 정리 be required to + 동사원형 ~하도록 요구 받다 sales performance 판매 실적 immediate supervisor 직속 상관 submit 제출하다, 제시하다 inform 알리다, 통보하다 postpone 연기하다

10. 정답 (D)

해설 이번 주에 야간 근무를 하는 사람들은 / 함께 사용해야 한다 / 직원 사무실을 경호원과

해설 목적어 뒤에 있는 전치사 with와 사용이 자연스러운 동사는 (D)로, '경호원과 직원 사무실을 함께 사용하다'라는 자연스런 해석이 되므로 (D)가 정답이다. 여기서 share A with B는 'A를 B와 공유하다'라는 뜻이다.

(A), (B)는 to 부정사를 목적 보어로 취하는 5형식 동사, (C)는 A to B의 어울림을 갖는다.

표현 정리 security guard 경호원 permit 허락하다, 허용하다 relocate 재배치하다 share 공유하다, 나누다 share A with B A를 B와 공유하다

법칙 73 to 부정사나 동명사, 명사절을 목적어로 하는 3형식 동사

◎ 유형을 파악해 봐
1. (B)   2. (C)   3. (C)

1. 정답 (B)

해설 Ms. Devon은 보고 싶어 한다 / 그녀의 의사를 / 즉시 / 그녀의 등 통증 때문에

해설 빈칸 뒤에 to 부정사가 있고, 보기 중에 '응큼쟁이' 동사인 wish가 있기 때문에 우선 대입해 본다. 'Ms. Devon은 그녀의 의사를 보고 싶어 한다'가 가장 자연스럽기 때문에 (B)가 정답이다. (A)는 목적 보어로 to 부정사를 갖는 동사, (C)는 동명사를 목적어로 취하는 동사, (D)는 provide A with B의 형태로 전치사와의 어울림을 갖는 동사이다.

표현 정리 immediately 즉시, 직후 pain 고통, 통증 require ~를 필요로 하다, 요구하다 mind 명심하다 provide 제공하다, 공급하다

2. 정답 (C)

해설 치료사는 추천했다 / 운동하는 것을 / 적어도 한 시간 / 매일

해설 빈칸 뒤에 exercising 동명사가 있고, 보기 중에 동명사를 목적어로 취하는 회장아들 동사가 있기 때문에 우선 대입해 본다. '치료사는 운동하는 것을 추천했다'가 자연스럽기 때문에 (C)가 정답이다. (A), (B), (D)는 주로 명사절을 목적어로 취하는 동사들이다.

표현 정리 therapist 치료사 exercise 운동하다 announce 발표하다, 알리다 recommend 추천하다 claim 주장하다, 요구하다

3. 정답 (C)

해설 Genome 사의 CEO는 발표했다 / 회사는 지금 위기 상황이라고

해설 'that S+V'을 목적어로 취하는 (C)를 대입해 해석해 보면 'CEO는 발표했다'라는 말이 잘 어울린다. (D)는 1형식 동사이므로 목적어를 가질 수 없다.

표현 정리 critical situation 위기 상황 secure 확보하다, 보장하다 announce 발표하다, 알리다 occur 발생하다, 일어나다

◎ 실전에 적용해 봐
1. (A)   2. (D)   3. (D)   4. (A)   5. (B)   6. (C)   7. (B)
8. (A)   9. (D)   10. (B)

1. 정답 (A)

해설 이사들은 했다 / Flex Production 사와 거래하기로 / Flex Production 사가 생산하도록 하기 위해 / 그들의 제품을

해설 빈칸 뒤에 to 부정사가 있고, 보기 중에 '응큼쟁이' 동사인 decide가

있기 때문에 우선 대입해서 해석하면 '이사들은 Flex Production 사와 거래하기로 했다'는 자연스러운 말이 되므로 (A)가 정답이다. (B)도 to 부정사를 목적어로 가질 수 있으나 '그들의 제품을 생산하기 위해서'라는 말과 맞지 않는다.

표현 정리 make a deal with ~와 거래하다, ~와 타협하다 in order to ~하기 위해서 reject 거절하다, 거부하다 inform 알리다, 통보하다

2. 정답 (D)

해석 Ms. Miller는 꺼려하지 않을 것이다 / 당신이 손님 목록을 정리하는 것을 돕는 것을 / 다가오는 세미나를 위한 / 그녀는 현재 할애할 시간이 있기 때문에

해설 빈칸 뒤에 동명사인 helping이 있고, 보기 중에 동명사를 목적어로 취하는 '회장아들' 동사 mind가 있기 때문에 우선 대입해 본다. '당신이 손님 목록을 정리하는 것을 돕는 것을 꺼려하지 않을 것이다'가 자연스럽기 때문에 (D)가 정답이다.

표현 정리 organize 정리하다, 체계화하다 upcoming 다가오는 spare 할애하다

3. 정답 (D)

해석 보고서로 미루어볼 때 / Graham 사는 고용할 예정이다 / 10명의 직원들을 더 / 올해 / 공석을 채우기 위해 / 인사부에

해설 빈칸 뒤에 to 부정사가 있고, 보기 중에 '응큼쟁이' 동사인 intend가 있기 때문에 우선 대입해 본다. 'Graham 사는 고용할 예정이다'라는 자연스러운 내용이 되기 때문에 (D)가 정답이다. (A)는 전치사 on과 덩어리로 사용하며, (B)는 주로 'that S+V'를 목적어로, (C)는 A as B 형태의 5형식 동사이다.

표현 정리 judge from ~으로 판단하다 vacancy 공석, 결원 rely 의존하다, 의지하다 regard 간주하다 intend 의도하다, 계획하다

4. 정답 (A)

해석 보고서를 살펴본 후에 / 다른 회사의 사업 계획들에 관한 / 이사들은 예상했다 / 시장에서 경쟁이 더 치열해질 것이라고 / 내년에

해설 빈칸 뒤에 'that S+V'가 왔으며, 보기 중에 '예상하다'라는 의미인 '생말예제' 동사 anticipate가 있기 때문에 우선 대입해 본다. '이사들은 시장에서 경쟁이 치열해질 것이라고 예상했다'가 자연스럽기 때문에 (A)가 정답이다. (B)는 that 다음에 will 대신 should가 와야 하고, (C)는 A for B의 어울림을 가지며, (D)는 to 부정사를 목적 보어로 취하는 5형식 동사이다.

표현 정리 competition 경쟁 fierce 치열한, 거센 anticipate 예상하다, 기대하다 request 요청하다 arrange 준비하다, 정리하다

5. 정답 (B)

해석 예상치 못한 일자리 제공은 / Solutions Tech로부터의 / 놀라게 했다 / Ms. Taylor를 / 일하는 것을 전혀 고려해 본 적이 없는 / 다른 IT 회사에서

해설 동명사 working이 있고, 보기 중에 동명사를 목적어로 취하는 '회장아들' 동사 consider가 있기 때문에 우선 대입해 본다. 'Ms. Taylor는 일하는 것을 고려해 본 적이 없다'가 자연스럽기 때문에 (B)가 정답이다.

표현 정리 unexpected 예상치 못한 surprise 놀라게 하다

consider 고려하다, 여기다 witness 보다, 증언하다 ensure 보장하다, 확보하다

6. 정답 (C)

해석 회원이 되기 위해 / 당신은 먼저 동의해야 한다 / 연회비 지불에 / 10달러 비용이 드는

해설 빈칸 뒤에 to 부정사가 있고, 보기 중에 '응큼쟁이' 동사인 agree가 있기 때문에 우선 대입해 본다. '당신은 먼저 연회비 지불에 동의해야 한다'가 자연스럽기 때문에 (C)가 정답이다. reply to 다음에는 명사가 와야 하며, permit은 목적어가 나오고 목적 보어 자리에 to 부정사를 써야 하는 동사이며, (D)는 to 부정사를 목적어로 취할 수는 있으나, '지불할 것을 요청해야 한다'는 말은 어색하다.

표현 정리 in order to ~하기 위해 annual membership fee 연회비 permit 허락하다 reply 응하다, 대답하다

7. 정답 (B)

해석 Ms. Browski는 수정할 필요가 있다 / 그녀의 보고서를 / 요청 받았기 때문에 / 명시할 것을 / 보고서에 관한 그녀의 연구가 / Canol 사에 의해 후원 받았음을

해설 빈칸 뒤에 'that S+V'가 왔으며, 보기 중 '명시하다'의 의미인 '생말예제' 동사인 specify가 있기 때문에 우선 대입해 본다. '그녀의 연구가 Canol 사에 의해 후원 받았음을 명시할 것'이란 말이 자연스럽기 때문에 (B)가 정답이다. (D)는 1형식 동사로 목적어를 취하지 않는다.

표현 정리 revise 개정하다, 수정하다 sponsor 지원하다, 후원하다 specify 명시하다, 구체화하다 allow 허락하다 proceed 진행하다

8. 정답 (A)

해석 이 사업 계획은 검토되어야 한다 / 회계부에 의해 / 분명히 하기 위해 / 사업계획이 예산을 초과하지 않는지

해설 보기 모두 'that S+V'를 목적어로 취하는 동사들이다. 단, (D)가 올 경우 'that S+V'에서 V는 (should) 동사원형이 온다. 따라서 (A), (B), (C) 중에서 의미상으로 답을 골라야 하는 문제이다. '사업계획이 예산을 초과하지 않는지 분명히 하기 위해서'라는 말이 자연스럽다. 따라서 (A)가 답이다.

표현 정리 Accounting Department 경리부, 경리과 exceed 초과하다 budget 예산 ensure 보장하다

9. 정답 (D)

해석 Royal 사와 파트너 관계임에도 불구하고 / Genuine Solutions는 거절했다 / 넘기는 것을 / 고객 데이터베이스 정보를 Royal 사에

해설 빈칸 뒤에 to 부정사가 있고, 보기 중에 '응큼쟁이' 동사인 refuse가 있기 때문에 우선 대입해 본다. 'Genuine Solutions는 고객 데이터베이스를 넘기는 것을 거절했다'가 자연스럽기 때문에 (D)가 정답이다. (B)는 to 부정사를 목적 보어로 취하는 5형식 동사, (C)는 'that S+V'를 목적어로 취하는 3형식 동사이다.

표현 정리 despite ~임에도 불구하고 hand over 인계하다, 양도하다 accept 받아들이다, 수용하다 permit 허용하다, 허락하다 refuse 거절하다, 거부하다

10. 정답 (B)

해설 얼마의 시간이 흘렀는지와는 상관없이 / 회의를 시작한 이후 / 참석자들은 토론을 계속했다 / 제기된 문제들에 대한 / 회의 동안

해설 빈칸 뒤에 discussing 동명사가 있고, 보기 중 동명사나 to 부정사 모두 목적어로 취할 수 있는 continue가 있기 때문에 우선 대입해 본다. '참석자들은 문제들에 대한 토론을 계속했다'가 자연스럽기 때문에 (B)가 정답이다. (A)는 예약 등을 확인할 때 사용하는 동사이고, (C)는 사람을 목적어로 취하는 동사이며, (D)는 행사 명이 목적어로 온다.

표현 정리 regardless of ~임에도 불구하고 attendee 참석자 confirm 확인하다, 공식화하다 remind 상기시키다, 생각나게 하다 organize 조직하다, 개최하다

법칙 74 '자동사+전치사' 묶음

◎ 유형을 파악해 봐
1. (A) 2. (C) 3. (D)

1. 정답 (A)

해설 사무실 전체 수리 비용이 / 대략 계산되었다 / 그래서 당신은 집중해야 한다 / 계산의 정확성을 올리는 것에

해설 빈칸 뒤의 on과 같이 덩어리로 쓸 수 있는 (A) focus를 대입해 해석하면, '당신은 올리는 것에 집중해야 한다'가 자연스럽기 때문에 (A)가 정답이다.

표현 정리 total cost 전체 비용 renovation 수리 roughly 대략 calculate 계산하다, 산출하다 focus on ~에 집중하다 accuracy 정확성

2. 정답 (C)

해설 Instar Corporation은 모든 비용을 부담한다 / 직원들을 위한 / 워크숍 프로그램에 등록하는

해설 빈칸 뒤의 in과 같이 덩어리로 쓸 수 있는 (C) enroll이 있으므로 대입해 해석해 본다. '워크숍 프로그램에 등록하는 직원들'이 가장 자연스럽기 때문에 (C)가 정답이다.

표현 정리 cover (비용을) 대다, 부담하다 enroll in ~에 등록하다 (= register for)

3. 정답 (D)

해설 사람들은 / 이번 주에 수업을 등록하는 / 30퍼센트의 할인을 받을 것이다

해설 빈칸 뒤의 for와 같이 덩어리로 쓸 수 있는 (D) register를 대입해 해석하면 '수업에 등록하는 사람들은'이 자연스럽기 때문에 (D)가 정답이다.

표현 정리 those who ~하는 사람들 register for ~에 등록하다 (= enroll in, sign up for)

◎ 실전에 적용해 봐
1. (A) 2. (B) 3. (A) 4. (C) 5. (D) 6. (D) 7. (B)
8. (B) 9. (C) 10. (A)

1. 정답 (A)

해설 Mr. Raynold가 휴가 중이기 때문에 / 그는 응답할 수 없을지도 모른다 / 당신의 대답에 / 즉시

해설 빈칸 뒤의 to와 같이 덩어리로 쓸 수 있는 (A) respond를 대입해 해석하면, '당신의 대답에 응답할 수 없을지도 모른다'가 자연스럽기 때문에 (A)가 정답이다. (B)는 to 다음에 동사원형이 와야 하며, (C)와 (D)는 A to B의 형태로 사용한다.

표현 정리 vacation 방학, 휴가 respond to ~에 대해 응답하다 reply 응답 immediately 즉시

2. 정답 (B)

해설 연례 도시 퍼레이드는 / 7번 가에서 열린 / 설명해 준다 / 엄청난 교통 체증의 이유를 / 6번 가에서 14번 가까지의

해설 빈칸 뒤의 for와 같이 덩어리로 쓸 수 있는 (B) accounts를 넣어 해석하면, '퍼레이드가 교통 체증의 이유를 설명해 준다'는 말이 자연스럽기 때문에 (B)가 정답이다.

표현 정리 annual 해마다 avenue 거리 account for ~의 이유를 설명하다 heavy 엄청난 traffic jam 교통체증

3. 정답 (A)

해설 만약 당신이 변경한다면 / 수취인 주소를 / 그것은 결과를 가져올 수 있다 / 배달 지연 / 주문된 물건의

해설 빈칸 뒤의 in과 같이 덩어리로 쓸 수 있는 (A) result를 넣어 해석하면, '만약 당신이 주소를 변경한다면 배달 지연의 결과를 가져올 것이다'가 자연스러워 (A)가 정답이다. (D)는 to와 같이 사용하여 '~한 결과를 낳다'라는 뜻이 된다.

표현 정리 recipient 수취인 result in ~의 결과를 야기하다 delay 지연 ordered 주문된

4. 정답 (C)

해설 Ms. Manning은 결정해야 한다 / 어느 것에 참석할지를 / 그녀의 직장 동료 결혼식 또는 세미나 / 날짜와 시간이 서로 겹쳤기 때문에

해설 빈칸 뒤의 with와 같이 덩어리로 쓸 수 있는 것은 (A), (C), (D)이다. (A)가 오면 '(규정 등을) 준수하다'이고, (D)가 오면 '~를 중단하다'이다. 반면에 (C)가 오면 '~와 동시에 일어나다'의 뜻이 되면서 '시간과 날짜가 서로 겹친다'는 의미가 된다. 따라서 (C)가 정답이다.

표현 정리 decide 결정하다 attend 참석하다 co-worker 직장동료 coincide with ~와 동시에 일어나다

5. 정답 (D)

해설 Reliable Investment는 사업을 이끌어왔다 / 34년 동안 / 투자 상담과 고객 관리를 전문으로 하는

해설 빈칸 뒤의 in과 같이 덩어리로 쓸 수 있는 (D) specializes를 넣고 해석하면 '투자 상담과 고객 관리를 전문으로 한다'가 자연스러워 (D)가 정답이다.

표현 정리 lead 이끌다, 안내하다 investment 투자 counseling 상담 customer management 고객관리

6. 정답 (D)

해설 Glec 사에서 프로젝트 관리자로 일하는 것은 / 기회를 제공한다 / 다양한 직업의 사람들과 상호작용할 / 다른 회사에 있는

해설 빈칸 뒤 with와 덩어리로 쓰일 수 있는 (D) interact를 넣어 해석하면 '다른 회사의 다양한 직업의 사람들과 상호작용할 기회'라는 말이 자연스러워 (D)가 정답이다. (B)는 to가 필요하다.

표현 정리 provide 제공하다 interact with ~와 상호작용하다, 소통하다 various 다양한 profession 직업, 종사자들 firm 회사

7. 정답 (B)

해설 Mr. Rodriguez는 그의 일을 끝내야 한다 / 그리고 준비해야 한다 / 회의실로 갈 / 저녁 회의에 참석하기 위해

해설 빈칸 뒤의 in과 같이 덩어리로 쓸 수 있는 (B) participate를 대입해 해석하면 '저녁 회의에 참석하기 위해서'가 자연스럽다. 따라서 (B)가 정답이다. (A) attend도 '참석하다'는 의미로 회의 앞에 쓸 수 있는 동사이지만, 3형식 동사이기 때문에 전치사 없이 목적어가 와야 한다. (D)는 타동사뿐 아니라 in과 사용할 수도 있으나 보통 이미 진행되고 있는 것에 '동참 혹은 합류한다'는 뜻으로 사용된다.

표현 정리 conference room 회의실 in order to ~하기 위해서 participate in ~에 참여하다

8. 정답 (B)

해설 3년 이상 경력이 있는 지원자들은 / 비슷한 분야에서 / 자격이 있다 / 기술 지원 엔지니어 직에

해설 빈칸 뒤의 for와 같이 덩어리로 쓸 수 있는 (B) qualify를 넣고 해석하면 '~한 지원자들이 기술 지원 엔지니어 자리에 자격이 있다'는 자연스런 말이 되기 때문에 (B)가 정답이다.

표현 정리 applicant 지원자, 후보자 experience 경력, 경험 relevant 유사한,비슷한 field 분야

9. 정답 (C)

해설 Genova 사는 여전히 진행 중이다 / 계약자와의 협상을 / 공급품들의 배송비에 관한

해설 (B), (C)가 모두 with와 같이 사용 가능하다. '계약자와 협상하는 과정'이란 말이 자연스러우므로 (C)가 정답이다.

표현 정리 process 과정 contractor 계약자 regarding ~에 관해서 shipping cost 배송비 supplies 공급품, 공급물

10. 정답 (A)

해설 매니저는 책임이 있다 / 신입 건설 근로자들을 교육시키는 것에 / 안전규정을 준수하기 위해

해설 빈칸 뒤의 with와 함께 덩어리로 쓸 수 있는 (A) comply를 먼저 대입해 해석하면, '안전규정을 준수하기 위해 신입 건설 근로자들을 교육시키는 것'이 자연스러워 (A)가 정답이다. (B)는 to와 같이 사용한다.

표현 정리 be responsible for ~에 책임이 있다, ~을 담당하다 training 교육, 훈련 construction 건설 worker 노동자 safety rule 안전수칙

법칙 75 '_____+목적어+목적 보어'이면 5형식 동사

◎ 유형을 파악해 봐
1. (A) 2. (C) 3. (D)

1. 정답 (A)

해설 Mr. Grit의 향상된 실적이 / 매니저를 기쁘게 했다

해설 빈칸 뒤 the manager가 목적어이므로 2형식 동사인 become은 탈락, 목적어 뒤의 pleased는 과거분사이다. 5형식 문장에서는 목적어 뒤 목적 보어의 역할로 p.p.가 올 수 있으므로 보기 중 5형식 동사인 (A)를 대입해 해석해 본다. '향상된 실적이 매니저를 기쁘게 했다'는 해석이 자연스럽기 때문에 정답이다. (C)는 5형식 동사로 사용시 목적 보어 자리에 to 부정사를 쓰는 동사이며, (D)는 동명사나 명사절을 목적어로 취하는 3형식 동사이다.

표현 정리 improved 개선된 performance 공연, 실적 manager 관리자

2. 정답 (C)

해설 회사 정책은 / 회사 차량의 적절한 사용을 설명한 / 유지한다 / 모든 직원들이 안전하게

해설 빈칸 뒤에 all employees라는 목적어가 있고, 그 뒤에 safe라는 목적격 보어가 있으므로 목적어와 형용사를 목적 보어를 취하는 (C) keeps가 정답이다. 해석도 '회사 정책은 모든 직원들을 안전하게 유지한다'가 자연스러우므로 (C)가 정답이다. (A)는 A from -ing의 형태로, (B)와 (D)는 'that S+V'를 목적어로 취하는 동사이다.

표현 정리 outline 개요를 서술하다 appropriate 적절한 keep 유지하다

3. 정답 (D)

해설 상점의 연장된 영업 시간은 / 고객들로 하여금 가능하게 한다 / 식사를 주문하는 것을 / 항상

해설 빈칸 뒤에 customers라는 목적어가 있고, 그 뒤에 to order라는 목적격 보어가 있으므로 목적어와 to 부정사를 목적 보어로 취하는 '결혼승낙' 동사인 (B), (C), (D) 중 '연장된 영업 시간은 주문하는 것을 가능하게 한다'는 뜻을 이루는 (D)가 가장 자연스럽다. (A)는 제안 등을 목적어로 취하는 3형식 동사이다.

표현 정리 extended 연장된 order 주문하다 allow 허용하다, 허락하다

◎ 실전에 적용해 봐
1. (D) 2. (B) 3. (A) 4. (C) 5. (B) 6. (A) 7. (B)
8. (A) 9. (C) 10. (D)

1. 정답 (D)

해설 급행 열차는 / Mr. Kerning을 도와주었다 / Kenmore에 제시간에 도착하도록 / 그가 참석할 수 있도록 / 지역 세미나에

해설 빈칸 뒤에 Mr. Kerning이라는 목적어가 있고, 그 뒤에 arrive라는 목적 보어가 있으므로 목적어와 to 부정사 또는 동사원형을 목적 보어로 취

하는 동사인 (D) helped가 정답이다. 해석도 '급행 열차는 Mr. Kerning이 Kenmore에 도착하도록 도와주었다'로 자연스럽다. (A)는 'A as B'나 'A to 동사원형'의 어울림을, (C)는 목적 보어 자리에 형용사나 -ing, p.p.가 필요한 동사이다.

표현 정리 express train 급행 열차 on time 제시간에 attend 참석하다 regional 지방의

2. 정답 **(B)**

해설 신중한 숙고 끝에 / 최고 관리자는 Mr. Will을 임명했다 / 최고 관리자로 / 그가 은퇴한 후에 일을 맡을

해설 빈칸 뒤에 Mr. Will이라는 목적어가 있고, 그 뒤에 as the executive manager가 목적 보어가 왔으므로 (B) appointed가 정답이다. 해석도 '최고 관리자는 Mr. Will을 최고 관리자로 임명했다'로 자연스럽다. (A), (C), (D)는 모두 'that S+V'를 목적어로 취하는 동사들이다.

표현 정리 careful 신중한 consideration 숙고 executive manager 최고 관리자 retire 은퇴하다 appoint 임명하다

3. 정답 **(A)**

해설 Kashi Corporation은 Mr. McKay가 회사 자동차를 사용할 수 있게 했다 / 공항으로 가는데 / 그의 외국 고객을 모시기 위해

해설 빈칸 뒤에 Mr. McKay라는 목적어가 있고, 그 뒤에 use는 목적 보어이다. 목적 보어로 동사원형을 취하는 사역동사 (A) let이 정답이다. (B)는 목적 보어 자리에 형용사, -ing, p.p.를, (C)는 to 부정사를 취하며, (D)는 3형식 동사이다.

표현 정리 automobile 자동차 in order to ~하기 위해서 foreign client 외국 고객 let 시키다

4. 정답 **(C)**

해설 Volume Music은 가능하게 한다 / 그들의 고객들이 스트리밍 서비스를 이용하는 것을 / 한 달에 10달러로

해설 빈칸 뒤에 its customers라는 목적어가 있고, 그 뒤에 to use가 목적 보어이다. 목적어와 to 부정사를 목적 보어로 취하는 '결혼승낙' 동사인 (C) enables가 정답이다. 'Volume Music은 고객들이 스트리밍 서비스를 이용하는 것을 가능하게 한다'는 해석도 자연스럽다.

표현 정리 enable 가능하게 하다

5. 정답 **(B)**

해설 장소를 찾는 것은 / 학장의 은퇴파티를 위해 적절한 / 더 어렵다 / 기대했던 것보다 / 모든 장소들이 / 내가 전화 한 / 예약이 꽉 찼기 때문에

해설 '은퇴파티를 위한 적절한 장소를 찾는 것'이란 말이 자연스러운데, 이 경우 find는 5형식이 아니고, 3형식 동사로 사용된다. 따라서 (B)가 답이다. (A)는 at이나 for와 같이 사용해야 목적어를 취할 수 있으며, (D)는 목적 보어로 to 부정사가 온다.

표현 정리 venue 연회장 appropriate 적절한 retirement party 은퇴파티 expect 기대하다, 예상하다 book 예약하다

6. 정답 **(A)**

해설 정기 보안 점검이 다음 주 수요일로 예정되어 있기 때문에 / 매니저는 상기시켰다 / 직원들 모두에게 / 그것에 대해 알고 있으라고

해설 빈칸 뒤에 all of the employees라는 목적어가 있고, 그 뒤에 은 to be가 목적 보어다. to 부정사를 목적 보어로 취하는 '결혼승낙' 동사인 (A) reminded, (C) allowed 중에 정답이 있다. '매니저가 직원들 모두에게 그것에 대해 알고 있으라고 상기시켰다'는 말이 자연스럽기 때문에 (A)가 정답이다.

표현 정리 regular security check 정기 보안 검사 employee 직원 be aware of ~을 알다 remind 상기시키다

7. 정답 **(B)**

해설 Ms. Packard는 Mr. Watanabi에게 전화했다 / 약속에 관해 / 그가 다시 일정을 잡고 싶어 했던

해설 빈칸 뒤에 Mr. Watanabi라는 목적어가 있고, 그 뒤에 전명구 수식어가 왔으므로 3형식 동사 자리이다. (A), (C)는 목적어 뒤 to 부정사를 목적 보어로 취하는 동사들이고, (D)는 목적어 다음 as 명사 또는 to 부정사를 목적 보어로 취하는 동사이므로 오답이다. 'Mr. Watanabi에게 전화했다'는 해석이 자연스럽기 때문에 (B)가 정답이다.

표현 정리 appointment 약속 want 원하다 reschedule 일정을 변경하다

8. 정답 **(A)**

해설 Ms. Jenkins는 전화를 받아야 했다 / 그녀의 보스로부터 / 그래서 그녀는 Mr. Olson을 남겨두었다 / 문에서 기다리도록 / 그가 그녀의 집을 방문했을 때

해설 빈칸 뒤에 Mr. Olson이라는 목적어가 있고, 그 뒤에 waiting이라는 목적격 보어가 있으므로 목적어와 형용사, -ing/p.p.를 목적 보어로 취하는 (A)가 답이다. (B)와 (C)는 to 부정사를 목적 보어로 취하는 동사이다.

표현 정리 receive 받다 waiting 기다리고 있는 leave 남겨두다, 있게 만들다

9. 정답 **(C)**

해설 투표가 실시된 후에 / Ms. Pill은 선출되었다 / 다음 이사회 멤버로

해설 빈칸 앞에 was가 있고, 보기가 전부 p.p. 형이므로 수동태이다. 빈칸 뒤에 as the next member란 전명구가 있다. 'as 명사'를 목적격 보어로 취하는 5형식 동사는 (C)이다. 5형식의 수동태는 be p.p. 다음에 목적 보어가 온다. 해석도 'Ms. Pill은 다음 멤버로 선출되었다'가 자연스럽기 때문에 (C)가 정답이다. (B)는 to 부정사를 목적 보어로 취하는 5형식 동사이다.

표현 정리 cast 던지다 board 이사회 elect 선출하다

10. 정답 **(C)**

해설 고객이 상담을 요청했기 때문에 / 투자 프로그램에 관해 / Bridge Solutions는 지정했다 / David Kean을 / 고객의 개인 상담가로

해설 빈칸 뒤에 David Kean이라는 목적어가 있고, 그 뒤에 o 부정사가 목적격 보어로 왔으므로 5형식 동사인 (A)와 (D)가 정답이 될 수 있다. 해석도 'David Kean을 개인 상담가로 지정했다'가 자연스럽기 때문에 (D)가 정답이다. 여기서 designate는 A as B로 주로 쓰이지만, 이렇게 목적 보어 자리에 to 부정사가 오기도 한다.

표현 정리 consultation 상담 investment 투자 personal 개인의 counselor 조언자 designate 지정하다

법칙 76 목적어가 없으면 1형식 동사

◎ 유형을 파악해 봐
1. (C)   2. (D)   3. (B)

1. 정답 (C)

해설 당신은 찾아야 한다 / 가장 짧은 길을 / 공항으로 가는 / 당신의 비행기가 / 출발할 것이기 때문에 / 7시에

해설 빈칸 뒤 전명구는 수식어이므로 빼내면 목적어가 없는 문장이므로 1형식 동사가 와야 한다. 3형식 동사인 (A), (B)는 오답이다. 1형식 동사인 (C), (D) 중 depart가 '출발하다'의 뜻으로 자연스러워 (C)가 정답이다. (D)는 '여행하다, 이동하다'의 뜻인데, 어디로 '여행, 이동'하는지가 나타나야 자연스럽게 된다.

표현 정리 shortest 가장 짧은 flight 비행, 비행기 여행 depart 출발하다

2. 정답 (D)

해설 당신의 회원 자격은 / 갱신되어야 합니다 / 그것이 만료되기 때문에 / 다음 주에

해설 빈칸 뒤의 next week는 부사이므로 목적어가 없는 문장이며, 따라서 빈칸에는 1형식 동사가 와야 하며, (D)가 정답이다. (A), (B), (C)는 목적어가 필요하다.

표현 정리 membership 회원자격 renew 갱신하다 expire 만료되다

3. 정답 (B)

해설 추가 여행 경비가 / 발생했다 / Mr. Bowman이 Norman Island를 방문한 후 / 그리고 그것은 포함되지 않았다 / 그의 계획에

해설 빈칸 앞에는 주어가, 빈칸 뒤에는 부사절과 형용사절이 나왔으므로 모두 수식어이며, 빈칸은 목적어를 취하지 않는 1형식 동사인 (B)가 와야 한다. (A), (C), (D)는 목적어가 필요하다.

표현 정리 additional 추가적인 travelling expenses 여행 경비 approved 승인된

◎ 실전에 적용해 봐
1. (D)   2. (A)   3. (C)   4. (A)   5. (B)   6. (B)   7. (D)
8. (C)   9. (D)   10. (A)

1. 정답 (D)

해설 분명히 하세요 / 당신이 끝내는 것을 / 첫 번째 보고서 원고를 / 오늘 / 마감 기한이 / 마지막 원고 제출을 위한 / 빠르게 다가오고 있기 때문에

해설 빈칸 앞의 부사는 수식어기 때문에 빼내면 현재진행형이며, 빈칸으로 문장이 끝나기 때문에 1형식 동사가 와야 한다. (D)는 1형식과 3형식으로 모두 사용할 수 있다. '마감일이 다가오고 있다'는 해석이 자연스러우므로 (D)가 정답이다. 나머지는 목적어가 필요하다.

표현 정리 make sure 명심하다 draft 원고 report 보고서 deadline 마감일 submission 제출 approach 가까워지다

2. 정답 (A)

해설 Riverside Bridge 건설은 / 예정되어 있다 / 시작되기로 / 7월 13일에 / 일단 계획들이 승인되면 / 시 공무원들에 의해

해설 빈칸은 to 부정사 자리로 동사원형이 와야 한다. 목적어가 없이 전명구가 왔기 때문에 3형식 동사인 (B), (C)는 오답이며, (A)는 '시작하다,' (D)는 '나아가다'의 뜻이다. '건설이 시작된다'는 내용이 자연스러우므로 (A)가 정답이다. proceed는 뒤에 with가 올 때 '진행되다'의 뜻을 갖는다.

표현 정리 construction 건설 be scheduled to ~할 예정이다 approve 승인하다 proceed 진행하다

3. 정답 (C)

해설 영업 이사는 발표했다 / 고객 수가 두 배로 증가했다고 / 회사가 새로운 상담 서비스를 도입한 후에

해설 빈칸 뒤에 수식어인 부사절이 왔기 때문에 빈칸은 목적어를 취하지 않는 1형식 동사의 자리이다. 1형식 및 3형식 동사인 (C)를 대입 후 해석해 보면 '고객들의 수가 두 배로 증가했다'는 말이 되어 자연스럽다. (A), (B), (D)는 목적어가 필요하다.

표현 정리 sales director 영업 이사 announce 알리다 introduce 도입하다 counseling service 상담 서비스 double 두 배로 되다

4. 정답 (A)

해설 지역 컨벤션 센터의 수리는 / 끝날 것이다 / 계획보다 한 달 뒤에 / 배수 시스템에 문제가 생겼기 때문에

해설 뒤에 목적어가 없기 때문에 1형식 동사가 정답이며, 목적어를 취하는 3형식 동사인 (B), (C), (D)는 오답이다. '배수 시스템에 문제가 발생했다'는 내용도 자연스럽기 때문에 (A)가 정답이다.

표현 정리 renovation 수선, 수리 planned 계획된 drainage 배수 emerge 나타나다, 출연하다

5. 정답 (B)

해설 비록 5년 이상 걸렸지만 / 전자공학에 관한 소규모 그룹 회의는 발달했다 / 신생 기술지원회사

해설 빈칸 뒤에 전명구가 왔기 때문에 목적어를 취하지 않는 1형식 동사 (B)가 정답이다. 3형식 동사인 (A), (C)와 5형식 동사인 '결혼 승낙' 동사 (D)는 오답이다.

표현 정리 electronic engineering 전자공학 startup 새로 시작하는

6. 정답 (B)

해설 Ms. Nervada는 기대된다 / CFO 자리를 넘겨받을 것으로 / 그녀가 가장 많은 수의 표를 받았기 때문에 / 최근 여론 조사에서

해설 빈칸은 to 부정사의 동사 자리로 뒤에 the CFO position이 목적어로 왔다. 'CFO 자리를 넘겨받다'는 말이 자연스럽기 때문에 (B)가 정답이다. (A)는 '은퇴하다,' (D)는 '포기하다'는 뜻이므로 뒤의 내용과 자연스럽지 못하며, (C)는 주로 뒤에 전치사 for나 at 등과 같이 쓰여 '~에 등록하다'는 뜻으로 사용된다. take over는 목적어 없이 1형식 동사로 사용되기도 하고,

지금처럼 3형식으로 사용되기도 하는 동사이다.

표현 정리 be expected to+동사원형 ~할 것으로 기대되다 vote 표, 표결 poll 여론조사, 투표 take over 인계 받다

7. 정답 (D)

해석 배송비는 / 다를지 모른다 / 당신의 지역에 따라 / 그리고 추가 금액이 청구될 것이다 / 먼 지역 배송에 대해서는

해설 빈칸 뒤의 depending on your region은 전명구이자 수식어이므로, 목적어를 취하지 않는 1형식 동사가 와야 한다. 해석도 '비용이 지역마다 다를지 모른다'는 내용이 자연스러우므로 (D)가 정답이다. 목적어를 취하는 (A), (B), (C)는 오답이다.

표현 정리 depending on ~에 따라 additional fee 추가인 비용 charge 청구하다 remote 외진, 먼 vary 다르다

8. 정답 (C)

해석 서면 통지서는 / 대략적인 날짜를 언급하고 있는 / 사무실 공사가 재개될 / 공지될 것이다 / 게시판에 / 정문 옆

해설 빈칸은 조동사 will 뒤의 동사원형 자리이고, 빈칸 뒤에는 아무것도 없기 때문에 목적어나 보어를 갖지 않는 1형식 동사 자리이다. 해석도 '사무실 공사가 재개될 것이다'라는 내용이 자연스럽기 때문에 (C)가 정답이다. 목적어를 취하는 동사인 (A), (B), (D)는 오답이다.

표현 정리 state 말하다, 진술하다 approximate 대략적인 renovation 수리, 보수 resume 재개하다, 다시 시작하다

9. 정답 (D)

해석 아마추어 작가는 심사숙고했다 / 공표하기 전에 / 어떤 비판도 받아들일 것이라고 / 그의 소설에 대한 / 그의 문체를 향상시키기 위해

해설 뒤에 전명구가 왔기 때문에 목적어를 취하지 않는 1형식 동사 자리이며, (D)가 정답이다. 해석도 '작가는 공표하기 전에 심사숙고했다'는 내용이 자연스러우므로 (D)가 정답이다. 목적어를 취하는 동사인 (A), (B), (C)는 오답이다.

표현 정리 author 작가 make an announcement 발표하다, 공표하다 criticism 비평 improve 향상시키다, 개선하다 offend 기분을 상하게 하다 deliberate 숙고하다

10. 정답 (A)

해석 50주년을 기념하기 위해 / 자동차 산업에서의 / Chez Auto는 소개했다 / 신형 자동차 모델을 / Velocity Vehicles와 협력하여

해설 빈칸은 its new car model을 수식하는 분사 자리이고, 전명구인 with 이하를 받는 1형식 동사 자리이다. collaborate with는 덩어리 동사로 '~와 협력하다'라는 뜻이며, 따라서 (A)가 정답이다. (D)는 1형식 동사로 사용 가능하나, 의미상 어울리지 않는다. 목적어를 취하는 B), (C), (D)는 오답이다.

표현 정리 commemorate 기념하다 automobile industry 자동차 사업 introduce 소개하다 collaborate with ~와 협력하다

법칙 77 목적어가 2개면 4형식 동사

◎ 유형을 파악해 봐
1. (A) 2. (C) 3. (A)

1. 정답 (A)

해석 Mannings Retailer Shop은 제안했다 / Daisy Manufacturing에게 1년 계약을

해설 빈칸 뒤 Daisy Manufacturing이 목적어, a one-year contract도 목적어이다. 목적어가 2개이므로 4형식 동사 자리이다. 4형식 동사가 아닌 (C), (D)는 오답이다. 남은 4형식 동사 (A), (B) 중 '1년 계약을 제안[제공]하다'는 어울림이 자연스럽기 때문에 (A)가 정답이다.

표현 정리 contract 계약 offer 제안하다

2. 정답 (C)

해석 매니저는 부여했다 / 고객 관리 팀에게 / 접근 권한을 / 고객 데이터베이스에 대한

해설 빈칸 뒤 the customer management가 목적어, access도 목적어이다. 목적어가 2개이므로 4형식 동사 자리이며, (C)가 정답이다. (D)도 4형식 동사지만, '고객 관리 팀에게 접근을 할당하다'라는 어색한 해석이 되며, 4형식 동사가 아닌 (A), (B)는 오답이다.

표현 정리 manager 관리자 customer management team 고객 관리 팀 access 접근; 접근하다 database 데이터베이스 grant 허가하다, 수여하다

3. 정답 (A)

해석 모든 직원들에게 알리세요 / 패션쇼가 취소되었다고

해설 빈칸 뒤에 all staff members라는 사람 명사가 왔고 이어 that S+V'가 왔기 때문에 빈칸에는 4형식 동사인 '인어노리' 동사가 와야 한다. '인어노리' 동사인 inform을 먼저 대입해 보면 해석이 자연스러우므로 (A)가 정답이다. (B)와 (C)는 3형식 동사이며, (D)는 to와 같이 덩어리로 사용하는 동사이다.

표현 정리 staff members 직원들 cancel 취소하다 inform 알리다

◎ 실전에 적용해 봐
1. (D) 2. (C) 3. (B) 4. (B) 5. (D) 6. (A) 7. (C)
8. (D) 9. (B) 10. (A)

1. 정답 (D)

해석 Ms. Knight의 보고서였다 / 그녀에게 노벨상을 안겨주고 / 글로벌 대중 의식을 고취시킨 것은 / 모금 캠페인들에 대한

해설 빈칸 뒤 her가 목적어, the Noble Prize도 목적어이다. 목적어가 2개이므로 4형식 동사인 (D)를 넣고 해석해 본다. '그녀에게 노벨상을 안겨주었다'는 어울림이 자연스럽기 때문에 (D)가 정답이다. 나머지는 3형식 동사들이다.

표현 정리 global 세계적인 public awareness 대중 의식 fundraising 모금 win 획득하다, 받다

2. 정답 (C)

해설 분명히 하세요 / 당신이 Mr. Miller의 고객에게 통보하는 것을 / 그가 사무실에 없을 것이라는 것을 / 내일부터 다음 주 목요일까지 / 출장 때문에

해설 빈칸 뒤 Mr. Miller's client라는 사람 명사가 오고, 이어 'that S+V'가 나왔기 때문에 빈칸에는 '인어노리' 동사가 와야 한다. '인어노리' 동사인 (C)를 넣어 해석하면 '고객에게 그가 사무실에 없을 것이라고 통보하라'는 내용이 자연스럽다. 따라서 (C)가 정답이다.

표현 정리 make sure ~할 것을 분명히 하다 from A to B A에서 B까지 business trip 출장

3. 정답 (B)

해설 만약 당신이 50세 이상이라면 / 질병 기록을 갖고 있는 / 그것은 비용이 들게 할 것이다 / 추가로 5퍼센트 / 보험을 가입하는데

해설 빈칸 뒤 you가 목적어, an additional 5%도 목적어다. 목적어가 2개이므로 4형식 동사인 (B), (D)를 먼저 대입해 본다. '추가로 5퍼센트 비용이 들게 하다'라는 해석이 자연스럽기 때문에 (B)가 정답이다.

표현 정리 over ~이상의 additional 추가적인 insurance 보험 cost 비용; 들게 하다

4. 정답 (B)

해설 환자의 요청대로 / 간호사는 / 그에게 가져다 주었다 / 더 많은 진통제를

해설 빈칸 뒤 him이 목적어, more pain relievers도 목적어이다. 목적어가 2개이므로 4형식 동사인 (B)를 먼저 대입해 본다. '그에게 더 많은 진통제를 주었다'는 해석이 자연스러우므로 (B)가 정답이다. (A)도 5형식 동사라 목적 보어 자리에 명사가 올 수 있는데, 그럴 경우 목적어와 목적 보어가 동격의 관계가 되어야 한다. him = pain relievers의 관계는 아니다.

표현 정리 request 요청하다; 요청 pain relievers 진통제 brought 가져다 주었다(bring의 과거)

5. 정답 (D)

해설 회사의 부채 비율이 눈에 띄게 낮은 상태였기 때문에 / 지난 몇 년 동안 / Local Industrial Bank는 대출해 주었다 / Prospect Energy에게 예상보다 더 많은 자금을

해설 빈칸 뒤 Prospect Energy가 목적어, more money도 목적어다. 목적어가 2개이므로 4형식 동사인 (D)를 대입하면 '~에게 더 많은 자금을 대출해 주었다'는 해석이 자연스럽다. 따라서 (D)가 정답이다. (B)는 4형식 동사일 때는 간접목적어에 사람이, 직접목적어에는 질문을 뜻하는 명사가 온다. (= He asked ma a question.)

표현 정리 debt rate 부채 비율 significantly 눈에 띄게 low 낮다 past 지난 expect 기대하다, 예상하다 lend 빌려주다

6. 정답 (A)

해설 멕시코 대사관은 Mr. Azek에게 취업 비자를 발급해 주었다 / 그가 Mexico에 머무르는 것을 허락하는 / 6개월 동안

해설 빈칸 뒤 Mr. Azrek가 목적어, a work visa도 목적어이다. 목적어가 2개이므로 4형식 동사인 (A)를 대입해 해석해 보면 'Mr. Azrek에게 취업 비자를 발급해 주었다'라는 자연스러운 말이 되므로 (A)가 정답이다. 나머지는 목적어를 취하는 3형식 동사이다. (B)의 경우는 to와 함께 덩어리로 사용하기도 한다.

표현 정리 work visa 취업 비자 issue 발급하다

7. 정답 (C)

해설 Ms. Frisen이 자기 자신을 주변 직원들에게 소개한 후에 / 그녀는 배정 받았다 / 그녀의 자리를 / 영업 팀 사무실에

해설 보기를 보면 모두 p.p. 형이기 때문에 빈칸은 수동태 자리이지만, 빈칸 뒤에 her seat라는 목적어가 왔기 때문에 4형식 동사 p.p.가 와야 한다. 4형식 동사는 (C)이며, 대입해 해석해 보면 '그녀는 그녀의 자리를 배정 받았다'라는 말이 자연스러워 (C)가 정답이다.

표현 정리 introduce 소개하다 employee 직원 assign 배정하다, 배치하다

8. 정답 (D)

해설 region's daily newspaper에 첫 출근한 날 / Mr. Clark는 받았다 / 두 개의 기사를 / 그가 비교하고 찾으라고 지시 받은 / 틀린 철자들을 / 기사 안에 있는

해설 보기를 보면 모두 p.p. 형이기 때문에 빈칸에는 수동태가 와야 하며, 빈칸 뒤에 two articles라는 목적어가 왔기 때문에 4형식 동사인 (D)를 대입해 해석하면 'Mr. Clark는 두 개의 기사를 받았다'가 자연스럽다. (A)도 4형식 동사의 기능이 있으나 '기사를 허락 받았다'는 말이 어색하다. 따라서 (D)가 정답이다.

표현 정리 article 기사 compare 비교하다 find 찾다 misspelled 철자가 틀린

9. 정답 (B)

해설 우리 회사의 정책에 따르면 / 직원들은 특별한 휴가를 받을 것이다 / 휴가 동안 그들은 일을 면제받는다 / 최대 15일 동안 / 특정 상황에서

해설 보기를 보면 모두 p.p. 형이기 때문에 빈칸은 수동태 자리이지만, 빈칸 뒤에 a special leave라는 목적어가 왔기 때문에 4형식 동사가 와야 하며, (B)를 먼저 대입해 해석해 보면 '직원들은 특별한 휴가를 받을 것이다'라는 자연스러운 해석이 되므로 (B)가 정답이다. (D)는 수동태가 되면 'that S+V'가 남아야 한다.

표현 정리 according to ~에 따르면 employee 직원 leave 휴가 certain circumstance 특정 상황 excuse 제외시키다, 면제하다 award 받다

10. 정답 (A)

해설 Relish Dining은 확신시켜 준다 / 고객들에게 / 회사는 단지 제공한다는 것을 / 가장 질 좋은 요리만을 / 가장 신선한 재료로 만들어진

해설 빈칸 뒤에 its customers라는 사람 명사가 왔고, 이어서 'that S+V'가 왔기 때문에 빈칸에는 '인어노리' 동사가 와야 한다. '인어노리' 동사인 assure를 먼저 대입해 해석해 보면 'Relish Dining은 단지 가장 질 좋은 요리만을 제공한다는 것을 확신시켜 준다'라는 자연스러운 말이 되므로 (A)가 정답이다. (C)도 4형식 동사이긴 하지만 'that S+V'를 직접목적어로 취하는 동사는 아니다.

표현 정리 the finest 가장 훌륭한 ingredient 재료 assure 보증하다

법칙 78 보어 자리에 형용사나 동격의 명사가 있으면 2형식 동사

◎ 유형을 파악해 봐
1. (C)　2. (D)　3. (B)

1. 　　　　　　　　　　　　　　　　정답 (C)

해설　필름 카메라는 더 이상 쓸모가 없는 상태가 되었다 / 디지털 카메라가 도입되자마자

해설　빈칸 뒤 obsolete는 형용사이다. 빈칸은 형용사를 보어로 취하는 2형식 동사 자리이다. (C)가 2형식 동사이므로 대입 후 해석해 보면 '필름 카메라들이 쓸모 없는 상태가 되었다'라는 글도 자연스럽기 때문에 (C)가 정답이다. 나머지 보기들은 모두 목적어가 필요한 동사들이다.

표현 정리　obsolete 더 이상 쓸모가 없는　introduce 소개하다, 출시하다

2. 　　　　　　　　　　　　　　　　정답 (D)

해설　너무 늦었다 / Ms. Pope가 알았을 때 / 무엇인가 잘못되었다는 것을 / 수술에서

해설　빈칸 뒤 wrong은 형용사이고, 빈칸은 형용사를 보어로 취하는 2형식 동사 자리이다. 보기에서 2형식 동사는 (A)와 (D)인데, '잘못 되었다고 판단했다'보다, '잘못 되었다'가 더 자연스러운 해석이므로 (D)가 정답이다. 여기서 go wrong은 '일 따위가 잘못되다'라는 표현으로 외우면 좋다.

표현 정리　realize 인지하다　operation 수술, 작전　prove 판명하다　go wrong (일이) 잘못되다

3. 　　　　　　　　　　　　　　　　정답 (B)

해설　뒤얽힌 파워 코드들은 / 문제가 있는 것으로 보인다 / 그것들이 만들기 때문에 / 건물 전체로의 파워 공급을 불안정하게

해설　빈칸 뒤 to be는 생략 가능하고, 남은 problematic은 형용사이다. 빈칸은 형용사를 보어로 취하는 2형식 동사 자리이다. (B)가 2형식 동사이므로 대입해 해석하면 '뒤얽힌 파워 코드들은 문제가 있는 것처럼 보인다'는 해석이 자연스럽기 때문에 (B)가 정답이다

표현 정리　tangled 뒤얽힌　problematic 문제가 있는　cause 야기하다, 일으키다　unstable 불안전한　power supply 파워 공급　entire 전체의　seem ~처럼 보이다

◎ 실전에 적용해 봐
1. (C)　2. (C)　3. (C)　4. (B)　5. (C)　6. (C)　7. (D)
8. (A)　9. (B)　10. (A)

1. 　　　　　　　　　　　　　　　　정답 (C)

해설　기조 연설에서 / Mr. Khan은 강조했다 / 회사의 꿈이 실현되게 하기 위해 / 모든 직원들은 가져야 한다고 / 구체적이고 성취 가능한 목표들을

해설　빈칸 뒤 true는 형용사이고, 빈칸은 형용사를 보어로 취하는 2형식 동사 자리이다. (C)가 2형식 동사이므로 먼저 대입해 해석하면, '회사의 꿈이 실현되도록 하기 위해서'가 자연스럽기 때문에 (C)가 정답이다.

표현 정리　keynote speech 기조연설　stress 강조하다　employee 직원　specific 구체적인　achievable 성취할 수 있는

2. 　　　　　　　　　　　　　　　　정답 (C)

해설　Mr. Johnson은 건강해졌다 / 입원한 후에 / 그의 부러진 다리 때문에 / 지난 2주 동안

해설　빈칸 뒤 well은 형용사이다. 빈칸은 형용사를 보어로 취하는 2형식 동사 자리이므로 2형식 동사인 (C)를 대입해 해석해 보면 'Mr. Johnson은 건강해졌다'가 자연스럽기 때문에 (C)가 정답이다.

표현 정리　get ~한 상태로 되다　after ~후에　hospitalize 입원시키다　broken 부러진

3. 　　　　　　　　　　　　　　　　정답 (C)

해설　두고 봐야 한다 / 올해 휴가 시즌 동안 매출액이 / 초과할지 아닐지는 / 지난해 판매량을

해설　빈칸 뒤 to be는 생략 가능하므로 생략해 보면 남아 있는 seen은 과거분사이고, 곧 형용사의 성격을 갖는다. 빈칸은 형용사를 보어로 취하는 2형식 동사 자리이므로 먼저 2형식 동사인 (C)를 대입해 해석해 보면 '~하는 것은 두고 봐야 한다'라는 해석이 자연스럽기 때문에 (C)가 정답이다.

표현 정리　remain to be seen 두고 보다　whether ~인지 아닌지　sales 판매량　holiday season 축제 시즌　exceed 초과하다

4. 　　　　　　　　　　　　　　　　정답 (B)

해설　많은 솔깃한 합병 제안들에도 불구하고 / 몇몇 다른 회사로부터 / Loyal 사는 파트너로 남았다 / LOK Corporation과

해설　빈칸 뒤 partnered는 과거분사, 즉 형용사이다. 형용사를 보어로 취하는 동사는 2형식 동사이고, 보기에서 2형식 동사인 (B)를 대입해 해석하면 '파트너로 남았다'라는 해석이 자연스러우므로 (B)가 정답이다.

표현 정리　notwithstanding ~에도 불구하고　tempting 솔깃한　merger 합병

5. 　　　　　　　　　　　　　　　　정답 (C)

해설　새로 설치된 소프트웨어는 판명되었다 / 효과적임이 / 컴퓨터 수를 줄이는 것에 / 바이러스들에 의해 감염된

해설　빈칸 뒤 effective는 형용사이다. 빈칸은 형용사를 보어로 취하는 2형식 동사 자리이므로, 2형식 동사인 (C)를 먼저 대입해 해석하면 '새로 설치된 소프트웨어는 효과적인 것으로 판명되었다'가 자연스럽기 때문에 (C)가 정답이다

표현 정리　newly 새로　the number of ~의 수　infected 감염된　prove 증명하다

6. 　　　　　　　　　　　　　　　　정답 (C)

해설　Ms. Sorenson은 초조해 보인다 / 의견을 들은 것에 / 그녀의 최근 제안에 대해 / 최고 관리자들로부터

해설　빈칸 뒤 to be는 생략 가능하므로 생략해 보면 남아 있는 nervous는 형용사이다. 빈칸은 형용사를 보어로 취하는 2형식 동사 자리이다. (E)와 (C)가 2형식 동사지만 to be를 좋아하는 것은 (C)이며, 대입해 해석해 보아도 '초조해 보인다'가 자연스럽기 때문에 (C)가 정답이다.

표현정리 nervous 불안해 하는, 초조해 하는 receive 받다 feedback 반응 executive manager 최고 관리자[경영자] appear ~처럼 보이다

7. 정답 (D)

해설 전 세계적으로 100만 부 이상의 판매량을 기록한 / 소설 'The Game of Swords'는 가장 잘 팔리는 소설 중 하나가 되었다 / 최근에

해설 빈칸 뒤 one은 명사이다. 소설이 가장 잘 팔리는 소설들 중 하나이므로 빈칸 앞뒤가 서로 같은 관계 즉, 동격이라고 볼 수 있다. 빈칸은 명사를 보어로 취하는 2형식 동사 자리이므로, (D)를 대입해 해석하면 'the novel 'The Game of Sword'는 가장 잘 팔리는 소설들 중 하나가 되었다'라는 내용이 자연스럽기 때문에 (D)가 정답이다. (A)는 'as 명사'를 목적 보어로 갖는 5형식 동사이고, (B)와 (C)는 3형식 동사이다.

표현정리 record 기록하다 million 100만 sales 판매량 around the world 전 세계적으로

8. 정답 (A)

해설 몇 번의 시도에도 불구하고 / 직원 복지를 향상시키려는 / Harrisburg 사는 하위권으로 남았다 / 다른 회사와 비교해 / 직원 만족도 면에서

해설 빈칸은 동사 자리이고, 뒤에 전명구가 왔기 때문에 목적어를 취하는 동사인 (B), (C), (D)는 답이 될 수 없다. 2형식 동사인 (A)의 뒤에 전명구가 보어로 온 형태이다. (A)를 대입해 해석해 보면 '하위권으로 남아 있다'는 자연스러운 해석이 되므로 (A)가 정답이다.

표현정리 attempt 시도 low rank 하위권 in terms of ~면에서 satisfaction 만족

9. 정답 (B)

해설 최근에 발견된 역사적인 유물들은 판명되었다 / 가장 오래된 로마 도자기의 전형으로 / 발견된 것들 중에

해설 여기서 remains를 동사로 보면 구조 파악이 안 되는 함정에 빠질 수 있다. remains는 주어, 빈칸이 동사 자리인데, remains는 곧 examples가 되는 관계이므로 동격의 관계라고 한다. 이때는 2형식 동사가 필요하다. 보기 중 to be를 매우 좋아하는 2형식 동사인 (B)를 대입해 해석해 보면 '역사적인 유물들은 판명되었다, 가장 오래된 로마 도자기들의 전형들이라고'라는 자연스러운 의미가 된다. 따라서 (B)가 정답이다.

표현정리 recently 최근에 example 본보기, 전형 pottery 도자기 discover 발견하다 turn out ~으로 판명되다

10. 정답 (A)

해설 동료 평가들은 필수사항들로 남아 있다 / 직원 성과 평가에서

해설 빈칸 뒤에 the essentials라는 명사가 나왔고, 동료 평가가 필수사항들이라는 주어와 빈칸이 서로 같은 관계, 즉 동격의 관계이므로 2형식 동사인 (A)를 대입해 해석해 보면 자연스런 의미를 이루므로 (A)가 정답이다.

표현정리 peer 동료, 친구, 동등한 것 essential 필수적인 것 performance 성과 evaluation 평가 remain 남아 있다

법칙 79 보기 중 1개라도 오답 처리해라

◎ 유형을 파악해 봐
1. (B)   2. (D)   3. (A)

1. 정답 (B)

해설 당신은 당신의 이름을 서명해야 한다 / 용지에 / 물건을 받기 위해서 / 당신에게 배달된

해설 빈칸 뒤 your name은 목적어이다. 목적어가 사람이 아니므로 (A)는 오답이다. 일단 (B)를 넣어 보면 '당신은 서명해야 한다'가 자연스럽기 때문에 (B)가 정답이다. 목적어를 갖지 않는 1형식이나 2형식 동사는 오답이다. (C)는 2형식 동사이므로 오답이다. 2형식 동사 뒤에 명사가 오는 경우는 you = your name의 관계일 때 가능하다. (D)는 A to B의 어울림을 좋아한다.

표현정리 sign one's name 서명하다 sheet 시트, 한 장 receive 받다 deliver 배달하다

2. 정답 (D)

해설 Realm Manufacture는 제품들의 생산을 늘릴 것이다 / 수요 증가 때문에

해설 빈칸 뒤에 the production이라는 목적어가 있기 때문에 1형식 동사인 (B)는 오답이다. 목적어를 취할 수 있는 (A), (C), (D) 중 하나를 넣어 해석해 보면 'Realm Manufacture는 생산량을 늘릴 것이다'가 가장 자연스럽기 때문에 (D)가 정답이다. (A)는 1형식일 때는 '자라다,' 2형식일 때는 '~되다.' 3형식일 때는 '키우다, 기르다'라는 뜻이므로 해석이 자연스럽지 못하다. (C)는 A to B의 어울림을 갖는다.

표현정리 production 생산, 생산량 goods 물건 due to ~때문에 demand 수요 increase 증가하다

3. 정답 (A)

해설 초대 강사는 여분의 시간을 요청했다 / 그의 강연 동안 / 청중들의 질문에 답하기 위해

해설 빈칸 뒤에 the audience's question이라는 목적어가 있기 때문에 to가 있어야 3형식 동사가 되는 (B)는 오답이다. 해석해 보면 '청중들의 질문에 답하기 위해'가 가장 자연스럽기 때문에 남은 3형식 동사들 중에 (A)가 정답이다.

표현정리 guest speaker 초청 강사 extra 여분의 lecture 강연 audience 청중

◎ 실전에 적용해 봐
1. (A)   2. (C)   3. (D)   4. (D)   5. (A)   6. (B)   7. (C)
8. (C)   9. (D)   10. (B)

1. 정답 (A)

해설 Mr. Schmitt는 요청했다 / 그의 비서에게 / 손님 리스트를 만들 것을 / 부사장의 은퇴파티를 위한 / 초대장이 발송되기 전에

해설 빈칸 뒤에 the guest list라는 목적어가 있기 때문에 1형식 동사인 (B)와 (C)는 오답이다. (A)와 (D) 중 '리스트를 준비하다, 편집하다'라는 해석이

자연스러우므로 (A)가 정답이다. (D)는 주로 '사람이나 직위를 인정하다'라는 뜻으로 쓰인다. 여기서 requested는 과거지만 compile 앞에 should가 생략되어 동사원형이 왔다.

표현 정리 request 요청하다 secretary 비서 guest list 손님 리스트 retirement party 은퇴 파티 send out 보내다 compile 준비하다

2. 정답 (C)

해설 B2B Tech Solutions는 Baycom 사에 조언했다 / 새로운 직원 복지 제도를 도입하라고 / 직원들의 사기를 높이기 위한

해설 빈칸 뒤에 a new ~ plan이라는 목적어가 있으므로 2형식 동사인 (D)는 제외시킨다. 나머지는 모두 3형식 동사들이므로 해석을 통해 가장 자연스러운 보기를 골라야 하는데, '직원들의 사기를 높이기 위한 복지 제도를 도입하다'가 가장 자연스럽기 때문에 (C)가 정답이다.

표현 정리 benefit plan 복지 제도 in order to ~하기 위해서 morale 사기 institute 도입하다

3. 정답 (D)

해설 기존의 안전 수준을 유지하기 위해 / G&W Electronics는 안전 검사를 시행한다 / 정기적으로 / 검사관의 엄격한 관리 하에

해설 빈칸 뒤에 safety inspections라는 목적어가 나오는데, (A) '안전 검사를 연장한다'는 말은 어색하며, (B)는 주로 5형식 동사로 사람 목적어에 to 부정사를 목적 보어로 취한다. 해석해 보면 'G&W Electronics는 안전 검사를 정기적으로 시행한다'란 뜻이 더 자연스럽기 때문에 (C)와 (D) 중 (D)가 정답이다.

표현 정리 maintain 유지하다 current 기존의, 현재의 safety level 안전 수준 inspection 검사, 검열 on a regular basis 정기적으로 strict 엄격한 supervision 감독 inspector 감사관 conduct 실시하다, 지휘하다

4. 정답 (D)

해설 Mr. Kemp의 지난 업무 경력은 / 그가 관리직을 맡았던 Gilson 사에서의 / 인정되었다 / 그리고 그는 제안 받았다 / Smith's Corp에서의 더 좋은 보수를 받는 직업을

해설 빈칸 뒤 목적어인 the managerial job이 있으므로 3형식 동사가 답이다. (A)의 경우 주로 목적 보어로 to 부정사가 필요한 5형식 동사로 사용한다. (B), (C), (D) 중 job이나 position을 목적어로 취하는 (D)부터 대입해 해석해 보면 '관리직을 맡았던 Gilson 사에서'라는 말이 자연스럽다. 따라서 (D)가 정답이다.

표현 정리 past 지난 work experience 업무 경력 managerial 관리직의 acknowledge 인정하다 better-paid 더 좋은 보수

5. 정답 (A)

해설 리투아니아 중앙 은행은 알렸다 / 그들의 계획들을 / 소규모 지역 회사들을 도울 / 창업자금 대출 금리를 낮춤으로써

해설 빈칸 뒤에 small local companies라는 목적어가 왔다. '계획 = 지역 소기업'의 관계, 즉 동격이 아니기 때문에 2형식 동사인 (B)는 제외하고, 나머지 3형식 동사들에서 결정한다. '소규모 지역 회사들을 돕기 위한 계획'이 가장 자연스럽기 때문에 (A)가 정답이다. (C)는 A from -ing의 어울림이, (D)는 'that S+V'를 좋아하는 동사이다.

표현 정리 announce 알리다 local 지역의 reduce 줄이다 interest rates 금리 loan 대출

6. 정답 (B)

해설 당신이 제공한 정보는 / 당신의 고객 등록 양식에 대해 / 은밀하게 취급될 것이다 / 그리고 사용될 것이다 / 오로지 정보를 제공하는 목적으로만

해설 수동태 형태이고, 빈칸 뒤에 목적어가 없기 때문에 3형식 동사의 p.p.를 고르는 문제이다. (C)는 5형식 동사이므로 수동태가 되면 'as 명사'가 남는다. 나머지 보기 중 '당신이 제공한 정보는 은밀하게 취급될 것이다'가 가장 자연스럽기 때문에 (B)가 정답이다.

표현 정리 provide 제공하다 registration form 등록 양식 confidentially 은밀하게 be used for ~를 위해 사용되다 informational 정보를 제공하는 handle 다루다

7. 정답 (C)

해설 General Pipelines 사는 개최할 것이다 / 회사 전체 오찬을 / 수요일에 / 뛰어난 성과를 기념하기 위해 / 매출 목표를 달성하는데

해설 빈칸 뒤에 its sales targets라는 목적어가 왔고, 따라서 목적어를 가지지 않는 1형식 동사인 (D)는 오답이다. '매출 목표를 달성한 성과를 기념하기 위해서'가 가장 자연스럽기 때문에 (C)가 정답이다. (A)는 주로 행사 뒤에, (B)는 to 부정사가 목적어로 오는 동사이다.

표현 정리 hold 개최하다 company-wide 회사 전체의 luncheon 오찬 commemorate 기념하다 outstanding 뛰어난 sales target 매출 목표 achieve 성취하다

8. 정답 (C)

해설 우리는 고객들에게 추천한다 / 스위트 룸을 미리 예약할 것을 / 방들이 모두 예약될 것이기 때문에 / 다가오는 휴가 시즌 동안

해설 빈칸 앞에 be 동사가 있고, 빈칸 뒤 목적어가 없기 때문에 수동태를 써야 하는 자리이다. 수동태가 돼도 목적 보어가 남는 5형식 동사인 (A)와 (B)는 일단 제외하고 '방이 모두 예약될 것이다'라는 의미가 앞에서 '예약을 미리 하도록 추천한다'는 말과 잘 어울리므로 (C)가 정답이다.

표현 정리 suite 스위트 룸 in advance 사전에 upcoming 다가오는 holiday season 휴가 시즌 reserve 예약하다

9. 정답 (D)

해설 유의하세요 / 우리가 이행할 수 없을지도 모른다는 것을 / 우리 고객들의 요구 사항들을 / 물품들의 배송에 대한 / 우리가 주문들을 처리하지 않기 때문에 / 수작업으로

해설 빈칸은 to 부정사의 동사원형 자리인 동시에 뒤에 온 목적어를 취하는 3형식 동사 자리이다. 따라서 1형식 동사인 (A)는 오답이다. '요청을 이행하다'라는 의미가 가장 자연스러워 (D)가 정답이다.

표현 정리 request 요청하다; 요청 delivery 배달 process 처리하다 receive 받다 order 주문 manually 수공업의, 손으로

10. 정답 (B)

해설 10년 넘게 Vox Motors에서 일해 온 / Mr. Eliot는 잘 알고 있다 / 심

지어 작은 부품들의 조각들도 / 대단히 중요하다는 것을 / 자동차를 조립하는데

해설 빈칸은 to 부정사의 동사원형 자리이면서 뒤에 목적어를 취할 수 있는 3형식 동사 자리이다. 따라서 1형식 동사인 (D)를 제외하고, 나머지 보기들을 대입해 해석해 보면, '조그만 부품조차도 차를 조립하는데 중요하다'라는 해석이 가장 자연스러우므로 (B)가 정답이다.

표현 정리 aware 알고 있는 component 부품 critical 중요한

법칙 80 제대로 해석해야 풀리는 동사 어휘 문제

◎ 유형을 파악해 봐
1. (C) 2. (B) 3. (A)

1.   정답 (C)

해설 갱신을 위한 당신의 요청에 따라 / 당신의 회원 만료일이 연장되었습니다 / 7월 20일로

해설 (A)와 (C)는 서로 반대말이므로 둘 중 하나를 대입해 해석해 본다. '갱신을 위한 요청이 있었기에 회원 자격이 연장되었다'고 해야 문맥상 맞다. 따라서 (C)가 정답이다. 1, 2형식 동사인 (D)는 수동태가 불가능하다.

표현 정리 request 요청하다, 요청 renewal 갱신 expiration date 만료일 extend 연기되다

2.   정답 (B)

해설 매출을 증가시키기 위해 / Dale 사는 추구해야 한다 / 효과적인 마케팅 전략을

해설 (A)는 주로 동명사나 to 부정사 목적어를 취하는 동사이고, (C)는 '인어노리' 동사로 사람 목적어를 취하는 동사이다. '매출을 증가시키기 위해 효과적인 전략을 추구해야 한다는 것이 논리적이므로 (B)가 정답이다.

표현 정리 sales 매출, 판매 effective 효과적인 strategy 전략 implement 실행하다 inform 알리다, 알아내다

3.   정답 (A)

해설 보석 가게의 빛나는 조명들은 증가시킨다 / 전시되어 있는 보석의 반짝거림을

해설 빈칸 뒤에 the glitter라는 목적어가 왔는데, 이 목적어는 주어인 the bright lightings와 동격이 아니기 때문에 2형식 동사인 (B)는 오답이다. '보석 가게의 빛나는 조명들이 보석의 반짝거림을 증가시킨다'가 자연스럽기 때문에 (A)가 정답이다.

표현 정리 lighting 조명 jewelry 보석 glitter 반짝거림 displayed 전시된 enhance 향상시킨다

◎ 실전에 적용해 봐
1. (D) 2. (B) 3. (C) 4. (A) 5. (D) 6. (A) 7. (B)
8. (B) 9. (D) 10. (C)

1.   정답 (D)

해설 TV 쇼에서 수석 주방장은 시연했다 / 만드는 과정을 / 인공 조미료 없는 건강식을

해설 빈칸 뒤에 the process라는 목적어가 있으므로 5형식 동사로 사용하는 (C)는 제외하고, 'TV 쇼에서 수석 주방장은 만드는 과정을 시연했다'가 자연스럽기 때문에 (D)가 정답이다.

표현 정리 head chef 수석 요리사 process 과정 healthy meal 건강식 artificial flavors 인공 조미료 demonstrate 보여주다, 시연하다

2.   정답 (B)

해설 Cescom Tech는 보았다 / 주가가 급등하는 것을 / 계획을 발표한 후 / L&P Electronics를 인수할

해설 빈칸은 뒤에 its plan이라는 목적어가 왔기 때문에 3형식 동사 자리이다. 1, 2형식 동사인 (C)를 제외하고 (A)와 (D)는 목적어와 to 부정사를 목적 보어로 취하는 5형식 동사들이다. '계획을 발표한 후'라는 해석이 잘 어울리므로 (B)가 정답이다.

표현 정리 sharp 급격한 increase 증가 stock price 주가 acquire 얻다 announce 알리다, 발표하다

3.   정답 (C)

해설 만약 당신이 지난 화요일의 워크숍을 놓쳤다면 / 알아두세요 / 우리가 해 온 활동이 / 요약되었고 / 3페이지짜리 유인물로 / 그리고 곧 배포될 것이라는 것을

해설 수동태의 형태에서 빈칸 뒤에 전명구 수식어가 왔기 때문에 수동태일 때 목적 보어를 가지는 5형식 동사인 (D)는 오답이다. '우리가 해 온 활동이 요약되었다'가 가장 자연스럽기 때문에 (C)가 정답이다.

표현 정리 miss 놓치다 handout 유인물 distribute 분배하다 summarize 요약하다

4.   정답 (A)

해설 회의실을 예약하기 위해서는 / 당신은 필요하다 / 우리에게 당신의 ID카드 또는 운전면허증을 제시하는 것이 / 그리고 그것은 당신에게 반환될 것이다 / 나갈 때

해설 빈칸 뒤에 a meeting room이라는 목적어가 있다. 간접목적어, 직접목적어를 가지는 4형식 동사인 (B)와 목적어를 갖지 않는 1형식 동사인 (C)는 오답이다. '회의실을 예약하기 위해'가 가장 자연스럽기 때문에 (A)가 정답이다.

표현 정리 require 요청하다 provide 제공하다 reserve 예약하다

5.   정답 (D)

해설 수리된 회의장은 확장되었다 / 정상 회담 이전에 / 50,000명까지 방문객들을 수용하기 위해

해설 빈칸은 to 부정사의 동사원형 자리이고, visitors를 목적어로 취하는 동사가 와야 하므로 1형식 동사인 (A) 오답이며, 3형식 동사로 쓰이면 '바르다'라는 뜻이 된다. (B)는 '방문객을 들어가다,' (C)는 '방문객을 세다'라는 해석이 어색하다. '방문객을 수용하다'라는 뜻의 (D)가 가장 자연스럽다.

표현 정리 renovate 보수하다 expand 연장하다 prior to ~이전에 summit 회담 accommodate 수용하다

118

6. 정답 (A)

해석 만약 이번이 당신의 첫 사무실 방문이라면 / 당신은 얻을 수 있다 / 방문자용 통행증을 / 안내 데스크에서 / 사무실에 출입할 수 있는 권한을 얻기 위해

해설 빈칸 뒤에 a guest pass라는 목적어가 있기 때문에 사람 목적어를 취하는 '인어노리' 동사인 (C)는 제외한다. you는 처음 방문하는 사람이므로 '방문자용 통행증을 얻는다'는 해석이 문맥상 적절하므로 (A)가 정답이다.

표현 정리 guest pass 방문자용 통행증 access 허가 allow 허락하다

7. 정답 (B)

해석 그녀의 제안에 대한 발표를 하기 전에 / Ms. Yamaguchi는 우선 유인물들을 배포했다 / 제안서의 주요 내용을 간략히 설명한

해설 빈칸 뒤에 the main points라는 목적어가 왔는데, 의미상의 주어인 the handouts와 동격이 아니기 때문에 2형식 동사인 (C)와 목적어로 주로 to 부정사를 갖는 (D)는 제외한다. 문맥상 발표를 하기 전에 나눠주는 것은 제안서를 간략하게 설명한 유인물이 적절하므로 (B)가 정답이다.

표현 정리 prior to ~이전에 deliver a presentation 발표하다 proposal 제안 distribute 배포하다 handout 유인물 outline 개요를 서술하다

8. 정답 (B)

해석 일단 우리가 수렴하는 것을 마치면 / 모든 직원들의 반응을 / 현재 근무 시간을 줄이는 것에 대한 / 우리는 CEO 승인을 얻기 위해 노력할 것이다 / 회사 정책을 수정하기 위한

해설 the company policy를 목적어 취하는 3형식 동사 자리이다. 1형식 동사인 (D)는 제외하고, '직원들의 근무 시간을 줄이는 것에 대한 반응을 수렴한 후, 회사 정책의 수정을 위한 CEO의 승인을 얻기 위해 노력한다'는 내용이 적절하므로 (B)가 정답이다.

표현 정리 once 일단 ~하면, ~하자마자 collect 수집하다 feedback 반응 approval 승인 accordingly 그에 맞춰 revise 개정하다

9. 정답 (D)

해석 만약 당신이 Alton 가의 웅장한 시계탑을 찾는다면 / 당신은 쉽게 우리 가게를 찾을 수 있을 것이다 / 근처에 위치한

해설 빈칸 뒤에 our store라는 목적어가 왔으므로 1형식 동사인 (B)는 오답이다. '시계탑을 찾으면, 우리 매장을 쉽게 찾을 수 있을 것'이라는 내용이 문맥상 적절하므로 (D)가 정답이다.

표현 정리 find 찾다 easily 쉽게 nearby 근처에 locate 찾다, 위치하다

10. 정답 (C)

해석 권장된다 / 당신이 백신 프로그램을 설치하는 것이 / 당신의 컴퓨터를 보호하기 위해 / 바이러스들과 웜으로부터

해설 모두 3형식 동사의 기능이 있으므로 문맥으로 해결해야 한다. 백신을 설치하도록 권유하는 이유는 컴퓨터를 바이러스로부터 보호하기 위해서이므로 (C)가 정답으로 적절하다.

표현 정리 recommend 추천하다, 권유하다 install 설치하다 vaccine program 백신프로그램

Chapter 10 명사 어휘 문제 (매월 4문제)

법칙 81 특정 전치사와 잘 어울리는 명사

◎ 유형을 파악해 봐
1. (B) 2. (A) 3. (A)

1. 정답 (B)

해석 최근 식료품 가격의 상승은 / 급격한 매출 하락을 가져왔다

해설 보기 중에서 빈칸 뒤 in과 함께 쓰이는 명사는 (B)이다. 이때 in은 '증감흥'이라고 불리며, '증가, 감소, 흥미'의 줄임말이다. '최근 스료품 가격의 상승'이라는 말도 자연스러우므로 (B)가 답이다. (A), (C)는 주로 뒤에 to가 온다.

표현 정리 recent 최근의 grocery 식료품 sharp 급격한 drop 하락, 감소 increase 상승

2. 정답 (A)

해석 우리는 사용하지 않을 것이다 / 당신의 답변을 / 우리의 설문 질문에 대한 / 다른 목적으로 / 당신의 허락 없이는

해설 보기 중에서 빈칸 뒤 to와 함께 쓰이는 명사는 (A), (B)이다. '당신의 허락 없이 우리의 설문 질문에 대한 당신의 답변을 사용하지 않을 것이다'라는 말이 자연스럽게 어울리므로 (A)가 답이다. (D)는 주로 앞에 under가 온다.

표현 정리 survey 설문조사 purpose 목적 permission 허락

3. 정답 (A)

해석 B_C 사는 계약했다 / 시 의회와 / Elga Bridge 건설에 관해

해설 보기 중에서 빈칸 뒤 with와 자연스럽게 어울리는 명사는 (A)이다. '시 의회와 계약을 했다'라는 말이 자연스러우므로 (A)가 답이다. (B)는 뒤에 to가, (D)는 into가 주로 온다.

표현 정리 make an agreement 협약을 맺다, 계약을 체결하다 city council 시 의회 approach 접근 initiative 계획 expansion 확장

◎ 실전에 적용해 봐
1. (D) 2. (C) 3. (B) 4. (D) 5. (B) 6. (D) 7. (C)
8. (D) 9. (C) 10. (B)

1. 정답 (C)

해석 만약 당신이 적어 / 당신의 기본 인적 사항을 / 제공된 서류에 / 제출한다면 / 접수처에 / 당신은 출입할 수 있을 것이다 / 건물을

해설 보기 중에서 빈칸 뒤 to와 자연스럽게 어울리는 명사는 (A)와 (D)이다. '기본 인적 사항을 적어 제출하면, 빌딩에 출입할 수 있다'는 말이 자연

스럽다. 따라서 (D)가 답이다. (B)는 주로 뒤에 on이 온다.

표현 정리 personal information 개인 정보, 인적 사항 submit 제출하다 reception desk 접수처 access 접근하다

2. 정답 **(C)**

해설 시 의원들은 개최할 것이다 / 긴급 회의를 / 오늘 아침에 / 논의하기 위해 / 급격한 상승에 대해 / 이란으로부터 수입한 오일 가격의

해설 보기 중에서 빈칸 뒤 in과 주로 쓰이는 명사는 (C)이다. 이때의 in은 '증감흥'이라고 불리며, '증가, 감소, 흥미'의 줄임말이다. '수입된 오일 가격의 급격한 상승'이라는 말이 자연스러워 (C)가 정답이다. 보통 (A)와 (D)는 바로 뒤에 of가 나오며, (B)는 to가 나온다.

표현 정리 council 의회 urgent 긴급한 dramatic 급격한 possibility 가능성 donation 기부, 기증 rise 증가 accumulation 누적, 축적

3. 정답 **(B)**

해설 당신이 연구실에서 일하는 동안 / 명심해야 한다 / 안전지침을 철저히 준수하는 것을

해설 보기 중 빈칸 뒤 with와 주로 쓰이는 명사는 (B)이다. '안전지침을 철저히 준수하는 것을'이라는 말이 자연스럽게 어울리므로 (B)가 정답이다. (C)는 주로 뒤에 to가 온다.

표현 정리 credibility 신뢰성 compliance 준수 contribution 공헌 specialty 전문

4. 정답 **(D)**

해설 Kemore Publication의 10주년을 기념하기 위해 / 창립 / 우리는 발표하고 영광을 돌립니다 / 사람들에게 / Kemore Publication에 지대한 공헌을 한

해설 보기 중 빈칸 뒤 to와 주로 쓰이는 명사는 (A)와 (D)이다. '지대한 공헌을 한'이라는 말이 자연스럽게 어울리므로 (D)가 답이다. (B)는 주로 뒤에 with가 온다. (C)는 'POWER' 명사로 뒤에 주로 to 부정사가 온다('법칙 57' 참고).

표현 정리 decennial 10년의 foundation 설립 contribution 공헌

5. 정답 **(B)**

해설 상품의 교환이나 반품에 관한 문의들은 / 이루어져야 한다 / 오직 전화로만 / 구매 후 7일 이내에

해설 보기 중 빈칸 뒤 about과 주로 쓰이는 명사는 (B)이다. '교환이나 반품에 관한 문의'가 자연스럽기 때문에 (B)가 답이다. (A)는 주로 뒤에 with가, (C)는 to가, (D)는 on이 온다.

표현 정리 purchase 구매 inquiry 문의, 질문 implication 영향, 암시

6. 정답 **(D)**

해설 Mr. Wales는 이직할 것이다 / 다른 회사로 / 최고 관리자로 20년간 근무한 후에 / Amerison 사에서

해설 보기 중에서 빈칸 뒤 as와 주로 쓰이는 명사는 (D)이다. '최고 관리자로 20년간 근무한 후에'가 자연스럽다. 따라서 (D)가 답이다.

표현 정리 move 이동하다 executive manager 최고 관리자 reputation 평판 reimbursement 환급

7. 정답 **(C)**

해설 Aramax Corporation은 채용했다 / 많은 수의 직원들을 / 국제부에 / 유럽 시장으로의 확장과 함께

해설 보기 중에서 빈칸 뒤 into와 잘 어울리는 명사는 (C)이다. (A)는 주로 뒤에 about이, (B)는 in이 온다.

표현 정리 recruit 채용하다 division 지사 enrollment 등록

8. 정답 **(D)**

해설 연례 직업박람회에서 / 많은 방문자들은 / 해외 고용에 큰 관심이 있는 / 신청했다 / 직무 자격 요건에 관한 정보를 얻기 위해

해설 보기 중에서 빈칸 뒤 in과 잘 어울리는 명사는 (D)이다. '해외 고용에 큰 관심 있는'이란 말이 자연스럽다. (B)와 (C)는 주로 뒤에 to가 오는 'POWER' 명사이다('법칙 57' 참고).

표현 정리 overseas 해외의 employment 고용 requirement 요구 조건, 필요 조건 authority 권한, 인가 opportunity 기회 effort 노력

9. 정답 **(C)**

해설 'The Story of Tom Carter'는 / 이번 주말에 출판될 / 가장 최신판이 될 것이다 / Jim Parker의 가장 최근 소설 시리즈

해설 보기 중에서 빈칸 뒤 to와 주로 쓰이는 명사는 (C)이다. '가장 최근 소설 시리즈의 최신판'이라는 말이 자연스럽게 어울린다. 따라서 (C)가 답이다.

표현 정리 publish 출판하다 addition 추가, 추가 작품

10. 정답 **(B)**

해설 만약 당신이 긴급한 서류를 갖고 있다면 / 즉시 배달되어야 할 / 우리 빠른 우편 서비스를 통해 보내세요 / 지연 없는 배달을 보장하는

해설 보기 중에서 빈칸 앞 without과 잘 어울리는 명사는 (B)이다. '우리 빠른 우편 서비스를 통해 지연 없는 배송을 보장하는'이라는 말이 자연스러우므로 (B)가 정답이다.

표현 정리 urgent 긴급한 immediately 즉시 ensures 보장하다

법칙 82 특정 명사와 잘 어울리는 명사

◎ 유형을 파악해 봐
1. (C) 2. (A) 3. (D)

1. 정답 **(C)**

해설 Arium Convention Hall은 예약되었다 / Belle 사 시상식을 위해 / 화요일에

해설 awards와 어울리는 복합명사는 (C)뿐이다. '시상식을 위해 예약되었다'는 해석도 자연스럽기 때문에 (C)가 정답이다.

표현 정리 reserve 예약하다 award ceremony 시상식 application 지원, 지원서, 신청서 product 제품, 상품

2. 정답 (A)

해설 높은 수준의 복지제도를 가진 회사는 / 더 높은 직원 생산성을 갖고 있다

해설 employee와 어울리는 복합명사는 (A)뿐이다. '더 높은 직원 생산성을 갖고 있다'는 해석도 자연스러워 (A)가 정답이다.

표현 정리 firm 회사 benefits 복지 혜택 employee productivity 직원 생산성 probability 개연성 feasibility 가능성 utility 유용성

3. 정답 (D)

해설 흔한 절차이다 / 제출하는 것이 / 당신의 사업제안서를 / 예산을 요청하기 전에

해설 business와 어울리는 복합명사는 (B), (C), (D)이며, 이들 중 문맥상 가장 자연스러운 말을 찾아야 한다. '사업제안서를 제출하는 것은 흔한 절차이다, 예산을 요청하기 전에'라는 해석이 가장 적절하므로 (D)가 정답이다.

표현 정리 common 흔한, 보통의 procedure 절차 submit 제출하다 budget 예산 entry 입구 merger 합병 partnership 동업자, 동반자 proposal 제안, 제안서

◎ 실전에 적용해 봐
1. (C) 2. (B) 3. (C) 4. (A) 5. (A) 6. (D) 7. (B)
8. (D) 9. (C) 10. (A)

1. 정답 (C)

해설 공사장 근처의 도로들은 폐쇄될 것이다 / 다음 주 금요일까지 / Gordon Bridge의 복원이 끝나는

해설 모두 construction과 복합명사로 사용 가능하다. '공사장 근처의 도로들은 폐쇄될 것이다'라고 해야 자연스럽게 어울리므로 (C)가 정답이다.

표현 정리 construction 공사, 건설 restoration 복원 management 경영, 관리 workforce 노동력 institute 기관, 협회

2. 정답 (B)

해설 우리는 수정할 것이다 / 우리의 안전 조치를 / 왜냐하면 우리가 최근에 설치했기 때문에 / 몇몇의 새로운 제조 장비를 / 매우 잘 작동하지만 위험할 수 있는 / 잘못 사용될 경우

해설 (C)를 제외하며, 모두 safety와 복합명사로 사용할 수 있는 명사들이다. 따라서 먼저 동사 revise와의 어울림을 보고, 이어서 as 다음을 확인한다. 안전 조치를 수정할 예정인데, 그 이유는 최근에 새로운 장비를 설치했기 때문이라는 문맥이다. 따라서 (B)가 답이다. (D)는 보통 for safety reasons(안전상의 이유로)라는 문구에 주로 사용된다.

표현 정리 safety measures 안전 조치 functional 실용적인 mishandle 잘못 처리[관리]하다 awareness 의식 estimates 추정, 견적서

3. 정답 (C)

해설 Royal Bank의 은행 대출 신청자 수가 / 3배 증가했다 / 작년과 비교해 / 월 김대로 증가 때문에

해설 loan과 같이 사용할 수 있는 복합명사는 (C)뿐이다. '대출 신청자가 3배 증가했다'가 자연스럽게 어울리므로 (C)가 답이다.

표현 정리 loan 대출 triple 3배가 되다, 3배로 만들다 compared to ~와 비교하여 increase in ~의 증가 monthly 매월의, 한 달에 한 번의 rent 집세, 임차료 applicant 신청자

4. 정답 (A)

해설 당신은 리허설 해야 한다 / 당신의 멀티 미디어 프레젠테이션을 / 미리 / 확인하기 위하여 / 모든 장비가 제대로 작동하는지

해설 rehearse는 공연이나 발표 등을 한번 해 보는 느낌의 동사이다. multimedia와 자연스럽게 어울리는 것도 (A)이므로 대입 후 해석해 보면 '멀티미디어 발표를 연습해야 한다'가 가장 적절하므로 (A)가 답이다.

표현 정리 rehearse 리허설 하다, 예행 연습하다 in advance 미리, 사전에 properly 제대로, 적절히 multimedia presentation 멀티미디어 프레젠테이션 stance 입장

5. 정답 (A)

해설 대중 교통을 이용하는 대부분의 차량 소유주들이 / 그들 자신의 차량 대신 / 출근하기 위해 / 상당히 증가했다 / 높은 연료 비용 때문에

해설 fuel과 잘 어울리면서, 높은 연료비 때문에 자신의 차량 대신 대중 교통을 이용하는 사람들이 증가했다는 내용과 잘 어울리는 (A)가 정답이다.

표현 정리 car owner 차주 public transportation 대중 교통 significantly 상당히 fuel cost 연료 가격 alternative 대안 receipt 영수증

6. 정답 (D)

해설 만약 당신이 받지 않았다면 / 여행일정표를 포함한 이메일을 / 우리가 당신에게 보낸 / 우리에게 알려 주세요

해설 travel과도 잘 어울리면서 이메일에 포함될 수 있는 내용은 복합명사인 (D) itinerary뿐이다.

표현 정리 receive 받다 contain 포함하다 equipment 장비 tension 긴장 itinerary 일정표

7. 정답 (B)

해설 Bell Airlines의 TV 광고는 / 미국의 세계적으로 유명한 관광 명소들을 보여주는 / 실제로 증진시켰다 / 관광 산업을

해설 tourism 및 promote와 잘 어울리는 (B)를 대입하여 해석해 보면 '관광 산업을 증진시켰다'라는 말이 자연스러워 (B)가 정답이다.

표현 정리 commercial 광고 world-famous 세계적으로 유명한 tourist spot 관광 명소 promote 증진하다, 홍보하다 tourism industry 관광 산업

8. 정답 (D)

해설 우리 회사의 연 수익 증가는 확실히 영업 직원 덕분이다 / 모든 국내 기업들보다 많이 판매한

해설 who 이하의 수식을 받으므로 사람 명사가 되는 복합 명사를 찾아야

한다. (D)를 대입하면 영업 직원이라는 사람을 가리키는 말이 되며, '연 수익 증가는 영업 직원 덕분이다'라는 자연스러운 말이 되므로 (D)가 정답이다.

표현 정리 revenue 수익 attributable ~가 원인인 outsell ~보다 많이 팔다 employment 고용 personnel 직원

9. 정답 (C)

해석 만약 당신이 구매하기를 원한다면 / 중국 향신료를 하나하나씩 각각의 맛으로 / 구매하기를 원할 것이다 / 소매점에서 / 도매시장보다는

해설 retail과 함께 복합명사를 구성하는 단어를 찾아야 한다. 장소와의 어울림을 갖는 (C)를 대입해 해석해 보면, '도매시장보다는 소매점에서 구매하기를 원할 것이다'라는 말이 자연스러워 (C)가 정답이다.

표현 정리 spice 양념, 향신료 flavor 맛 retail location 소매점 wholesale market 도매 시장

10. 정답 (A)

해석 안전 장비를 착용하는 것은 / 상당히 높일 수 있다 / 보호 수준을 / 충격과 신체적 손상으로부터 / 사고가 발생할 경우

해설 safety와도 잘 어울리면서 착용할 수 있는 의미를 포함하는 복합명사가 될 수 있는 것은 (A)뿐이다.

표현 정리 significantly 상당히 damage 손상 accident 사건 equipment 장비 guideline 가이드라인, 지침 caution 경고, 주의 evidence 증거

법칙 83 '사람 명사 및 to 부정사'와 잘 어울리는 명사

◎ 유형을 파악해 봐
1. (A)   2. (B)   3. (C)

1. 정답 (A)

해석 Elevated Tech 대변인은 오늘 발표했다 / 출시할 것이라고 / 인체공학적인 최첨단 의자를 / 다음 주에

해설 announced는 '생말예제' 동사이므로('법칙 73' 참고) 주어 자리에 사람 명사가 온다. (B), (C), (D)는 사람 명사가 아니므로 제외하고, (A)를 넣어 해석하면 'Elevated Tech 대변인은 발표했다'라는 말이 자연스럽게 어울리므로 (A)가 정답이다.

표현 정리 announce 발표하다, 알리다 launch 출시하다 state-of-the-art 최첨단의, 최신식의 ergonomic 인체공학의 spokesperson 대변인 reputation 명성, 평판 petition 진정[탄원]서 feedback 의견

2. 정답 (B)

해석 고객들은 / 우리의 판촉 행사에 참가하는 / 기회가 주어질 것이다 / 상을 받을

해설 빈칸 바로 뒤에 to 부정사가 왔으며, to 부정사의 수식을 잘 받는 (B)를 넣어 해석하면 '상을 받을 기회가 주어질 것이다'라는 말이 자연스럽게 어울리므로 (B)가 정답이다.

표현 정리 participate in ~에 참가하다 win 얻다, 타다 prize 상 arrangement 준비, 정돈, 배열 objection 이의, 반대 appointment 약속, 임명, 지명

3. 정답 (C)

해석 자선 행사의 목표는 향상시키는 것이다 / 자립능력을 / 그리고 근절하는 것이다 / 극도의 빈곤을

해설 be to 부정사와 잘 어울리는 명사는 '목표, 계획'의 뜻을 가진 명사이다. 따라서 (C)를 대입해 해석해 보면 '자선 행사의 목표는 향상시키는 것이다'라는 자연스러운 말이 되므로 (C)가 정답이다. (B)는 목표가 아니고 목적지라는 뜻이다.

표현 정리 charity 자선, 자선 단체 self-sustainability 자립능력 eradicate 근절하다 extreme 극도의 poverty 가난, 빈곤

◎ 실전에 적용해 봐
1. (D)   2. (D)   3. (B)   4. (A)   5. (D)   6. (D)   7. (B)
8. (D)   9. (C)   10. (C)

1. 정답 (D)

해석 'Exclusive Magazine'은 인하했다 / 구독료를 / 유지하기 위한 노력으로 / 독자들을 / 비싼 요금에 대해서 종종 불만을 보인

해설 빈칸 뒤에 to 부정사가 왔으므로 to 부정사의 수식을 잘 받는 (D)를 넣어 해석하면 '독자들을 유지하기 위한 노력으로'라는 자연스러운 내용이 되므로 (D)가 답이다. effort는 'POWER' 명사이다('법칙 57' 참고).

표현 정리 reduce 내리다, 인하하다 subscription 구독 in an effort to+동사원형 ~하기 위한 노력으로

2. 정답 (D)

해석 다수 이사들은 기꺼이 받아들일 것이다 / 후보자를 / 영업 부장 자리에 대한 / 그는 이미 5년의 경험을 갖고 있기 때문에 / 관련 분야에서

해설 because 다음에 he가 있는 것으로 보아 빈칸은 사람을 가리키는 말이 와야 한다. 사람을 나타내는 (A)와 (D) 중에서 '영업 부장 자리에 대한'이란 말의 수식을 받으려면 '후보자'라는 말이 와야 한다. 따라서 답은 (D)가 된다.

표현 정리 a majority of 다수의 board members 이사진 accept 받아들이다 related field 관련 분야 attendee 참석자 candidate 지원자, 후보자

3. 정답 (B)

해석 Foster 사가 Innovative Tech의 통제권을 넘겨받은 후로 / Foster 사는 터치스크린 기능을 사용할 권리를 보유하고 있다 / 처음 고안된 / Innovative Tech에 의해 / 휴대폰을 위해

해설 빈칸 바로 뒤에 to 부정사가 왔으며, to 부정사의 수식을 잘 받는 (B)를 넣어 해석하면 '터치스크린 기능을 사용할 권리를 보유하다'라는 말이 자연스러워 (B)가 정답이다. right는 'POWER' 명사이다('법칙 57' 참고). 또한 reserve the right는 '권리를 보유하다'라는 숙어로 외워두는 것도 좋다.

표현 정리 reserve 보유하다, 확보하다, 예약하다 right to+동사원형 ~할 권리 initially 처음에 devise 고안하다, 창안하다 budget 예산 inquiry 문의, 문의 사항

4. 정답 (A)

해석 당신이 First Security 사가 최근에 개발한 보안 프로그램을 이용할 때 / 당신의 컴퓨터에 / 모든 미확인 시도가 / 당신의 은행 계좌에 접근하려는 / 자동적으로 차단될 것이다

해설 빈칸 바로 뒤에 to 부정사가 왔으며, to 부정사의 수식을 잘 받는 (A)를 넣어 해석하면 '당신의 은행 계좌에 접근하려는 미확인 시도'라는 자연스러운 말이 되므로 (A)가 정답이다. attempt는 'POWER' 명사이다('법칙 57' 참고).

표현 정리 recently developed 최근 개발된 security program 보안 프로그램 unidentified 미확인의, 정체불명의 bank account 은행 계좌 automatically 자동으로 block 막다, 차단하다

5. 정답 (D)

해석 기술자에 따르면 / 우리 사무실에 왔던 / 프린터를 점검하기 위해 / 오늘 아침에 / 프린터는 교체될 필요가 있다 / 새 것으로

해설 빈칸 뒤에는 선행사가 사람일 때 쓰는 주격관계대명사 who가 있다. 따라서 빈칸은 사람 명사가 와야 한다. '프린터를 점검하기 위해 사무실에 온' 사람이므로, (A), (B), (D) 중에서 '기술자'라는 뜻을 가진 (D)가 가장 적절하다.

표현 정리 inspect 점검하다 replace 교체하다, 대치하다 generator 발전기 accountant 회계사 estimate 추정, 견적, 견적서

6. 정답 (D)

해석 심사 위원단이 / 연례 세계 요리 경연을 위한 / 소개되었다 / 청중들에게 / 행사의 개막식에서

해설 청중에게 소개가 되려면 사람을 가리키는 말이 필요하다. 위원단의 뜻을 가진 (D)를 대입하면 뒤의 judges와도 잘 어울리고, 청중에게 소개되었다는 말과도 의미가 이어지므로 (D)가 정답이다.

표현 정리 judge 심사위원 audience 관중 opening 개막식, 개회식 advantage 유리한 점 account 계좌 extent 범위, 정도, 넓이

7. 정답 (B)

해석 Mr. Dobb는 의심할 여지없이 바람직한 지원자이다 / 직책에 대해 / 국제사업부 / 그는 보유하고 있기 때문에 / 4가지 언어를 유창하게 말할 능력을

해설 빈칸 바로 뒤에 to 부정사가 왔으며, to 부정사의 수식을 잘 받는 명사인 (B)를 넣어 해석해 보면 '4개 언어를 유창하게 말할 능력을 보유하고 있다'라는 자연스러운 말이 되므로 (B)가 정답이다. ability는 'POWER' 명사이다('법칙 57' 참고).

표현 정리 undoubtedly 의심할 여지가 없이 desirable 바람직한 candidate 지원자, 후보자 possess 소유하다 tendency 성향, 기질 property 재산, 부동산, 소유물

8. 정답 (D)

해석 Wellbeing Food는 소개했다 새로운 인스턴트 면류 식사를 / 빠른 식사를 원하는 사람들을 목표로 한

해설 빈칸 뒤에 사람을 선행사로 취하는 주격관계대명사 who가 있으므로 빈칸은 사람 명사가 와야 한다. (D)를 대입해 해석해 보면, '빠른 식사를 원하는 사람들을 목표로 하는'이라는 내용이 자연스럽기 때문에 (D)가 정답이다. individual은 형용사로만 알고 있기 쉬운 단어이지만, '사람, 개인'이라는 뜻의 명사로도 잘 쓰이는 단어이다.

표현 정리 introduce 소개하다 instant 즉각적인, 인스턴트의 supplies 비품 instructions 지침 individuals 개인

9. 정답 (C)

해석 Williams Convention Center에서 줄을 서서 기다리는 사람들 중에 / 직원은 허락했다 / 초대된 게스트만 / 비공개 쇼에 입장할 수 있도록

해설 빈칸 앞 invited은 빈칸의 명사를 수식하는 분사이다. 초대된'은 사람을 수식하는 말이므로 사람 명사를 답으로 골라야 한다. '초대된 게스트만 비공개 쇼에 입장할 수 있도록 허락했다'는 내용이 되므로, '초대되는' 사람은 (A) 승객들'보다는 (C) '손님들'이라는 말이 더 자연스러우므로 (C)가 정답이다.

표현 정리 individual 개인; 개인의 wait in line 줄을 서서 기다리다 allow 허용하다 private 사적인, 개인적인

10. 정답 (C)

해석 Wellness Fitness Center는 제공한다 / 신입 회원에게 / 요가 수업을 등록할 수 있는 기회를 / 무료로

해설 빈칸 바로 뒤에 to 부정사가 있으며, to 부정사의 수식을 잘 받는 경우는 (A)와 (C)이다. 신입 회원들(newcomers)에게 요가 수업에 등록할 '기회'를 제공한다는 해석이 자연스러우므로 (C)가 정답이다.

표현 정리 provide A with B A에게 B를 제공하다 newcomer 신입회원 sign up for 등록하다 for free 무료로 involvement 관여, 연루

법칙 84 특정 단어와 잘 어울리는 기타 명사들

◎ 유형을 파악해 봐
1. (D)   2. (A)   3. (C)

1. 정답 (D)

해석 존 지배인은 결정했다 / 개최하기로 / 환영회를 / 기조 연설자의 발표 후에

해설 빈칸 앞의 hold(개최하다)는 행사 명사를 목적어로 취하는 동사이므로 '환영회'라는 뜻의 (D)가 hold의 목적어로 적합하다. '환영회를 개최하기로 결정했다'라는 내용도 자연스러우므로 (D)가 답이다. 나머지 보기들은 hold(개최하다)와 어울리지 않는다.

표현 정리 general manager 사장, 총 지배인 hold 개최하다 keynote speaker 기조연설자 presentation 발표 association 협회, 연합, 조합

2. 정답 (A)

해석 Home n' Shop에서 / 우리는 제공한다 / 아주 다양한 인테리어 소품들을

해설 빈칸 앞에 관사 a가 있으므로 불가산명사인 (B)는 우선 오답 처리한다. 빈칸 앞 a wide와 빈칸 뒤 of가 있으므로 a wide ~ of 형태로 잘 쓰이

는 (A)를 넣어 해석해 본다. '아주 다양한 인테리어 장식품을 제공한다'라는 자연스러운 내용이 되므로 (A)가 정답이다. a variety of는 '다양한'이라는 뜻이며, variety 앞에 wide, broad, large, diverse 등의 형용사가 들어가면 '아주(매우) 다양한' 이라는 표현이 된다.

표현 정리 a (wide) variety of (아주) 다양한 merchandise 물품, 상품 approach 접근하다, 접근, 가까움 allocation 할당, 배당

3. 정답 (C)

해설 알려졌다 / Mr. Mitch가 은퇴할 것이라는 소식은 / 실제로는 사실이 아닌 것으로

해설 빈칸 뒤에 that과 완전한 문장이 왔다. 이것을 동격의 that 절이라고 한다. 보기 중에 동격의 that과 잘 쓰이는 명사는 (C)이다. 'Mr. Mitch가 은퇴할 것이라는 소식은 실제로는 사실이 아닌 것으로 밝혀졌다'는 내용이 적절하므로 (C)가 정답이다.

표현 정리 resign 사임하다 actually 실제로 assessment 평가 criticism 비판, 비난

◎ 실전에 적용해 봐
1. (A) 2. (C) 3. (C) 4. (D) 5. (C) 6. (A) 7. (D)
8. (A) 9. (B) 10. (D)

1. 정답 (A)

해설 Wagner IT 사는 워크숍을 준비하고 있다 / 멀티미디어 컴퓨터 사용에 대한 / 모든 신입사원들의 참석이 의무적인

해설 빈칸 앞의 is organizing은 행사 명사를 목적어로 취하는 동사이므로 (A)가 is organizing의 목적어로 적합하다. '워크숍을 준비하고 있다'라는 내용이 자연스러우므로 (A)가 정답이다.

표현 정리 organize 준비하다, 조직하다 mandatory 의무적인, 강제의 recruit 신입사원, 신입생 attend 참석하다

2. 정답 (C)

해설 Mr. Loon은 요청했다 / 건축가가 제공할 것을 / 서면 견적서를 / 전체 비용이 포함된 / 그의 집을 리모델링 하는 / 리모델링 시작 일주일 전에

해설 빈칸 앞에 있는 written(쓰여진)과 관련 있는 것은 (C)와 (D)인데, 빈칸 뒤에 '비용에 대한'이라는 말이 있으므로 '견적서'라는 의미의 (C)가 적합하다. '건축가가 전체 비용에 대한 서면 견적서를 제공한다'라는 내용 역시 적절하므로 (C)가 정답이다.

표현 정리 architect 건축가 written estimate 서면 견적서 total cost 총 비용 involved 포함된 tender 입찰 recommendation 추천, 추천서

3. 정답 (C)

해설 Stationery Depot는 / 복사 용지, 메모장, 도장, 그리고 다른 비품들을 파는 / 대량으로 / 이상적인 공간이다 / 집필 도구들을 위한 / 알맞은 가격으로

해설 일단 앞의 동사는 sells이므로 판매할 수 있는 단어로 가야 한다. 빈칸 앞에는 빈칸과 같은 성격의 단어들이 열거되었다. 복사 용지, 메모장, 도장 등을 포괄적으로 부르는 단어인 '비품'이란 뜻의 (C)가 정답이다.

표현 정리 copy paper 복사 용지 memo pad 메모장 stamp 도장 bulk 대량량(의) ideal 이상적인 implement 도구 at affordable price 적절한(알맞은) 가격으로

4. 정답 (D)

해설 그의 연설에서 / Neilson 박사는 덕분으로 돌렸다 / 그의 최근 연구 결과물에 관한 긍정적인 반응을 / 그의 조교들에게

해설 빈칸 앞 positive(긍정적인)와 concern(걱정, 우려)이라는 말은 서로 어울리지 않으므로 (C)는 우선 오답 처리한다. 조교에게 그 공로를 돌리려면 긍정적인 평가를 나타내는 말이 필요하다. 따라서 (D)가 정답이다. (A)와 (B)는 공로의 성격을 가진 단어가 아니다.

표현 정리 attribute A to B A를 B의 덕분(탓)으로 돌리다 positive 긍정적인 findings 조사결과물 assistant 조수, 조교 concern 걱정, 염려

5. 정답 (C)

해설 만약 당신이 직접 올 계획이라면 / Best Rivervill Hotel에 / 당신이 공항에 도착하면 / 픽업 서비스를 이용 가능하다 / 추가 요금으로

해설 for an additional과 잘 어울리는 charge를 대입해 해석해 본다. '추가 요금으로 픽업 서비스를 이용 가능하다'는 말이 자연스럽기 때문에 (C)가 답이다. (A)는 불가산명사라 앞에 관사를 쓸 수 없고, (D)는 '견적서'라는 말인데 구매자로부터 가격 의뢰가 있을 시 판매자가 발행해 주는 것이 견적서이다.

표현 정리 directly 직접 pickup service 픽업 서비스 available 이용 가능한 additional 추가의, 여분의 charge 요금

6. 정답 (A)

해설 예상치 못한 상황의 결과 / Delipop Company의 많은 직원들은 / 정리 해고를 당했다 / 지난 달에

해설 unforeseen과 잘 어울리는 circumstances부터 대입해 해석해 본다. '예상치 못한 상황의 결과 정리 해고를 당했다'는 말이 자연스러우므로 (A)가 정답이다. 나머지 보기들은 unforeseen과 어울리지도 않고, 해석도 자연스럽지 않다.

표현 정리 as a result of ~에 대한 결과로 unforeseen 예측하지 못한, 뜻밖의 lay off 정리 해고하다 circumstance 상황, 여건 qualification 자격, 능력 categorization 범주화

7. 정답 (D)

해설 Ms. Flora는 기뻤다 / 받았을 때 / 그녀가 선택되었다는 소식을 / 해외 지사로 파견될 직원들 중에 한 명으로

해설 that 뒤에 완전한 문장이 오는 경우, 앞의 명사는 동격의 that과 어울리는 명사 자리이다. '그녀가 선택되었다는 것'은 생각이 아니고, 소식이라고 보는 것이 맞으므로 (D)가 정답이다.

표현 정리 employee 직원, 사원 dispatch 파견하다, 보내다 overseas 해외의, 국외의 promotion 승진

8. 정답 (A)

해설 Home Service Support는 제공한다 / 아주 다양한 가사 서비스들

을 / 집을 청소하는 것부터 잔디를 깎는 것까지 / 우리의 고객들을 위해

해설 빈칸 앞 a broad와 빈칸 뒤 of가 있으므로 a broad ~ of 형태로 잘 쓰이는 (A)를 넣어 해석해 본다. '아주 다양한 가사 서비스를 제공한다'는 내용이 적절하므로 (A)가 정답이다. a range of는 '다양한, 많은'이라는 뜻이며, range 앞에 wide, broad, large, diverse 등의 형용사가 들어가면 '아주(매우) 다양한'이라는 표현이 된다.

표현 정리 a broad range of 아주 다양한 housekeeping 가사 mow (잔디를) 깎다, (풀을) 베다 lawn 잔디 point 의견, 요점 width 폭, 너비

9. 정답 (B)

해설 의회 조정자인 Ms. O'Connell는 취소했다 / 모든 그녀의 약속을 / 이번 주 목요일 / 기념식에 참석하기 위해 / 50주년을 기념하여 열리는 / Local Aboriginal Land Council의

해설 빈칸 앞뒤로 attend와 held가 있다. 빈칸에는 행사를 나타내는 명사가 오는 것이 자연스러우므로 (B)가 정답이다. (D)는 '행사 장소'라는 뜻이다.

표현 정리 coordinator 진행자, 조정자 cancel 취소하다 appointment 약속, 예약, 임명, 지명 attend 참석하다 in honor of ~를 기념하여 anniversary 기념일, (몇) 주년 aboriginal 호주 원주민의 ceremony 의식, 기념 venue (행위의) 장소, 현장

10. 정답 (D)

해설 다행스런 일이었다 / Ms. Spears가 받은 것은 / 간단한 경고를 / 그녀가 저지른 작은 실수들에 대해 / 추정하는데 있어 / 전체 수입을 / 우리 회사의 / 재무 보고서 상에서

해설 minor와 잘 어울리면서, 동시에 뒤의 made와도 잘 어울리는 명사는 (D)이다. 대입해 해석해 보면 '그녀가 저지른 작은 실수에 대해'라는 말이 자연스럽다. 따라서 (D)가 정답이다.

표현 정리 fortunate 다행스러운 warning 경고 estimate 추정하다 revenues 매출, 수입 financial statement 재무제표

법칙 85 올바른 해석으로 풀어야 하는 명사 어휘 문제

◎ 유형을 파악해 봐
1. (A) 2. (D) 3. (B)

1. 정답 (A)

해설 기상악화에 대비해 / 우리는 모든 경로를 따르지 않을 수도 있다 / 여행 일정표에 나타난

해설 보기 모두 여행이라는 말과 사용할 수 있는 단어들이다. 빈칸 주변 내용을 해석해 보면, '여행 ~에 나타난 모든 경로들을 따르지 않을 수도 있다'고 했으므로 (A)를 답으로 고르는 것이 적합하다.

표현 정리 indicated 나타난 itinerary 여행 일정 agency 기관 destination 목적지

2. 정답 (C)

해설 경제 위기 때문에 / BC&M 사의 주식은 급락했다 / 주식 시장에서

해설 빈칸 주변만 보면 주식과 어울릴 수 있는 말이라 혼동될 수 있는 문제인데, 주가가 떨어졌다는 말로 보아 (D)가 정답임을 추론할 수 있다.

표현 정리 economic crisis 경제 위기 sharply 급격하게 stock market 주식 시장

3. 정답 (B)

해설 많은 사람들이 생각한다 / 텔레비전이 / 가장 훌륭한 현대의 발명품이라고

해설 modern 다음에 온 빈칸에는 모든 보기들이 사용 가능하다. 따라서 문맥상으로 정답을 골라야 한다. consider는 5형식 동사로 to be 앞과 뒤가 서로 같은 내용이 나와야 하며, 'television = 발명품'의 관계이므로 (B)가 정답이다.

표현 정리 consider 간주하다 modern 현대의 invention 발명품 technology 기술

◎ 실전에 적용해 봐
1. (B) 2. (C) 3. (A) 4. (B) 5. (D) 6. (C) 7. (B)
8. (D) 9. (A) 10. (C)

1. 정답 (B)

해설 최근 연구에 따르면 / 많은 인구가 주요 도시에 살고 있다 / 오직 20퍼센트 인구만이 교외나 외딴 지역에 사는 반면에

해설 보기들이 빈칸 앞 large와 모두 어울리기 때문에 해석을 통해 단서를 찾아야 하는 문제이다. 뒤에서 20퍼센트의 인구가 산다는 말이 나오므로 빈칸도 비율을 나타내는 말이 와야 한다. 따라서 (B)가 답이다.

표현 정리 suburban 교외의 remote 외딴

2. 정답 (C)

해설 Revive Motors은 수행해 왔다 / 엔진의 내구성을 강화하는 방법에 관한 연구를 / 오래 지속되는 힘을 가지고 있는 엔진을 생산하기 위해

해설 빈칸 앞만 봐서는 정답을 고르기 쉽지 않은 문제이다. 뒤에 '오래 지속되는 힘을 가지고 있는'이란 말이 나오므로 보기 중에서 '내구성'의 뜻을 가진 (C)가 정답으로 적절하다.

표현 정리 flexibility 유연성 complacency 안주, 만족감 durability 내구성 volatility 휘발성

3. 정답 (A)

해설 소비자들의 구매 습관이 자동으로 기록되는 데이터베이스 개발은 / 가져왔다 / 상당한 변화를 / 전통적인 마케팅 기법에

해설 빈칸 앞만 봐서는 정답을 고르기 쉽지 않은 문제이다. 소비자들의 구매 습관이 자동으로 기록되는 시스템이 개발됨에 따라 전통적인 마케팅 기법에 큰 변화가 왔다고 해야 문맥상 맞으므로 '변화, 이전'을 뜻하는 (A)가 정답이다.

표현 정리 development 개발 automatically 자동으로 significant 상당한 traditional 전통적인 shift 변화

4.   정답 (B)

해설 Mega Sales는 환불해 준다 / 생산 과정에서 일어난 결함이 있는 상품들에 대해 / 그러나 구매자들의 단순 변심에 의한 반품에 대해서는 안 된다

해설 빈칸 앞만 봐서는 정답을 고르기가 쉽지 않은 문제이다. '단순 반품은 안되지만 결함이 있는 제품에 대해서는 환불해 주겠다는 내용이므로 (B)가 정답이다.

표현 정리 defect 결함 create 일으키다, 만들다 production process 생산 공정, 생산 과정

5.   정답 (D)

해설 대부분의 직원들이 여전히 개정된 직원 복지에 만족하지 않기 때문에 / 시스템은 필요로 한다 / 더 철저한 점검을

해설 빈칸 앞만 봐서는 혼동되기 쉬운 문제이다. 개정된 직원 복지에 여전히 만족하지 않기 때문에 복지 시스템은 철저한 점검이 필요하다고 해야 맞으므로 (D)가 정답이다.

표현 정리 majority 대부분의, 주요한 be dissatisfied with ~에 불만족하다 employee benefits 직원 복지 revision 개정, 수정 overhaul 점검

6.   정답 (C)

해설 영업 부장 직을 위한 각 후보자들은 / 수행해야 할 미션을 제공받았다 / 간략한 모의 제품 시연 / 채용 면접의 일부로

해설 빈칸 주변만을 보고 풀기는 어려운 문제이며, '간략한 모의 제품 시연을 하도록 미션을 받았다'는 말을 통해 (C)가 답임을 유추할 수 있다. (D)는 면접관을 뜻하는 말이다.

표현 정리 conduct 수행하다 mock 모의 candidate 지원자

7.   정답 (B)

해설 일단 중요한 정책 결정 과정이 본사에서 끝나면 / 자회사들은 책임이 있다 / 명령을 따라야 할 / 경영진이 보낸

해설 빈칸 주변만 봐서는 안 풀리는 문제이다. 본사에서 정책 결정 과정이 끝나면 본사가 내린 명령을 따라야 한다는 내용이 적절하므로 (B)가 정답이다. 올바른 정답으로 고르기 위해서는 보기들의 의미도 잘 알고 있어야 하는 문제이다.

표현 정리 headquarter 본사 orders 명령 executive 경영의 subsidiary 자회사

8.   정답 (D)

해설 자선 단체 World Dream의 설립자로서 / Mr. Harper는 주도할 것이다 / 재활센터 자금 지원을 / 장애인을 위한

해설 center만 보고는 답을 고를 수 없는 문제이다. 앞의 문맥에서 자선 단체 이야기가 나왔고, 장애인을 위한 센터에 자금을 지원하는 일을 주도하겠다고 했으므로 정답은 (D)가 되어야 한다.

표현 정리 charity organization 자선 단체 the disabled 장애인 rehabilitation 재활

9.   정답 (A)

해설 제공되는 신용등급은 / Investment Watch에 의해 / 신뢰할 수 있는 지표들이다 / 회사 가치를

해설 빈칸 앞의 reliable만 보고는 풀 수 없는 문제이다. 앞의 문맥에서 신용등급이란 말이 나왔고, 뒤에서는 '회사 가치를'이란 말이 나왔으므로 지표를 뜻하는 (A)가 가장 잘 어울린다.

표현 정리 credit rating 신용등급 reliable 신뢰할 수 있는 indicator 지표

10.   정답 (C)

해설 경영자는 거절했다 / 프로젝트에 대한 Mr. Harding의 계획을 / 왜냐하면 그것이 필요로 하기 때문에 / 과다한 지출을 / 회사가 제한된 예산을 보유하고 있는 반면

해설 빈칸 앞의 heavy만 보고는 풀 수 없는 문제이다. 앞에 프로젝트에 대한 계획을 거절했다는 말과 뒤에 예산이 제한적이라는 말을 통해 프로젝트가 과다한 지출을 필요로 함을 알 수 있다. 따라서 (C)가 정답이다.

표현 정리 executive 경영자 require 요구하다 heavy 과한 expenditure 지출

Chapter 11 형용사 어휘 문제(매월 3문제)

법칙 86 특정 명사와 잘 어울리는 형용사

◎ 유형을 파악해 봐
1. (D)   2. (D)   3. (D)

1.   정답 (D)

해설 PC 업계의 경쟁이 더욱 심화되기 때문에 / 더 많은 컴퓨터들이 제공되고 있다 / 점점 합리적인 가격에

해설 price와 자연스럽게 어울리는 형용사는 (D)이다. '합리적인 가격에 제공된다'는 내용이 어울리므로 (D)가 정답이다.

표현 정리 competition 경쟁 industry 업계 intensive 집중적인, 철두철미한 increasingly 점점 더

2.   정답 (D)

해설 Life Partner Insurance는 / 업계에서 선두주자로 남아 있다 / 20년이 넘도록 / 회사의 뛰어난 서비스 덕분에

해설 보기 중 service와 어울리는 형용사는 (D)인데, 대입해 해석해 보면 '탁월한 서비스 덕분에 선두주자로 남아 있다'는 말이 자연스러우므로 (D)가 정답이다.

표현 정리 remain 남다 industry 업계 thanks to ~덕분에 outstanding 뛰어난

3.   정답 (D)

해설 당신의 인적 사항을 기입하세요 / 제공된 공간에 / 무료 특별 판촉 할

인을 받기 위해

해설 일단 information과 가장 잘 어울리는 형용사인 (D)를 대입해 해석해 보면 '인적 사항을 제공된 공간에 기입하세요'라는 말이 자연스럽기 때문에 (D)가 정답이다.

표현 정리 space 공간 receive 받다 promotional 홍보의 personal 개인의

◎ **실전에 적용해 봐**

1. (A) 2. (B) 3. (C) 4. (B) 5. (A) 6. (C) 7. (D)
8. (B) 9. (D) 10. (A)

1. 정답 (A)

해석 Sunrise Hotel / 스위트룸에서 머무는 고객들은 / 제공 받는다 / 무료 룸서비스를 / 그리고 그것은 포함한다 / 무료 식사를 / 요청할 경우에는

해설 일단 '룸 서비스'와 가장 잘 어울리는 (A)를 대입해 해석해 본다. '무료 룸서비스를 제공 받는다'는 내용이 자연스러워 (A)가 정답이다.

표현 정리 suite 객실, 스위트룸 provide A with B A에게 B를 제공하다 meal 식사 upon request 요청 시에 complimentary 무료의

2. 정답 (B)

해석 판매 부장은 이메일을 보냈다 / 일정표에 관한 자세한 정보를 포함하는 / 고객 각자에게 / 최근에 구매한 / 그 스스로의 패키지 투어를

해설 일단 information과 가장 잘 어울리는 형용사 (B)를 먼저 대입해 해석해 보면, '상세한 정보를 포함한 이메일을 고객 각자에게 보냈다'는 내용이 적절하므로 (B)가 정답이다.

표현 정리 sales manager 판매 부장 contain 포함하다 itinerary 일정표 recently 최근에

3. 정답 (C)

해석 인사부는 선호한다 / 관련 근무 경력이 있는 직원을 팀에 갖는 것을 / 그들은 많은 훈련을 필요로 하지 않을 것이기 때문에

해설 일단 work experience와 가장 잘 어울리는 형용사 (C)를 대입해 해석해 보면 '관련 근무 경력이 있는 직원들'이라는 말이 자연스럽다. 따라서 (C)가 정답이다.

표현 정리 Human Resources Department 인사부 prefer to ~을 선호하다 work experience 근무 경험 relevant 관련 있는

4. 정답 (B)

해석 깨지기 쉬운 상품들이 있다면 / 그 사실은 표시되어야 한다 / 상자 위에 / 배달원에게 알리기 위해 / 특별한 주의를 할 필요가 있다는 것을

해설 일단 items와 자연스럽게 어울리는 (B)나 (C)를 먼저 대입해 해석해 보면, 특별한 주의를 기울이기 위해서라는 말이 있으므로 (B)가 더 자연스럽다는 것을 알 수 있다. 따라서 (B)가 정답이다.

표현 정리 fact 사실, ~라는 점 indicate 표시하다, 가리키다, 암시하다 notify 알리다 deliverymen 배달원 take care of ~을 돌보다, 주의하다 suspicious 의혹을 갖는 fragile 깨지기 쉬운 innovative 획기적인

5. 정답 (A)

해석 We Fit Sporting Goods 영업 부장은 보냈다 / 사과 편지를 / 불만을 제기한 고객들에게 / 결함이 있는 상품들에 대한 / 판매되고 있는

해설 일단 items와 자연스럽게 어울리는 (A)를 먼저 대입하여 해석하면, '결함이 있는 상품들에 관한 불만을 제기한 고객들'이라는 말이 자연스럽다. 따라서 (A)가 정답이다.

표현 정리 sales manager 영업 부장 file a complaint 불만을 제기하다 defective 결함 있는 demanding 까다로운 avoidable 피할 수 있는

6. 정답 (C)

해석 Global Eco Energy에 투자하기 전에 / 종합적인 검토가 / 회사의 재정 상태에 관한 / 요구된다

해설 일단 review와 잘 어울리는 comprehensive를 먼저 대입하여 해석하면, '회사의 재정 상태에 관한 종합적인 검토'라는 말과 잘 어울리므로 (C)가 정답이다.

표현 정리 diligent 부지런한 extreme 극도의, 지나친 comprehensive 포괄적인, 종합적인 utmost 궁극의

7. 정답 (D)

해석 증거의 부족 때문에 Dr. Birdman 연구 팀은 / 잠정적인 결론을 내렸다 / 직원 개인의 성격이 연관이 있다는 / 회사의 전반적인 생산성과

해설 일단 conclusion과 잘 어울리는 (D)를 우선 대입해 해석해 보면, '증거의 부족 때문에 잠정적인 결론을 내렸다'는 내용이 자연스럽기 때문에 (D)가 정답이다. (C)는 사람과 어울리는 말이다.

표현 정리 permanent 영구적인 irreversible 되돌릴 수 없는 tolerant 관대한 tentative 잠정적인

8. 정답 (B)

해석 Ms. Combs는 완전히 지쳤다 / 엄격한 훈련으로 / 그녀의 개인 트레이너에 의한

해설 일단 training exercises와 잘 어울리는 (B)부터 대입해 해석하면 '트레이너에 의한 엄격한 훈련으로 지쳤다'는 말이 자연스럽기 때문에 (B)가 정답이다.

표현 정리 exhausted 기진맥진한 spacious 넓은 rigorous 엄격한, 철저한 generous 관대한 single 단수의, 한

9. 정답 (D)

해석 워크숍 참석자들은 / 그들만의 벤처 사업을 할 계획이 있는 / 배웠다 / 성공을 위한 핵심 요소들을 / 모범적인 사례를 분석함으로써

해설 일단 case와 잘 어울리는 (D)를 먼저 대입해 본다. '모범적인 사례를 분석함으로써 성공을 위한 핵심 요소를 배웠다'는 내용이 적절하기 때문에 (D)가 정답이다. (C)는 주로 사람이 '~를 알고 있다'는 뜻으로 be aware of나 'that S+V'의 형태로 사용한다.

표현 정리 attendant 참석자 analyze 분석하다 permanent 영구적인 reliant 의존하는 aware 알고 있는 exemplary 모범적인

10. 정답 (A)

해설 불리한 시장 상황은 / Watson Tech로 하여금 지연시키도록 했다 / 회사의 신형 컴퓨터 모델의 출시를 / 최종 개발 단계에 있음에도 불구하고

해설 일단 market conditions와 잘 어울리는 (A)를 먼저 대입해 해석해 보면, '불리한 시장 상황이 신형 컴퓨터 모델의 출시를 지연시켰다'는 내용이 자연스러우므로 (A)가 정답이다.

표현 정리 market conditions 시장 상황 delay 연기하다 unfavorable 불리한 encouraged 장려된 impartial 공정한

법칙 87 특정 전치사와 잘 어울리는 형용사

◎ 유형을 파악해 봐
1. (B)   2. (C)   3. (A)

1. 정답 (B)

해설 판매 사원은 / 주로 책임진다 / 재고품 관리를

해설 빈칸 앞 be 동사와 빈칸 뒤 for와 어울리는 형용사를 고르는 문제이다. be responsible for은 '~에 대해 책임지다'는 뜻으로 '직원은 재고품 관리를 책임진다'라는 말이 자연스러우므로 (B)가 정답이다. (A)는 주어가 사람일 때는 쓰지 않고, (C)는 사람이나 제품이 신뢰할 만할 때 사용한다. (D)는 가주어/진주어와 잘 쓰이는 형용사다.

표현 정리 explainable 설명할 수 있는 responsible 책임이 있는 reliable 믿을 수 있는 advisable 권할 만한, 바람직한

2. 정답 (C)

해설 직원들은 채택하기를 열망한다 / 새로운 회사 정책을 / 그리고 그것은 더 나은 업무 환경을 보장할 것이다

해설 빈칸 앞 be 동사와 빈칸 뒤 to 동사원형과 어울리는 형용사를 고르는 문제이다. 'be eager to 동사원형'은 '~하기를 열망하다'는 뜻이므로 (C)가 가장 적절한 정답이다. (A)와 (B)는 to 뒤에 명사가 오고, (D)는 to 동사원형이 가능하지만 '~하도록 유혹되다'라는 뜻으로 자연스럽지 못하다.

표현 정리 susceptible 민감한 prone 하기 쉬운 eager 열렬한 tempt 유혹하다, 유도하다

3. 정답 (A)

해설 신입 직원들은 / 회계 용어에 익숙하지 않은 / 어려움이 있을 수 있다 / 재무제표에 대해

해설 빈칸 앞 be 동사와 빈칸 뒤 with와 어울리는 형용사를 고르는 문제이다. be unfamiliar with는 '~에 익숙하지 않다'는 뜻으로 '회계 용어에 익숙하지 않은 신입 직원들은'이라는 말이 자연스러우므로 (A)가 정답이다.

표현 정리 accounting 회계 term 용어 financial statements 재무제표

◎ 실전에 적용해 봐
1. (A)   2. (B)   3. (C)   4. (C)   5. (D)   6. (D)   7. (A)
8. (A)   9. (B)   10. (C)

1. 정답 (A)

해설 조건들은 / 당신의 보험 설계와 관련한 / 통보 없이 변경될 수 있다

해설 빈칸 앞 be 동사와 빈칸 뒤 to 명사 혹은 동사원형과 어울리는 형용사를 고르는 문제이다. (A)와 (C)가 있는데, 'be subject to 명사'가 오면 '통보 없이 변경될 수도 있다'는 뜻으로 사용되므로 (A)가 정답이다. (B)는 be 없이 바로 opt to 동사원형 형태로 '~을 선택하다'라는 뜻이고, (C)는 주어가 사람일 때 사용한다.

표현 정리 condition 조건 insurance 보험 without notice 통보 없이 be willing to+동사원형 기꺼이 ~하다

2. 정답 (B)

해설 소설 'Seven Treasures'는 / 역대 가장 훌륭한 걸작 중 하나로 여겨지는 / 작가 John Schouten를 대표하는 작품이다.

해설 빈칸 앞 be 동사와 빈칸 뒤 of와 어울리는 형용사를 고르는 문제이다. be representative of는 '~를 대표하다'라는 뜻으로 '작가 John Schouten을 대표하는'이라는 말이 자연스러우므로 (B)가 정답이다. (C)는 be proud of '~을 자랑으로 여기다'의 뜻으로 쓰이며, (D)는 be reliant on의 형태로 쓰인다.

표현 정리 all time 역대의 exemplary 모범적인, 본보기를 보이는 representative 대표적인, 대표하는 reliant 의존하는

3. 정답 (C)

해설 IT 회사에서 일하는 것에 관심 있는 구직자들은 / 모의 취업 면접에 신청하도록 권장된다 / E&T Solutions가 개최하는

해설 in과 자연스럽게 어울리는 (C)부터 대입해 해석해 본다. 'IT 회사에서 일하는 것에 관심 있는 구직자들은'이란 말이 자연스럽다. 따라서 (C)가 정답이다. (A)는 뒤에 in을 쓸 경우 '~에 동봉된'이라는 말이 되는데, 그럴 경우 주어가 사람이 될 수는 없다.

표현 정리 be interested in ~에 흥미가 있다 be encouraged to ~하도록 권장되다 mock-job 모의 취업 hold 개최하다

4. 정답 (C)

해설 명백했기 때문에 / Mr. Decker의 팀이 회사의 전체 매출에 적게 공헌한 것이 / 다른 팀보다 / 그의 팀은 판매 보고서를 제출하는 것을 꺼려했다

해설 빈칸 앞 be 동사와 빈칸 뒤 to 동사원형과 어울리는 형용사를 고르는 문제이다. (C)가 가능하므로 대입하여 해석해 보면, '다른 팀보다 기여도가 낮은 것이 명백해서 판매 보고서를 제출하는 것을 주저했다'는 말이 자연스럽다. 따라서 (C)가 정답이다. (A)와 (D)는 to 명사가 오며, (B)는 'It is possible that/to ~.'와 같은 가주어/진주어 용법으로 사용된다.

표현 정리 obvious 분명한, 명백한 contribute 기여하다 applicable 해당되는

5. 정답 (D)

해설 3년 동안 결근 없이 일한 직원들은 / 자격이 있다 / 최대 한 달 동안의 휴가를 받을

해설 'be ~ for'와 어울리는 것은 (D)이다. '휴가를 받을 자격이 있다'는 내용이 자연스러워 (D)가 정답이다. (A)는 be exempt from의 형태로, (B)와

(D)는 사람이 주어로 올 때 쓴다.

표현정리 absences 부재, 결근 up to ~까지 exempt 면제되는 variable 다양한 receivable 수령할 수 있는 eligible 자격 있는

6. 정답 (D)

해설 이미 같은 세션을 마친 Ms. Parker는 / 면제 받았다 / 필수 교육 워크숍 참석을 / 신입 직원들을 위한

해설 빈칸 앞 be 동사와 빈칸 뒤 from과 어울리는 형용사를 고르는 문제이다. be exempt from은 '~로부터 면제되다'라는 의미로 빈칸에 가장 잘 어울리므로 (D)가 정답이다. (A)는 'be liable to 부정사'나 'for 명사'의 형태로 쓰이고, (B)와 (C)는 to 명사가 온다.

표현정리 attend 참석하다 liable 법적인 책임이 있는 applicable 해당되는 exempt 면제된

7. 정답 (A)

해설 오늘날의 첨단 IT 기술은 / Silicon Valley에서 발달한 산업에 기반을 두고 있다.

해설 빈칸 앞 be 동사와 빈칸 뒤 on과 어울리는 형용사를 고르는 문제이다. be based on은 '~에 기반을 두고 있다'는 의미이며, '첨단 IT 기술이 Silicon Valley에서 발달한 산업에 기반을 두고 있다'는 내용이 자연스러워 (A)가 정답이다. (B)는 agree on이 수동태가 되면 be agreed on 다음에 수식어가 따라 오고, (C)는 'be delivered to 명사'의 형태로 사용된다.

표현정리 state-of-the-art 최신의 base on ~에 기초하다

8. 정답 (A)

해설 매장 직원실은 / 이용 가능하다 / 풀타임 직원만 / 그들 자신의 ID 카드를 소지한

해설 빈칸 앞 be 동사와 빈칸 뒤 to와 어울리는 형용사를 고르는 문제이다. 'be accessible to 사람 명사'는 '사람이 주어를 이용할 수 있다, 접근할 수 있다'는 의미이다. '회사 직원 ID 카드를 소지한 정규직 직원들만 이용할 수 있다'는 내용이므로 (A)가 정답이다.

표현정리 accessible 이용 가능한 full-time clerk 정규직 직원 possess 소유하다

9. 정답 (B)

해설 LM Electronics는 새로 추가하게 되어 자랑스럽다 / 출시된 모델을 / 휴대용 장치 시리즈에 / 그것으로 회사가 잘 알려진

해설 빈칸 앞 be 동사와 빈칸 뒤 to 부정사와 어울리는 형용사를 고르는 문제이다. 'be proud to 동사원형'의 형태로 사용해 '~하는 것이 자랑스럽다'라는 뜻을 가진 (B)가 정답이다. (A)는 가주어/진주어에 주로 사용하고, (C)는 뒤에 'to 명사'가 붙어 '~에게 친절하다'는 듯으로 사용한다.

표현정리 released 출시된 portable 호환 가능한 apparent 분명한 incremental 증가의

10. 정답 (C)

해설 그녀가 Compa Design에서 일한 첫 날이었기 때문에 / Ms. Murray는 능숙하지 않았다 / 다양한 디자인 도구를 이용해 일하는 것에 / 그녀에게 모두 새로웠던

해설 빈칸 앞 be 동사와 빈칸 뒤 at과 어울리는 형용사를 고르는 문제이다. 먼저 be poor at을 넣어 해석해 보면 '그녀에게 새로운 다양한 디자인 도구들로 작업하는 것에 능숙하지 않다'는 내용으로 (C)가 정답이다. (A)와 (B)는 뒤에 about을 좋아하고, (D)는 뒤의 내용과 상충된다.

표현정리 tool 도구 confident 자신감 있는 optimistic 낙관적인 professional 전문적인

법칙 88 사람에 답이 되는 형용사

◎ 유형을 파악해 봐
1. (D)   2. (B)   3. (A)

1. 정답 (D)

해설 Mr. Fowler는 가장 경험이 있는 지원자이다 / 그가 7년의 경력을 갖고 있기 때문에 / 관련 분야에

해설 빈칸 뒤 applicant는 '지원자'라는 뜻으로 사람을 지칭하는 명사이다. 사람을 수식할 수 있는 형용사는 (C)와 (D)이다. '가장 경험 있는 지원자'라는 말이 자연스러우므로 (D)가 정답이다. (A)는 날씨 등이 화창할 때 쓰고, (B)는 회사 등이 인수되었을 때 쓰며, (C) '까다로운'이란 뜻은 자연스럽지 못하다.

표현정리 applicant 지원자 relevant 관련 있는 field 분야 pleasant 즐거운, 기분 좋은 acquired 획득한, 습득한 demanding 까다로운 experienced 경험이 있는, 능숙한

2. 정답 (B)

해설 최고 관리자는 승진시키도록 했다 / 가장 자격을 갖춘 직원을

해설 빈칸 뒤 employee는 '직원'이라는 뜻으로 사람을 지칭하는 명사이므로 사람을 수식할 수 있는 형용사를 골라야 한다. '가장 자격을 갖춘 직원'이라는 말이 자연스러우므로 (B)가 정답이다. 나머지는 사람과 거울리지 않는다.

표현정리 executive 간부의, 임원의 promote 승진시키다 highly 매우 mandatory 의무적인 qualified 자격 있는, 적격인 intentional 의도적인 probable 있음직한, 그럴듯한

3. 정답 (A)

해설 Kolm 사는 약속했다 / 더 많은 성과금을 주기로 / 직원들에게 / 그들의 급여에 만족하지 않는

해설 빈칸 앞 employees는 '직원들'이라는 뜻으로 사람을 지칭하는 명사이므로 사람을 수식할 수 있는 형용사를 골라야 한다. (A)와 (B) 중 빈칸 뒤 with와 어울리는 형용사는 (A)이다. '그들의 급여에 만족하지 않는 직원들'이라는 말이 자연스럽다.

표현정리 promise 약속하다 incentive 성과금 salary 급여 dissatisfied 불만족하는 attached 동봉된

◎ 실전에 적용해 봐
1. (B)   2. (A)   3. (A)   4. (A)   5. (D)   6. (B)   7. (C)
8. (C)   9. (C)   10. (C)

1. 정답 (B)

해석 많은 재정 분석가들은 낙관적이다 / 주식 시장의 상승 추세에 / 안정적인 경제 여건 때문에

해설 빈칸은 be 동사 뒤에 온 보어 자리이다. 주어 analysts는 '분석가'라는 뜻으로 사람을 지칭하는 명사이므로 주어를 보충해 줄 수 있는 형용사를 골라야 한다. 일단 about과 자연스럽게 어울리는 (A)와 (B) 중에서 뒤에 안정적 경제 여건이라는 말이 있으므로 낙관적이라고 보는 (B)가 정답이다. (A)는 '의심스러운'이란 뜻이고, (C)는 be aware of나 'that S+V' 형태로 사용한다.

표현 정리 doubtful 의심하는 optimistic 낙관적인 aware 알고 있는 common 흔한, 공통의

2. 정답 (A)

해석 KM Resources Design은 지명되었다 / 100개의 가장 바람직한 직장 중 하나로 / 좋은 작업 환경을 제공하는 / 직원들을 위한

해설 빈칸 뒤 working environment는 사물을 지칭하는 명사이므로 사물을 수식할 수 있는 형용사를 골라야 한다. 이상적인 작업 환경을 제공한다고 한 것으로 보아 '유쾌한'이란 뜻을 가진 (A)가 가장 자연스럽다. (B)는 '도전적인,' (C)는 '깨지기 쉬운'이란 뜻으로 '작업 환경'을 수식하기에 어색하다.

표현 정리 name 명명하다, 이름을 붙이다 desirable 바람직한, 호감 있는 workplace 작업장, 근무 현장 challenging 도전적인, 어려운 fragile 깨지기 쉬운 cautious 조심스러운

3. 정답 (A)

해석 Grand Royal Hotel 안내원으로서 / Ms. Tomoya는 / 주로 책임진다 / 고객들을 돕는 것을 / 체크인과 체크아웃 하는

해설 빈칸은 be 동사 뒤의 보어 자리이다. 주어인 Ms. Tomoya를 보충해 줄 수 있는 형용사를 골라야 한다. be responsible for라는 어울림을 고려해 (A)를 먼저 대입해 본다. 'Ms. Tomoya는 고객들을 돕는 것을 주로 책임진다'라는 말이 자연스러우므로 (A)가 정답이다.

표현 정리 receptionist 접수 담당자 mainly 주로 assist 돕다 reliable 믿을 수 있는 desirable 바람직한, 호감이 가는 feasible 이행 가능한

4. 정답 (A)

해석 Mr. Pearson은 영어와 스페인어를 말하는 것에 자신이 있었기 때문에 / 그는 일자리에 지원했다 / 통역사로서의

해설 빈칸은 be 동사 뒤의 보어 자리이다. 주어인 Mr. Pearson을 보충해 줄 수 있는 형용사를 골라야 한다. 일단 사람과 잘 어울리는 (A)를 먼저 대입해 해석해 보면, '영어와 스페인어 둘 다 말하는 것에 자신이 있다'는 말이 자연스러우므로 (A)가 정답이다. confident 다음엔 in이 생략되어 있다. (C) exhaustive는 '철저한'이란 의미로 exhausted(기진 맥진한, 지친)와 다른 의미이다.

표현 정리 interpreter 통역사 confident 확신하는, 자신감 있는 personal 개인적인, 개인의 exhaustive 철저한 practical 현실적인, 실용적인

5. 정답 (D)

해석 그는 현재 프로젝트 매니저로 일하지만 / Mr. Green은 가장 다재다능한 직원 중 한 명이다 / 우리 회사에 근무하는 / 그래서 그는 어떤 위치에 투입될 수 있는

해설 형용사의 최상급 자리이며, 빈칸 뒤 employees를 수식할 수 있는 형용사를 골라야 한다. 일단 사람과 잘 어울리는 (D)부터 대입해 해석하면, '어떤 자리로든 배정될 수 있는 가장 다재다능한 직원 중 한 명이다'라는 말이 자연스러워 (D)가 정답이다. versatile은 사람, 사물 모두 수식하며, 두 가지 의미로 모두 출제된 적이 있다.

표현 정리 assign 배정하다, 맡기다 varying 바뀌는, 가지각색의 arguable 논의의 여지가 있는 consistent 한결같은 versatile 다재다능한

6. 정답 (B)

해석 양사 이사회는 / T&E Chemicals와 Wells Energy의 / 계약을 연장하고자 하는 바람이 같았다

해설 빈칸은 be 동사 뒤의 보어 자리이다. 주어인 The board of directors는 사람이므로 사람을 보충해 줄 수 있는 형용사를 골라야 한다. '이사회는 계약을 연장하고자 하는 바람이 같았다'는 말이 자연스러우므로 (B)가 정답이다. (A)와 (C)는 사람을 수식하는 형용사가 아니다.

표현 정리 unanimous 만장일치의, 모두 뜻이 같은 obvious 분명한 speculative 이론적인

7. 정답 (C)

해석 해결하기 위해 / 우리 소프트웨어의 복잡한 문제들을 / 숙련된 기술자가 문제점을 점검하게 할 필요가 있다

해설 빈칸은 관사 뒤, 명사 앞의 형용사 자리이다. 빈칸 뒤 engineer는 사람을 지칭하는 명사이므로 사람을 수식할 수 있는 형용사를 고르는 문제이다. 사람과 잘 어울리는 (C)를 먼저 대입해 해석해 보면, '숙련된 기술자가 점검하게 할 필요가 있다'는 말이 자연스러우므로 (C)가 정답이다. (A)와 (D)는 사람보다는 사물과 더 자연스럽게 사용되는 형용사이다.

표현 정리 complicated 복잡한 inspect 점검하다, 검사하다 powerful 강력한, 영향력 있는 skilled 숙련된 major 주요한

8. 정답 (C)

해석 Mr. Roland는 좋은 평판을 갖고 있다 / 그의 회사 신입 직원들 사이에서 / 매우 사려 깊다고 그들에게 알려져 있기 때문에 / 심지어 그들이 사소한 실수를 할 때에도

해설 빈칸은 be 동사 뒤의 보어 자리이다. 주어인 he를 보충해 줄 수 있는 형용사를 골라야 한다. 일단 사람과 잘 어울리는 (C)부터 대입해 해석하면, '그는 매우 사려 깊다고 알려져 있기 때문에'라는 말이 자연스러우므로 (C)가 정답이다. (A)는 전치사 on과 함께 '의존하는'의 의미로 쓰이며, (B)와 (C)는 사물을 수식하는 형용사들이다.

표현 정리 reputation 명성, 평판 hire 직원; 고용하다 be known to ~로 알려지다 dependent 의존하는 detectable 감지할 수 있는 considerate 사려 깊은, 신중한 informative 유익한

9. 정답 (C)

해설 비록 피곤한 일이었지만 / 새로운 사업 계획을 구상하는 것은 / 최고 관리자의 긍정적인 피드백은 / 그들의 아이디어에 관한 · 팀이 활력이 넘치게 만들었다

해설 render의 목적 보어 자리에 feeling이 왔으며, 빈칸은 feeling의 보어 자리이다. 목적어인 the team은 사람을 지칭하는 명사이고, 이를 보충해 줄 수 있는 형용사를 골라야 한다. 사람과 잘 어울리는 (C)를 대입해 해석하면, '피드백은 팀이 활력이 넘치게 만들었다'는 의미가 되므로 (C)가 정답이다.

표현 정리 exhausting 기진맥진하게 하는 conceive 구상하다 positive 긍정적인 feedback 의견, 피드백 render 만들다, 주다 severe 극심한 invigorated 활력이 넘치는 intricate 뒤얽힌, 엉클어진

10. 정답 (C)

해설 Ms. Nagoya가 Turbo Auto에서 일을 시작한 이래 / 그녀는 아는 것이 많아졌다 / 기술에 대해 / 차를 제조할 때 사용되는

해설 빈칸은 become 동사 뒤의 보어 자리이므로 주어인 she를 보충해 줄 수 있는 형용사를 골라야 한다. 일단 사람과 잘 어울리는 (C)와 (D) 중 (C)를 먼저 대입해서 해석하면, '그녀는 자동차 회사에서 일을 시작한 이래 자동차 조립 기술에 대해 많이 알게 되었다'는 의미가 되므로 (C)가 정답이다. (A)와 (B)는 주로 사물을 수식한다.

표현 정리 manufacture 제조하다, 생산하다 extensive 광범위한 infrequent 드문 knowledgeable 아는 것이 많은, 정통해 있는 optimistic 낙관적인

법칙 89 가주어, 진주어에 잘 어울리는 형용사

◎ 유형을 파악해 봐
1. (C) 2. (D) 3. (A)

1. 정답 (C)

해설 중요하다 / 당신이 안전 규칙을 준수하는 것은 / 일할 때

해설 'It is ~ that' 형식의 완전한 문장으로 가주어/진주어 문장이다. 가주어/진주어와 잘 어울리는 형용사인 (C)가 정답이다. (A)는 전치사 to 또는 by와 잘 어울리는 형용사, (B)는 사람을 수식하는 형용사이다.

표현 정리 comply with ~를 준수하다 instruction 지시, 규칙 at work 일할 때, 회사에서 crucial 중요한

2. 정답 (D)

해설 명백해졌다 / Ms. Jenson이 그녀의 약속에 늦을 것이라는 것은 / 버스가 제 시간에 오지 않았을 때

해설 'It became ~ that' 형식의 완전한 문장으로 가주어/진주어 문장이다. 가주어/진주어와 잘 어울리는 형용사인 (A)와 (D) 중에서 that 절 안에 should가 없다. 따라서 '요번주의 명제'인 (A)보다는 (D)가 어울린다('법칙 28' 참고). 따라서 (D)가 정답이다.

표현 정리 on time 제시간 obsolete 쓸모가 없는 prerequisite 전제 조건 apparent 명백한

3. 정답 (A)

해설 젊은 소비자들은 종종 깨닫는다 / 온라인으로 쇼핑하는 것이 훨씬 쉽다는 것을 / 오프라인 소매점에서 쇼핑하는 것보다

해설 find의 목적어 자리에 가목적어 it이 온 문장이다. 가목적어/진목적어와 잘 어울리는 형용사인 (A)가 정답이다. (B)와 (C)도 가목적어/진목적어와 어울릴 수 있으나 much는 비교급을 수식하는 부사이다.

표현 정리 often 종종, 자주 find 알다, 깨닫다 online 온라인의, 온라인으로 retail 소매 profound 엄청난, 깊은

◎ 실전에 적용해 봐
1. (C) 2. (B) 3. (A) 4. (D) 5. (B) 6. (B) 7. (D)
8. (A) 9. (B) 10. (C)

1. 정답 (C)

해설 유용할 것이다 / 회의 참석자들이 / 데이터를 이해하는 것이 / 만약 멀티미디어 발표가 더 많은 그래프들을 포함한다면

해설 'It will be ~ to 동사원형' 형식의 완전한 문장으로 가주어/진주어 문장이다. 가주어/진주어와 잘 어울리는 형용사인 (C)가 정답이다. (A)는 사람을 수식하는 형용사이다.

표현 정리 attendees 참석자들 diagram 도형, 그래프 qualified 자격이 있는 plausible 그럴듯한 tangible 분명히 보이는

2. 정답 (B)

해설 인사부 직원이 분명히 이해하는 것은 중요하다 / 우리 회사의 임무와 목표를 / 적절한 인사 정책을 시행하기 위해

해설 'It is ~ that S+V' 형식의 완전한 문장으로 가주어/진주어 문장이다. 가주어/진주어와 잘 어울리는 형용사인 (B)가 정답이다. (D)는 사람을 수식한다.

표현 정리 implement 시행하다 competitive 경쟁력 있는 vital 중요한

3. 정답 (A)

해설 최고 관리자가 아마 우리에게 공지할 것 같다 / 수요일에 있을 오찬에 관해 / 그의 임시 휴가로부터 돌아오는 날인

해설 'It is ~ that S+V' 형식의 완전한 문장으로 가주어/진주어 문장이다. 가주어/진주어와 잘 어울리는 형용사인 (A)가 정답이다. (B)는 사람을 수식하는 형용사이다.

표현 정리 probable 있을 것 같은 flexible 신축성 있는 relative 관련 있는

4. 정답 (D)

해설 Daily & Store는 깨달았다 / 정기적으로 홍보 이벤트를 여는 것이 유익하다는 것을 / 정해진 시간에 다른 시간보다 더 많은 고객을 유치하기 위해

해설 found의 목적어 자리에 가목적어 it이 온 문장이다. 가목적어/진목적어와 잘 어울리는 형용사인 (D)가 정답이다.

표현 정리 find 알다, 깨닫다 forcible 강제적인 abundant 풍부한

beneficial 유익한, 도움이 되는

5. 정답 (B)

해설 자동차 제조업체는 한때 / 직원들이 자동차 부품을 수동으로 생산하도록 하게 한 반면에 / 지금은 더 효율적이다 / 그들이 기계로 부품들을 만들게 하는 것이

해설 'It is ~ to 동사원형' 형식의 완전한 문장으로 가주어/진주어 문장이다. 가주어/진주어와 잘 어울리는 형용사인 (B)가 정답이다. (D)도 가능하긴 하나 앞의 내용과 상충된다.

표현 정리 offensive 모욕적인 efficient 능률적인 convertible 전환 가능한 outdated 구식인

6. 정답 (B)

해설 비교적 흔한 일이다 / 신생 기업이 보조금을 받는 것은 / 정부로부터 / 자본이 적은 기업들을 지원해 주는

해설 'It is ~ to 동사원형' 형식의 완전한 문장으로 가주어/진주어 문장이다. 가주어/진주어와 잘 어울리는 형용사인 (B)가 정답이다. (A)는 주로 사람이 주어로 오고, (D)는 복수 명사를 수식할 때 사용한다.

표현 정리 relatively 비교적 startup enterprise 신생 기업 subsidies 보조금 small-capital 소자본 common 흔한 even 균등한

7. 정답 (D)

해설 난방시스템을 고치는 것은 필요하다 / 이 건물에서 / 왜냐하면 그것은 자주 전기가 나가기 때문에

해설 'It is ~ to 동사원형' 형식의 완전한 문장으로 가주어/진주어 문장이다. 가주어/진주어와 잘 어울리는 형용사인 (D)가 정답이다. (A)와 (B)도 가주어/진주어와 어울리나 진주어 자리에 'that S+V'가 오는 형용사들이다.

표현 정리 repair 수리하다 frequently 빈번히 apparent 명백한 absolute 절대적인 obvious 분명한 necessary 필수적인, 필요한

8. 정답 (A)

해설 합리적이다 / 반바지들이 판매된 것은 / 최대 50퍼센트까지 할인되어 / 여름 시즌이 끝났기 때문에

해설 'It was ~ that S+V' 형식의 완전한 문장으로 가주어/진주어 문장이다. 가주어/진주어와 잘 어울리는 형용사는 (A)이다. (C)는 수나 양이 충분할 때 사용한다.

표현 정리 shorts 반바지 up to ~까지 reasonable 합리적인 punctual 시간을 지키는

9. 정답 (B)

해설 Harold 사의 대부분의 직원들은 / 시골에 위치하고 있는 / 회사 사택에 거주한다 / 그들에게 더 편리하기 때문에

해설 it is more _____ for them 뒤에 to live in company housing이 생략되었다고 보는 것이 좋다. 가주어/진주어 문장이다. 가주어/진주어와 잘 어울리는 형용사인 (B)가 정답이다. (A)는 as 다음이 이유가 되므로 편리하기 때문에 사는 것이지, 선택 사항이기 때문에 사는 것은 아니고, (C)는 복수 명사를 좋아한다.

표현 정리 employee 직원, 사원 rural 시골의 optional 선택적인 convenient 편리한 comprehensive 포괄적인, 종합적인

10. 정답 (C)

해설 연구를 수행하는 것이 쉬워질 것이다 / 일단 Dr. Harlan의 팀이 더 많은 자금을 받는다면 / 연구장비를 구입할

해설 'It will be ~ to 동사원형' 형식의 완전한 문장으로 가주어/진주어 문장이다. 가주어/진주어와 잘 어울리는 형용사인 (C)가 정답이다. (B)는 진주어로 'that S+V'를 좋아한다.

표현 정리 conduct 수행하다 research 연구 fund 자금, 기금 equipment 장비 volatile 변덕스러운

법칙 90 올바른 해석으로 풀어야 하는 형용사 어휘 문제

◎ 유형을 파악해 봐
1. (B)   2. (B)   3. (D)

1. 정답 (B)

해설 매니저는 Ms. Lee를 방문했다 / 간단한 의견을 주기 위해 / 그녀에 제안서에 관해 / 휴식 동안에

해설 빈칸 뒤 명사를 수식해 주는 형용사 어휘 문제이다. 의미상 서로 반대되는 말이 보기로 제시되면 둘 중 하나를 대입해 해석해 본다. 의미상 (B)와 (D)가 반대 의미이므로 먼저 (B)를 넣어 해석하면, '휴식 동안 그녀의 제안서에 관해 간결한 의견을 주기 위해'라는 의미가 되므로 (B)가 정답이다.

표현 정리 call on 방문하다 comment 의견, 논평 proposal 제안, 제안서 break time 휴식 시간 dissatisfied 불만족스런 brief 간결한 unanimous 만장일치의, 뜻이 같은 lengthy 길이가 긴

2. 정답 (B)

해설 우리는 주문해야 한다 / 여분의 선반을 / 충분히 튼튼한 / 다수의 책들을 넣을 수 있는 / 현재 선반에 놓을 수 없는

해설 빈칸 앞 명사를 수식해 주는 형용사 어휘 문제이다. 현재 선반으로는 충분하지 않은 다수의 책들을 넣을 수 있는 튼튼한 선반을 주문할 필요가 있어야 하므로 (B)가 정답이다.

표현 정리 order 주문하다, 지시하다 extra 추가의 a bunch of 다수의 place 놓다, 두다 current 기존의, 현재의 qualified 자격 있는, 적격인

3. 정답 (D)

해설 만약 용지함이 비어 있다면 / 당신은 적당한 양의 A4 용지를 안에 넣어야 한다 / 다음 사람이 사용할 수 있게

해설 빈칸은 be 동사 뒤의 보어 자리로 주어와의 어울림을 보는 형용사 어휘 문제이다. 의미상 (A)와 (D)가 반대의미이므로 먼저 (D)를 넣어 해석하면, '만약 용지함이 비어 있다면, 다음 사람이 사용할 수 있게 적당한 양의 용지를 넣어야 한다'는 내용이 자연스러우므로 (D)가 정답이다.

표현 정리 tray 상자 a handful of 한 줌의, 소수의 full 가득 찬 stuck 갇힌 outdated 구식인 empty 비어있는, 빈

◎ 실전에 적용해 봐
1. (D) 2. (C) 3. (A) 4. (B) 5. (A) 6. (A) 7. (D)
8. (D) 9. (B) 10. (A)

1. 정답 (D)

해설 BNM International Air는 정해야 한다 / 최대 수하물 무게를 / 각 승객들이 짐으로 부칠 수 있는 / 혼란을 초래하지 않기 위해

해설 빈칸 뒤의 명사를 수식해 주는 형용사 어휘 문제이며, '혼란을 초래하지 않기 위해 최대 수하물 무게를 정해야 한다'는 내용이 자연스러우므로 (D)가 정답이다.

표현 정리 weight 무게 passenger 승객 check in (짐을) 부치다, 체크인하다 luggage 수하물, 짐 in order not to ~하지 않도록 cause 초래하다 enormous 거대한, 막대한 average 평균의 inaccurate 부정확한 maximum 최대의

2. 정답 (C)

해설 이번 달 / 시 의회는 의무적으로 만들었다 / 지역 학교나 회사들이 / 대피 훈련을 정기적으로 실시하도록 / 발생한 빈번한 지진 때문에

해설 빈칸 뒤 명사를 수식해 주는 형용사 어휘 문제이다. 의미상 서로 반대되는 말이 보기로 제시되면 둘 중 하나를 대입해 해석해 본다. (A)와 (C)가 반대 의미이므로 먼저 (C)를 넣어 해석하면, '빈번한 지진들 때문에 정기적으로 의무적인 대피 훈련을 실시하게 했다'라는 의미가 되므로 정답이다.

표현 정리 city council 시 의회 mandatory 의무적인 evacuation drill 대피훈련 earthquakes 지진 occur 일어나다, 발생하다 rare 드문 ancient 고대의

3. 정답 (A)

해설 세계에서 가장 번창하는 회사 중 하나인 / Glory는 항상 유지했다 / 낙관적인 이윤을

해설 빈칸 뒤의 명사를 수식해 주는 형용사 어휘 문제이다. 의미상 (A)와 (C)가 반대 의미이므로 먼저 (A)를 넣어 해석하면, '세계적으로 가장 번창하는 회사 중 하나인 Glory는 항상 낙관적인 이윤을 유지했다'는 내용이 되므로 (A)가 정답이다. (D)는 앞의 내용과 상충된다.

표현 정리 name 명명하다, 이름 짓다 prosperous 번영한, 번창한 maintain 유지하다 profit 이익 margin 수익 positive 낙관적인 rare 드문 negative 부정적인 limited 제한된

4. 정답 (B)

해설 CEO는 결정했다 / 최근에 개발된 전자기기를 출시하기로 / 임원들의 강한 반대에도 불구하고

해설 빈칸 뒤의 명사를 수식해 주는 형용사 어휘 문제다. 보기가 모두 명사 앞에 사용할 수 있으므로 문맥상 적절한 정답을 골라야 한다. (A)와 (B), (C), (D)가 서로 반대의 어감을 갖고 있으므로 (B)를 먼저 넣어 해석하면, 'CEO는 임원들의 강한 반대에도 불구하고 최근에 개발된 전자기기를 출시하기로 결정했다'는 말이 자연스러우므로 (B)가 답이 된다.

표현 정리 launch 출시하다, 개시하다 recently 최근에 developed 개발한 electronic device 전자기기 regardless of ~에 상관없이

objection 이의, 반대 executive 임원, 간부 mere 단지 bearable 참을 만한

5. 정답 (A)

해설 Dr. Moore는 조언했다 / 환자에게 운동을 포함시키도록 / 최소한 30분 동안 / 그의 일상생활에서

해설 빈칸은 소유격 뒤의 형용사 뒤 명사 자리이다. 형용사인 daily와 어울림이 자연스러운 명사를 골라야 하는데, 보기 모두 사용이 가능하므로 문맥을 통해 적절한 정답을 고른다. '환자의 일상 생활에서'라는 의미가 알맞으므로 (A)가 정답이다.

표현 정리 advise 충고하다, 조언하다 patient 환자 routine 일상 incident 일, 사건

6. 정답 (A)

해설 비록 후보자는 상당한 노력을 기울였지만 / 연설하는 것에 / 청중들은 반응이 없었다 / 그의 공약에 / 그리고 그들은 공약이 설득력이 없음을 알았다

해설 빈칸은 2형식 동사(remained) 뒤 보어 자리이다. 주어(the audiences)와의 어울림을 보는 형용사 어휘 문제이며, 부사절 문두에 역접의 연결어 although가 왔으므로 주절은 상반되는 내용이 되야 한다. 따라서 (A)를 넣어 해석하면, '비록 후보자는 그의 연설에 상당한 노력을 기울였지만, 청중들은 반응이 없었다'가 어울리므로 (A)가 정답이다.

표현 정리 candidate 후보자 considerable 상당한, 많은 deliver one's speech 연설하다 audience 청중 remain ~이다, 남다 pledge 공약, 맹세 convincing 설득력 있는, 확실한 unresponsive 반응이 없는 excited 흥분한 attentive 주의를 기울이는 obligatory 의무적인

7. 정답 (D)

해설 그가 Spix Design에 단 1주일 근무했다는 것을 고려하면 / 만만찮은 일이다 / Mr. Davis가 이름을 암기하는 것은 / 그와 사무실을 함께 사용하는 50명의 직원들의

해설 빈칸 뒤의 명사를 수식해 주는 형용사 어휘 문제이다. '그가 Spix Design에 단 1주일 근무했다는 것을 고려하면, Mr. Davis가 50명의 이름을 외우는 것은 만만찮은 일이다'로 해석하는 것이 적절하므로 (D)가 정답이다.

표현 정리 considering that ~를 고려하면 formidable task 만만찮은 일, 힘에 겨운 일 memorize 암기하다 minimal 최소의

8. 정답 (D)

해설 시상식에서 / Ms. Jamison은 칭찬받았다 / 그녀의 뛰어난 능력에 대해 / 팀을 관리하는 / 그녀의 지휘 하에 있는

해설 빈칸 뒤의 명사를 수식해 주는 형용사 어휘 문제이다. 'Ms. Jamison은 팀을 관리하는 그녀의 뛰어난 능력으로 칭찬을 받았다'는 내용이므로 (D)가 정답이다. 나머지는 job과의 어울림이 좋지 않다.

표현 정리 award 상, 시상식 praise 칭찬하다, 찬미하다 manage 경영하다, 관리하다 under one's supervision ~의 감독 하에 trifling 사소한 insignificant 중요하지 않은 synthetic 인조의, 합성의

superb 훌륭한, 뛰어난

9. 정답 (B)

해설 레스토랑은 / 7번 출구에서 한 블록 떨어진 곳에 위치한 / Almond Station쪽으로 가장 가까운 장소이다 / 비즈니스 오찬을 개최할 수 있는

해설 빈칸 뒤의 명사를 수식해 주는 형용사 어휘 문제이며, 문맥상 의미를 파악해 정답을 골라야 하는 문제이다. 7번 출구에서 한 블록만 떨어졌으므로 역 쪽으로 가장 가깝다고 할 수 있다. 따라서 (B)가 정답이다.

표현 정리 locate 위치하다 away from 떨어진 venue 장소 luncheon 오찬, 점심

10. 정답 (A)

해설 꽤 자주 생긴다 / Ms. Bacon이 식사를 거르는 일이 / 그녀의 바쁜 일정 때문에

해설 빈칸 뒤의 명사를 수식해 주는 형용사 어휘 문제로, 해석을 통해 정답을 골라야 한다. because of 앞에 '식사를 거른다'는 이유가 제시되었으므로 뒤에는 그 원인을 나타낼 수 있는 표현이 필요하다. 문맥상 바쁜 일정 때문에 식사를 거르는 일이 생긴다고 보아야 하므로 (A)가 정답이다.

표현 정리 happen 일어나다, 발생하다 quite often 꽤 자주 skip 거르다, 건너뛰다 empty 비어있는, 빈 detailed 상세한, 자세한 specific 구체적인

 Chapter 12 부사 어휘 문제(매월 3문제)

법칙 91 특정 시제와 잘 어울리는 부사

◎ 유형을 파악해 봐
1. (B) 2. (C) 3. (A)

1. 정답 (B)

해설 Voltech Solutions는 / 지금 모집하고 있다 / 신입 사원을 / 엔지니어 자리의

해설 동사의 시제는 현재진행시제(is recruiting)이며, 현재진행시제와 잘 어울리는 부사는 (B)이다. '지금 모집하고 있다'는 내용이 어울리므로 (B)가 정답이다. 다른 부사들은 딱히 특정 시제와 어울리는 것이 없다.

표현 정리 recruit 모집하다 new employee 신입 사원

2. 정답 (C)

해설 Host Hotel은 최근에 보수되었다 / 설립 30년 후인

해설 동사의 시제는 현재완료시제(has been renovated)이며, 현재완료시제와 잘 어울리는 부사는 (C)이다. '최근에 보수되었다'는 내용이 어울리므로 (C)가 정답이다. (B)는 주로 현재진행 및 현재시제, (D)는 현재시제와 쓰인다.

표현 정리 renovate 보수하다, 개조하다 primarily 주로 currently 현재, 지금 recently 최근에 usually 보통, 대개

3. 정답 (A)

해설 그 책의 영문판은 / 곧 이용 가능할 것이다.

해설 동사의 시제는 미래시제(will be available)이며, 미래시제와 잘 어울리는 부사는 (A)이다. '곧 이용 가능할 것이다'라는 말이 어울리므로 (A)가 정답이다. 다른 부사들은 딱히 특정 시제와 어울리는 것이 없다.

표현 정리 version 판 available 이용할 수 있는

◎ 실전에 적용해 봐
1. (C) 2. (D) 3. (B) 4. (C) 5. (D) 6. (A) 7. (A)
8. (D) 9. (D) 10. (B)

1. 정답 (C)

해설 우리는 고객에게 권한다 / 패키지 투어를 선택하도록 / 호주의 / 여름철 / 날씨는 보통 더 좋으므로 / 그 기간 동안

해설 동사의 시제는 현재(is)이며, 현재시제는 반복/습관적 사실을 나타내므로 빈도부사 (C)가 잘 어울린다. '날씨는 그 기간 동안 보통 더 좋으므로'라는 말도 자연스럽다. (B)는 주로 전명구 앞에 잘 쓰이는 초점 부사이고, (D)는 주로 미래시제와 쓰인다.

표현 정리 encourage 장려하다, 격려하다 season 계절 favorable 좋은, 호의적인 possibly 아마 exactly 정확하게 usually 보통, 대개 shortly 곧

2. 정답 (D)

해설 현재 Mr. Dawson의 감독 하에 일하는 직원들은 / 지시를 받을 수도 있다 / 최고 관리자의 / 다음 주 월요일부터

해설 동사의 시제는 현재진행시제(are working)이며, 현재진행시제와 잘 어울리는 부사는 (D)이다. '현재 Mr. Dawson의 감독 하에 일하는 직원들은'이라는 말이 자연스럽게 어울리므로 (D)가 정답이다. (A), (C)는 주로 과거나 현재완료와 쓰인다.

표현 정리 supervision 감독 executive officer 고위 임원, 최고 관리자 previously 이전에 significantly 상당히, 크게 recently 최근에 currently 현재, 지금

3. 정답 (B)

해설 지원자들을 철저하게 면접한 후 / 한 명씩 / 매니저는 마침내 결정했다 / 그가 누구를 고용할 것인지

해설 After와 짝으로 잘 어울리는 부사는 (B)이며, 대입해 해석하면 '철저하게 면접한 후 마침내 결정했다'는 내용이 자연스러우므로 (B)가 정답이다. (A)와 (C)는 주로 문두에 오는 부사들이며, (D)는 원급의 형용사나 부사를 수식하는 부사이다.

표현 정리 intensively 강하게, 철저하게 one by one 한 명씩 decide 결정하다 meanwhile 그 동안에 mostly 대개는 extremely 매우

4. 정답 (C)

해설 전에는 작은 국내 회사였던 / Genetic Auto는 다국적 기업이 되었다 / 자동차를 전 세계적으로 판매하는

해설 명사 앞은 전치사 자리라고 생각해 무조건 전치사 (B)와 (D)를 고르지 않도록 한다. (C)는 명사 앞에도 올 수 있는 부사인데 '전에는 작은 국내 회사였던 Genetic Auto는'으로 해석되며, 여기서 Formerly는 Formerly known as의 줄임말이라고 생각하면 쉽다.

표현 정리 domestic 국내의 multinational 다국적인 automobile 자동차 worldwide 전 세계적으로

5. 정답 (D)

해설 가격이 바뀔 예정인 상품들이 / 홍보 기간이 끝난 후에 / 틀림없이 발표될 것이다 / 이번 주말에

해설 this week와 결합하여 '이번 주말 경에'의 뜻을 갖는 (D)가 정답이다. later this month는 '이번 달 말 경에,' later today는 '오늘 늦게'와 같은 형태로 사용된다.

표현 정리 be subject to ~의 대상이다 promotion 홍보 announce 발표하다 formerly 이전에

6. 정답 (A)

해설 바로 먹을 수 있도록 준비된 식사는 / 원래 의도되었다 / 구매를 촉진시키기 위해 / 1인 가구들의 / 하지만 인기를 얻게 되었다 / 또한 대가족들 사이에서도

해설 동사의 시제는 과거시제(were intended)이며, 과거시제와 주로 잘 어울리는 부사 (A)를 대입해 해석하면, '바로 먹을 수 있는 식사는 원래 의도되었다'가 어울리므로 (A)가 정답이다. (B)는 교통량 등이 원활하게 이동할 때, (C)는 증가/감소의 표현들과 사용되며, (D)는 주로 현재 또는 현재진행시제와 쓰인다.

표현 정리 meal 식사 stimulate 자극하다 household 가정 originally 원래, 본래 smoothly 원활하게 significantly 상당히 currently 현재, 지금

7. 정답 (A)

해설 상점에서 판매되는 대부분의 의류가 / 이전에는 제작되었다 / 수작업으로 / 드물다 / 수작업으로 제작한 의류를 보기란 / 기계로 제작되는 의류들 사이에서 / 요즈음

해설 동사의 시제는 과거시제(were made)이며, 과거시제와 주로 잘 어울리는 부사는 (A)이다. '상점에서 판매되는 대부분의 의류들이 이전에는 수작업으로 제작되었다'라는 말이 자연스러우므로 (A)가 정답이다. (B)는 주로 현재 또는 현재진행시제와 쓰이고, (C)는 뒤에 시점이 오고, (D)는 미래시제와 쓰인다.

표현 정리 garment 의류, 옷 rare 드문 previously 이전에 currently 현재, 지금

8. 정답 (D)

해설 우리는 정기적으로 점검한다 / 모든 컴퓨터들을 / 우리 회사의 / 바이러스에 대비해 / 시스템 고장을 방지하기 위해

해설 빈칸은 현재시제인 check를 수식하는 부사 자리이다. 현재시제 및 check 동사와 잘 어울리는 부사는 (D)이다. (A)는 주로 과거시제, (B)는 현재완료 또는 과거시제와 쓰이고, (C)는 증가 감소의 표현과 어울리는 부사이다.

표현 정리 check 점검하다 failure 고장 originally 원래 significantly 상당히 recently 최근에

9. 정답 (D)

해설 Ms. Miranda가 현재 시내에 거주하고 있지만 / 그녀는 곧 이사할 것이다 / 사택으로 / GK Design에서 일하기 시작하자마자

해설 live는 상태를 나타내는 현재시제이며, 상태를 나타내는 현재시제와 잘 어울리는 부사 (D)를 먼저 대입해 해석해 보면, '현재 시내에 거주하고 있지만'이라는 말이 자연스러우므로 정답이다. (A)와 (B) 모두 주로 현재완료나 과거시제와 쓰이고, (C)는 주로 형용사나 부사를 수식하는 부사이다. currently를 현재진행시제에만 사용한다고 알고 있었다면 함정에 빠질 수 있는 문제이다.

표현 정리 downtown 시내 company housing 사택 recently 최근에 once ~하자마자 currently 현재

10. 정답 (B)

해설 차트에 있는 이들 수치를 참고하면 / 당신은 알 것이다 / 밀의 가격이 분명히 인상되었음을 / 지난 3년 동안

해설 '밀의 가격이 분명히 인상되었다'라는 해석이 적절하다. 현재완료시제만 보고 recently를 답으로 고르지 않도록 하자. recently는 과거나 현재완료시제와 사용하지만, 구체적인 기간과는 어울리지 않는다. '지난 3년 동안'이라는 표현이 있으므로 recently는 오답이다.

표현 정리 figure 수치 wheat 밀 increase 인상하다 monetarily 화폐로, 금전상으로

법칙 92 특정 형용사와 잘 어울리는 부사

◎ 유형을 파악해 봐
1. (B)   2. (D)   3. (D)

1. 정답 (B)

해설 Hobb 사의 웹사이트는 / 접근하기 어려웠다 / 거의 이틀 동안

해설 숫자도 형용사이므로 숫자와 잘 어울리는 숫자 수식 부사는 (B)이다. '거의 이틀 동안'이란 말이 자연스럽기 때문에 (B)가 정답이다. (A)는 주로 impossible, correct, right 등의 형용사와 어울리고, (C)와 (D)는 동사의 빈도를 나타내는 빈도 부사이다. 특히 (D)는 준부정어라고 하며, 동사를 부정한다.

표현 정리 inaccessible 접근하기 어려운 absolutely 전적으로, 틀림없이 frequently 빈번하게, 자주 rarely 드물게, 좀처럼 ~하지 않는

2. 정답 (C)

해설 Mr. Song은 이미 매우 성공한 저자이다 / 그의 신작이 베스트셀러 명단에 올랐기 때문에

해설 빈칸 뒤에 형용사가 있다. 부사 중에서 특히 형용사 앞에 잘 오는 부사는 정도 부사인 (D)이다. '매우 성공한 저자이다'라는 내용으로 봐서도 (C)가 정답이다. (B)는 주로 전명구와 쓰이고, (C)는 주로 문두에서 문장 전체를 수식한다.

표현 정리 author 저자 elegantly 우아하게, 고상하게 mainly 주로, 대부분 fortunately 운 좋게도 highly 크게, 대단히

3. 정답 (D)

해설 매년 / 단체는 개최한다 / 일주일에 걸친 워크숍을 / 그리고 참석을 많이 한다 / 지역 사업가들이

해설 부사 중에서 특히 형용사 앞에 잘 오는 부사는 정도 부사. 정도 부사 중 p.p.를 좋아하는 부사는 (D)이다. (A)와 (B)는 주로 원급의 형용사나 부사를 수식하는 정도 부사로 사용된다.

표현 정리 enormously 엄청나게, 대단히 adversely 반대로, 역으로

◎ 실전에 적용해 봐
1. (A)   2. (C)   3. (B)   4. (C)   5. (A)   6. (D)   7. (A)
8. (D)   9. (B)   10. (A)

1. 정답 (A)

해설 HB Bank의 이자율은 / 올랐다 / 약 5% 가량

해설 숫자도 형용사이므로 숫자와 잘 어울리는 숫자 수식 부사는 (A)이다. '대략 5퍼센트'란 말이 자연스러우므로 (A)가 정답이다. (B), (C), (D)는 주로 일반적인 형용사 앞에 잘 쓰이는 정도 부사이다.

표현 정리 interest rate 이자율 roughly 대략 relatively 비교적 slightly 약간, 조금 fairly 꽤

2. 정답 (C)

해설 우리의 자선행사를 위해 / 모든 종류의 지원은 / 기부의 형태로든, 아니면 자원봉사 형태로든 / 매우 감사히 여겨진다.

해설 정도 부사 중 p.p.를 좋아하는 부사는 (C)이다. '매우 감사히 여기다'라는 해석 또한 어울리므로 (C)가 답이다. (A)와 (B)는 증감 부사('법칙 94' 참고)이므로 증가나 의미를 가진 동사와 어울린다. (D)는 주의 깊게 읽거나 검토할 때 사용한다.

표현 정리 fundraising event 자선행사 donation 기부 appreciate 고맙게 생각하다 gradually 서서히 deeply 깊이 carefully 주의하여, 조심스럽게

3. 정답 (B)

해설 전문 CAD 디자이너를 위한 적성검사는 / 물어 본다 / 100가지에 이르는 다양한 질문들을

해설 숫자도 형용사이므로 숫자와 잘 어울리는 숫자 수식 부사는 (B)이다. '100가지에 이르는 다양한 질문들을'이란 말이 어울리므로 (B)가 정답이다.

표현 정리 aptitude 적성 professional 전문적인 along with ~와 함께

4. 정답 (C)

해설 그녀의 제안이 거절된 후 / Ms. Walter는 다소 우울해 보였다 / 그리고 회의에서 많이 이야기하지 않았다

해설 형용사나 p.p.의 정도를 표시하는 부사는 (C)이다. (A)와 (B)는 주로 과거시제의 경험을 나타내는 말로 seemed 보다 앞에 위치하는 것이 좋다.

표현 정리 proposal 제안 turned down 거절하다 depressed 우울한 previously 이전에 somewhat 다소 officially 공식적으로

5. 정답 (A)

해설 비록 Loonie Store가 다리 건너에 있지만 / Mr. Farrell의 집으로부터 / 항상 다리에 심한 교통 체증이 있기 때문에 / 몇 마일 떨어져 있는 Farmers Shop이 비교적 접근하기 쉽다.

해설 부사 중에서, 특히 형용사 앞에 잘 오는 부사는 정도 부사인 (A)이다. '몇 마일 떨어져 있는 Farmers Shop이 비교적 접근하기 쉽다'라는 내용이 어울리므로 (A)가 정답이다. (B)는 '손상된'이란 뜻의 형용사를 수식할 때, (C)는 협조하여 작업하거나 면밀히 조사할 때 사용하고, 준부정어인 (D)는 동사의 빈도를 나타내는 빈도 부사이다.

표현 정리 heavy traffic 극심한 교통량, 교통 체증 relatively 상대적으로

6. 정답 (D)

해설 Ms. Tylor는 Sunpick Inn의 단골 고객이었기 때문에 / 그녀는 특별 쿠폰을 받았다 / 하루 숙박을 제공하는 / 30퍼센트 정도 할인된 가격에

해설 숫자도 형용사이므로 숫자와 잘 어울리는 숫자 수식 부사는 (D)이다. '30퍼센트 정도 할인된 가격에'라는 내용이 어울리므로 (D)가 정답이다. (A)는 of와 함께 전치사로 사용하며, (B)는 '명사 and 명사'를 취하는 부사이고, (C)는 접속사이다.

표현 정리 regular guest 단골 고객 regardless 관심 없는, 개의치 않은 as much as ~만큼

7. 정답 (A)

해설 사치품들의 특징은 / 가격을 매우 높게 책정하는 것이다 / 오직 제한된 수의 고객들만이 그것들을 소유할 수 있도록

해설 빈칸 뒤에 형용사가 있다. 부사 중에서, 특히 형용사 앞에 잘 오는 부사는 정도 부사인 (A)이다. (B)는 문장의 맨 앞이나 뒤에 위치하고, (C)는 널리 퍼져있거나 알려져 있을 때 사용하며, (D)는 앞에 after 등의 표현이 올 때 자연스럽게 어울리는 부사이다.

표현 정리 characteristic 성격 luxury 사치 limited 제한된 extremely 매우, 극도로 accordingly 따라서, 그러므로 widely 널리, 폭넓게 finally 마침내

8. 정답 (D)

해설 대략 30명 이상의 멤버가 / 필요할 것이다 / 다가오는 매장 행사에

해설 숫자도 형용사이므로 숫자와 잘 어울리는 숫자 수식 부사는 (D)이다. (A)는 주로 과거 또는 현재완료시제와 쓰이는 시제 부사, (B)와 (C)는 동사의 빈도를 나타내는 빈도부사이다. 특히 (B)는 준부정어라고 하며 동사를 부정한다.

표현 정리 require 필요하다 upcoming 다가오는 approximately 대략, 거의

9. 정답 (B)

해설 채소를 소비하는 것은 / 정기적으로 / 의심할 여지없이 좋은 습관이다 / 하지만 이것에 심하게 의존하는 것은 / 방해할 가능성이 높다 / 단백질

이나 다른 필수 영양소의 섭취를 / 당신의 몸에

해설 정도를 나타내는 부사인 heavily는 p.p. 앞이니 의존하다' 유형의 표현과 잘 어울린다. (B)를 대입해 해석하면, '~는 좋은 습관이다. 그러나 심하게 의존하는 것은 좋지 않다'는 말이 자연스럽다. 따라서 (B)가 정답이다.

표현 정리 consume 소비하다 on a regular basis 정기적으로 undoubtedly 의심할 여지없이 prevent 방해하다 ingestion 섭취 protein 단백질 nutrients 영양소

10.   정답 **(A)**

해석 메릴랜드 연례 주택 전시회는 항상 매우 인기 있었기 때문에 / 우리는 권장한다 / 당신이 17회 박람회 티켓을 구입할 것을 / 훨씬 미리

해설 in advance와 같이 사용해 '훨씬 이전에'라는 표현을 나타내는 (A)가 정답이다. (C)와 (D)는 이미 '사전에'라는 뜻을 포함하고 있어 in advance와 중복된다.

표현 정리 fair 박람회 eventually 궁극적으로 beforehand 사전에

법칙 93 전명구와 잘 어울리는 부사

◎ 유형을 파악해 봐
1. (C)   2. (B)   3. (B)

1.   정답 **(C)**

해석 등록 기간은 / 스페인어 수업 / 연장되었다 / 특히 수강료를 납부하지 않는 사람을 위해

해설 빈칸 뒤에 전명구가 있다. 전명구와 잘 어울리는 부사는 초점 부사인 (C)이다. '특히 수강료를 납부하지 않는 사람을 위해'라는 말이 자연스럽기 때문에 (C)가 정답이다. (A)는 증감 부사('법칙 94' 참고)이므로 증가나 의미를 가진 동사와 어울리고, (B)는 beneficial과 같은 형용사를 수식한다. (D)는 주로 현재시제와 함께 사용하는 부사이다.

표현 정리 registration 등록 period 기간 extend 연장하다 noticeably 두드러지게, 현저히 mutually 서로, 상호간에 annually 일년에, 한번

2.   정답 **(B)**

해석 회원 카드는 / 독점적으로 제공된다 / 고객들에게만 / 매달 500달러 이상 구매한

해설 빈칸 뒤에 전명구가 있다. 전명구와 잘 어울리는 부사는 초점 부사인 (B)이다. '회원 카드는 고객들에게만 독점적으로 제공된다'라는 말이 자연스럽기 때문에 (B)가 정답이다.

표현 정리 firmly 단호히, 확고히 exclusively 배타적으로, 독점적으로 hopefully 바라건대

3.   정답 **(B)**

해석 이 이메일을 보내주세요 / 직접 / 인사 부장에게

해설 빈칸 뒤에 전명구가 있다. 전명구와 잘 어울리는 부사는 방식을 나타내는 부사인 (B)이다. '이 이메일을 직접 인사 부장에게 보내 주세요'라는 말이 자연스럽기 때문에 (B)가 정답이다. (A)와 (D)는 주로 형용사 앞에 쓰이는 정도 부사이고, (C)는 점검하거나 읽는 동사와 어울린다.

표현 정리 forward 보내다 director 부장 Personnel Department 인사부 absolutely 전적으로, 틀림없이 directly 직접 thoroughly 철저히 relatively 상대적으로, 비교적

◎ 실전에 적용해 봐
1. (D)   2. (A)   3. (A)   4. (C)   5. (D)   6. (C)   7. (B)
8. (A)   9. (B)   10. (D)

1.   정답 **(D)**

해석 Ms. Giambi는 문제를 다뤘다 / 계속해서 논의되어 왔던 / 특히 회계부 직원들에 의해

해설 빈칸 뒤, 명사 앞에 올 수 있는 부사는 초점 부사인 (D)이다. '특히 회계부 직원들에 의해'라는 내용 또한 어울리므로 (D)가 정답이다. (B)는 숫자와 잘 어울리는 부사이다.

표현 정리 address 다루다, 고심하다 discuss 논의하다, 토론하다 Accounting Department 회계부 economically 경제적으로 randomly 임의로, 무작위로

2.   정답 **(A)**

해석 Sharp Corporation은 결정했다 / 그들의 주 고객층을 변경하기로 / 작은 회사 오너들로 / 주로 신생 업체를 운영하는

해설 빈칸 뒤에 전명구가 있다. 전명구와 잘 어울리는 부사는 초점 부사인 (A)이다. '주로 신생업체를 가진 사람들로'라는 말이 자연스럽기 때문에 (A)가 정답이다. (B)는 주로 형용사 앞에 쓰이는 정도 부사이다.

표현 정리 start-up business 신생 업체 primarily 주로 relatively 상대적으로 comparatively 비교적으로

3.   정답 **(A)**

해석 Ms. Mill은 정확히 같은 메뉴를 주문했다 / 그녀가 주문하곤 했던 / 5년 만에 방문한 레스토랑에서

해설 초점 부사는 전명구 앞에도 잘 오지만, 명사 앞에도 온다. '정확히 같은 메뉴'라는 해석이 적절하므로 (A)가 정답이다. (B)는 숫자 수식 부사, (C)는 형용사, (D)는 형용사나 p.p. 앞에 오는 정도 부사이다.

표현 정리 order 주문하다 exactly 정확하게 approximately 대략적으로 timely 시기 적절한 uncommonly 드물게, 희저하게

4.   정답 **(C)**

해석 지원자들 중 / 프로젝트 매니저 자리에 지원하는 사람들은 / 면접을 볼 것이다 / 다른 지원자들과 별도로

해설 빈칸 뒤에 전명구가 있다. 전명구와 잘 어울리는 부사는 방식을 나타내는 부사인 (C)이다. '다른 지원자들과 별도로'라는 말이 자연스럽기 때문에 (C)가 정답이다. (B)는 주로 과거시제나 현재완료시제와 쓰이고, (D)는 숫자를 수식하는 숫자 수식 부사이다.

표현 정리 applicant 지원자 apply for ~에 지원하다 stably 안정되게, 견고하게 recently 최근에 separately 별도로, 따로따로 nearly 거의

5. 정답 (D)

해설 각각의 조사에서 / 소비자 만족에 관한 / 우리는 응답을 얻는다 / 이상적으로는 100명 이상으로부터 / 신뢰할 만한 결과를 산출하기 위해

해설 전명구 앞에 와서 문장 전체에 영향을 미치는 부사는 (D) ideally이다. '이상적으로는 100명 이상으로부터 신뢰할 만한 결과를 산출하기 위해'라는 내용 또한 자연스럽다.

표현 정리 abruptly 갑자기, 불쑥 critically 비판적으로 rarely 드물게, 좀처럼 ~하지 않는 ideally 이상적으로

6. 정답 (C)

해설 Mr. Gill은 이유를 말하지 않았다 / 그의 결근에 대한 / 지난 회의 때 / 그러나 그는 미팅에 불참했던 것 같다 / 아마도 그의 병원 예약과 일정이 겹쳐

해설 전명구 앞에 와서 전명구를 수식하는 부사인 (C)를 먼저 대입해 해석하면, '불참 이유를 말하진 않았지만 아마도 그의 병원 예약과 일정이 겹친 것이 이유인 것 같다'는 말이 자연스럽다. 따라서 (C)가 정답이다. (A)는 주로 현재시제, (D)는 주로 well과 같은 부사를 수식할 때 사용한다.

표현 정리 conditionally 조건부로 exceptionally 유난히, 예외적으로

7. 정답 (B)

해설 Ms. Lace는 불편한 것 같다 / 사적인 질문에 답하는 것이 / 특히 그녀의 결혼생활에 대해 / 동료 앞에서

해설 빈칸 뒤에 전명구가 있다. 전명구와 잘 어울리는 부사는 초점 부사인 (B)이다. '특히 그녀의 결혼생활에 대해'라는 말이 자연스럽기 때문에 (B)가 정답이다. (C)는 증감 부사('법칙 94' 참고)이므로 증가나 의미를 가진 동사와 어울린다. (D)는 형용사나 부사의 정도를 묘사하는 정도 부사이다.

표현 정리 appropriately 적당하게 particularly 특히 significantly 상당히 unusually 대단히, 평소와 달리

8. 정답 (A)

해설 Mr. Hall에게 주어졌다 / 마지막 경고가 / 그의 상사로부터 / 그가 그의 서류작업을 끝냈기 때문에 / 계속해서 예정보다 늦게

해설 (A)를 대입하면 전명구와도 잘 어울리고, '최종 경고를 받았는데, 계속해서 일정보다 늦게 끝냈기 때문에'라는 해석도 적절하다. (B)와 (C)는 경고를 받았다는 말과 상충되며, (D)는 최종 경고라는 말과 상충된다.

표현 정리 consistently 계속해서, 지속적으로 rarely 드물게 punctually 정각에, 시간대로

9. 정답 (B)

해설 승무원의 안내 방송이 전달된 후에 / Amsterdam으로 향하는 비행기는 / Istanbul International Airport에서 출발했다

해설 after와 잘 어울리는 부사는 (B)이다. '승무원의 안내 방송이 전달된 후에'라는 내용 역시 자연스러워 (B)가 정답이다. (A)는 위치를 묘사할 때 사용하며, (C)와 (D)는 현재시제와 어울린다.

표현 정리 depart 출발하다 immediately 즉시 commonly 흔히, 보통 usually 보통, 대게

10. 정답 (D)

해설 Maxx Tech의 엔지니어 구인 광고는 / 명시하고 있다 / 회사는 고용한다고 / 오직 경력직 지원자만을

해설 여기서 빈칸은 experienced applicants를 수식하는 자리이다. 따라서 명사 수식 기능이 있는 초점 부사 (D)가 정답이다. (A)는 과거시제와 사용하고, (B)는 숫자를 수식하며, (C)는 미래시제와 어울린다.

표현 정리 job advertisement 구인 광고 state 명시하다 hire 고용하다

법칙 94 특정 동사와 잘 어울리는 부사

◎ 유형을 파악해 봐
1. (C)   2. (A)   3. (D)

1. 정답 (C)

해설 팀의 동기부여가 급격하게 증가되었다 / 매출이 최고치를 기록한 후

해설 빈칸은 동사를 수식해 주는 자리이므로 increase와의 어울림을 봐야 한다. '증가[감소]하다' 류의 동사와 어울리는 증감 부사인 (C)가 정답이다. (A)는 '적극적으로'라는 뜻으로 '대응하다' 류의 동사와 어울리고, (B)는 '열망하여'라는 뜻으로 '기대하다' 류의 동사와 어울리며, (D)는 현재진행시제나, 현재시제와 어울리는 부사이다.

표현 정리 aggressively 적극적으로 eagerly 열망하여, 열심히 dramatically 극적으로 currently 현재

2. 정답 (A)

해설 Mr. Trey는 명령했다 / 그의 비서에게 / 철저히 이메일을 검토하도록 / 스팸을 걸러내기 위해

해설 빈칸 앞의 to 부정사를 수식해 주는 부사 자리이므로 review와의 어울림을 봐야 한다. '검토하다' 류의 동사와 어울리는 (A)가 정답이다. (B)는 '견고하게'라는 뜻으로 '잡고 있다' 류의 동사와 어울리고, (C)는 '열망하여'라는 뜻으로 '기대하다' 류의 동사와 어울리는 부사이다. (D)는 '과도하게'라는 뜻으로 주로 형용사를 수식한다.

표현 정리 filter out ~을 걸러내다 thoroughly 철저히

3. 정답 (D)

해설 매니저로부터 들은 대로 / 영업 사원은 빠르게 응답했다 / 고객 문의에

해설 빈칸은 앞의 동사를 수식해 주는 자리이므로 respond와의 어울림을 봐야 한다. '응답하다'의 동사와 어울리는 (D)가 정답이다. (A)는 '견고하게'라는 뜻으로 '잡고 있다' 류의 동사와 어울리고, (B)는 '점차'라는 뜻으로 '증가[감소]하다' 류의 동사와 어울리고, (C)는 '심히, 깊이'라는 뜻으로 '감사하다' 류의 동사와 어울리는 부사이다.

표현 정리 respond 응답하다 inquiry 문의 quickly 빠르게

◎ 실전에 적용해 봐
1. (B)   2. (C)   3. (D)   4. (A)   5. (A)   6. (D)   7. (C)
8. (D)   9. (C)   10. (A)

1. 정답 (B)

해설 반드시 주의 깊게 읽어 주세요 / 기계의 작동 설명서를 / 사용하기 전에

해설 빈칸은 완전한 문장 뒤에 오는 부사 자리이다. 앞의 동사를 수식해 주는 자리이므로 read와의 어울림을 봐야 한다. '읽다'의 동사와 어울리는 (B)가 정답이다. (A)는 '열망하여'라는 뜻으로 '기대하다' 류의 동사와 어울리고, (C)는 '이전에'라는 뜻으로 주로 과거시제와 어울리며, (D)는 원급의 형용사나 부사를 수식하는 정도 부사이다.

표현 정리 manual 설명서 carefully 주의 깊게

2. 정답 (C)

해설 당신의 급여는 점차 인상될 것이다 / 연수에 비례하여 / 이 회사에서 당신이 근무한

해설 빈칸은 조동사와 동사원형 사이에서 동사를 수식해 주는 자리이므로 increase와의 어울림을 봐야 한다. '증가하다'는 뜻으로 '증감[감소]하다' 류의 동사와 어울리는 '증감 부사인' (C)가 정답이다. (A)는 '주의해서', (B)는 '철저하게'라는 뜻인데, 둘 다 '검토하다' 류의 동사와 어울린다.

표현 정리 in proportion ~에 비례하여 gradually 점차

3. 정답 (D)

해설 본사에서 온 지시 사항은 요청했다 / 지점장이 재고조사를 실시할 것을 / 가능한 빨리

해설 as와 as 사이는 원급 형용사나 부사가 오는데, 앞의 문장이 완전하므로 빈칸은 부사 자리이다. 내용상 부정으로 가는 (B)와 (C)를 제외하고, '실시하다'라는 동사와 어울림이 좋은 보기는 (A)와 (D)가 있다. 가능한 한 빨리 실시할 것을 요청했다는 말이 적절하므로 (D)가 정답이다.

표현 정리 headquarters 본사 require 요구하다, 요청하다 inventory 재고 gradually 점차 inadvertently 부주의하게

4. 정답 (A)

해설 교통은 오후 7시쯤에 항상 좋지 않기 때문에 / Mr. Chang은 이 시간에 사무실을 거의 떠나지 않고 / 대신 선호한다 / 오후 5시에 나가는 것을

해설 앞에서 동사를 수식해 주는 부사 자리이므로 leaves와의 어울림을 봐야 한다. '좀처럼 떠나지 않다'라는 의미로 일반 동사 앞에 쓰이는 준부정어 (A)가 정답이다. (B)는 현재완료시제 및 과거시제와 어울리고, (C)는 '아마'라는 뜻으로 문장 전체를 수식하며, (D)는 '자주, 빈번히'라는 뜻의 부사이다

표현 정리 seldom 좀처럼 ~않은 recently 최근에 frequently 빈번히

5. 정답 (A)

해설 불행한 일이다 / 저소득 가구를 위한 기부가 올해에 급격히 줄었다는 것은 / 경제 불황 때문에

해설 동사를 수식해 주는 부사 자리이므로 have dropped와의 어울림을 봐야 한다. '증가[감소]하다' 류의 동사와 어울리는 증감 부사인 (A)가 정답이다. (B)는 형용사로 사용되며, (C)는 '유창하게'라는 뜻으로 '말하다' 류의 동사와 어울리고, (D)는 형용사를 수식한다.

표현 정리 recession 불황 sharply 급격히 timely 적시의 eloquently 유창하게 desirably 바람직하게

6. 정답 (D)

해설 Resil Manufacturing Company에서 생산된 상품의 품질은 상당히 향상되었다 / 회사가 직원들을 더 충원한 후에

해설 빈칸은 has been과 p.p. 사이에서 동사를 수식해 주는 자리이므로 be improved와의 어울림을 봐야 한다. be improved는 '향상되다'의 뜻으로 '증가[감소]하다' 류의 동사이며, 이와 어울리는 증감 부사인 (D)가 정답이다. (A)는 '견고하게'라는 뜻으로 '잡고 있다' 류의 동사와 어울리고, (B)는 '특색이 없이', (C)는 '일반적으로, 보통은'이라는 뜻의 부사이다.

표현 정리 firmly 확고히 indistinctively 특색이 없이 typically 보통, 전형적으로 considerably 많이, 상당히

7. 정답 (C)

해설 Kelleher Furniture Shop은 / 배송비를 거의 청구하지 않는다 / 상품에 대해서는 / VIP 멤버인 소비자로부터 주문 받은

해설 주어와 동사 사이에서 동사를 수식해 주는 부사 자리이므로 charges와의 어울림을 봐야 한다. 'VIP 멤버인 소비자로부터 주문 받은 상품에 대해서는 배송비를 거의 청구하지 않는다'라는 의미로 일반 동사 앞에 쓰이는 준부정어 (C)가 정답이다. (B)는 '빠르게'라는 뜻으로 '변화하다, 접근하다' 류의 동사와 어울리고, (D)는 '우세하게'라는 뜻의 부사이다.

표현 정리 rapidly 급격히 rarely 드물게, 좀처럼 dominantly 지배적으로

8. 정답 (D)

해설 불안정한 경제 상황 때문에 / 많은 회사들은 그들의 사업을 점점 축소한다 / 위험을 줄이기 위해

해설 be -ing 사이에서 동사를 수식해 주는 부사 자리이므로 downsizing과의 어울림을 봐야 한다. '축소하다'는 뜻으로 '증감[감소]하다' 류의 동사와 어울리는 증감 부사 (D)가 정답이다.

표현 정리 diversely 다양하게 timely 시기 적절한 availably 구할 수 있게, 시간적인 여유가 있어서 increasingly 점점 더

9. 정답 (C)

해설 최근 가뭄은 악영향을 끼쳤는데 / 보리 생산에 / 그 수확량은 단지 예상의 절반에 이르렀다

해설 빈칸은 has와 p.p. 사이에서 동사를 수식해 주는 부사 자리이므로 affected와의 어울림을 봐야 한다. '반대의 영향을 미쳤다'의 의미를 이루는 (C)가 정답이다. 긍정적인 의미의 (A)와 (B), 그리고 (D)는 문장 내용과 상충된다.

표현 정리 favorably 호의적으로 valuably 소중하게 adversely 역으로, 반대로 positively 긍정적으로

10. 정답 (A)

해설 영화 'Chicago Dance'의 3분짜리 예고편은 만들어졌다 / 많은 영화 팬들로 하여금 / 간절하게 기대하도록 / 영화의 공식 개봉을

해설 동사를 수식해 주는 부사 자리이므로 anticipate와의 어울림을 봐야

한다. '기대하다'는 뜻과 어울리는 부사 (A)가 정답이다. (B)는 '마지막으로'라는 뜻으로 주로 문두나 문미에 사용되어 문장 전체를 수식한다.

표현 정리 moviegoer 영화 관람객 official release 공식 개봉 eagerly 간절히 lastly 마지막으로 abruptly 갑자기

법칙 95 올바른 해석으로 풀어야 하는 부사 어휘 문제

◎ 유형을 파악해 봐
1. (A)   2. (C)   3. (B)

1. 정답 (A)

해설 우리는 드물게 사용한다 / 인공 조미료와 방부제를 / 우리 요리에 / 그래야 당신이 더 건강하게 먹을 수 있으니까

해설 내용상 서로 반대되는 말이 보기로 제시되는 경우 둘 중 하나가 답이면 다른 하나는 틀리게 되어 있다. 비교적 뜻이 나머지와 반대인 (A)를 넣어 해석하면 내용이 자연스러우므로 정답이다.

표현 정리 artificial flavor 인공 조미료 preservation 방부제 dish 요리 healthily 건강하게 sparingly 드물게 substantially 상당히

2. 정답 (C)

해설 그들은 요청 받았다 / 명확하게 답변하도록 / 면접관들의 질문에

해설 빈칸은 동사(answer)를 수식해 주는 부사이므로 먼저 (C)를 넣어 해석해 보면, '면접관들의 질문에 명확하게 답변하도록 요청 받았다'는 내용이 논리적이므로 (C)가 정답이다.

표현 정리 reservedly 터놓지 않고, 삼가서 doubtfully 미심쩍게, 불확실하게

3. 정답 (B)

해설 연극은 영어로 완벽하게 번역되었고, 호의적인 반응을 얻었다 / 청중들에 의해

해설 be 동사와 p.p. 사이에서 과거분사를 수식해 주는 부사 자리이므로 translated와의 어울림을 봐야 한다. (B)를 대입해 해석해 보면, '완벽하게 번역되었다'가 논리적이므로 (B)가 정답이다.

표현 정리 be translated into ~로 번역되다 perfectly 완벽하게 manually 손으로, 수공으로

◎ 실전에 적용해 봐
1. (B)   2. (A)   3. (A)   4. (D)   5. (C)   6. (C)   7. (B)
8. (D)   9. (D)   10. (A)

1. 정답 (B)

해설 업무량을 배분하고 / 업무를 적합한 직원에게 할당하는 것이 중요하다 / 사업을 효율적으로 하기 위하여

해설 문장이 완전하므로 빈칸은 동사를 수식해 주는 부사 자리이므로 'do business'와의 어울림을 봐야 한다. 문맥상 '효과적으로'라는 내용의 (B)가

정답이다.

표현 정리 workload 업무량 appropriate 적절한 do business 사업을 하다 incrementally 증대하게 spontaneously 자발적으로

2. 정답 (A)

해설 유명 회사인 Bell 사 CEO는 아낌없이 기부했다 / 그의 총 재산의 절반을 / Share Hopes Society에 / 지난 달

해설 주어와 동사 사이에서 동사를 수식해 주는 부사 자리이므로 donate와의 어울림을 봐야 한다. 문맥상 (A)가 가장 적절한 정답이다. (D)는 '지속적으로 기부했다'는 내용이 되어 '지난 달 총 재산의 절반을 기부했다'는 내용과 어울리지 않는다.

표현 정리 generously 아낌없이, 후하게 indecisively 우유부단하게 consistently 지속적으로

3. 정답 (A)

해설 주문 제작한 액세서리들은 / 보통 회사 웹사이트에서만 구매 가능하다 / 하지만 일시적으로 가능할 것이다 / 오프라인 매장에서 / 다음 주 동안

해설 빈칸은 be 동사와 형용사 사이에서 형용사를 수식해 주는 부사 어휘 문제이다. 빈칸 앞에 but이라는 역접의 연결어가 있으므로 상반되는 내용이 와야 하므로 (A)를 넣어 해석하면, '다음 주 동안에는 오프라인 매장에서 일시적으로 가능할 것이다'는 자연스런 내용이 되어 (A)가 정답이다. (B)는 형용사나 부사를 수식하는 정도 부사이며, (C)와 (D)는 뒤의 내용과 상충된다.

표현 정리 custom-made 주문 제작한 temporarily 일시적으로, 임시로 accordingly 따라서

4. 정답 (D)

해설 사적인 내부 보고서는 익명으로 제출되었다 / 그리고 주장했다 / GRT 사의 많은 직원들이 연루되었다고 / 위법 행위에

해설 문장은 완전하므로 빈칸은 동사를 수식해 주는 부사 자리이며, was submitted만으로는 답을 고를 수 없다. 사적인 내부 보고서는 말 그대로 익명성을 가지고 있다고 보는 것이 가장 적절하다. 따라서 (D)가 정답이다. (B)는 be 동사 뒤에 오며, 주로 현재시제와 어울린다.

표현 정리 internal 내부의 wrongdoing 위법 행위 respectfully 공손하게 anonymously 익명으로

5. 정답 (C)

해설 High-Tech Electronics의 생산 매니저는 계속 강조했다 / 신형 웨어러블 기기의 내구성의 중요성을 / 3겹의 티타늄으로 코팅된

해설 주어와 동사 사이에서 동사를 수식해 주는 부사 자리이므로 stress와의 어울림을 봐야 한다. 문장에서 부정어가 올 내용은 없는 상태이므로 (B)와 (D)는 제외하면, (C)가 문맥상 가장 잘 어울린다. (A)는 긴밀하게 일하거나 볼 때 사용하는 부사이다.

표현 정리 stress 강조하다 durability 내구성 wearable 착용이 적합한, 웨어러블 layer 레이어, 층 titanium 티타늄

6. 정답 (C)

해설 정책은 명확히 명시한다 / 반품이나 교환은 허용되지 않는다는 것을

/ 구입 30일 후에는

해설 주어와 동사 사이에서 동사를 수식해 주는 부사 자리이므로 states와의 어울림을 봐야 한다. state는 '명시하다, 서술하다, 적다'라는 의미의 동사인데, 이 동사를 앞에서 수식하기에 적합한 부사로는 (C)가 가장 적절하다.

표현 정리 ambiguously 애매모호하게 indefinitely 막연히, 애매하게 explicitly 분명하게 allegedly 주장한 바에 의하면

7. 정답 (B)

해설 Ms. Titus는 정확하게 알지 못했다 / 그녀의 매니저가 정확하게 무엇을 의미했는지 / 그가 미용 제품 매장들에 대해 대략적으로 언급했을 때

해설 refer to만으로는 문제를 풀 수가 없고, 문맥상으로 판단해 정답을 골라야 하는 문제이다. (B)를 제외한 보기의 부사들은 (A) 명확하게, (C) 분명하게, (D) 직접의 뜻으로 모두 의미가 확실하지만, (B) broadly는 '대략'이라는 뜻의 부사이므로 문맥과 가장 잘 어울린다.

표현 정리 broadly 대략 obviously 분명하게 directly 직접

8. 정답 (D)

해설 긴급 회의가 / 5시간 이상이 걸린 / 악영향을 끼쳐 / 그녀의 가족 여행에 / 취소해야 했다.

해설 주어와 동사 사이에서 동사를 수식해 주는 부사 자리이므로 affected와의 어울림을 봐야 한다. 문장 뒤의 내용에서 취소해야 했다고 했으므로 가족 여행에 부정적인 영향을 끼쳤다고 봐야 하므로 (D)가 정답이다.

표현 정리 urgent 긴급한 adversely affect 악영향을 미치다 precisely 정확하게

9. 정답 (D)

해설 웹사이트는 견딜 수 없어 / 평소와 달리 많은 수의 방문자들을 / 다운되었다

해설 빈칸은 형용사 앞에서 형용사를 수식해 주는 부사 자리이므로 large와의 어울림을 살펴야 하며, 내용상 평상시와 달리 너무 많은 사람들이 접속해 웹사이트가 다운되었다는 내용이므로 (D)가 정답이다.

표현 정리 sustain 지탱하다, 견디다 go down 쓰러지다, 넘어지다, 다운되다 obviously 분명히 sufficiently 충분히 unusually 평소와 달리

10. 정답 (A)

해설 당신은 임상실험의 결과를 믿어도 된다 / 이 화장품들에 관한 / 실험이 꼼꼼히 실시되었기 때문에 / 피부과 전문의에 의해

해설 빈칸은 동사를 수식해 주는 부사 자리이므로 conducted와의 어울림을 봐야 하지만 동사만으로는 정답을 고르기가 쉽지 않은 문제이다. 내용상 피부과 전문의에 의해 실험이 꼼꼼히 실시되었기 때문에 믿어도 된다는 내용으로 봐야 하므로 (A)가 정답이다. (C)는 숫자나 '말하다' 계열의 동사 또는 문장 전체를 수식하는 부사이다.

표현 정리 clinical trial 임상 실험 dermatologist 피부과 전문의 meticulously 꼼꼼하게

Chapter 13 빈칸 문장만으로는 풀 수 없는 파트 6 문제 (매월 9문제)

법칙 96 알맞은 문장 넣기 문제는 앞뒤 흐름을 파악

◎ 유형을 파악해 봐
131. (C) 132. (A) 133. (D) 134. (B)

문제 131-134는 다음 공지 사항을 참조하시오.

Wills Technology 프로젝트 리더들께

여러분께 알려드리고자 합니다 / 곧 있을 교육에 대한 예비 회의가 개최될 것임을 / 목요일에 / 모든 프로젝트 리더들은 참석해야 합니다 / 그 회의에 / 그 회의에서 / 각 강좌에 대한 구체적인 지침이 / 제공될 것입니다 / 그 교육을 담당하고 있는 모든 구성원들이 / 명확히 알 수 있도록 / 그 교육의 절차를 / 우리는 생각합니다 / 전체 절차에 대한 적절한 이해가 / 모든 구성원들 사이에 공유된 / 교육의 성공에 중요하다고 / 그러나 / 당신이 그 회의에 참석할 수 없다면 / 알려주십시오. ―134―.

여러분의 지원에 감사드립니다.

표현 정리 preliminary 예비의 training session 교육 강좌 specific 구체적인 in charge of ~를 담당하고 있는 procedure 절차 proper 적절한 critical 중요한 alternative 대안 precede ~에 앞서다, 선행하다

131. 정답 (C)

해설 be동사와 to부정사 사이에 들어갈 advise의 알맞은 형태를 고르면 된다. "be advised to부정사"의 형태로 "~하도록 충고 받다, 권고 받다" 의미를 가진 표현으로 쓰이므로 (C)가 정답이다.

132. 정답 (A)

해설 교육 절차에 대해 적절히 이해하는 것(proper understanding)이 중요하다는 빈칸 바로 다음 문장을 통해서도 빈칸에 적절한 단어는 문맥상 "know"가 되어야 함을 알 수 있다.

133. 정답 (D)

해설 교육을 위한 예비 회의의 취지에 관해 설명한 후에 참석고· 반대 경우인 참석 불가한 경우 알려 달라는 내용이 나오고, 빈칸 뒤가 "should"로 시작하는 조건절이므로 빈칸에는 접속 부사인 "however"가 적절하다. (C) since는 접속사이므로 접속 부사 자리에 올 수 없다.

134. 정답 (B)

해설 (A) 그렇게 하는 것은 도울 것입니다 / 우리가 더 나은 해결책을 찾는 것을 / 다음의 이유로 (B) 우리는 당신에게 연락할 것입니다 / 개별적으로 / 대안을 논의하기 위해서 (C) 교육 훈련이 선행될 것입니다 / 미팅보다 (D) 우리의 고객들은 도착할 것입니다 / 그 회의 시간에 맞춰 * 밑줄 앞은 '예비미팅에 참석해야 하며, 참석하지 못하는 경우엔 알려달라'는 내용이므로 이어질 흐름은 그에 대한 해결방책이 필요하다. 따라서 (B)가 정답이다. (A)는 다음의 이유가 무엇인지 열거가 되어야 하며, (C)는 미팅이 교육훈련

보다 먼저이므로 앞의 내용과 모순된다. (D)는 meeting과 client를 연상시켜 오답으로 유도하는 전체 내용과 아무런 관련 없는 내용이다.

법칙 97 시제 문제는 나중에 푼다

◎ 유형을 파악해 봐
131. (A)   132. (B)   133. (C)   134. (B)

131-134번은 다음 공지 사항을 참조하시오.

> 우리는 알리게 되어 기쁩니다 / Dr. Dawson이 합류했음을 / Dr. Norris의 연구 팀에 / 이번 주 화요일에
>
> Dr. Dawson은 전에 National Institute of Biotech Research에서 일했습니다 / 그렇지만 Dr. Norris의 연구를 돕기로 했습니다 / 그녀의 요청에 따라
>
> —133—. 그의 전문지식과 경력을 고려하여 / Dr. Dawson은 연구 팀과 팀의 프로젝트를 공동으로 이끌 것입니다 / Dr. Norris와 함께 / 내년까지
>
> Dr. Dawson의 감독 하에 / 팀은 이미 뚜렷한 진척을 보이고 있습니다 왜냐하면 팀이 최근에 가능성을 발견했기 때문에 / 손상된 인간의 혈관을 건강한 돼지의 혈관으로 대체할

표현 정리 be pleased to +동사원형 ~하게 되어 기쁘다, 참가하다 join 가입하다 previously 이전에 upon request 요청에 따라 in light of ~에 비추어, ~을 고려하여 expertise 전문지식, 기술 co-lead 공동으로 이끌다 supervision 감독 make a progress 진전을 보이다 possibility 가능성 replace 대체하다 damage 손상시키다, 손해를 입히다 blood vessel 혈관 biotechnology 생명공학 contribution 공헌 asset 자산

131. 정답 (A)
해설 시제 문제이다. 134번에서 Dr. Dawson의 감독 하에 팀이 이미 진척을 보이고 있다고 했으므로 Dr. Dawson은 이미 연구팀에 합류했다고 볼 수 있다. 따라서 과거시제인 (A)가 정답이다. 빈칸 뒤에 목적어가 있으므로 수동태 (C)는 탈락.

132. 정답 (B)
해설 134번의 마지막 문장에서 손상된 혈관을 돼지의 혈관으로 대체할 수 있는 가능성을 발견했는데, 그것이 Dr. Dawson의 감독 하에 이루어진 것이므로 연구를 도와주겠다는 말이 적합하므로 (B)가 정답이다. 목적어로 'Dr. Norris의 연구'라는 말이 왔으므로 사람을 목적어로 갖는 (A)는 탈락.

133. 정답 (C)
해설 (A) 불행하게도 / Dr. Dawson은 우리를 떠날 것입니다 / 다른 프로젝트를 수행하기 위하여 (B) Dr. Dawson의 도움으로 / 연구팀은 이미 완료하였습니다 / 프로젝트를   (C) Dr. Dawson은 / 거의 15년의 경험을 가지고 있습니다 / 생명 공학 분야에서 (D) 연구팀에 대한 그의 기여를 고려하면 / Dr. Dawso은 우리에게 중요한 자산입니다. * 빈칸 뒤의 내용에서 Dr. Dawson이 전문성과 경력을 가지고 있어서 연구팀과 프로젝트를 이끌 것이라고 하므로, 빈칸 내용은 Dr. Dawson의 경험에 대해 언급하고 있는

(C)가 적합하다. (A), (B)는 빈칸 앞 뒤의 내용과 연결성이 없고, (D)는 공지의 마지막 부분과 관련이 있다.

134. 정답 (B)
해설 연구 결과가 놀라운 만한 내용이므로 (B)가 자연스럽다. (D)는 항상 the same의 형태로 사용한다

◎ 실전에 적용해 봐
131. (B)   132. (D)   133. (A)   134. (C)   135. (A)   136. (C)
137. (B)   138. (B)   139. (C)   140. (D)   141. (D)   142. (A)
143. (D)   144. (D)   145. (C)   146. (A)

문제 131-134번은 다음 광고를 참조하시오.

> 신생 기업을 위한 새로운 보험
>
> 우리는 알고 있습니다 / 신생 기업은 차별적인 보장을 필요로 함을 / 특별한 위험에 대처할 / 그 기업이 직면하는 / 따라서, Schmann Insurance에 새로운 보험 상품이 마련되어 있습니다 / 고객들이 가입할 수 있도록
>
> 이 보험 상품은 다양한 혜택들을 포함합니다 / 초기 창업 비용의 보장을 포함해서 / 따라서 고객은 폭넓은 보장을 받게 됩니다 / 선택하고 추가할 수 있는 / —133—. 직원 건강 보험료의 할인과 같은 혜택들은 없습니다 / 다른 보험 상품에서는
>
> 다른 특별한 혜택들 또한 있습니다 / 상품들에 있어서 / 다른 규모와 목적을 가진 사업체들을 위한 / 따라서 고객이 운영하는 사업의 종류와 상관없이 / 우리는 추천할 수 있습니다 / 적합한 보험 상품을
>
> 만약 당신이 관심이 있다면 / 3,000명의 고객들 중 한 명이 되는데 / 이미 이 보험에 의해 보장을 받고 있는 / 오늘 전화주세요 / 0888-330-3399로

표현 정리 insurance 보험 startup 시작하는, 신생의 coverage 보장 client 고객 apply for ~에 신청하다 benefit 혜택, 이익 initial 초기의 efficient 효율적인 a wide range of 폭넓은, 다양한 cover 보장하다 enhanced 강화된 exclusive 전용의, 독점적인 specialize in ~을 전문으로 하다 set apart from ~에서 구별하다 regardless of ~와 상관없이 on top of 는 ~이외에도, 게다가

131. 정답 (B)
해설 빈칸이 포함된 문장만 봐서는 정답을 고르기 어려운 고난이도 시제 문제이다. 지문 마지막 문장에서 3,000명이 이미 가입했고, 보험에 가입하는 것에 관심이 있다면'이라는 말을 통해 보험은 현재 가입 가능한 상태라고 봐야 한다. 따라서 현재완료시제인 (B)가 답이다.

132. 정답 (D)
해설 다음 문장에서 '고객은 선택하고 추가할 수 있는 폭넓은 보장을 받게 됩니다.'라는 말이 나오므로 '다양한, 폭넓은'이란 뜻의 (D)가 가장 자연스럽다.

133. 정답 (A)
해설 (A) 그런 혜택들 중 몇몇은 / 또한 해당됩니다 / 이 특별한 보험 상품에만 (B) 우리는 전문으로 합니다 / 적합한 보험 상품을 제안하는 것을 / 어떤 사업체를 대상으로 (C) 그 혜택들이 아닙니다 / 이 보험을 다른 보험

과 구별하는 것은 (D) 그 고객은 고려하고 있습니다 / 더 특별한 혜택들을 추가할지를 * 빈칸 뒤의 내용에서 직원 의료 보험료 할인과 같은 혜택들은 다른 보험 상품에는 없다고 하는 것으로 보아, 이 보험 전용의 혜택이 있음을 말하고 있는 (A)가 적합하다.

134. 정답 (C)

해설 명사 앞에 빈칸이 있고, 콤마 다음에 문장이 이어지므로 빈칸은 전치사 자리이다. 전치사 (C)와 (D) 중, 사업의 종류와는 상관없이 적합한 보험 상품을 추천할 수 있다가 자연스럽다. On top of는 '~이외에도, 게다가'라는 뜻인데, 추가 되기 전과 추가되는 것이 서로 같은 성격이 와야 한다.

문제 135-138번은 다음 이메일을 참조하시오.

> Mr. Devon 씨께,
>
> 우리의 기쁨입니다 / 당신을 단골 고객으로 모시고 있는 것은 / 그리고 우리는 항상 헌신적입니다 / 당신에게 최고의 서비스를 제공하는 것에 대해 / 우리가 제공할 수 있는
>
> 유감스럽게도 / 당신의 연간 회원권은 이번 금요일에 만료됩니다 / 그래서 우리는 유감입니다 / 우리가 당신을 더 이상 도와줄 수 없어 / 유효한 회원이 아니면
>
> 만약 당신이 우리의 서비스를 계속 받기를 원하신다면 / 간단한 신청서를 작성해 주십시오 / 이 메일에 첨부된 —137—. 당신의 신청서를 보낼 주소는 / 회원권 갱신 요금과 함께 / 고객 서비스팀, Rendleman Bldg., 309호, 우편함 776.
>
> 우리는 진심으로 당신에게 서비스를 제공하기를 희망합니다 / 한 해 더

표현 정리 loyal customer 단골 고객 be dedicated to -ing ~하는데 전념하다 tempt 유혹하다 opt 택하다, 고르다 unfortunately 유감스럽게도, 불행하게도 assist 도와주다 active 유효한 expire 만료되다 fill out 작성하다 brief 간단한 attach 첨부하다 exempt 면제하다 permanent 영구적인 enclose 동봉하다 promptly 지체없이 otherwise 그렇지 않으면 in person 직접 renewal 갱신 sincerely 진심으로

135. 정답 (A)

해설 동사 어휘 문제지만, 문법으로도 풀 수 있는 문제이다. 보기 중 'to -ing' 형태로 쓸 수 있는 동사는 (A)뿐이다. (B)는 'in -ing' 형태를, (C)와 (D)는 'to 동사원형'의 형태를 취한다.

136. 정답 (C)

해설 이미 만기가 되었다면 (A)를, 만기가 될 예정이라면 (C)를 써야 하는데, 다음 문장에서 계속 서비스를 받기를 원하면, 갱신을 요청하라는 내용이 있으므로 아직 만기가 되지 않았음을 알 수 있어 (C)가 답이다.

137. 정답 (B)

해설 (A) 당신은 면제받을 것입니다 / 갱신 요금을 / 갱신의 영구 회원권 때문에 (B) 그리고 나서 동봉하세요 / 20달러의 갱신 요금을 / 그리고 보내주세요 / 완성된 양식을 (C) 우리는 매우 기쁩니다 / 당신이 지체없이 지불해서 (D) 그렇지 않으면, 당신은 방문해야 할 것입니다 / 우리를 직접 / 그리고 지불해야 할 것입니다 / 당신의 벌금을 * 빈칸 앞에서 첨부된 신청서를 작성하라고 하는 것과 빈칸 뒤에서 갱신 요금과 함께 신청서를 보낼 주소를 언급하고 있는 것으로 보아 갱신 요금을 동봉하여 완성된 신청서를 보내라고 하는 (B)가 적합하다.

138. 정답 (B)

해설 앞 단락에서 연간 멤버십이라고 했고, 이메일 전체 내용 또한 멤버십 갱신을 권하는 내용이므로 뒤의 year를 수식해 미래의 의미를 갖는 (B)가 답이 된다.

문제 139-142번은 다음 이메일을 참조하시오.

> 직원들에게,
>
> 여러분 모두에게 감사 드립니다 / 훌륭한 준비를 해 준 것을 / 은퇴식을 위한 / Mr. Everett의 / 그의 마지막 날에 / Cenmora 사에서의 / Mr. Everett는 진정으로 은퇴를 즐겼으며 / 여러분 개개인에게 그마워했습니다 / 그의 마지막 날을 채워준 것에 대해 / 잊지못할 순간들로
>
> Mr. Everett는 매우 열정적이고 부지런한 사람이었습니다 / 그의 헌신 없이 / 회사는 도달하지 못했을 것입니다 / 회사의 지금 위치에 / —141—. Cenmora, Inc.는 항상 기억할 것입니다 / 그의 서비스와 기여를
>
> 비록 Mr. Everett가 회사를 떠났지만 / 그의 정신은 Cenmora 사에 남아 있을 것입니다 / 성원합시다 / 그의 계속 진행중인 지원을 / Cenmora, Inc.에 대한 / 우리는 탁월함을 위해서 애쓰고 있으니까요.

표현 정리 retirement party 은퇴식 upcoming 다가오는 ultimate 궁극적인, 최후의 unforgettable 잊을 수 없는 preferably 오히려 가급적 gradually 서서히 truly 정말로, 진심으로 passionate 열정적인 farewell 작별 resume 다시 시작하다 dedication 헌신 contribution 기여 remain 남다 strive for ~을 얻으려고 노력하다

139. 정답 (C)

해설 다음 문장에서 '은퇴 파티를 즐겼고, 고마움을 전하고 싶어 했다'는 말이 나오므로 이미 은퇴 파티가 열렸음을 알 수 있으며, 따라서 (C)가 정답이다.

140. 정답 (D)

해설 Mr. Everett가 그의 인생에서 잊을 수 없을 시간이었다고 말한 것으로 보아 그는 '진심으로 파티를 즐겼'음을 알 수 있어, 정답은 (D)가 된다.

141. 정답 (D)

해설 (A) 그의 협조 덕분에 / 우리는 연장할 수 있을 것이다 / 우리의 협력 관계를 (B) 그러므로 / 우리는 모두가 참석하기를 원한다 / 은퇴식에 / 작별인사를 하도록 (C) 그는 떠나 있을 것이다 / 오래 동안 / 그가 다시 시작할 때까지 / 그의 일을 / 여기서 (D) 그는 성실히 봉사하였다 / 회사에 / 영업 담당 고위 관리자로서 / 30년 동안 * Mr. Everett의 헌신 없이 회사가 지금의 위치에 있지 못했을 것이라는 빈칸 앞의 내용으로 보아, 그가 오랜 기간 회사를 위해서 성실히 일했다는 (D)가 적합하다. (B)는 은퇴식과 관련이 있기는 하지만 은퇴식은 이미 과거에 진행되었으므로 맞지 않는 내용이다.

142. 정답 (A)

해설 은퇴 파티가 열린 것은 과거의 일이므로 회사를 떠났다고 봐야 한다. (A)와 (D) 중에서 '떠나고 지금 없다'는 느낌을 주어 현재와의 연결고리를 갖는 시제는 (A) 현재완료이다.

문제 143-146번은 다음 기사를 참조하시오.

Cherryville 시는 알립니다 / Supreme Techno Plaza의 개장을 3월 15일은 새로운 문화 공간의 개장을 기념했습니다 / Cherville에서 / 특별 기념식이 개최되었습니다 / 오전 10시에 / 그리고 이어졌습니다 / plaza의 공식적인 개장이 / 오전 11시에 / 1,000명 이상의 내빈이, 주로 지역 주민들이 참석했습니다 / 그 기념식에 ―144―.
Supreme Techno Plaza의 설립은 첫 번째 단계입니다 / 지역을 개발하기 위한 계획의 / 복합 문화 중심지로 / 그리고 운영됩니다 / 문화부에 의해서
"Cherryville시는 들떠 있습니다 / 자체 문화 공간을 소개하게 되어서 / 시민들에게 / 마침내" / 문화부의 책임자가 말했습니다 / 개장식에서 / "Supreme Techno Plaza는 지역 주민들에게 제공할 것입니다 / 많은 기회를 / 풍성하고 다양한 문화 생활을 즐길"

표현 정리 mark 기념하다 cultural space 문화 공간 official 공식적인 resident 주민 acknowledged 인정받는 official 관료 remark 말, 논평, 언급 establishing 설립하다 region 지역 multicultural 다문화의 hub 중심지 thrilled 신이 난 varied 다양한

143. 정답 (D)

해설 이어서 나오는 문장에서 특별 기념식이 개최 되었고 개장식이 열렸음을 알 수 있으므로 과거시제가 와야 한다. 따라서 (D) 가 정답이다.

144. 정답 (D)

해설 (A) 다시 말하면, 손님의 숫자는 10명 입니다 / 평균적으로 / 하루에 (B) 손님들은 자랑스러워 합니다 / 이 공간이 세계적으로 인정받는 것을 (C) 이 손님들 중 다수가 계획하고 있습니다 / 플라자에 입장하기를 / 기념식 직후에 (D) 지역사회 지도자들과 관리들 / 또한 방문해서 / 한마디씩 남겼습니다. * 빈칸 앞의 기념식과 개장식에 1000명 이상의 손님들이 참석했고 대부분이 지역 주민들이었다고 하는 내용에 자연스럽게 이어지며, 기사의 후반부에 개장식에서 문화부 책임자의 발언 내용이 나오는 것으로 보아 지역사회 지도자들과 관리들도 참석해서 한마디씩 남겼다는 (D)가 적합하다.

145. 정답 (C)

해설 파트 6에서도 문법 문제는 여전히 절반 가량 출제된다. 빈칸은 주어 자리이므로 명사가 필요한데, 첫 번째 단계 = 설립' 관계이므로 (C)와 (D) 중에서 (C)가 와야 한다. establishing은 동명사도 되고, 명사도 되는 단어이다. (D)는 사람을 가리키는 말이다

146. 정답 (A)

해설 빈칸은 문미에 오는 부사 자리이다. yet는 부정문이나 의문과 사용하며, though는 접속사이며, 때로는 구어체에서 '그래도, 그렇지만'이라는 의미의 부사로 사용되기도 한다. however는 문두에 사용하는 부사이다. (A)는 문미에 올 수 있으며, '마침내 문화 공간을 갖게 되어 기쁘다'는 말로서 자연스럽다.

법칙 98 연결어 문제는 밑줄 앞뒤를 요약하라

◎ 유형을 파악해 봐
135. (D) 136. (B) 137. (C) 138. (A)

문제 135-138번은 다음 편지를 참조하시오.

독자 여러분께
'Trends Magazine'은 노력해 왔습니다 / 우리 독자들에게 제공하기 위하여 / 읽을 가치가 있는 기사들을 / 적당한 가격으로 / 지난 20년 동안
유감스럽게도 / 최근에 대부분의 택배 회사들이 / 그들의 배송비를 인상해서 / 우리는 여러분에게 잡지를 배달하는 것이 어렵게 되었음을 알았습니다 / 지금과 같이 / 따라서 / 우리는 인상할 수 밖에 없었습니다 / 연간 구독료를 / 다음달부터 적용되도록
인상된 구독료에 대한 자세한 사항은 / 이 편지와 함께 동봉된 서류에 있습니다 ―138―.
당신의 지원에 감사드립니다 / 수년 동안의 / 그리고 우리는 보답하기를 희망합니다 / 그 충실성에 / 앞으로의 많은 시간동안

표현 정리 strive to +동사원형 ~을 위해 노력하다, 애쓰다 provide A with B A에게 B를 제공하다 worthy ~을 받을 만한 reasonable 적당한 in addition 게다가 therefore 그러므로 on the contrary 그와는 반대로 have no choice but to + 동사원형 ~할 수 밖에 없다 subscription 구독, 구독료 enclose 동봉하다 appreciate 고마워하다 affordable (가격이) 알맞은 loyalty 충성, 충실

135. 정답 (D)

해설 빈칸이 포함된 문장만으로 정답을 고를 수 있는 문제이다. 문미에 for the last 20 years라는 말이 온 것으로 보아 지난 20년 동안 계속 일을 해오고 있음을 알 수 있으므로 현재완료진행시제 (D)가 정답이다.

136. 정답 (B)

해설 빈칸 앞에는 운송회사가 요금을 인상했다는 내용. 뒤에는 연간 구독료를 인상하기로 했다는 내용이 나오므로 원인과 결과의 관계를 나타내는 (B)가 정답이다.

137. 정답 (C)

해설 인상된 구독료에 관련된 상세한 내용이 동봉되어 있다고 해야 문맥이 일치하므로 (C)가 정답이다.

138. 정답 (A)

해설 (A) 저희는 매우 죄송합니다 / 그리고 희망합니다 / 이것이 귀하의 지속적인 구독에 영향을 주지 않기를 (B) 저희는 감사히 여깁니다 / 귀하의 지적을 / 우리의 현재 구독료에 대한 (C) 그 편지는 이유를 설명해야만 합니다 / 왜 귀하가 취소하기 원하는지 / 귀하의 구독을 (D) 저희는 기쁩니다 / 저희가 이제 저희 잡지를 제공할 수 있어서 / 더욱 알맞은 가격에 * 빈칸 앞의 내용에서 인상된 구독료에 대해 언급하고 있으므로, 인상된 구독료가 독자의 지속적인 구독에 영향을 주기 않기 바란다는 (A)가 적절하다. 구독료 인상을 독자들에게 알리고, 그에 대해 양해를 구하고 있는 것이 이 편지의 전체 내용으로 (B)의 독자의 구독료에 대한 지적, (C)의 독자가 구독을

취소하기 원하는 것은 내용과 관련이 없다.

◎ 실전에 적용해 봐
131. (D) 132. (A) 133. (C) 134. (C) 135. (C) 136. (B)
137. (A) 138. (D) 139. (C) 140. (C) 141. (D) 142. (B)
143. (C) 144. (C) 145. (B) 146. (A)

문제 131-134번은 다음 공지 사항을 참조하시오.

> 전 직원들은 주목해 주세요.
>
> 우리는 알게 되었습니다 / 일부 직원들이 / 다시 발급된 직원ID 카드를 아직 수령하지 않았다는 것을
>
> 만약 여러분이 아직 ID 카드를 찾아가지 않았고 / 다음 주 전에 필요하다면 / 인사부를 방문해 주십시오 / 업무 시간 동안 / ID카드를 수령하러 / 그렇지 않으면 / 모든 남은 카드들은 각 부서로 보내질 것입니다 / 다음 주 수요일에 / 그때 여러분은 ID 카드를 받으실 수 있습니다
>
> 또한 유념하세요 / ID카드 재발급이 무료로 제공된다는 것을 / 처음 발급 요청해 대해서만 / 그리고 10달러의 발급 비용이 든다는 것을 / 다음에 발급을 요청할 경우에 / 여러분은 간단한 발급 요청서도 작성해야 합니다 / ID 카드를 재발행 받기 전에 ―134―

표현 정리 attention 주목, 주의 extra 여분의 reissue 재발급 하다 Human Resources 인사부 remaining 남아있는 consequently 결과적으로 otherwise 그렇지 않으면 in addition 게다가 note that S + V that 이하를 알아 두다 latest 최근의, 최신의 missing 없어진 advisable 권할 만한, 바람직한 respective 각각의

131. 정답 (D)

해설 공지문의 끝부분에서 ID 카드의 재발급이 이번에만 무료라고 한 것으로 보아, ID 카드가 재발급 된 것을 알 수 있으므로 (D)가 정답이다.

132. 정답 (A)

해설 찾아 가지 않은 ID 카드는 다음 주 수요일에 한꺼번에 각 부서로 보낸다고 했으므로 다음 주 전, 즉 정확히 말하면 다음 주 수요일 전에 인사팀을 방문해 찾아가면 되므로 (A)가 정답이다

133. 정답 (C)

해설 ID 카드가 필요한 사람들은 인사부를 방문해 찾아가라고 했고, 빈칸 다음 문장에서는 다음 주 수요일에 한꺼번에 각 부서로 보낸다고 했으므로 빈칸에는 '그렇지 않으면'의 뜻을 갖는 (C)가 정답이다.

134. 정답 (C)

해설 (A) 다시 한번 / 이번주 말은 최근의 가능한 때입니다 (B) 우리는 희망합니다 / 이것이 당신이 찾는 것을 도울 수 있기를 / 당신의 잃어버린 ID 카드를 (C) 그러므로 / 항상 권할 만합니다 / 당신이 주의하기를 / 당신의 ID카드를 잃어버리지 않도록 (D) 당신의 협조에 감사드립니다 / ID카드들을 돌려주는데 있어서 / 각각의 주인에게 * 빈칸 앞의 내용이 ID카드의 재발급은 처음만 무료이고 그 다음부터는 10달러의 비용이 들며, 발급 요청서도 작성해야 한다는 카드 발급 관련 주의 사항에 대한 것이므로 카드를 분실하지 말라고 권하고 있는 (C)가 적합하다. (A)는 이

공지에서 카드 수령 기간에 대해 언급하고 부분의 내용과 맞지 않으며, (B)와 (D)는 카드 분실과 관련된 것으로 카드 재발급과는 관련이 없다.

문제 135-138번은 다음 이메일을 참조하시오.

> To: 모든 의회 구성원
> From: 조지 맥퀸, 부장
> Date: 5월 14일
> Subject: 연례 지역 경제 포럼
>
> 연례 지역 경제 포럼이 / 열릴 예정입니다 / 이번 주 토요일에 / 지난번 포럼이 개최되었던 곳과 같은 장소인 / Millsworth Town의 Huntington Hall, 2층에서 / 그러나 올해는 / 포럼이 3시간 동안 진행될 것이기 때문에 / 정오부터 오후 3시까지 / 무료 점심 제공될 것입니다 / 모든 참석자들에게 / 짧은 휴식시간 동안에 /
>
> 따라서 / 모든 의원들은 이메일에 답장해 주십시오 / 포럼에 참여할 것인지를 통보하는 / 늦어도 이번 주 목요일까지 / 그래야 식사가 참석자 수에 맞게 사전에 준비될 수 있기 때문입니다. ―138―.
>
> 미리 감사드립니다 / 귀하의 신속한 회신에 / 우리는 귀하를 뵙기를 고대하고 있습니다 / 토요일에

표현 정리 annual 매년의, 연례의 economic forum 경제 포럼 hold 개최하다 attendee 참석자 council 의회 indicate 나타내다, 암시하다 accordingly 따라서 otherwise 달리, 그렇지 않으면 ultimately 궁극적으로 nonetheless 그럼에도 불구하고 no later than 늦어도 ~까지 beforehand 사전에, 미리 prompt 신속한

135. 정답 (C)

해설 문장에 동사 하나는 꼭 있어야 하므로 준동사인 (D)는 탈락한다. This Saturday는 부사이므로 목적어가 될 수 없으므로 수동태가 아닌 (B) 역시 탈락이다. 그런데 바로 다음 문장에서 포럼이 3시간 동안 계속될 것이라고 했으므로 미래시제인 (C)가 정답이다.

136. 정답 (B)

해설 빈칸 뒤에 however가 온 것으로 보아 매번 반복되는 내용이 다닌 올해에만 해당되므로 (B) This가 어울린다. (C)의 First는 항상 앞에 the를 써야 하며, (D)는 반복습관적인 사실을 나타내어 현재시제와 어울린다.

137. 정답 (A)

해설 무료 점심 식사가 제공된다는 것이 원인이고, 참석 여부를 알려야 한다는 것이 결과라고 볼 수 있다. 원인과 결과를 연결하는 (A)가 정답이다. (C)는 '궁극적으로, 마침내'라는 뜻으로 앞에 일련의 일들이 일어났음을 전제하여 최종적인 결과를 나타낼 때 사용한다.

138. 정답 (D)

해설 (A) 우리는 또한 추천합니다 / 모든 회원들이 그 새 요리를 맛보시기를 / 우리의 식당에서 (B) 그러므로, 우리는 여분의 식사를 준비할 것입니다 / 당신이 회신을 주지 않을 경우에 대비해서 (C) 지난해의 포럼은 두 시간 동안 진행되었고 / 점심 시간이 없었습니다. (D) 또한 회신에서 말씀해 주십시오 / 채식 식사가 필요한 경우라면 * 식사 사전 준비 관계로 포럼 참석 여부를 이메일 회신으로 알려 달라는 빈칸 앞의 내용에 이어서 채식 식사가 필요한 경우에도 회신에서 알려 달라고 하는 (D)가 적절하다. (B)는 빈칸 앞

의 내용과 상반되며, (C)는 내용의 흐름상 적합하지 않다.

문제 139-142는 다음 안내 사항을 참조하시오.

> 회사 오버헤드 프로젝트의 사용
>
> 회사 소유의 오버헤드 프로젝트는 사용이 가능합니다 / 신청에 의해 / 하지만 오직 사무실내의 미팅을 위한 목적으로만 / 게다가 / 동호회 미팅 또는 3명 이하 직원들의 소그룹 미팅에 대한 사용은 / 허용이 안 될 수 있습니다 / 다른 요청이 있다면 / 더 큰 공식적 미팅을 위해 사용하겠다는
>
> 이것은 관리하기 위함 입니다 / 우리가 가지고 있는 한정된 수의 프로젝터들이 / 그것들이 긴급한 필요를 충족시키기 위해 주로 사용될 수 있도록 하기 위해서 입니다 / 그러나 당신이 프로젝터를 필요로 하고 / 빌려야 하는 타당한 이유를 가지고 있다면 / 당신은 프로젝터를 사용할 수 있습니다 / 위에 언급된 요건에 상관없이 / 당신이 당신의 부서장으로부터 승인을 받은 한에서는 / 프로젝터를 빌리기 위해서는 / 신청 양식을 작성해서 제출해 주세요 / 총무부의 Mr. Callaway에게 ─142─.

표현 정리 issuance 배포, 발행 consequently 따라서 likewise 똑같이, 비슷하게 in addition 게다가 given that ~을 고려하면 disapprove 승인을 거절하다 manageable 관리할 수 있는, 처리할 수 있는 limited 한정된 primarily 주로 satisfy 충족시키다 urgent 긴급한 valid 타당한 requirement 요건, 필요 조건 approval 승인 fill out 작성하다 submit 제출하다 General Affairs Department 총무부

139. 정답 (C)

해설 upon과 잘 어울리는 명사 (C)와 (D) 중에서 요청하면 회사가 보유하고 있는 프로젝터를 사용할 수 있다는 내용이므로 (C)가 정답이다.

140. 정답 (C)

해설 빈칸 앞은 사무실 미팅 용도로만 사용해야 한다는 것, 빈칸 뒤는 동호회 미팅 또는 3명 이하의 미팅에는 사용 허락이 안 된다는 내용이므로 앞의 내용에 이은 추가적인 내용 이라고 볼 수 있어서 (C)가 정답이다. (D)는 접속사이다.

141. 정답 (D)

해설 we have는 '우리가 가지고 있는'이란 뜻의 형용사 절이므로 수식어로 빼내면, 빈칸은 정동사 자리이다. this는 앞의 문장 내용을 가리키므로 뒤에는 그에 대한 이유를 나타내는 말이 이어지는 것이 자연스러워 (D)가 정답이다.

142. 정답 (B)

해설 (A) 그러나 당신의 요구는 거절될 수 있습니다 / 다음의 이유로 (B) 게다가 적어도 이틀은 잡으십시오 / 당신의 요청이 승인되는 데는 (C) 그러므로, 당신이 그에게 말할 수 있습니다 / 더 많은 프로젝터들을 구입하는 것에 관하여 (D) 또한 승인을 받으십시오 / 그로부터 / 프로젝터를 빌리기 위해서는 / 사적인 미팅을 위해 * 프로젝터를 빌리려면 신청서를 작성해서 총무부에 제출하라는 내용 다음에는 요청에 대한 승인이 날때까지 이틀은 잡으라는 (B)가 오는 것이 문맥상 자연스럽다. (C)는 프로젝터 추가 구입에 대한 요청으로 프로젝트 사용 신청을 안내하고 있는 전체 내용과는 관련이 없고, (D)는 이 안내의 도입부에서 사적 미팅을 위한 프로젝트 사용은 허용이

안될 수 있다고 언급되어 있으므로 적절하지 않다.

문제 143-146은 다음 공지 사항을 참조하시오.

> Abby Road 건설 공사에 대한 소식
>
> Abby Road의 공사는 11월 30일에 완료되기로 일정이 잡혀 있었습니다. 하지만, 연례 추수감사절 축제가 / 지난 수요일부터 일요일까지 개최된 / 불가피하게 5일간의 지체를 초래하였습니다 / 공사 일정에 있어서 ─145─. 상가나 주거지로의 진입은 허가될 것입니다 / 공사기간 동안 / 한편, 북쪽 방향 Meiland Avenue는 계속 연결될 것입니다 / Olympic Boulevard로 / 반면에 동쪽방향 도로들이 / Southern Bay Avenue에 있는 / 영구적으로 폐쇄될 것입니다 / 7th Street와 8th Stress 사이의 모든 차량들에 대해 / 프로젝트 일정에 대한 다른 소식들은 확인 가능하고 최신으로 게재되고 있습니다 / 마을 웹사이트 www.cityofrey.org에서
>
> 감사 드립니다 / 여러분의 인내와 이해에 / 공사기간 동안의

표현 정리 construction 공사 annual 매년의, 연례의 inevitably 불가피하게, 피치 못하게 cause 야기하다, 원인이 되다 revision 개정, 수정 advance 전진, 진보 access to ~로의 진입 residence 주거지 permit 허가하다 meanwhile 한편으로는 regrettably 유감스럽게도 alternatively 그 대신에 northbound 북쪽 방향 permanently 영구적으로 patience 인내

143. 정답 (C)

해설 주어가 단수이므로 복수 동사인 (D)는 탈락. schedule은 to 부정사를 목적어로 쓰는 동사가 아니고, be scheduled to와 같이 수동태일 때 to 부정사를 동반하는 동사이다. 따라서 (A)와 (C)가 가능하다. 그런데 다음 문장에서 기존의 일정에 변경이 생겼음을 알 수 있으므로 과거시제인 (C)가 와야 한다.

144. 정답 (C)

해설 11월 30일에서 12월 5일로 지연된 것이므로 (C)가 정답이다

145. 정답 (B)

해설 (A) 따라서, Abby Road는 영구적으로 폐쇄될 것입니다 / 이 지점부터 (B) 결과적으로, Abby Road는 개통될 것입니다 / 12월 5일에 / 공사가 끝나는 (C) 지역 주민들은 참석할 수 없습니다 / 그 축제에 / 추가 공지가 있을 때까지 (D) 천천히 운전하십시오 / 공사 구간을 지나는 동안 * 빈칸 앞의 내용에서, 11월 30일에 예정되었던 도로 공사 완료가 추수감사절 축제 때문에 5일 지연되었다고 하므로, 예정된 일정보다 5일 후인 12월 5일에 공사가 끝난다고 하는 (B)가 적절하다.

146. 정답 (A)

해설 공사 연장기간 동안 지역 상가나 주거지로의 진입은 가능하다는 내용 다음에 도로 이용 상황에 대한 내용이 이어지고 있으므로 화제를 전환하는 의미를 가지고 있는 접속 부사 (A)가 정답이다.

법칙 99 대명사 문제는 문법적 소거 후 가리키는 말을 확인

◎ 유형을 파악해 봐

139. (D) 140. (C) 141. (D) 142. (C)

문제 139-142번은 다음 편지을 참조하시오.

> 12월 21일
> Shelby Sheraton
> 52 Street, Central Valley
> Newtown Land, CA
> Ms. McCarthy 씨에게,
> 우리의 대여 서비스에 대해 문의해 주셔서 감사합니다 / 최근에 출시된
> 당신은 우리에게 문의하셨습니다 / 모델 GX-780의 월 대여료를 / 매월 100달러에서 130달러로 제공되는 / 풀 옵션과 함께 / 올해 —141—.
> 만약에 당신이 아직 GX-780의 대여에 관심이 있다면 / 우리에게 회신해 주세요 / 추가적인 도움을 위해 / 또한 / 알아 두세요 / 대여료가 달라질 수 있다는 것을 / 내년에는 / 위에 언급된 요금대는 올해에만 제공 되고 있는 것으므로 / 판촉 행사로

표현 정리 inquiry 문의 launch 출시하다 installation 설치 guarantee 보장하다 reply 회신 assistance 도움, 지원 in addition 게다가 note that ~를 알아 두세요 fee 요금 vary 달라지다 range 범위

139. 정답 (D)
해설 소유격 다음은 명사 자리이다. (B)와 (D) 중에서 우리의 서비스에 대한 당신의 문의에 감사한다고 했으므로 (D)가 정답이다.

140. 정답 (C)
해설 빈칸과 year가 함께 부사의 기능을 해야 하는데, 지문 마지막 문장에서 '위에 언급된 가격은 올해에 한정된 것이고, 내년에는 달라질 수 있다'는 내용이 언급되었으므로 140번 문제에서 제시되는 가격은 올해의 가격이라고 볼 수 있다. 따라서 (C)가 답이 된다.

141. 정답 (D)
해설 (A) 당신은 가지게 될 것입니다 / 편안한 시간을 / 곧 (B) 우리의 대여 서비스는 이용 가능할 것입니다 / 다음주에 (C) 설명 드리겠습니다 / 왜 우리가 제공할 수 있는지 / 무료 설치 서비스를 (D) 우리는 보장합니다 / 이 대여료는 가장 저렴합니다 / 지역에서 * 빈칸 앞에서 GX-780의 월 대여료에 대해 언급하고 있으므로 대여료에 대해서 추가적으로 언급하고 있는 (D)가 적당하다. (A)는 전혀 관련성이 없는 내용이며, (B)과 (C)는 대여료에 대해서만 언급하고 있는 편지의 전체 내용과 관련이 없다.

142. 정답 (C)
해설 GX-780을 대여하는 것에 관심이 있다면 회신을 달라고 하는 문장과 그 다음에 오는 이미 언급된 대여료는 올해만 유효하고 내년에 바뀔 수 있음을 알고 있으라는 문장을 자연스럽게 이어지도록 하는 접속부사는 (C)이다.

◎ 실전에 적용해 봐

131. (C) 132. (C) 133. (A) 134. (D) 135. (C) 136. (D)
137. (D) 138. (C) 139. (C) 140. (B) 141. (D) 142. (C)
143. (C) 144. (C) 145. (B) 146. (B)

문제 131-134는 다음 편지를 참조하시오.

> Ms. Chen 께,
> —131—. 우리는 성공적으로 모금했습니다 / 우리의 목표 금액을 / 지난해보다 증가된 금액인 백만달러인
> 우리는 우리의 목표에 도달할 수 없었을 것입니다 / 당신의 기부가 없었더라면 / 당신이 기부한 상당한 금액은 큰 도움이 되었습니다 / 우리의 성공에 / 이 모금에 있어서
> 2년 동안 모금된 금액은 / Education For Children에 기부될 것입니다 / 우리가 이전에 약속한 바와 같이 / 우리는 진심으로 약합니다 / 당신을 다시 기부자로 모실 수 있기를 / 우리의 다음 캠페인에 / 개최될 / 내년 초에
> 다시 한번 감사 드립니다

표현 정리 inquire 문의하다 research grant 연구비 contribution 기부 fundraiser 모금 행사 reminder (해야할 일 등을) 상기 시켜주는 편지 regarding ~에 관한 successfully 성공적으로 raise 모금하다 donation 기부 distribution 분배, 분포 significant 상당한 sincerely 진심으로 donor 기부자, 기증자 incident 일 사건 strategy 전략

131. 정답 (C)
해설 (A) 문의하고자 합니다 / 어떻게 제가 연구비를 받을 수 있는지를 (B) 축하합니다 / 수필 경연 대회에서 우승하신 것을 (C) 감사합니다 / 당신의 기부에 / 우리의 모금 행사에 대한 (D) 이것은 상기시켜드리는 중요한 편지입니다 / 우리의 자선 기금과 관련하여 * 편지의 내용이 전반적으로 Ms. Chen의 모금 행사에 대한 기부에 감사하는 내용이므로 이 편지의 도입 문장으로는 (C)가 적합하다.

132. 정답 (C)
해설 134번 문제 앞의 문장에서 2년 동안 모금된 금액은 기부될 것이라고 했으므로, '작년부터 모금된 금액'이라고 봐야 한다. 따라서 (C)가 답이다. second는 앞에 the를 써야 한다.

133. 정답 (A)
해설 '기금모금 행사, 백만 달러, 기부하다' 등의 표현들을 통해 단서를 찾을 수 있다. '기부'의 뜻을 가진 (A)가 정답이다.

134. 정답 (D)
해설 전체적으로 기부와 관련된 내용이므로 fundraising campaign들을 가리키는 (D)가 맞다.

문제 135-138은 다음 공지 사항을 참조하시오.

> 우리는 알려드리게 되어 유감입니다 / 우리 고객들에게 / 상품 Blooming Flower Cushion(상품 번호 67542)은 현재 재고가 없음을 / 우리가 두배로 늘렸음에도 불구하고 / 그 상품의 생산을 / 그 쿠션들은 신속히 팔려 나갑니다.
>
> 4월 8일 전에 주문이 이루어진 물품에 대한 배송이 / 내일부터 시작될 것입니다 / 하지만 그 후에 이루어진 주문들은 / 취소될 것입니다 / 그리고 고객들은 전액 환불을 받을 것입니다.
>
> 이에 대해 사과하기 위해서 / 우리는 제공할 것입니다 / 할인 쿠폰을 / 주문을 한 고객들에게 —138—.
>
> 만약 당신이 통보 받기를 원한다면 / 그 상품이 재 입고되었을 때 / 우리에게 연락하세요 / 883-3333으로 / 다시 한번 죄송합니다 / 불편을 드린 점에 대해서 / 그리고 감사드립니다 / 당신의 이해해 주심에 / 미리

표현 정리 inform 알리다 malfunctioning 제대로 작동하지 않는 out of stock 재고가 없는 irreplaceable 대체할 수 없는 double 두 배로 만들다 sell out 팔리다 rapidly 신속히 forward 보내다, 전달하다 clearance sale 재고 정리 세일 household items 가정용품 valid 유효한 defective 결함이 있는 refund 환불 restock 다시 채우다 inconvenience 불편

135. 정답 (C)

해설 문장이 '유감이다'라는 말로 시작하므로 부정적인 어감이 필요하다. 138번 다음 문장에서 '물품이 입고될 때 통보 받기를 원하면'이란 말이 단서가 된다. 따라서 '재고가 바닥난'이란 뜻의 (C)가 정답이다.

136. 정답 (D)

해설 '4월 8일 전에 주문된 물품들에 대한 배송은 가능하지만, 그 이후에 이루어진 주문들은 취소되어 환불될 것이다'라는 내용이 전체 문맥과 어울린다. 따라서 (D)가 정답이다.

137. 정답 (D)

해설 빈칸은 4월 8일 이후에 주문한 주문들을 말한다. 따라서 those orders라고 해야 한다. their를 쓰면 아무 고객이나 할인 쿠폰을 받는 셈이 된다.

138. 정답 (C)

해설 (A) 우리는 열고 있습니다 / 대규모 재고 정리 세일을 / 가정용품에 대한 (B) 주문 상품은 배달될 것입니다 / 이번주 말까지 (C) 그것들은 유효합니다 / 모든 구매 상품에 대한 10%의 할인에 대해 (D) 고객들은 요청 받습니다 / 결함이 있는 상품에 대해 알려주도록 * 빈칸 앞에서 할인 쿠폰이 발급된다고 언급되어 있으므로 할인 쿠폰을 가리키는 대명사 they로 시작하여 할인 쿠폰이 어떻게 적용되는지를 설명하고 있는 (C)가 적합하다.

문제 139-142는 다음 공지 사항을 참조하시오.

> 모든 고객분들은 주목해 주세요.
>
> 최근에 우리는 발견했습니다 / 일부 기술적인 문제들을 / 우리 온라인 상점의 웹사이트와 관련된
>
> 일부 고객들은 불만을 표했습니다 / 우리 웹사이트에 접속할 수 없는 것에 대해 / 그리고 문제를 분석한 후에 / 우리는 알아냈습니다 / 웹사이트가 자동적으로 막는다는 것을 / 일부 접속을 / 방문자들에 의한 —141—.
>
> 우리는 현재 최선을 다하고 있습니다 / 그것의 원인을 찾기 위해 / 하지만 지금까지 웹사이트는 모든 방문자의 접속을 허용합니다 / 만약 그들이 Plasm 브라우저를 사용하면 / 따라서 만약 당신이 우리 웹사이트에 접속하는데 문제가 있다면 / Plasm-based 브라우저를 사용하세요.
>
> 협조에 감사 드립니다.

표현 정리 recently 최근에 discover 발견하다 multiple 많은, 다수의 social 사회적인 access 접속하다, 접근하다 analyze 분석하다 determine 알아내다, 밝히다 automatically 자동적으로 block 막다, 차단하다 have a hard time + 동명사 ~하는데 어려움을 겪다 currently 현재, 지금 find out 발견하다 in advance 사전에 accordingly 따라서 so far 지금까지

139. 정답 (C)

해설 전체 문맥을 파악해야 정답을 고를 수 있는 문제이다. 기술적인 오류와 관련된 내용으로 보는 것이 적절하므로 (C)가 답이다.

140. 정답 (B)

해설 지문 후반 내용에서 Plasm 브라우저로는 접속이 가능하다고 했다. 따라서 모두를 뜻하는 (A)나 (D)는 탈락. other는 some이 먼저 언급된 후에 나올 수 있다. 따라서 '약간, 몇몇'을 뜻하는 (B)가 정답이다.

141. 정답 (D)

해설 (A) 방문자중 아무도 / 접속하는데 어려움이 없었습니다 / 우리 온라인 상점에 (B) 우리는 새로운 광고를 게재했습니다 / 우리의 웹사이트에 (C) 온라인 구매는 이용 불가 합니다 / 당신의 지역에서는 (D) 우리는 사과합니다 / 불편에 대해서 / 이 문제가 야기한 * 웹사이트 접속이 왜 불가한지 분석해 보니, 웹사이트 몇몇 접속을 자동으로 차단하고 있다는 것을 알아냈다는 빈칸 앞의 내용에 대해 고객들에게 사과의 말을 전하는 (D)가 적합하다. (A)는 상반된 내용이며, (B)와 (C)는 관련이 없는 내용이다.

142. 정답 (C)

해설 지금까지 Plasm 브라우저로 접속하는데 문제가 없으므로 그것을 이용해 보라는 내용으로 현재완료시제 혹은 현재시제와 잘 어울리는 표현은 (C)이다. (D)는 과거시제나 현재완료시제와 어울린다.

문제 143-146번은 다음 광고를 참조하시오.

> 오래된 전화를 반납하세요 / 새 Moby Phone을 가지기 위해 / 더 싸게!
>
> 우리의 설립 10주년을 기념하여 / Moby Electronics는 지금 제공하고 있습니다 / 새로 나온 Moby phone을 / 특별 가격에 / 한정된 기간 동안
>
> 만약 당신이 중고폰을 가져 온다면 / 제조사와 상관없이 / 당신은 최대 20퍼센트까지 할인 받을 수 있습니다 / 최신의 Moby Phone 중 하나를 구매하는데 대해 / 이것들은 포함합니다 / Moby 4와 Moby Mini를 / 꼭 서두르세요 / 제공 행사는 다음 주에 끝나니까요. —145—.
>
> 우리 웹사이트 www.mobyphones.com를 방문하세요 / 자세한 정보를 얻기 위해 / 이 특별 제안을 이용할 수 있는 모델들에 대한

표현 정리 celebration 축하 anniversary 기념일 foundation 설립 remaining 남아있는 limited 제한된 regardless ~에 상관없이 manufacturer 제조자, 제조회사 purchase 구매 extend 연장하다 sell out 매진되다 availability 유효성 direct ~에게 보내다 cutting edge 최첨단의 attract 끌다 share 공유하다

143. 정답 (C)
해설 다음 문장에서 이러한 제공이 다음 주에 끝날 예정이므로 서두르라는 말이 나온다. 따라서 '한정된 기간 동안'이란 의미의 (C)가 자연스럽다.

144. 정답 (C)
해설 빈칸은 주어 자리로 최신 폰들의 종류를 가리키는 지시대명사 (C)가 정답이다. (B)는 부사, (D)는 형용사이다.

145. 정답 (B)
해설 (A) 이 특별한 제공은 연장될 수도 있습니다 / 2주 더 (B) 그 모델들 중 몇몇은 조기에 매진될 수도 있습니다. (C) 어떠한 문의도 / 그것의 유효성과 관련된 / 전해져야 합니다 / 우리 인사부장에게 (C) 우리의 최첨단 전화기들은 끌고 있습니다 / 많은 주목을 * 최신 Moby Phone의 특별 제공 행사가 다음주에 끝나므로 서두르라는 내용 다음에 오기 적절한 것은 (B)이다. (A)는 빈칸 앞 문장과 상반되는 내용이며 (C)는 전혀 관련이 없는 엉뚱한 내용이고, (D)는 전화기에 대한 내용으로 특별 제공 행사와는 관련이 없다.

146. 정답 (B)
해설 이러한 특별 제공이 적용되는 모델에 대한 상세한 정보를 얻으려면 웹사이트를 방문하라고 했으므로 (B)가 정답이다. (A)를 대입하면 정보를 공유하기 위해 오라는 말이 되는데, 이미 정보를 알고 있는 상태는 아니므로 어색하다.

법칙 100 어휘 문제는 논리적 근거로 마무리한다
(동사/명사/형용사/부사 어휘)

◎ 유형을 파악해 봐
143. (A) 144. (A) 145. (B) 146. (B)

문제 143-146은 다음 이메일을 참조하시오.

> To: 성산부 전직원
> From: 데이비드 맥스웰, 생산 관리자
> 날짜: 6월 20일
> 제목: 안전 검사
>
> —143—. 회사 정책에 따라 / 정기 안전 점검이 실시될 예정입니다 / 이들 말에
>
> 여러분이 잘 알고 있듯이 / 안전 점검은 방지하는데 도움이 됩니다 / 근로자들이 다치는 것을 / 작업장에서 / 그것은 부정적으로 영향을 미칩니다 / 전반적인 생산성에
>
> 모든 기계들의 전원을 반드시 켜 두기 바랍니다 / 여러분이 사용을 마친 후 / 다음 주 수요일에 / 이전 점검 때 했던 것과 같이 / 점검은 시작될 것입니다 / 모든 직원들이 퇴근한 직후에
>
> 덧붙이자면 / 점검 받는 기계들은 사용 가능할 것입니다 / 오후 9시 이후에 / 목요일에

표현 정리 inform A of B A에게 B를 알리다 bear in mind 명심하다 production 생산, 생산량 take part in 참여하다 install 설치하다 regulation 규정 in compliance with ~에 따라 regular 정기적인 documentary 기획물, 다큐멘터리 safety inspection 안전 점검 conduct 실시하다 at the end of ~의 말에 be aware 알다 overall 전반적인 productivity 생산성 previous 이전의 additionally 추가적으로 undergo 받다, 겪다

143. 정답 (A)
해설 (A) 여러분에게 알리기 위해서 메일을 씁니다 / 여러분이 명심하고 있어야만 하는 것을 / 생산 라인과 관련하여 (B) 이것은 여러분에게 알리기 위한 것입니다 / 생산량이 많이 증가되었음을 (C) 여러분에게 요청하기 위해서 메일을 씁니다 / 세미나에 참석하도록 / 새로 설치된 기기들에 대한 (D) 이것은 여러분 모두에게 상기시키기 위함 입니다 / 안전 규정을 따를 것을 * 이메일이 직원들에게 생산 라인의 정기 안전 점검과 그에 대비하여 해야할 것들을 상기시키는 내용이므로, 도입 문장으로서 (A)가 적합하다.

144. 정답 (A)
해설 다음 문장에서 '이전 검사 때 한 것과 마찬가지로'라는 내용이 언급된 것으로 보아 안전 점검은 정기적으로 실시되고 있음을 알 수 있어 (A)가 정답이다.

145. 정답 (B)
해설 did를 수식해 줄 수 있는 부사 (B)가 정답 이다.

146. 정답 (B)
해설 문맥상 '점검 중인 기계들'이란 내용으로 빈칸 뒤에 있는 machines를 수식해 주는 (B)가 정답이다.

◎ 실전에 적용해 봐
131. (C) 132. (C) 133. (C) 134. (B) 135. (D) 136. (D)
137. (C) 138. (D) 139. (B) 140. (D) 141. (B) 142. (B)
143. (D) 144. (A) 145. (A) 146. (D)

문제 131-134 번은 다음 회람을 참조하시오.

From: 크리스 벤틀리, 생산부 관리자
To: 공장 전직원
Date: 9월 24일
Subject: 단독 방문 알림

당신도 알다시피 / Carson Auto의 이사인 Mr. Cyrus가 / 연례 방문을 할 예정입니다 / 생산 공장을 / 다음 주 월요일 / 우리의 사기를 복돋우기 위해

따라서 / 전 직원들은 모일 것을 권합니다 / 세미나실에 / 월요일 오후 5시까지 —133—.

이사님의 간략한 격려사 후에 / 연회가 열릴 것입니다 / 구내식당에서 / 또한 알아 두십시오 / 올해 방문은 지연되었다는 것을 / 4일 가량 / 그리고 다음 방문은 예정되어 있습니다 / 내년 9월 20일로

모두 세미나실에서 봅시다 / 다음 주 월요일에

표현 정리 executive 중역, 이사 informal 비공식적인 annual 연례의, 매년의 abrupt 갑작스런 boost 복돋우다 morale 사기, 의욕 accordingly 따라서 accommodate 수용하다 participant 참가자 be supposed to + 동사원형 ~하기로 되어 있다 assign 맡기다, 배정하다 self-development 자기 개발 brief 간단한 farewell 작별 encouragement 격려 gratitude 고마움 banquet 연회

131.   정답 (C)

해설 회람의 끝 부분에서 매년 있는 계획된 방문임을 알 수 있으므로 (C)가 정답이다.

132.   정답 (C)

해설 advise는 to 부정사를 목적 보어로 취하는 동사이므로 'be advised to 동사원형' 형태로 사용된다. 따라서 (C)가 정답이다. (D)는 가주어, 진주어에 잘 어울리는 형용사로서 '~하는 것이 권장된다'라고 말할 때 사용한다.

133.   정답 (C)

해설 (A) 그 방은 수용할 수 없다 / 모든 참석자들을 (B) 당신은 논의하기로 되어있다 / 그 문제들을 / 그 방에서 (C) 밤 근무를 맡은 사람들도 참석해야 한다 / 또한 (D) 자기 개발에 대한 강의가 있을 것이다. * 모든 직원들이 월요일 오후 다섯시까지 세미나실에 모일 것을 권장하는 빈칸 앞의 내용과 문맥상 적절히 이어질 수 있는 것은 (C)이다. (A)와 (B)는 세미나 룸에 관련된 내용으로 보여, 정답으로 오인할 수 있으나, 글의 전체 흐름에서 보면 적절하지 않을 내용이다.

134.   정답 (B)

해설 첫 번째 문장에서 '직원 사기를 올리기 위해서'라는 내용이 언급되었으므로 '격려, 고무'를 뜻하는 (B)가 정답이다

문제 135-138번은 다음 편지를 참조하시오.

날짜: 1월 25일
제목: 룸 무료 업그레이드
Ms. Lynn 께,

단골 손님이 돼 주셔서 감사합니다 / Riverside Hotel의 / 이 편지는 귀하에게 알리기 위한 것입니다 / 귀하는 자격이 있습니다 / 객실 업그레이드를 받을 / 무료로 / 다음 방문시에 —136—.

무료 객실 업그레이드는 가능합니다 / 만약 귀하가 딜럭스 또는 그보다 넓은 방을 예약한다면 / 만약 귀하가 딜럭스 방을 예약한다면 / 귀하의 방은 업그레이드 될 것입니다 / 스위트 또는 비즈니스 객실로

만약 당신이 이 제안에 관심이 있다면 / 첨부된 양식을 작성해서 / 우리에게 보내 주세요 / 월말까지

우리는 고대하고 있습니다 / 곧 당신을 뵐 수 있기를 / 그리고 희망합니다 / 귀하가 좋은 시간을 가지기를 / 업그레이드된 객실에서

표현 정리 regular guest 단골 손님 inform 알리다 suitable 적합한 eligible 자격이 있는 rate 요금 renovate 개보수 하다 spectacular 장관을 이루는 miss out on ~을 놓치다 deluxe 고급의, 호화스러운 reserve 예약하다 browse 둘러보다 fill out 작성하다 attach 붙이다, 첨부하다

135.   정답 (D)

해설 편지를 보내는 이유는 곧 that 이하의 내용을 전하기 위한 것이다. 첫 문장에서 단골 고객이 된 것에 대해 감사의 뜻을 전하고 있고, 두 번째 문장의 that절에서는 '다음에 방문할 때 무료로 방을 업그레이드 할 수 있다'고 했으므로 빈칸에 들어갈 단어는 (D)가 가장 적절이다. (C)는 be suitable to(~에 적합하다) 형태로 사용되는데, '귀하는 방을 업그레이드 받기에 적합하다'는 내용은 쓰임이 어색하다.

136.   정답 (D)

해설 (A) 알아 두십시오 / 숙박료가 인상될 것을 / 다음 달에 (B) 식당이 보수 공사 중이며 곧 다시 문을 열 것입니다. (C) 저희 호텔은 잘 알려져 있습니다 / 멋진 한강의 전망에 대해 (D) 이 좋은 기회를 절대 놓치지 마십시오 / 아래의 상세한 정보를 확인함으로써 * 편지를 쓴 목적이 객실 무료 업그레이드에 대해 알리기 위한 것이라는 빈칸 앞의 내용에 이어 (D)가 언급되어야 무료 업그레이드를 받는 방법을 알려주고 있는 뒤 따르는 내용과 흐름이 맞게 전개된다.

137.   정답 (C)

해설 빈칸 앞 문장에서 무료 업그레이드는 deluxe room부터 가능하다고 했는데, 업그레이드는 방을 예약하거나 숙박을 할 때 적용이 되므로 빈칸에는 '예약하다'라는 내용의 (C)가 오는 것이 적절하다

138.   정답 (D)

해설 '~에 관심이 있다'는 be interested in이다. 주절(please ~)이 미래시제나 명령문일 때 조건 부사절에서는 현재가 미래를 대신하므로 (D)가 정답이다.

문제 139-142번은 다음 발표를 참조하시오

Regina Residences 주요 공지 사항

최근에 / 우리는 더 많은 건수의 불평을 접수해 왔습니다 / 층간 소음에 관하여 / 우리의 거주민들로부터

알아 두십시오 / 세탁기를 가동하는 것은 큰 방해가 될 수 있다는 것을 / 다른 사람들에게 / 그러므로 허락되지 않는다는 것을 / 오후 10시 이후에는 / 마찬가지로 / 높은 볼륨으로 라디오를 듣거나 TV를 시청 하는 것은 강력하게 제지됩니다 / 밤에 —141—.

Regina Residences는 아파트입니다 / 50명 이상의 주민들이 공유하는 / 우리는 감사하겠습니다 여러분이 저희에게 협조해 주시면 / 반드시 규칙과 규정에 따라 주십시오 / 여러분이 준수하겠다고 동의한 / 입주하실 때

표현 정리 lately 최근에 complaint 불평, 불만 crack 갈라진 틈 dispute 분쟁, 분규 disturbance 방해, 폐해 discourage 막다, 좌절시키다 relatively 비교적 landlord 임대주 revise 수정하다, 개정하다 regulation 규정 moreover 더욱이 premises 구내, 단지내 designated 지정된 besides 게다가 key deposit 보증금 resident 거주자, 주민 appreciate 고마워하다 cooperate 협력하다 comply with 준수하다, 지키다

139. 정답 (B)

해설 빈칸 다음 문장에서 세탁기를 가동하는 것이 큰 방해가 되기 때문에 10시 이후에는 사용하지 말아 달라는 내용과 함께 TV와 라디오의 높은 볼륨도 크게 하지 말아 달라고 부탁하는 것으로 보아 (B)가 정답임을 유추할 수 있다.

140. 정답 (D)

해설 바로 앞 문장에서 세탁기 사용은 오후 10시 이후에는 자제해 달라고 부탁했고, 이어 다른 금지 사항을 추가하고 있으므로 강조의 부사 (D)가 오는 것이 적절하다.

141. 정답 (B)

해설 (A) 따라서, 임대주는 개정할 것입니다 / 규칙과 규정들을 / 이 아파트의 (B) 더욱이, 어떤 악기도 연주되어서는 안됩니다 / 아파트 구내에서는 / 어떤 때라도 (C) 추가로, 모든 쓰레기는 버려야 합니다 / 지정된 장소에 (D) 게다가, 보증금은 환불되지 않습니다 / 당신이 퇴거하기 전에는 * 오후 10시 이후 세탁기 사용 금지, 라디오와 TV소리 줄이기와 같이 소음 문제와 관련하여 입주민들이 지켜야하는 규칙들을 언급하는 내용이 오는 것이 적절하므로 (B)가 정답이다. (C)와 (D)도 규칙에 해당되지만, 소음 문제와는 관련이 없다.

142. 정답 (B)

해설 공지 사항을 나열한 후에 마지막으로 협조를 구하는 내용이므로 (B)가 정답이다. 타동사인 (A)와 (D)는 목적어가 없어 탈락이다.

문제 143-146은 다음 정보를 참조하시오.

The Arizona Natural Environment Foundation은 회원제 기반의 환경 단체이다 / 해결하는 것을 목적으로 하는 / 국제적인 문제들을 / 공기, 물, 토양 오염에 관한

이 단체는 전념하고 있다 / 광범위한 연구를 실시하는데 / 해결책을 찾기 위하여 / 세계 도처의 문제에 대한 / 이 단체는 특별히 관여해 오고 있다 / 해결책을 찾는데 / Ghana의 심각한 가뭄과 중국의 황사에 대한 / 2007년 설립 이후로

비록 이 단체는 사립 비영리 기관이지만 / 수립해 왔다 / 폭넓은 동맹과 협력 관계를 / 다양한 기관들과 함께

—146—.

표현 정리 organization 기관, 단체 aim ~을 목표로 하다 resolve 해결하다 controversial 논란이 많은 connective 연결하는 be committed to ~에 전념하다, 헌신하다 throughout 도처에 be involved in ~에 관련되다 specifically 분명히, 명백하게 solution 해결책 drought 가뭄 foundation 설립 illegal 불법적인 widespread 널리 퍼진 extensive 광범위한 alliance 동맹 cooperative 협력하는 institution 기관 convert 전환시키다 strive 분투하다 internal 내부의 establish 설립하다

143. 정답 (D)

해설 빈칸 다음 문장에서 '전세계에 걸쳐 문제의 해결책을 찾기 위해 연구 활동을 하고 있다'라고 하므로 오염에 대한 '국제적인 문제들'로 보는 것이 적절하므로 (D)가 정답이다. (B)를 답으로 하기에는 어떤 논쟁의 소지가 있는지에 대한 단서가 전혀 없는 상태이다.

144. 정답 (A)

해설 빈칸은 동사 자리이므로 (D)는 탈락이다. involve는 목적어가 필요한 동사이므로 수동태는 be involved in의 형태로 써야 한다. 따라서 (A)가 답이다. (B)와 (C)는 능동태이므로 목적어가 필요하다.

145. 정답 (A)

해설 지문 첫째 줄에서 membership-based, 즉 회원제를 기초로 하는 단체라고 했으므로 (C)보다는 (A)가 문맥상 어울린다.

146. 정답 (D)

해설 (A) 이러한 동맹을 형성함으로써, 이 단체는 전환될 것이다 / 공공 단체로 (B) 이 단체는 분투해 왔다 / 원인을 찾기 위하여 / 내부적 문제의 (C) 그 기관들은 지역 사무소를 개설해 왔다 / 전세계적으로 (D) 이러한 동맹을 통하여 / 이 단체는 더 잘 달성할 수 있을 것이다 / 그것의 목표를 / 국제적 환경 문제를 해결하려는 * '아리조나 자연 환경 재단이 다양한 기관들과 동맹과 협력관계를 맺어오고 있다'라는 내용 다음에 이어질 내용으로 가능성이 있는 것은 (A)와 (D)인데 이 글의 도입부에서 '재단의 목표는 국지적 오염 문제들을 해결하는 것'이라고 했으므로, 이와 관련 지어 보면, (D)가 적합하다.

누구라도 5세트면 시험에 완벽하게 적응한다!
신토익 전면 개정판 출간!

차별점 1 | 하루에 1세트씩 5일이면 필요한 문제를 다 볼 수 있다!

실전 유형과 난이도를 반영한 고품질 실전 모의고사 5회분을 제공합니다. 출제율을 바탕으로 가장 자주 출제되고 점수 상승에 필요한 문제만 뽑았습니다.

차별점 2 | 신토익을 완벽하게 반영한 문제!

10년만에 개정되는 신토익 유형을 분석해서 완벽하게 문제에 반영했고, 책의 전체 내용을 완전히 개정했습니다.

차별점 3 | 명쾌하고 친절한 해설집 무료 제공!

학습하는 수험생들을 위해 파트 별 전문 저자들이 만든 친절하고 명쾌한 해설집을 무료로 제공합니다.

초보 토익커도 이해하기 쉬운
단계별 과외식 학습

유형 확인 → 풀이법 확인 → 함정 확인 → 실전 적용

❶ **8년간 저자가 직접 시험을 보며 정리한 출제율**
저자가 직접 시험을 보며 8년간 정리한 출제율을 기반으로 이 책을 구성했습니다. 실제 확실히 나오는 유형만 출제 빈도로 정리했습니다.

❷ **우선 순위 대로 학습하는 효율적 학습**
요즘처럼 취업이 힘든 시기에 수험생들은 할 일이 너무 많습니다. 효율적인 학습을 위해 우선 순위 대로 학습할 수 있게 했습니다.

❸ **실전 감각을 길러주는 실전테스트 8회분 추가 제공!**
책을 학습한 후 실전을 앞두고 실전 감각을 더 기르고 싶은 수험생을 위해 3회분 실전테스트를 제공하고, 본문 문제로 재구성한 5회분 실전테스트를 추가로 제공합니다.

▶ 1회 문제를 제외한 내용은(2~3회 문제, 1~3회 해설, 본문 문제 재구성 5회분) 모두 홈페이지에서 내려받을 수 있습니다. 본문 문제 재구성 5회분의 해설은 따로 제공하지 않고 해당 법칙의 본문 해설로 확인하실 수 있습니다. (www.gilbut.co.kr)

시나공 토익 출제 순위 파트 5, 6
Crack the Exam! – Statistics TOEIC Part 5, 6

값 15,000원

ISBN 979-11-5924-051-5